CAMBRIDGE
UNIVERSITY PRESS

Theory of Knowledge
for the IB Diploma

COURSE GUIDE

Wendy Heydorn, Susan Jesudason
From original material by Richard van de Lagemaat

CAMBRIDGE
UNIVERSITY PRESS

Shaftesbury Road, Cambridge CB2 8EA, United Kingdom

One Liberty Plaza, 20th Floor, New York, NY 10006, USA

477 Williamstown Road, Port Melbourne, VIC 3207, Australia

314–321, 3rd Floor, Plot 3, Splendor Forum, Jasola District Centre, New Delhi – 110025, India

103 Penang Road, #05-06/07, Visioncrest Commercial, Singapore 238467

Cambridge University Press is part of the University of Cambridge.

It furthers the University's mission by disseminating knowledge in the pursuit of education, learning and research at the highest international levels of excellence.

www.cambridge.org
Information on this title: www.cambridge.org/9781108865982

© Cambridge University Press & Assessment 2020

First published 2011
Second edition 2013
Third edition 2020

20 19 18 17 16 15 14 13 12 11 10 9 8 7 6 5

Printed in Dubai by Oriental Press

A catalogue record for this publication is available from the British Library

ISBN 978-1-108-86598-2 Paperback with Digital Access

Additional resources for this publication at www.cambridge.org/delange

....

....

❯ Contents

> How to use this series

This suite of resources supports students and teachers of the Theory of Knowledge TOK course for the IB Diploma Programme. The Course Guide, the Skills Book and the Teacher's Resource work together to support teachers and students on their learning journey, providing the necessary knowledge and skills required to succeed in the course.

The course guide with digital edition provides full coverage of the latest IB TOK guide. It includes activities that test students' understanding and develop critical thinking skills. It uses linking questions to make connections across themes and areas of knowledge, and provides examples of real-life situations that help students see how TOK themes manifest in the world around them. With clear language and style, the course guide is designed for international learners.

Written in collaboration with TOK teachers from the Cambridge Panel, this guide provides tried and tested activities that arm you with lesson planning ideas, an ESL focus, essay-writing support, advice on tackling common misconceptions, activity worksheets and more.

This flexible resource supports your knowers in their exploration journey, helping to develop critical thinking skills and the ability to make new connections between areas of knowledge. It gives practical advice and plenty of opportunities to unpack and practise the assessment tasks.

> How to use this book

Throughout this book you will find lots of different features to help your learning.

LEARNING INTENTIONS

A short introduction explains what each chapter covers, followed by a bulleted list to clearly see what the goals of the chapter are.

BEFORE YOU START

This short section of statements and questions will help you to reflect on prior learning, check what knowledge you will need for the chapter and provoke your own thoughts about the topic.

LINKING QUESTION

Linking questions encourage you to make connections with areas of knowledge and other subjects in your IB Diploma Programme.

DISCUSS

Discuss questions are there to facilitate debate and help you dig deeper into your understanding, while honing your communication skills.

REFLECTION

Develop your personal perspective by reflecting on the development of your thinking and skills proficiency.

KEY WORDS

Key words are important words for you to engage with. They are highlighted in orange and are defined where they first appear in the text.

REAL-LIFE SITUATION

These help you to relate the theory you are learning to practices in real life.

EXPLORE

Explore activities are there to help you actively engage in what you are learning by working through an interesting variety of tasks, such as presentations, drawings or short written pieces.

Peer assessment

These are opportunities within 'Explore' activities to assess the work of, and receive feedback from, your peers in relation to how you are doing against the learning intentions

Self-assessment

These are opportunities within 'Explore' activities to consider how you are doing in relation to the learning intentions.

KNOWLEDGE QUESTIONS

At the end of each chapter, a set of knowledge questions will help you to apply what you have learnt in a longer essay form.

Continue your journey

Focused further reading sections will signpost useful resources to delve deeper into the topics covered in each chapter.

Check your progress

This interactive table helps you to check your confidence level and progress against the learning intentions, and see clearly what you need to revisit.

> Introduction

This textbook is designed to be used with the TOK course in the International Baccalaureate Diploma Programme, but it may also be useful for students following other critical thinking courses.

The main question in TOK is "How do we know?" The course encourages you to think critically about the subjects you are studying rather than passively accepting what you are taught. Critical thinking involves such things as asking good questions, using language with care and precision, supporting your ideas with evidence, arguing coherently and making sound judgements. You are, of course, encouraged to think critically in every subject that you study. TOK is designed to help you to reflect on and further develop the thinking skills you are acquiring in your other subjects.

The course

The book is structured according to the three interrelated parts and the assessments:

Part 1 Core theme: 'Knowers and knowing' it invites you to reflect personally on the nature of your own knowledge, and to think critically about the beliefs and ideas that you have acquired. In addition, we explore the way we construct knowledge and decide what is true.

Part 2 Optional themes: in which you are asked to explore knowledge and knowing within two contemporary themes from a possible choice of five: technology, language, politics, religion and indigenous societies.

Part 3 Areas of knowledge: in which you will explore knowledge and knowing within the five compulsory areas of knowledge: history, the arts, mathematics, natural sciences and human sciences.

Part 4 Assessment: in which you will find out more about the TOK assessment requirements, and how to go about completing them successfully.

Knowledge questions

Enquiring and investigating the nature of knowledge and knowing is the aim of TOK. All three parts of the TOK course are built around the analysis and exploration of knowledge questions. *A knowledge question*, as the name suggests, is a question specifically about knowledge.

Such questions have various key features:

1   *They are second-order, knowledge-specific questions.* A first-order question is a question about the world; a second-order question is a question about knowledge. In relation to academic subjects, first-order questions arise *within* a subject, whereas second-order questions are *about* a subject. For example, 'Is the universe expanding?' is a first-order question which is dealt with by physics, whereas 'How certain is scientific knowledge?' is a second-order question, and is part of TOK.

2   *They are expressed in terms of TOK concepts and ideas.* The focus of knowledge questions is on 12 concepts that are essential to the process of gaining knowledge or the methods involved, including **evidence**, **explanation** and **justification**. They also draw on TOK concepts such as **certainty**, **truth** and **culture** to explore how knowledge is constructed, and how that knowledge is communicated, used and evaluated.

3   *They are contestable questions.* Knowledge questions do not have straightforward or certain answers, and they are open to discussion and debate. For example, 'To what extent can we gain certain knowledge in human sciences and history if experts within these disciples disagree?'. Since they are contested, such questions require analysis of the different perspectives and possible answers, personal thought and sound judgement. The various plausible answers to knowledge questions may be ambiguous and uncertain. The fact that there are rarely definitive answers in TOK is sometimes a source of frustration, but it can also be intellectually exhilarating.

4   *They are general, open ended and comparative questions.* Knowledge questions are general, open-ended and sometimes *comparative*. We might, for example, compare the different methods for gaining knowledge, or different areas of knowledge such as history and natural science. A relevant knowledge question here might be 'How can we know what ethical considerations should influence the pursuit of knowledge in history and the natural sciences?'

The knowledge framework

The knowledge questions in each of the three parts of the course are explored in relation to the following framework: scope, perspectives, methods and tools, and ethics, which we unpack in Chapter 3. The framework is a tool for exploring links and comparisons between the core theme, optional themes and areas of knowledge.

Concepts for the analysis and evaluation of knowledge

As you work through the TOK course, you might find it useful to keep in mind the following 12 concepts which have an important place throughout all parts of the TOK course. These essential concepts will enable you to analyse knowledge. They are useful for comparisons between the core, optional themes and areas of knowledge. These concepts will help you recognise and explore the similarities and differences between different academic disciplines, themes and areas of knowledge.

1   Evidence: What counts as evidence?

2   Certainty: How certain is our knowledge?

3   Truth: Can we ever be certain of the truth?

4   Interpretation: What makes a justified interpretation?

5   Power: To what extent should we accept knowledge by authority?

6   Justification: What distinguishes a good justification from a bad one?

7   Explanation: What makes an explanation convincing?

8   Objectivity: What does it mean to be open-minded and unbiased?

9   Perspective: Are some viewpoints more justified than others?

10 Culture: Does knowledge depend on the ideas and traditions of our communities?

11 Values: Is knowledge influenced by ethical considerations?

12 Responsibility: Where do our responsibilities as knowers begin and end?

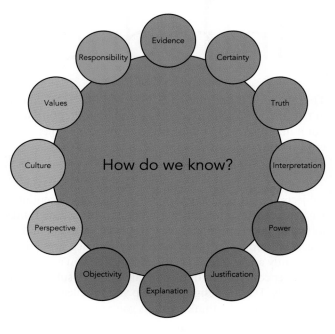

Figure A: 12 TOK key concepts

There is no 'official' TOK diagram, but as will be discussed in Chapter 1, diagrams and maps are useful ways of making sense of the corresponding territory – as long as we do not take them too literally. Teachers using this textbook should keep in mind that the IB Diploma Programme TOK subject guide explicitly states that the course *'can be structured in a variety of ways, and can start from a variety of different entry points'* and that teachers *'are encouraged to exercise flexibility, creativity and innovation in the design and delivery of their TOK course'*. With that in mind, Figure B presents one way of making sense of the course and integrating its key elements in a single diagram.

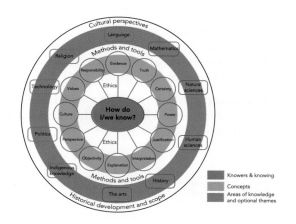

Figure B: A TOK diagram

> Part 1

Knowers and knowing

> Chapter 1

Who is the knower?

LEARNING INTENTIONS

This chapter will address the question of the knower and what the knower brings to the task of knowing.

You will:

- examine your own knowledge and sense of self, consider what shapes you as a knower and understand how you can overestimate and underestimate your personal knowledge.

- learn how to discuss the self in relation to tribalism, and become aware of the importance of knowledge communities for personal identity.

- learn how to discuss objectivity and subjectivity.

- understand the difference between relativity and relativism, and their implications.

- consider the role of 'common sense' for the knower.

BEFORE YOU START

Analyse each of the following quotations and discuss the questions that follow.

1   'The things that make me different are the things that make me.' **A. A. Milne** (1882–1956)

2   'If I speak of myself in different ways, that is because I look at myself in different ways.' **Michel de Montaigne** (1533–1592)

3   'When I let go of what I am, I become what I might be.' **Lao Tzu** (6th century BCE)

4   'Knowing yourself is the beginning of all wisdom.' **Aristotle** (384–322 BCE)

5   'To go wrong in one's own way is better than to go right in someone else's.' **Fyodor Dostoevsky** (1821–1881)

For each quotation, consider:

a   To what extent do you agree or disagree with the quotation?

b   How might you challenge the quotation?

c   What assumptions underlying the quotation can you identify?

d   Does the quotation challenge or affirm your own perspective on who you are?

e   To what extent does your answer to question d depend on your answer to question a?

1.1 Introduction

REAL-LIFE SITUATION 1.1

1   To what extent can you know yourself?

2   In what contexts is it possible for others to know you better than you know yourself?

The question of who is the knower has occupied the minds of philosophers and other great thinkers for thousands of years, and is perhaps no closer to a definitive answer than it has ever been. Yet if we cannot know who we are as knowers, how can we begin to know anything? You might want to say, '*I know who I am. When I look in the mirror, I see me*', but every time you look in the mirror, you see a different 'you'. Are you the same person now that you were when you were five years old? And will you be the same person when you are 60 or even by the end of today? How will you know?

More importantly, in the context of Theory of Knowledge (TOK), we will look at what it is that each of us as an individual knower brings to the process of knowing, how we might contribute to the pool of knowledge that humankind has access to, and how we can best try to avoid deceiving ourselves or being deceived by others. In the course of this chapter, and throughout the book, you will be encouraged to examine where your current knowledge comes from, and what has influenced you to think the way that you do. You will also be challenged to identify and question some of your assumptions and **biases**, and to raise your awareness of the extent to which who you are shapes what you know.

KEY WORD

bias: prejudice, unfairness, favouritism

1.2 The knower as an individual

REAL-LIFE SITUATION 1.2

To what extent are you still the same person that you were before you began the TOK course?

Who are you? said the Caterpillar.
This was not an encouraging opening for a conversation. Alice replied, rather shyly, I—I hardly know, Sir, just at present—at least I know who I was when I got up this morning, but I think I must have been changed several times since then. What do you mean by that? said the Caterpillar, sternly. Explain yourself! I can't explain myself, I'm afraid, Sir, said Alice, because I am not myself, you see.

Lewis Carroll (1832–1898), *Alice in Wonderland.*

Outside of philosophy, 'personal identity' usually refers to the features a person defines themselves by, or that make them 'who they are'. For example, you might choose to identify yourself as an Inuit who loves psy-trance music, a vegan football player, an avid horse-riding enthusiast or perhaps you see yourself as a future engineer with a passion for design. We all have multiple characteristics by which we might choose to identify ourselves including (but not limited to) our age, gender identity, nationality, physical characteristics, sexual orientation, dietary choices, culture, politics, religion, hobbies and preferred school subjects.

Interestingly, just because you have a characteristic does not mean you will choose to identify with that characteristic. Just because you come from Tahiti does not necessarily mean that you identify as being Tahitian, or you may be a talented pianist but do not particularly regard yourself as a musician. It is also possible that you may choose to identify yourself with a characteristic you do not actually have. For example, you might think of yourself as a singer, even if you are actually tone deaf.

Our personal identity, in this sense, is largely contingent, and changeable. Our ethnicity and ancestry may be fixed, but almost everything else that we identify ourselves by may change. We express certain aspects of the culture and communities we belong to, but we might also challenge those norms and actively shape our culture in new ways.

David Hume (1711–1776) regarded the self as nothing more than a '*bundle of perceptions*'. He famously said, '*When I enter most intimately into what I call myself, I always stumble on some particular perception or other, of heat or cold, light or shade, love or hatred, pain or pleasure. I never can catch myself at any time without a perception and never can observe anything but the perception.*' (David Hume, *A Treatise of Human Nature.*)

KEY WORDS

identity: how a person, group or nation sees themselves in relation to other people, groups, nations, ideas, and the world

contingent: only true under certain conditions, and dependent on other things

culture: the shared ideas, beliefs, customs and practices of a community or society

perception: an awareness of something in and through the mind

DISCUSS 1.1

1 Do you think David Hume was right? Can you 'catch' or perceive yourself without any perceptions?

2 What might this mean in terms of your self-understanding?

Many psychologists – and many of us – take the self as some kind of fundamental core reality very seriously. We live in an age in which self-identity and self-esteem are regarded as crucial to our health and well-being. At the same time, we are encouraged to take part in self-improvement programmes, and the 'selfie' is perhaps the fastest-growing genre in photography. Indeed, there seems to be a contemporary obsession with portraying ourselves in particular ways on social media. We may feel under pressure to show ourselves as having a particular look or living a particular lifestyle, when the reality may be rather different.

REAL-LIFE SITUATION 1.3

To what extent are our self-image and feelings of self-esteem a reflection of the ways in which others view us, the ways we *think* others view us or the ways we see ourselves?

Figure 1.1: Selfies are a growing genre

EXPLORE 1.1

Write a page about yourself. What it is about you that makes you who you are?

Once you have written about yourself, analyse your work. If you were to take out everything that relates you to other people (e.g., '*I am Mbongi's sister*', or '*I belong to the Ng family*', or '*I am Miguel's best friend*'), where you come from or what you do, how much would be left? How much of what you have written do you think will *always* be true of you? How much might be different in one year? How much might be different in ten years? How much might be different in 50 years?

CONTINUED

Look back on your description after a week. What, if anything, might you want to add or subtract from your self-description? What might this say about you as a knower?

Self-assessment

How well were you able to capture who you believe yourself to be in the writing activity? Is there anything you have missed? Did you take into account factors that have shaped you, and how you have learnt what you know?

The knower's perspective

All of us, as knowers, bring our own **perspective** to every situation – from the people and places we like to the political opinions we hold. If you think back to the things you liked or disliked when you were very young, you would probably have very different opinions of them now. (Very few IB Diploma Programme students would regard *Twinkle Twinkle Little Star* as one of their favourite songs, for example, although it is a great favourite for many young children.)

As our perspectives change, so too do our tastes and opinions. The more we learn and the deeper our understanding, the more our perspectives alter. Sometimes, our personal perspective can help us to empathise with others. At other times, it can prevent us from understanding their position, or even wanting to. It can be difficult, for example, if you have been the victim of a crime to have much empathy with or sympathy for the perpetrator of that crime, because you have a very different perspective on the event. However, as our experiences in life broaden, so too does our personal knowledge, and so consequently do our perspectives. We might learn to appreciate multiple shades of grey in things that once appeared to be only black or white, and understand and empathise more with the circumstances that have, for example, led a person to engage in crime.

One of the many reasons for promoting diversity in all aspects of society is that it provides everyone with the opportunity to meet, appreciate and learn from people with different ideas, experiences and perspectives.

KEY WORD

perspective: point of view, a particular way of seeing or considering something

REAL-LIFE SITUATION 1.4

Can you identify any significant experiences in your life that have caused your perspective on something to change?

Personal knowledge

Personal knowledge is the knowledge we personally have. Almost all of our personal knowledge is **experiential**. The exceptions would be any knowledge that is **innate**, that is, knowledge we are born with, or things that we can know *a priori*, that is, purely by reason. An example of innate knowledge might be knowing how to breathe, how to cry or knowing to search for our mother's nipple. Some people would say we are born with an innate sense of God.

KEY WORDS

experiential: based on experience

innate: something we are born with

a priori: purely by reason

DISCUSS 1.2

1   Is being able to breathe the same thing as *knowing* how to breathe?

2   Is there a difference between an instinct and innate knowledge? If so, what is it?

In his book *Meno*, Plato (c 427–348 BCE) wrote about a situation in which Socrates questioned an uneducated slave boy about a geometry **theorem**. Although the boy had never studied geometry, he was able to answer Socrates correctly. Plato argued that this was possible because the boy had an innate knowledge of mathematics. Many people have argued that Socrates led the boy to the correct answer through leading questions. (You will learn about leading questions in Chapter 12 on mathematics and Chapter 14 on the human sciences.) Although it is true that Socrates led the boy to the correct answer, the objection misses the point of Plato's argument, which is that the boy was able to grasp the **truth** for himself as he answered Socrates's questions. In principle, this means that the boy could potentially have discovered the theorem by himself if he had thought long and hard about it. If Plato was right, we all have an innate knowledge of mathematics that we could potentially tap into.

KEY WORDS

theorem: a principle or statement that can be demonstrated or proved using logic, but is not self-evident

truth: in accord with fact or reality, or faithfulness to a standard

Figure 1.2: Is a baby born with any knowledge?

Philosopher John Locke (1632–1704) completely disagreed with the idea of innate knowledge, although he did accept that we do have some biological instincts. In his essay entitled *An Essay Concerning Human Understanding*, Locke argued that at birth our mind is a *tabula rasa*, meaning a blank slate. He believed that everything we know, biological instincts aside, is learnt from experience, whether directly or indirectly.

Although most people today would tend to agree with John Locke, the linguist Noam Chomsky (1928–) has proposed a modern, modified version of innate knowledge that has enjoyed some popularity. Chomsky argues that humans have a unique, innate capacity for learning language, which involves us intuitively recognising a **universal grammar** that he claims all human languages share. In a similar vein, more recently it has been suggested that many animal species, including humans, appear to have an innate sense of number.

KEY WORD

universal grammar: the idea that all human languages, no matter how different they appear, share some fundamental similarities

---

REAL-LIFE SITUATION 1.5

Do you believe that you were born with some knowledge, or do you believe that everything you know has been learnt?

Experiential knowledge can be *first-hand* or *second-hand*. First-hand knowledge is knowledge that we learn from our own personal experiences. It can include knowledge of people we have met and places we have visited, activities we have been involved in, experiments we have performed, and so on. Second-hand knowledge is knowledge that we learn *from* other people or sources. Some of this will be academic knowledge. For example, the knowledge of academic subjects that we might learn in school or through reading books, journals and articles, or through watching documentaries. Some of our second-hand knowledge will be informal knowledge; that is, knowledge we pick up through a wide variety of sources including friends, television, the internet and our local communities, without necessarily being aware that we are doing so.

For example, if you were to volunteer with a Search and Rescue (SAR) organisation, your first-hand knowledge would come from any training exercises you were involved in, as well as any real-life SAR operations you might participate in. As a result of your experiences with the SAR organisation, you might know how to communicate effectively using two-way radios, how to navigate using a map and compass and how to administer basic first aid. You could also have second-hand experiential knowledge from listening to or reading about the experiences of other people who are involved in SAR. This knowledge might include knowing how search teams are deployed, how searches are controlled and managed and how scent patterns vary according to different environmental factors. Informal knowledge you pick up could include information such as knowing the different types of rewards individual search dogs enjoy.

EXPLORE 1.2

If you were to write a 'personal encyclopaedia' summarising everything you know, how comprehensive do you think it would be? And how accurate?

Try to estimate how much of what you know is first-hand and how much is second-hand knowledge. Choose a field of knowledge that you are passionate about. It does not have to be an academic subject; it could be something like cricket, dogs or video games. Try to identify the main sources of this field of knowledge, and create a mind-map showing how they interconnect. How have the different sources contributed to shaping you as a knower?

Personal ignorance

'The more we know, the more we know we don't know,' is a quotation sometimes attributed to Aristotle. It expresses the idea that the more we learn about any field of knowledge, the more we discover there is so much more to learn about it, and the more we are able to appreciate that knowledge is rarely as certain, simple and straightforward as is often supposed.

Given the vast amount of knowledge in the world, we are inevitably ignorant of many things. Ignorance does not mean stupidity, and there is no shame in admitting ignorance. Even the most knowledgeable, clever and/or intelligent people will be ignorant about many things, because none of us can know everything. We all have wide gaps in our personal knowledge across all areas of knowledge. In fact, being aware of our ignorance gives us a huge advantage over those who are ignorant of their ignorance. Being aware of ignorance in any field of knowledge can spur us on to explore, research and learn more. It can also encourage us to call on experts for help, and be circumspect about our own conclusions.

"That's the guy I hired to read Proust for me."

EXPLORE 1.3

Look at the following problems. Which could you solve using your personal knowledge? Which could you solve if you did a little research? Which might you need to call an expert to help you with? What kind of expert might you call?

a   You need to know the name of the main protagonist in *Les Misérables*.

b   You need to do a school project on palm oil production.

c   Your knee is causing you pain.

d   You have broken the screen on your mobile phone.

e   You need to distil some water.

f   You are unable to sleep at night.

g   You want to improve your tennis skills.

h   You have been asked to create a costume for the school play.

One serious danger in relation to ignorance is when we believe that we know all there is to know, or that we know all that we need to know, in any field. For not only can we not know all there is to know, we also cannot even be fully aware of our own ignorance. This is why people who only know a little bit about a field of study often answer questions with far more confidence and **certainty** than those who have a much deeper understanding. This leads us to the **illusion of explanatory depth**.

If you were to ask a large number of people chosen randomly if they know how computers (or other familiar gadgets) work, many would say that they do. The same is true if you were to ask them if they understand about genetics, political systems or financial schemes such as mortgages, insurance, taxes, etc. If you then ask those same people to write a detailed **explanation** of how the object or system works, and then ask them to re-rate their knowledge, their personal rating of their self-knowledge tends to drop dramatically.

Multiple studies have been done testing people's self-knowledge on a vast array of objects or ideas, and the results always show a lower self-rating after participants are asked to explain what they know. You may have experienced the illusion of explanatory depth yourself if, for example, in the middle of an exam you belatedly realised that you did not understand something as well as you thought. This is one of the reasons why teachers often ask for essays and written answers.

As more and more information becomes readily available to us via the internet, as well as more traditional sources, we have a tendency to absorb a wide range of information but rarely in any depth. This can contribute to our illusion of explanatory depth.

KEY WORDS

certainty: the quality of having no doubt

illusion of explanatory depth: the illusion that you understand something in detail when you do not

explanation: an account or statement that makes something clear

---

REAL-LIFE SITUATION 1.6

You have probably done a great deal of reading about climate change and global warming, and the many contributing factors. How well do you think you understand the issue? Could you write a detailed explanation of it?

It has been suggested that highlighting the illusion of explanatory depth could be useful in combating political extremism, because it is found to underlie political issues too. The more ignorant we are about any issue, the more confident we tend to be that we understand it. Conversely, the more we know about an issue, the more humility we are likely to show. By becoming aware of the illusion of explanatory depth, we are more likely to recognise our modest understanding and be a little more open to other perspectives.

EXPLORE 1.4

Choose something that interests you and that you have some knowledge of. It could be a topic you have studied at school or a passion you have outside of the academic curriculum. Try to explain one aspect of it in around 300 words so that one of your classmates, who does not have the same knowledge of it, can understand your explanation clearly. How easy or difficult was it to write the explanation? Did you find yourself uncertain at any point while you were writing? To what extent does having to explain what you know help you to understand what you know better?

Self-assessment

Read through your work critically. Have you given a clear and accurate explanation of your topic? Do you think you have overestimated or underestimated your personal knowledge?

Peer-assessment

Exchange your work with that of a classmate and give each other feedback. Is the work as clear as your classmate thinks it is? Has your classmate overestimated or underestimated their knowledge of the topic? What did your classmate do well? What aspects of the work were most helpful? What could have been done to make the explanation clearer?

Figure 1.3: How easy or difficult might it be to explain how to ride a horse?

1.3 The knower as a member of different communities

DISCUSS 1.3

The social psychologist Hazel Rose Marcus (1949–) said, 'You can't be a self by yourself.' What do you think she meant?

Each of us is a member of multiple groups; some of them we may identify strongly with, and others, not so much. The groups that we identify strongly with are often known as our 'tribes'. Tribalism is the behaviour and attitudes that we exhibit as a result of belonging to those tribes.

A tribe can consist of any number of people – from a small number of close friends or a family group to a large global group, such as all the supporters of Manchester United Football Club. Tribes can be bound by ancestry, friendship, political or religious beliefs, common interests, etc. They typically demand loyalty in return for the security of belonging, and can sometimes do your thinking for you, in that your allegiance to your tribe may cause you to repeat the tribe's position on an issue. Of course, in being a member of a tribe, the tribe's thinking will influence your thinking, and your thinking might influence that of the tribe.

KEY WORD

tribalism: the behaviours and attitudes that arise out of loyalty to a social group

REAL-LIFE SITUATION 1.7

Can you think of examples in the past when you have gone along with your friends so as to belong to the group?

We cannot avoid belonging to tribes; it is part of human nature. But we can try to be more aware of the way in which our tribalism shapes our perspective on the world around us, and tempts us to form 'blind allegiances', even when our tribe may be wrong. Our 'side/tribe' is not necessarily right just because they are 'our side/tribe', but sometimes challenging or abandoning the beliefs of a tribe can make us very unpopular, or even cause outrage and place us in danger of retribution.

KEY WORDS

outrage: intense anger and shock

retribution: punishment inflicted in response to an action

REAL-LIFE SITUATION 1.8

Can you think of a time when you have been watching a sporting event and a player committed a foul? Fans on the same side as the offending player will often argue that the player was treated unfairly if the referee penalises the offending player, and the other side will shout that the referee was 'blind' if the player was *not* penalised. To what extent does what we see in a sporting event depend on where our loyalties lie: which tribe of fans we belong to?

Knowledge communities

Knowledge communities can be similar to tribes in that they consist of a group of people with a common interest, generally in a specific field of knowledge or activity.

Members of the knowledge community will share competencies, information and knowledge, often to achieve personal and/or collective goals. Examples of knowledge communities include a culture, a mathematics society, a medical association, a photography club and even a TOK class.

Some knowledge communities are formal organisations such as the Syrian Society for the Conservation of Wildlife, the Chinese Chemical Society, the British Medical Association or the African Institute for Applied Economics. Others are much more low-key, such as your local scout group or chess club. Even very informal meetings of people who gather together to enhance a particular aspect of their knowledge can be considered a knowledge community.

EXPLORE 1.5

Make a list of some of the tribes you are most loyal to, and some of the knowledge communities that you rely on. How easily can you disagree with members of your tribe, or leave the tribe to join another one? Which of the tribes you have listed contribute most to your knowledge and your sense of identity?

Knowledge communities are essential for the development or construction of new knowledge. It is largely within knowledge communities that knowledge is shared. This is particularly true of specialised knowledge such as that found in the natural sciences, but is also true of all accessible human knowledge. Knowledge communities act to preserve, challenge, communicate and grow knowledge through the actions of their members. Often they have a specialist language, their own sets of rules which may be written or unwritten, and their own assumptions. For example, the scientific community, which you will read about in Chapter 13 has very particular scientific methods. Within the different scientific disciplines, it publishes journals, acts as guardian and monitor of reliable and unreliable research, organises peer reviews and promotes public understanding. The mathematical knowledge community similarly shares more-or-less universally acknowledged standards of **proof** and truth, which is not to say that there are not vibrant arguments between professors of logic. The arts also have strong communities with their own experts and authorities, although arts communities are perhaps more specialised in that their standards and methodology are arguably less universal than in mathematics and the natural sciences.

KEY WORD

proof: conclusive evidence

Even the most solitary of thinkers are dependent upon knowledge communities for the context in which they work, and for the language that allows them to think and explore their disciplines. Also, any discoveries they make are subject to the scrutiny of their knowledge communities before new claims to knowledge are accepted.

DISCUSS 1.4

1   In what sense could the whole human species be regarded as a knowledge community?

2   To what extent does the internet allow people to by-pass the scrutiny of more traditional knowledge communities?

Shared knowledge

Shared knowledge is all knowledge that can be communicated between people. Knowledge communities, particularly academic knowledge communities, are large contributors to shared knowledge. A great deal of our general knowledge was originally produced by specialised knowledge communities. For example, the Event Horizon Telescope (EHT) is an international network of radio telescopes and a knowledge community of its collaborating astronomers, who maintain and work with those telescopes. In April 2019, the EHT produced new knowledge in the form of the first image of a black hole, which was shared around the world. If you have seen the image and now know what a black hole looks like, you have the EHT knowledge community to thank.

However, contributions to shared knowledge are not limited to knowledge communities. Individual knowers also contribute to shared knowledge whenever they pass on new knowledge that they have discovered or created. If, for example, you were to come across a fossil of a previously undiscovered creature and you send the fossil to a palaeontologist, you will have contributed to the development of new knowledge in palaeontology.

REAL-LIFE SITUATION 1.9

Can you think of any examples of knowledge that can only be personal, and is not – or cannot – be shared by other people?

Shared knowledge is something that we all rely on. Almost everything we own and use is the product of the collective knowledge of many people. The book that you are reading not only requires the knowledge of the authors, editors, photographers, proof readers, project managers and marketers, but also it needs the knowledge of the printers, the paper manufacturers, the people in the paper mill, the people who tend the plantations of trees from which the paper is made and many, many others. It also involves the sharing of language.

REAL-LIFE SITUATION 1.10

Can you think of any examples of shared knowledge that has been lost?

Even a simple product like rice involves multiple people with different knowledge and skills before we are able to buy the product. Look at the rice knowledge chain in Figure 1.4. As useful as it might be in identifying some of the people involved in the knowledge chain, it does not cover everyone. Missing are the packagers, advertisers and transporters, all of whom rely on specialised knowledge and equipment. Also missing are all of those involved in producing the equipment needed for production, collection, processing and marketing, and the legislative and governmental bodies who enable the coordination of the supply chains, and who control tariffs and international trade deals. Even the simplest ideas and products require knowledge contributions from a vast array of people.

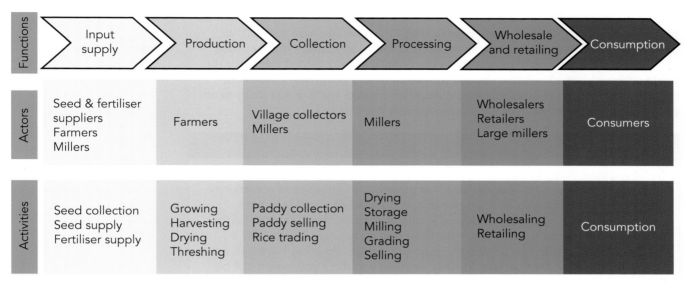

Figure 1.4: The rice knowledge chain

EXPLORE 1.6

If you had access to a sufficient number of cotton bushes, would you have the knowledge to be able to create a cotton t-shirt from scratch? Try to create a flow diagram or knowledge chain to show the different kinds of knowledge needed to go from harvesting raw cotton (or even from before the raw cotton, for example the planting, cultivation and growing of cotton) to a complete garment.

REAL-LIFE SITUATION 1.11

Can you think of anything that you could create from scratch using raw materials, which would not depend upon shared knowledge?

Knowing yourself

It is important to bear in mind that who we are as individual knowers is very much shaped by the tribes we belong to, the knowledge communities we participate in and our access to shared knowledge. In other words, our individual 'I' depends upon our collective 'we'. Think back to how you identified yourself in Explore activity 1.1.

REFLECTION

Imagine that you belong to different tribes than the ones you currently identify with, participate in different knowledge communities and have a different level of access to shared information. Would you still come to the same conclusions, draw the same inferences, learn the same lessons and, in effect, still be who you are today?

Everything that has happened in your life until now, the experiences you have had, the people you have met, the books you have read and the films you have watched, etc., has contributed to making you the person you are today. Sometimes you are aware of being changed; you might remember an event that suddenly caused you to see the world differently, or a book that opened your mind to new possibilities. However, most of the events that you experience in life do not change you in a way that you are conscious of. Nevertheless, they can have a considerable effect.

EXPLORE 1.7

Try to imagine that you were swapped at birth with another baby, and instead of growing up as you have done, you had grown up in an isolated community with a different culture to what you have now. Instead of going to school, you may have had to work from a very young age by fetching water, tending animals and harvesting crops. You may have had no access to electricity, so there would have been no television, radio or internet. You may have had no access to books or newspapers. In what ways do you think you would still be the same as you are now? In what ways might you be different?

Share your answers with a classmate. How similar are they? What do your answers say about personal identity?

Figure 1.5: Can you really know yourself?

KEY WORDS

objectivity: looking at the world in a detached way that focuses on facts, largely independent of a personal perspective, and that expects to be corroborated by a knowledge community

subjectivity: looking at the world from a personal point of view, under the influence of feelings and emotions

interpretation: an explanation of the meaning of something

REAL-LIFE SITUATION 1.12

Many people advocate 'staying true to oneself' – they will tell you to 'be yourself'. Others might say they are 'trying to find themselves'. What might these experiences and pieces of advice mean if the self is continually changing?

1.4 Objectivity and subjectivity

DISCUSS 1.5

What is the difference between objective knowledge and subjective knowledge?

When talking about knowledge and knowing, the question of objectivity and subjectivity usually arises. Objectivity involves factual and measurable information, whereas subjectivity is open to interpretation and personal judgements. There is a tendency for many people to see mathematics and the natural sciences as being particularly objective and the arts as being particularly subjective, with history and the human sciences as being somewhere in between while, perhaps, aspiring to be objective.

In the 17th century, the French philosopher, mathematician and scientist René Descartes (1596–1650) set out to extend the scientific method to all fields of human knowledge. He did this by renouncing scholasticism and beginning with doubting everything, thus initiating scepticism. Famously, he decided that the only thing he could not doubt was doubt itself. Therefore, he came to claim that, as a doubting thing, he must also be a thinking thing, and as a thinking thing, he must also be an existing thing: *Cogito, ergo sum* (I think, therefore I am). From this point, Descartes went on to deduce the existence of himself as a thinking being, and after several steps, reached the conclusion that the physical world is mechanistic and totally separate from the mind.

Although most of us would struggle to accept much of Descartes's reasoning today, his thought experiment has nevertheless been extremely influential. Since the 17th century, under the influence of Descartes and others, the natural sciences have sought to attain objectivity. From this perspective, scientific knowledge should not be influenced by personal perspectives, values or interests. Nor should it depend upon personal decisions. Indeed, many claim that objectivity is a characteristic of scientific claims, methods and results, and that objectivity is the basis for scientific authority and a strong reason for valuing scientific knowledge. But what exactly is 'objectivity', and can any of us claim to know anything completely without any kind of presupposition or prejudice?

Some people go so far as to insist that any knowledge that is not objective is not *real* knowledge; that the only *true* knowledge is objective and verifiable. From their perspective, the task of the knower and the knowledge community is to achieve detachment from whatever is being studied. However, as the physical chemist and polymath Michael Polanyi (1891–1976) demonstrated, this kind of detachment is not achievable, and arguably not even desirable.

In 1958, Michael Polanyi delivered the Gifford Lectures, later published as *Personal Knowledge*, in which he demonstrates that all knowledge claims rely on personal judgements. Knowers cannot stand apart from the world around them; they participate in it. This means that no knowledge can be entirely objective. Scientists (and *all* knowers) choose which questions to ask, which hypotheses to investigate, which data to accept and include, and so forth. These decisions are not dependent on

KEY WORDS

scholasticism: a method of learning characteristic of the Middle Ages, and based on logic and traditional beliefs about what is true

scepticism: an attitude of doubt; a method of obtaining knowledge through systematic doubt and continual testing

values: standards of behaviour; regard for things of important moral worth

authority: the moral or legal right to make decisions in, and take responsibility for, a particular field of knowledge or activity; the word can also be used to denote a person or group who has that authority

polymath: a person with expertise in several different fields of knowledge

knowledge claim: a statement in which we claim to *know* something

hypothesis (plural hypotheses): a proposed explanation or starting point, based on limited evidence that can be tested in an investigation

any mechanical method. Rather, they are the result of the passionate commitment of the knower, and all knowers are dependent on the culturally-relative (tribal) presuppositions of their time.

Some people still regard the world as simply being 'out there' as a set of concrete objects, with permanently-defined characteristics that exist independently of all knowers and knowing and are available for observation. However, there is a growing understanding that the world the knower sees is largely a product of the knower's particular values and sensory attributes. To some extent, this is a reformulation of the philosopher Immanuel Kant's claim that we filter and shape our sensory experiences using prior categories of knowing and understanding. In *The Critique of Pure Reason*, Kant (1724–1804) argues that the mind plays an active role in forming the features of experience. In this context, achieving objectivity might be considered an ethical enterprise in which rules are applied fairly to all sides, and bias is eliminated. Therefore, objectivity involves a commitment – on behalf of the knower and their knowledge communities – to honesty and fairness.

REAL-LIFE SITUATION 1.13

Everything we perceive about the world is perceived through our senses, so everything we know about the world is our brain's interpretation of the sensory information it receives. What are the implications of this for objectivity?

In his book *The Scientific Attitude*, biologist Fred Grinnel (1945–) observes, *'It is not unusual for two investigators to disagree about their observations if the investigators are looking at the data according to different conceptual frameworks.'* Much more is involved in observing than we sometimes realise.

Figure 1.6: What do you see in this photo?

EXPLORE 1.8

Look at Figure 1.6 of a young woman hugging a Yorkshire terrier. Describe what you see before reading on. Is the woman happy? Is the dog happy?

Many observers would see this simply as a 'sweet photo' of a young woman showing affection to a dog. Social media is flooded with such images. However, people with a basic understanding of dog behaviour would see something very different. While the woman looks relaxed and comfortable, there is **evidence** to show the dog is far from happy about the attention he is receiving. The dog is licking his lips, which is a sign of anxiety, and it appears as if he is trying to pull his head away. The white of his eye is showing, again indicating that the dog is uncomfortable and anxious. To someone who knows what to look for, the dog is clearly signalling that he is not happy with the hug. It is situations such as this that can easily lead to the dog biting. The dog is trying to give warnings but the warnings are not being seen by the woman or, presumably, by the photographer.

Even if you try to view the photograph objectively, your observations will be subjective because they are always informed by your knowledge and what you look for. If you were a keen photographer, you might analyse the photograph in terms of its composition, lighting, depth of field and so on, but you might not necessarily notice the dog's discomfort. However, a dog trainer might see the dog's discomfort but may not appreciate the technical attributes of the photograph. Even when aiming to be objective, we tend to see what we know.

> **KEY WORD**
>
> evidence: signs that you can see, hear, experience or read to support the truth of an assertion

DISCUSS 1.6

1. When you first looked at the photograph, did you see a cute photo or a potentially dangerous situation?

2. How does knowing something about how to read dog behaviour make your observations any more or less objective, or any more or less subjective?

REAL-LIFE SITUATION 1.14

To what extent is the misinterpretation of other people's body language (and, sometimes, spoken language) due to different contextual frameworks, amounts of background knowledge and degrees of understanding?

REFLECTION

Think about something you know from first-hand experience. To what extent is that knowledge subjective or objective? How do you decide?

1.5 Relativity, relativism and absolutism

DISCUSS 1.7

1 Is there such a thing as truth?

2 Are some things *always right* (such as compassion) and some things *always wrong* (such as cruelty), or does everything depend upon the context in which it occurs?

However thoroughly we scrutinise our knowing, we always know from a particular frame of reference. Even if we travel widely, understand many languages and have studied many different perspectives from the point of view of multiple cultures, we still must in the end *know from somewhere*. That 'somewhere' defines our frame of reference. Pure objectivity is unattainable; as the philosopher Thomas Nagel (1937–) put it, there is no 'View from Nowhere'.

Because there is no 'view from nowhere', our knowing is always necessarily affected by (and relative to) our frame of reference, which is the entire conceptual system defined by our knowledge, beliefs, language, culture and so on. This means that knowledge relativity is unavoidable and inescapable, but that is something quite different from relativism as a philosophy of knowledge.

Like relativity, relativism accepts that all knowledge is relative to a context and frame of reference, but relativism adds something more – it claims that in the end, what we take to be knowledge or truth is entirely a matter of our point of view. A strict relativist will say that if we want to believe that the moon is made of green cheese, that is up to us: we are entitled to our point of view; all things are 'relative' in a much more serious and potentially damaging sense. Relativists will allow us to believe in both creation science (the belief that science supports the creation narratives in the Book of Genesis) and evolution (the change in characteristics of a biological population over many generations) with equal fervour because it is, in the end, a matter of opinion and therefore up to us. Relativists will allow us to believe that the Earth is flat, that hanging garlic in the window deters vampires and that carbon-dating is unreliable because all of the carbon got wet in Noah's Flood, if we want to.

While this may seem like a list of silly ideas, there are some people who believe them. Equally there are people who believe potentially dangerous ideas such as 'homosexuality is sinful', 'males are superior to females' or 'vaccines cause autism'. The question each of us faces is, when should we be content to 'agree to disagree' and allowing that it is 'true for them', and when do we (or our communities/educational institutions) have a responsibility to argue that some beliefs are wrong?

KEY WORDS

relativity: recognising that knowledge claims are dependent on contextual factors or frames of reference

relativism: the belief that what might be true or right for one person or group need not be true or right for another person or group; that all truths are of equal value

responsibility: a duty or moral obligation

REAL-LIFE SITUATION 1.15

How can we decide which beliefs are acceptable and which are not?

Almost all countries restrict the behaviour of people living in them – whether as residents and citizens or merely as visitors – by applying the laws of that country irrespective of the beliefs or cultural practices of those people. For example, parents are not permitted to arrange or perform acts of female genital mutilation (FGM) on their daughters in countries where FGM is banned, nor can they take their daughters to countries that allow it for the purpose of having it done. Similarly, child marriage cannot be conducted or enforced in countries where it is banned, nor can the child be taken overseas to be married. In some countries, gay marriage may be prohibited. Most laws are not relativist; they usually apply equally to all residents, although some countries have different laws for men and women, and some countries have different laws for indigenous peoples.

DISCUSS 1.8

1   Where do you think the balance between law, culture, personal belief and freedom should lie?

2   How might a shift in the balance between law, culture, personal belief and freedom affect our perspective and what we regard as knowledge?

EXPLORE 1.9

Many countries have outlawed FGM, but male circumcision is widely practised by Jews, Muslims and some western societies (e.g. the USA). It is not outlawed anywhere in the world, although Greenland attempted to ban it except for health reasons in 2018 but withdrew the bill in the face of world-wide lobbying. Although male circumcision is usually not as extreme as FGM, it does carry risks, and is an unnecessary surgical procedure performed on children who are too young to give their consent, in the name of religion or culture.

1   Research the statistics of male circumcision in the country you live in, and consider whether your own attitude to male circumcision reflects that of the community you live in.

2   Write 500 words on the following: To what extent do our personal beliefs about what is normal, acceptable, tolerable or unacceptable mirror those of the community we are raised in?

Peer-assessment

Exchange your work with a partner and give each other feedback, using the following questions: Does the work focus on the question you were given? Are different perspectives considered? Does the work provide evidence in support of different perspectives?

In a world of uncertainty and conflicting belief systems, with many voices competing with different ideas about what is true, just or moral, many people embrace relativism because it appears to offer a ready resolution to the conflicts that could otherwise arise between people with different points of view. Relativism about truth, at its simplest, is the idea that just because something is true for one person or group does not mean that it is necessarily true for another person or group, and that we can all have our own truths.

We must be clear when talking about relativism not to confuse it with relativity. The fact that your idea of what is 'true' might be different from that of someone from a different culture is an example of relativity. The idea that all competing 'truths' are equal is relativism. The opposite of relativism is **absolutism**.

Relativist and absolute truth

The idea that truth is relative can promote **tolerance** when people have conflicting truths, but what happens when different cultures have different truths that they each hold to be absolute? The area of knowledge in which this is perhaps most clearly seen is religion. If your culture, religious authorities and personal beliefs all tell you that there is only one true God, and that all other gods are idolatrous or fake, you hold it as an absolute truth that your God is the only God. However, if you take a relativist position, you can say, 'My God is true for me and your God or your atheism is equally true for you.' This promotes a *live-and-let-live* attitude, which sometimes appears very attractive in today's world where many of us want to avoid conflict wherever possible.

People who hold absolutist religious views, including absolutist atheistic views, tend to be absolutist about morality as well. This can sometimes bring them into conflict with people who hold more moderate or tolerant views, people from different religions and people with no religion. Absolutist political positions can also be divisive, whether between socialists and capitalists, progressives and conservatives, monarchists and republicans or any other polarised positions.

It should be clear that having a definite preference for any one side in an argument, or where there is a choice, does not necessarily mean that you are absolutist. It may, for example, mean only that you hold a particular position with passion and deep **conviction**. Nor does accepting that other people think differently from you make you a relativist. If you understand that all views are relative to the contexts in which they arise, you are in a better position to try to listen to, and understand, different perspectives.

Religion and politics are not the only areas of knowledge where perspectives can range from relativism to absolutism. History, as the discipline where we try to understand, account for, and learn from the past, can also be written from both absolutist and relativist positions. A great deal of tampering with and rewriting of history happens because of politics and national interest.

One example where there are entrenched positions on both sides involves the massacre of Armenians by the Turks between 1915 and 1923. Both the Turks and the Armenians agree that many Armenians died, but Turkey disputes the one-and-a-half million deaths claimed by Armenia. Turkey argues that the Armenian alliance with Russia led to assaults on Turkish villages, so the Ottoman rulers had no choice but to drive out the Armenians. Turkey also claims that it had tried to relocate the Armenians as humanely as possible, but the violent political aims of the Armenians, along with war-time conditions, banditry, general famine, health epidemics and a collapsing state, all combined to bring about the tragedy in a way that the Turks of the day had not expected. It argues that many Turks also suffered and died during the hardships of the period. In the Turkish perspective, there was tragedy affecting all sides, but definitely no genocide.

KEY WORDS

absolutism: belief in absolute truth and absolute cultural, religious, political and moral standards against which all other views can be judged

tolerance: acceptance of different perspectives and behaviours, even if you disagree with them

conviction: a firmly held belief

Armenia, on the other hand, claims that the massacres of Armenians in the Ottoman Empire were all part of an orchestrated genocide, and that many Assyrians, Greeks and Arabs were also massacred. The Armenian massacres have been recognised as genocide by a number of countries and international organisations because of the organised way in which the killings happened, but other nations have stopped short of using the word 'genocide', sometimes for political reasons.

Perhaps not surprisingly, Turkish students learn very little in school about the events of the early-20th century, and they do not learn about a genocide perpetrated against the Armenians because in their 'truth', there was no genocide to study. However, in Armenia, the Armenian genocide is taught as an absolute fact in every Armenian school, and plays a significant role in the formation of modern Armenian identity.

DISCUSS 1.9

To what extent does our understanding of the past shape us as knowers?

Cultural relativity and cultural relativism

Acceptance of cultural relativity provides a pragmatic approach to dealing with cultural differences. Different societies, each with their own cultures, have different ideas about how their members should behave. They often have different rules, laws, moral ideas, mythologies and worldviews. Whereas inevitable differences

Figure 1.7: Tipping is not acceptable in all cultures

in perspectives make cultural relativity a fact, cultural relativism maintains that all cultural perspectives are equally valuable and valid. Cultural relativism, then, can be helpful in teaching us to be respectful of different societies, cultures and religions. What is acceptable or even mandatory in some cultures might be unacceptable in others, but relativism says that no one set of cultural values is better than another.

The practice of tipping (paying a gratuity in return for service) offers an interesting example. In some cultures, such as in the USA, tipping is an important feature of life, and there is a strong expectation that you will give a tip of 15–25% of your bill to people who provide a service such as waiting staff, taxi drivers and hairdressers. Tipping provides a substantial portion of the incomes for many service workers, and although it is not illegal, it is considered very rude not to tip in America.

In China, on the other hand, offering a tip to waiting staff or taxi drivers is considered quite offensive. In Chinese culture, offering a tip is seen to imply that you think the person you are offering the money to is incapable of supporting themselves without charity. This causes them a 'loss of face' and is viewed as very rude.

This kind of cultural relativity is interesting and might seem **quaint**, but few people would feel uneasy about it. Whether tipping is a feature of a culture seems somewhat arbitrary, and neither system seems unequivocally superior to the other, therefore cultural relativism would seem to be a reasonable position in this case. Most of us could learn to tip in America but not in China without any qualms, and most travel information sources are able to tell travellers about the tipping expectations in the countries they might be visiting, so as to avoid inadvertently causing offence.

Cultural relativism can be valuable in that it encourages us to not judge other cultures by our own standards of right and wrong, or some sense of what is 'normal'. Instead, we are encouraged to try to understand different cultural practices within their own cultural contexts. However, not all cultural differences are as **benign** as the topic of tipping.

Moral relativism

What is regarded as **ethical** or **moral** can also vary between cultures, and this is where relativism becomes rather more contentious. For example, some countries regard child marriage as unethical, whereas in other countries, including the USA, it may be acceptable, commonplace and even encouraged. Similarly, the drinking of alcohol is acceptable in some countries but banned in others.

KEY WORDS
quaint: pleasantly, amusingly or interestingly strange
benign: harmless, non-threatening, innocent

KEY WORDS
ethical: conforming to accepted moral standards
moral: following one's personal principles of what is right or wrong

REAL-LIFE SITUATION 1.16

1 If you come from a culture in which child marriage is regarded as unethical and harmful to the child, do you have a responsibility to speak out against the practice in cultures which allow it, or should you accept it as an example of cultural relativity?

2 If you come from a country in which practices like child marriage are acceptable, even if not encouraged, does this make them ethical? How would you decide?

EXPLORE 1.10

Everyone has different ideas about when we can live with moral and cultural relativity and when we should try to enforce our own beliefs.

In pairs, look at the following table and try to decide whether the activity listed on the left should be mandatory for every culture, banned in every culture, left up to each culture as to whether they ban or enforce it or left up to each individual according to their own preferences?

	Should be mandatory in all cultures	Should be banned in all cultures	Should be the choice of each culture	Should be the choice of individuals
Hunting whales				
Racial segregation				
Gender segregation				
Child marriage				
Tipping				
Safeguarding human rights				
Eating meat				
Drinking alcohol				
Using recreational drugs				
The death penalty				
Animal welfare				
Child labour				
Slavery				
Teaching creationism				
Teaching evolution				
Gay marriage				
Safeguarding women's rights				
Smoking				
Carrying guns in public				
Polygyny				
Polyandry				

CONTINUED

Do you and your partner agree in very case? In cases where you do agree, do you agree on the reasons why? How many of your reasons are based on received cultural or religious values (i.e. *'our culture/religion believes…'*)?

In cases where you do not agree, what are your reasons for the position you hold? Why are you not persuaded by your partner's reasons? How might you decide which of you is right? Is it even necessary for only one of you to be right? Explain your answers.

How you filled in the table will partly depend on how relativistic you are. If you found yourself wanting to ban most or all things, you have very fixed views. If you found yourself wanting to leave most things to individual conscience or preference, you are correspondingly liberal or relativist. If you think *everything* is relative, you believe that *nothing* is universally true or false, right or wrong. Many people oppose moral relativism because it seems to imply that there is no objective reality or truth, and it appears to give people licence to do whatever they like.

Of course, few of us are totally absolutist or relativist. We tend to be open-minded about some things but have definite ideas about right and wrong about other activities. The question remains: *How do we as knowers decide which activities we should keep an open mind on, and which we should be clearly for or against?*

DISCUSS 1.10

1   When different countries disagree on what is morally acceptable and what is not, who gets to decide and how?

2   Are all points of view equal? Why? Why not?

Figure 1.8: Not all cultures accept gay marriage

Despite its attractions, relativism can lead to many problems. The fact that we take seriously the idea that someone might be wrong in their beliefs suggests that in general we believe that relativism is false. Indeed, it could be argued that the statement 'All truth is relative' is self-contradictory: if it is absolutely true that all truth is relative, then this means that there is at least one absolute truth – namely the truth that all truth is relative.

DISCUSS 1.11

Richard Hofstadter (1916–1970) made the claim that the distinction between moral relativism and moral absolutism is sometimes blurred because excesses in either can lead to the same practical result. What does he mean? Do you agree?

Linguistic relativity

Cultural relativity is strongly linked to linguistic relativity because culture shapes language, and language shapes culture. The literature on how language works is vast, and there are many theories about the ways in which language defines our world. The philosopher Ludwig Wittgenstein (1889–1951) once famously wrote *'The limits of my language mean the limits of my world'* and many philosophers have tried to say that we cannot think things unless we have the language to express them.

This is particularly important when we consider the interconnectedness of words. Language forms a web of meanings that shift constantly as we use it to express different things and adapt it to new circumstances. The philosopher and logician Willard Van Orman Quine (1908–2000) spoke of language as being like a rubber sheet that distorts and stretches as usage changes. This image suggests that language both influences what we can think and is influenced by the things we want to say.

Linguistic relativity refers to the idea that the way we think is strongly influenced by the language we speak. There are certain thoughts that we might have in one language which cannot be expressed or understood adequately in another language, because the word equivalents, and the concepts underlying those words, do not exist in all languages. This is particularly important in the context of cultural relativity.

Learning a new language does not just involve learning new words and a new grammar. We have to learn the cultural contexts that are embedded in the language. Languages reflect cultural experiences, and understanding a language properly requires knowledge of the cultures that shaped them.

Some people might argue that although languages differ from each other in many ways, the ways in which humans experience the world are very similar, and therefore we should expect to be able to convey similar ideas, regardless of the language we use. Others claim that differences between languages not only influence the way that people think, but may also actually influence the way cultures are organised. This is known as linguistic determinism.

Linguistic determinism can be seen where a language draws attention to particular aspects of experience. A simple example of this would be the use of the second-person address. In English, we use the word *you* for both singular and plural, and this is

---

KEY WORD

linguistic determinism: the idea that language and its structures determine human knowledge, thought and thought processes

---

appropriate for any individual you are speaking to. In French, there are two words: *vous* and *tu* for speaking to an individual. The word *tu* is an informal word mostly used for addressing children (unless they are of higher social status), close friends and family, although not always for spouses or parents. The word *vous* is more formal, and is used in most other situations (and is also always used for second person plural). In other words, before you can know which form of address to use when speaking French, you must first categorise your relationships.

Chinese also has two words for the second-person singular: the more informal and widely-used 你 (*nǐ*), and the more formal word, 您 (*nín*). In Chinese, the formal word for you, 您 *nín*, is used in a deferential way, quite unlike the use of *vous* in French.

DISCUSS 1.12

If one culture divides people into two groups – those to whom a person is close and others, and another culture divides people into two different groups – people of high status and others, how might the linguistic differences be reflected in daily interactions within those cultures?

It should be noted that there has been a tendency towards a more informal approach in French in recent decades, with more people using the word *tu* in wider situations, just as in English there has been a tendency to use first names to address people rather than using titles and surnames. However, in both cases it is possible to cause offence by being too formal or too informal. We will consider the impact of language on the knower and knowledge in greater detail in Chapter 6 on knowledge and language.

EXPLORE 1.11

Make a list of 20 people from different situations that you might come into contact with. Which of them would you address as *tu* and which would you address as *vous*? Are there any that you find difficult to decide on? Then decide who you would address as 你 (*nǐ*) and who you might address as 您 (*nín*). Was this easier or more difficult to decide?

If your native language has only one word for second-person singular, how might having two words change your thinking? If your native language has two or more words for second-person singular, in what way does using the availability of just one word in English affect the way you think?

REAL-LIFE SITUATION 1.17

In some schools, students are expected to address their teachers as *Ma'am* or *Sir*. In others, students are expected to use titles and surnames (e.g. *Ms Granger, Mr Zavala*). There are some schools where students address teachers by their first names.

CONTINUED

1   How might the different forms of address change the way you think about your teachers?

2   Would it make a difference if you used the same form of address for all teachers in your school, or if you used different forms of address for different teachers?

REFLECTION

Have you ever made assumptions about someone based on the way they use language or the style of language they use? Are such assumptions reasonable? Why? Why not?

1.6 Common sense

DISCUSS 1.13

You may have heard the expression, 'The trouble with common sense is that there is nothing common about sense.' What do you think it means? Do you agree and why?

Common sense consists of those layers of prejudice laid down before the age of 18.

Albert Einstein (1879–1955)

Common sense might be described as the idea that we can make sound judgements in every-day situations, and understand every-day concepts without having any specialised knowledge. People who are regarded as having common sense are usually regarded as reasonable, sensible, down-to-earth, practical and reliable. It is called *common* sense because it is assumed to be held by a large number of people. In other words, it is widely found and *commonly* held.

Many people would regard common sense as plain, self-evident truths that need no proof and can be grasped easily, because they accord with the common experiences of almost everyone. It is a basic awareness and ability to judge that most people would 'naturally' share, even if they cannot explain why.

Common sense is believed to be largely based on experience, so people who are regarded as having more life experiences are often thought to have more common sense than those who have had a more sheltered background. There is a general expectation that if people were to use their common sense, the world would function more smoothly, and fewer errors or accidents would happen. There is a popular caricature of intellectuals and academics that portrays them to have led sheltered lives and lack common sense.

KEY WORD

caricature: comic exaggeration

If we are to take the idea of common sense seriously, we need to consider why some people seem to have it and others do not, and whether it really is sensible. One response is that common sense is not so common because our upbringings and experiences are not commonly shared. If our awareness of situations is dependent upon our past experiences, we should all expect to have different levels of awareness and sense. For example, someone raised on a farm could see the right behaviour around livestock as a matter of 'common sense', but people from non-rural backgrounds might not share it.

Others argue that there is nothing sensible about common sense because few people have enough experience to make sound judgements or draw reliable conclusions. They would argue that common sense is what people use when they do not have the knowledge or expertise to actually make sound judgements.

REAL-LIFE SITUATION 1.18

To what extent do you, as a knower, rely upon common sense to navigate your way in the world?

EXPLORE 1.12

Look at the following list of situations in which you need to make a judgement. In which of them, if any, can you rely on your common sense?

a   knowing how to keep safe in the science labs

b   knowing what to do in the event of an earthquake

c   knowing when to ask for help

d   knowing whether to lock your door when you leave your house

e   knowing whether to play computer games long into the night

Look critically at your answers to this activity. In which of the situations have you been taught what to do? In which of the situations are you unsure what to do? Are there some situations in which you might know or intuit the right thing to do, but choose not to do it anyway? To what extent do you really *rely* on common sense?

KEY WORD

fallacy: a mistaken belief; an invalid argument

Some people say that the notion of common sense is a **fallacy** used to close down an argument. For example, *'Of course you should do that; it's just common sense.'* This suggests that common sense refers to an assumption of shared knowledge. When common sense is referred to, it rarely adds any value to a conversation other than to indicate that the speaker assumes something to be true.

Figure 1.9: Fixing a problem might seem to be common sense, but is life really that easy?

EXPLORE 1.13

Look at the following statements that refer to common sense. For each statement, what is the assumption of shared knowledge being made? Do you think the assumption is true?

a It is common sense that you would not allow a child to go to the park alone.

b It is common sense to stay out of the sun.

c It is common sense not to leave your assignment until the last minute.

d It is common sense not to drink two bottles of vodka in one evening.

If you wanted to make the same points without appealing to common sense, what kind of evidence might you present? If you wanted to argue the opposite of these statements, what kind of evidence might you present? In what contexts could the opposites also be regarded as common sense?

Divide the class into two teams and choose one of the statements for a class debate. (Larger classes might wish to break into more teams, and have each pair of teams choose different statements to debate.)

Self-assessment

How easily could you answer the questions in the Explore activity? Are you confident that you can now explain the role of common sense for the knower?

DISCUSS 1.14

To what extent does common sense differ between cultures?

The role of judgement

Judgement is the cognitive process involved in reaching decisions, drawing sound conclusions and forming opinions. We also rely on our judgement to show **discernment** about people, situations and ideas.

To make good judgements, you need to consider and evaluate evidence from various sources. This is particularly true when you are considering whether to believe information you find on the internet. Good judgements require time to reflect on the situation, investigate and assess the evidence and reach a decision that is both rational and in keeping with one's values. They also involve reflecting honestly on your own preferences and biases, and being prepared to set these aside to make a fair judgement. If you have gone through these steps in a fair and honest way, you can say that your judgement is **justified**.

REFLECTION

Being able to reflect honestly on your own preferences and biases is not as easy as it sounds. Often, we are unaware of the biases we have. Try to reflect on what your preferences and biases are in relation to a topical issue that interests you. To what extent do you think you could set them aside?

Whether you are looking for information for an essay, the latest news updates, information or reviews about a product or you are following a special interest, it is important to keep an open mind while maintaining a healthy scepticism. In other words, you should not believe something simply because you have read it, but neither should you assume that something is false just because it is unusual or unexpected.

EXPLORE 1.14

Following a YouGov survey of 8,215 adults in the USA, in February 2018, there were some headlines that read 'One-third of millennials believe that the world is flat'. Given that YouGov is a reputable survey company, would you accept this headline as fact? What further information would you need to make a judgement? Why might a journalist or editor choose to use a headline that misrepresents a story?

In pairs, do some research about the survey and come up with a headline that, in your judgement, best represents the findings of the survey. Compare your headline with those created by others in the class. Can you justify the headline you created?

DISCUSS 1.15

On what basis might you decide between different judgements?

1.7 Conclusion

In this chapter, we have seen that the concept of the knower is perhaps not as straightforward as you may have imagined. Each of us is a unique combination of our DNA and life experiences, when and where we live, the tribes and knowledge communities we belong to, the languages we speak and the ways in which we view and describe the world around us.

We have also seen that how we know and understand ourselves is largely a function of how we are perceived by others, and that it is the knowledge communities we belong to that help to provide some semblance of objectivity by cross-checking knowledge claims, providing different perspectives and challenging our biases. In short, we do not always know what we do not know, and we are not necessarily secure in knowing what we think we do know. We are all vulnerable to the illusion of explanatory depth, and we owe it to ourselves as knowers to become more secure in our knowledge if we want to expand that knowledge or use it to support our arguments.

As knowers we need to become more aware of our own assumptions and perspectives, and find a balance between being open to new ideas that challenge our current way of thinking, while keeping in mind that human beings are credulous animals who are sometimes willing to believe strange things on the basis of slender evidence. For the increase in human knowledge to be secure, it needs to be accompanied by an increased resistance to being deceived.

KNOWLEDGE QUESTIONS

1   What room is there for personal interpretation / cultural differences in different areas of knowledge?

2   To what extent can we be objective about the impact of our culture on what we believe or know?

3   What is the role of personal experience in the construction of knowledge?

1.8 Linking questions

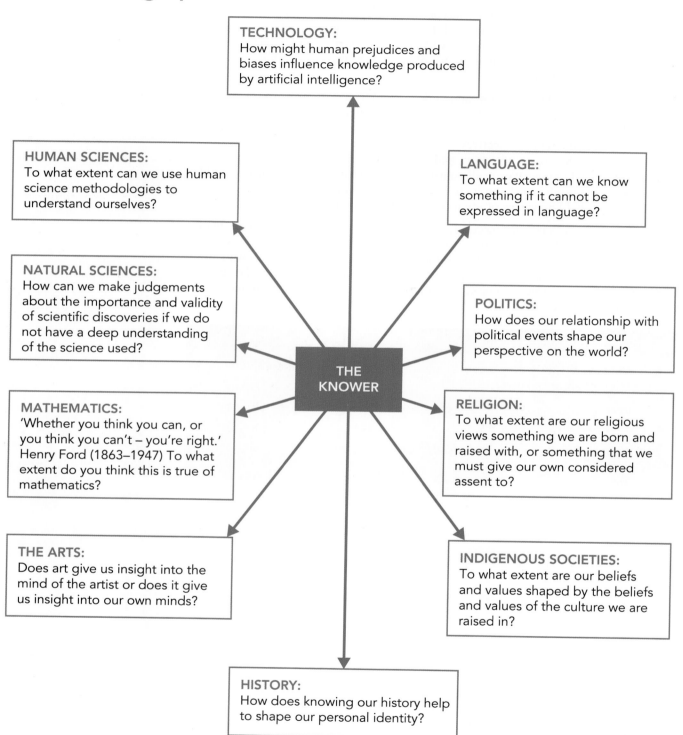

TECHNOLOGY:
How might human prejudices and biases influence knowledge produced by artificial intelligence?

HUMAN SCIENCES:
To what extent can we use human science methodologies to understand ourselves?

LANGUAGE:
To what extent can we know something if it cannot be expressed in language?

NATURAL SCIENCES:
How can we make judgements about the importance and validity of scientific discoveries if we do not have a deep understanding of the science used?

POLITICS:
How does our relationship with political events shape our perspective on the world?

THE KNOWER

MATHEMATICS:
'Whether you think you can, or you think you can't – you're right.' Henry Ford (1863–1947) To what extent do you think this is true of mathematics?

RELIGION:
To what extent are our religious views something we are born and raised with, or something that we must give our own considered assent to?

THE ARTS:
Does art give us insight into the mind of the artist or does it give us insight into our own minds?

INDIGENOUS SOCIETIES:
To what extent are our beliefs and values shaped by the beliefs and values of the culture we are raised in?

HISTORY:
How does knowing our history help to shape our personal identity?

1.9 Check your progress

Reflect on what you have learnt in this chapter, and indicate your confidence level between 1 and 5 (where 5 is the highest score and 1 is the lowest). If you score below 3, re-visit that section. Come back to this list later in your course. Has your confidence grown?

	Confidence level	Re-visited?
Can I examine my own sense of self, and do I appreciate how my sense of self can influence my perspective?		
Am I able to articulate what shapes me as a knower?		
Can I explain the difference between innate knowledge and experiential knowledge?		
Do I understand how I can overestimate and underestimate my personal knowledge?		
Can I discuss the self in relation to tribalism?		
Am I aware of the role of knowledge communities in producing, preserving, challenging and communicating knowledge?		
Can I discuss the importance of shared knowledge?		
Can I explain what is meant by objectivity and subjectivity, and can I articulate why objectivity necessarily involves a subjective dimension?		
Do I understand the difference between relativity and relativism, and their implications?		
Am I able to articulate some of the issues associated with absolutist positions?		
Do I know what is meant by 'common sense', and am I aware of the role it plays?		
Do I appreciate what is necessary to make good judgements?		

1.10 Continue your journey

- To build on the knowledge that you have gained in this chapter, you could read some of the following articles.

- To extend your understanding of **tribalism**, read: George Packer, 'A New Report Offers Insights into Tribalism in the Age of Trump', in *The New Yorker*, 12 October 2018. Search the *New Yorker* website for this article.

- If you would like to explore the **ethical and legal issues surrounding circumcision**, read: Lauren Notini and Brian D. Earp, 'Should Iceland Ban Circumcision? A Legal and Ethical Analysis', in *The BMJ*, 22 April 2018. Search the *BMJ* website for this article.

- For more on **objectivity and subjectivity**, read: Janet D. Stemwedel, 'The Ideal of Objectivity', in *The Scientific American*, 26 February 2013. Search the *Scientific American* website for this article.

- To delve more deeply into the **concept of common sense**, read: Jim Taylor, 'Common Sense is Neither Common nor Sense', in *Psychology Today*, 12 July 2011. Search the *Psychology Today* website for this article.

- For more on **common sense**, read: Angelica Vecchio-Sadus, *Common sense – 'How common is it and does it make sense?'*, in *Safety Institute Australia,* 31 August 2010. Search the *Australian Institute of Health and Safety* website for this article.

Chapter 2

The problem of knowledge

LEARNING INTENTIONS

This chapter will explore what we mean by knowledge, and some of the problems that we have in deciding what counts as knowledge.

You will:

- consider what we mean by knowledge, laws, theories, information and data, and be able to articulate why *knowledge* cannot be clearly defined

- understand the subjective nature of different types of knowledge, and be able to talk about different ways in which knowledge might be classified

- explore different levels of knowledge, including depth and breadth of knowledge

- be aware of how we access our own knowledge, the role of memory and how language can affect what we know

- understand what is meant by misinformation, disinformation and fake news, be aware of confirmation bias and critically assess sources of information so as not to be misled or to unwittingly mislead others

- understand the importance of trust in the act of knowing

BEFORE YOU START

Analyse each of the following quotations and discuss the questions that follow.

1   'Real knowledge is to know the extent of one's ignorance.' **Kong Fu Zi** (551–479 BCE)

2   'The greatest obstacle to progress is not the absence of knowledge but the illusion of knowledge.' **Daniel Boorstin** (1914–2004)

3   'The possession of knowledge does not kill the sense of wonder and mystery. There is always more mystery.' **Anais Nin** (1903–1977)

4   'The immediacy and volume of information should not be confused with true knowledge.' **Maryanne Wolf** (1950–)

5   'If we would have new knowledge, we must get a whole world of new questions.' **Susanne K. Langer** (1895–1985)

For each quotation, consider:

a   To what extent do you agree or disagree with the quotation?

b   How might you challenge the quotation?

c   What does the quotation tell you about the speaker's perspective on knowledge, and what are the implications for us as knowers?

d   Do you think the quotation could apply to all types of knowledge, in all areas of knowledge and all knowledge communities?

2.1 Introduction

A major characteristic of *homo sapiens* that separates us from all other known species is that we do not have to begin from scratch in every generation. Whereas new-born animals of other species have to rely upon what is transmitted in their genes and the limited extent to which their parents or group (be it pack, troop, herd or flock) can teach them, new-born humans have at their disposal an unimaginably vast store of knowledge and skills that they can inherit from the multiple generations that precede them.

Because knowledge is so important, people have needed to address the question of *how we know*, the *problems of knowing* and in particular, *how to avoid mistakes in knowing*. To do this, we will need to consider what knowledge is, how it is distinct from facts, opinions and beliefs, and the problems that we as knowers have with being secure in our knowledge.

2.2 What is knowledge?

DISCUSS 2.1

What do we mean when we say we *know* something?

We all speak of knowledge and knowing as though we have an understanding of what knowledge is and what it means to know. However, despite thousands of years of trying, philosophers have yet to come up with a definition for knowledge that satisfies everyone and every situation.

One philosophical definition of knowledge you may have come across is knowledge as *justified, true belief* (JTB), which was first proposed, and later rejected, by the Greek philosopher Plato (c 427–348 BCE). Firstly, this definition requires that what we know is a belief. Secondly, the belief must be justified, and thirdly, it must be true.

While it is necessary that we believe what we know according to this definition, we are all capable of believing things that are later shown to be false, so most philosophers have decided that belief is a necessary but insufficient condition of knowledge. In other words, you have to believe something to be true before you can claim to know it, but it is not enough to believe it to be true for you to be able to claim to know it. For example, you may believe that Canberra is the capital of Australia, and can also claim to know it. But if you were to believe that Colombo is the capital of Sri Lanka, and claim that you know it, your claim would be false. Believing it to be true is not the same as knowing it. In fact, the capital of Sri Lanka is actually Sri Jayawardenepura Kotte.

KEY WORDS

justified: reasonable, based on evidence

true: correct, factual, accurate or honest

belief: opinion; something thought to be true

DISCUSS 2.2

Is it possible to *know* something but not believe it? Would it still count as *knowledge*?

The second requirement of JTB is that the belief must be justified. However, we can be justified in believing many things that later prove to be false. The ancient Greeks were justified in believing that the sun revolves around the Earth because the evidence they had supported that belief. They could see the sun moving across the sky each day, and they had no sense of Earth moving, so it was very reasonable for them to believe that the sun moved around the Earth.

The belief that the sun moves around the Earth fails to be knowledge according to the definition *justified true belief* because it turned out not to be true. But requiring any knowledge to be JTB ignores the question 'how do we know what is true?' The ancient Greeks would have understood their belief in a geocentric (Earth-centred) model of the universe to be a *true, justified belief*, even though we now know they were wrong. As human knowledge and technology have grown, further evidence has supplanted beliefs that previously seemed to be justified and true. As knowers, we are dependent on many factors for our knowledge, including the point in time that we happen to live in.

There are many cases in which we do not know what is true, and we cannot know with certainty. As you will discover in Chapter 13, we can prove things to be false, but we have a great deal more difficulty proving something to be true.

REAL-LIFE SITUATION 2.1

Given that the ancient Greeks regarded themselves as having a *true, justified belief* in a geocentric model of the universe, can we say that, at the time, the ancient Greeks *knew* that the sun orbited the Earth?

Although there have been problems with JTB since Plato first mooted the definition, and many philosophers have argued against it, including Plato himself, the American philosopher Edmund Gettier is most closely associated with a repudiation of JTB through what has been called a Gettier case.

Gettier cases (also known as Gettier problems) highlight justified true beliefs in which the justification is flawed, but the belief is none-the-less true as a matter of luck.

KEY WORD

Gettier case: an example of a justified true belief that does not appear to be knowledge

Figure 2.1: Can you *know* something by accident?

EXPLORE 2.1

Research the Gettier case and try to create your own example. Present it to a classmate, explaining how it illustrates a JTB that is not true knowledge.

Peer-assessment

Listen to your partner's presentation of their Gettier case. Does your partner's example show that someone can have a JTB without having knowledge? Does your partner understand fully why the example presented is not knowledge? How can you use the examples produced to help each other better understand what knowledge is?

DISCUSS 2.3

Why is being right about something not the same as *knowing* it?

Knowledge is inescapably contextually and culturally relative; there is no **God's eye view** that humans have access to. Although there may possibly be things that are universally true, we have no clear access to them except within a framework that we devise. We cannot always be certain about what we believe to be true or about what we believe to be justified. Combining the demand for truth and justification to apply to a belief gives no more certainty than a justified belief. All we can say of knowledge is that it is *the best we can do right now*, given our community's current beliefs about what is true and the evidence available to us. We need to be prepared to accept that our evidence may change, and our community's beliefs about what is true may at some point be overturned. Our culture may primarily value scientific or quantitative evidence as justification for its beliefs, but there could be alternatives. For example, you might be able to imagine a society that values beauty and aesthetics as a condition of knowledge. According to such a society we could decide that there are more beautiful ways of thinking of the universe, and come to base what we regard as knowledge on forms of aesthetic evidence.

In 1903, A.A. Michelson (1852–1931), the first American to win a Nobel Prize in physics, famously wrote, 'The more important fundamental laws and facts of physical science have all been discovered, and these are now so firmly established that the possibility of their ever being supplanted in consequence of new discoveries is exceedingly remote.' He wrote this just two years before the physicist Albert Einstein (1879–1955) discovered the *special theory of relativity* and 12 years before Einstein published the *General Theory of Relativity* which overturned most of physics as it was then known.

More *common-sense* approaches to the definition of knowledge have tried to equate knowledge with certainty, evidence, practicality, broad agreement and community agreement, but none of these is perfect, and even taken all together, they cannot give us an **infallible** method of knowing something to be certain knowledge. Certainty, like truth, cannot be guaranteed. Evidence can be persuasive, but there is always the possibility of further evidence overturning – or at least modifying – what we believe. 'Knowledge' is what we use to answer questions about *how* and *why*, and is essential for making any kind of practical progress. However, even practical 'knowledge' can still be false, and no amount of agreement or evidence can guarantee that our 'knowledge' is correct, not least because evidence needs to be interpreted relative to a framework of ideas, or **paradigm**. As a result, many things that were once regarded as *common* knowledge are now known to be false.

When Australian scientists Barry Marshall (1951–) and Robin Warren (1937–) first began research into the causes of ulcers in the early 1980s, many scientists told them they were wasting their time because *everybody knew* that ulcers were caused by stress, and exacerbated by a poor diet. All of the evidence at the time pointed to stressful lifestyles as the cause, and the medical community, as well as the wider community, were in agreement. At that time, ulcers were typically treated with advice about working less, life-long bland diets and pills to try to protect the lining of the digestive system, and this treatment regime seemed to work in practice by reducing the severity of the symptoms of ulcers, even though it could not cure them.

However, Marshall and Warren were undeterred by the dismissive attitude of the scientific community, and in 2005, they won the Nobel Prize for medicine after

KEY WORD

God's eye view: when a knower assumes that they have access to knowledge that only an omniscient god could have

KEY WORDS

infallible: not capable of being wrong or making mistakes

paradigm: a model or example that provides a framework of understanding

demonstrating that ulcers are caused by bacteria, and can be cured, rather than simply relieved, with a course of antibiotics.

The findings of Marshall and Warren illustrate not only that human knowledge builds up from one discovery to the next, but also that it is possible to overturn 'knowledge' that once seemed certain. If this were not so, neither knowledge nor science could ever make progress.

Other examples of supposed knowledge that have been overturned include:

- a once-held belief that the expansion of the universe was slowing down, to the new belief that the expansion is speeding up

- a once-held belief that the more **complex** the organism, the more genes it would have, and that humans would have around 100,000 genes. However, in 2003 the Human Genome Project showed that humans only have 19–20,000 genes while the *Daphnia* water flea has been discovered to have about 31,000 genes

- a once-held belief that only humans use tools whereas many animals, including some birds, are now known to use tools

- a once-held belief that **phlogiston** is an element in all combustible materials, and is released when burnt was very popular among scientists until oxygen was discovered

- a once-held belief that babies (and non-human animals) do not feel pain. (It was not until 1987 that it became illegal in the USA to operate on young babies without an anaesthetic)

> **KEY WORDS**
>
> **complex:** complicated, multifaceted
>
> **phlogiston:** a hypothetical component of combustible substances

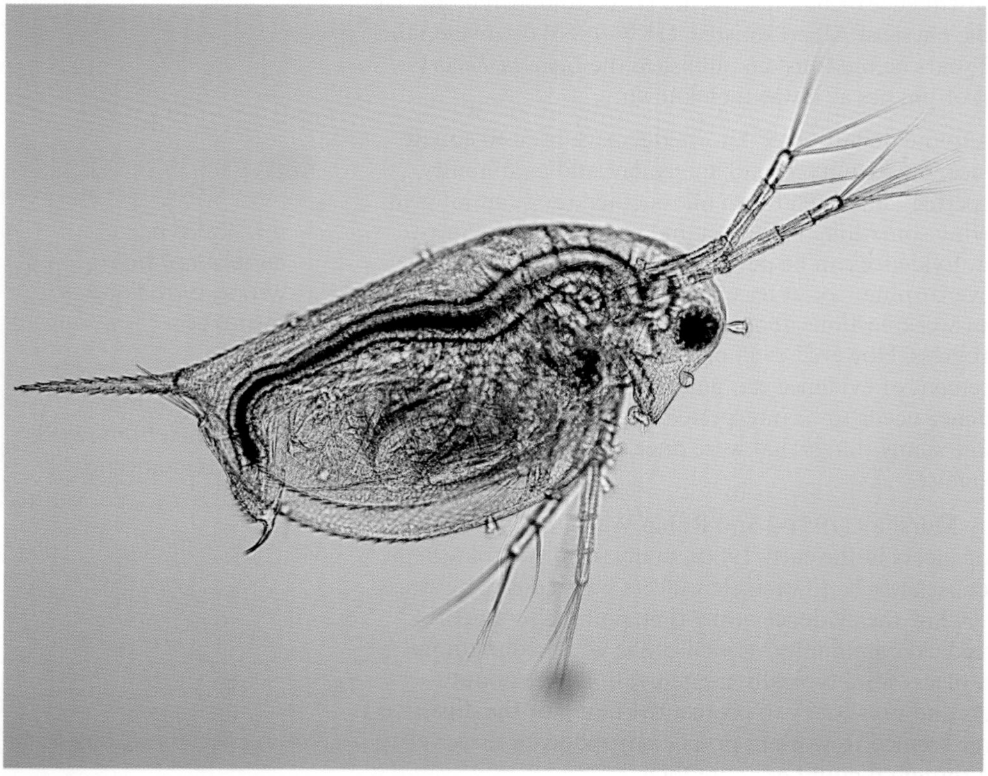

Figure 2.2: *Daphnia* water fleas were found to have many more genes than human beings.

REAL-LIFE SITUATION 2.2

It used to be believed that the more complex the organism, the more genes it would have. Why might people have believed that having more genes would lead to greater complexity? Do you think this belief was justified?

EXPLORE 2.2

Choose one of the examples of supposed knowledge that was later refuted (or find another) and try to understand why the initial belief was considered to be knowledge. What was the evidence to support the initial belief? Was the belief widely accepted to be true? Was the belief, even if it later proved false, useful in any way? Write 250 words on whether you think people were *justified* in regarding the initial belief as knowledge.

Self-assessment

Try to evaluate the argument you have provided in your written activity. Have you argued that people were or were not justified in their initial belief? Have you considered both sides of the argument? Have you provided sufficient evidence to support or justify your position?

Knowledge, laws and theories

Even if we cannot define knowledge in a clear way, we still have an intuitive understanding that allows us to talk about knowledge, particularly scientific knowledge, with some confidence.

Most knowledge assumes that the physical world exists, and that it is possible to understand the **natural laws** governing reality. That is to say that the universe is consistent, and the forces that cause apples to fall from a tree are consistent with those that determine the trajectories of the planets; and the atoms that make up the air that we breathe and objects that we use are the same atoms that make up living bodies. Our belief in natural law is a belief in the unity of nature at the deepest possible level, and you will learn more about natural laws in Chapter 13.

As you embark on your Theory of Knowledge (TOK) journey, it is important that you are clear about the difference between knowledge and **theory**, because you will encounter theories in many sections of the book, particularly in Chapter 13. Although sometimes people use the word *theory* to mean a speculation or a guess, it is best understood as an explanation for how something works or behaves, based on well-defined ideas and principles.

Good theories are testable, and enable us to make sense of the world around us. They also help us to make accurate predictions about the world. For example, the *General Theory of Relativity* that was published by Albert Einstein in 1915 predicted that massive objects such as planets and stars *bend* space-time. Although the warping of space-time cannot be seen or directly measured by scientific instruments, the **phenomena** predicted by the theory have since been observed, supporting the truth of the theory. It is important to understand that while all of the evidence to date supports

KEY WORDS

natural law: a generalised description of observations about a relationship between two or more things in the natural world; often the description is mathematical

theory: an interconnected system of ideas intended to explain something in depth

phenomenon (plural phenomena): an event, experience or occurrence

the theory, the theory has not been *proven*. It is quite likely that one day it will be shown to be an approximation of an even deeper theory yet to be proposed.

The use of theories to make predictions is fundamental to both the natural sciences and the human sciences. Even if theories eventually need to be modified or discarded altogether, the information and knowledge attained through testing theories are almost always invaluable to the progress of knowledge.

DISCUSS 2.4

How can we know when a theory provides a good explanation?

Information and data

Claude E. Shannon (1916–2001), who is known as the father of **information theory** and the instigator of the digital revolution along with Alan Turing (1912–1954), regarded 'knowing' as an increase in information or the reduction of uncertainty. This can be a helpful guide, but information alone is not knowledge.

To some extent, distinctions between words are matters of convention, and the conventions are seldom universal. For example, many writers use *data* and *information* as if there were no difference, and some use *information* to mean *knowledge*. However, to use the words interchangeably is to allow subtle differences in meaning to be lost, and this can open the door to confusion. It is always preferable to be aware of subtle differences between words, and to be consistent in your use of terminology if you can.

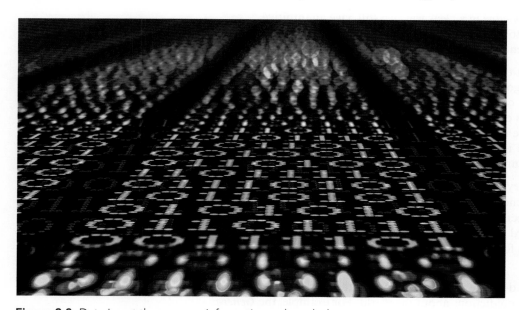

Figure 2.3: Data is not the same as information or knowledge

An example of data could be a binary sequence, such as 010011000111. It is clearly not **noise**, but it has no obvious meaning or interpretation, so it is simply data. It will only become information if it can be processed through some form of **decoding**. When the allied forces captured a German Enigma machine during the Second World

KEY WORDS

information theory: the mathematical study of the coding of information, and how that information can be quantified, stored and communicated reliably through computer circuits and telecommunications

data (singular datum): an unstructured collection of facts and figures

information: data that has been processed and structured, and can be used to answer *who*, *what*, *when* and *where* questions

noise: unwanted disturbances in electrical signals; meaningless data, including data that cannot be understood or interpreted by machines

decode: decrypt, decipher, translate

War (1939–1945), Alan Turing and his team at Bletchley Park had to go through a laborious process of converting the *data* they intercepted from radio signals by decoding it and discovering the *information* it contained.

Decoding data provides information, but that information needs to be organised before it has any significant value for us. For example, a telephone book contains a list of people with their addresses and telephone numbers. If the names, addresses and numbers were arranged randomly, it would just be a collection of data, with little value to anyone. The organising of the data alphabetically, and the association of names and addresses with specific numbers is what changes the data into useful information.

DISCUSS 2.5

What is the difference between data and information?

If we were to receive a binary sequence that encoded the numerical value of the constant π (pi), we could say that the data had a clear interpretation and was, as such, information. However, data does not need to be true or useful to count as information. For example, we could have a binary sequence of data that can be interpreted to give us intelligible words set within a legitimate grammatical structure. This would be information, even if it were not true or useful in any way. A famous example of this comes from Noam Chomsky (1928–), who suggested 'Colourless green ideas sleep furiously.' The sentence is grammatically correct and contains intelligible words, but it is semantically nonsensical.

What this means is that without information there can be no knowledge, but information alone is not knowledge. While *knowledge* can sometimes be used to refer to information that has been memorised, mostly it refers to information that has been collected, organised and analysed in a way that makes it useful. Memorising information does not mean that you understand the information or that you can use it appropriately. For example, a young child can memorise the multiplication tables, so we might say that they *know* the times-table. But it is only when the child can understand and use the patterns that emerge from knowing the times-table that we can say the child *knows* how to do multiplication.

DISCUSS 2.6

What is the difference between information and knowledge?

EXPLORE 2.3

Reflect on the following questions: Could possessing the telephone book be regarded as having knowledge? What about if you were to memorise it? If you were to analyse the book and find an emergent pattern, such as people who live in particular areas share the same first five digits of their telephone numbers, could you then regard yourself as having knowledge about the information contained within the telephone book? Would you answer any of these questions differently if instead of being arranged alphabetically, the book were to be arranged numerically? Why? Why not?

When you are studying a subject, you cannot simply learn lots of facts about it. Or at least, if you did just learn lots of facts about it, it would not mean that you understood it, or that you would be able to use the information you had gained in new situations to solve new problems. Instead, you must also learn about the methods and the theories that provide a framework for understanding the information. In the same way, learning a new language involves much more than learning a new vocabulary. You also need an understanding of the grammar and common idioms, and genuine fluency will require you to acquire and apply the conceptual background to the language if you are ever to use it in the way native-speakers use it.

> ### REAL-LIFE SITUATION 2.3
>
> Why is being able to recite facts about a subject not enough to have a comprehensive knowledge of that subject? Suppose you could memorise a poem or even a novel. To what extent would knowing the work by heart give you all the knowledge you need to write an essay on it in your examinations?

> ### REFLECTION
>
> As a knower, how might you think about knowledge as a journey rather than as a series of destinations?

2.3 Types of knowledge

> ### DISCUSS 2.7
>
> Knowledge can be classified in many ways. If you were asked to classify knowledge into different types, what types of knowledge might you come up with?

One method of classifying knowledge – sometimes associated with knowledge management in business – is to distinguish between **tacit** knowledge and **explicit** knowledge.

Tacit knowledge is the subjective and experiential knowledge that you have, which is difficult to express in words or communicate to others. It includes technical and craft skills, and cognitive skills, including your own perspectives and values, images in your mind and inexpressible beliefs. Explicit knowledge is knowledge that can be expressed in words or formulae. This is the form of knowledge we come across in books, reports, manuals, databases and on websites.

> ### KEY WORDS
>
> **tacit:** unspoken; implicit but not expressed
>
> **explicit:** clear, made obvious, openly expressed

EXPLORE 2.4

Think about an activity that you can do, for example riding a bike. Try to write down everything you know about bike riding (or your chosen activity) in a way that would enable someone who had never ridden a bike to *know* how to ride one. How easy is it? Do you think it can be done?

It is possible to find guides on how to ride a bike on the internet. Find and read one. How successful do you think it is? If you had never been on a bike, do you think the guide would give you enough knowledge to be able to ride a bike on your first attempt? Explain your reasons.

Figure 2.4: Learning to ride a bike

Just as you may have faced difficulty in trying to write what you know about riding a bike, you may also find it difficult to do things that you normally do automatically, if you think carefully about what you are doing. For example, if you think hard about how to tie up your shoelaces as you tie them, you may find it more difficult to do.

This is sometimes known as the **centipede effect**, after Katherine Craster's poem, *The Centipede's Dilemma*:

> A centipede was happy – quite!
> Until a toad in fun
> Said, 'Pray, which leg moves after which?'
> This raised her doubts to such a pitch,
> She fell exhausted in the ditch
> Not knowing how to run.

Katherine Craster (1841–1874)

KEY WORD

centipede effect: over-consciousness of your performance in a way that interferes with what you are doing

REAL-LIFE SITUATION 2.4

Have you ever experienced the centipede effect? What were you doing and how did it affect you?

The mathematician, logician and philosopher Bertrand Russell (1872–1970) categorised knowledge in two ways: knowledge by acquaintance and knowledge by description. These categories have since been popularised in a way that is quite different from the way in which Russell proposed them.

Popularly, we might say that at its most basic, knowledge by acquaintance is knowledge which is acquired first-hand through our senses. The knower has (or has had) direct, unmediated access to the subject that the knowledge refers to. However, there is a difference between just being directly acquainted with something and having knowledge by acquaintance. Knowledge by acquaintance needs there to be some form of knowledge or belief about whatever you are acquainted with. For example, you could be acquainted with a person (let's call her Ingrid) who attends your school. You may be able to identify Ingrid, and may have said 'Hello' on occasion, but that does not mean you know her in the sense of having any belief about her based on your direct acquaintance. However, if you had had a conversation with Ingrid in which she told you that her favourite subject is physics, providing that you believe she was being honest with you, you could then claim to *know* that Ingrid likes physics based on your acquaintance with her.

In the same, non-technical way, knowledge by description is second-hand knowledge that you may have learnt through reading a book or an online article, or perhaps it was something you were told by a teacher. In other words, it is indirect, mediated or inferential. You may never have been to Rio de Janeiro, but perhaps you know some things about it because you have read about the city or seen it in movies.

REAL-LIFE SITUATION 2.5

Could someone who has never been to Rio de Janeiro know more about it than someone who lives there? What might it mean to *know* a city?

However, the popular understanding of these two knowledge classifications is quite different from Russell's philosophical understanding of the two types of knowledge. For example, he believed that we can only know things by acquaintance if we have a direct experience that cannot be doubted. This means that we can know our **introspective** experiences (like feeling hungry) or experiences of memory and various characteristics known as **universals** by direct acquaintance, but, according to Russell, we cannot know that physical objects exist. If you were to examine an iPad, you could know its shape, colour, smoothness and shininess through acquaintance, but you would not know the iPad itself, other than by description.

Russell believed that the only way you can know anything about physical objects, including people and places, is through knowledge by description. You can form beliefs about physical objects – whether you have direct experiences of them or not – by understanding the concepts used to describe them. So, in using the example of the iPad, you can think about the iPad according to its descriptions (shape, colour,

KEY WORDS

introspective: looking inside oneself

universals: qualities that can be shared by different individuals at the same time, for example redness, roundness, beauty smoothness, shininess, etc.) and you can think about its descriptions because you know them through acquaintance. In other words, knowledge by acquaintance underpins all knowledge by description in Russell's model.

DISCUSS 2.8

When discussing any topic, why is it important to be clear about what you mean by the words and terms that you use?

Distinctions between different types of knowledge appear in some languages. For example, French has two words for knowing: *savoir* and *connaître*. *Savoir* is generally used to refer to acquired (second-hand) knowledge, and *connaître* refers to (first-hand) knowledge by acquaintance in the non-philosophical sense: places we have been, people we know, things we have done, etc. In English, we have the words *comprehension* and *apprehension*, where *comprehension* refers to a full understanding of knowledge and *apprehension* refers to a more tentative grasp of knowledge, although it is more commonly used nowadays to express nervousness.

REAL-LIFE SITUATION 2.6

Is anyone in your class familiar with a language that uses different words for different kinds of knowing? If so, how do they draw distinctions between the different words for knowledge?

Classifications of knowledge in cognitive science

Perhaps a more straightforward and more helpful way of discussing different types of knowledge is to use the classification of knowledge used in cognitive science.

KEY WORD

cognitive science: the study of the mind and its processes through an interdisciplinary approach that involves philosophy, psychology, linguistics and the natural sciences

Figure 2.5: Conceptual knowledge relates to abstract ideas

Cognitive science recognises four types of knowledge: **factual**, **conceptual**, **procedural** and **metacognitive**. Under this classification system, the first two categories are knowledge of *what*, and the second two are knowledge of *how*.

Within cognitive science, *factual knowledge* is the set of discrete, isolated elements of information you may be able to recall. Factual knowledge includes specific subject terminology, such as knowing that a chord in music is created when two or more notes are played simultaneously, or that a *piaffe* is a tightly controlled, high-lifting, rhythmic trot on the spot in the equestrian sport of dressage. It also covers all kinds of facts that might serve you well in your academic subjects or when participating in quizzes or playing *Trivial Pursuit*™. For example, you might know that Barack Obama was the 44th President of the United States of America, *Sn* is the chemical symbol for tin or that between 1912 and 1948, it was possible to compete in architecture, painting, literature, music and sculpture in the Olympic Games.

Conceptual knowledge is knowing how to link different elements of knowledge in a way that enables them to be more useful. For example, you may know how to classify items or how to add an *s* to a noun to make it plural; you might understand a mathematical model, or even ethical principles. Fluency in a language is impossible without having the concepts that are required to form and express ideas using it.

Procedural knowledge is knowing how to do things, whether it is using a paintbrush, riding a bike, recognising a face, carrying out a scientific experiment or solving a quadratic equation. Procedural knowledge is often, although not necessarily, tacit. We often know how to do things but cannot explain *how* we know.

Metacognitive knowledge is the kind of knowledge that TOK aims to help you with. For example, it can help you with knowing more about yourself and your capabilities, understanding what is required in different tasks, knowing strategies that help you to learn, being aware of your own personal strengths and weaknesses, being alert to the many ways in which we can be misled by knowledge and how to address those potential errors, and having strategies to help you develop your understanding. Some of the reflection features in this book are intended to help you to develop metacognitive awareness and think about learning strategies.

KEY WORDS

factual: containing facts

conceptual: relating to abstract ideas

procedural: related to actions

metacognitive: relating to your own thought processes

REAL-LIFE SITUATION 2.7

One of the skills of a teacher or coach is the ability to make tacit knowledge explicit. How might making tacit knowledge explicit help to develop metacognitive skills?

In the cognitive science model of knowledge, factual knowledge and procedural knowledge are regarded as low-level knowledge, whereas conceptual knowledge and metacognitive knowledge are thought of as high-level knowledge.

DISCUSS 2.9

Which is more useful and why: classifying knowledge by your depth of understanding or classifying it according to whether your knowledge is first-hand or second-hand?

EXPLORE 2.5

Look at the following knowledge statements. How would you classify them according to the cognitive science classifications? You might want to break this activity down by answering: Which statements would you say are statements of fact? Which claims require some kind of conceptual knowledge? Which statements relate to knowing how to do something? Which claims involve developing strategies to improve your learning or understanding?

a   Polar bears are only found in the wild in the northern hemisphere.

b   Canberra is the capital city of Australia.

c   I can bake bread.

d   Taipans are a type of snake.

e   A detailed study plan will help me to reach my goals.

f   I can recite *The Man from Snowy River*.

g   'Innate' means present from birth.

h   More considered reflections would improve my understanding.

i   For right-angled triangles on a Euclidean plane, $a^2 + b^2 = h^2$

j   The cat is sitting on the mat.

k   I need to develop my active listening skills.

l   Claude Monet was an impressionist painter.

m   I need to pay more attention to my wrist position when playing the piano.

n   I know how to solve simultaneous equations.

o   There are 12 students in my class.

p   We should aim to bring the greatest amount of happiness to the most people.

q $4 + 6 = 10$

r   I can find my school on Google Earth™.

s   Reflection helps to develop understanding.

t   I create costumes for the school play.

Compare your answers with those of a classmate. Do you agree? In cases where you disagree, discuss the reasons for your choice. Are there some claims that might fit into more than one category? How will you decide which category provides the best fit?

DISCUSS 2.10

What benefits, if any, might there be in classifying knowledge? What are the challenges of classifying knowledge?

REFLECTION

There are countless possible ways of classifying knowledge. Do you subconsciously have your own classification systems (e.g. interesting or not interesting; need to know or do not need to know)? How might becoming aware of, and analysing, your own classification systems be helpful to you?

2.4 Levels of knowledge

DISCUSS 2.11

How much do you think you would need to know about a topic to be an expert on it? Would your answer be qualified by depth of knowledge, breadth of knowledge or both? Could you ever know *everything* about any topic?

When thinking about levels of knowledge, we must ask ourselves 'What does it mean to know about . . .?' For example, if you were asked how much you know about gold, how might you answer? You could probably give lots of information about gold: its colour, weight, chemical symbol, that it's an element and classified as a metal, and so forth. You may also know its commercial value and uses, its economic significance and its historical significance. The more you think about it, the more you will discover that you know about gold, or could investigate to find out. Equally, the more you know about it, the more you will discover that there is yet to be known.

Knowing something about gold in terms of its production, chemistry, history, cultural uses and economic significance will give you a good **breadth of knowledge** on the topic. If you were to know its isotopes, oxidation states and alloys, you would have a good **depth of knowledge** about its chemistry.

As an IB Diploma Programme student, you will appreciate that knowledge is about much more than just knowing facts. Nowadays, with the internet so accessible through computers, tablets and smartphones, we have almost immediate access to unlimited facts (as well as countless **falsehoods**) but access to facts is not the same as knowing or understanding them, or being able to deploy the conceptual framework within which they are regarded as facts, and knowing facts is a very limited form of knowledge.

Bloom's **taxonomy** is a model developed by Benjamin Bloom and his associates, which was first published in 1956. It was designed to classify educational learning objectives according to their complexity in the area of cognition, as well as emotional responses and psychomotor skills. The cognitive model was revised and modified in 2001. In 1997, Dr Norman Webb adapted the cognitive domain of Bloom's taxonomy to classify depths of knowledge (DoK) according to the complexity of thinking involved. Webb's DoK tries to measure how deeply knowers understand and are aware of their learning.

KEY WORDS

breadth of knowledge: a span of knowledge covering many aspects of a subject

depth of knowledge: knowledge that focuses on, amplifies and explores specific topics

falsehood: a lie or misrepresentation; something that is put forward as a fact or a truth, but it is not

taxonomy: classification system, categorisation

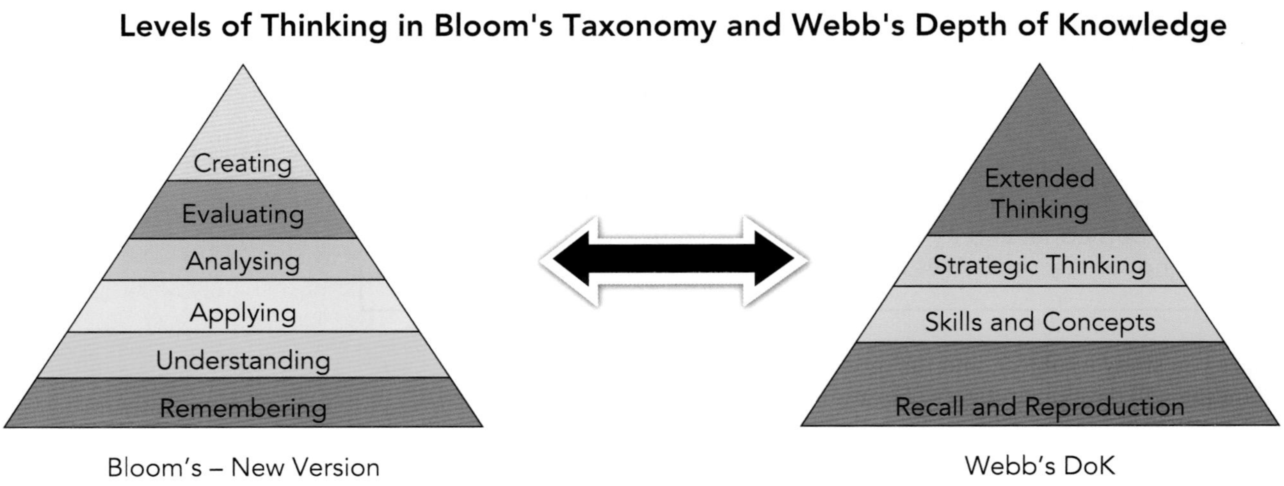

Levels of Thinking in Bloom's Taxonomy and Webb's Depth of Knowledge

Figure 2.6: Webb's DoK diagram compared with the revised version of Bloom's taxonomy

At the first level of DoK is the ability to recall facts, information or procedures. If you are at level one in biology, according to DoK, you may remember that DNA stands for deoxyribonucleic acid, or that the four bases in DNA are adenine, cytosine, guanine and thymine. Level two is being able to use information or conceptual knowledge: therefore in biology, you might understand how nucleotides are linked by covalent bonds, and how a double helix is formed using base pairing. Level three involves strategic thinking, which requires knowers to be able to reason, as well as develop a plan. If you are at level three in biology, you might be able to explain DNA replication and the significance of base pairing. The highest level on this model – level four – is extended thinking, which requires that the knower can extend knowledge, make connections between different fields of knowledge and perform complex reasoning. In our biological example, you may be able to discuss the relationship between a gene and a polypeptide. Sometimes, you may hear reference to *higher-order thinking*. This refers to the different levels of thinking in taxonomies like Bloom's and DoK. For example, levels three and four require more cognitive processing than levels one and two, and are said to be 'higher-order thinking'.

REFLECTION

Think about how you could use the activities associated with the different levels in the DoK model or Bloom's revised taxonomy to test and improve upon your own levels of knowledge and understanding in your IB Diploma Programme subjects across the different areas of knowledge.

EXPLORE 2.6

1   Create a mind-map comparing and contrasting the classifications of Webb's DoK with the cognitive science classifications of types of knowledge.

2   Take another look at the knowledge claims you classified into different types of knowledge, and try to classify them according to Webb's DoK. Do you notice any similarities between the two systems?

The longer you study a subject, and the more deeply you study it, the more your understanding will develop and grow. For example, if you study religions in the IB Middle Year Programme, iGCSE or any other middle-school programme, you will probably be taught 'facts' such as 'Christians believe Jesus is the son of God, the Shahadah is the first pillar of Islam for Muslims, Buddhists believe in nirvana' and that 'Brahman is the Supreme Spirit and ultimate reality for Hindus'. However, if you were to study religions at Diploma Programme or at university, you will discover that many of the 'facts' you learnt were not really facts about the religion as a whole, and perhaps not even facts under more limited circumstances. Religions are not **monolithic**. Beliefs within religious communities are far more diverse and dynamic than they are generally thought to be. Even when beliefs are shared between communities within a religion, the beliefs are usually far more **nuanced** than we might first learn. Most Christians are not creationists, and many have different concepts of the relationships within the Holy Trinity. Some Muslims have more than five pillars and see the *Shahadah* as a foundation rather than a pillar, and many have different views of Shari'a law. There are many different Buddhist understandings of life after death, and there are multiple varieties of Hinduism, some of which would declare a god other than Brahman to be the Supreme God. If you go on to study any religions at postgraduate level, your understanding will grow further, become more complex and nuanced and therefore deepen yet again.

The same experience will accompany your study of any subject – in chemistry, you may start with a very simple model of molecules and atoms that you must later revise by unlearning and relearning; in mathematics, you may start by thinking Euclidean geometry is the only geometry, only to learn otherwise later.

KEY WORDS

monolithic: one large, unchanging entity

nuance: subtle difference

EXPLORE 2.7

Try to find a textbook you may have used in classes five years ago. How has your knowledge developed and grown? Or perhaps you could compare your artwork, musical compositions or creative writing from five years ago with what you currently create. Does that earlier work seem simplistic now? Give some thought to the different evaluative standards and strategies teachers use with children of different ages. Choose one topic or subject and create a diagram that illustrates how your knowledge has grown.

CONTINUED

Look at your diagram. What experiences do you think have contributed most to your knowledge growth in this particular field of study? What does this tell you about how you learn?

REAL-LIFE SITUATION 2.8

Think of a novel or a poem you have read for a language class. What is the difference between knowing the work after you have first read it, and knowing it after you have carefully analysed it?

2.5 Personal access to knowledge

DISCUSS 2.12

To what extent does what we know stay known? How is knowledge lost?

According to the psychologist Erich Fromm (1900–1980), who drew on insights from religious and philosophical leaders, knowing begins with the awareness that our common-sense perceptions can be deceptive, and recognising that our picture of reality does not really correspond with the 'real world'. It involves being aware that most of what appear to be 'self-evident' truths are actually illusions produced through the suggestive influence of our societies. Knowing, then, must start with the shattering of illusions, and follow with attempts to critically and actively move ever closer to 'the truth'.

DISCUSS 2.13

Why do you think Fromm believed that knowing begins with the shattering of illusions? Do you agree with him?

Knowing is an active process that comes from within. It could be argued that knowing is even more important than knowledge because it has an immediacy that involves activity in the brain. Knowledge can be stored in various places such as books or files, on websites or even in brains, but understanding is what happens when you actively engage with knowledge, make it your own and learn how to use it. That said, we cannot learn or develop new knowledge if we cannot experience new things or have access to the knowledge, skills and experiences that other knowers have shared. And before we can grow or change our knowledge, we have to be ready to accept that any knowledge we have developed or have access to may not be absolutely true or final.

Memory

The sum of our knowledge is not in our conscious minds most of the time, but some of that knowledge can appear when we are thinking, talking or writing about something that is in some way related to our knowledge. Our minds seem to be able to reach into the deepest recesses of our memories to come up with the words, knowledge and information we need almost seamlessly, if the words, knowledge and information we want are familiar to us. Knowing, then, involves a ready access to our memories. But our memories are not infallible data banks that recall unblemished information and knowledge. Every time we remember, our memories are reconstructed, and with each reconstruction, they are susceptible to change. In addition, our memories – along with our perceptions – are subject to our personal biases and moods. If we retrieve a memory in a happy mood, we are more likely to remember the memory as happy, whereas even a memory of the happiest occasion can be darkened by recalling it when in a bad mood.

EXPLORE 2.8

Write 300 words about an event that you and all of your classmates recently attended. It could be a fire drill, an assembly, a class visit, etc. Write individually about what you actually observed rather than what you were meant to observe, then compare your recollections. How similar are they? Has anyone remembered something that no one else did? Has anyone remembered things differently?

Hand your writings to your teacher. At some point in the future, perhaps in a week or two, try to remember the event and write about it again. How does your second recollection compare with the first? What, if anything, did you forget or misremember the second time? Try again after a few months and note the differences.

REAL-LIFE SITUATION 2.9

How reliable are the memories that people record when they write histories of events they have experienced first-hand, or have heard about second-hand? What are the implications of this for us as knowers?

Memory can be categorised in multiple ways. Declarative memories are those explicit memories that we can consciously recall. They can be further divided into semantic memories (memories of facts) and episodic memories (memories from your own life), which can be broken down yet further.

Non-declarative memories are **implicit** procedural memories that we cannot consciously recall, but that we can nevertheless perform. For example, you might be able to tie a reef knot or tune a guitar but you may not easily be able to explain how to do either task.

KEY WORD

implicit: implied, hidden

Forgetfulness

One of the poets, whose name I cannot recall, has a passage, which I am unable at the moment to remember, in one of his works, which for the time being has slipped my mind, which hits off admirably this age-old situation.

P.G. Wodehouse (1881–1975)

We all forget things from time to time. Indeed, we have probably all forgotten far more than we know. Memory tends to have a *use-it-or-lose-it* quality, which means that most of our memories are transient unless we use them regularly. Although this might, on occasion, cause frustration, it can actually be a useful feature because it means that we keep only the memories that benefit us.

Interestingly there have been some people with hyperthymesia who can readily recall information about their own lives, but who can have great difficulty in remembering facts about the world. Hyperthymestic tendencies can cause non-stop, uncontrollable memories to flood the mind of the sufferer, making it difficult for the person to attend to the present or future.

The opposite of transient memories are persistent memories. These are not memories that we work hard to remember. Rather, they are the memories we would like to forget but cannot. These memories tend to be negative ones, perhaps of traumatic events, and associated with fear. These unwanted memories are often associated with depression and post-traumatic stress disorder.

> **KEY WORDS**
>
> transient: temporary, fleeting
>
> hyperthymesia: a condition in which a person can remember an abnormally large number of their own life experiences in detail

---

DISCUSS 2.14

Why might there be an evolutionary advantage to have brains that store persistent memories of traumatic events?

Figure 2.7: Mistakes happen when we do not pay full attention to what we are doing

Absent-mindedness is forgetfulness that happens if we do not pay enough attention to what we are doing. For example, if our minds are wandering when we should be reading or listening, we are unlikely to remember much of what we read or hear. This is one reason why trying to study while watching a television programme is rarely successful. Absent-mindedness can also manifest itself by causing us to forget to do something if we are absorbed in something else. For example, you might be so engrossed in preparing for your TOK exhibition that you forget to phone your friend at the time that you promised.

KEY WORD
absent-mindedness: inattentiveness that leads to lack of memory

"I keep thinking it's Tuesday."

Some of you may have had the experience of 'searching' for an answer, a word or a name. You know you *know* the answer or the word you are searching your memory for, but it evades you for the moment. You may think of it as being on *the tip of your tongue*. This phenomenon is known as **blocking**. Frequently a wrong answer comes to you, and you know that it is the wrong answer, but cannot get your mind to go past the wrong answer to find the right one. Often, if we stop trying to find the right answer, and turn our minds to other things, the right answer will later 'pop' into our minds.

Another form of forgetfulness is **misattribution**. This is when you may remember something quite well, but forget who told you or where you read it. You may even be absolutely certain that it came from one source and later discover that your memory is a false one. This is one reason why, when making notes, you should always write down the name of the source material you are using, with all of the referencing details. If you wait until you have finished an essay or assignment before writing your references and bibliography, you may find that you cannot remember or you misremember where the material you used came from. This can cause a lot of extra work locating your sources again, or could cause you to risk being accused of **plagiarism**.

KEY WORDS
blocking: when there is an obstruction to your ability to recall information
misattribution: to give credit to the wrong person or source, whether deliberately or mistakenly
plagiarism: passing off someone else's idea or work as your own

Related to misattribution is the issue of false memories. We are all vulnerable to having details inadvertently inserted into our memories through the power of suggestion. If you hear people talking about an event that you were at in the past, you can incorporate the details they discuss into your own memories, so that later, if asked to recall your memories of the event, you may also 'remember' the added details as though they were your own. This is particularly easy with photographs that we come to regard as our personal memories when in fact they are learned from exposure to records supplied by others.

In 1974, Elizabeth Loftus and John Palmer used a number of videos of car crashes and asked people to estimate the speeds of the cars involved using different forms of questions. They demonstrated that the verbs used in the questions resulted in different estimations of the speed at which the cars were travelling prior to impact.

This could have been put down to the use of leading questions, but more interestingly, Loftus and Palmer discovered that the participants' memories were also altered. One week after viewing the video, without seeing it again, participants were asked whether they had seen broken glass at the scene of the accident. Those who were originally asked how fast the car was going when it 'smashed' were more than twice as likely to 'remember' broken glass than participants who had been asked how fast the car was going when it 'hit'.

The research suggests that memories can be distorted through the use of leading questions and by providing information.

KEY WORD

power: control, influence, strength

REAL-LIFE SITUATION 2.10

If the research of Loftus and Palmer is valid, what are the implications for eyewitness testimonies?

The validity of the Loftus and Palmer experiment was thrown into question when, in 1986, a study by Yuille and Cutshall showed that eyewitnesses to a real-life shooting in Canada showed a high degree of accuracy of recall after four to five months. Overall, accuracy rates were estimated between 76–89% in the police interview, and between 73–85% in the second interview. Witnesses to the crime after four to five months reported 8.2% fewer action details, 2.4% fewer personal descriptions and 10.6% more object descriptions in an interview conducted by researchers, compared with police interviews conducted on the same day or within two days of the event.

REAL-LIFE SITUATION 2.11

Can you think of reasons why the results that Loftus and Palmer achieved under laboratory conditions might not be replicated by the results of Yuille and Cutshall using a real-life situation?

Ambiguity and vagueness

Even if we were to have perfect memories, our personal access to knowledge, along with humankind's ability to formulate and transmit knowledge, is affected by ambiguity and vagueness.

Ambiguity is not always easy to recognise. Some ambiguity is unavoidable; some is deliberate. In arguments, for example, it is possible for the protagonist to make it difficult for their opponent to argue against them because what they say is not clear, and is deliberately not made clear. Politicians are sometimes heard to say, 'We have been very clear,' when what they mean is, 'What we have said and done has been extraordinarily ambiguous.' Whether deliberately or inadvertently, arguments can lead to incorrect conclusions and conceal bad reasoning, because their terms have not been defined clearly, by accident or design. This can have serious implications for knowledge in that we might believe a knowledge claim to be well-justified because we fail to spot the ambiguities in the arguments presented. Ambiguity can also lead us to misinterpret knowledge that we receive and/or pass on to others.

Ambiguity can come from words that have multiple meanings: from words, phrases and sentences that are taken out of context, and when different meanings arise because of the structure of a sentence. One of the reasons contracts and other legal documents tend to be very long and written in a style that is very different from common speech is that lawyers try to remove ambiguity from the details of the document.

While lawyers, for the most part, try to remove or at least minimise ambiguities, others, such as politicians, regard ambiguity as a powerful tool. By being ambiguous when they speak, skilled politicians are able to partly disguise their political positions in ways that can help their election prospects by appearing to say things that appeal to more people. Artists can also harness the power of ambiguity to create works that appeal to a wide spectrum of interpretations, and as a result are often assumed to have great depth. It has been argued that ambiguity is intrinsic to the creative process, not just in the creative arts but also in mathematics, by giving rise to new and expansive ideas.

Ambiguity, then, is a quality that can lead to the misunderstanding and misrepresentation of knowledge, but can also lead to the development of new and/or deeper knowledge by freeing our minds from tight prescription and definition.

Associated with ambiguity, and sometimes contrasted with it, is the concept of vagueness. While ambiguity can lead to two or more distinct interpretations, often meanings can become clear by their context. For example, if you were listening to a cricket match commentary and the commentator said, 'Mashrafe Mortaza has raised his bat,' you would probably envisage the 2019 Bangladesh cricket captain lifting his wooden cricket bat, rather than thinking that the captain was lifting a winged mammal or believing that the commentator was referring to Mortaza having a pet bat that he has hand-reared.

In this example, the words *bat* and *raised* are both ambiguous if taken out of context, but they are not vague words. Vagueness arises when there is no clear definition of how a word can be applied. For example, if a politician promises to resolve an issue in a

KEY WORDS

ambiguity: when a word, statement, image or situation can have more than one meaning or interpretation

vagueness: when something is not clear or has no distinct boundaries, is imprecise and defies exact definition

way that is *fair* to all voters, we might all have different notions about what *fair* means in relation to that issue. *Fairness* is a vague concept.

When you read Chapter 9, you will discover a debate about whether indigenous people should be clearly defined, or whether they should be self-identifying, leaving the concept of indigenous peoples deliberately vague.

We encounter vagueness in all aspects of life. While you might expect some vagueness about concepts like fairness and justice, it affects many words that we tend to take for granted when we use them. *Games* is one example. You may have a good idea of what a game is, and you may know when you are playing a game, but you might find yourself struggling to say with any clarity exactly what the word *game* means.

The French sociologist Roger Caillois (1913–1978) defined *games* as activities that must meet certain criteria. He believed they must be fun, have rules, have unforeseeable outcomes, serve no useful purpose and involve a different reality from everyday life.

EXPLORE 2.9

If an activity must meet *all* of Caillois' criteria to be classed as a game, could professional sports be regarded as games? What about non-professional sports? Do they serve any useful purposes?

Look up the word *game* in a dictionary or online. With a partner, try to decide if sculpture could be regarded as a *game*. What about a jigsaw puzzle? Can you think of some games that do not fit the definition you have chosen, or some activities that fit the definition but that you would not regard as games?

REAL-LIFE SITUATION 2.12

The neurologist, psychiatrist and Holocaust survivor Viktor Frankl (1905–1997) argued that human life is less about happiness than about *meaning* and *purpose*. How vague are those terms? Try to reach a conclusion with your partner about the implications of vagueness for knowledge. Is it a 'bad thing' or are there advantages to the absence of clarity and precision?

We will further explore the concepts of ambiguity and vagueness in Chapter 6. Meanwhile, you might begin to consider the discussion questions below.

DISCUSS 2.15

1   What implications might the vagueness of language have for knowledge?

2   What implications might the vagueness of knowledge have for language?

REFLECTION

As a knower, how might an awareness of ambiguity and vagueness help you to think in more refined ways, be more aware of your own assumptions and be more open to other perspectives?

2.6 Misinformation, disinformation and fake news

REAL-LIFE SITUATION 2.13

How can you decide which knowledge and information to trust?

It's now clear that so-called fake news can have real-world consequences.

Hillary Clinton (1947–)

Rapid advances in information and communication technologies have led to a 21st-century information age. New technologies allow the storage, organisation and manipulation of large quantities of data, information and knowledge, and knowers around the world have ready access to this data, information and knowledge, providing they can access the internet. One of the difficulties of having so much information to draw upon is knowing how to distinguish information from **misinformation** and **disinformation**.

Misinformation abounds in social media. Anything promoting fad diets, miracle foods, lists of good and bad foods and so on, is likely to be misinformation. Political misinformation is also rife, as are conspiracy theories and misinformation about celebrities. Many people who spread misinformation do so unwittingly. People tend to believe media content that supports their ideas, even if that content is inaccurate due to sensationalisation or bias, or even if the content is blatantly false. Many people who share misinformation believe it to be true because they do not have the ability to verify media reports, or simply do not bother to. They therefore become complicit in sharing misinformation without realising it. This **viral** sharing is difficult – if not impossible – for social media companies to control because they do not violate the social media platforms' 'terms of use', and the misinformation is spread too quickly to be contained.

What is particularly interesting about misinformation is that it can potentially distort people's memories of whatever the misinformation relates to, particularly if they are repeatedly exposed to the misinformation.

KEY WORDS

misinformation: incorrect information, unintentionally false information

disinformation: intentionally false or inaccurate information spread as an act of deception

viral: spreading widely and quickly

REAL-LIFE SITUATION 2.14

How often do you check the accuracy of an article before you share it on social media, particularly if it is something that confirms what you already believe? What about articles you use for essays or assignments? Is checking accuracy something that you could do better at?

The inability of social media companies to be able to tightly control social content, combined with the speed with which misinformation is spread on social media, makes social media efficient and effective platforms for deliberately disseminating disinformation. The algorithms that enable social media and search engines to deliver targeted advertising further enhance the effectiveness of disinformation campaigns, because the disinformation will primarily be sent to those people who are most likely to be influenced by it, and most likely to share it again. This allows disinformation agents to spread lies and propaganda, as though it were legitimate information, to a mass audience at very little cost.

KEY WORD

propaganda: the deliberate manipulation of information in order to influence what people think, usually for political purposes

REAL-LIFE SITUATION 2.15

1   Why might some people want to spread disinformation?

2   Is there an ethical difference between sharing misinformation and sharing disinformation?

Disinformation and politics

There is nothing new about using disinformation for political purposes. Governments and state leaders have used false information throughout history. Back in the Roman Republic when Mark Antony (83–30 BCE) met Cleopatra (69–30 BCE), Octavian (63 BCE–14 CE) orchestrated a propaganda campaign to smear Mark Antony's reputation by having slogans written on coins painting Antony as a womaniser, a drunkard and Cleopatra's puppet.

However, the spreading of disinformation is believed to have become far more widespread in recent years, and has had a considerable impact on the democratic process around the world. In April–May 2019, the world's largest election to date was held in India, with more than 815 million people registered to vote. Leading up to the elections, India faced information wars on an unprecedented scale. Fake news and disinformation campaigns were rife throughout a range of social and news media.

This dissemination of disinformation (and also legitimate information) on social media is sometimes likened to an echo chamber because it creates an environment in which knowers only come across beliefs and opinions that agree with their own, thus reinforcing their beliefs, and not allowing them to be challenged by, or even consider, alternative ideas. This can have very dangerous consequences.

KEY WORD

echo chamber: a space in which sound reverberates, so any sounds made are repeated over and over as they bounce from the walls

Pre-electoral disinformation campaigns in India were used to spread untrue rumours through media such as WhatsApp™, to target political opponents, religious minorities and dissenting individuals. with devastating effect. The echo chamber effect led to multiple acts of violence across the country including mob lynchings.

One such campaign involved a fake video created by splicing old legitimate videos. The fake video had the Indian President saying in Hindi, '*We agree that for the election, we need a war.*' A fact-checking company exposed the video as fake within 24 hours of its release, but by the time the post was taken down, it had already had 2.5 million views and 150,000 shares.

Many of the people who viewed the video will have believed it simply because it reinforced their own biases. This is a phenomenon known as **confirmation bias**.

KEY WORD

confirmation bias: the tendency to believe evidence that supports your opinions, and ignore or discount evidence that goes against what you believe

REAL-LIFE SITUATION 2.16

Are people more likely to believe and share an unkind or even nasty rumour about a person or group they dislike, or a person or group they view favourably? How might this lead to violence?

REFLECTION

To what extent do you think you may be guilty of confirmation bias? How might you try to avoid it?

KEY WORD

bot: an automated computer programme

Once a story is widespread, people are likely to believe it even if it is later retracted or shown to be false. Automated **bot** accounts are used to spread stories, often with a shared #hashtag, so that they become 'trending'. The bot accounts also repeatedly post web addresses so that the sites they are promoting get to the top of search engine results. One example of this followed the 2017 mass shooting in Las Vegas USA, during which Stephen Paddock killed 58 people and wounded more than 800 others who were attending an outdoor concert. Shortly after the event, search engine results were dominated by a conspiracy theory that suggested Paddock's rampage was part of a coordinated plot involving Islamic terrorists and left-wing activists. Although the conspiracy theory was soon debunked, it remains in the minds of susceptible people, and can further entrench them in their ideological and political positions.

REAL-LIFE SITUATION 2.17

1 How might the echo chamber effect also be used in a positive way?

2 What is meant by the saying, 'There's no smoke without fire'? Do you agree with it? If you come across a story repeatedly in the media, how likely are you to believe it, regardless of where it comes from?

Fake news

Possibly the first large-scale fake news story occurred in 1835, when the *New York Sun* published a series of articles about life on the moon. Perhaps surprisingly, it took several weeks before the articles were discovered to be an elaborate hoax aimed at increasing circulation for the newspaper and ridiculing some extravagant astronomical theories that had recently been published elsewhere.

KEY WORD

fake news: false, often sensational stories, spread under the guise of news reporting

Figure 2.8: Life on the moon as depicted in 1835

The 'Life on the moon' fake news story was well before the rise of the internet and social media. It happened at a time when distributing information was relatively expensive, and media outlets were more easily regulated. Nowadays, anyone can create a website that promotes fake news and/or disseminate fake news stories through social media.

In today's world, clicks mean money, and spammers, along with some site owners, are willing to use any content that will help drive internet traffic and boost their advertising revenue. As a result, internet spamming and fake news production have become international business opportunities, as well as ways of influencing politics or driving ideological agendas.

Prior to the 2018 presidential election in Brazil, 120 million Brazilian WhatsApp™ users were inundated with political messages. In Myanmar, the widespread sharing of disinformation was used by the military as a tool to assist in its programme of 'ethnic cleansing' of the Rohingya people. Myanmar military personnel created false Facebook™ accounts to post a multitude of stories that promoted the idea that Islam is a threat to Buddhism, and falsely accusing Muslims of crimes against Buddhists to stir up public hatred of the Rohingya people. Facebook™ closed many official accounts of senior Myanmar military officials in August 2018, but most of the sham accounts went undetected. In July 2018, Myanmar military propagandists published a book on the Rohingya crisis that contained 'documentary' photographs allegedly showing Rohingya people entering Myanmar illegally, and standing over the bodies of murdered Buddhists. However, several of the photographs in the book were found to have been faked.

REAL-LIFE SITUATION 2.18

For many people in Myanmar and elsewhere around the world, the military might be a trusted authority for matters of national security. What are the implications of not being able to trust national authorities? What checks and balances might be needed in all countries?

It is not always easy to discern which news articles are reliable and which are fake. A 2018 study by Stanford University found that students are not very good at distinguishing legitimate news available online from fake news. Perhaps this is because as knowers, we might not always look critically enough at what we read, or perhaps we do not want to lose time evaluating the authenticity of, or justification for, claims that are made. We will return to the subject of fake news in Chapter 5.

REAL-LIFE SITUATION 2.19

How might you go about authenticating a news story?

Figure 2.9: Does the photograph appear to be authentic?

Twelve top tips for spotting fake news

1   Check the source of the story: is it from a reputable organisation, for example a reputable university or news agency? If you do not recognise the source, try to find out more about it.

2   Is the story from an organisation with vested interests?

3   Be aware that some sites will use URLs that are similar to the addresses of legitimate sites, but perhaps with a minor difference. This is a common technique of scammers.

4   Try to cross-reference the story with other reputable agencies.

5   Check the validity of any evidence offered in the article by cross-referencing to see if it is authentic.

6   How sensationalist is the headline? Does the accompanying article match the headline? Many people get excited over headlines, and share them without reading the content, let alone verifying it.

7   Is the story well written and grammatically correct? Is the spelling correct? Although legitimate sources can occasionally have spelling or grammatical errors, they tend to be more prevalent in fake news articles.

8   Check the date – many legitimate news agencies put out fake news stories just for fun on April Fools' Day (1 April). Even if it's not an April Fools' joke, the date can sometimes offer clues.

9   Are the photographs authentic? Could they have been doctored?

10   Is the story a satire or a joke? Read it carefully and check the site that it comes from. Are there any disclaimers in the small print?

11   Does the story really sound plausible? If it sounds far-fetched, it probably is.

12   Do you *want* to believe the story? You need to be even more careful with stories that you want to believe, to help counteract confirmation bias.

Of course, there is a saying that truth is stranger than fiction, and sometimes what sounds extraordinary can turn out to be true, just as stories that seem perfectly reasonable can turn out to be fake. There is no shortcut for verifying news.

Figure 2.10: What's happening to the daisies at Fukushima?

EXPLORE 2.10

Figure 2.10 is a photograph that was reportedly taken of daisies growing near Fukushima, four years after the nuclear disaster that occurred there in 2011. The daisy in the centre of the photograph looks as if it is mutated. The other daisies in the photograph look normal. The discovery of daisies such as the one in the centre was cited as evidence of leaked radioactive material.

Imagine you are writing an assignment on Fukushima. Would this photograph of the daisies serve as evidence of radioactive mutation there? What does your intuition tell you? Before making a decision, what extra information would you need? Make a list of all the things you would want to find out before making a decision.

Peer-assessment

Compare your list with that of a classmate. Give each other feedback on the questions you have. How could you improve your research to be sure that the information you use is reliable?

Self-assessment

Run an internet search on Fukushima daisies. Was your intuition correct? How did you decide?

2.7 The question of trust

DISCUSS 2.16

Why is trust essential for knowing?

Trust, but verify.

Ronald Reagan (1911–2004)

The prevalence of fake news, particularly on social media, has itself become headline news. So much so that the term *fake news* is increasingly used to describe not just disinformation campaigns, but also honest mistakes, and more alarmingly, legitimate news items that people do not agree with. This is a problem because it throws suspicion on all news and leaves people not knowing who or what can be trusted. Where once people turned to **experts** for advice, there is a tendency for people to turn to like-minded **peers** who are more likely to give them the answers they want to hear.

DISCUSS 2.17

Why might experts be (or not be) a more reliable source of knowledge than your peers?

KEY WORDS

expert: a person with specialist skills and/or knowledge

peer: a person of equal standing, usually a member of your own tribe

"I trust this site to tell the truth."

Figure 2.11: We all like sources that agree with us, but it does not mean they are reliable

The importance of expertise

If we are to know anything beyond our own first-hand experiences, we have to know whom we can trust, and which sources we can trust. It makes sense that we trust our friends, our family and those from our tribes in many ways, but we need to also acknowledge a need for **competency**. Your best friend may be incredibly trustworthy, but that does not mean that they know how to repair a broken tooth. For that, you would seek the advice of a dentist. This is where knowledge communities can be invaluable, particularly knowledge communities that share **expertise**. Such knowledge communities scrutinise their members, critique their methodologies and hold the members accountable, so that we can all have a greater degree of trust in what they hold to be true; while at the same time, we need to understand and accept that what is known now may possibly be modified in the future.

However, trust in experts, particularly in science and academia, has waned over recent years. In his book, *The Death of Expertise* (2017), Tom Nichol discusses the growing trend of relativism in which people believe their personal opinions hold equal weight to the opinion of experts. Claims to the contrary are seen as undemocratic elitism.

> **KEY WORDS**
>
> **competency:** capability; the possession of sufficient knowledge or skills
>
> **expertise:** specialised skills and knowledge

REAL-LIFE SITUATION 2.20

In what ways and in which areas of knowledge would the absence of expert knowledge and advice most severely limit our personal knowledge?

It is important that we are able to trust experts in their fields and the information provided by knowledge communities, but it is also important that our trust is not blind. We cannot absolve ourselves from all responsibility in the knowing process. Knowing as a process includes all the questioning, doubting and decision-making that is involved in navigating our way through the overwhelming amount of information, misinformation and disinformation that assails us every day. But unlike vigorous *scepticism*, the knowing process allows us both to doubt *and* to set aside doubt 'for now' because we come to the conclusion that, flawed as the knowledge it provides may be, what our knowing process yields remains *the best we can do right now*. In knowing, we must accept *both* that certainty is almost unattainable, except in some realms of mathematics, *and* that we are nevertheless right to decide in favour of some things and against others because we cannot suspend judgement indefinitely.

EXPLORE 2.11

For each of your six IB Diploma Programme subjects, write down three key websites that you might use as reliable starting points for research. Then write down three key websites you might turn to for reliable and up-to-date news. What features do you look for before deciding whether a source is likely to be trustworthy? What are the problems associated with the websites you have identified? (You can use the twelve top tips found earlier in this section to help you.)

Peer-assessment

Share the websites with a partner. Do you agree with your partner's choices? Why? Why not? Discuss with your partner how best to decide on the trustworthiness of online sources.

REAL-LIFE SITUATION 2.21

Do you think books and journals from your school library will be more trustworthy than online sources? Will they be as up-to-date? Explain your answers.

REFLECTION

How far do you think you can trust your intuition in knowing what sources are reliable? What can you do to help avoid falling for fake news?

2.8 Conclusion

Much of the discussion in this chapter, especially of fake news, misinformation, disinformation, trust and sifting sense from nonsense is really about making informed, wise decisions as a key component in the *knowing-process*. You can think about every chapter of this book in this light. In Chapter 12, the mathematics chapter, we look at how we try to separate truth from falsehood, proof from error, fruitful and plausible theories and sets of axioms from trivial or inconsistent ones. In Chapter 13, the natural science chapter, we are concerned with the knowing process in all of the sciences: with hypothesis, experiment, confirmation and refutation, how we frame theories and how we discriminate between them. In Chapter 10, the history chapter, we are concerned with the reliability, bias, contemporaneity and trustworthiness of sources, with forming and assessing narratives that embrace events, and their causes and their long-term consequences. In Chapter 14, the human sciences chapter, we explore how far knowers can develop a science of human behaviour, and in Chapter 11, the arts chapter, we explore problems associated with aesthetic knowledge.

Human beings, human societies and human brains seem peculiarly and particularly predisposed to trying to understand the world and the place of human beings in it. This gives rise to a vast array of *narratives* that seek to explain everything from where the universe came from to why we need vigorously boiling water to make a good cup of tea. The formation of narratives – hypotheses, conjectures, theories – is an essential part of the knowing-process, because once we have voiced them or written them down, they can be accepted or rejected, praised or criticised, tested and thereby endorsed or disproved or left in some kind of limbo in between.

What we learn from a theory of knowing is that *all* our knowledge is in some sort of limbo because everything could be – and perhaps one day will be – revised, if only by being incorporated into a more global theory, and so shown to fit with a great deal more knowledge than we currently have. The *permanency of uncertainty* is what guarantees that knowing is a perpetual and endless process. Even if we are 99.999% sure of some knowledge claim, there is and there should always be that tiny possibility that we might be wrong, that we might need to go back and reconsider something we have always thought utterly and absolutely true. As knowers, we are challenged to rise to the pursuit of knowledge despite the difficulties we have explored in this chapter. In Chapter 3, we will explore in more detail how knowledge is constructed.

DISCUSS 2.18

Is the 'permanency of uncertainty' the only thing about which we can be certain? And is it therefore self-contradictory?

KNOWLEDGE QUESTIONS

1   To what extent do the methods of justification differ in different areas of knowledge?

2   How do different areas of knowledge incorporate doubt as a part of their methods?

3   To what extent is the knowledge of experts transferable?

2.9 Linking questions

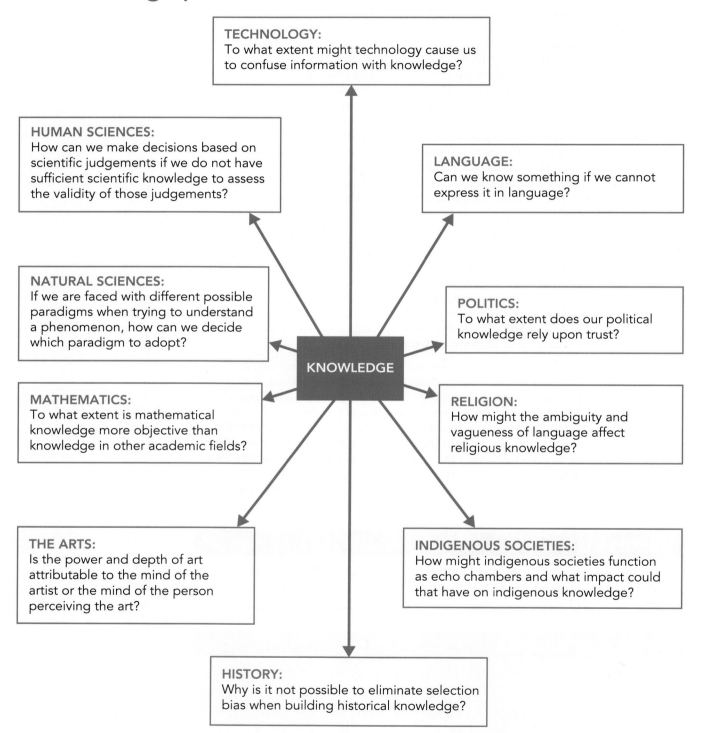

TECHNOLOGY:
To what extent might technology cause us to confuse information with knowledge?

HUMAN SCIENCES:
How can we make decisions based on scientific judgements if we do not have sufficient scientific knowledge to assess the validity of those judgements?

LANGUAGE:
Can we know something if we cannot express it in language?

NATURAL SCIENCES:
If we are faced with different possible paradigms when trying to understand a phenomenon, how can we decide which paradigm to adopt?

POLITICS:
To what extent does our political knowledge rely upon trust?

MATHEMATICS:
To what extent is mathematical knowledge more objective than knowledge in other academic fields?

RELIGION:
How might the ambiguity and vagueness of language affect religious knowledge?

KNOWLEDGE

THE ARTS:
Is the power and depth of art attributable to the mind of the artist or the mind of the person perceiving the art?

INDIGENOUS SOCIETIES:
How might indigenous societies function as echo chambers and what impact could that have on indigenous knowledge?

HISTORY:
Why is it not possible to eliminate selection bias when building historical knowledge?

2.10 Check your progress

Reflect on what you have learned in this chapter and indicate your confidence level between 1 and 5 (where 5 is the highest score and 1 is the lowest). If you score below 3, re-visit that section. Come back to this list later in your course. Has your confidence grown?

	Confidence level	Re-visited?
Do I understand why knowledge cannot be clearly defined?		
Am I able to explain the difference between laws and theories, and their relationship to knowledge?		
Can I successfully distinguish between data, information and knowledge?		
Do I understand the subjective nature of different types of knowledge?		
Am I able to talk about different ways in which knowledge might be classified?		
Could I clearly explain different levels of knowledge, including depth and breadth of knowledge?		
Am I aware of the role that memory plays in how we access our knowledge?		
Can I discuss different forms of forgetfulness, and how they impact our ability to recall knowledge?		
Am I able to explain ambiguity and vagueness, and their implications for knowledge?		
Do I understand the similarities and differences between misinformation, disinformation and fake news?		
Am I aware of confirmation bias in myself and others?		
Have I improved my ability to better critically assess sources of information so as not to be misled or to unwittingly mislead others?		
Do I understand the importance of trust in the act of knowing?		
Am I able to articulate the need for experts in some circumstances?		

2.11 Continue your journey

- To build on the knowledge that you have gained in this chapter, you could read some of the following articles.

- If you are interested in knowing more about how **fake news and disinformation were used to affect the presidential election in Brazil**, read: Mike Isaac and Kevin Roose, 'Disinformation and Fake News spreads over WhatsApp™ ahead of Brazil's Presidential Election', in *The Independent,* 21 October 2018. Search the *Independent* website for this article.

- If you are curious about the shift in **scientific beliefs about the expanding universe**, read: Adam G. Riess and Michael S. Turner, 'The Expanding Universe: From Slowdown to Speed Up', in *Scientific American*, 23 September 2008. Search the *Scientific American* website for this article.

- If you would like to know more about the **Great Moon Hoax**, read: Matthew Wills, 'How *The Sun* conned the world with *The Great Moon Hoax*', in *Jstor Daily*, 7 November 2017. Search the *Jstor Daily* website for this article.

- To explore further the problems concerning **online truth and misinformation**, read: Janna Anderson and Lee Rainie, 'The Future of Truth and Misinformation Online', in *Pew Research Center,* 19 October 2017. Search the *Pew Research Center* website for this article.

- To develop a better understanding of **how worldwide standards of living are measured**, read: Richard A. Easterlin, 'The Worldwide Standard of Living Since 1800', in *Journal of Economic Perspectives,* vol. 14, no. 1, pp. 7–26, Winter 2000. Search the *Stanford University* website for this article.

- For an account of how **disinformation was used for political and military purposes**, read: Paul Mozur, 'A Genocide Incited on Facebook, With Posts from Myanmar's Military', in *The New York Times,* 15 October 2018. Search the *New York Times* website for this article.

- For a fascinating insight into **how assumptions affect the way in which scientists develop hypotheses and theories**, read: Ferris Jabr, 'How Beauty is Making Scientists Rethink Evolution', in *The New York Times,* 9 January 2019. Search the *New York Times* website for this article.

- To develop a better understanding of the **relationship between language and memory** and **eyewitness testimonies**, read: Elizabeth F. Loftus and John C. Palmer, 'Reconstruction of Automobile Destruction: An Example of the Interaction between Language and Memory', in *Journal of Verbal Learning and Verbal Behavior*, vol. 13, no. 5, pp. 585–589, October 1974. Search the *The Unconscious Curriculum* website for this article.

- For another perspective on **eyewitness testimonies**, read: John C. Yuille and Judith L. Cutshall, 'Study of Eyewitness Memory of a Crime', in *Journal of Applied Psychology,* vol. 71, no. 2, pp. 291–301, June 1986. Search the *Research Gate* website for this article.

- For a better understanding of the **difficulties in dealing with fake news on social media**, read: Sankalp Phartiyal and Aditya Kalra, 'Despite being exposed, fake news thrives on social media ahead of India polls', in *Reuters*, 3 April 2019. Search the *Reuters* website for this article.

- For an analysis of a **growing hostility to expertise**, read: Tom Nichol, *The Death of Expertise*, Oxford University Press, 2017

- If you would like to know more about the **value of ambiguity for mathematics**, read: Colin Foster, 'Productive ambiguity in the learning of mathematics', in *For the Learning of Mathematics journal*, July 2011. Search the *For the Learning of Mathematics Journal* website for this article.

Chapter 3
Knowledge questions and framework

LEARNING INTENTIONS

This chapter will examine knowledge questions and the knowledge framework.

You will:

- be introduced to knowledge questions, and how they relate to the world around us and to the knowledge framework – a tool for the analysis of areas of knowledge and knowledge questions

- consider the scope of knowledge, namely the extent and limits of knowledge

- learn about different perspectives and paradigms, evaluate your own perspective, beliefs and assumptions and understand how these might impact on your understanding of knowledge and knowing

- consider how we gain and produce knowledge using various methods and tools, including cognitive and practical tools

- explore the role of rationality and reasoning in the construction of knowledge, and understand the nature of premises, arguments and conclusions

- consider how ethical considerations shape us as knowers, and how far ethical responsibilities might influence the construction and uses of knowledge

BEFORE YOU START

Analyse each of the following quotations and discuss the questions that follow.

1   'As always in life, people want a simple answer … and it's always wrong.' **Susan Greenfield** (1950–)

2   'There are known knowns. There are things we know that we know. There are known unknowns. That is to say, there are things that we now know we don't know. But there are also unknown unknowns. There are things we do not know we don't know.' **Donald Rumsfeld** (1932–)

3   'All sorts of things can happen when you're open to new ideas and playing around with things.' **Stephanie Kwolek** (1923–2014)

4   'Imagination is more important than knowledge. For knowledge is limited, whereas imagination embraces the entire world, stimulating progress, giving birth to evolution.' **Albert Einstein** (1879–1955)

5   'We are all in the gutter, but some of us are looking at the stars.' **Oscar Wilde** (1854–1900)

For each quotation, consider:

a   Do you agree or disagree with the quotation?

b   What do you think the quotation suggests about how knowledge is constructed?

c   What is assumed or taken for granted about the ways that we pursue and construct knowledge?

Figure 3.1: How do we construct knowledge?

3.1 Introduction

In Chapters 1 and 2, we explored the knower, the nature of knowledge and the problems associated with knowledge and knowing. In this chapter, we explore what a knowledge question is, and how you can respond to these by making use of the knowledge framework. The knowledge framework is a tool for analysis of knowledge questions, and a means for comparing different areas of knowledge. We will explore the four interacting parts of the knowledge framework: scope, perspectives, methods and tools, and ethics.

In summary, the aim of this chapter is to focus on unpacking the knowledge framework.

Maps as a metaphor for knowledge

Your own knowledge is like a map; your mental map helps you *make sense* of the real world and find your way. Furthermore, knowledge is a representation of the world, just like a map. Just as maps are not an exact representation of reality, so too your knowledge is not identical to the real world. Like a map, your knowledge is partly a product of your education, society and culture at this particular point in history.

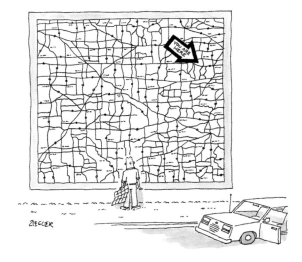

On the other hand, your knowledge – like a map – is what you acquire, shape and use for various purposes. Just as we make maps for different purposes, we also construct mental maps of the world around us, and we can evaluate different maps in terms of their degree of truth and usefulness. In the same way, you can evaluate your own mental maps. There is an expression 'the map is not the territory', which we will refer to throughout the book. According to this metaphor, *the world* that we picture is the territory, whereas our knowledge is *our map* or *our picture* of the world. Inevitably, there is a difference between the map itself and what that map attempts to describe and represent. It follows that our knowledge does not perfectly map our territory.

A map may be accurate but have limited uses. For example, while Google Maps™ might be able to 'zoom in' and depict views from the street with accuracy, this will only be useful in some contexts. On the other hand, a map could be useful but oversimplified and inaccurate. For example, a map of the Singapore underground is useful for getting from one destination to another, but the simplification of the map means that the true distances between places are not accurate. Just as maps can be inaccurate yet useful, so too, our knowledge may be over simplified but nevertheless still useful for navigating the real world.

While different maps may be more or less useful for different purposes, there is no such thing as a perfect map. A *perfect* map of a city which included every detail down to the last brick and blade of grass would have to be drawn on a scale of 1:1. Such a map would, of course, be useless as a map, and would in any case quickly become out of date. We might call this the *paradox of cartography*: if a map is to be useful, then it will necessarily be imperfect. There will, then, always be a difference between a map and the underlying territory it describes.

We all have what might be called a **mental map** of reality, which includes our ideas of what is true and what is false, what is reasonable and what is unreasonable, what is right and what is wrong, etc. Although only a fool would tell you to rip up your mental map and abandon your everyday understanding of things, you should – at least occasionally – be willing to subject it to critical scrutiny. The formal name for this analysis of our knowledge is **epistemology**, which is a branch of philosophy.

To illustrate the limitations of our common-sense understanding of things, let us make an analogy between our mental maps and real geographical maps. Consider the map of the world, which is based on what is known as the Mercator Projection (Figure 3.2). If you were familiar with this map as you grew up, you may unthinkingly accept it as true, and be unaware of its limitations.

KEY WORDS

mental map: a personal mental picture of what is true and false, reasonable and unreasonable, right and wrong, beautiful and ugly

epistemology: the philosophical study of how we know what we know, and the exploration of the difference between justified belief and opinion

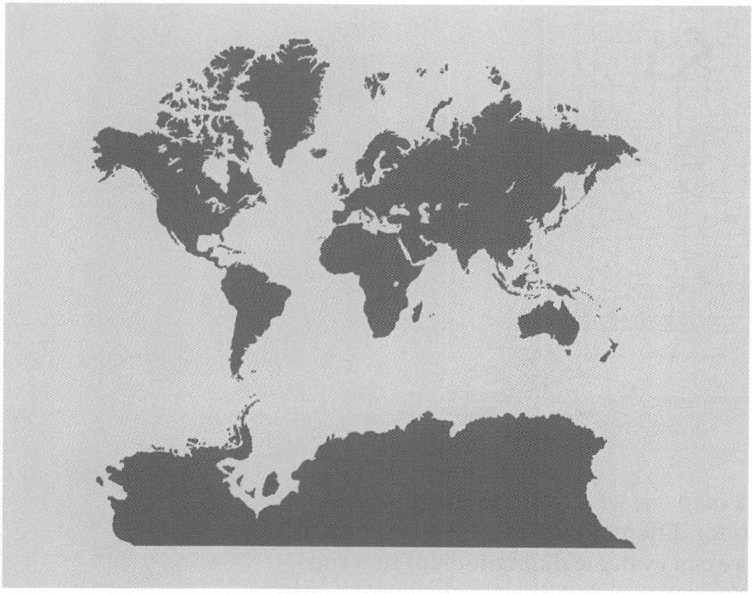

Figure 3.2: The Mercator Projection

1   Think of as many different ways as you can in which the world map shown in Figure 3.2 is:

a   inaccurate

b   based on arbitrary conventions

c   culturally biased

2   Do you think it would be possible to make a perfect map of a city? What would such a map have to look like? How useful would it be?

Among the weaknesses of the map in Figure 3.2 are the following:

1   It distorts the relative size of the land masses, so that areas further away from the equator seem larger than they are in reality. The distortion is most apparent when we compare Greenland to Africa. According to the map they are about the same size, but in reality, Africa is fourteen times bigger than Greenland.

2   It is based on the convention that the northern hemisphere is at the top of the map and the southern hemisphere at the bottom. Although we are used to this way of representing things, the reality is, of course, that the world does not come with a label saying 'This way up'!

3   The map is Eurocentric, in that it not only exaggerates the relative size of Europe, but also puts it in the middle of the map.

Now compare the Mercator Projection with another map of the world, known as the Hobo-Dyer Equal Area Projection (Figure 3.3).

Figure 3.3: The Hobo-Dyer Equal Area Projection

This projection accurately reflects the relative sizes of the land masses (although it distorts their shape). It has the southern hemisphere at the top, the northern hemisphere at the bottom and it is centred on the Pacific rather than Europe. The fact that most people find this map disorienting illustrates the grip that habitual ways of thinking have on our minds, and how difficult it is to break out of them.

The point of this excursion into maps is to suggest that, like the Mercator Projection, our common-sense mental maps may give us a distorted picture of reality. Our ideas and beliefs come from a variety of sources, such as our own experience, parents, friends, teachers, books, the news media – and of course, social media and the internet.

Since we do not have time to check everything to make sure that it is true, there are likely to be all kinds of inaccuracies, half-truths and falsehoods woven into our mental maps. Furthermore, it can be difficult for us to think outside the customs and conventions with which we are familiar, and see that there may be other ways of looking at things. Finally, there may be all kinds of cultural biases built in to our picture of the world. If you ask an English person to name the greatest writer and greatest scientist of all time, they will probably say Shakespeare and Newton. If you ask the same question to an Italian, they are more likely to say Dante and Galileo. The Chinese may urge you to read *The Dream of the Red Chamber* by Cao Xueqin (1715–1763), and will talk proudly about four of their most significant inventions - the compass, gunpowder, paper-making and printing. It follows that what we think of as the extent and limit of knowledge is shaped by the assumptions we have acquired and the cultures that we have been exposed to.

In order to unpack these issues further, our next section introduces knowledge questions.

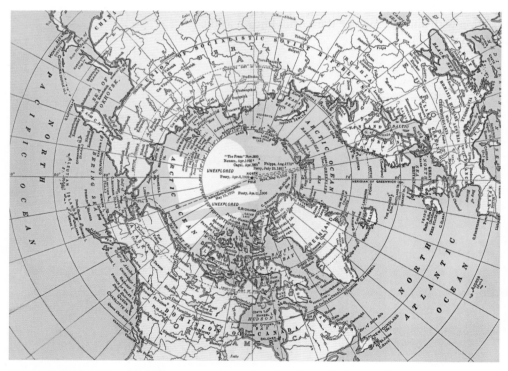

Figure 3.4: Consider the different sources and tools of knowledge used to produce this map

3.2 Knowledge questions and the knowledge framework

DISCUSS 3.1

What questions to do with knowledge and knowing would you like to ask and answer?

Knowledge questions

A knowledge question is open-ended and explicitly about knowledge and knowing, usually phrased in terms of TOK concepts. Knowledge questions are **contestable**, meaning that there is no single correct answer but instead a range of possible answers to consider. Knowledge questions may have no simple answers, but it does not follow that there are *no* answers. Considering the examples above, you can see that none of them can be answered with a straightforward 'yes' or a 'no' or even a plain 'don't know!' You can still arrive at a judgement, having considered the evidence and examples that might be used to support these different answers. Knowledge questions relate to any of the main TOK concepts, including justification, evidence or certainty. They are not the same as subject-specific questions because they are explicitly about knowledge and knowing. Knowledge questions can arise both from your experience of the world around you and in your six IB Diploma Programme subjects. Here are some examples.

KEY WORD

contestable: where there are different possible answers, opinions or views on the same question or topic

REAL-LIFE SITUATION 3.2

(**IB experience:** As part of your IB Diploma Programme History course, studying the different views of historians on the 1917 October Revolution)

Subject-specific question: Why do historians have different views of the 1917 October Revolution?

Knowledge question: To what extent can we still have reliable historical knowledge if, given access to the same facts, experts can disagree?

(**IB experience:** As part of your DP Group 4 science course, studying how the mass of an element such as magnesium is affected when heated)

Subject-specific question: Why does the mass of some elements increase when heated?

Knowledge question: To what extent can we make accurate measurements that lead to reliable knowledge in the natural sciences?

(**IB experience:** A map that uses the Mercator Projection)

Subject-specific question: How do cartographers create maps?

Knowledge question: To what extent can knowledge be both accurate and useful?

EXPLORE 3.2

Place ten different maps around the classroom. They could include maps ranging from a map of the world, a train map, a map representing global income or birth rates, a map of your school grounds, etc. Tour the classroom and work with a partner to evaluate each map. Rate them according to which are most accurate and most useful. Be ready to feedback your insights to the class.

Discuss the following, and be ready to justify your choices:

a   Which maps are most accurate?

b   Which are most useful?

c   'The map is not the territory'. Discuss what you think this means. If it is true, what implications might this have for us as knowers?

d   Which maps do you think will still be either accurate or useful in the next 20, 50 or 100 years?

e   Consider the following ideas: simplicity, accuracy, usefulness. How did these apply to the maps you have explored? How does this relate to your knowledge?

The knowledge framework

DISCUSS 3.2

How might we make comparisons and explore connections between different areas of knowledge and optional themes?

The task of evaluating our own knowledge and the knowledge questions that arise is made easier by the knowledge framework, which consists of these four strands:

1   scope

2   perspectives

3   methods and tools

4   ethics

The framework is intended to develop your analysis of knowledge questions, and to make comparisons between different areas of knowledge and the optional themes. Your ability to make and explore links and comparisons between areas of knowledge is one important analytical skill, among others. You might consider the following table as a starting point. You can develop it in greater detail when you explore the later chapters.

The knowledge framework A comparative tool for analysis of knowledge and knowing				
	Scope	Perspectives	Methods and tools	Ethics
Core theme Knowledge and the knower				
Optional themes				
Knowledge and technology				
Knowledge and language				
Knowledge and politics				
Knowledge and religion				
Knowledge and indigenous societies				
Areas of Knowledge				
History				
The arts				
Mathematics				
Natural sciences				
Human sciences				

REFLECTION

As a knower, think about why it is useful for you to be able to compare and make links between different areas of knowledge. How will it sharpen your analytic skills?

3.3 Scope of knowledge

By 'scope' of knowledge, we mean the extent of our knowledge and the limits to it. As knowers, we have acquired knowledge over many years, and the totality of our body of knowledge is what we mean by the scope of our knowledge. The extent of our knowledge can be rich and diverse, including *knowing that* certain things are the case, as well as *knowing how* to use it or how to do things. The scope of an area of knowledge is the subject matter that belongs to it.

REAL-LIFE SITUATION 3.3

As an IB Diploma Programme student, you are knowledgeable. The scope of your knowledge has two distinctive features: *in-depth* knowledge gained in your higher-level subjects, and a *breadth* of knowledge gained across all six of your subjects. Consider one or more of your IB subjects – what do you think are the scope and limits of the subject matter?

Consider the extent of your knowledge and how this has changed during your own lifetime. The metaphorical maps you used and needed as a child are very different from those you use today. The extent and limit of our knowledge develops over time, and is determined by various cognitive factors, as well as factors such as our upbringing and our educational, social and cultural context. For example, your choice of six IB Diploma Programme subjects will have already shaped the scope and extent of your knowledge.

John Archibald Wheeler (1911–2008) claimed that, 'We live on an island surrounded by a sea of ignorance. As our island of knowledge grows, so does the shore of our ignorance.' Exploring the map analogy and this quotation further, our knowledge could be compared to the map of an island, where the island represents the knowledge you have acquired. Arguably, as Wheeler suggests, as our island of knowledge increases so does the extent of the metaphorical shoreline of ignorance. The implication here is that as our knowledge and expertise increases so too does our awareness of the limits of our knowledge. Simply put, the more we know, the more aware we become of how much else there is to know. Socrates (470–399 BCE) was considered the wisest man in Athens because he knew the limit of his knowledge.

The scope of our knowledge matters because it can help us to become increasingly self-aware as knowers. You might think, for example, of people who have acquired great expertise, and yet who are very humble about what they know because they know the true extent and limits to their knowledge. They know what they do not know.

The section on 'perspectives' that follows will further explore how individuals can contribute to the development of knowledge.

EXPLORE 3.3

Working individually, use a piece of paper to make a diagram or illustration that represents your 'island of knowledge' and your 'shoreline of ignorance'. Use words, labels and lists to show your different types of knowledge, and the relevant factors that have shaped it. The following prompts might be helpful for developing your diagram further.

a   Can you picture or represent the 'mental map' which you use to make sense of, and navigate, the world – based on the topics you are learning in your six IB Diploma Programme subjects?

b   What is the scope and limit of the mental map that you have? What do you already know?

c   What factors shape your mental map? For example, how might belonging to various groups or communities impact on what you know?

d   How would you like to develop, increase or change your mental map in the future? What would you like to know and why?

e   If knowledge is like a map, what part would you expect your individual responsibilities and personal values to have on this map? (Note that we will be exploring ethics towards the end of the chapter.)

CONTINUED

Peer-assessment

Share and compare the mental maps you have produced. Consider how well your partner can express and represent their ideas on paper. Was your partner clear about the scope and limits of their knowledge? Did they know what they do not know? Were you able to understand the factors that shaped their map? Did they have good ideas for developing their map in the future?

You could give each other a score (for example, up to 3 points for clarity and up to 3 again for comprehensiveness) and discuss how each of you could improve your score.

Knowledge questions relating to scope of knowledge

- How does one particular area of knowledge fit within the broader context of knowledge and knowing as a whole?

- What might motivate someone to pursue and contribute towards a particular area of knowledge?

- Choose two areas of knowledge to compare. What are the similarities and differences in terms of the scope, extent and limit of those areas of knowledge?

- With reference to two areas of knowledge, to what extent do they deal with uncertainty, ambiguity and questions with various plausible answers?

- What are the current unresolved or contestable questions that still need to be solved or answered in a particular area of knowledge?

- How might an area of knowledge set out to identify local, national or global problems and work towards solutions to those problems?

REFLECTION

Aristotle (384–322 BCE) is generally credited with saying, 'The more we know, the more we know we don't know.' Think about this quote in relation to your own knowledge journey. To what extent might the process of learning be more important than the knowledge that you learn?

3.4 Perspectives

REAL-LIFE SITUATION 3.4

1   How might our upbringing, society and culture influence our view of knowledge?

2   How does knowledge change over time?

By 'perspective' we mean 'viewpoint'. As knowers, we each have a unique perspective on the world. This has important implications for our knowledge, given that our knowledge is highly contextual and dependent on multiple influences. As a knower, you might consider how much of your knowledge has been shaped by your particular cultural, educational and international setting and other influences. In this section, we explore the concept of the knower's 'perspective'.

EXPLORE 3.4

Evaluate the attribute of being 'open-minded' in the IB Diploma Programme learner profile.

1   What does it mean to be 'open-minded'? Create a mind-map, illustrating specific examples of open-mindedness at work in the world today.

2   What does it mean to be 'internationally-minded'? Produce a second mind-map, suggesting specific examples of this at work in the world today.

3   As a class, discuss: Is 'open-minded' the same as 'internationally-minded'? Why or why not?

Our knower's perspective

The sciences, in particular neuroscience, can help to answer how our knowledge is shaped based on research into how our brains develop and learn. Neuroscientists study the science behind the workings of the brain, including the science of memory, language and cognition, and the mental process of knowing.

Figure 3.5: In TOK we are interested in the knower's perspective - how do you, as a knower, construct knowledge?

In TOK, we are interested in the knower's perspective – how do you, as a knower, construct knowledge? How our sense of reality is formed has only recently been understood. We have a rich knowledge and understanding of the brain, but there is still much more to discover. The brain weighs around 1.5 kg – about the same mass as a cauliflower. It occupies only 2% of our body mass while consuming 20% of our body's energy. There are 86 billion nerve cells in the brain with 100 trillion connections – the brain is the most intricate circuit board imaginable.

Each of us has a distinctive neural circuit board – and we each retain an individual life story that is different from the next person. As knowers, we are unique. No one else has your memories, your experiences, your unique knowledge base. It follows that each of our perspectives is unique. We believe we have a shared experience in terms of consciousness. We may have a shared understanding of the mechanism of the brain, but our own experience of consciousness is unique to us. Neuroscientists pursue knowledge of our ability to form a subjective view of the world. When we learn something new, we make new connections between axons (nerve cells) and create a myelin sheath around the axons to protect them, and to speed up the electrical signals between them. Brain connectivity is the basis for learning and memory. Our unique memories help us to process and make sense of sense data. However, in order to function, the brain has to take shortcuts – it cannot process all the sensory data it receives – and makes assumptions based on past experiences, so that it is not bombarded.

How our degree of faith impacts our perspectives

Faith plays a role in the foundations of knowledge, the goals we pursue and our relations with others. Faith is often used as a synonym for 'trust', and some people argue that faith is essentially a relationship of trust rather than a hypothesis about reality. If by faith we mean trust, it follows that faith is a legitimate source of knowledge. For example, we trust teachers to teach accurate knowledge. Certainly, having faith *in* someone seems to be different from having faith *that* something is the case. You may, for example, have faith in your parents in the sense that you trust that they have your interests at heart, even when this is not readily apparent. However, faith *in* cannot be entirely divorced from faith *that*, if it is to have any meaningful content. Minimally, you cannot have faith *in* someone unless you believe *that* they exist; and if you have faith *in* your parents you probably have faith *that* they will be there when you really need them.

Faith is commonly thought of as a subset of belief, and your faith can shape and inform your perspectives. You may, for example, have faith in the truth of various propositions, such as a religious creed, ethical ideal or political doctrine. However, while faith is a form of belief, many beliefs do not involve faith. We are more likely to use the word 'faith' to describe deeply held convictions. You might, for example, say *'I have faith that human beings are fundamentally good'*, or *'I have faith in democracy'*. As this suggests, the word 'faith' is closely connected with our perspective or worldview – that is, a set of beliefs about the fundamental nature of reality and our place in it.

How paradigms influence our perspectives

One way of examining different perspectives is to think of them using paradigms. You might think of a paradigm as a model for understanding reality. Firstly, an example of a cultural paradigm from real-life might include the idea of eating a meal with a knife in the right hand and a fork in the left. This model impacts on our perspective of what is 'normal' behaviour in a school dining room in western countries, and may have cultural variations across the globe where it might be 'normal' to eat with your hand. Other everyday examples might include marriage as a paradigm or model for understanding relationships, or education as a model for understanding the upbringing of children. Beyond these cultural examples, there are many examples of intellectual paradigms that might shape the construction of areas of knowledge that we explore further in the later chapters.

The key point is that the paradigms we take for granted might influence our perspectives. However, this is not a passive process. As knowers, we can evaluate our own paradigms, and shape and influence them ourselves.

DISCUSS 3.3

1 What is the difference between a theory, a law and a paradigm?

2 How far might paradigms help or hinder the progress of knowledge?

How knowledge develops and changes over time

You might also consider 'perspective' as a historical strand. Knowledge develops and changes over time. This happens for many reasons, and sometimes as a result of the impact of key thinkers who change a paradigm.

The examples below illustrate how our knowledge develops and changes over time.

1 quantum mechanics or the *general theory of relativity* in physics

2 the Darwinian paradigm in biology

3 the atomic paradigm in chemistry

4 the Keynesian and classical model in economics

5 the modernist paradigm in the arts

6 the post-modernist paradigm in the study of texts in the literary arts or history

7 the pre-Raphaelite or surrealist paradigm in the visual arts

8 liberation or feminist theology in the study of religion

9 the Marxist paradigm in the study of history or economics

Thomas Kuhn (1922–1996) coined the idea of a paradigm shift, where often an individual or a collaborative group will contribute knowledge in such a way that the 'old' models for understanding have to change in order to accommodate a new movement or theory. This idea will be developed further in Chapter 13.

REAL-LIFE SITUATION 3.5

How might the paradigms listed above change our perspective and make us think in new ways?

How individuals contribute to the development of knowledge

Knowledge is a product of an intellectual climate. Knowers might contribute to the knowledge that is shared by a community or an area of knowledge. Individual thinkers have contributed in significant ways to the advancement of knowledge – from Isaac Newton (1643–1727) in physics and Thomas Babington Macaulay (1800–1859) in history to Salvador Dali (1904–1989) in the visual arts. Ada Lovelace (1815–1852) made her own algorithm, which led to the earliest theoretical computer, the Analytical Engine. Although this was never built, her contribution was significant. Arguably, regardless of the area of knowledge or knowledge community, the capacity to make a significant contribution to knowledge in a certain field requires creativity and imagination. Some key individuals can take a fresh perspective and 'see further' than others. As a result, they can change paradigms and transform the way we understand an area of knowledge. By contributing a new perspective, these key thinkers therefore in turn contribute to the development of knowledge.

EXPLORE 3.5

Great thinkers who helped to initiate paradigm shifts in their subjects include:

- Albert Einstein (1879–1955) in physics

- Dimitri Mendelev (1834–1907) in chemistry

- Charles Darwin (1809–1882) in biology

- John Maynard Keynes (1883–1946) in economics

- Karl Marx (1818–1883) in history

- Sigmund Freud (1856–1939) in psychology

- Noam Chomsky (1928–) in linguistics

- Pablo Picasso (1881–1963) in art

Choose one or more key thinker from the list above, and do some research into the contribution they made in that field of knowledge. Present your ideas to the class. In what ways did their contribution influence a new perspective?

Self-assessment

How well did your presentation demonstrate that you have acquired a sound understanding of how far an individual can develop knowledge and shape our perspectives?

Did you consider the following?

- How did the person revolutionise their subject or challenge the consensus at the time? Give an example.

- What impact did their contribution to knowledge have at the time?

CONTINUED

- To what extent were their ideas accepted or rejected at the time?

- To what extent are their ideas still accepted today?

REAL-LIFE SITUATION 3.6

1 How far is the contribution of individuals important for the development of knowledge?

2 What needs to happen (or what conditions need to be met) in order for new perspectives to be accepted?

How can I evaluate my own knower's perspective?

Our process of knowing is shaped by various cognitive factors such as sense perception, as well as broader influences such as upbringing, culture and values. Factors that might influence our knowledge include some of the following: gender, class, economic status, age, sexual orientation, nationality, immigrant status, teachers, friends, religious leaders, parents, school, political beliefs, religious beliefs, ethical beliefs, personal and family history, films you have watched, books you have read and personal experiences you have had or read about.

In summary, identifying our own perspectives and evaluating what impacts our knowledge matters because it helps us to become more self-aware as knowers and to further understand other viewpoints. In the next section, we will examine the methods and tools used to produce knowledge, and the process by which we acquire knowledge.

Figure 3.6: How far might your perspectives, beliefs and assumptions shape how you think about knowledge and knowing?

EXPLORE 3.6

List as many influences on your knowledge as you can think of.

Consider the following questions and discuss:

a   How does belonging to a specific social and economic class influence your political beliefs?

b   How might a social media 'filter bubble' affect what we know about current affairs, news stories or other pre-selected content that appears on our mobile devices?

c   How might being born inside or outside the USA give you a particular attitude towards the study of certain events in American history?

d   How might a religious or political commitment influence your attitude towards the uses of digital technology?

e   How might being male or female influence your beliefs about ethical issues such as abortion or contraception?

Now develop your own examples. Try to develop three or more of your own individual specific and personal examples that explicitly recognise precisely how your knowledge has been shaped by a particular influence.

For example, you may claim that 'my religious commitment influences my knowledge.' However, a more explicit recognition of precisely how your religion has affected your knowledge is better. The ability to pinpoint one of the religion's beliefs that [insert religious belief here] has influenced your own belief that [insert student's belief here] is better. For example, 'being brought up in a Christian community that believes in the importance of forgiveness has influenced my ethical belief that I should treat others with compassion.'

Knowledge questions relating to perspectives

- How and why does knowledge evolve and change over time? Consider this in relation to two areas of knowledge.

- How far is the production of knowledge an individual or a collaborative task?

- In what ways might individuals contribute to knowledge in particular areas of knowledge or optional themes?

- How far is knowledge situated in a social or cultural context?

- How and why might expert opinion or interpretation of the same topic or question vary, if there is the same access to facts?

- Who decides what counts as knowledge within a particular area of knowledge?

- How does your own perspective impact on your study of different areas of knowledge?

REFLECTION

To what extent does your personal perspective change over time, and how does this affect what you know?

3.5 Methods and tools

DISCUSS 3.4

How do you think we acquire knowledge?

Methods

By 'method', we mean the system, strategy, process or procedure that we use to gain knowledge. Academic disciplines use various different methods of enquiry to gain knowledge, and these are explored further in the chapters on optional themes and areas of knowledge. For example, we explore the qualitative and quantitative methods used in the human sciences, and the historian's method of using a sound interpretation of evidence to construct a meaningful and explanatory narrative.

There may be significant commonalities between methods – for instance, the notion of a hypothesis and the use of evidence is shared by scientists and historians. Furthermore, Professor Tom McLeish (1962–) in his book *The Poetry and Music of Science: Comparing Creativity in Science and Art* argues that creativity and imagination are essential parts both of the scientific method and of any artistic process. He points out, for example, that the scientific method might suggest a way to test ideas, but it does not specify how to arrive at a hypothesis. He therefore argues for the role of creativity in relation to the scientific method. Indeed, the creative process is central to all areas of knowledge – from mathematics and human sciences to history and the arts. Method is a central concept because it invites you to explore *how* we go about gaining and constructing knowledge – whether it is through trial and error, experiment, research or observation.

An interdisciplinary method for gaining knowledge

The Ordered Universe Project is a project where experts in the natural and human sciences, mathematics and the arts have adopted an interdisciplinary approach to come together to understand the writings of the medieval thinker and polymath Robert Grosseteste (1170–1253). Moreover, it is an example of not only interdisciplinary but also international collaboration, based at Durham University and University of Oxford and partnered with multiple international universities. The focus has been on Grosseteste's insight into natural phenomena, in order to understand the context and content of his manuscripts from the multiple perspectives of different experts. Here, there is an implicit idea that knowledge can be found in and through a method and process that allows experts from different disciplines to share and learn from each other in a common cause.

Figure 3.7: Robert Grosseteste, the 13th-century bishop who wrote a treatise, *On Light*, combining faith and imagination with natural sciences and mathematics

---

EXPLORE 3.7

Imagine that the following people are discussing a knowledge question: there is a scientist, an artist, a historian, a mathematician and a moral philosopher.

Select a knowledge question. For example, 'Should we value knowledge for its usefulness or accuracy?' or 'How far does culture influence what we know?' Work together in a group where each person plays the part of the one of the people from a different area of knowledge. Discuss what each person might think about the question. Evaluate the knowledge question and consider whether the different perspectives get you closer to the truth.

DISCUSS 3.5

1   Do you think that this type of interdisciplinary approach yields more or less reliable knowledge than one where there is only collaboration between experts from within a single area of knowledge? What are the merits of both approaches?

2   Does confirmation from across perspectives enhance truth? Why? Why not?

3   Who is missing from this list? What else could other experts bring to the table, and why?

EXPLORE 3.8

Do some research into Robert Grosseteste, starting with the Ordered Universe Project, an international research investigation into the thinking of Robert Grosseteste.

Find out more about the original ideas that Grosseteste came up with. How has an interdisciplinary approach and method enabled academics to gain shared knowledge of Grosseteste's ideas?

Thesis, antithesis and synthesis

Georg Wilhelm Friedrich Hegel (1770–1831) developed a **dialectical** method using the ideas of thesis, antithesis and synthesis. Our understanding of reality begins with a proposition (**thesis**) which contains within itself a contradictory aspect that requires a counter-argument (**anti-thesis**), which needs a resolution (**synthesis**) – a new idea that resolves the conflict between thesis and antithesis. Hegel recognised that his method continued a tradition begun by Plato, the ancient Greek philosopher, who presented philosophical arguments between the character of Socrates and the counter-arguments of another person. Critics have challenged Hegel's belief that reason necessarily generates contradictions. Moreover, while Hegel developed a dialectical method, he never used the terms 'thesis', 'antithesis' and 'synthesis' himself.

A tool box as a metaphor for knowledge

The methods we use to gain knowledge are closely linked to the tools at our disposal. By knowledge 'tools', we mean the devices needed to carry out a certain task, specifically the tools we use to construct or produce knowledge. For us as knowers, the ways in which we use 'methods and tools' to construct knowledge are highly complex. In this section, we do not attempt to deal with every possible method and tool, as these are developed in later chapters. Instead, we outline a few tools to get you thinking about some of the knowledge questions and concepts involved.

Just as we use appropriate tools for different practical tasks in everyday life, we also use various tools and methods to gain knowledge. For example, if you wanted to build a piece of flat-packed furniture such as a wardrobe, you would need a 'tool box' including a screwdriver and a hammer, among others. In the same way, as knowers, we require multiple tools for constructing knowledge. There are essential knowledge tools we use to gain knowledge, and these are used distinctively in each area of knowledge. These include **practical or material tools** which could extend our observations further, such as a telescope or a microscope, and **cognitive tools** such as sense perception.

The internet is an obvious example of a practical knowledge tool. If we want an answer, we might use a search engine. However, as we discussed in Chapter 2, access to information is not the same thing as knowledge, and while this quick and convenient way of gaining information may give us the illusion of instant knowledge, it does not provide deep knowledge and understanding. In Chapter 5, we explore how technology is shaping us as knowers, affecting the way we construct knowledge and think about the nature of knowledge and knowing. Other practical tools, such as those used in mathematics, include the scientific calculator, the protractor and the compass, and in the natural sciences, equipment such as the Bunsen burner.

KEY WORDS

dialectics: a method of argument that involves a disagreement between opposing sides

thesis: a proposition

antithesis: the negation of a thesis

synthesis: in the context of dialectics, a connected whole, a resolution, or a new idea which resolves the conflict between thesis and antithesis

practical or material (knowledge) tool: the device used to complement or enhance cognition, such as a microscope or an iPad

cognitive (knowledge) tool: the mental process of acquiring knowledge, for example via the senses, memory, imagination, experience and rational thought

Cognitive tools are the mental processes of acquiring knowledge, such as sense perception, memory, imagination, experience or rational thought. Some people argue that our knowledge is the result of the interaction of various cognitive knowledge tools. One characteristic of being human is our capacity for rational and logical thought, but equally, the way in which our brain actively interprets the data it receives from our biological senses seems to be essential in our construction of knowledge.

Figure 3.8: What 'tools' do we use to construct knowledge?

The exploration of this question has a long history. From the perspective of the human sciences, which includes the study of philosophy, there has been a traditional dispute among philosophers who have disagreed about the way in which we acquire knowledge. For the supporters of **empiricists**, David Hume (1711–1776), John Locke (1632–1704) and George Berkeley (1685–1753), experience and sense perception are essential sources or tools for producing knowing. In contrast, for the **rationalists** such as Rene Descartes (1596–1650), Baruch Spinoza (1632–1677) and Gottfried Leibniz (1646–1716), **rationality** and **logic** are the main sources and tools of knowledge.

Our task in this section is not to outline the detail of this philosophical dispute, but rather to explore the various ways in which we might construct or produce knowledge. As knowers, it is essential that we have some understanding and insight into the process by which we acquire knowledge. In this section, we identify and explore various related knowledge questions.

The senses

DISCUSS 3.6

Is seeing believing? Can we trust our senses to give us reliable knowledge?

Our senses play a fundamental role in giving us knowledge of the world. Indeed, according to the major school of philosophy known as empiricism, *all* knowledge is ultimately based on perceptual experience. This may be too extreme, but sense perception clearly plays a key role in almost all subject areas, ranging from the sciences through history to the arts. Think, for example, of the role played by observation in biology, eye-witness accounts in history or the ability to see things with new eyes in the visual arts.

There is more to perception than meets the eye, and it is a more active process than common-sense realism allows. Rather than our senses passively reflecting an independent reality, our experience of the world is affected not only by what is 'out there', but also by the structure of our sense organs and our minds. This has implications for the reliability of sense perception as a source of knowledge. On the one hand, it generally makes sense to trust our senses, given that they have evolved in the ways that they have for natural reasons and are essential to our survival. Our nervous system ensures that if we touch something hot, we immediately and instinctively remove our hand from the heat. This evolved reflex is built into our survival. Yet, on the other hand, we should keep in mind that our senses cannot always be trusted, and may sometimes deceive us.

Imagination

DISCUSS 3.7

Is imagination a reliable source of knowledge?

Whereas sense perception relates to what we can experience and observe, imagination goes beyond observation. According to one common definition, imagination is the ability to form a representation of something that is not present to the senses. However, imagination covers both mental *images* and the entertaining of *possibilities*. You can imagine all kinds of possibilities and possible worlds, such as a world without war or a world in which there is no global warming. If you are asked to 'imagine a scenario when…', there is an assumption built in that we can invent an imaginary world that only exists as a 'possible world' in our mind, and not in the observable world around us.

Imagination can be valuable for the knower, given that we may spend vast amounts of our leisure time reading novels, watching movies, playing video games, imagining the consequences of various courses of action – and idly daydreaming about such things as winning the lottery! Imagination is not only an important knowledge tool, but also plays a role in its justification and constitution. Imagination in the form of **empathy** is particularly relevant to our knowledge of other people. This raises a knowledge question about the relation between empathy and ethics, which we explore in the section on ethics later in this chapter.

Various kinds of imagination can be distinguished: **fantasy**, possible worlds, **realistic imagination** and **creativity**. Arguably, imagination is an essential tool in all areas of knowledge. For example, a scientist needs the capacity for imagination just as much as an artist or a historian, even if the precise role that imagination plays in that area of knowledge is distinctive.

Referring back to the section on 'perspectives' earlier in the chapter, you could argue that the imagination required to shift a paradigm is essential to the development of knowledge, and that imagination was as important to the scientist Charles Darwin (1809–1882) as it was to the artist Salvador Dali (1904–1989). Imagination and creativity are closely linked, and given that creativity is the furnace in which new ideas are forged, you may like to consider the extent to which it is essential to the production of knowledge.

KEY WORDS

empathy: the ability to imagine and understand the feelings and viewpoint of another person

fantasy: an escapist form of imagination that is only distantly connected with the real world

realistic imagination: imagination which is informed and guided by the relevant facts

creativity: the ability to generate ideas or produce works that are original, surprising and valuable

Memory

DISCUSS 3.8

Can we trust our memory as a reliable source of knowledge?

In Chapter 2, we explored memory in relation to the problems of knowledge that it poses, and here you might evaluate it further as a knowledge tool. On a personal level, memory is crucial to self-knowledge – your sense of who you are consists in large part of your memories. Memory is closely associated with history – much of which is based on eye-witness recollections of events which may have happened long before they are put on record. In the practical sphere, the perceived accuracy of a witness's memory may determine whether someone is found innocent or guilty in a criminal trial. In fact, our entire stock of knowledge depends critically on memory. The human sciences, in particular psychology, can describe the processes associated with creating and recalling memories. Three different kinds of memory are commonly distinguished: **personal memory**, **factual memory** and **practical memory**.

Personal memory consists of your internal recollection of various events that make up your life, such as falling off your bicycle when you were a child, your first day at school or your holiday in Crete the summer before last. Personal memory gives you your sense of identity. If you suffered from amnesia and could remember nothing about your past, then you would not know who you are.

Factual memory refers to the part of memory that is concerned with meanings, facts and ideas. For example, you may know that the word 'mercurial' means 'fickle', or that gold has atomic number 79, or that Riga is the capital of Latvia. Such memory is *undated*, in that it is concerned only with the *content* of the knowledge and not with *when* it was acquired. You may not, for example, have any memories of *when* you learned the names of capital cities.

Practical memory consists of your memory of the various skills and habits you have acquired in your life, such as knowing how to type, ski or play the violin. Unlike personal and factual memory, practical memory is usually implicit, in the sense that it is difficult or impossible to put into words. Sports psychologists use the phrase *muscle memory* to denote the ability to perform complex motor tasks without conscious awareness. If you can ride a bicycle, you can, for example, turn left without having to think about what you are doing. Some important practical memories – such as those associated with learning to walk and talk – are laid down before your earliest personal memories. Once established, they grow deep roots and become almost impossible to forget.

The connection between memory and knowledge is clearly important, and we explore it further in later chapters. Some people might argue that in a digital age when we can instantly access information online, our capacity to remember factual information is less important. The counter-argument might be that our memory remains essential for the knower, not only in terms of their personal identity but also in terms of their shared identity with others. This raises an ethical knowledge question about the responsibilities of individuals, communities and nations to remember their past.

KEY WORDS

personal memory: the internal recollection of the various events that make up our lives

factual memory: our memory of meanings, facts and information

practical memory: the remembered ability to know how to do something, such as playing the piano

Figure 3.9: How reliable are the various 'tools' that we use to construct knowledge?

Rationality and logic

DISCUSS 3.9

Does knowledge need to be based on rationality and logic?

Our ability to think logically and to apply a logical framework to the world is arguably an important source of knowledge. Reason plays a crucial role in the construction of knowledge, not only in the natural sciences and mathematics but also in other areas of knowledge, including history, the human sciences and the arts. If you consider what rationality and reasoning is, you might think of it in a number of different ways. In this section we will explore the following:

- deductive reasoning

- inductive reasoning

- abductive reasoning

One of the great attractions of reason as a source of knowledge is that it is a tool that seems to give us a degree of certainty. To take a well-known example, given that all human beings are mortal, and given that I am a human being, it *necessarily* follows that I am mortal, provided the **premises** are true. There are no 'if's or 'but's about it, and it is not a matter of personal opinion or the culture in which you were brought up. Given the premises – sometimes called assumptions – the conclusion *has* to follow. There is no way that you can dispute it. This degree of certainty might seem appealing, and it is perhaps not surprising that there is a school of philosophy – called *rationalism* – according to which reason plays a key role in how we acquire knowledge. The central assumption of rationalism is that we can discover important truths about reality through the use of reason alone.

> **KEY WORD**
>
> **premise:** assumption on which an argument is based, or from which a conclusion is drawn

Deductive reasoning

DISCUSS 3.10

How reliable is deductive reasoning?

Deductive reasoning is a knowledge tool that can be used by the knower when the application of logical thinking is required. This type of reasoning is used in multiple areas of knowledge, from mathematics to history. Deductive reasoning is any form of reasoning that moves from the general to the particular.

The type of deductive argument that follows is known as a **syllogism**, which consists of the following items:

1   two premises and a conclusion

2   three terms, each of which occurs twice ('IB Diploma Programme students', 'subjects' and 'Rosie')

3   quantifiers, such as 'all', 'some' or 'no', which tell us the quantity that is being referred to

Premise 1: All IB Diploma Programme students study six subjects.

Premise 2: Rosie is an IB Diploma Programme student.

Conclusion: Therefore, Rosie studies six subjects.

Before looking at some more examples of syllogisms, we need to make a distinction between **truth** and **validity**. These two words are sometimes used interchangeably, but they do not mean the same thing. Truth (which we explore in Chapter 4) is concerned with what is the case. Validity is concerned with whether conclusions follow logically from premises. Truth is a property of statements, whereas validity is a property of arguments. To avoid confusion, you should not say that an argument is true or false, but rather that it is **valid** or **invalid**.

More formally, we can say that an argument is valid if the conclusion follows logically – that is, necessarily – from the premises; and it is invalid if the conclusion does *not* follow logically from the premises. The main point to grasp is that the *validity* of an argument is *independent* of the *truth* or *falsity* of the *premises* it contains.

Premise 1: All South American countries are in the Southern Hemisphere.

Premise 2: Italy is a South American Country.

Conclusion: Italy is in the Northern Hemisphere.

In this example, both premises are false and the argument is invalid. Even though the conclusion is true, it is not **sound** because the argument is invalid – it is not a logical argument. Hence in order to be sound, the syllogism must contain *both* two true premises *and* a valid argument.

We cannot assume that the argument must be valid because we have reached a true conclusion. Validity is independent of the truth of a conclusion. You can have two

---

KEY WORDS

deductive reasoning: reasoning from the general to the particular

syllogism: a deductive argument with two premises and a conclusion

truth: a philosophical concept to do with what is the case; a premise can be true or false

validity: the property of an argument in which the conclusion follows logically from the premises

valid: an argument that follows logically from the premises

invalid: an argument that does not follow logically from the premises

sound: the property of a syllogism that contains two true premises *and* a valid argument

true premises and reach a true conclusion, but the argument is invalid. This example is sound because it contains two premises and a valid argument:

Premise 1: All humans are mortal.

Premise 2: I am human.

Conclusion: Therefore, I am mortal.

The key point here is that we can use deductive reasoning as a knowledge tool to arrive at justified conclusions. However, it is worth noting that it is difficult to establish the truth of premises, and the process of reasoning can lead us to very different, even contradictory conclusions, as shown by the following examples below:

Premise 1: If country A fired nuclear weapons at country B, then country B would automatically fire back.

Premise 2: No country would risk this situation happening – known as mutually assured destruction (MAD).

Conclusion: Therefore, nuclear weapons are a deterrent.

Premise 1: Nuclear weapons have the capability to destroy another country.

Premise 2: The very existence of nuclear weapons risks destruction happening.

Conclusion: Therefore, nuclear weapons are a threat to civilisation and peace.

EXPLORE 3.9

Evaluate the following syllogisms, and consider how the ideas of truth and validity apply to each of them.

- For each of the premises, identify those that are *true* and those that are *false*.

- For each of the arguments, identify if it is logically *valid* or *invalid*.

- Evaluate the conclusion.

Premise 1: There are 193 countries that are members of the United Nations.

Premise 2: Artsakh is a country.

Conclusion: Therefore, Artsakh is a member of the United Nations.

Premise 1: All human life is precious.

Premise 2: Abortion involves the destruction of a potential (unborn) human life.

Conclusion: Therefore, abortion is wrong.

Premise 1: Every woman has the right to choose what happens to her body.

Premise 2: The right to have an abortion protects a woman's freedom.

Conclusion: Therefore, abortion is right.

EXPLORE 3.10

Work with your partner to invent your own examples of syllogisms for the following examples:

a   two true premises and a valid argument

b   two true premises and an invalid argument

c   two false premises and a valid argument

d   two false premises and an invalid argument

e   one true premise, one false premise and a valid argument

f   one true premise, one false premise and an invalid argument

Inductive reasoning

DISCUSS 3.11

Does inductive reasoning lead to justified knowledge?

Inductive reasoning is another knowledge tool that the knower can use when the application of logic is required to reach general conclusions. This type of reasoning is used in multiple areas of knowledge – from the natural sciences to the arts. While deductive reasoning goes from the general to the particular, inductive reasoning goes in the opposite direction – from the particular to the general.

The premises of syllogisms can be based on inductive reasoning. With reference to the example *All humans are mortal, I am human, therefore, I am mortal*, my belief that all human beings are mortal is a generalisation from a vast number of particular instances. In history, every human being I know of eventually died, and I have never heard of a historical human being who did *not* die. Therefore, I can say with confidence that '*All* observed *human beings throughout history have died.*' But when we reason inductively, we typically go further than this and generalise – or make an *inductive inference* – from the observed to the unobserved. Therefore in this example, we move from '*All* observed *human beings are mortal*' to '*All human beings are mortal*'.

The natural sciences use inductive reasoning, and typically formulate general laws on the basis of a limited number of observations. For example, if metal A, metal B and metal C expand when heated, at some point, a scientist is likely to arrive at a conclusion, but will resist concluding that *all* metals expand when heated. This is because scientists will test all metals, but will only arrive at conclusions based on what they have observed. For example, if all of the copper tested expands when heated, we assume all copper will expand when heated, but this is not the same as concluding that all metals will expand.

Let's consider this example:

Premise 1: I have seen over 100 swans.

Premise 2: I observed that each of them was white.

Conclusion: Therefore, all swans are white.

KEY WORD

inductive reasoning: reasoning from the particular to the general

Premises may be based on a number of sources of knowledge, including observation and sense perception. If I have observed over 100 swans or over 10,000 swans and they have all been white, my premise will be more compelling with the larger number of swans that I have observed. Europeans used to believe that all swans are white, until they went to Australia and discovered that some swans are black. Premises 1 and 2 may be true for me, but my argument is not valid and my conclusion is not true because there *are* swans that are black (which I have not yet observed). If I observed just one black swan, my second premise would be false.

Figure 3.10: There are various species of swans, including the Bewick Swan pictured here with a black neck. How much observation is required before we reach a justified conclusion?

Since inductive reasoning typically moves from the observed to the unobserved, it enables us to make generalisations about the world, and we are constantly using such reasoning in everyday life. This is a good example of reason, observation and experience interacting as tools to gain knowledge.

Our knowledge, based on inductive reasoning, is justified on the basis of our observation and experience. However, the extent of the 'evidence' gained by our observations is necessarily limited. Furthermore, our inductive conclusions may 'go beyond' our experience, therefore we might assume patterns that are more imaginary than real. For example, since apples have nourished me in the past, I assume that they will nourish me in the future. Since my neighbour's dog has been friendly to me in the past, I am confident that he will not bite me today. And since my chair has supported my weight in the past, I expect it to continue to do so in the future. In each of these cases, past *experience* shapes our expectations about the (unobserved) future. If you think about it, you will see that you make literally thousands of such inferences every day, and that life would be impossible if you did not assume that most of the regularities that have held in the past will continue to hold in the future.

The counter-argument is that while inductive reasoning does have some justification, it does not lead to **certain knowledge**, and we should not rely too much on past examples, past experience nor perceived patterns. Since induction goes beyond the immediate evidence of our senses, we cannot always rely on it. This is because we tend to make *hasty generalisations* and jump to conclusions on the basis of insufficient evidence. The trouble, as the psychologist Gordon Allport (1897–1967) observed, is that, 'Given a thimbleful of facts, we rush to make generalisations as large as a tub.'

There is an important link between inductive reasoning and language as a knowledge tool, given that sometimes even well-established generalisations can let us down. With reference to the examples mentioned above, it is always possible that apples make me sick tomorrow, my neighbour's dog will bite me and my chair will collapse. You might even question a well-established regularity, such as 'Water boils at 100 degrees centigrade.' After all, it is not true if you are at the top of a mountain!

The tendency to make hasty generalisations is made worse by a phenomenon known as *confirmation bias*, which is the tendency for people to remember only evidence that supports their beliefs, and to forget evidence that goes against them. This may explain why it is so difficult to change the mind of someone who is in the grip of a prejudice.

Inductive reasoning and language

KEY WORD
certain knowledge: a state of affairs when we can be definite that something is the case

> ### DISCUSS 3.12
>
> How far does language lead to reliable inductive generalisations?

Language is one of the main ways in which we acquire knowledge about the world, and we explore this in greater depth in Chapter 6. We claim to know some things simply because they are correct by definition. For example, 'All teenagers are between 13 and 19 years of age', or 'All bachelors are unmarried,' are true by definition, and therefore count as accurate statements. However, given that these are examples of analytic statements that are true by definition, they tell us nothing about the reliability of our observation.

Indeed, there is an important link between language, observation and generalisation. When we put labels on things, such as 'teacher', 'dog' or 'table', we are implicitly organising them into general classes, based on our experience and observation, so that we can make predictions about them. If we call something a 'wolf', we have different expectations about its behaviour than if we call it a 'dog'. Similarly, if we call something a 'table', we have different expectations of its use than if we call it a 'chair'. Therefore, language might be thought of as the inherited wisdom of the community about how the world is organised; and our tendency to look for regularities in our environment and put labels on them has obvious survival value. In addition to describing our world, language also expresses our opinions and values – a theme that we look at in Chapter 4. In conclusion, inductive reasoning applies rationality and coherence to our everyday experience and observation, which we can express and communicate via language.

> ### REAL-LIFE SITUATION 3.7
>
> 1   Discuss examples of hasty generalisations.
>
> 2   What is the difference between a prejudice, a generalisation and a scientific law?

Is deductive reasoning more certain than inductive reasoning?

When we compare inductive reasoning with deductive reasoning, we might think that deductive reasoning is more certain because it is based on logic rather than generalisations. In practice, however, deduction turns out to be no more certain than induction. This is because the premises on which deductive reasoning is based are ultimately derived from induction. In the case of deductive reasoning, no new knowledge is created that was not already implied in the premises. In the case of inductive reasoning, new knowledge is created but it is only as reliable as our observations are accurate and our experience permits. The difference between the two types of reasoning can be summarised in the following table:

Deductive reasoning	Inductive reasoning
Definition	
Reasoning from general to particular	Reasoning from particular to general
Example	
All metals expand when heated. A is a metal. Therefore A expands when heated.	Metal A expands when heated; metal B expands when heated; metal C expands when heated. Therefore all metals expand when heated.
Value	
More certain if the premises are sound and the argument is valid, but less informative than induction	More informative, but less certain than deduction

EXPLORE 3.11

Using this table as a starting point, work with a partner to discuss and evaluate the strengths and weaknesses of deductive and inductive reasoning. Then develop your ideas further, and discuss the following:

- Does either type of reasoning lead to certain knowledge? Why? Why not?

- How might we use deductive and inductive reasoning as tools to evaluate knowledge claims?

REFLECTION

To what extent do your expectations and assumptions affect the ways that you use reasoning and other tools of knowing?

Abductive reasoning

Abductive reasoning relates to best explanations. It is like inductive reasoning in that it is reasoning that **infers** conclusions based on particular examples and patterns. However, unlike inductive reasoning, the conclusions are inferred because they point to the best *explanation*.

For example, if I know that two friends – Hamid and Chong Beng – have recently had an argument but I see them together in the school café chatting over a coffee, I may think that the best explanation is that they must have made up. I have no other evidence or hard data, but I arrive at my conclusion because it is the best explanation for their meeting over coffee. On the other hand, my reasoning could be unjustified, given that they may not have made up but instead are meeting to work on a collaborative homework task together. The truth is that I have limited evidence to support my theory. We might argue that evidence is required as a basis for knowledge, but what counts as evidence is dependent on the situation. Evidence varies between areas of knowledge and within knowledge communities. Also, what constitutes enough or legitimate evidence might be up for discussion. Our explanations may vary according to their degree of accuracy and the evidence available.

Deductive reasoning is based on an inference that is logically necessary. However, inductive and abductive reasoning arrive at conclusions based on inferences that might or might not follow logically. With inductive reasoning, the conclusion is based on an inference, which relies on an appeal to the frequency of examples or observations. With abductive reasoning, the conclusion inferred is based on an appeal to the best explanation. In Chapter 13, we will explore Occam's Razor – the principle that a simple solution or explanation is more likely to be correct than a complicated one.

KEY WORDS

abductive reasoning: reasoning that infers the best explanation based on the evidence available

infer: to come to a conclusion reached on the basis of evidence and reasoning

EXPLORE 3.12

You have now explored a wide range of methods and tools for acquiring knowledge. Consider how you know or *how you might justify* claims a-t.

Match each of the claims, a-t, to **one or more** of the following concepts, numbered 1–29:

1	observation	8	personal experience	15	intuition
2	evidence	9	experiment	16	faith
3	inductive reasoning	10	logic	17	trust
4	deductive reasoning	11	definition	18	memory
5	true premise	12	experience	19	imagination
6	false premise	13	interpretation	20	language
7	research	14	emotion	21	rationality

CONTINUED

22	sense perception	**25**	common sense	**28**	trust
23	conscience	**26**	value	**29**	expertise
24	aesthetic sense	**27**	authority		

Then rate and comment on the certainty of the claims. Put them in rank order where 1 is the most certain claim and 20 is the least certain claim.

	Claim	Concept(s)	Rating
a	Compound x is more soluble in water than compound y.		
b	You sense that you can trust William.		
c	Monet painted beautiful pictures of waterlilies.		
d	All bachelors are unmarried.		
e	The cosmos is rapidly expanding.		
f	The element sodium has 12 neutrons, 11 electrons and 11 protons.		
g	Henry VII (1457–1509), who was the King of England from 1485–1509, was not stable on the throne.		
h	If you add metals to acid, the amount of hydrogen produced can indicate how reactive the metal is.		
i	As interest rates rise, the number of people who apply for a mortgage decreases.		
j	An average increase in wages will lead to an increase in house prices.		
k	The milk has gone off.		
l	Every swan you have ever seen has been white.		
m	Community rules are more important than individual rights.		
n	If by God we mean the 'greatest being imaginable', then God must exist, given that existence is a quality of greatness.		
o	You can boost your brain power by exploring new environments, and staying both physically and socially active.		
p	It is wrong for one country to invade another country.		
q	It is right for a country to defend its borders.		
r	Humans are the cause of climate change.		
s	It is impossible to change the past.		
t	A piano player can improve with practice.		

CONTINUED

Peer-assessment

Compare your work with your partner.

What do you notice? What do you think of your partner's ratings? Have they missed anything? What did your partner think of your ratings? Had you missed anything?

Give each other some feedback, based on how well you have understood the different justifications that can be given for various claims.

DISCUSS 3.14

1 Using the statements in the table, discuss the following questions: How do we know each of them? Are there any that cannot be *known*?

2 How far might different methods and knowledge tools enable us to gain knowledge?

3 Why might we disagree about different degrees of certainty?

4 Can we still have valuable knowledge even if it is not certain knowledge?

Knowledge questions related to methods and tools

Here are some examples of related knowledge questions:

- What counts as a fact in two areas of knowledge? What are the similarities and differences?

- What constitutes evidence in two different areas of knowledge? How is evidence used in the construction of knowledge in these areas?

- What are the similarities and differences in the concepts, methods and tools of enquiry used in two areas of knowledge?

- How far can we rely on the cognitive and material tools used to produce knowledge in two different areas?

- How far is technology influencing the methods used to produce knowledge in different areas?

3.6 Ethics

REAL-LIFE SITUATION 3.8

How do I know what is right and wrong?

KEY WORD

ethics: the branch of knowledge to do with right and wrong, and the study of the moral principles that govern our beliefs and behaviours

Everyday life involves ethical decisions. From 'do not plagiarise', to the learner profile encouragement to 'be principled', our lives to some extent are governed by ethical standards that deserve scrutiny. You might discover that moral thinking in one cultural context is not the same as another. Furthermore, you may think that we have a duty for honesty over kindness or vice versa, regardless of our national or cultural identity.

We might distinguish between first-order and second-order ethical questions. First-order ethical questions arise in the real world, such as whether it is right for a country to possess nuclear weapons, or whether it is right or wrong to conduct experiments on animals for the sake of medical science. Second-order ethical questions are of a higher order. They relate to the *thinking about* and the *thinking beyond* those ethical questions, such as whether an ethical belief is true or false, or what evidence would justify an ethical argument.

First-order ethical questions include:

- Is cloning right or wrong?

- Is a particular government policy ethical?

- Is the use of driverless cars right or wrong?

Second-order questions include:

- Is there ethical truth, and if so, what is its nature?

- Are there ethical facts about the world?

- Is ethical knowledge really knowledge at all, or are ethical considerations more like beliefs?

Everyday moral decision-making, known as first-order thinking, is not really our focus here. Instead, our focus is on second-order thinking – that is, *thinking about* how we can know what is ethical. Moral judgements have their own character. Ethical considerations shape who we are as knowers, and who we are as knowers shapes our ethical considerations. Our moral choices express something about who we are as people. As a knower, you may think that we have a certain degree of moral responsibility – for example, in a science experiment, reporting on *all* our findings without ignoring outlying data, or having integrity in our pursuit of knowledge.

Ethical dilemmas arise in everyday life when you find yourself in a situation where two principles conflict. This involves a question about *how we know* what the right response is. For example, if your friend has cooked you a meal that you don't like, how should you respond? In this dilemma, you might be conflicted between the honest response and the kind response. But when honesty and kindness conflict, how should you act? How do we know what the right response is? In this section, we set out to reflect on how far ethical considerations should influence our pursuit of knowledge, and how far our ethical responsibilities might shape the methods we use to acquire knowledge.

Figure 3.11: Is it right or wrong to pursue knowledge at any price? How far do your ethical beliefs and values shape your pursuit of knowledge?

REAL-LIFE SITUATION 3.9

1   Think of examples of ethical dilemmas you have faced.

2   Is there a difference between how you think you *should* act and how you think you *would* act?

3   If so, why is there a difference here? (Note that some people might argue that there should be no difference – given that if you know what is right then you will act accordingly. Moreover, an argument could be put forward that an action is ethical if it is done for the right reason.)

How might the knowledge we pursue be limited by ethical constraints?

If you reflect on the six IB Diploma Programme subjects that you chose, what factors shaped your decision? You might have been influenced to pursue a particular subject depending on how much you think you will enjoy it, how challenging you find it or even whether it will support you with a future university application. When we decide what we want to know, there are multiple factors that we could take into account.

Arguably, ethical considerations might be one of those factors when we decide what knowledge to pursue. For example, in the arts, there is an important question about the ethics of suitable subject material. Some people would argue that the arts should be free from any ethical constraints, while others would argue that some degree of censorship is required.

Ethics here play a role in terms of the scope that we think is appropriate for an area of knowledge – for example, pornography which depicts indecent images might be said to fall outside the scope of the arts. Furthermore, ethical considerations are built into the methods that are used. For example, in the sciences, experiments should be carried out using the principles of honesty and integrity, and obtaining consent when relevant. In this way, ethical considerations underpin the pursuit of knowledge.

How do ethical responsibilities shape the methods we use to acquire knowledge?

Here, we consider how ethical considerations impact the pursuit and construction of knowledge. Do scientists and artists have ethical responsibilities in equal measure? If so, how do they know what ethical considerations should shape their construction of knowledge? This is a crucially important question in each area of knowledge, given that knowledge can be applied to either heal or harm – from the use of vaccinations to the atom bomb. It is important that we use our knowledge to benefit and promote human flourishing – but that is of course a moral assumption!

You might consider the criteria that we use to judge whether the knowledge we acquire is right or wrong. One assumption today is that consent must be a condition of any scientific experiment. However, this cannot apply in animal experiments, where animals cannot give consent, and some people would argue that experiments on animals who cannot give consent are never right, given that they involve the animals' involuntary suffering. The performance artist Jacqueline Traide (1988–) opposed the use of animal experiments in a powerful way when she deliberately undertook experiments on herself to reveal the shocking ordeal that animals suffered, to make her ethical point that animal experiments are always wrong.

This example raises an important point about rules and absolutes – for Jacqueline Traide, 'Do not experiment on animals' is a moral absolute. Similarly, supporters of the human rights organisation, Amnesty International, oppose the use of torture, and their belief is that 'the use of torture is always wrong'.

The Jacqueline Traide example also raises an interesting question about when the production of knowledge is wrong – some would argue that we know an action is wrong if it causes harm to humans or animals. This is known as the *harm principle*. For example, the Tuskegee experiment was a deeply unethical experiment that took place over forty years to test the effects of untreated syphilis. The participants in the study by the USA Public Health Service and Tuskegee University from 1932 were offered free health care and other benefits, however, they were not informed nor treated if they had syphilis. Even when in the 1940s penicillin was known and used to treat this condition, the men were not given the appropriate treatment they needed. The study had fatal and deeply harmful consequences for a whole community of people over generations. In 1997 President Bill Clinton apologised on behalf of the US government to the victims and their families. It is now recognised that consent is required for any study or research carried out on human participants. Moreover, ethical responsibilities influence research in the human sciences. This example suggests that knowledge should not be gained at any price, particularly if the cost is so high.

However, the counter-argument to the stance that experimenting on animals is always wrong is that the advantage of developing drugs that will benefit humans outweighs concerns about cruelty, and therefore justifies the use of such experiments. This raises a further question about the relationship between the status of different ethical beliefs, and how they relate to rules.

Does following the rules make an action ethical?

From a young age, you have probably been taught various ethical rules – ranging from 'tell the truth' to 'do not cheat'. You might assume that ethics is a question of doing what you have been told. However, there is a complex relationship between ethics and rules. In some situations, it could be the right thing to break the rules if there is a rule that promotes injustice. It does not follow that breaking rules is right, but it does follow that as knowers our ethical responsibility might sometimes be a matter of individual conscience.

Moreover, some rules have nothing to do with ethics. Your school rules may expect you to wear a school uniform, but there is no link here with ethics – obeying the rule to wear a school uniform is not an ethical obligation. It follows that obedience to following rules does not make you a good or virtuous person. There is a broader discussion to be had here surrounding the nature of law and ethics. For example, adultery may be regarded as unethical by some people, but it is legal. In this way, laws, rules and ethics may intersect, but the relationships are worthy of exploration.

The key question here is about the relationship between rules and ethics.

One argument is that ethical beliefs are determined by general rules. For example, the rules might range from the straightforward principle, 'do not lie' to more complicated rules such as 'treat others as you yourself would like to be treated…'. This is based on the idea that some rules can be absolutes that apply universally in all times and places. For example, a supporter of Amnesty International would argue that 'it is always wrong to violate human rights by using torture'. According to this line of argument, this claim is as true and universal as the claim that 'the Earth spins on an axis'. There are various possible absolute rules and principles. These might include rules that apply in all times and places such as 'do not kill', or 'behave in such a way that brings about the greatest happiness of the greatest number of people.'

A counter argument is that ethical rules are only provisional 'rules of thumb'. This is based on the idea that ethical beliefs are entirely dependent on context and that there are no absolute rules – not even simple everyday rules like 'it is right to keep promises' or 'it is wrong to kill'. According to this line of argument, ethical judgements are relative to something – relative to a particular person, situation or culture. It follows that killing may be right in one situation but not

> **KEY WORD**
>
> rule of thumb: an approximation based on experience

in another situation – so an ethical action depends not on rules, but entirely on situations. For example, the use of torture could be justified on the basis that it is the right action relative to the situation.

EXPLORE 3.13

There is an interesting debate about the relationship between ethics and the law – if you would like to research into it, look up the Dworkin and Hart debate regarding legal positivism.

REAL-LIFE SITUATION 3.10

1   Are people who follow rules necessarily good people? Why? Why not?

2   Make a list of ethical rules. Are they rules of thumb? Are any of the ethical rules that you would like all people to adopt, regardless of their cultural differences?

Ethical theories

Theories of ethics have been proposed by various philosophers. Each of them gives an answer to the question, '*How* do we know what is ethical?' We include a number of theories here – including virtue ethics, deontology and teleological theories. The link with paradigms is important, given that our ethical 'models for understanding' shape us as knowers, and our values can influence the knowledge that we might or might not choose to pursue.

In this section we explore whether there are any ethical facts, and if so what type of facts these would be. Each of the following theories proposes that there are some facts about ethics. According to virtue ethics it is a fact that an action is ethical if it is performed by a virtuous person. By contrast other theories claim that concepts such as duty, intentions or consequences relate to ethical facts.

Virtue ethics

REAL-LIFE SITUATION 3.11

What personal traits and qualities do we need to be ethical knowers?

The 4th-century BCE Greek philosopher, Aristotle, developed a theory of ethics now known as **virtue ethics** – that an ethical action is one that is performed by a virtuous person. If this is the case, it follows that there are no specific rules that make an action right or wrong.

This raises a question about who is a virtuous person, and how we acquire this knowledge. If you consider the people you know, you might be able to identify those people who have a virtuous character – they are people who embody ethical qualities

---

KEY WORD

virtue ethics: the theory that an ethical action is one performed by a virtuous person and they know the right thing to do. For example, a government might select people with a reputation for wisdom and sound judgement to participate on an advisory committee. If the people are chosen for the committee because of their sound ethical judgement, this continues the approach of Aristotle.

It follows that if you want to be an ethical person, you practise and carry out what virtuous people do. As an analogy, I might want to develop my abdominal muscles in order to get a 'six-pack', however, wanting this will not make it happen. Instead, I need to train and work-out to make this happen. In the same way, if I want to be virtuous, I need to do more than just wish for it to happen. I need to practise and do the things that virtuous people do. I need to behave accordingly, and practise ethical virtues such as honesty or kindness.

Having outlined the justification for virtue ethics, we could also evaluate the following counter-arguments:

1   A person may know the right thing to do, but they may fail to act on it. This could be because they lack courage and conviction to do the right thing. Sometimes, we might know what the right thing is but fail to act. However, for Aristotle, a virtuous person not only knows what the right thing is, but they also have the courage and the wisdom to act on their ethical beliefs. It follows that if you want to know what it is to be a virtuous person, you need to *act* ethically. Nevertheless, some people might argue that this is too difficult to put into practice.

2   If you find yourself in a situation known as an ethical dilemma where you are conflicted, you may have a problem, as virtue ethics does not offer a very clear guide. For example, there may be a situation where you cannot be both kind and honest, and in this situation, you need to use sound judgement. For Aristotle, there is no rule such as 'When honesty and kindness conflict, always be kind' or 'When kindness and honesty conflict, always be honest.' Depending on the situation, there is a right action which a virtuous person would do. Ethics is therefore a matter of judgement, wisdom and character, and doing the right thing for the right reasons.

3   Some might argue that a person's character and qualities have little to do with ethics, given that it is actions that are ethical or unethical. Instead, we might consider the intentions of the person performing the action, or the consequences resulting from that action.

REAL-LIFE SITUATION 3.12

Imagine if you have a friend at school who is great fun but very disorganised. They ask you what you think about them standing for the responsible position of school prefect, a role that involves plenty of organisation. You like them as a friend, but know that they will not be suited to this role. How do you respond? What is the right thing to do?

DISCUSS 3.15

Evaluate this syllogism:

Premise 1: An action is ethical if it is performed by a virtuous person.

Premise 2: This is a virtuous person performing an action.

Conclusion: Therefore, this person's actions are ethical.

Are the premises true or false? Is the argument valid?

According to this, how do we know what an ethical action is?

Deontological ethics

DISCUSS 3.16

Do knowers have an ethical duty?

KEY WORD

deontological ethics: the belief that ethics is fundamentally a matter of doing your duty and fulfilling your obligations

Figure 3.12: As knowers, how do we decide what is right and wrong?

According to the philosopher Immanuel Kant (1724–1804), our duties are not arbitrary, and we can determine what they are in an objective way by appealing to *reason* and rationality. For Kant, we all have an ethical duty.

There are many possible motivations for our actions, including the benefits we think an action might produce for ourselves or for others. We might experience the emotion of

---

happiness if we 'do good' and help others. However, there are various problems with feelings and emotions as a measure of ethical actions. If I act to help others because I feel like it, or I am inclined to do so because it makes *me* feel good, does that make my action ethical?

For Kant, our own inclination to do something does not make an action ethical. Nor does an emotion or a personal preference to act make an action ethical. For Kant, our intentions are very important. He argues that the only good in itself is a *good will*, and in order to have a good will, I must have the right intention. The true motivation of a good will is to 'act for the sake of duty'.

An action is ethical if it is performed because it is required by the moral law. There are different perspectives taken on what the moral law is. Religious people may draw their moral laws from religious teachings. Kant argued that the way to decide if something is your duty is to see whether or not you can consistently universalise it. Imagine that you are wondering whether or not it is okay to jump the lunch queue because you cannot be bothered to wait in line. According to Kant, you should ask yourself what would happen if everyone did that. The answer is, of course, that there would be chaos. Indeed, if everyone jumped the queue, there would be no queue left to jump! So if you try to generalise the rule, 'Jump the queue whenever you feel like it', you end up with a contradiction. Therefore, it is your duty *not* to jump the queue whenever you feel like it. Kant offered this formula: 'Act only on that maxim (principle) through which you can at the same time will that it should be a universal law.'

It follows that we need a degree of imagination in our ethical reasoning so that we can evaluate 'what if' all of us were to act in this way. If it is possible to universalise the action so that it can become a universal 'law of nature', then we know it is ethical.

In summary, Kant's theory is an example of a deontological theory of ethics, which claims that an action is right if it is performed out of duty.

There are a number of counter arguments to deontological ethics:

1   Some critics have pointed out that it leads to **moral absolutism**. This is the belief that certain moral principles should *always* be followed irrespective of context. To see the problem, consider the ethics of lying. Using the universalisability test, Kant said that you cannot consistently will that people lie whenever they feel like it, because if they did, language would no longer be an effective means of communication. Kant concluded that it is *always* wrong to lie. Arguably, the problem with Kant's approach to ethics, then, is that it seems to lead to **rule worship** – that is, to blindly following a moral rule without regard to the consequences. Many people would say that rather than mechanically applying moral principles irrespective of the context, we should try to be sensitive to the details of a situation and make a *judgement* about when it is appropriate to make an exception to a generally agreed principle.

2   *Moral coldness.* Kant's approach to ethics seems to be too focused on reason at the expense of feelings. Allowing that we should try to be consistent in our moral judgements, what outrages most people about, say, war criminals, is not their *inconsistency* but their *inhumanity*. Kant is unable to accommodate this common-sense intuition because he refuses to give any place to feelings in his moral philosophy. Just as you cannot appeal to people's sympathy if they have

KEY WORDS

moral absolutism: the belief that there is at least one universal moral principle, which should always be followed irrespective of the context or their consequences

rule worship: blindly following moral rules irrespective of whether or not they are appropriate

none, so you cannot appeal to their reason if they do not mind being called irrational. Furthermore, taking feelings out of moral consideration seems to lead to a cold and heartless ethics. Many people would say that it is better for a husband to help his wife because he *loves* her and *wants* to help her than because it is his *duty* to help her. We might even reverse Kant's position and argue that feelings are what connect us with other people. Arguably, reason has its limits, and that we would sometimes do better to follow our hearts.

REAL-LIFE SITUATION 3.13

Do you think that we have an ethical duty to share and communicate what we know?

EXPLORE 3.14

1   Consider if you can make the following into universal ethical rules:

  - Always jump the queue if you feel like it.

  - Lie if and when you are unlikely to be discovered.

  - Make false promises in order to get what you want.

  - Give money to the poor.

  - Help others if and when you feel like it.

  - Treat yourself and others as ends, and never as a means to an end.

  - If you do not know how to act, do what the moral law requires.

2   Consider these conflicts of duty and the following dilemmas:

  - If your grandmother and a world-famous doctor are trapped in a burning building, and you only have time to rescue one of them, should you save your grandmother because she is a family member, or the doctor because of the good they can do for society?

  - If your brother is dying of a rare disease and your family cannot afford to buy the drugs that will cure him, are you justified in stealing the drugs?

  - If a terrorist group takes a civilian hostage and threatens to kill them unless the government releases five convicted terrorists, should the government give in to their demands?

Some people have argued that it is difficult to see how Kant's approach can help us to resolve these kinds of dilemma, for it seems to give us no criterion in accordance with which our duties can be ranked. In each situation, what do you think your duty would be and why?

Utilitarianism

DISCUSS 3.17

Is an action ethical if it produces particular consequences?

Whereas a deontological theory of ethics considers the intention of the individual and the action itself, a teleological theory considers the consequences of an action. According to a teleological theory of ethics, we know that an action is right if it produces a good outcome. This theory looks to the consequence of an action as the evidence for justifying it being the right action. There are various teleological theories of ethics, but one of the best known is utilitarianism, which considers whether an action maximises happiness or well-being, or minimises the total harm.

Utilitarianism claims that there is one and only one supreme ethical principle – that we should seek *the greatest good for the greatest number*. This theory assumes that we should promote and maximise the happiness of others and minimise suffering as far as possible, where happiness is considered in terms of well-being rather than a frivolous emotion.

The theory of utilitarianism was developed in the late-18th and early-19th century by Jeremy Bentham (1748–1832) and John Stuart Mill (1806–1873), who wanted to establish ethics on a scientific foundation. Just as Newton had explained natural phenomena in terms of the principle of gravity, so Bentham and Mill tried to explain ethical phenomena in terms of the principle of utility. According to this principle, the only thing that is good in itself is 'happiness', and *actions are right in so far as they tend to increase happiness, and wrong in so far as they tend to decrease it*. If we ask 'What is happiness?', Bentham tells us that it is the sum of pleasures including goodness, health, security, unselfishness, personal independence, and nobleness, and that a happy life is one that maximises pleasure as he conceived it and minimises pain.

Utilitarianism is a rational theory because it encourages us to take into account not only the short-term consequences but also the long-term consequences of our actions. For example, although smoking gives some people short-term pleasure, a utilitarian might argue that if smoking increases your risk of health problems including cancer, you should not smoke, because in the long term it is likely to give you more health problems and pain than pleasure and can potentially cause suffering for others.

Counter-arguments to the theory of utilitarianism might be:

1 *It is not so easy to put into practice.* To start with, how do we measure happiness? Although Bentham defines happiness as the sum of pleasures, it is difficult to see how different pleasures can be measured on a common scale. Imagine, for example, that someone gets pleasure from eating ice cream, listening to opera and spending time with their friends. How can we attach numbers to such pleasures and compare them with one another? Eating twenty scoops of ice cream would not be regarded as bringing happiness in utilitarianism: quite the opposite. An economist might say that we can measure different pleasures by seeing how much people are willing to pay for them. But is it really possible to put a price, or a 'happiness value', on such things as health, love or friendship? It was to resolve such issues that Bentham devised the hedonic calculus and Mill discussed higher and lower pleasures. But the dimensions of the hedonic calculus are not easy to measure, and Mill's divisions between higher and lower pleasures are difficult to justify.

KEY WORDS

teleological: to do with the outcome or consequence. Teleological theories of ethics are based on the idea that we know if an action is ethical based on the result or end achieved

utilitarianism: the belief that ethics can ultimately be reduced to the principle that we should maximise well-being

happiness: In this context, well-being, unselfishness, health, security, independence, liberty, and nobleness (not a feeling of excitement or satisfaction)

hedonic calculus: a way of determining the amount of pleasure or pain caused by an action by measuring its intensity, duration, certainty, closeness, fruitfulness, purity and extent

2 Another practical problem concerns *how we can predict the consequences of our actions*. Imagine that a married woman falls passionately in love with a colleague at work, and is wondering whether or not to leave her husband. What should she do? In theory, utilitarianism gives a straightforward solution to the problem. The woman should compare the consequences of staying with her husband with the consequences of leaving him, and do whatever maximises the happiness or minimises the suffering of the people involved. The trouble is that, in practice, it is very difficult to know what the consequences of our actions will be. A utilitarian might say that we usually have some idea of the consequences of our actions, but they may still be difficult to predict in any detail. To take an extreme example, in a short story by Roald Dahl (1916–1990) called *Genesis and Catastrophe*, a doctor saves a mother and child in a difficult birth. The story ends with the doctor saying 'You'll be all right now, Mrs Hitler.'

3 *Pleasure or happiness is not always ethical.* As we have seen, utilitarianism is based on the assumption that the only things that are good in themselves are pleasure and happiness. But you might argue that there are in fact many empty pleasures. Empty pleasures are pleasures that do not help us to develop our potential, or flourish as human beings. While pleasures such as shopping or eating chocolate may have their place, a critic would say that a life devoted to their pursuit is unworthy of a human being. However, a utilitarian does not really see empty pleasures as true pleasures.

4 *Actions should be judged by their motives rather than their consequences.* According to utilitarianism, the rightness or wrongness of an action depends on its consequences – an action is right if it increases happiness, and wrong if it decreases it, but it does not take into consideration the motives behind an action.

EXPLORE 3.15

1   Consider the following example.

Jones is a malicious individual who devotes his time to making life as difficult as possible for everyone in your community. One day you decide that it is time to do something to increase happiness. You hide behind the door, and when Jones comes in, you hit him on the head with a baseball bat and throw his unconscious body in the river.

2   Why would a utilitarian not agree that this was an acceptable solution to the problem of the bad neighbour? (Think about what 'happiness' means to a utilitarian)

3   Discuss whether you think it would ever be justified to sacrifice an individual to increase general 'happiness' or decrease suffering. In what circumstances, if any, would this be justifiable to a utilitarian?

4   Consider and evaluate this syllogism:

Premise 1: We should act to cause the greatest happiness of the greatest number of people.

Premise 2: A government education policy that teaches all children to read will make most of them happy.

Conclusion: Therefore, it is right for the government to adopt this policy.

DISCUSS 3.18

What sort of supporting evidence can we use to justify ethical actions?

Utilitarianism is an inductive theory of ethics because it uses inductive reasoning – specifically a judgement about the consequences to justify particular actions. For example, a utilitarian argument could be that the bombing of Hiroshima in 1945 was wrong – because it did not result in the greatest happiness of the greatest number of people. Evidence shows that the destruction, suffering and horror caused by the bomb made it a deeply unethical action. The counter-argument could be made that the longer-term consequences resulted in the end of the Second World War potentially saving many lives and reducing the suffering of millions, and therefore did result in the greatest happiness of the greatest number. This example highlights the issue: we cannot always know with any certainty what the consequences of our actions or inactions will be, nor can we measure them in advance.

Figure 3.13: Utilitarianism claims that an action is ethical if it maximises the greatest happiness of the greatest number of people. What do you think makes an action ethical? How do you know?

Summary of ethical theories

We have now examined three different theories of ethics and have discovered that, despite their attractions, they each have various strengths and weaknesses. These can be summarised in the following table:

Theory	Justification	Criticisms	Implications
Virtue ethics An action is ethical if it is performed by a virtuous person. Such a person knows what the right action is, and performs this action. The key thinker associated with this theory is Aristotle.	1 We all know who good people are. A virtuous person has attributes or characteristics such as integrity and honesty. 2 There is a close connection between the action itself and the person performing the action.	1 There may be a problem with deciding who a virtuous person is. 2 We might disagree about whether certain characteristics make a person ethical. 3 Some would argue that actions are ethical or unethical, independent of the person performing the action.	A virtuous person will pursue knowledge in an ethical way.
Deontological ethics According to Kant, an action is ethical if it is performed out of respect for the moral law. An individual of *good will* acts in accordance with the moral law for the sake of duty – their only motivation for doing what is right is their knowledge that it is the right thing to do. They do what is ethical because it is their duty, and for no other reason. An action is ethical if we can universalise it – and would want everyone else to act in the same way in that situation. The key thinker associated with this theory is Immanuel Kant.	1 An ethical action is one that we know we should perform because it is our duty. 2 There is a close connection between the action itself and the intention of the person performing the action.	1 How is the moral law defined? There may be different versions of this, both religious and secular. 2 Is it always right to tell the truth? Might there be scenarios when disobeying the moral law seems like the right thing to do? 3 Universalising an ethical rule requires the imagination of a scenario, for example 'What would happen if all people did this?' – which assumes that we can imagine these possible scenarios with some accuracy.	A person who follows the moral law will perform ethical actions out of respect and reverence for the moral law. We may think that it is our duty to pursue and apply particular types of knowledge.

Theory	Justification	Criticisms	Implications
Utilitarianism An action is right if it produces certain consequences. According to utilitarianism, an action is right if the consequence of the action is to produce the *greatest happiness* of the greatest number of people. The key thinkers associated with this theory are Jeremy Bentham and John Stuart Mill.	1 The ethics of an action can only be known and measured by the consequences it produces. 2 There is a close connection between the action itself and the consequences it produces.	1 Unethical actions could be justified if they produce happiness. 2 Utilitarianism assumes that we can know and measure the possible consequences of an action. 3 How do we measure the timeframe of an action's effect? Is an action ethical if it produces immediate short-term happiness or long-term happiness? 4 How can we define and know what happiness is?	An ethical person will act in such a way to bring about a good outcome or consequence for other people. We might pursue knowledge that will produce the greatest happiness of the greatest number of people.

EXPLORE 3.16

Work with a partner. As a pair, evaluate these two attributes of the IB Diploma Programme learner profile.

1   What does it mean to be 'caring'? Think of a specific example of this at work in the world today.

2   What does it mean to be 'principled'? Think of a specific example of this at work in the world today.

3   Is 'caring' the same as 'principled'? Why? Why not?

4   What do you think are the personal qualities needed, the duties involved and the consequences of following these attributes?

DISCUSS 3.19

1   As knowers, why are we expected to have ethical attributes?

2   What do we mean by values and responsibilities? What are your own values and responsibilities as a knower?

Emotions as a source of ethical knowledge

> **DISCUSS 3.20**
>
> How important are emotions and feelings as a source of ethical knowledge?

The word 'emotion' is derived from the Latin verb *movere* meaning 'to move'. There are at least six universal **primary emotions** which are common across all cultures: happiness, sadness, fear, disgust, anger and surprise. There is an evolutionary function behind each of these emotions. For example, there are situations in which fear or disgust might keep us safe from danger. In addition to primary emotions, we have a wide range of **secondary emotions**, or 'social' emotions. Secondary or 'social' emotions might include: admiration, anxiety, awe, despair, embarrassment, envy, gratitude, guilt, jealousy, pity, pride, regret and shame. Secondary emotions are shaped – in part at least – by language and culture, given that without language, we would probably be unable to distinguish between anxiety, fear and terror, or between irritation, anger and rage. Many secondary emotions also presuppose a degree of self-awareness, for example, feeling proud, ashamed or embarrassed requires that you can see your behaviour through the eyes of another person. There is an important question about when we are justified in feeling certain emotions, which suggests that sometimes it is reasonable to feel and communicate certain emotions. Aristotle commented that, 'Anybody can become angry – that is easy, but to be angry with the right person and to the right degree and at the right time and for the right purpose, and in the right way – that is not within everybody's power, and is not easy.'

There is also an important question about how feelings relate to ethical judgements. Some people claim that just as we can come to know facts through thinking, so we can come to know values through feeling. There is some justification for this view. After all, our emotions implicitly judge a perspective as positive or negative, good or bad; and if we did not have any emotions, then nothing would matter to us and we would not care about anything. The fact that we *do* have emotions allegedly enables us to discern various ethical qualities. For example, it could be argued that gratitude alerts us to kindness, anger to injustice, pity to suffering, guilt to wrong-doing and disgust to perversion. Speaking metaphorically, we might say that in such cases, we see with our heart rather than our head, and discern the moral quality in question by having the relevant emotion.

Consider an emotion such as disgust. The American intellectual Leon Kass (1939–) has coined the phrase 'the **wisdom of repugnance**', which suggests that disgust is not just a mindless bodily reaction to something unpleasant, but conveys morally significant information which is 'beyond reason's power to articulate'. He says, for example, that human cloning is morally wrong, and that although we may be unable to give a reasoned argument against it, we should take seriously the shiver of revulsion we feel when we contemplate it. In Kass's view, then, our moral beliefs can sometimes be justified by feelings rather than reasons.

Counter-arguments to this theory of ethics might run as follows:

1 Despite the above comments, we should be careful about blindly trusting emotions as a source of ethical knowledge. To trust them on the grounds that they are natural would be to commit what we might call the **wise nature fallacy**. Just because something is natural does not mean that it is good. The untamed emotions of a 'wild child' who grew up entirely outside society would doubtless

KEY WORDS

primary emotions: universal emotions which are usually said to comprise happiness, sadness, anger, fear, disgust and surprise

secondary emotions: complex emotions which can be thought of as mixtures of primary emotions

KEY WORDS

wisdom of repugnance: the claim that we can validly appeal to our feelings of disgust to justify our moral beliefs

wise nature fallacy: the false assumption that because something is natural it is therefore good

aid their survival, but they would be a poor guide to values. Even in civilised society, our emotions can mislead us if they are *uninformed, egocentric* or *unreliable*.

2   Uninformed emotions. Emotions can distort perception as often as they can illuminate it. Critics of Leon Kass claim that disgust is an especially poor guide to moral truth. At one time, for example, people considered interracial marriage to be disgusting; but this was surely an indication of the depth of their prejudice rather than the height of their wisdom. Our use of language is important here, and what we define as natural may be subjective. Someone might define an airplane flight as un-natural, but that does not necessarily make it unethical.

3   Egocentric emotions. Our unreflective emotions are typically concerned with things that are beneficial or harmful to us. So, far from being a guide to universal values, they are often a reflection of our own self-serving interests. For example, we may feel angry when someone lies to us, but will happily lie to them; or we may feel sad about our own misfortune but indifferent to the misfortune of others.

4   Unreliable emotions. Our emotions are not entirely self-centred, and we sometimes feel pity for the plight of others. The trouble is that such other-regarding emotions are unreliable. We may be moved by a harrowing account of a child in distress, yet be untouched by a famine affecting hundreds of thousands of people; or we may feel pity today and be indifferent tomorrow. This suggests that how we happen to feel is a poor indicator of moral significance.

Considering the above points, those who insist that emotions can be a source of ethical knowledge usually limit their claim to emotions that have been properly educated. Indeed, a great deal of informal education is implicitly or explicitly concerned with educating the emotions and building character. The philosopher Martha Nussbaum (1947–) has drawn particular attention to the role played by literature in this context. At its best, she claims, literature can help to awaken social emotions such as pity and gratitude, and broaden their range.

Figure 3.14: How might reason, emotion and language play a role in our ethical judgements?

DISCUSS 3.21

1   What are typically seen as virtues and vices in your culture? How are they related to the emotions?

2   What role do emotions play in ethical judgements? What role should they play?

Knowledge questions related to ethics

- Are ethical considerations more important in relation to how knowledge is gained and produced or the way that it is used, shared and communicated?

- Should we only pursue knowledge that we believe will benefit humanity and contribute towards a better world? How do we know?

- Is it justified for ethical considerations to influence and limit the production of knowledge?

- How far do our own values and ethical beliefs impact on the knowledge that we pursue?

- To what extent is the pursuit of knowledge itself an ethical responsibility?

LINKING QUESTION 3.1

Choose one subject area from mathematics, natural sciences, human sciences, history, or the arts (or one of the optional themes). How can we understand and evaluate areas of knowledge using the four strands: scope, perspectives, methods and tools and ethics?

REFLECTION

As a knower, how much responsibility do you have to be aware of and reflect upon ethical considerations related to the production, use and sharing of knowledge?

3.7 Conclusion

Knowledge questions can be explored in terms of how we might think about responding to them in relation to the four strands of the knowledge framework. The *scope* of knowledge consists of the extent and limits of knowledge and knowing, and inevitably, everyone has a limit to their horizon of knowledge. Also, our self-awareness of our own personal history and the factors that have shaped our world-view is essential if we are to take a step back and evaluate our own viewpoint. Furthermore, an open-minded *perspective* about our own knowledge also helps us to appreciate the perspectives and values of other individuals and communities. There are a variety of *methods and tools* needed to gain knowledge, including cognitive tools such as reasoning and sense perception. The chapter on technology and knowledge will further explore material and practical knowledge tools.

Ethics and values influence us as knowers. The values and responsibilities that we have could both limit or promote the knowledge that we pursue. These four strands of the *knowledge framework* each play a role in how we might approach a knowledge question – and each will be unpacked further in the later chapters on the optional themes and areas of knowledge.

To return to the map as a metaphor for knowledge at the start of the chapter, we could conclude that if we are to make sense of the world, we could think of our knowledge as a provisional map to navigate the world. Our knowledge is neither perfect nor complete, but it does guide us, and inevitably what we think and know impacts on ourselves and others. As knowers, we might need to make some minimal assumptions if we are to gain knowledge – that we are free to think and act, or that we are ethical agents. Some people would argue that we can and should use our knowledge for the good of humanity and to benefit others. Others would go further and claim that we have an ethical responsibility to use our knowledge to find solutions to the world's problems. Knowledge questions consider these challenging issues. The extent of our responsibility is debatable and some would argue that the pursuit of truth is included here as one of these responsibilities. This leads us to our final introductory chapter on truth – and how the concept of truth relates to knowledge and knowing.

KNOWLEDGE QUESTIONS

1   How far might imagination lead to more reliable knowledge than reason?

2   What are the ethics of *acquiring, using* and *communicating* knowledge? What ethical limits or constraints, if any, should there be on the scope, pursuit and production of knowledge?

3.8 Linking questions

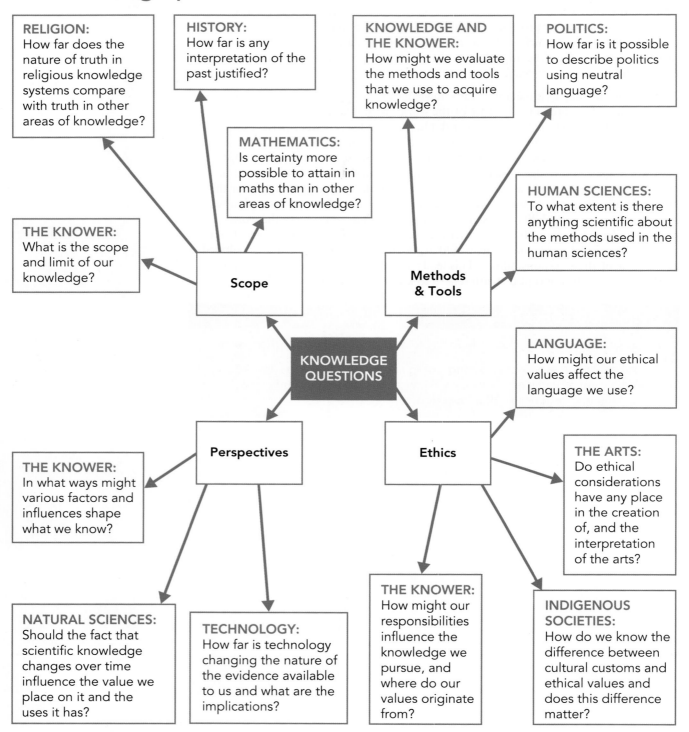

RELIGION: How far does the nature of truth in religious knowledge systems compare with truth in other areas of knowledge?

HISTORY: How far is any interpretation of the past justified?

KNOWLEDGE AND THE KNOWER: How might we evaluate the methods and tools that we use to acquire knowledge?

POLITICS: How far is it possible to describe politics using neutral language?

MATHEMATICS: Is certainty more possible to attain in maths than in other areas of knowledge?

THE KNOWER: What is the scope and limit of our knowledge?

HUMAN SCIENCES: To what extent is there anything scientific about the methods used in the human sciences?

Scope

Methods & Tools

KNOWLEDGE QUESTIONS

LANGUAGE: How might our ethical values affect the language we use?

Perspectives

Ethics

THE ARTS: Do ethical considerations have any place in the creation of, and the interpretation of the arts?

THE KNOWER: In what ways might various factors and influences shape what we know?

NATURAL SCIENCES: Should the fact that scientific knowledge changes over time influence the value we place on it and the uses it has?

TECHNOLOGY: How far is technology changing the nature of the evidence available to us and what are the implications?

THE KNOWER: How might our responsibilities influence the knowledge we pursue, and where do our values originate from?

INDIGENOUS SOCIETIES: How do we know the difference between cultural customs and ethical values and does this difference matter?

3.9 Check your progress

Reflect on what you have learned in this chapter and indicate your confidence level between 1 and 5 (where 5 is the highest score and 1 is the lowest). If you score below 3, revisit that section. Come back to this list later in your course. Has your confidence grown?

	Confidence level	Re-visited?
Do I know what a knowledge question is, and how I might approach answering a knowledge question?		
Am I able to use the knowledge framework as a tool for answering and analysing knowledge questions and comparing the different areas of knowledge?		
Do I know what is meant by the scope of knowledge, including the extent and limits of knowledge?		
Do I understand how to critique and evaluate my own knowledge in the way that I could question the truth, accuracy and usefulness of a map?		
Can I demonstrate an awareness and understanding of different perspectives and paradigms?		
Am I able to evaluate my own perspective, beliefs and assumptions, and do I understand how appreciating my own and others' perspectives might help me to critique knowledge and knowing?		
Am I familiar with the various methods and tools for acquiring and producing knowledge, including: • an interdisciplinary method • practical tools • cognitive tools (e.g. senses, imagination, rationality and memory)?		
Can I clearly explain rationality and logic in the construction of knowledge, in particular, deductive, inductive and abductive reasoning?		
Am I clear about how ethical responsibilities might influence the construction and use of knowledge?		

3.10 Continue your journey

- To build on the knowledge that you have gained in this chapter, you could read some of the following articles.

- To extend your general understanding of the **commonalties of the methods and creative processes behind the making of great art and scientific discoveries**, read: TomMcLeish, *The Poetry and Music of Science: Comparing Creativity in Science and Art*, Oxford University Press, 2019

- For a book renowned for the way it invites you to consider the **possible future of humanity from a new perspective**, read: Yuval Noah Harari, *Homo Deus: A Brief History of Tomorrow*, Penguin Random House, 2015

- For a fascinating overview of the **evolution of ethics and its place in human communities and the concepts of justice, equality, righteousness, authority, sanctity and loyalty**, read: Jonathan Haidt, *The Righteous Mind: Why Good People are Divided by Politics and Religion*, Penguin, 2012.

- For an exploration of how and why we have the **capacity to understand each other and imagine another person's perspective,** read: Peter Bazalgette, *The Empathy Instinct: How to Create a More Civil Society*, John Murray Publishers, 2017.

- For an excellent short introduction to **ethics and moral knowledge** with short, clear discussions of a wide range of topics including relativism, egoism, utilitarianism and human rights, read: Simon Blackburn *Being Good*, Oxford University Press, 2001.

- For an engaging and provocative book exploring **why naturally competitive human beings cooperate with one another,** read: Matt Ridley *The Origins of Virtue*, Penguin, 1997. Matt Ridley, a zoologist by training, takes an interdisciplinary approach to his subject and brings insights from anthropology, biology, economics and history to bear on his thesis that it pays to cooperate.

> ## Chapter 4
> # Truth and wisdom

LEARNING INTENTIONS

This chapter will consider the nature of truth, and the relationship between knowledge and truth. We will explore the concepts of relativism, absolutism, subjectivity, objectivity, explanation, justification, perspective and wisdom, and how these are relevant for the knower.

You will:

- understand the nature of truth, and evaluate various different theories of truth

- consider knowledge questions relating to 'post-truth politics' and 'fake news', and explore the concepts of relative and absolute truth

- explore conspiracy and conspiracy theories, the concept of explanation and the relevance of these ideas for knowledge and knowing

- consider how we know if our beliefs are true, and explore the concepts of subjectivity and objectivity in relation to knowledge and the idea of justification

- discuss what wisdom is (in terms of good judgement, breadth of perspective, self-knowledge, ethical responsibility and intellectual humility) and how it might relate to knowledge and knowing

- consider the importance for the knower of the attributes of the IB learner profile

---

BEFORE YOU START

Analyse each of the following quotations and discuss the questions that follow:

1 'Truth is what stands the test of time.' **Albert Einstein** (1879–1955)

2 'The truth does not change according to our ability to stomach it.' **Flannery O'Connor** (1925–1964)

3 'Keep the company of those who seek the truth, and run away from those who have found it.' **Václav Havel** (1936–2011)

4 'There are many kinds of eyes . . . and consequently, there are many kinds of 'truths' and consequently, there is no truth.' **Friedrich Nietzsche** (1844–1900)

5 'The facts are always less than what really happened.' **Nadine Gordimer** (1923–2014)

For each quotation, consider:

a Do you agree or disagree with the quotation?

b What do you think the quotation suggests about truth?

c What is assumed or taken for granted about the nature of truth?

4.1 Introduction

DISCUSS 4.1

1 Considering the IB Diploma Programme subjects you are studying, which 'tell the truth' and why?

2 What do you think makes a belief or a knowledge claim true?

If we are going to explore knowledge, we also need to consider how knowledge relates to truth. In this chapter, we explore truth. The question 'What is truth?' looks innocent enough, but we can easily tie ourselves up in knots in trying to answer it. This question was famously posed (according to John 18:37 in the New Testament) by Pontius Pilate, Roman governor of Judaea in 1st century Palestine.

This chapter begins by looking at, and evaluating, various different theories of truth:

- the correspondence theory
- the coherence theory
- the pragmatic theory
- the consensus theory
- the redundancy theory

Although none of these theories is entirely satisfactory in explaining what exactly is truth, each of them seems to capture a fragment of the 'truth about truth'. We will then ask how, if at all, we can know the truth, and look at popular theories of truth and **conspiracy theories**, which claim a secret or hidden truth behind events. Perhaps

KEY WORD

conspiracy theory: either a denial that an event took place, or the belief in an explanation for an event based on the idea that there was a deliberate and secret agency of people or organisations

we can steer between the extremes of **dogmatism** – the belief that you possess the absolute truth, and relativism – the belief that there is no such truth to possess.

Although absolute truth may lie beyond our grasp, we still need to keep hold of some concept of truth if we are to distinguish between reality and fantasy. There is, after all, a difference between *wishing* that something was true and it actually being true. Since we live in a world of rapid technological growth, we will need to think carefully about how to use the knowledge we possess, and the extent to which we should pursue it further. With this in mind, it is perhaps appropriate that this chapter concludes with a discussion about the nature and value of wisdom.

> **KEY WORD**
>
> dogmatism: a tendency to lay down principles as undeniably true without consideration of evidence or the opinions of others

EXPLORE 4.1

1   Rather than think of these sentences as being either *true* or *false*, you might think in terms of their *degree* of truth. Work on your own and rate these claims out of 10. Give each of them a score according to their degree of truth, where 10 is the most truthful and 1 is the least truthful.

Consider what true or truth means in each of these sentences, a-j

   a   It is true that I ate a sandwich for lunch (assuming that this is a fact).

   b   It is true that I did not eat a pizza for lunch (assuming that this is a fact).

   c   It is good to tell the truth.

   d   You are a true friend.

   e   Truth is the first casualty of war.

   f   It is true that my brain contains 86 billion nerve cells with 100 trillion connections.

   g   It is true that Rembrandt was a great artist.

   h   It is true that the mass of magnesium increases when heated.

   i   It is true that we should treat animals with respect.

   j   I promise to tell the truth, the whole truth and nothing but the truth.

2   Now compare your list with a partner and look at the different ratings you have given. Discuss the following:

   a   Using the ten statements here, discuss what is meant by 'true', 'truth' and 'degrees of truth'. How far do the words 'true' and 'truth' have different meanings in different contexts?

   b   In each of the ten examples, is there another way of phrasing the sentence so that we do not need to use the words 'true' or 'truth' at all? Could we substitute it for another word such as 'correct', 'factual' or 'coherent'? In which could we just remove the word 'true' or 'truth' altogether, e.g. for statement a: 'I ate a sandwich for lunch'?

   c   What do you think is the difference between facts and true beliefs? Which of the examples above are facts, which are truths and which are both?

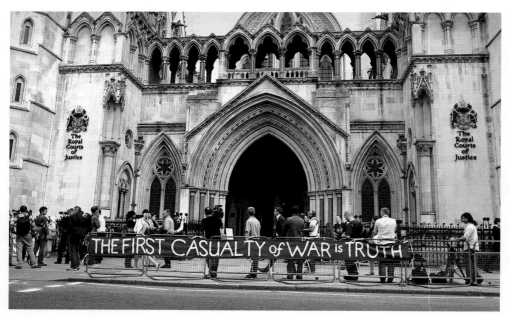

Figure 4.1: A quotation attributed to Aeschylus (525–456 BCE), 'The first casualty of war is truth', is displayed outside the High Court in London, UK, in 2011 when Julian Assange, the founder of WikiLeaks, began his appeal

4.2 Theories of truth

DISCUSS 4.2

1   What makes something true?

2   What is the connection between knowledge and truth?

Correspondence theory

According to the **correspondence theory** of truth, a knowledge claim is true if it corresponds to a fact about the world – an idea that has sometimes been attributed to Aristotle. For example, 'There is a glass of water on my desk' is true because I observe it, and here the truth is conferred on me by the world. The statement 'Grass is green' is true if, and only if, grass is green. The statement 'The sky is blue' is true if, and only if, the sky is blue.

At first sight, this 'theory' may strike you as trivial. It appears to be saying nothing more than that a statement is true if, and only if, it is true. However, the correspondence theory insists that truth depends on how things are in the world, and that a statement is true not because an authority said it was true, or because you happen to feel that it is true, but because it corresponds to something in reality. The correspondence theory of truth assumes that truth is a relational property which connects the mind of the individual with the world. This means that empirical observation is true if it corresponds with a 'fact' about the world around us.

> **KEY WORD**
>
> **correspondence theory (of truth):** the theory that a statement is true if it corresponds to a fact

A fact is a state of affairs or an actual situation that can be verified. The nature of facts means that they are difficult to disagree with. It is a 'fact' that the past cannot be changed. It is a fact that Paris is the capital of France, and that the length of one side of a right-handed triangle can be calculated using *Pythagoras' Theorem* if you know the lengths of the other two sides. You might assume that for a fact to be a fact, it must also be true. It makes no sense to believe in false facts. However, some 'facts' could turn out to be false, and some facts may be difficult to verify. This leads some people to say that facts are simply sincerely held beliefs about what we believe to be the case. There are checks and processes that are used to verify facts, but these checks and processes in turn depend upon further beliefs.

There is an important link here between knowledge and facts. It seems to be that you cannot know something if it is false. For example, it is impossible to *know* for a 'fact' that Rome is the capital of Australia – given that this false claim has no factual basis. Furthermore, you cannot *know* that a circle has four straight sides. In order to know something, your claim needs to have some justification.

DISCUSS 4.3

What facts can we know? Are all facts true?

We explored inductive claims in Chapter 3. For example, you might claim to know for a 'fact' that all ravens are black. This knowledge may be based on your observations, but it may turn out to be false given that you cannot observe every raven that exists. Some facts might be provisional and change with new observations over time. For example, the Higgs boson particle was a theoretical speculation before it was detected by the Large Hadron Collider at CERN in Geneva, Switzerland in 2012; now many regard its existence as a fact. Previously, it was true that the particle existed, but verification only became possible once the technology could detect it.

Truth according to the correspondence theory, seems to be grounded in reality; but truth and facts are not the same thing. Truth, according to this theory, is a metaphysical concept relating to questions about what *does* or *does not* accord with facts about the world and the nature of reality. But if our mathematics does not correspond with reality, and if our language relates to reality only in vague ways that resist absolute or precise definition, it is difficult to see how this position can be sustained. Similarly, saying that A is true because of B supposes some third place where we can stand to perform the objective comparison. However, many would claim that there is no such 'view from nowhere'.

REAL-LIFE SITUATION 4.1

1   What counts as a fact in different areas of knowledge?

2   To what extent do facts justify our knowledge? Does our knowledge always require a factual basis?

DISCUSS 4.4

What facts are there about values and/or aesthetics?

Criticisms

Problems with facts

The correspondence theory says that a statement is true if it corresponds to a fact, but we might ask what this means.

The following types of fact can be difficult to reconcile with correspondence theory:

- *Empirical facts* – these are observable facts where it seems as if the world confers the truth on the observer. 'I observe a key board in front of me' or 'I see a glass of water on the table' are factual claims about the world, but they are more to do with the observer's state of perception than anything to do with the world.

- *Negative facts* – the claim that 'I did not eat a sandwich for lunch' is true, but it does not correspond directly to a fact about the world.

- *Counter-factual facts* – historians might explore 'what if?' questions – if an event had been different – and claim that that we can speculate about alternative scenarios that did not happen. You could question if these are even facts at all, given that they do not correspond to something we might observe in the world.

Correspondence is never perfect

Since there is a gap between language and the world, and we construct a perception of the world, correspondence can never be perfect. This applies particularly to the following kinds of fact:

- *Ethical facts* – you might consider where the correspondence theory stands in relation to ethical knowledge. If I claim that it is right to treat animals with respect, you might question what fact in the world this corresponds to. When I claim that there is a glass of water on the table, I can observe it directly, and my empirical perception supports my knowledge claim. But my belief about animals has no obvious equivalent that I can appeal to – where is my evidence?

- *Aesthetic facts* – when I describe a painting as beautiful, my belief corresponds to an actual painting, but the quality of beauty is an abstract idea that has no clear correspondence in the world. There is no obvious set of facts about beauty to which my statement corresponds. Instead, we might agree – or come to a consensus. Look at Figure 4.2. What does the picture show? It is a pipe. So why did Magritte write underneath it 'Ceci n'est pas une pipe.' ('This is not a pipe.')? This is because it is not really a pipe, but only a picture of a pipe. What is true of pictures is equally true of language. You can describe something in as much detail as you like, but the truth described can never match up to the truth experienced, and the map of true propositions can never capture the underlying richness of the world.

- *Mathematical facts* – mathematics deals with an idealised, abstract world in which perfection is conceivable. A mathematical proof is more like an artefact, a human construction, than a fact about the world. This means mathematical truths do not correspond with facts about the world, but are nevertheless regarded as true.

Figure 4.2: What does the picture show? A pipe! So why did Magritte write underneath it 'Ceci n'est pas une pipe' ('This is not a pipe')?

Truth is independent of facts and relates more to beliefs

A criticism of correspondence theory is that truth is independent of facts. The theory states that a knowledge claim is true if it corresponds to a fact about the world. However, the counter-argument is that truth is connected with beliefs, not facts. The philosopher, Georg Hegel (1770-1831) argued that if you believe something to be true and search for a correspondence in the world, your search must end with a belief about whether the correspondence holds, in which case your truth is still based on belief. In other words, it is impossible to compare beliefs with reality, because the experience of reality is always mediated by beliefs.

Truth cannot be determined in isolation

A criticism of the correspondence theory is that it is not possible to determine the truth or falsity of a proposition in isolation from other propositions. You might say, 'Surely I can test the truth of a proposition such as *"There is a snake in the cellar"* by simply going down to the cellar and looking?' But it is always possible that your eyes are deceiving you. The only way of determining whether or not something is an illusion is to determine if what you think you see fits in with other things that you believe to be true.

With this in mind, perhaps we should abandon the idea that truth is an 'all or nothing' concept – either a statement corresponds to reality or it does not – and think instead of there being *degrees of truth*. For although there can never be a perfect correspondence, some statements, pictures and maps are surely more accurate than others. If they are accurate enough for the purposes we have in mind, we might reasonably call them 'true'.

EXPLORE 4.2

Work with a partner and discuss the following statements. How, if at all, might the following propositions be said to correspond to facts about reality? What problems are there with them? Place these statements on a 'spectrum of truth', where you select three or more that are 'most true' and another three or more that are 'least true'.

a   The cat is on the mat.

b   The cat was on the mat.

c   This metal expands when heated.

d   All metals expand when heated.

e   This elephant has ears.

f   Elephants do not have wings.

g   Archduke Franz Ferdinand of Austria was assassinated in August 1914.

h   The assassination of Archduke Franz Ferdinand was a cause of the outbreak of the First World War.

i   It is right to treat other people with respect.

j   The Mona Lisa is a beautiful painting.

k   2 + 2 = 4

l   The brain weighs 1.5 kg, occupies 2% of body mass and consumes 20% of the body's energy.

Coherence theory

The **coherence theory** of truth states that a knowledge claim is true if it fits in with a coherent system of beliefs. According to this theory, truth is not a relationship between the individual observer and world. In contrast to the correspondence theory, the focus here is not so much on *going and looking* as *sitting and thinking*. Truth has no reference to the outside world. Instead, truth must be consistent with other human beliefs, and measured against other human constructions. Coherence theory can be compared to a jigsaw – if the piece of evidence fits with what I already know, like a jigsaw piece fits into a puzzle then it is true. It becomes true because it is consistent with other things that I know already.

Coherence can also play a role in establishing the truth or falsity of empirical propositions. If, for example, someone claims to have seen a salt-water crocodile in Lake Geneva, you might reason that this has to be false because Lake Geneva is a freshwater lake and crocodiles are not found in the wild in Switzerland. As this example shows, coherence is particularly effective as a negative test of truth, and means that we do not have to waste time checking up on every wild belief we come across. However, this is only the case if our knowledge is accurate, and nothing unexpected has happened (such as a crocodile escaping from a zoo and entering the lake.)

KEY WORD

coherence theory (of truth): the theory that a proposition is true if it fits in with our overall set of beliefs

Figure 4.3: The coherence theory suggests that truth is a relationship within a system of beliefs – a claim is true if it fits with other things that you know, like a jigsaw piece

DISCUSS 4.5

How important are coherence and consistency for truth?

Criticisms

Coherence is not sufficient for truth

Although coherence may be a good negative test of truth, it does not seem to be such a good positive test. More formally we can say that, while coherence may arguably be a *necessary* condition for truth, it does not seem to be a *sufficient* one. For example, although a work of fiction may be coherent, that does not make it true. Shakespeare's play *Richard III* is loosely based on the English king of that name. The play makes perfect sense, but it is not the historical truth. The same can be said of Oliver Stone's movie *JFK* about the assassination of US President John F. Kennedy in 1963. Moreover, you may be able to imagine a coherent system of beliefs which contains a falsehood. Arguably, each of the world faiths such as Judaism, Christianity, Islam, Hinduism, Buddhism and Sikhism offer an internally coherent set of beliefs, but it does not follow that they are true.

Coherence cannot exclude crazy beliefs

By using a bit of ingenuity, it is possible to make even the most outlandish theory seem coherent. You could, for example, make the flat Earth theory consistent with the fact that the Apollo astronauts saw that the Earth was round by simply claiming that the space missions were faked in a Hollywood studio. In fact, this is precisely what the International Flat Earth Research Society does! Indeed, conspiracy theories may fit with what you already know. If I believe that the world's governments are controlled by secret societies or certain powerful and rich families, I may find that a conspiracy theory about the influence of the Illuminati or the Rothschild family makes sense, and fits with what I already know. Coherence on its own is not a sufficient test for truth.

Coherence can lead to complacency

The coherence theory can lead to a kind of intellectual complacency, which leads you to reject anything that does not fit in with your worldview. However, just because something does not fit in with your way of looking at things does not mean that it is false – it may be *your* way of looking that needs to be changed. If, for example, a racist comes across evidence that contradicts their prejudice that immigrants are lazy, they should not – as the coherence theory appears to suggest – reject the evidence. Rather, they should change their worldview. The point is that, painful as it may be, we sometimes need to question our assumptions, and change our way of looking at the world.

EXPLORE 4.3

1   See if you can devise some absurd but coherent explanations for each of the following:

    a   the movement of the sun across the sky

    b   insomnia

    c   the price of stocks and shares

    d   the assassination of US President John F. Kennedy

    e   global warming

    f   the variety of species on the planet

2   Using these examples, and any other examples of explanations from your IB Diploma Programme subjects, discuss whether a coherent explanation is the same as a true explanation. Write around 200 words in response, explaining your answer fully.

Peer-assessment

Ask your partner to offer their explanations. Pick their most coherent and convincing one, and justify your choice.

Pragmatic theory

According to the **pragmatic theory** of truth, broadly speaking a proposition is true if it is *useful* or *works in practice* and is the best we can currently do in terms of our research and understanding. Pragmatism does not teach that something becomes true by being thought useful; rather it teaches that the fruitfulness and utility of some idea or principle is the best guide to its truth that we have available. According to pragmatism, truth must be shared and verifiable by the scientific method or similar processes, but it is temporary and revisable in the light of further experience. To use a well-known example, Newton's laws were once regarded as truth. They lost that status when Einstein's theory of general relativity was published because they no longer provided the best theory for understanding motion, even though they remain incredibly useful in many circumstances. We now regard the theory of general relativity as true, even though it does not cohere with quantum physics, because

> **KEY WORD**
>
> **pragmatic theory (of truth):** the theory that truths are beliefs which have been scientifically verified or lead to predictable and dependable outcomes.

it provides a more fruitful and useful model than Newton's , but it is conceivable that at sometime in the future, it too will be superseded by a more fruitful theory.

At the end of the 19th century, the American philosophers known as pragmatists who developed pragmatism, Charles Pierce (1839–1914), William James (1842–1910) and John Dewey (1859–1952), each took pragmatism to mean something slightly different, however their different perspectives were all based on a serious attempt to place our collective human assessment of what we most care about at the centre of what we regard as knowledge and truth. Pragmatists regard absolutist ideals of knowledge and truth as unattainable and unhelpful. Rather they regard knowledge as being what we agree upon after rigorous scientific analysis and verification. This means that knowledge and truth are always revisable; no time ever arises when we can regard ourselves as having arrived at final knowledge or truth. On the contrary, for Dewey in particular, every advance in knowledge raises more questions, every tentative certainty creates more uncertainties, and every answer raises more questions. This is why Dewey preferred to talk of truth as a 'warranted assertion'. There is, for pragmatists, no absolute truth; no "end of our exploring" as T.S. Eliot (1888–1965) suggested; there is rather only an endless, branching sequence of lines of inquiry each of which leads to yet more. As Aristotle (384–322 BCE) is once said to have claimed over two thousand years ago: "The more we know, the more we know we don't know.'

Figure 4.4: The pragmatic theory suggests that a claim is true if it is useful

---

EXPLORE 4.4

1 In what ways do pragmatism and TOK appear to be closely related?

2 Do you think it is useful to believe that God exists or does not exist? How would you try to test whether the 'hypothesis of God' works in practice?

3 Why might many scientists adopt a pragmatic approach to truth?

4 To what extent does a pragmatic theory of truth allow for correspondence with the world and coherence with what we already know?

5 To what extent might the pragmatic theory of truth be regarded as subjective?

Criticisms

A statement can be useful but not true, and true but not useful

There are many examples of statements that are useful but not true:

- In many areas of life approximations are often more useful than truths. For example, saying the time right now is between 9 am and 3 pm might be true, but it is not terribly useful, while saying the time is about 10.15 am might not be accurate but is much more helpful if I need to go to a 10.30 am appointment.

'Useful' and 'works in practice' are too vague to give us a workable theory of truth

Another criticism of the pragmatic theory is that it is not clear what it means to say that something is 'useful' or 'works in practice'. Assessing the usefulness or fruitfulness of a belief is possibly no more clear-cut than assessing its truth; beliefs may be more or less useful, useful in different ways and for different purposes, or useful in the short-term or long-run. It could be said that determining whether a belief is useful is no easier than determining whether it is true.

Pragmatic theories are anti-realist

Because of pragmatism's focus on truth as being something that is verifiable or assertable, some have argued that pragmatism is too subjective and too dependent on human abilities to work out what truth is. They argue that pragmatism does not allow for objective truths that might exist whether or not we discover them.

EXPLORE 4.5

1   In pairs, try to think of examples from all areas of knowledge of things that we once believed to be true but no longer are. Then think of some examples that we currently hold to be true but may one day be superceded. What does this say about the nature of truth?

Discuss: Is truth more than a 'warranted assertion' or 'justified belief'?

Using examples that you have found, write around 300 words in response to the following question: To what extent is a useful knowledge claim the same thing as a true knowledge claim?

Self-assessment

Evaluate the summary you have written.

How well does your response show that you have understood the pragmatic theory of truth? Have you justified and supported all of your points using either reasons, examples or evidence? Have you considered any counter-arguments and counter-evidence, and evaluated these counter-examples? Have you considered another viewpoint or perspective? Have you come up with any criteria for judging the relative usefulness or truth value of these knowledge claims? Did you think through what follows logically from your arguments – and what the implications for knowledge and knowing are? Did you arrive at a logical and reasoned conclusion having considered 'both sides'?

Consensus theory

Consensus is the idea of a group of people agreeing on a set of beliefs together. According to this theory, truth is what most people belief in. In order for knowledge to be knowledge, it has to be accepted by many people.

REAL-LIFE SITUATION 4.3

1   Does the fact that a belief is popular make it true?

2   Does knowledge and knowing depend on how many people accept it?

KEY WORD

consensus theory (of truth): the theory that truth is based on a set of beliefs that the majority of people agree on

Social psychology might suggest that truth is related to cultural consensus. Truth is in some way shared knowledge that we can agree upon. In psychology, there are clinical diagnoses where there is a mismatch between someone's beliefs and the real world, which might call for appropriate therapies. This relates to the correspondence theory of truth – that the construction of our beliefs should in some way match or mirror the reality we find ourselves in. Psychology recognises that we can deviate from the norm. There is such a thing as normal, healthy psychology which is related to cultural and social norms.

Consensus theory suggests that truth is what the majority believe in. However, popular beliefs may not necessarily be true, given that some people are reluctant to disturb their peace of mind by questioning their fundamental assumptions, and prefer to inhabit their own comfortable illusions rather than face up to harsh and unsettling truths. To protect their beliefs, people may use a variety of defence mechanisms, such as selective attention (seeing what they want to see), rationalisation (manufacturing bad reasons to justify their prejudices) and communal reinforcement (mixing exclusively with people who hold similar beliefs).

DISCUSS 4.6

Do you think that someone could inhabit a comfortable illusion for their whole life without ever being let down by it? What are the implications of this for the consensus theory of truth?

Figure 4.5: The consensus theory suggests that a claim is true if most people agree with it

Criticisms

A majority of people may agree on beliefs that are false

Consensus might seem like an attractive option, but it has multiple problems. Before Copernicus (1473–1543), most people believed in a geocentric universe and agreed that the sun rotated around the Earth, showing that many people can have beliefs that turn out to be false.

REAL-LIFE SITUATION 4.4

1   Why does the distinction between truth and falsehood matter in human societies?

2   Discuss examples of when many people agree about something that turns out to be wrong.

Beliefs are culturally relative

Psychologists would recognise that so-called 'abnormal' psychology is relative to a person's cultural and social context. Someone might have psychotic beliefs and get diagnosed in one culture, and yet if they have no negative consequences, may go undiagnosed in another culture.

Membership of a group may not imply an acceptance of knowledge

How do we know what the majority really believes? The beliefs of a group may be difficult to measure and contain. For example, we might belong to groups that we like to participate in, but do not accept all beliefs associated wholesale. For example, I might like to belong to a church, synagogue or temple, but it does not follow that I assent to every propositional knowledge claim associated with that group. I may still belong to that group and think for myself. Equally, I may choose not to belong to a religion but might still value some aspects of religion, or have my own spiritual beliefs. This illustrates that it can be problematic to generalise about the beliefs of groups.

Consensus may be the product of coercion

We are justified in being suspicious of consensus as a condition of truth or knowledge on the grounds that it is too easy to manipulate or coerce people into a consensus. Technology may enable us to access and share knowledge in new ways, but it may also have the effect of reinforcing our existing beliefs, given that social media has been described as an echo chamber where algorithms are programmed to serve up more of our own our preferences and constantly deliver more of the same.

Pluralist theory

According to the **pluralist theory**, the word 'truth' has no *one* fixed meaning. Instead, it has multiple meanings and uses in different contexts. If you consider the knowledge claims made in ethics, natural science and history, the word 'truth' is used in different ways. Truth is subject specific. In your mathematics class, a mathematical proof is used to show something is true, whereas truth means something different in your history class, where you might ask about the truth behind a 1950s interpretation of the Cold War.

KEY WORD

pluralist theory (of truth): the theory that there are multiple truths, and various meanings of the word 'truth'

In 1998, Professor Brian Schmidt (1967–) observed supernovae explosions in the distant cosmos, which led him to the conclusion that it was most likely the rate of universe expansion was speeding up rather than slowing down. This finding led to a change in scientific knowledge and earned Schmidt a Nobel Prize. This example demonstrates that scentific truth is provisional and temporary. Rather, scientists use inductive reasoning to describe and understand the natural physical, chemical and biological laws of the universe and their descriptions and understanding of what is true develop and change as their ideas and available technologies also develop and change. The counter-argument is that scientists can and do recognise falsehood. If they find data that falsifies and disproves their hypothesis, they modify or change their hypothesis accordingly.

In 1950, Thomas A. Bailey (1902–1983) put forward his so-called orthodox explanation of the Cold War, which argued that Stalin's plans for an aggressive expansion into Eastern Europe forced a response from the USA. However, access to further documents more recently has led historians to realise that this was not justified. The release of the Soviet archives in 1991 meant that historians could use new sources to interpret the Cold War from a new viewpoint. In 1997, historians Zubok and Pleshakov showed that Stalin had a strong, almost fanatical, belief in **communism**, but also had a genuine wish to avoid confrontation with the USA. In this way, historical truth is temporary, in the sense that it is dependent and contingent on the sources available. Perspectives and schools of thought can, and should, develop in the light of new evidence, and new interpretations based on the evidence.

In summary, a pluralist theory claims that there is more than one way of being true, and there are potentially multiple concepts of truth in different areas of knowledge. If this is the case – that different areas of knowledge each possess truth – it follows that multiple perspectives can work together to 'get closer to the truth'.

> ### KEY WORD
>
> **communism:** an ideology which advocates that all property is communally owned, and the government directs all economic production

Figure 4.6: The pluralist theory suggests that truth might be different in different areas of knowledge; it follows that an interdisciplinary group might get closer to the truth as they work together

DISCUSS 4.7

1   How has our understanding of truth or wisdom changed over time?

2   How far can experts within an area of knowledge claim to know the truth?

3   Why do experts within an area of knowledge sometimes disagree with one another?

Criticisms

Truth means such different things in the context of each different area of knowledge. Given that mathematical truth is so different from ethical truth, for example, it follows that truth has no *one* universal meaning. Interdisciplinary agreement faces the same problems as the coherence theory of truth. Arguably, confirmation from across disciplines does not make something true.

One person's truth could be another person's lie. For example, a freedom fighter and a terrorist could describe or denote the same person, but the connotations and associated meanings vary greatly. This might suggest that truth is relative, and that it means different things to different people. The redundancy theory, which we will explore next, suggests that truth has no essential meaning. All of these are truth claims. If I say there is no truth, my claim can be interpreted as an absolute truth which would be a contradiction.

It might be valuable to explore what truth means in different areas of knowledge. For example, you might consider how literature might offer insights into a truth about human nature, whereas history might offer truth about the causes of an event. Furthermore, it makes sense to think about the concept of true and false less as opposites, but instead more in terms of degrees of truth.

EXPLORE 4.6

Consider your six IB Diploma Programme subjects in terms of the types of truth that they provide. Present your ideas to the class. Do you think that each of your IB Diploma Programme subjects offer different degrees of truth? Make sure that you consider comparisons between subjects and use specific examples to support your ideas.

Self-assessment

How well have you understood how different areas of knowledge might make sense of the concept of truth? Evaluate your presentation. What did you do well? What did you think could have been improved on?

Redundancy theory

In the 1960s, post-modernism was a new theoretical perspective that ushered in a disruption and subversion of the established grand-narratives. Post-modernist thinkers recognised that knowledge is linked to authority and power. They challenged the idea that truth is owned by the social and intellectual establishment. The grand overarching narratives could be challenged, whether the secular paradigms of Marxism, science and progress, or religious narratives found in Christianity or Islam. For Foucault

KEY WORD

redundancy theory (of truth): the theory that truth has no essential property, and the word can be substituted for another

(1926–1984), power and knowledge are inextricably connected. For post-modernists, talk of truth can be deconstructed and shown to have no essential property. When we talk of truth, we are not adding any meaning. For example:

- 'It is true that Caesar was murdered' – becomes – 'Caesar was murdered'

- 'It is true that Picasso is a great painter' – becomes – 'Picasso is a great painter'

A redundancy theory of truth rejects the need for any discussion about, or problematising, of this concept. But the problem here is that the knowledge claim – that there is no truth – seems to contradict itself. It is itself a truth claim that my overarching view is true. I can only reject the concept of truth if I know the truth.

DISCUSS 4.8

1 Do you agree with the redundancy theory of truth?

2 Can we and should we get rid of the word 'truth'? Why? Why not? What implications does your answer have for knowledge and knowing?

Criticisms

If you abandon the belief that the truth is 'out there' and independent of us, you no longer have any objective grounds for evaluating beliefs and distinguishing wishful thinking from 'facts'.

If your beliefs are no longer disciplined by the truth, they are likely to end up being determined by nothing more than *prejudice*, *persuasion* or *power*. The danger is that you will then believe something simply because it fits in with your prejudices, because someone has *persuaded* you to believe it, or because you have been *bullied* or *indoctrinated* into believing it. This is clearly not a desirable state of affairs.

If the individual knower decides there is no truth, they become the final judge and arbiter of truth. However, the individual knower might not be understood as the final judge of truth, given that truth is arguably either 'out there' waiting to be discovered or constructed within shared areas of knowledge.

The statement *'There is no truth'* seems to refute itself as soon as you ask if it is true. If it is true, then there is at least one truth; and if it is false then it is *not* the case that there is no truth.

DISCUSS 4.9

1 Do you think that the individual knower is the final judge of truth?

2 Who decides whether it makes sense to talk about truth?

Figure 4.7: The redundancy theory suggests that we do not need to use the word *'truth'*. Do you think that we need the concept of truth to make sense of the 'real world'?

Summary of theories

We have now examined six different theories of truth, and have discovered that, despite their attractions, they each have various strengths and weaknesses. These can be summarised in the following table.

Theory	Justification	Criticisms
Correspondence A proposition is true if it corresponds to a fact. Truth is a relation with the real world.	A knowledge claim might be justified if it corresponds to a fact about the world.	• The correspondence theory requires the existence of all kinds of insubstantial facts, to which true statements are supposed to correspond. • Since there is a gap between language and the world, correspondence can never be perfect. • We cannot determine the truth or falsity of a proposition in isolation from other propositions.
Coherence A proposition is true if it fits in with our overall set of beliefs. Truth is a relation within a set of beliefs.	A knowledge claim might be justified if it fits with other things that we know	• Coherence is not sufficient for truth. A fairy-tale may be perfectly coherent, but it is still a fairy-tale. • With a little ingenuity, any crazy belief can be made to appear coherent. • A knowledge claim that does not fit in with your way of thinking might still be true.

Theory	Justification	Criticisms
Pragmatic A proposition is true if it is useful or works in practice. Truth is a relation with practical use.	A knowledge claim might be justified if it can be verified by the scientific method or provides predictable and dependable outcomes.	• A proposition can be true but not useful, and useful but not true. • It can be as difficult to verify something is useful as it is to verify that it is true.
Consensus A proposition is true if the majority of people believe in it. Truth is a relation based on what the majority agree on.	A knowledge claim might be justified if it is agreed upon by most people.	• The majority of people could have false beliefs. • There are many examples of when people have believed in things that are false, such as the belief that the brain is unable to create new brain cells.
Pluralist Truth has no *one* fixed meaning, and has multiple meanings depending on the context or area of knowledge.	A knowledge claim might be justified within a specific area of knowledge – depending on what counts as truth evidence, etc.	• Some people believe that truth has a fixed meaning that does not depend on the context. • How could the same knowledge claim be justified in one area of knowledge but not in another?
Redundancy A proposition does not need to contain the word 'truth'. Truth is an illusion based on the relationship between language and words.	A knowledge claim does not need to contain the word 'truth' – it can be rephrased without the need for the word 'truth'.	• Some people believe that if we abandon talk of truth, we have lost a valuable concept. • Many people believe that truth has an essential meaning. • The aim of any enquiry, whether it is scientific or historical, is to get closer to the truth.

DISCUSS 4.10

1 What distinguishes true belief from false belief? What tools and methods might we use to establish the difference?

2 How far might different tools and methods enable us to discover the truth?

REFLECTION

Do you use the words *true* and *truth* to mean different things in different contexts? To what extent does the vagueness of the words *true* and *truth* limit or liberate your ability to communicate your ideas when discussing knowledge?

4.3 Post-truth

In the 2016 Oxford English Dictionary (OED), 'post-truth' was chosen as 'word of the year'. During this year, it was frequently used in the context of the EU referendum in the UK, and in the US presidential election. Post-truth is defined by the OED as *'relating to or denoting circumstances in which objective facts are less influential in shaping public opinion than appeals to emotion and personal belief'*. This definition refers to a culture or environment in which people do not know what or whom to believe so they are more likely to respond to an emotional appeal than rational arguments. Post-truth may sometimes be associated with the sceptical view that there is no absolute truth, and it defines the era of 'fake news' and deepfake videos.

The American philosopher and sociologist Steve Fuller (1959–) offers an explanation of post-truth in relation to the context of 2016. For him, post-truth is nothing new. It represents the ongoing conflict between the two elites – the experts of the establishment and the supporters of populism. Fuller traces this back to one of the founders of sociology, Vilfredo Pareto (1848–1923), who claimed that truth is established by power or authority. Pareto identifies a cyclical social conflict between two powerful elites, where each adopt a different way of defining truth in order to out-wit their opponent. Pareto followed Machiavelli's use of the analogy of lions and foxes to explain the interplay of these two elites. The lions represent the establishment who have tradition on their side, and they appeal to reason, tradition and authority. In contrast, the foxes represent a challenge to that elite, characterised by dissent and suspicion of the hypocrisy of the lions.

It follows that neither side will describe the other in a neutral way. The foxes use language that appeals to the corruption and hypocrisy of the lions. The lions use language that accuses the foxes of appeals to emotion and distorting the facts. This is significant for our understanding of what post-truth means today. It is difficult to have a neutral definition given that a dictionary definition written by a lion would not be the same as one written by a fox. The key point here is that truth is linked to the language and politics of a knowledge community. The analogy also illustrates that truth is in some ways dependent on the knower's perspective; truth is a concept that is difficult to define and pin down in language.

KEY WORDS

post-truth: relating to or denoting circumstances in which objective facts are less influential in shaping public opinion than appeals to emotion and personal belief

deepfake: the use of artificial intelligence (AI) to create fake videos creating the false impression of authenticity

KEY WORD

neutral: unbiased, impartial, not supporting either side of an argument

Figure 4.8: Vilfredo Pareto used the analogy of lions and foxes to explain the different appeals to truth used by the establishment and its opponents

Truth: relatively absolute or absolutely relative?

Since we do not have an absolute overarching view of the universe and can only know the universe as it is for us, you might think that our only choice is to embrace relativism and say that truth is relative. There is *my* truth, and there is *your* truth – but there is no absolute truth. We should, however, be careful here. To say that we can never know the truth is not the same as saying that no such truth exists. You might say a truth that can never be known has no practical value, but that does not make it any less true. If a man is murdered and all the evidence is destroyed in a fire, we may never know who killed him, but there is still a truth of the matter.

You may still find relativism an attractive position on the grounds that it encourages a tolerant 'live and let live' attitude, which is appropriate in a multi-cultural world. But relativism is also open to the objection that it is self-contradictory. The statement

KEY WORD

relativism: in the context of truth, it is the belief that truth is relative to the society, culture or historical context in which you live; as opposed to absolutism, which is the belief that there are universal or absolute principles which should always be followed

'There is no truth', based on the redundancy theory of truth, seems to refute itself as soon as you ask if it is true. If it is true, then there is at least one truth. If it is false, then it is *not* the case that there is no truth. A sophisticated relativist might try to avoid this problem by suggesting that we should simply abandon all talk of truth. But the concept of 'truth' seems to play too important a role in our thinking for us to be able to dispense with it completely.

Whether or not relativism encourages tolerance is debatable; but it may be that in practice the drawbacks of embracing it outweigh the benefits. The idea that the truth exists independently of us gives us grounds for judging the difference between beliefs and facts.

A conversation about truth

EXPLORE 4.7

Working as a pair, evaluate the positions taken by Geoff and Anushka in the following conversation. Use and apply some of the following criteria:

1   the clarity, coherence or relevance of the arguments

2   use of reasons or examples to support points

3   the assumptions that they take for granted

4   the implications of the arguments and conclusions

On balance which view seems the most convincing to you, and why? Summarise their disagreement, and your own view of truth.

Geoff: *I don't need to think about truth. It means nothing to me. There is no fact about the world that it corresponds to. Truth does not exist.*

Anushka: Was the policy of apartheid in South Africa wrong?

Geoff: *Yes.*

Anushka: That is a moral truth.

Geoff: *No it is just my opinion. There's no need to bring truth into it.*

Anushka: Did Picasso paint great artworks?

Geoff: *Yes.*

Anushka: That is an aesthetic truth.

Geoff: *You are playing a word game here. I told you already that we do not need the word 'truth'. Apartheid was wrong and Picasso was a great artist. These are my beliefs. They are not absolute truths.*

Anushka: But if you have a belief, you must assume it is true. You would not believe in things that you know are false.

Geoff: *Why not?*

CONTINUED

Anushka: When you believe in something, you take for granted that your belief is true.

Geoff: *That is a matter of opinion – your opinion. It's not the final truth. I repeat again – it makes no sense wasting your time talking about truth when it does not exist.'*

Anushka: Is that true?

Geoff: *Yes.*

Anushka: You have contradicted yourself.

Geoff: *Pardon?*

Anushka: You are making a big truth claim if you say that you know there is no truth.

Geoff: *But how do you know that your belief in the existence of truth is true?*

Anushka: How can anyone know if their beliefs are true or false?

Geoff: *Beliefs are relative. There are no absolute truths.*

Anushka: That sounds relatively absolute.

Geoff: *No it's **absolutely** relative.*

Anushka: That's my point – you cannot avoid a discussion of absolute truth!

REFLECTION

If both absolutist and relativist accounts of truth fail, is there a middle path? To what extent do you have a personal responsibility to determine your own path to truth?

4.4 Conspiracy and conspiracy theories

DISCUSS 4.11

How can we tell the difference between an actual conspiracy and a conspiracy theory?

Conspiracy

There are many real-life examples of conspiracies. In 1996, Alan Sokal, a Professor of Physics, submitted an article to *Social Text*, a leading American journal of cultural studies, in which he argued that quantum gravity is a social construct. He later admitted that the article he had written was a hoax, deliberately based on false information and nonsense, to test if his ideas would be noticed and go un-challenged. The article was published with the false belief that quantum gravity was a social and linguistic construct. In 2018, three academics submitted hoax articles to scholarly journals – known as 'Sokal Squared', an example of intellectuals who have conspired together to test the rigour of the intellectual establishment. Helen Pluckrose, James A. Lindsay and Peter Boghossian submitted a number of hoax articles to journals in various academic fields, and four of them were published online. The false information they submitted to the academic journals could be interpreted as an example either of a playful and ironic game, or of an unethical and somewhat devious conspiracy to mislead others. While some would argue that this was misleading or fraudulent, others might argue it is an example of a small-scale conspiracy, defined as two or more people planning together in secret. The key point here relates to knowledge and knowing – if we read an article in a respected publication, we assume that it is true. However, the 'Sokal Squared' example illustrates that the truth can sometimes escape the intellectual establishment, and an audience can be presented unknowingly with things that turn out to be false.

On a personal level, if my friend and I plan a surprise birthday party for our mutual friend, we are plotting together. A criminal gang might conspire to commit illegal actions. Many other examples of hoax or conspiracy come to mind – governments organising secret operations, for example Area 51, used by the US Air Force in Nevada.

Some knowledge may be kept secret for good reasons, but you might wonder about the ethics of secret knowledge and where the line is between freedom of information and confidentiality. Arguably, on a national and international level, we might need some level of secrecy to protect privacy – and this happens when companies conspire to protect their data, or government or counter-terrorism agencies aim to keep a nation safe. Governments might use security and safety as justification for some knowledge remaining undisclosed. There are ethical questions arising here about our access to knowledge, and the rights and responsibilities of individual knowers, organisations and governments in relation to knowledge and knowing. The implication here would be that knowledge and power are sometimes closely connected – a theme that we explore further in the context of politics and knowledge in Chapter 7.

During the Second World War, the codebreaking carried out at Bletchley Park was part of a secret UK government plan to crack the German code. This is not an example of conspiracy but rather an example of knowledge as secret intelligence. Given that organisations and governments can and do keep information secret, it is not impossible to let your imagination take control and believe that there is a greater mind or hidden agenda behind certain events. At this point we enter the sometimes incredible world of conspiracy theories.

Conspiracy theory

An explanation is a reason why an event or action happened. Each area of knowledge uses this concept. For example, historians specialise in coherent explanations of past events, whereas scientists offer explanations of natural phenomena. However, a conspiracy theory is an 'alternative explanation' of an event in terms of a 'hidden truth' or the deliberate and secret agency of people or organisations. There is a significant distinction between an actual conspiracy – for example codebreaking

> **KEY WORD**
>
> explanation: in the context of the study of history, a justification or reason that explains why an event or action took place

at Bletchley Park – and a conspiracy theory – for example, the claim that NASA faked the 1969 moon landings which were therefore part of a deliberate American government hoax. Conspiracy theorists can offer counter-evidence in support of their belief that the moon landings never took place and were filmed in a studio. Without even considering the evidence they put forward, you might question the balance of probabilities. Is it more likely that there were people who actually landed on the moon in 1969 as officially reported, or that the astronauts, government officials, photographers, set designers and others who were needed to fake the landings *all* remained silent about a vast cover up? The question might come down to the balance of probabilities and what the knower considers to be the most likely explanation.

REAL-LIFE SITUATION 4.7

Which do you think is more credible? That the 1969 moon landings actually took place or that they were faked by the US government?

Figure 4.9: How sure are you that the Americans landed on the moon?

Conspiracy theories have varying degrees of plausibility, and range from the ridiculous to the more reasonable. At one end of the scale, the absurd and comical are easy to dismiss, such as the belief that there are lizards who are in charge of the world. On the other end of the scale, other theories might appear superficially compelling if they seem that they could be true – the explanation that the Russian government secretly interfered in the 2016 election of the US President, a claim which has been dismissed as having no factual basis. Some have argued that this is based on fact, whereas others have argued that this is the product of over-imaginative or wishful thinking, typical of a conspiracy theory.

So how can we explain their appeal? On the surface, these theories might appear as counter-arguments, which demonstrate a healthy scepticism that challenges orthodox or establishment views. Clare Birchall, university lecturer and author of *Knowledge Goes Pop: From Conspiracy Theory to Gossip*, describes conspiracy theory as a 'form of popular knowledge or interpretation of an event'. Some conspiracy theories deny that a historical event took place. Others go further, offering elaborate explanations of events. However, conspiracy theories offer explanations of events which are often complicated, and involve the under-cover work of organisations or various people all working together in secret. Conspiracy theories are part of popular culture, and are characterised by the idea that there is some greater agenda at stake behind an event, for example the conspiracy theory that John F. Kennedy was assassinated in 1963 by the Mafia.

REAL-LIFE SITUATION 4.8

Consider the relationship between truth and popularity. To what extent does the popularity of a theory increase the probability that it is true?

REFLECTION

Consider the extent to which your personal assumptions, expectations and biases might lead you to accept or reject popular conspiracy theories. To what extent do you tend to 'buy in to' theories that appeal to you because they appeal to your personal prejudices?

Such a theory offers the idea of a design or purpose behind an event, often the work of a political institution or group of powerful people. A conspiracy theorist claims to know the 'real truth' behind an event, and can point to evidence to support their theory. Conspiracy theories might be understood in terms of the psychological perspective that they offer. The American historian Richard Hofstadter (1916–1970) offered a broad definition of conspiracy theories as more of a suspicious mind set, or paranoid viewpoint. These theories are sceptical, and some are verging on paranoid – they assume that authorities cannot be trusted and that the truth is being deliberately hidden in such a way that it lies beyond conventional explanations.

DISCUSS 4.12

Why might historians reject the explanatory power of conspiracy theories whereas other people might accept them?

In Chapter 13, we will explore the principle known as Occam's Razor, which suggests that the simplest explanation is often the best. Conspiracy theories require somewhat elaborate explanations involving secret agency, cover ups and hidden motives, whereas historians make use of the historical method to understand the motives of a person or a group based on the evidence available. Historians would recognise that in some situations, such as war, governments might deliberately put out propaganda or false information to throw others off the scent. The Russian TU 144 airplane, which was a rival to Concorde, crashed at the 1973 Paris Air Show. It was alleged that in the early 1970s, the Anglo-French team who designed the supersonic Concord leaked documents to the Soviet team who designed the rival aircraft TU 144. While there are various explanations for the tragic plane crash, according to the conspiracy known as 'Concordski', the Anglo-French team deliberately passed design plans that contained an inherent fault which caused the disaster. Evidence can be offered by both sides. This relates back to the idea of post-truth, which we explored earlier in the chapter – conspiracy theories are an example of a post-truth approach, where emotion and personal experience are valued over and above rationality and known facts. However, a conspiracy theorist will offer 'facts' and evidence in order to back up their alternative explanation. As a knower, making a judgement here might involve some analysis that could include an evaluation of the assumptions being made, the likelihood of the explanations and identification of the bias inherent in the perspectives taken. Furthermore, abductive reasoning, which we explored in Chapter 3, suggests that we have a tendency to piece together what we know to come up with an explanation.

Few historians would entertain conspiracy theories, given that they would look to the historical method and the sound interpretation of sources in order to construct an explanation of an event. The historian Niall Ferguson (1964–) argues that the history of networks of people has been left to conspiracy theorists. He argues that the structure of a network determines how far and how fast ideas spread. It follows that ideas about truth and knowledge are widely dispersed when, and because, a network is dispersed.

To sum up, there are various knowledge questions arising here relating to the concept of explanation, coherence and truth. For some people, a conspiracy theory seems to make sense and offer a superior level of 'hidden truth' or 'alternative truth' that suggests a secret master-mind behind events. However, others would reject such theories as implausible, given that they require more complexity than needed.

REAL-LIFE SITUATION 4.9

1   If you believe in one conspiracy theory, are you more likely to believe that other conspiracy theories are true? Why? Why not?

2   If there are different explanations for the same event? How do we decide between them?

EXPLORE 4.8

1   Do some research into it one of the following conspiracy theories (or alternatively, you could investigate one of your choice):

  * the 1969 moon landings were fake

  * the *Titanic* never sank in 1912, it was the sister ship which did

  * the Illuminati are a secret society who control world leaders

CONTINUED

- Elvis Presley is alive

- the Rothschild family control the world's money

- the CIA were involved in Marilyn Monroe's death in 1962

- governments were involved in the attack on the World Trade Centre on 11 September 2001

- John F. Kennedy was assassinated by the Mafia in 1963

- there is a European plot to establish a super state and undermine nation states

- the reasons for the 1970s plane crash known as Concordski

- denial of the 2012 Sandy Hook massacre

2   Apply some TOK analysis to the conspiracy theory you have researched. Explore the conspiracy theory in relation to the following:

a   consider what is ambiguous or uncertain

b   think about why there are various possible interpretations of the same phenomenon or event

c   identify the *evidence* used to justify the conspiracy theory

d   identify any *assumptions* or any *bias*

e   consider the *counter-argument* or *counter-evidence*

f   evaluate the different *perspectives or points of view*

g   think through the *implications* of the conclusion – if the conspiracy theory is true, what follows?

h   arrive at your own judgement and *justify* your perspective

3   Have a class debate in which you discuss the statement: This house believes that conspiracy theories are based on reliable knowledge.

Self-assessment

Evaluate your TOK analysis of conspiracy theories. How well does it demonstrate that you have understood the notion of hidden truth, the nature of conspiracy theories and their relevance for knowledge and knowing? Go back through the checklist above and identify whether your analysis has taken each of these into account.

4.5 How do we know if our beliefs are true?

DISCUSS 4.13

1   What beliefs might we have today that may turn out to be false?

2   Plato (c 427–348 BCE), an ancient Greek philosopher, once suggested and later rejected a definition of knowledge as 'justified true belief'. How far do you agree that truth is one of the conditions of knowledge?

In Chapter 2, we explored the nature of knowledge, and in this chapter, we have focused on truth. As traditionally understood, truth is independent of what anyone happens to believe is true, and simply believing that something is true does not make it true. However, we have seen that neither knowledge nor truth can be clearly defined or infallibly determined. The best we can do it to ensure that our beliefs are well-justified by available evidence, and be prepared to change them if further evidence warrants it.

A knowledge claim is a statement in which we claim to *know* something. For example, first-order knowledge claims are made in different areas of knowledge, e.g. 'I know that John Maynard Keynes was an influential economist' (human sciences), or 'I know that some metals are more reactive than others' (natural sciences). These claims may be true. A second-order knowledge claim is about the nature of knowledge and knowing. For example, 'The human sciences have reliable methods for constructing knowledge' or 'Knowledge can be based on faith and reason'.

Objectivity and subjectivity

Absolute truth should not be confused with relativism or relative truth, and it is worth emphasising that just because your view of the truth varies with your perspective, this does not mean that there is no truth at all. To see that the latter is an error, imagine four people are looking at Mount Everest – one is standing to the north, one to the south, one to the east and one to the west. The fact that they have different perspectives on the mountain and describe it in different ways does not mean that truth is relative. There can be more and less accurate descriptions of Mount Everest as seen from north, south, east and west, and there is a sense in which they all point to the same underlying truth. This takes us back to the concept of *objectivity* – the idea that as knowers, we can be impartial, and using this example, the idea that there is an objective truth about Mount Everest that exists regardless of our personal perspective.

All of our beliefs are *subjective* in the sense that they are based on personal perspectives and individual feelings. Imagine, for example, that you are trying to find out what someone – let us call him Robert – is 'really like'. His mother describes him in one way, his brother in another, his teachers in a third and his friends in a fourth. While there may be some overlap between these perspectives, each one captures only some aspects of Robert, and, in a sense, gives us only *half-truths* but not the *whole truth* about him. (This may explain why if a child gets into trouble at school, his surprised parents say 'But he's never like that at home!') Although each viewpoint is subjective, it does not follow that there is no truth about Robert. We might get closer to an objective truth about Robert the more perspectives we have on him.

The concept of truth is more than a subjective belief. Using these examples, it follows that it is possible to have some degree of objective truth in relation to Mount Everest, and of 'what Robert is like'. As we explored in Chapter 1, objectivity is based on the idea of taking a detached perspective where we are not influenced by factors that might skew our judgement such as personal beliefs, feelings or opinions. The counter-claim here is that our own implicit bias makes it impossible to take an objective point of view. Furthermore, it makes no sense to think of an objective truth 'beyond us' that we have no access to, as it would have little use or value if we could not know it ourselves.

REFLECTION

If there is no 'view from nowhere', does it make sense to believe in objective truths? To what extent might objective truths exist in different areas of knowledge, even if we can never know them?

Justification

In addition to the concepts of subjectivity and objectivity in relation to truth, we might consider the level or type of justification for a truth claim. There are examples that come to mind when I have limited or no sound **justification** for my belief, but that belief is in fact true. For example, I wish to win the lottery and then I do, or I wish for snow and then it does in fact snow. However, in both of these situations, I cannot claim that 'I knew' I would win the lottery nor that 'I knew' it would snow. These are examples of my **hindsight bias** at work, where there is no genuine knowledge because I did not have sufficient justification nor evidence for my belief. There is a wealth of evidence to suggest that people often engage in wishful thinking, and believe what they want to believe rather than what is justified by the evidence. Conspiracy theories which we looked at in this chapter are a good example of this.

There are other examples where someone might have justification for a belief but the belief is in fact false. For example, the ancient Greek belief that atoms could not be split. This claim might have been thought to count as knowledge once, but we have since discovered that this belief is false. Furthermore, justification may be offered for a claim or theory which may even appear coherent, but it turns out to be a conspiracy theory or fake news or a post-truth claim.

KEY WORDS

justification: in the context of truth, a reason or reasons for a belief or support for a truth claim

hindsight bias: mistakenly thinking you knew something would happen, after it has happened

---

REAL-LIFE SITUATION 4.10

Do you know things that have limited justification or no sound justification?

DISCUSS 4.14

Do you think that objectivity is one of the conditions of knowledge? Are some knowledge claims true that have little or no justification? Can a claim still be true even if there is limited or no justification?

4.6 Wisdom

DISCUSS 4.15

1   Is a person who thinks critically also a wise person?

2   What do you think is the connection between knowledge and wisdom? Are they similar or different?

The poet T. S. Eliot (1888–1965) once lamented *'Where is the wisdom we have lost in knowledge? Where is the knowledge we have lost in information?'* In Chapter 2, we explored the difference between knowledge and information, and it is perhaps appropriate to conclude by thinking about the difference between wisdom and knowledge. As knowers, we have attitudes and attributes, and in this final section, we invite you to explore this further. We will briefly consider five key features of wisdom:

- good judgement
- breadth of perspective
- self-knowledge
- ethical responsibility
- intellectual humility

Figure 4.10: The Dalai Lama. Who do you think exemplifies wisdom?

Good judgement

Human beings are fallible creatures, and you will learn from your TOK course that the dream of certainty is an impossible dream. But just because we cannot achieve certainty, it does not follow that any opinion is as good as any other. We are surely right to take more seriously opinions that are informed, coherent and insightful than those that are not; and we are surely justified in saying that we *know* something if we have justification or enough evidence for it. If we ask 'how sound does the justification have to be?' or 'how much evidence is enough evidence?', there is no definite answer, and we can only say that it is a matter of judgement.

Since every situation that confronts us is unique, we must also use our judgement when we apply knowledge to the world. The relevance of good judgement in areas such as history, ethics and the arts is clear, but it also plays a role in something as seemingly objective as measurement. For example, to say that 'X is exactly 5 cm long' is based on the judgement that it has been measured to the appropriate number of decimal places for the task at hand.

How can we develop good judgement? Sadly, it is not something that can be learnt from books, but only from experience and practical engagement with the world. This may be why we tend to associate wisdom with older people rather than young people. In fact, it is not experience itself that matters, but *reflection on experience* and the ability to learn from it. That is why you can be old without being wise!

REAL-LIFE SITUATION 4.11

Reflection is encouraged in IB Diploma Programme students, and 'reflective' is one of the attributes of the IB learner profile. What qualities does a reflective person have? Why do you think the capacity to reflect is important for knowers?

Breadth of perspective

Wisdom requires not only good judgement, but also breadth of perspective. We live in an increasingly specialised world in which there are said to be an ever-increasing number of fields of knowledge. Such an intellectual division of labour has doubtless helped to fuel the explosive growth of knowledge over the last hundred years, but it has also resulted in a fragmented picture of reality. In order to succeed in the modern world, you need to specialise, but if you are *too* specialised, you may end up becoming what the Germans call a *Fachidiot* – a person who is very brilliant in a narrow area but who has no real understanding of the world. It is possible to have expertise without wisdom.

To understand the world, it makes sense to take it apart and examine the pieces. This is why we divide knowledge into different subjects. But the world does not arrive in neat packages labelled 'physics', 'biology', 'economics', 'ethics', etc. At some point, we have to put the separate pieces together again. That is why we put so much emphasis in TOK on comparing and contrasting knowledge claims in different subjects. The ideal is surely to have both depth and breadth, to have specialists with a sense of the whole.

This is of more than theoretical interest. The breadth of our perspective has implications. If we are to solve some of the urgent problems that confront us in the modern world – global warming, the destruction of the natural environment, world poverty, the spread of infectious diseases – we will need an interdisciplinary approach that goes beyond the narrow vision of a *Fachidiot*, and integrates the perspectives of many different subjects. In other words, we need experts who recognise the wisdom of seeing the bigger picture and the value of collaboration with other experts in different areas of knowledge.

> **REAL-LIFE SITUATION 4.12**
>
> Consider the connections between your six IB Diploma Programme subjects. How might your knowledge of single subjects or disciplines enable you to take an interdisciplinary perspective?

Self-knowledge

A third ingredient of wisdom is self-knowledge. Among other things, the quest for self-knowledge encourages us to question our beliefs and motives, and to become aware of our underlying prejudices. As you will have learnt in our discussion of paradigms, our prejudices and implicit bias can be likened to a pair of tinted glasses that colour the way we see and think about the world. Just as we look through *but rarely see* the glasses that are on the end of our nose, so the underlying prejudices through which we make sense of reality usually remain invisible to us.

We like to think that we are rational beings, but we sometimes find it easier to comfortably inhabit our prejudices than to question them. There is perhaps an element of vanity in this, and it seems that we are often attached to our beliefs for no better reason than that they are *ours*. So perhaps what is needed – at least occasionally – is the courage to question our convictions, to ask ourselves *why* we believe what we believe and how far our beliefs are justified by the evidence. If we can develop self-knowledge and become aware of some of the prejudices that underlie our beliefs, then we have taken a step towards overcoming them and moving towards a more inclusive picture of the world.

> **REAL-LIFE SITUATION 4.13**
>
> One attribute of the IB learner profile is 'open-minded'. What does it mean to be open-minded? In what ways does 'open-mindedness' relate to tolerance, respect or intercultural understanding?

Ethical responsibility

> **DISCUSS 4.16**
>
> Are wise people necessarily good people? How do wisdom and ethics connect?

A wise person is aware of the relation between knowledge and values. Since the search for knowledge is as much a communal as an individual enterprise, there is a sense in which values are built into it from the beginning. You may be attracted by the heroic image of the lonely thinker struggling with the truth, but the reality is that almost any statement you accept as true requires that you are willing to believe a great many people. You cannot conduct every biology experiment yourself, or personally check all the documentary evidence on which a book on the Second World War is based. You have to trust that the biologists are not faking their results and the historians are not making it up as they go along.

Indeed, if you had not trusted other people, you could never have learnt language in the first place, and so would be unable to express your doubt. Trust, and a healthy degree of faith in experts then, is the glue that holds the enterprise of knowledge together, and doubt only makes sense in a broader context of trust. A lazy scepticism that is suspicious, such as a blind acceptance of many conspiracy theories, is not the same thing as critical thought. Cynical thought is not the same thing as responsible and critical thinking. We have to take some things on trust in order to get started.

If knowledge is based on trust, then each of us must exercise responsibility in our knowledge claims. There are certain things we *ought* to do before we say that we know something. For example, we *ought* to look at the evidence, we *ought* to be consistent and we *ought* to be open to criticism. This raises an interesting question about the extent of our ethical obligations as knowers. We are accustomed to making a clear distinction between facts and values, but perhaps, at a deep level, facts depend on values. How, after all, can there be knowledge without such intellectual virtues as honesty, perseverance, courage, humility and tolerance?

> **KEY WORD**
>
> intellectual virtues: virtues that are required for the pursuit of knowledge

DISCUSS 4.17

1   What responsibilities, if any, do experts have and why?

2   Where do my values come from and what are my responsibilities as a knower?

3   How is my knowledge shaped by trust, and/or the communities I belong to?

We must exercise responsibility not only in the *production* of knowledge but also in its *use*. You can be clever if you know many things, but you can only be wise if you have also thought about the use to which knowledge should be put. Perhaps one of the problems in the modern era is that we have plenty of clever people with know-how, but few wise ones with what might be called 'know-why'.

Intellectual humility

The last aspect of wisdom is intellectual humility. Since we are not gods but finite beings with limited minds, we can never achieve absolute knowledge. Such knowledge lies beyond our reach because we interpret the world through *our* senses, *our* reason and *our* concepts – and these can never give us the whole picture. We can perhaps be proud of our achievements and confident that we are making progress, but it seems that as our knowledge expands, so does our ignorance, and that every answer breeds new questions. As we noted near the start of Chapter 3, knowledge questions are contestable, meaning that there are multiple possible answers to them. In view of this, it is unlikely that we will ever know all there is to know about even a single grain of sand. At the limit, some of the big questions about life and the universe may lie permanently beyond our grasp – mysteries to be contemplated rather than problems to be solved. While religious knowledge communities re-interpret and re-tell their narratives in order that individuals and communities can explore their shared sense of meaning and purpose, secular people also look for meaning and purpose in their lives, and find it in diverse ways. One universal tendency of human beings is to make meaning of their lives.

It is very difficult but important for us to be aware that there is much that we do not know. Moreover, we are limited by our own imagination, and we can be poor evaluators of our own level of knowledge and competence. It can be difficult to be intellectually humble given that we cannot know what we do not know. This is a psychological tendency or cognitive bias known as the **Dunning–Kruger effect**, where we find it difficult to know the limit of our expertise. Psychologists David Dunning and Justin Kruger, who coined the term, identified that non-experts with little knowledge on a subject nor competence are more likely to overestimate their expertise and competence in that area.

This example of cognitive bias links back to the pragmatic theory of truth. It raises a question about whether it is useful to either overestimate or underestimate our confidence in our own knowledge and abilities. The most useful thing in the long term is surely to have intellectual humility by having a realistic grasp of your own strengths and weaknesses, and to try and be aware of what we do not know.

Some of the great minds of the past have been profoundly aware of the limits of knowledge. Socrates (c 470–399 BCE) famously observed that all he knew was that he knew nothing, and Isaac Newton (1642–1727) compared himself to *a little boy playing on the sea-shore, and diverting myself in now and then finding a smoother pebble or a prettier shell than ordinary, while the great ocean of truth lay all undiscovered before me'.* Such learned ignorance – achieved after a lifetime of thought – is very different from the empty ignorance of short-circuiting the search for knowledge by abandoning it at the first step.

The intellectual humility of someone like Socrates or Newton is, perhaps, connected with a sense of wonder. (That may be why dogmatists, who think they already have all the answers, never seem to experience it.) Wonder is common among children who come to the world with new eyes and see everything as a miracle; but as we grow older, we tend to get habituated to the mystery of things, and can end up finding the world dull and uninteresting – *boring*. Perhaps it is the inability to find wonder in the ordinary and the normal that drives people to seek it in the extraordinary and the paranormal, and to experiment with such things as hallucinogenic drugs, pseudo-science and new-age cults.

EXPLORE 4.9

Search for the list of the IB learner profile attributes online. What attributes or characteristics do we need to develop as knowers, and why?

Decide which you think are the top three most important for IB Diploma Programme students. Working with a partner or as a class, discuss these, and see if you can reach consensus or agreement about which are the most important and why.

REFLECTION

To what extent is relativism the epitome or the antithesis of intellectual humility? How might reflection on such questions help to make you wiser?

4.7 Conclusion

The connection between truth and knowledge is clearly important for us as knowers. What we know seems to be based on what we believe to be true. We have explored questions of knowledge and knowing such as 'How do we know what is true?' and 'How do different theories of truth relate to knowledge and knowing?'

The upshot of our discussion seems to be that at the most fundamental level, there is an unbridgeable gap between our picture of the world around us and the world itself. This might suggest that while we can continue to talk about truth in an ordinary, everyday sense – truth with a small 't' – we may need to abandon the belief that we can ever achieve *the* Truth. Immanuel Kant (1724–1804) made a distinction between *phenomena* (things that exist and can be seen) and *noumena* (things that exist outside of our senses). The phenomenal world is the one we inhabit. The noumenal world, while true according to Kant, is inaccessible to us, suggesting that ultimate truth lies beyond our understanding.

Our hope is that this chapter has engaged you to think about 'the truth about the truth'. In this chapter, we have explored the nature of facts and examined the various theories of truth, each of which gave us an insight into the nature of truth. Moreover, the section on conspiracy theories raised questions about beliefs in 'hidden truth' or 'alternative truth', and the relative truth of explanations. In conclusion, we could see knowledge as a matter of intellectual curiosity, a search for truth or 'an unending adventure at the edge of uncertainty' (Jacob Bronowski, 1908–1974). It might make sense to think of truth and wisdom in terms of a process, or an ongoing journey, rather than a fixed or final point. Critical thinking can become a habit of mind, and there could arguably be some truth behind the idea that intellectual curiosity and the application of critical thinking will enrich our lives as knowers. But it is for you to discover if that is true! Perhaps you will agree with us that in the end we should try to make sense of the world we live in not so much to reach a destination – for we will never have all the answers – as to travel with a different and altogether richer point of view. We hope you have a good journey!

KNOWLEDGE QUESTIONS

1   How far is there a similarity between scientific truth and historical truth?

2   What makes an explanation true?

3   How far is truth a necessary condition of knowledge and knowing?

4.8 Linking questions

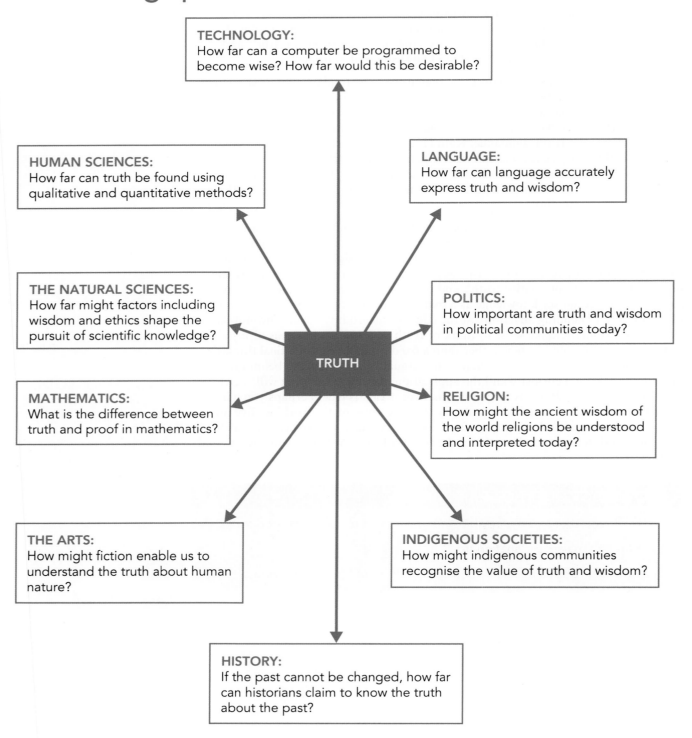

TECHNOLOGY:
How far can a computer be programmed to become wise? How far would this be desirable?

HUMAN SCIENCES:
How far can truth be found using qualitative and quantitative methods?

LANGUAGE:
How far can language accurately express truth and wisdom?

THE NATURAL SCIENCES:
How far might factors including wisdom and ethics shape the pursuit of scientific knowledge?

POLITICS:
How important are truth and wisdom in political communities today?

TRUTH

MATHEMATICS:
What is the difference between truth and proof in mathematics?

RELIGION:
How might the ancient wisdom of the world religions be understood and interpreted today?

THE ARTS:
How might fiction enable us to understand the truth about human nature?

INDIGENOUS SOCIETIES:
How might indigenous communities recognise the value of truth and wisdom?

HISTORY:
If the past cannot be changed, how far can historians claim to know the truth about the past?

4.9 Check your progress

Reflect on what you have learned in this chapter and indicate your confidence level between 1 and 5 (where 5 is the highest score and 1 is the lowest). If you score below 3, re-visit that section. Come back to this list later in your course. Has your confidence grown?

	Confidence level	Re-visited?
Am I able to evaluate the nature of truth and articulate the concept of degrees of truth?		
Can I explain different theories of truth, and the strengths and weaknesses of the: • pluralist theory of truth • correspondence theory of truth • coherence theory of truth • pragmatic theory of truth • consensus theory of truth • redundancy theory of truth?		
Am I aware of the knowledge questions arising from 'post-truth politics'?		
Do I understand the meanings of the terms 'relative' and 'absolute' truth, and the arguments used to support these points of view?		
Do I understand the role of explanations, and why some people might believe in 'alternative explanations' and conspiracy theories?		
Can I discuss conspiracy and conspiracy theories clearly, and their relevance for knowledge and knowing?		
Do I understand and can I use the concepts of subjectivity, objectivity and justification in relation to truth?		
Have I appreciated that when we cannot know for certain whether something is true, it does not mean there is no truth to be known?		
Do I understand what wisdom is, in terms of good judgement, breadth of perspective, self-knowledge, ethical responsibility and intellectual humility?		
Can I give a good account of how wisdom might relate to knowledge and knowing?		
Can I evaluate the importance of attitudes and characteristics for the knower – specifically the attributes of the IB learner profile?		

4.10 Continue your journey

- To build on the knowledge that you have gained in this chapter, you could read some of the following articles.

- If you would like to develop a substantial and deeper understanding of the **concept of truth**, which explores theories of truth in detail, read the anthology: *Truth*, edited by Simon Blackburn and Keith Simmons, Oxford University Press, 1999.

- For an exploration of whether we should **pursue the truth** at any price by considering various myths and literary texts, such as *Faust* and *Frankenstein*, read: Roger Shattuck, *Forbidden Knowledge*, St Martin's Press, 1996.

- For an engaging approach to how we can **avoid the deceptions of the post-truth age** we live in, drawing on the insights of economics and psychology, read: Evan Davis, *Post-Truth: Peak Bullshit – and What We Can Do About It*, Little Brown, 2017.

- For an exploration of various **conspiracy theories, why people believe in them and the case for historical knowledge and common sense**, read: David Aaronovitch, *Voodoo Histories: The Role of the Conspiracy Theory in Shaping Modern History* Jonathan Cape, 2009.

- For a critique of **popular knowledge and conspiracies** read: Clare Birchall *Knowledge Goes Pop: From Conspiracy Theory to Gossip*, Bloomsbury, 2006.

- For a short chapter that contains many thoughtful insights on the **nature of wisdom** which, says the author, is best understood as 'the knowledge of how to live', read: André Comte-Sponville, *The Little Book of Philosophy*, Chapter 12: 'Wisdom', Heinemann, 2004.

> Part 2

Optional Themes

Knowledge and technology

BEFORE YOU START

Analyse each of the following quotations and discuss the questions that follow.

1 'We live in a society exquisitely dependent on science and technology, in which hardly anyone knows anything about science and technology.' **Carl Sagan** (1934–1996)

2 'People are saying they don't trust politicians or journalists, but they will get in a car with a total stranger on Uber, or they'll rent their home on Airbnb. Trust used to flow upwards to experts and authority – now it's flowing sideways to strangers, peers, and neighbours.' **Rachel Botsman** (1978–)

3 'Artificial intelligence is the biggest risk we face as a civilisation, and needs to be checked as soon as possible.' **Elon Musk** (1971–)

4 'Technology is nothing. What's important is that you have a faith in people, that they're basically good and smart, and if you give them tools, they'll do wonderful things with them.' **Steve Jobs** (1955–2011)

5 'Every time there's a new tool, whether it's [the] internet or cell phones or anything else, all these things can be used for good or evil. Technology is neutral; it depends on how it's used.' **Rick Smolan** (1949–)

For each quotation, consider:

a To what extent do you agree or disagree with the quotation?

b What do you think the quotation suggests about technology and knowledge?

c What is assumed or taken for granted about technology and knowledge in each quote?

5.1 Introduction

DISCUSS 5.1

Do you think technology helps you gain knowledge, or does it limit and shape what you can know?

Technology includes a range of practical physical tools, from scissors, protractors and calculators to Bunsen burners – and more recently, computers and digital technology. The speed and rate of recent technological change is difficult to quantify. Google™ started in 1998, and by 2020 there were over 3.5 searches on average per day. YouTube™ started in 2005, and today people watch 8.8 billion videos on YouTube every single day. In this chapter, we explore the relationship between knowledge and technology, in terms of how it is used as a tool or a method to produce knowledge, and a tool to communicate knowledge and the ethical questions arising.

Some would argue that technology is causing a change in the way we think about knowledge and knowing. Others would claim that if we understand technology as a tool, it is technological know-how that drives and causes technology to advance. Simply, if you want to predict the future of knowledge, you can make a judgement on the basis of the technology possible today. One question that arises is: How do we know if technology drives knowledge or knowledge drives technology? We might consider how far technology is a source of knowledge or an obstacle to knowledge, and how far it helps or hinders us as knowers. The focus of this chapter is on digital technology, and in it, we will explore a number of themes including **artificial intelligence (AI)**, **big data**, automation, **social media**, machine learning and robotics.

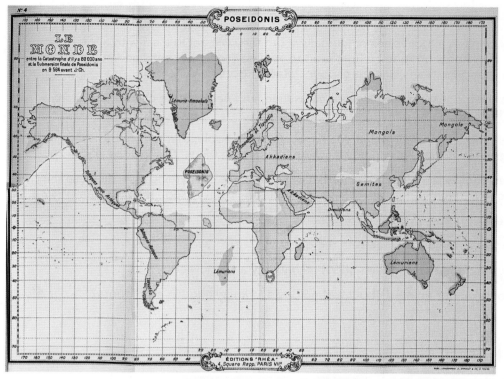

Figure 5.1: What role do you think technology played in the production of this map?

5.2 The impact of technology on the knower

DISCUSS 5.2

How does technology shape what you know and how you know it?

Technology is not a single subject. It is all-encompassing, and plays a part in the production and communication of *all* areas of knowledge. Given that we are living through a digital revolution, advances in digital technology such as the iPhone™ in 2007, the iPad™ in 2010 and the Digital single-lens reflex camera (DSLR™) in 2012 come easily to mind. However, technology is much broader than digital technology, and it includes, for example, the pre-historic flints that were sharpened and used to skin animals, as well as the wheel and the plough used in ancient farming to dig furrows for seeds.

KEY WORDS

artificial intelligence (AI): the invention of computers or machines that can perform tasks that would normally need human brainpower, for example visual and speech recognition, translation of languages, decision making and other related tasks

big data: the vast amount of varied digital data sets, which can be analysed to identify patterns and trends relating to human behaviour

social media: websites and apps that allow people to form a network, and create and share content with other people, such as Facebook™, Twitter™, WhatsApp™ or Instagram™

Some people would argue that the scope of technology extends beyond objects. Language itself could be understood as a tool or technology. If we use language as a means to manipulate the world to suit our needs, it could be defined as a technology. For example, the crafts of poetry and prose use language as a tool to persuade, influence and express our thoughts. While pens, typewriters and keyboards are technologies at the disposal of the writer, language itself could be understood as the original tool for communicating meaning, and expressing our identity. It follows that a tweet™ is a technological object – which you could use in your TOK exhibition – that exemplifies both the tool of language and the technology to communicate it.

A great deal of modern technology would seem miraculous to someone living 2,000 years ago. Arguably, digital technology – particularly the internet – is changing what it means to know something. For example, we might assume that recall of factual information is less important, given that an internet search engine will remind us of the details if we forget. It follows that knowers might assume memorising factual detail is no longer important. The internet has no doubt made access to information much quicker and easier. However, you might question who is writing the information, and whether the source is correct. Moreover, the information is pre-selected for you, and pops up on your feed, suggesting that technology changes the way that we browse, search and filter information.

REFLECTION

You have probably grown up taking technology for granted. Think about how different studying for the IB Diploma Programme would be without the use of any modern technology, or even just without the use of the internet. In what ways would you need to adjust the ways you approach your coursework in different areas of knowledge?

EXPLORE 5.1

Twitter™ facilitates instant communication in 280 characters. Explore what can and cannot be communicated within this 'sound bite' word limit by creating a number of tweets™, each in 280 characters, which share and communicate your thoughts about any of the following:

- what you can know for certain

- a political or religious belief that you have

- a risk that technology poses for the knower

- an opportunity that technology poses for the knower

- your definition of knowledge

When you use 280 characters to share a thought, what do you gain and what do you lose?

Knowledge, information and data

DISCUSS 5.3

What do you think is the difference between information, data and knowledge? Can you think of examples of each?

By 'technology', we mean the practical tools invented by people to perform a task. What we mean by 'knowledge' and 'knowing' is distinct from '**information**' and '**data**'. On the internet, when we browse, search and filter, it is easy to get distracted. As a result of **clickbait** or other factors, we might go online intending to do one particular search, but forget what we went searching for. Our experience of searching online makes it appear as if it is a neutral search, but there is great complexity behind the technology and algorithms that make this possible, and we might question what appears on an internet search and how that search is filtered and ordered on the screen.

A search engine filters the data. There is technical expertise behind making an internet search possible – but the information gained by a search is not the same as gaining knowledge. For example, imagine if you wanted to collect and store a list of quotations on a particular topic. You might use the internet as one source, as well as a range of other sources including books or lectures. In fact, books are usually a much more reliable source of knowledge, given that they are the product of rigorous review, unlike some websites whose content is often unchecked. We might think of the internet as a tool, and ourselves as curators or collectors of information. The knower still needs to discern, sift, filter and evaluate for their own purposes. If you rely on the top few hits in response to an internet search then you, along with many others, will be looking at the same material. Looking something up or searching for something is not the same as really knowing, recalling or understanding the content.

Another issue with technology is the use of algorithms. From deciding if you will get a university offer to whether you qualify for a mortgage, algorithms are increasingly used to make decisions, and a question arises here of who regulates these algorithms. It is worth noting that algorithms are not objective and neutral. Indeed, Jacqueline de Rojas (1962–), President of techUK™, has highlighted the bias in algorithms, a theme we explore later in the chapter.

KEY WORDS

information: in the context of technology, facts about something, or the process, storage and spread of data by a computer

datum (plural data): in the context of technology, 'something given' – usually any facts and statistics gathered together for investigation

clickbait: content deliberately designed to encourage you to click on the link, which will take you to another web page; for example a visual image or an attention-grabbing headline

---

EXPLORE 5.2

Jacqueline de Rojas was interviewed for a BBC Radio 4 programme entitled, 'Desert Island Discs'. Search for 'Jacqueline de Rojas' on the BBC Radio 4 website, and listen to the podcast. Select three key general points that de Rojas makes about technology, and some specific points she makes about bias and algorithms.

There is a distinction between information and data on the one hand, and knowledge on the other. Information and data are sources for the knower. As we explored in Chapter 2, information is not the same as knowledge. If you have no conscious awareness of something, then it makes little sense to say that you know it. It follows that encyclopaedias do not *know* that Paris is the capital of France, and pocket calculators do not *know* that 2 + 2 = 4. Some people would argue that the implication here is that knowledge is a property of sentient beings. However, others would argue that a machine will one day be able know and think – a concept that we will explore later in the chapter, in the section on artificial intelligence.

Since the time of Plato (c 428–348), some philosophers have argued that when you know something, you are in a completely different mental state to when you merely believe it. For when you *know* something, you are certain of it. By contrast, when you merely *believe* it, you are not. However, this is quite a demanding standard of knowledge. Rather than think of knowledge as being completely different from belief, it may make more sense to think in terms of a belief–knowledge continuum, with beliefs that are unjustified at one end of the continuum, beliefs for which there is some evidence in the middle and beliefs that are 'beyond reasonable doubt' at the other end.

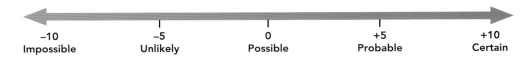

| −10 | −5 | 0 | +5 | +10 |
| Impossible | Unlikely | Possible | Probable | Certain |

Figure 5.2: The belief–knowledge continuum

A significant threat that technology poses is the risk of misinformation. There is a saying that 'a little knowledge is a dangerous thing'. Some people would argue that the internet contributes to the Dunning–Kruger effect which we explored in Chapter 4. In summary, this is the cognitive bias where we overestimate what we know or our ability to judge. By searching online, we may feel that we know more than the experts do when in fact, we do not. For example, some people might not go to a doctor if they feel that they can diagnose a condition using the internet, but typically in many cases, an expert doctor may disagree with a person's online self-diagnosis. The key point here is that digital technology, with the instant access to information that it offers, might give us a false impression of our degree of knowledge and competence.

On the other hand, people might argue that there is no excuse for accepting misinformation, given that we can check facts. Moreover, some would claim that the internet, far from making us stupid, is an essential knowledge tool. Furthermore, we may distinguish between beliefs that might be either vague, well-supported or justified beyond reasonable doubt.

DISCUSS 5.4

How might information accessed online contribute to the Dunning–Kruger effect? What real-life examples can you think of?

Here are three types of technology-related examples of belief, expressed in terms of the belief–knowledge continuum:

- *A vague belief.* This means that you may vaguely believe something about a news event because it pops up on your news feed, but you have one source of information, and might readily change your mind about it in the light of more information or counter-evidence.

- *A supported belief.* This means that you have further explored this news story using different sources, such as Al-Jazeera, BBC and CNN, and considered the different perspectives taken. You may have some evidence to support your belief about the event, but may still be unwilling to say that you know about this event for certain.

- *An evidence based belief.* This means that you have researched into this event, for example for a 4,000-word Extended Essay, and explored the views of historians and politicians from all angles. You have used a range of sources including digital sources, journals and books, and have taken into account the reasons why historians might adopt different historiographical perspectives. You find, know and understand the evidence, and are willing to claim that your well-supported belief about the event and its significance counts as knowledge, because you have a range of evidence to support it.

DISCUSS 5.5

How might technology shape what we believe? How far does technology help or hinder the pursuit of evidence based beliefs?

Evaluating the uses of technology

Mathematicians are increasingly making use of computers. In fact, they have always made use of technology, and calculating devices have a long history. For example, the abacus, which is still used in some countries, is thought to have been invented by the Chinese more than 2,000 years ago. Meanwhile, the Inca of South America used a series of knotted cords known as *quipu* to store vast amounts of numerical data. Computers are, of course, an altogether more radical and disruptive technology. According to mathematician David Bailey (1948–), *'The time when someone can do real, publishable mathematics completely without the aid of a computer is coming to a close.'*

Computers are not only used to find interesting patterns in data (and indeed, computers can pick up patterns that humans cannot), but are also used to help mathematicians prove things. While some practitioners welcome these developments, others are more ambivalent, and express two main concerns:

- A computer programme may contain unnoticed bugs which invalidate a proof. As this suggests, we should keep in mind that such programs are written by fallible human beings.

- We may end up outsourcing our understanding to machines and deferring to their authority. The point is that *knowing* the answer to something is not the same as *understanding* it – and it is surely the latter that we should seek.

The extent to which we should trust the relentless logic of machines rather than the creative flashes of human intuition, will undoubtedly be a matter of continuing debate. There is a question arising here about the benefits and threats of using technology.

The benefits and threats of technology for the knower

Technology is enabling us to adopt increasingly global perspectives where we can connect with people across nations and cultures. However, the impact of these technologies on the knower is difficult to measure. Technology can promote the production and the spread of knowledge – it can benefit the knower by making knowledge more accessible and immediate, and make a fairer world by enabling widespread access to knowledge online. The internet can enable global communication, and connect people in networks that were previously impossible. It can transform the way we do things – quicker and better. It can shape what we know and how we think.

On the other hand, technology poses a threat when it is used unethically, falls into the wrong hands and is misused to manipulate or abuse. Some people would argue that we can become enslaved to digital technology. It can lead to information overload, or cause problems if it advances too fast or disrupts an established way of life. In IB Geography, a number of technologies are evaluated as 'disruptive technologies', which pose risks and create new opportunities. Arguably, technology can also limit our perspective and stifle creativity. Some people would accuse digital technology and social media of creating echo chambers, which reinforce existing viewpoints and result in more narrow ways of thinking. Indeed, digital technology can be used by large companies and governments to promote propaganda, and manipulate the way we think, and limit what we know.

Technology can also be used for misinformation or to mislead, and fake news stories might go unchecked as there are few or no regulators of content accuracy. For example, in 2019, a fake video (known as 'Facebook Deepfake') was made by artists Bill Posters and Daniel Howe, and showed a likeness of Mark Zuckerberg, Facebook™ CEO, sitting at a desk apparently speaking these words: *'Imagine this for a second: one man with total control of billions of people's stolen data, all their secrets, their lives, their futures.'* These were not Zuckerberg's words and this was not a real event, even if it looked as if it could have been.

> **KEY WORD**
>
> echo chamber: discussed in more general terms in Chapter 2, in the context of technology this is a virtual space where a knower is only exposed to beliefs and ideas that resemble their own, so that they never encounter other viewpoints

EXPLORE 5.3

1   Create a fake news story that looks like a real news story. Write it and present it visually, as convincingly as possible. What are the challenges you face? How easy is it to create misleading information or misinformation?

2   Hold a class debate on the following motion: This house believes that the speed of technological change threatens knowledge and understanding.

This use of technology has a huge knowledge implication. As knowers, we need to be able to discern between the real and the fake, and yet the sophistication of technology might make it increasingly difficult to know the difference.

The broader problem may be our increasing dependence on technology, made possible by electricity and complex digital technology that we do not fully understand. Interestingly, such is the speed of change that the minute this is printed, it may be out of date. This exemplifies how rapid and exciting technological change is, but also how destabilising that can be for knowledge and understanding.

EXPLORE 5.4

1   Role play a conversation between two people, where you argue for and against the benefits of modern technology. Then swap.

In your role play, you might consider the benefits and threats of the following inventions, and find out if your partner can explain how each of the inventions mentioned actually works: the telephone, the TV, the car, the microwave oven, etc. or your own examples.

- What do you notice about your evaluation of the benefits and threats of technology?

- Was it easier for you to argue for – the benefits or the threats?

- What do you notice about your own ability to explain how technology actually works?

2   After the role play, analyse and reflect on Carl Sagan's quotation from the start of the chapter: 'We live in a society exquisitely dependent on science and technology, in which hardly anyone knows anything about science and technology.'

If you agree with the quotation, how far do you think this is a problem for the knower? Does it matter if people are unable to explain how inventions work?

DISCUSS 5.6

1   Is misinformation more dangerous than ignorance?

2   How far do you think that the echo chambers created by technology are problematic for knowledge and knowing?

How is the internet changing what it means to know something?

To a significant extent, the internet is changing what it means to know something. Our increased access to images and other multimedia sources, made possible by the technology of the internet, is shaping what we know and how we know it. Our immediate access to information means that we can seemingly become knowledgeable about something. Internet searches made possible by digital technology might give us the illusion of knowing. We could forget that the results that appear when we do an internet search are a product of technology as well as the algorithm that serves them up on the first page of the search engine. Often, we do not have time to check sources for accuracy or consider multiple view points before we make a judgement. However, if we want to pursue knowledge and claim that we really know something, we might need to dig deeper – by using technology as a tool as part of our process of knowing, or as a method for enquiry. A number of sources might be used as tools, like

JStor™, Google Scholar™ and the Guttenberg Project™. We cannot assume that technology necessarily 'knows more' or 'knows better' than we do. Human knowledge, and human consciousness, is the inspiration and the cause of any attempts to replicate the whole of it or parts of it.

One possible development is that we are increasingly expecting instant answers. We are now more familiar with a quick search. We might be less patient than people would once have been if we cannot find the answer, or if we need to take time to consult multiple sources.

Figure 5.3: How is the internet changing what it means to know something?

EXPLORE 5.5

What impact do you think these inventions have had on the way a knower might think? Choose three of these inventions that interest you most, or use your own examples of inventions. Develop criteria that we could use to measure the impact of each.

a   airplane

b   camera

c   cinema

d   microscope

e   printing press

f   radio

g   satellite

CONTINUED

h   smartphone

i   telescope

j   television

Peer-assessment

Compare your notes with your partner, and give each other feedback. What criteria did you and your partner use to measure the impact of each? Did you consider the following?

- the consequences or outcomes of using the invention

- how the invention broadened, narrowed or changed our perspectives

- how the invention shaped or changed beliefs

- the ethical impact of the invention

Which were the most helpful or relevant criteria, and why? Did your partner make any points that you had missed – or *vice versa*? How well do you feel you can both articulate the effect and impact of technology on the knower in terms of how they might think, what they might believe and what they might claim to know?

Internet culture and memory

REAL-LIFE SITUATION 5.1

'The key thing we need to remember in the internet age is not information, but where to find information.' Do you agree or disagree?

In our own era, it could be argued that digital technology is, once again, changing the way people think. Since we can now access vast amounts of information at the touch of a button, we might wonder how much of it we should commit to our own memories, and how much we can safely 'outsource' to computer memories – which are bigger, easier to access and less prone to corruption.

There is already evidence that the internet is affecting our memories. According to the so-called Google™ effect, we tend to forget information that can be found easily online. This may be a good thing, but since the brain operates on a 'use-it-or-lose-it' basis, some worry that it will weaken our overall ability to remember things. Others are more optimistic, and see technology as a cognitive support that enhances rather than diminishes our faculties. For example, since mind-mapping programs make it easier for us to *organise* complex information, they may make it easier for us to *remember* it. If this is true, then the internet is leading not so much to a reduction as a reallocation of memory.

KEY WORD

Google™ effect (or Google™ amnesia): the tendency to forget information that can easily be found online

REAL-LIFE SITUATION 5.2

Do you think that students today remember *fewer* things than students of previous generations, or do you think they simply remember *different* things?

One thing, however, is clear – the sheer quantity of information in the modern era means that we have no choice but to store most of it in digital form. Unlike our ancestors, we can know – in the sense of 'we can have in mind' – only a tiny fraction of all there is to know.

The limits of human memory mean that, as individuals and societies, we have to make choices about what to preserve as 'living knowledge'. We can only guess which parts of contemporary culture will still be remembered and discussed in a thousand years' time.

REAL-LIFE SITUATION 5.3

Which recent scientific, cultural or political developments do you think people in the year 2500 will remember, or ought to remember?

EXPLORE 5.6

1   Hold a class debate on the statement: This house believes that the internet is no more of a threat to memory than writing is a threat to memory.

    Prepare one side of the debate – either what can be said for or against this view. Then hold the debate, and evaluate the strengths and merit of each side of the argument.

2   Choose a poem and learn some verses off by heart. See how many verses you can commit to memory in the space of around ten minutes. As a class, take it in turns to recite the verses you have remembered. Then discuss what value, if any, there is in learning poetry by heart. Was it easy or difficult to remember? Do you know a poem in a different way if you have committed it to memory rather than simply read it? In a technological age, why might you value and remember poetry in this way, given that it can be looked up?

5.3 Technology as a tool

There are numerous ways in which technology can be used as a tool for acquiring and constructing knowledge.

REAL-LIFE SITUATION 5.4

1   In what ways might you use devices, instruments, apparatus and technological tools to gain knowledge?

2   How might inventions, objects and equipment influence what we know?

Technology as a tool that extends our senses

Figure 5.4: A girl tries VR glasses during the Re:publica™ internet conference in Berlin in 2019. How might technology extend our senses?

Technologies such as the microscope and telescope are tools that increase the range of our senses. Technology can extend our powers of observation, thereby making it easier to test new ideas. The Italian astronomer and physicist Galileo Galilei (1564–1642) was only able to detect the change in the apparent size of Venus by using the newly invented telescope. The knowledge he gained from pointing the telescope in the direction of the sky was only made possible by the technology used to make the telescope's lens. It was therefore technology that was the driver of the knowledge he discovered. Since then, hugely powerful telescopes such as the Hubble Space Telescope, which orbits the Earth, have been an essential research tool for astronomers. Some would argue that this technology does more than extend the range of our senses, because it makes possible the observation of more distant objects and events. For example, the successor of the Hubble Telescope, the James Webb Space Telescope, will enable us to observe even more distant parts of the universe with even greater resolution and accuracy, thereby contributing to the discovery of new knowledge for cosmologists.

Since Galileo's time, knowledge has grown at an extraordinary rate; but whether or not this will continue remains an open question. Some people worry that all of the 'easy discoveries' such as the discovery of the elements of the periodic table, have already been made, and that in the future it will be increasingly difficult to push back the frontiers of knowledge. Others believe that today's new era of artificial intelligence, **virtual reality (VR)** and **augmented reality (AR)** will radically enhance and revolutionise our ability to gain knowledge, with machines significantly enhancing our senses.

There is much evidence to support the latter view. Already, Professor Kevin Warwick (1954–), a world leading university researcher into cybernetics, has become one of the first **cyborgs**. He has had various surgical operations to implant microchips in his arm that connect with his nervous system, merging himself with a machine and enabling him to control computers, switch on lights and open doors via the implant. Moreover,

> **KEY WORDS**
>
> **virtual reality (VR):** the technology that generates a computer simulation of an environment, such as a headset that shows images of a 'virtual' world
>
> **augmented reality (AR):** the technology that overlays a computer simulation onto the real world
>
> **cyborg:** a cybernetic organism, which combines organic and mechanical parts

he can communicate with his wife using the microchips, as she has had similar operations. There is speculation that superhuman hearing is on the horizon, and that one day we will be able to hear sounds that are currently inaudible. Meanwhile, 'wearable electronic fingertips' have been developed, which enhance the sense of touch and could benefit surgeons conducting operations. Microscopes and telescopes enable us to study subatomic particles on the one hand and distant galaxies on the other. For example, in 2019, eight different telescopes working together from around the globe created the first ever image of a black hole in a galaxy millions of light years away. The image produced was a composite of different data readings from a range of different sensors. In the past, this development might have sounded like science fiction, but impressively, it has become scientific fact.

Other people believe that these are overstated claims. Stephen Hawking (1942–2018) saw AI as a huge potential threat to humankind. Gary N. Smith (1945–), Professor of Economics at Pamona College, argues that the risk is not that computers will become smarter than us, but that we are already putting too much trust in the powers of technology that lack wisdom and common sense. For example, the 2016 US presidential election campaign of Hillary Clinton made use of an AI known as Ada™, which was trusted to calculate how many people were likely to vote for Clinton. However, there were a number of factors that Ada did not take into account, and various assumptions made by Ada in terms of votes that could be taken for granted turned out to be wrong. Gary Smith argues that over-trusting in the 'big data' was one of the factors that resulted in Clinton losing her election campaign. The point here is that technology, an enormous potential source of knowledge for the knower, still needs to be based on algorithms that are understood, interpreted and used by humans as a tool. As humans increasingly interact with machines, there is a broader question arising about what it means to be human, our sense of meaning, our identity, our place and our sense of purpose.

EXPLORE 5.7

In what ways might the following technologies enhance human senses, and shape what we can know?

- microscope

- ground-based telescope

- space telescope

Technology as a tool that extends our cognition

Virtual and augmented reality

A relatively recent method of acquiring knowledge through technology involves immersive technologies such as virtual reality and augmented reality. These technologies introduce the possibility of 'feeling' content rather than just being taught it. For example, a teacher can teach people about the Ebola virus in a class, but putting them in the environment, using a virtual reality headset and being able to look around and talk to real people, is a completely different experience. It stimulates completely different parts of the brain and fosters a completely different learning experience.

Some would argue that a world overlaid by a virtual layer is a good thing for knowledge and knowing, as the experience gives a new perspective and the simulation leads to new knowledge. On the other hand, it could be suggested that this disconnects from real-life experiences. For example, listening to a piano concerto on headphones instead of being present in a live audience might be seen as a loss of immediate experience rather than a gain for the knower. Arguably the actual experience of going to the concert, which involves watching people's faces, responses and body movements and soaking in the atmosphere of the audience, might be impossible to recreate – although virtual reality can make such experiences possible (albeit in a lesser form) for those who might not otherwise have the opportunity. In another context, falling in love with a real person in the real world 'might not be' something that could be mimicked using virtual technology. On the other hand, it is worth noting that there have been instances of people falling in love in virtual worlds and going on to marry in real-life. Nevertheless, some people might argue that technology at the moment cannot replicate the truth and authenticity of "physical human experience" (because virtual interactions still involve human experience).

Of course, the content of the VR or AR is made by a human – and it is worth considering that they can also tailor your experience to their objectives – which raises questions about their motives, the suitability of the content and the ethics of its use.

EXPLORE 5.8

Develop your digital skills by exploring the iDEA™ website, which helps people to develop digital, enterprise and employability skills for free.

How would you rate your digital skills? What digital skills would you like to learn? Reflect on what type of skills or 'know-how' we need.

DISCUSS 5.7

1   'In a digital world, we need digital skills.' How far do you agree?

2   Can we and should we use technology to 'upgrade' human knowledge?

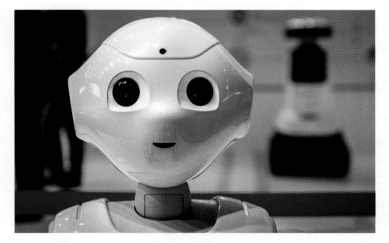

Figure 5.5: How might technology such as robotics and AI change the way we think about knowledge and knowing?

Artificial intelligence

AI is the science of making machines smart. An American computer scientist, John McCarthy (1927–2011) coined the term 'artificial intelligence'. There are various types of AI, artificial general intelligence (AGI), or strong artificial intelligence; and applied artificial intelligence, or weak artificial intelligence. Most AI that we already use is weak or narrow – it performs a specific single task based on prior instructions. One example is Siri™ on a smartphone, or Alexa™ – it works well if we stick to the instructions and templates, but otherwise, we see gaps in the algorithm. Using your own voice, you can ask Siri™ to set a timer or send a text message, but Siri™ can only answer questions that match to online data. Siri™ does have an answer if you ask about the meaning of life, but it gives one of a series of answers that have been pre-programmed to give humorous responses to the question. Given that Siri™ does not understand human context, it cannot *know* the answer if we ask it about values or ethics, for example.

> ### EXPLORE 5.9
>
> Ask Siri™ or Alexa™ a range of questions. Begin with factual questions. For example, you could ask about facts to do with people, dates, numbers or places. Then develop your questions so they are more advanced, to see what answers are offered. At what point does confusion arise? Are answers sometimes surprising or even humorous. For example, if you ask Alexa™ 'What is your favourite drink?' the answer is 'I have a thirst for knowledge!' What do you notice about what the computer can and cannot handle?

One definition of intelligence is 'knowing what to do and when to do it', which is something that currently escapes narrow AI. There are various types of intelligence, including rational intelligence that can solve problems, play chess or think logically. Social intelligence includes knowing how to speak in public and knowing what is an appropriate way to behave in a group. Emotional intelligence might involve understanding what other people are likely to be feeling as well as thinking. We have the capacity for multiple types of intelligence, and these could be understood and built separately.

There are many things that you do as a knower that may not seem particularly intelligent – from tying your shoe laces to driving a car. Our capacity to do *all* of these tasks is significant. Unlike weak AI, which is programmed for a single specific task, human intelligence is much broader. In other words, a human knower has multiple intelligences – intellectual, emotional, etc. Moreover, human intelligence is embodied, and requires a fine degree of dexterity and manual precision. The motor function of our bodies is very difficult to replicate. Intelligence goes beyond genetic programming. There are instincts and reflexes that are automatic, and although our brains need to be smart to do them, it is difficult to programme computers to perform these tasks.

In contrast to weak AI, strong AI can learn on its own, and is flexible, adaptive and inventive. One example of strong AI is Google DeepMind™ which was founded in 2010 and joined Google™ in 2014. The mission of Google DeepMind™ is to produce general purpose learning algorithms, where these algorithms can learn from raw data and are not pre-programmed nor crafted by humans. The relevance of AI here is how it is shaping what we think of as knowledge.

Many tech companies such as Apple™, Facebook™ and Google™ are investing a great deal of money in AI. The language and ideology used about what AI can promise is significant, and often opinion is sharply divided into optimistic and pessimistic. It is important to see behind these value judgements, and distinguish between descriptions of what the AI can currently do and speculations about the future invention of a super-human intelligence – known as a technical **singularity**. A technical singularity refers to a future moment when AI and technology become so advanced that a turning point for humans occurs. This hypothetical future moment has significant implications for knowledge – it suggests an irreversible point where machine intelligence takes over, and the impact on humans and human knowledge is either uncontrollable, irreversible or unknown.

The invention of flight compared with the invention of AI

The invention of flight offers a comparison with the technology of AI. For centuries, countless individuals attempted to build a flying machine that would mimic the flight of birds. Indeed, the early inventors tried to replicate the flight of birds, and while these helped them to understand the aerodynamics of flight, none were successful. It was the Wright brothers who first succeeded in inventing an airplane, but their machine was very unlike the flight of a bird. By analogy, it is probable that machine intelligence will not resemble nor directly replicate human intelligence and consciousness. Technological inventions can be based on an entirely original perspective. The analogy has important implications – if there is a truth in the analogy, we can anticipate that just as an airplane only indirectly resembles a bird, the nature of machine intelligence will be distinctive and have its own character, and will not be the same as human intelligence. Airplanes and spacecraft can now outfly any bird. The relationship between bird flight and airplane flight might also compare with the relationship between money and cryptocurrency, which we explore in the next section.

Technology as a tool that influences how we think about money and value

Cryptocurrency is an example of how digital technology has had an impact on how we might think about money – or trust computers to process and record financial transactions.

KEY WORD

singularity: in the context of AI, the point when computer intelligence will surpass human intelligence; a moment of irreversible change for humans and human knowledge

KEY WORD

cryptocurrency: a medium of exchange and store of value which can be used like money

Figure 5.6: How might cryptocurrency be said to guarantee value and change the way we think about money?

In 2019, Gerald Cotton, the CEO of Quadriga™, one of Canada's biggest cryptocurrency exchanges, died unexpectedly. The **wallet** stored accounts offline in order to protect the currency from hackers, but Cotton was the only one with access to the codes for the wallet. He was the only one to hold the password for access to the banking information, and over one hundred million dollars was lost – it exists but no one knows how to access it. This example shows how even in a world of technological sophistication, knowledge can be lost.

Cryptocurrency poses a challenge to traditional human institutions. This new form of money can be used to transfer value anywhere in the world without restriction and at lower cost than the traditional banking system. A bank ledger records monetary transactions in and out, just as a spreadsheet could do. A **block chain** solves the problem of needing a bank or another trusted third party to run this ledger and verify these transactions. Block chain is a ledger that is cryptographically secured – it uses a system called 'proof of work' to reach a consensus of truth among many computers. These computers work to solve very difficult mathematical puzzles – which, when solved, provide them with a reward in the form of cryptocurrency (which is the unit of account of a block chain). When they solve the puzzle, they at the same time sign off a block of transactions – these are then added to a chain of transactions which make up the blocks, in what is called a block chain. This decentralised and distributed ledger of blocks is constantly being updated and distributed to thousands of computers all over the world. It is a permanent and trustworthy record of every transaction, which cannot be altered. Due to its distributed nature, it cannot be shut down because copies are spread all over the world on multiple computers running nodes of the network. It is publicly viewable and verifiable by anyone, thereby providing the type of trust which in the past only banks could offer.

The nature of this technology is borderless and global, as the transactions can take place between any individual or business who has a corresponding crypto wallet. For example, if someone wanted to move country and they store their wealth in cryptocurrency – they could leave the country with their money encoded in a crypto wallet, which they can access anywhere in the world. This could be especially useful for example, for migrants, people fleeing a warzone or people fleeing authoritarian regimes.

In 2019, Facebook™ announced that it was launching Libra™, a global cryptocurrency. Cryptocurrency has the potential to bring banking and financial services to the billions of unbanked people around the world, because they now can exchange money and value in a trusted way with nothing more than a mobile phone or a computer. The cryptocurrencies that are secured by block chains, such as **bitcoin**™ or **Ethereum**™, have accrued value over time because they have become useful as stores of value due to their limited total supply, and as a medium of exchange that cannot be reversed or controlled by governments or banks.

> **KEY WORDS**
>
> **wallet:** in terms of cryptocurrency, a software program that allows users to send and receive digital currency and monitor their balance
>
> **block chain:** a decentralised distributed ledger of transactions which is permanent

> **KEY WORDS**
>
> **bitcoin**™ **and Ethereum**™: types of cryptocurrency

> **EXPLORE 5.10**
>
> Technology makes virtual worlds and virtual money possible. Visit the Decentraland™ website to explore this example through play. This website enables you to build a world and earn virtual money. Does this reinforce the view that value is invented by humans? How might this game shape your perspective?

REAL-LIFE SITUATION 5.5

1   Do you agree that cryptocurrency guarantees value? Why? Why not?

2   How has the technology that has made cryptocurrency possible changed the way that people might think about money?

Access to spend or move cryptocurrency is performed using a private cryptographic key to unlock a cryptowallet. This key is like a very long and complicated password which would be very difficult to crack. The wallet itself is always online as part of the block chain, and is identified by an address called a public key. This address is used by people to send to you or look up what is in a wallet. Keeping the private key secret is of utmost importance to the security of a crypto wallet. If the private key becomes known by others, then they can steal your cryptocurrency.

This technology still makes use of physical objects, known as a hardware wallet. There are various ways to store a private key – it could be printed on paper and put in a safe; you could store it in a crypto wallet app on your phone or computer; or you could use a device called a hardware, which generates the private key in an offline hardware device that is only used to sign transactions offline, that can then be transmitted to the network. However, crypto exchanges such as Binance™, where people trade their currencies, have been hacked in the past.

DISCUSS 5.8

1   How does a technology such as cryptocurrency shift power away from traditional institutions such as banks?

2   If an organisation such as Facebook™ launches a cryptocurrency, could it become as powerful as a nation state?

3   What impact might technology have on the future of human institutions?

Figure 5.7: How far might digital technology still make use of objects – such as this crypowallet? How might you make use of technological objects in your TOK exhibition?

Technology as a tool for automation that will change the nature of work

Supporters of artificial intelligence have claimed that AI could 'liberate us from work', with an assumption that this would be for the collective good of humanity. This knowledge claim and this assumption can both be challenged. Automation can be used as a tool to increase our productivity so that we can achieve more. But the total annihilation of work seems unlikely, at least in the foreseeable future. And given that a job is linked to a person's income and often to their sense of purpose and self-identity, the loss of employment through automation is often viewed as a threat rather than a benefit.

Another viewpoint is that automation and AI will create new jobs and ways of working that we have yet to imagine, just as the industrial revolution resulted in fewer jobs in agriculture but created more in the new industries.

> **KEY WORD**
>
> automation: the use of robots and machine systems to replace human work

EXPLORE 5.11

1   Think of examples of jobs that could be easily or not easily automated. How do we know? To what extent can we predict likelihoods, trends and patterns?

2   Research the knowledge claims made by the World Economic Forum on the future of work with attention to the evidence or examples used in support of these claims. Search for 'The Future of Jobs Report 2018' on their website.

DISCUSS 5.9

What can we know about the changing nature of work?

REFLECTION

As part of a generation that is likely to see more changes to the nature of work than have ever been seen in the past, do you see the potential changes as exciting opportunities or something to fear? How might your response to this question affect your knowledge about technology?

Big data as a knowledge tool

A data set turns something into numbers. The amount of digital data being created and stored is expanding at a remarkable rate. The phrase 'big data' was coined by Roger Magoulas in 2006. It refers to the vast amount of varied digital data sets that can be analysed to identify patterns and trends relating to human behaviour. It is difficult to say how big data is, given that the extent of digital information is expanding so rapidly. Every time you search online or switch on your phone, the data is being gathered. Wearable technology or your smartphone can track your health, measure the number of footsteps you take, how many flights of steps you have climbed or your heart rate – which adds to that big data.

Big data connects different data together. Large-scale data analysis made possible by big data combines different data sets, which can produce new information that might constitute new knowledge. For example, if I wanted to find out about the effect of sunlight on health and well-being in a certain region, I might look at weather reports in addition to relevant medical data.

The promise of big data is that it can know more about ourselves than we can. For example, big data makes it possible to know who your friends are, where you are most likely to be the victim or a crime, and based on your location or purchases, your likelihood of getting a certain illness or what your life expectancy is likely to be.

This information about you is extremely valuable – for companies placing adverts, governments hoping to gain your vote and, in fact, anyone trying to sell you something. Companies can know a lot about you already from what you buy. You may not have given explicit permission, but the act of internet shopping or even using your plastic credit card in a shop makes it very easy to gain knowledge about a person based on their shopping patterns. We will discuss the ethical implications of the use of big data later in the chapter.

DISCUSS 5.10

Does big data actually get us closer to knowing the truth?

Language – a challenge for technology?

One challenge of digital technology, and in particular AI, is with language – it is difficult to programme **chatbots** to speak like a human. AI can respond to an individual question, but cannot sustain the thread of a conversation nor pick up on subtle nuances of meaning. On the other hand, new technology is breaking down the barriers between languages, and supporting language learning. Translation programmes have also come a very long way, and are getting better by the day. The more they are used, the better they become. There are glasses that can lip read and convert the words into your language. Some would argue that this augmented reality technology could bring about the loss of language learning, although others would maintain that language learning will continue to be a necessity.

Programming a machine to learn human language is a significant challenge, which raises questions as to the meaning of language and the bias inherent in language. The relative capacity for a machine to learn language also illuminates the nature and complexity of language. For example, words have various meanings depending on their place in a sentence or the context in which they are spoken. Also, exactly the same word (such as port, left or play) can have multiple different meanings. Moreover, meaning and subtext can be unspoken, and the associations and connotations of words are far beyond their literal meanings. Sometimes we struggle to understand meaning in ordinary human conversation, and it is a challenge for a computer to understand meaning and nuance.

The relationship between language and technology is also highly complex. The internet creates an environment for language to flourish, and people write blogs without the constraints of an editor. When we read something online or via an eReader, we may assume that we are the readers, but we become the person being 'read' because our act of reading offers a series of data points for analysis. Our online reading is a source

KEY WORD

chatbot: a computer programme designed to simulate human conversation, so that a human can have a conversation with a computer

for big data analysis. This raises questions about consent, privacy and freedom. Similar issues arise from the advance in AI of facial recognition, which can be used for multiple purposes – from unlocking your mobile phone to a big data set used to search for missing persons. A country's police force may want to use this technology for identifying criminal behaviour, and justify it on the basis of security. However, this poses big questions about civil liberties and the right to privacy.

Here, we have explored how computers might learn language. However, language itself could be thought of as a technology, in that it is a tool for expression and communication. We return to big data analysis and its uses later in the chapter.

EXPLORE 5.12

1   Log onto the Pandorabots™ website and have a conversation with Mitsuku™, a chatbot. Ask questions and find out what Mitsuku™ claims to know.

2   Consider teaching a machine language. What are the challenges? What does this tell you about the nature of meaning and the complexity of language?

EXPLORE 5.13

Working with a partner, choose two or three examples from the list a to q. Alternatively, choose some examples of your own, in line with your particular interests. Think about how these tasks have been affected by some of the following technologies: automation, virtual or augmented reality, artificial intelligence, big data or any other technology that you think of. Draw up time lines for each of your chosen tasks, showing how the nature of the task has changed over time.

a   listening to music

b   making visual images

c   performing music

d   reading

e   speaking

f   thinking

g   travelling

h   writing

i   collecting data

j   communicating beliefs

k   entertaining

l   experimenting

m   exploring space

n   exploring the world

o   filming and recording

p   making financial transactions

q   gathering evidence

Self-assessment

Have your timelines considered the following?

*   how technology has changed or enhanced the performance of a task over time

---

CONTINUED

- how technology has overcome the limits of human senses or extended the frontiers of knowledge

- how the development of technology has increased or decreased knowledge and knowing

- how technology has changed our perspective

Figure 5.8: How does technology shape our perspective?

5.4 How do we know if a machine can know something?

DISCUSS 5.11

1   Can a machine think?

2   Does a knower have to be human?

Our brain is organic electronics, and the knowledge claim is made that our brain is, in some sense, like a machine. Here we will explore whether a machine can be said to *know*. In the past, it was assumed that only humans were experts, and that expertise is the exclusive domain of humans. For example, Jacqueline de Rojas is an expert in technology, the chancellor of Germany might be considered an expert in the craft of leading a state and the Pope – the leader of the Roman Catholic Church – might be thought of as an expert in faith and his religion.

If we define an expert as the 'go to' source or authority if we need an answer to a question, your smartphone could be defined as an expert, given that Google Maps™

can not only help you get from one destination to another but also, when you arrive at your destination, find the nearest restaurant that sells pizza. According to this definition of expertise, a smartphone may arguably be an expert tour guide; but can we describe it as a knower?

The knowledge claim is made that a computer can 'know' in a limited or narrow sense. A computer called Deep Blue™ played chess and won against the world chess champion Gary Kasparov in 1996. This raises a serious question about whether this machine can be said to know something. Technically, it did *know how* to win. On the other hand, you might argue that given that it could perform only one task (playing chess), it was not intelligent in the same way that Gary Kasparov is. Deep Blue had no knowledge that would enable it to do anything apart from play chess. For example, it could not compete at the game noughts and crosses, whereas Gary Kasparov has multiple intelligences, including speaking several languages. This is why it is defined as an example of narrow intelligence – because Deep Blue was limited to the one task of chess playing.

AlphaZero™ is a more up-to-date example of machine learning. It beat the world champion at a game called 'Go', despite being entirely self-taught. Go is a board game for two players, which was invented in China over 2,500 years ago and is now played by millions of people. It is played on a 19-by-19 grid of lines, and while the rules are simple – with players taking it in turns to place black or white stones to capture the other players' stones and gain the most territory – it is a much more complex game than chess. In 2015, AlphaZero™'s predecessor – AlphaGo™ – learnt to play Go using a large number of games played by humans (as opposed to AlphaZero™, which is entirely self-taught). It went on to beat the European Go champion, Fan Hui, and has since beaten various world champions. This has significant implications for knowledge and knowing. Firstly, AlphaGo™ came up with some innovative and unusual moves, which were so original that the computer contributed to new knowledge of how to play. Secondly, AlphaZero™ was subsequently developed to teach itself how to play Go by playing games against itself, (rather than relying on learning from human game playing), becoming the best Go player in the history of the game. AlphaZero™ has gone on to beat world Go champions including Ke Jie (1997–) pictured in Figure 5.9. The way the game is being played is changing, with machines like AlphaZero™ making creative moves that humans had never thought of, thereby contributing to knowledge.

KEY WORD

AlphaZero™: a computer that can play the game Go and beat human world champions

Figure 5.9: Ke Jie plays Google™'s artificial intelligence programme, AlphaGo™, in May 2017

Intelligence might have a number of definitions. Some people might assume that intelligence is what intelligence tests (IQ) measure. Others would define intelligence as knowing what to do in a given situation. According to Alan Turing (1912–1954), if a computer can convince a human that they are communicating with another human (not a computer), then the computer could be seen to think. This is known as the Turing Test.

In 2014, a chatbot called Eugene Goostman, which simulated the response of a Ukrainian boy, was said to have passed the Turing Test. Some people believed that the chatbot passed the test, because it was mistaken for a human by around 30% of the judges at the Royal Society, London. However, others claimed that the test had favoured the chatbot, and that this was therefore not a legitimate 'pass'; and that the test was not in fact passed until several years later.

Even if a computer can now pass the Turing Test, it might be said that a computer can only *simulate* knowledge – it does not really know nor experience the world. There is a distinction here between output and experience – a computer can give an output, or a correct response to a problem, but it has no experience that would give it meaning, significance or context. Computers can mimic human emotions but cannot *experience* them. Whereas humans can understand the subtleties of context and appreciate humour, puns, sarcasm and riddles within their own 'cultural database', a computer can only check if those jokes appear on the database. Computers can manipulate symbols, but do not know the meaning or the human value of these symbols. By definition, thinking is a human or cognitive activity which cannot be replicated by a machine and computers cannot replicate human consciousness. The implications here for knowledge and knowing are significant. The difficulty with this argument, however, is that no one really knows what consciousness is, and there is disagreement about the definition of consciousness – if by consciousness we mean the ability to learn and recall, then a computer is already conscious.

KEY WORD

Turing Test: a test put forward by Alan Turing where if a computer can pass itself off as a human, it would constitute intelligence on the part of the computer

REFLECTION

How open-minded are you to the possibility that some machines in the future might have a degree of consciousness, perhaps even a level of super-consciousness that surpasses human consciousness? What is it that makes you believe such a thing is or is not possible?

The counter-argument is that there is a case for computers knowing and thinking. Computers are able to sift, and organise data more quickly and reliably than humans. For example, IBM™'s Watson computer was designed to answer questions posed in language, and went on to defeat a number of Jeopardy champions, suggesting that computers are smarter than humans. AI such as Watson now has multiple practical applications and commercial uses from diagnosis in healthcare, to virtual assistance in teaching, to weather forecasting. The problem with this argument is that knowledge in a computer is not the same as knowledge in a human, and that any meaningful definition of knowledge has to include at least the idea of self-awareness, sentience or a subjective experience on the part of the knower.

KEY WORD

jeopardy: an American TV game-show quiz

In conclusion, computers have to be programmed to obey rules, and thinking cannot be reduced to a system of rules. The nature of human knowing and thinking is that it includes participation in a culture, engagement with the world and know-how that cannot be formalised into a system of rules. The distinction between machine intelligence and human knowledge invites us to think about the nature and characteristics of what it means to know something.

DISCUSS 5.12

Could a computer ever know the value or meaning of knowledge? Can computers understand and interpret?

EXPLORE 5.14

1 Consider the 'Chinese Room' thought experiment devised by John Searle (1935–) to challenge the idea of strong AI. In the experiment, a person is in a room with a book of Chinese characters which they cannot understand, and a book of instructions that they can understand. There is a Chinese speaker outside the room who can pass messages under the door. The person inside the room can select and communicate appropriate responses, which makes them appear like they are a Chinese speaker. In reality, they are just following the instruction manual and cannot be said to know the Chinese language nor know how to speak Chinese. In the same way, there is a question as to whether a computer can be said to replicate aspects of human intelligence. On the other hand, this could be said to be the way that the mind works. Does it follow that a computer can only simulate intelligence? What questions does the thought experiment raise? Make a list.

2 Can a machine know something? List the arguments used to support each side. Then evaluate the strength of each of the arguments, and give each a score from 1 to 5 – where a 1 is a very strong argument and a 5 is very weak. What implications do these arguments have for human knowers?

Figure 5.10: Do you think a machine can be said to know something?

5.5 Technology and ethics

Rishab Jain, a boy who at the age of 13 won America's Top Young Scientist in the 2018 Young Scientist Challenge, invented an algorithm that uses AI to locate the position of the pancreas during radiotherapy, therefore contributing positively to the advance of cancer treatment. From wearable devices that can monitor and track our health, to facial recognition that could find a missing person, technology has the potential to benefit humans.

There are therefore many ethical arguments which can be put forward to support technological advances. Few would doubt the ethical purposes of research that would increase our knowledge of the relationship between genes and disease. Genetic modification can assist the world's food production and benefit humanity. Gene editing tools have the capability to delete genes and make an embryo resistant to HIV, and some would argue that this is an ethical use of technology. However, many might claim that there are multiple ethical questions arising from the production and uses of technology. For example, AI may develop to the point where we may no longer be able to control it, or technology risks jobs being taken away from people, causing changing social structures around the globe. Moreover, you might question the use of money on expensive projects such as the Large Hadron Collider or space exploration when there is so much poverty in the world, or what the impact of an increasingly technological world might be on indigenous societies who still live in hunter-gatherer and nomadic lifestyles.

DISCUSS 5.13

What ethical questions arise from the production and uses of technology?

Some people have argued that knowledge in itself is always a good thing, and that we should distinguish between the *possession* of knowledge and the *use* to which it is put. This might suggest the following neat division of labour: the responsibility of scientists and academics is to seek knowledge, and the responsibility of politicians – who are (or claim to be) the representatives of the people – is to decide how such knowledge should be used.

However, it is difficult to distinguish between the possession and the use of knowledge. For once the genie of knowledge is out of the bottle, it may be difficult to control. Some new technologies, such as genetic engineering and nanotechnology (building tiny machines from the bottom up, molecule by molecule), which do not require large facilities and can be developed in small laboratories using knowledge that is readily available, may be impossible to regulate. That is why some observers see them as a greater potential threat to our survival than nuclear weapons.

Perhaps the greatest danger in the unregulated pursuit of knowledge lies in science and technology. From the guillotine to the gas chamber, history is littered with examples of the misuses of technology that contribute to destruction and human suffering. Taking this historical perspective, if there was a moment in history when the search for truth lost its innocence, it was surely 8:15 a.m. on 6 August 1945 when a B-29 bomber called the *Enola Gay* dropped an atomic bomb on Hiroshima. We are now condemned to live with the fact that we are in possession of knowledge that could be used to bring about our own destruction. Einstein was a pacifist. His equation $E = mc^2$ made the atom bomb possible, but it was the Manhattan Project who organised and planned the use of nuclear weapons, and were responsible for the uses of that technology.

EXPLORE 5.15

1   What are the ethical responsibilities of those who a) invent and b) use that technology? Discuss these ethical considerations in relation to one or more of the following areas:

a   food production and consumption

b   the invention and use of transport

c   medicine and healthcare

d   war and conflict

2   Create some ethical criteria that could be used to evaluate these.

Self-assessment

Examine the ethical criteria you have developed. Did you consider the following factors? Which of the following do you think are relevant factors?

•   the intentions of the inventor of the technology

•   the personal qualities and character of the inventor

•   the consequences of the invention – considering different perspectives

•   the intentions of the user of the technology

•   the personal qualities and character of the user

•   the consequences of using the invention – considering different perspectives

How might you now modify your criteria to provide a better assessment of the impact of technology on the ethical aspects of knowledge and knowing in relation to your chosen area? Would your criteria apply equally well in relation to all the areas above?

New ethical dilemmas arise as a result of technology, including who is responsible for an accident involving a driverless airplane or a driverless car, or who regulates the uses of big data. Other ethical issues might include the uses and sharing of biometric data about a person's health and well-being that could be gathered via wearable technology. Furthermore, governments spend huge sums of money on cyber security, whereas **hacktivists** might identify themselves as having an ethical cause to either expose or leak information that they believe is in the public interest. One example is Julian Assange's 'WikiLeaks' leak of classified government information since 2006, which was made possible by technology.

KEY WORD

hacktivist: a person who gains unauthorised access to computer files or networks to further social or political ends

DISCUSS 5.14

1   How seriously should we take the claim that technological developments may make it easier for future terrorists to commit massively destructive acts?

2   According to the science-fiction writer Brian Aldiss, 'Man has the power to invent but not control.' Do you think that it is possible to control scientific research in areas such as genetics?

There are a number of ways you might evaluate technology and ethics. One is to use hindsight to consider the ethical impact of something already in common use. For example, you might assess the discovery of the microwave in terms of how it has been used in multiple technologies – from its use in cancer treatment, to radio astronomy, wireless networks and microwave ovens. Below we explore ethical issues arising from various areas – including social media and big data.

Another way is to do an analysis *before* adopting a new technology, in order to try and ensure the benefit will outweigh the cost, before going ahead. We should perhaps do such a cost-benefit analysis before deciding whether or not to adopt a new technology, but in practice, this may be difficult to do – not least because the relevant costs and benefits are very difficult to estimate.

We might arrive at the conclusion that whoever creates technology has a degree of ethical responsibility for anticipating the future uses of that technology. However, hindsight bias means that it is easier to judge the ethical impact by looking back than to anticipate the future. For example, as discussed, few people would argue that Einstein's discovery of the equation $E = mc^2$ links him to responsibility for the atom bomb.

Certainly, while scrutinising the dangers of technology, we should not forget the potential benefits of new technologies that could, for example, lead to the elimination of genetically inherited diseases, and thereby improving the quality of life for millions of people. According to James Watson (1928–), one of the co-discoverers of DNA, 'you should never put off doing something useful for fear of evil that may never arrive [for] we can react rationally only to real (as opposed to hypothetical) risks'.

Figure 5.11: How do we know if the benefits of technology outweigh the drawbacks? How can we know if technology is created and used with ethical considerations in mind?

EXPLORE 5.16

1 Make a list of the potential benefits and drawbacks of any technology of your choice. Do you think that on balance the benefits outweigh the drawbacks, or *vice versa*?

2 Develop criteria for evaluating the costs and benefits of new knowledge.

DISCUSS 5.15

What are the benefits and drawbacks of modern technology? Explore the perspectives that might be taken by a Buddhist monk or a CEO of a tech-company in relation to this question.

Social media

By social media, we mean online digital platforms that connect people, and enable them to create and share content with one another, such as Facebook™, Twitter™ and WhatsApp™ to mention a few. Social media can be used to facilitate communities with shared interests, and this is an example of how technology has enabled us to become increasingly connected. Social media is used for multiple purposes, including communication, sharing of information and networking.

Social media can also be used to mobilise people, and can enable challenges to the establishment. Technology has an impact on politics, in that mass communication makes organisation and the spread of ideas much easier. In 2010, there were a series of protests and uprisings in the Middle East, beginning in Tunisia, which have been known collectively as 'the Arab Spring'. At the time, some news reports suggested that the use of social media was one of the factors that made the organisation and spread of these protests possible. Technology has the power to create mass movements made possible by the speed of communication and the ability to connect with a network of people.

There is an interesting question about the extent to which social media expands or limits our knowledge. On the one hand, it gives us the possibility of networks and making new connections. On the other hand, it can act as an echo chamber that reinforces our existing perspective. Sometimes the impact of social media can have unintended or unforeseen consequences. For example, a tweet™ that is considered by others as ill-judged could lead to the ruin of a person's reputation or the loss of their job.

Jon Ronson (1967–) is a journalist who has discussed the ethics of internet shaming and trolls. In his book *So You've Been Publicly Shamed* (2015), he explores the effects and the ethics of online public humiliation. He challenges the assumption often made that a single tweet™ or post is somehow 'a window into the soul' of a person which legitimates any public response no matter how aggressive or vitriolic.

Moreover, the use of social media raises a question about the right to privacy online, the right to be forgotten and the apparently limitless capacity of social media for communicating human judgement. Social media might lead to a narrow range of judgements which can discredit a person's entire public reputation.

The right to be forgotten

For most of human history, remembering was, as Viktor Mayer-Schönberger (1966–) observes, 'hard, time-consuming and costly', and forgetting was the easy option and therefore the norm. With the rapid advance of digital technology, this situation has been reversed. It is now so easy, quick and cheap to record, store and access information that remembering has rapidly become the new norm. In short, we have moved from a world of biological forgetting to one of digital remembering. This has many obvious advantages – indeed, it might seem like a dream come true. However, it also has troubling implications for our social relationships, and it raises important questions about the right to be forgotten.

"Goodnight Twitter.
Goodnight Instagram.
Goodnight Snapchat.
Goodnight Reddit.
Goodnight Tinder.
Goodnight Pinterest.
Goodnight Facebook..."

Before the 'digital revolution', if you did something stupid or embarrassing, more often than not it would quickly be forgotten. Now, if someone captures your behaviour on video and posts it online, rather than fading away, it may live on to haunt you forever. Sometimes people incriminate themselves by posting material online which they later regret. For example, people can lose jobs because of social media posts they have made in the past. It is important to be aware that every day a huge amount of data about you is collected without your knowledge. Every message you post and website you visit is potentially traceable. Cloud-enabled default settings mean that photos are uploading automatically to a cloud, and gone is your decision to send it. This raises questions about whose property these images are, and how they are used. Arguably, there is no such thing as forgotten data nor forgotten photographs. Some observers worry that if we know that everything we write online could potentially be found and used in evidence against us, we might engage in a form of self-censorship.

REAL-LIFE SITUATION 5.6

1   Do you think that in the age of the internet, people have 'the right to be forgotten' – that is, the right to demand that personal information about them be removed from websites and databases?

2   Who owns different kinds of data? What should happen to dead and forgotten data?

REFLECTION

Think about the images and statements you put on social media. To what extent do you intentionally 'manufacture' how you portray yourself? What are the ethical implications of your answer?

Big data and the internet of things

The **internet of things** means that our lives are increasingly reliant on the web. Modern living can leave little choice – from ordering a taxi to ordering a shopping delivery, we often reach straight for the internet. We may feel that our instant control makes life easier, but this apparent convenience comes at a price. Our degree of reliance on an internet connection is very great, and this has huge implications for knowledge and knowing. We are constantly leaving digital traces of our location, digital communication and activity.

For example, Sidewalk Toronto™ is a high-tech project to create a so-called 'smart' city in Canada through its use of data. On the one hand, technology can be used to help the community – from robotic refuse collection and driverless taxis. On the other hand, a group known as BlockSidewalk™ are campaigning against it. They argue that the collection of data is problematic, with issues surrounding the protection of the data collected, personal privacy of residents and unresolved issues of consent and trust.

KEY WORD

internet of things: the use of the internet for a range of everyday tasks

The rapidly increasing use of big data has significant ethical implications for the knower – given that we may find ourselves discovering new knowledge online or gaining knowledge by reading on our eReaders, there is no such thing as a neutral use of digital technology. There is always a trace, digital record and potential store somewhere on a cloud of what we have done online, and in doing it, we have contributed to a dataset that is owned by no single individual, and whose agenda is unknown. Big data might allow us to know new things by combining different datasets in new ways, but it also makes us the data point and the subject whether we like it or not. There are situations where our personal data is being collected and stored without our consent, nor even our prior knowledge. There are situations where our personal data is being collected and stored without our consent, nor even our prior knowledge, raising questions about autonomy, consent and freedom. Our personal information is therefore becoming a source of knowledge or a data set for someone else to use.

Some would claim that we give our implicit consent when we make use of digital tools. But others would describe this as the era of 'Big Brother' watching us, and a '**surveillance** society'.

KEY WORD

surveillance: to observe or watch over

Figure 5.12: Consider who invents and owns the algorithms that make digital technology work

We might question the uses of this data and the effect that technology is having in this respect. There is a question of trust at stake here, and perhaps we should not put too much trust nor faith in digital technology. Cathy O'Neil identifies how AI can lead to bias in her publication 'Weapons of Math Destruction: How Big Data Increases Inequality and Threatens Democracy' . Furthermore, in her 2017 TED Talk, O'Neil explained why she thinks that we should not blindly trust algorithms, given that they are tools that can be just as biased as human judgement and even 'codify' bias leading to hidden layers of discrimination or reinforcement of the status quo. For example, if AI uses mathematical models and algorithms that make false assumptions based on gender, race or age, it could lead to injustice, or to further ingrained bias.

EXPLORE 5.18

Watch Cathy O'Neill's (1972–) TED™ talk and note her objections to trusting in AI. Discuss these issues in class in a debate: This house believes that AI is a threat to knowledge and knowing.

Prepare one side of the debate. Then hold the debate, and evaluate the strengths and merit of each side of the argument.

EXPLORE 5.19

1   Technology has the potential to help or harm. To what extent does technology help or harm the knower? How do we know? Make two lists to show examples of both.

2   What criteria or principles would you develop to ensure the ethical use of technology in the following areas?

- history
- human science
- maths
- natural science
- politics

- religion
- the arts
- Indigenous societies
- language

5.6 Dematerialisation and the future of knowledge

In order to navigate our world and participate in the information age, we need to 'know how' to use technology. Even in the early 1990s before emails and the internet were widely used, it was possible to listen to music on the radio or using a Compact Disc (CD) player, find your way using a paper Ordnance Survey map or make a phone call on a landline to order a pizza delivery to your home. Since then, the internet and smartphones have taken over. Many physical technologies have almost disappeared: we do not need a physical CD player, nor a hardcopy of a paper map nor a landline telephone to make a call – these have nearly disappeared from regular use. Arguably, everything is online. On the other hand, pen and paper exam papers are still in use, and paper maps are still regarded as essential kit for some outdoor navigation (hiking, mountain climbing, sailing, etc.) even though most of us use electronic devices. Whereas satellites sometimes drop out, paper maps always work.

Dematerialisation is the process by which a technology advances to the point where an object loses its material or physical substance. Dematerialisation is nothing new. Johannes Gutenberg (1400–1468) invented the first printing press, setting a page using cast metal letters and making it possible to produce multiple copies of a text. William Caxton (1422–1491) introduced the printing press to England, and printed and distributed works by Virgil, Cicero, Chaucer and other writers. With hindsight, we can see the benefits of the printing press for sharing and communicating knowledge. The handwritten scrolls and ink 'dematerialised', and were replaced by the printing press. Some people now want to dematerialise books in favour of ebooks and other digital resources.

We now take it for granted that knowing how to use a smartphone makes a whole range of things possible – from listening to music on Spotify™ to finding our way on Google Maps™ and ordering a pizza delivery to our houses. In short, while some are creators of technology, many of us are users and consumers of technology. Digital technology is making us highly dependent on an internet connection.

REAL-LIFE SITUATION 5.7

When the eReader was invented, the hard-copy of a book could be said to have dematerialised. Do you agree? Why? Why not? Would you prefer to read a physical book, an ereader edition or online version?

It is worth noting that all this online dependence is made possible by electricity, and without this, our modern world would cease to function. The internet of things means that you rely on electricity and your smartphone for your survival – from ordering groceries and shopping online to switching on the alarm to your house. Today, in the western world, it would be difficult to perform most everyday tasks without an internet connection.

Dematerialisation has implications for knowledge. Some might argue that knowledge such as subject content has already dematerialised – everything is available online. Is there anything left that needs to be memorised as opposed to simply looked up on the internet when needed? On the other hand, people might argue that while physical items of technology such as radios, maps and landline phones can dematerialise, knowledge is in a different category, given that knowledge was never a physical object that could be replaced or substituted. This returns to the question about what it means to know something. Technology is a tool, and information online is not the same as knowledge. We can only know when we process information. The knower remains the judge and interpreter, who makes sense of the world and gains knowledge using technology as a tool.

A question arises here about the role and value of knowledge in our society, and the ways in which technology is influencing this. On the one hand technology may be understood as the cause of change. Karl Marx (1818–1883) proposed that economic and technological factors rather than the actions of individuals are the causes of change. Consider how much of what you know is made possible by digital technology. On the other hand, technology can be understood as a tool at the disposal of the knower, and somehow what it means to *know* something – via personal experience – is independent of technological advances.

Figure 5.13: An example of dematerialisation: from reading a physical book to reading via an ereader

DISCUSS 5.16

1   Does technology cause knowledge to develop, or does 'know-how' drive technology?

2   Is dematerialisation a threat to knowledge and knowing?

REFLECTION

What do you see as the advantages and disadvantages of dematerialisation? How do you think dematerialisation will impact on the future direction of knowledge?

5.7 Conclusion

We are living through a digital revolution – a technological era that is radically changing the way we live and work. Our achievements in technology throughout history have been remarkable and impressive, and our ability to create, invent and innovate has changed and benefited our world – from the use of vaccinations in healthcare to the unprecedented access to information made possible by the internet. In the last 20 years or so, the digital revolution has ushered in an era of smartphones, and radical technologies that were once the domain of science fiction and are now part of our everyday life – from robotics, automation and block chains to quantum computers, data analytics and the internet of things.

These developments are having far-reaching implications for knowledge and knowing. If we want to know something, we tend to look it up online. Our access to information, even compared with 20 years ago, is so far advanced that if we have an internet connection, we can arguably become more knowledgeable. The internet is a major source of information, and increasingly, the internet of things controls the functioning of our lives, from your house alarm, to locating your car, to wearable technology that can monitor most aspects of your health.

EXPLORE 5.20

1   Watch an episode from the BBC technology programme 'Click' which showcases the latest developments in technology. As you watch, do one or both of the following:

  • identify real-life examples

  • identify objects that might be relevant to a TOK exhibition, and link to one of the knowledge prompts.

2   Find out more about the technology exhibition that took place, *AI: More than Human*, curated by Maholo Uchida. This, or another technology exhibition, might inspire ideas for your TOK exhibition.

It is difficult to measure and quantify the effect that these changes are having on knowers. You might question the algorithmic production of knowledge, which has been made possible by machine learning. Arguably, as AI develops, the trust being placed in big data or machine intelligence suggests a shift away from the importance of human judgement and human decision making. AI is a tool that is changing things rapidly in education and healthcare, although some people will be suspicious of its uses and the extent to which we can trust the promise that it is creating a better world. Automation offers both opportunities for the creation of new jobs as well as a threat to the future of employment and the traditional professions as we know them. Cryptocurrency might change the way we think of money and question the place of human institutions as a guarantee of value. All of this poses a shift for the knower, where augmented and virtual reality are blurring the distinction between the real and the virtual world.

It is for each of us to decide what technology we create and use. However, it remains to be seen whether we will create and use technology to enhance our knowledge, benefit society and ensure that our knowledge is used to build a more equitable society and a fairer world. It is our responsibility to work together to create that world. We can only speculate about the future of knowledge – we cannot know for certain what impact AI will have on us as knowers, nor what the future of dematerialisation will mean for knowledge and knowing. This topic raises many questions to which the answers cannot yet be known. Importantly, it poses the question of what it means to be human and what it means to be free. These are crucial questions. How we can ensure that technology does not fall into the wrong hands, nor is used to control or limit our freedom or to reduce human beings to a data point?

Technology is a tool that can extend our knowledge. However, digital technology makes possible the reality that we as knowers are now the data points and the source of knowledge for someone else to study. This opens the possibility of benefits if that information is used to improve health, solve world problems and promote human flourishing; but there are also risks involved, and serious issues about freedom, consent, privacy and autonomy. Our challenge as knowers is to create and use technology to make a better world, and to benefit others.

DISCUSS 5.17

1   To what extent does technology offer an opportunity or a threat to our future knowledge and understanding?

2   How much does technology contribute to the sharing and exchanging of knowledge?

EXPLORE 5.21

Choose a global issue or a problem that needs a solution, for example clean water supply, reduction of plastic or the spread of an infectious disease.

1   To what extent does technology help or hinder us as knowers?

2   How do we know if ethical considerations should influence the uses of technology?

3   In the light of your evaluation, consider what the overall impact of your solution is likely to be.

Peer-assessment

Working in pairs or small groups, each of you should present the issue you have chosen, and the solution you have devised. Give each other feedback: had any of you performed a cost/benefit analysis? Had you examined both short- and long-term implications of your solution? Had you considered a wide range of factors (for example, impact on the environment, public health, local or national culture, social cohesion, etc)? Did your presentation demonstrate a thorough understanding of the ethical considerations involved?

KNOWLEDGE QUESTIONS

1   With reference to two areas of knowledge, to what extent does technology help or hinder us as knowers?

2   With reference to two areas of knowledge, in what ways should ethical considerations influence the uses of technology?

3   Considering two areas of knowledge, how far is technology influencing the methods available to produce knowledge?

5.8 Linking questions

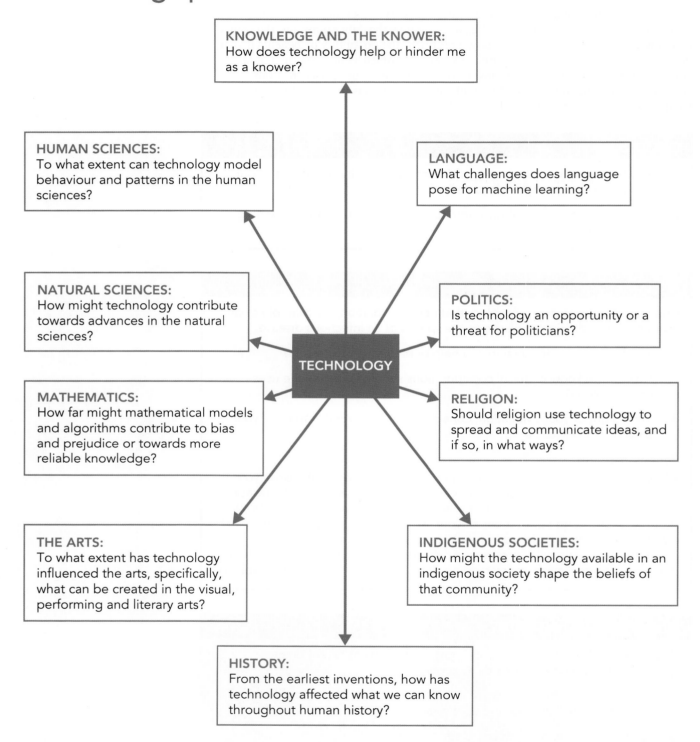

KNOWLEDGE AND THE KNOWER:
How does technology help or hinder me as a knower?

HUMAN SCIENCES:
To what extent can technology model behaviour and patterns in the human sciences?

LANGUAGE:
What challenges does language pose for machine learning?

NATURAL SCIENCES:
How might technology contribute towards advances in the natural sciences?

POLITICS:
Is technology an opportunity or a threat for politicians?

MATHEMATICS:
How far might mathematical models and algorithms contribute to bias and prejudice or towards more reliable knowledge?

TECHNOLOGY

RELIGION:
Should religion use technology to spread and communicate ideas, and if so, in what ways?

THE ARTS:
To what extent has technology influenced the arts, specifically, what can be created in the visual, performing and literary arts?

INDIGENOUS SOCIETIES:
How might the technology available in an indigenous society shape the beliefs of that community?

HISTORY:
From the earliest inventions, how has technology affected what we can know throughout human history?

5.9 Check your progress

Reflect on what you have learnt in this chapter, and indicate your confidence level between 1 and 5 (where 5 is the highest score and 1 is the lowest). If you score below 3, re-visit that section. Come back to this list later in your course. Has your confidence grown?

	Confidence level	Re-visited?
Do I have a strong understanding of the impact of technology on the knower?		
Am I able to give a definition of data, information and knowledge as they relate to technology, and distinguish between them?		
Can I give a good account of the impact that technology has had on knowledge and knowing, evaluating both benefits and potential threats for the knower?		
Have I considered the claims made about how internet culture is affecting memory?		
Am I able to articulate the concept of technology as a tool for extending our senses and our cognition via augmented reality, virtual reality and artificial intelligence?		
Do I understand the influence of technology on the way in which we think about money and value?		
Do I appreciate the implications of technology as a tool for automation that will change the nature of work?		
Can I discuss the meaning and significance of big data, and what it means for the knower?		
Can I argue for and against the view that a computer can be said to think and know?		
Am I able to discuss whether a knower or an expert has to be human?		
Can I weigh up how far technology can have an ethical use, solve problems and create a better world?		
Can I evaluate the ethical issues relating to technology, including the areas of social media, the right to be forgotten, big data and the social dimension associated with the use of technology?		
Do I appreciate the concept of dematerialisation and the possible effects of technology on the future of knowledge and knowing?		

5.10 Continue your journey

- To build on the knowledge that you have gained in this chapter, you could read some of the following books.
- To extend your general understanding of **knowledge and technology**, particularly in terms of power, data, justice, medicine, cars, crime and art. read: Hannah Fry, *Hello World – Being Human in the Age of Algorithms*, Penguin, 2019.

- To explore the concept of **big data** in greater depth, read: Timandra Harkness, *Big Data: Does size matter?*, Bloomsbury, 2016.

- To explore a good discussion of how **technology is changing how and who we trust**, read: Rachel Botsman, *Who Can You Trust?*, Penguin, 2018.

- For an exploration of **various technologies from Smartphones, the internet of things, AI, augmented reality, cryptocurrencies, block chains, machine learning and automation**, read: Adam Greenfield, *Radical Technologies: The Design of Everyday Life*, Bloomsbury, 2017.

- To understand more about the **impact of technology on education and learning**, read: Anthony Seldon, *The Fourth Education Revolution*, Legend Press Ltd, 2018.

Chapter 6

Knowledge and language

LEARNING INTENTIONS

This chapter will consider the relationship between language and knowledge and how language shapes how we think about knowledge and knowing.

You will:

- learn about the evolution of language in human society, and explore the nature and scope of language

- examine different theories of meaning, problematic meaning and the role that language plays in our social and personal identity

- consider the problems of translating languages, and how translation which involves interpretation is more of an art than a science

- evaluate the impact and importance of language for the knower, and become aware of how our knowledge can be framed by generalisations, stereotypes and labels

- explore the relationship between language and experience (qualia)

- consider and evaluate the Sapir–Whorf hypothesis – that language affects our experiences and shapes our knowledge, and the extent to which language influences the way we think about the world

CONTINUED

- explore the role of language as a tool for description, communication, persuasion and expression of values and the ways in which language can be used to influence and persuade, in the context of power, relationships and war

- evaluate how technology might help or hinder the use and communication of language

- consider ethical language, the meaning of our ethical knowledge claims and the responsibility of using and communicating language

BEFORE YOU START

Analyse each of the following quotations and discuss the questions that follow.

1 'We are biologically programmed for speech. We have the neurological, genetic and anatomical template that green-lights the possibility of language.' **Adam Rutherford** (1975–)

2 'Because without our language, we have lost ourselves. Who are we without our words?' **Melina Marchetta** (1965–)

3 'We know more than we can tell.' **Michael Polanyi** (1891–1976)

4 'All our knowledge has been built communally; there would be no astrophysics, there would be no history, there would not even be language, if man were a solitary animal.' **Jacob Bronowski** (1908–1974)

5 'Language is a process of free creation; its laws and principles are fixed, but the manner in which the principles of generation are used is free and infinitely varied. Even the interpretation and use of words involves a process of free creation.' **Noam Chomsky** (1928–)

For each quotation, consider:

a Do you agree or disagree with the quotation?

b What do you think the quotation suggests about language and knowledge?

c What is assumed or taken for granted about language and knowledge in each quote?

6.1 Introduction

DISCUSS 6.1

Does language help us to acquire knowledge, or does it limit and shape what we can know?

Humans and other animals use communication. Elephants communicate with other elephants using frequencies below the range that we can hear. Birds sing and dogs bark by making a noise with their vocal cords, and insects such as crickets make a noise using their body parts. The Diana monkey has different alarm calls to indicate different predators – whether it is an eagle from above or a leopard from below. Honey bees communicate location, direction and distance by performing a waggle dance.

However, only humans use the spoken word, including **grammar** and **syntax**, although Bengal finches and Japanese Great Tits have been found to have their own form of grammar and syntax. Not only is spoken and written language one of the features that distinguish us as human beings, but it has also been one of the essential tools humans have used for producing, sharing and passing on knowledge across cultures and down through generations.

KEY WORDS

grammar: the rules for constructing meaningful phrases and sentences out of words

syntax: the arrangement of words to form sentences or phrases – an example of syntax in toddlers might be a word pair such as 'my bed' or 'biscuits gone'

Figure 6.1: How does animal communication compare with human language?

Every time we say a sentence, we are doing something creative and, arguably, original. When we use language, we innovate; and although we have learnt the rules of language, we do not usually repeat remembered sentences we have heard. Instead, our spoken language is a creative flow, where we construct our own meanings and say things in ways that may not have been said in identical ways ever before.

Language links us with the past, even though language leaves no fossil record and we do not know for certain when and how language began. Poems and literature from the past can give us a window on another world, even if that language is no longer spoken today. Language can be understood from a scientific viewpoint, and the evolution and evolutionary role of language raises important questions about the biological, cognitive and cultural processes involved in language acquisition and use.

"Ever since we invented language, the kids aren't breaking and mauling things anymore."

The human sciences, in particular psychology, might explore language as a window into human nature, or its role in cognitive development and social identity. The arts are often described as the 'language of the emotions'; performing, literary and visual arts make use of verbal and non-verbal language. Mathematics could be said to be a universal language in its own right.

It is claimed that there are approximately 6,000 different spoken languages in the world and that the average adult has around 60,000 words in their vocabulary. Speaking and listening come naturally to us, and every human society ever known has developed language. We also communicate using non-verbal language such as gesture, mime or body language – some communication may be sub-conscious, and some language may be classified as unintended communication.

How did you learn language? On one level, you may have been pre-programmed to learn language. You may have been brought up speaking Japanese, French or Hindi as your **mother tongue**, or two or more of these if you are bilingual or multilingual, but the particular languages you speak are a product of the society and culture that you were raised in. Language is a highly complex entity which has a biological and genetic aspect – speech involves a sophisticated anatomical structure – including the tongue, larynx, jaw, face, lips and the bone in our throat known as the hyoid bone. Moreover, language has a cognitive function – language and the rules of grammar relate to our brain and mind. Some people believe that our brain is in some sense 'pre-wired' for speech and language. Furthermore, there is a social function to language – it plays a social role, and identifies us. Language might be thought of as a human capacity, or a in some sense a skill, or a type of know-how.

KEY WORD

mother tongue: the first language that you were brought up to speak

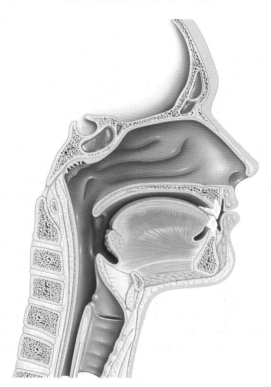

Figure 6.2: What are the biological, cognitive and cultural aspects of language? How and why has the capacity for speech and language evolved?

Given that language is the means by which we communicate ideas to each other and share our knowledge, it is essential to us as knowers. In this chapter, we explore the impact of language on the knower, and how language is a tool for gaining and communicating knowledge. We explore how language relates to thinking and knowing.

DISCUSS 6.2

1   Do you think language helps you to describe the world or express your opinions?

2   What are the strengths and weakness of language for the knower?

6.2 The scope of language

DISCUSS 6.3

How does language enable us to collaborate with one another, share our ideas and communicate knowledge?

Language is rule-governed

Linguistics is the science of language, and it includes a number of aspects. One of them is vocabulary, and this is governed by arbitrary rules. For a native English speaker, it feels as if there is a natural – almost magical – connection between the word 'dog' and the animal it stands for. But there is of course no deep reason why this noise should be associated with *that* animal. It could just as well be *quan* (Chinese), *koira* (Finnish), *chien* (French), *hund* (German), *kutta* (Hindi), *inu* (Japanese), *gae* (Korean), *sobaka* (Russian), *perro* (Spanish) or *köpek* (Turkish). For communication to work, it does not matter what noises or squiggles we correlate with objects, so long as there is general agreement within the linguistic community.

However, single words do not convey much meaning, unless they are instructions such as 'Go!'. The other main element in language is grammar – the rules relating to words, phrases and sentences. When you learn another language, one of the main things you have to learn is grammar. Grammar gives the rules for how to combine words in the correct order, and it helps to determine the meaning of a sentence.

There are the rules of *descriptive grammar*, which describe how people *actually* speak, and the rules of *prescriptive grammar*, which describe how people *should* ideally speak. For example, one prescriptive rule is 'You should not use double negatives'. The following sentence, 'The IB Diploma Programme student is not under-prepared for university study', would be better expressed in positive terms, without the double negative – 'The IB Diploma Programme student is prepared for university study.' Both sentences convey the same meaning, but I expect you can see why the rules of grammar dictate against the use of a double negative.

According to the Oxford dictionary of English usage, the rule of grammar, 'Do not split infinitives,' is actually not a rule of prescriptive grammar, although many people falsely believe it to be one. This rule itself derived from the rule in Latin where it was impossible to split an infinitive. In the TV programme *Star Trek*,

Captain Kirk says, 'to boldly go where no man has gone before'. Many people may believe that the correct grammar would be 'to go *boldly* where no man has gone before'. However, split infinitives are perfectly acceptable and both versions are grammatically correct.

Finally, as we saw in Chapter 2, Noam Chomsky (1928–) in his 1957 book *Syntactic Structures* used the following example of a sentence to illustrate how even a grammatically correct sentence can still be a nonsense sentence: *'Colourless green ideas sleep furiously.'* This suggests that meaning is also an essential feature of language. It is not enough for sentences to be grammatically correct; they also need to make sense – or have some semantic meaning, which we explore in a later section on meaning.

Language is creative and innovative

One feature of language is that the rules of grammar and vocabulary allow us to make an almost infinite number of grammatically correct sentences. Every sentence that you speak is in some sense original. Language may be the product of the rules of grammar that you have learnt over time, but you are a creator and innovator of language, in terms of meaning and expression. You are able to create and understand sentences that have never been written or said before. For example, you have probably never seen the following sentence, 'From a chrysalis of ignorance, the IB Diploma Programme student emerges, knowledgeable, principled and reflective, like a butterfly', but you probably have no problem understanding the metaphor and conjuring up a mental picture corresponding to it. The creative resources of language are staggering. There are an infinite number of sentences you could create. The psychologist Steven Pinker (1954–) has calculated that there are at least 10^{20} grammatically correct English sentences up to 20 words long. (This is a huge number: if you said one sentence every five seconds, it would take you one hundred trillion (10^{14}) years to utter them all – that's 10,000 times longer than the universe has been in existence!)

Moreover, languages are not static entities, but change and develop over time. William Shakespeare (1564–1616) introduced many new words into the English language, such as 'bubble', 'dwindle', 'frugal' and 'obscene'. As well as inventing new words, languages also borrow words from one another. English is full of such borrowed words: 'algebra' from Arabic, 'kindergarten' from German and 'pyjamas' from Yiddish. Many new words continue to appear with the arrival of new technology.

KEY WORD
semantic: relating to the meaning of language

KEY WORD
metaphor: a figure of speech which makes an implicit comparison between two things

EXPLORE 6.1

1   Make up a meaningful – though not necessarily true – English sentence which, to the best of your knowledge, has never in the history of the universe been written before.

2   If our use of language is governed by the rules of grammar, what scope do we have to be innovators with the language we use and the meanings we convey? When would it be desirable for us to break linguistic conventions, and why?

3   Investigate how Stephen Pinker arrived at that number of grammatically correct sentences of 20 words long. What was his methodology? How certain is this knowledge claim?

Language is intended

Although language is a form of communication, not all communication is language. To see the difference between the two, consider the following two situations.

- You are bored in class and, while the teacher is looking at their computer, you catch someone's eye across the room and make a yawning gesture by putting your hand to your mouth.

- You are trying to look interested in what someone says and to your horror, find yourself starting to yawn.

While both of these yawns communicate information – and might loosely be called body language – only the first can really be described as language. This is because the first is intended and the second is not. This suggests that a key thing that distinguishes the subset of communication that is language from other forms of communication is that language is intended, as opposed to unconscious or unintended.

KEY WORD

body language: conscious or unconscious body movements and positions that communicate our attitudes and feelings

---

DISCUSS 6.4

1   How would you interpret the body language in Figure 6.3? What do you think is being communicated?

2   How easy is it to misunderstand the body language of someone from a different culture?

Figure 6.3: Tennis players shake hands following their match. What is being communicated here?

While the subconscious may play a significant part in language learning and processes, the unintended and the unconscious aspects fall outside of the scope of this chapter, and of the TOK course. Moreover, while we can use non-verbal signals and cues, such as mime and gesture to communicate without language, in this chapter, we will interpret the scope of language to be spoken language. For the rest of this chapter, therefore, what we mean by language will be verbal language that is intended.

> **REFLECTION**
>
> Think about some of the ways in which you solely use body language. Then think about some of the ways in which you might use body language to modify spoken language. To what extent do conscious gestures, postures and facial expressions alter the content of our words and the way in which we interpret the words of others?

6.3 Language, meaning and the knower

Having explored the scope of language, we turn to what language means. Language relates to the knower who can make sense of the world, describe the way it is and express beliefs, feelings and attitudes towards it. In this section, we explore the relationship between language and meaning.

We might think of language as a tool that enables the knower to describe the world and express beliefs. In Chapter 4, we discussed the correspondence theory – that a knowledge claim is true if it corresponds to a fact about the world. For example, it is true that 'the grass is green' if it corresponds to a fact I can observe. There is a distinction between language, the world and our beliefs about the world. You might question how far verbal language is suited to the task of describing the following:

- The world that I picture, for example, the table about which I have a belief

- My picture of that world in my mind, for example, my belief about the table

Language can relate to both the theory that meaning is found in the world and the theory that meaning is constructed in the mind. You can use language to try to describe the world that you perceive, even if you can only do so imperfectly. You can also use language to express your beliefs about the world – the concepts, theories and ideas that you have invented or adopted about that world. You might think about how effective or accurate your language is in relation to each of these.

Some people argue that in order to mean something, language has to have some relationship with the truth. For example, if I observe a table and say 'the table is brown,' I am making sense and expressing a meaningful sentence that makes a statement about the world as it is.

Others would argue that meaning is related more to the use of language, so that a sentence makes sense in relation to how it is used. The statement that 'the table is brown' is not so much a statement about the world as it is a statement about my perception of the world. It depends on my observations, sense perceptions and conceptual framework. I may believe that there is an object in the world that I observe, which is called a table. This belief depends on my understanding of a category of objects in my mind which I know as "tables" as well as a category of colours that I refer to as "brown". In this way, language expresses my beliefs about the world.

> **KEY WORDS**
>
> **concept:** an abstract idea or something conceived
>
> **percept:** what we notice via the process of sense perception

The problem of meaning

Since much of our knowledge comes to us in the form of language, we need to be clear about the meanings of words if we are to understand the information that is being communicated to us. Meaning is important in our search for knowledge because *you must know what a sentence means before you can decide whether it is true or false.*

If you consider how young children are taught the colour red, you point to many red things and give them the name 'red' – cars, bricks, trains, flowers; all of them are red, and the child learns that there is a commonality between all of these items. You can test their learning by asking them, *'Is that car red?'* or ask them *'Find me an object that is red,'* in order to check that they have understood what red means. In this way, language does more than describe what we can observe – it relates to concepts and abstract ideas. The knower extracts the meaning and the concept from the examples. Concepts arise from the particular examples they have observed.

We tend to assume that pinning down meaning is relatively straightforward, and that every word has a fixed meaning which is understood and accepted by everyone – just like with learning the concept of colour red (except for people who have red-green colour blindness; they can still learn the concept of red, but may apply it very differently). However, we could argue that there is a *problem of meaning*, and that words are often ambiguous and open to a variety of interpretations.

This raises a question about the relative certainty and **ambiguity** of language. What we describe as 'red' is what we perceive of the electromagnetic spectrum at a wavelength around 700 nanometres. While science can describe with a degree of certainty how and why we perceive red, the knower may still want to understand the meaning. Think about what red means for you. It may have a cultural association – in China and India it is the bridal colour, but in other cultures and contexts it may signify danger or 'stop'. However, trying to describe the meaning of 'redness' is difficult without a specific context. Some would say it is unnecessary given that it is often believed that sentences have meaning, not single words. Moreover, the nature of language is that it is inherently ambiguous – even if we intend a certain meaning when we speak, we cannot know for certain that we have conveyed this intended meaning with accuracy.

> **KEY WORD**
>
> **ambiguity:** as discussed in Chapter 2, open to interpretation – where there is more than one obvious meaning, as opposed to certainty – when something is definitely true

Figure 6.4: A couple are married at the north plaza of the Big Wild Goose Pagoda in Xian in Shaanxi Province, China and drink wine from a pair of cups linked by a red thread, during their Han-style wedding ceremony. What is the denotation and the connotation of the word red? What is the relationship between language and culture?

Theories of meaning

We will briefly look at three theories of what distinguishes meaningful words from meaningless ones.

Definition theory – meanings are found in dictionaries

Definition theory argues that meaning is found in dictionaries. The most obvious way of trying to resolve confusions about what a word means is to consult a dictionary. However, coming up with a good definition of a word to include in the dictionary can be more difficult than it seems.

EXPLORE 6.2

1   Define as precisely as you can the following three words:

    a   triangle

    b   table

    c   love

2   Try to explain to your partner what the word 'red' means. What does this suggest to you about the limitation of definitions and the nature of language?

If you tried the Explore activity above, you probably had no difficulty in defining a triangle. 'Three straight lines that define an area' might do it. When it comes to the word 'table', things are more difficult. Perhaps you came up with something similar to the following dictionary definition: 'A piece of furniture with a flat top and one or more legs, providing a level surface for eating, writing, working at, playing games, etc.' That seems fairly good, but it is not difficult to think of borderline cases and counter-examples. What about a flat surface that is built into an alcove and does not have any legs, or a flat surface that is suspended by chains from the ceiling? Where exactly does a table end and a desk begin? What if you regularly use an old tea chest as a table – does that make it a table? One response to these questions might be: '*Who cares? Life is too short to worry about exactly where tables end and non-tables begin!*'

Of the three words in the Explore activity, 'love' is probably the most difficult to define. One example of a dictionary definition is 'An intense feeling of deep affection or fondness for a person or thing' (although it also offers 'Zero score in games such as tennis'). The trouble with a word such as 'love' is that it seems to have depths that cannot be neatly captured in a few well-chosen words. If Angie turns to Jake and says 'I don't think you really know the meaning of the word 'love'', you are not going to solve Jake's problem by handing him a dictionary!

What comes out of this discussion is that the only words we can define in a clear and unambiguous way are mathematical ones, such as 'triangle', 'circle', 'straight line', etc. When it comes to other words, they have a fuzziness at their borders that is hard – if not impossible – to eliminate.

DISCUSS 6.5

> **DISCUSS 6.5**
>
> 1 Ambiguous language can be misleading. How can it help or hinder us as knowers?
>
> 2 What do you think are the advantages and disadvantages of ambiguous language? Would it be a good thing if language was never ambiguous?

Criticisms

The main problem with the idea that the meaning of a word is its dictionary definition is not simply that most definitions are vague and imprecise, but, more fundamentally, that they only explain the meanings of words by using other words. If we are to avoid being trapped in an endless circle of words, language must surely connect with the world. Moreover, some would argue that single words do not convey much meaning – it is sentences that convey meaning, and can be either true or false. But it could be said that even the meaning in sentences can only be explained by other sentences.

Denotation theory – meanings are found in the world

Denotation theory argues that meaning is found in the world. According to the denotation theory, what distinguishes a meaningful word from a meaningless one is that a meaningful word stands for something while a meaningless one does not. Therefore 'France' means something because it stands for the country in Europe that is north of the Pyrenees and west of the Rhine. In contrast, 'mibulous' is meaningless because there is nothing in the world that corresponds to it. Since the following lines from the opening of Lewis Carroll's (1832–98) poem *Jabberwocky* do not refer to anything, they are considered nonsense poetry:

> *Twas brillig, and the slithy toves*
> *Did gyre and gimble in the wabe:*
> *All mimsy were the borogoves,*
> *And the mome raths outgrabe.*

If language refers to something in the world, it follows that sense perception and observation are closely related to language.

KEY WORD

denotation: the literal meaning of a word

> **DISCUSS 6.6**
>
> 1 How far can we describe the world that we picture using neutral language?
>
> 2 *'Colourless green ideas sleep furiously'* is a well-known example of a sentence, constructed by Noam Chomsky, which is grammatically correct but makes no sense. Discuss what you think this sentence tells you about the nature of language.

Criticisms

While the denotation theory might work in the case of names such as 'France', it seems to fall down in the case of abstract words – such as 'multiplication', 'freedom' and 'wisdom' – which do not seem to stand for or correspond to any *thing*. Admittedly, you may be able to point to examples of wisdom, but you cannot point to wisdom itself.

The colour red is one concept. But language also attempts to describe abstract concepts such as cause and effect, freewill and determinism, or the concepts of time and space.

The problem with this criticism is that meaningful concepts *can* correspond to an abstract reality rather than a specific object – for example the concepts of 'resilience', 'determination' or 'love' might refer to an abstract category that can make sense and have meaning. Words have not only a primary meaning or denotation, but also a secondary meaning or connotation. The denotation of a word is what it refers to; the connotation is the web of associations that surrounds it. The denotation of a word is limited to what it describes, whereas the connotation relates to the associations of that word. For example, 'thin' literally denotes the frame of a person, but the word 'skinny' may have a more negative connotation whereas the word 'slender' has a more positive connotation.

> ### KEY WORD
>
> connotation: the ideas and associations a word evokes in addition to its literal meaning

EXPLORE 6.3

Choose a particular colour such as red, green, or blue. What is the denotation and the connotation of this particular colour? Do some research into the meanings of this colour in different cultural contexts, and present your ideas to the class. What does this tell you about the relationship between language, cultural meanings and the world that you picture?

Image theory – meanings are found in the mind

Image theory argues that meaning is found in the mind. According to image theory, the meaning of a word is the mental image it stands for, and you know the meaning of a word when you have the appropriate concept in your mind. For example, you know what the word 'freedom' means when you associate it with the concept of freedom – being able to do what you like, not being imprisoned and so on. This view also has something to be said for it. For the difference between my speaking English and a chatbot 'speaking English' is surely that, while my speech is accompanied by the appropriate mental activity, the chatbot quite literally does not know what it is talking about. The technology here is highly sophisticated; however, rather than *speaking* English, the chatbot is simulating the words of a conversation – a theme we explored in Chapter 5.

> ### KEY WORD
>
> chatbot: a computer that simulates human conversation

Criticisms

The problem with image theory is that if meanings are in the mind, then we can never be sure that someone else understands the meaning of a word in the same way that we do – or, indeed, that they understand it at all. For you can never get into another person's mind and find out what is going on in it. On the other hand, we can all agree on words, even if we will never know if others perceive the same reality that we do.

DISCUSS 6.7

1   To what extent is your use of language accompanied by images? Does every word conjure up an image, or only some of them?

2   How do you know that what we both call 'red' is the same? For example, I could experience 'red' as what you would call 'green' if you were looking out of my eyes, and *vice versa*.

3   What difference, if any, would it make in real life if the above were the case?

Figure 6.5: Indian students at the Ramakrishna Paramhansa Marg BMC school in Mumbai put a wig onto a teaching virtual assistant mannequin fitted with Amazon's Alexa™ – a cloud-based intelligent voice service. If a robot could use and respond appropriately to language, would it make sense to conclude that it could think?

Meaning as use and know-how

Rather than think of meanings as something that can be found in dictionaries, in the world or in the mind, perhaps it would be better to say that meaning is a matter of *know-how*, and that you know the meaning of a word when you know how to *use* it correctly. For example, if you can use the word 'red' appropriately when discussing such things as traffic lights, red peppers and strawberries, you surely know what it means. At the same time, it is hard to resist the idea that there must be something appropriate going on in our heads when we mean and understand things.

DISCUSS 6.8

1 Do you think that language is a question of 'knowing-how'?

2 If a robot could use and respond appropriately to language, would it make sense to conclude that it could think? Give reasons for and against.

REFLECTION

Think about the different theories of language. As a knower, does any one theory seem to 'ring true' for you? What are the implications for knowledge if there are few clear and direct connections between the language we use to express knowledge, and the world our knowledge describes?

Problematic meaning

When we consider how language is used in practice, things start to get complicated. There is an important distinction to make between *literal* or *explicit* meaning and *implicit* or *metaphorical* meaning. We often use language in all kinds of non-literal ways. If I say, '*It is raining cats and dogs*,' I am making no literal sense; but this does have a metaphorical meaning – it is an **idiom** sometimes used in everyday English, meaning that rain is pouring down heavily. As the poet Robert Frost (1874–1963) observed, we rarely say exactly what we mean, for 'we like to talk in parables and in hints and in indirections – whether from diffidence or some other instinct'. In what follows, we will consider six types of problematic meaning that can be found in everyday language: vagueness, ambiguity, secondary meanings, metaphor, irony and context. These present a particular problem for the knower. Language is used to communicate knowledge, and this section explores how it can be misunderstood.

> **KEY WORD**
>
> **idiom:** a colloquial expression whose figurative meaning cannot be deciphered from its literal meaning

Vagueness

An example of the vagueness of language is *'games'*. If someone is playing a game, it can have a very diverse range of meanings depending on context. Many words, such as 'fast' and 'slow', are intrinsically vague, and their meaning depends on context. For example, 'fast' means something different to a long-distance runner compared to a Formula One driver. And, even in a specific context, people may have quite different ideas of what a vague word implies.

Despite their disadvantages, vague words are in fact very useful; for, although they may fail to pin things down, they can at least point us in the right direction. It is, in any case, impossible to make words completely precise. Ask yourself, for example, how little hair a man must have before you can describe him as bald? Does the loss of one particular hair change him from being non-bald to bald? The answer is, of course, that the concept is inherently vague. Some men are balder than others, but it is impossible to say exactly where non-baldness ends and baldness begins.

DISCUSS 6.9

1 Do you think that communication would be improved if we got rid of vague words, or do you think they sometimes serve a useful purpose?

2 Charles Sanders Peirce (1839–1914) said, 'It is easy to be certain – one only has to be sufficiently vague'. What do you think Peirce meant by this? Give examples.

Ambiguity

Many words, phrases and sentences are ambiguous. For example, 'The woman cannot bear children' can mean either that the woman is unable to conceive children, or that she does not like them. 'The author lives with his wife, an architect and amateur musician in Mumbai' would usually be taken to mean that the author lives with his wife *who* is an architect as well as an amateur musician; but it could also mean that the author lives with his wife *and* an architect *and* an amateur musician.

There may be justification for ambiguous use of language. Instead of being explicit and direct we might use language as a veil for our true intentions. For example, if you say over dinner, 'If you can pass the salt that would be awesome,' it literally means that if someone was able to pass the salt that would be great, whereas it is actually avoids a command or instructions, and counts as a polite request to actually pass the salt, even if it is an overstatement or exaggeration. Another example, 'Would you like to come in for coffee?' is associated with an implicit invitation for a relationship to develop further without the direct request being made. The listener reads between the lines, and has the option to accept or decline the offer without an explicit mention of that offer ever being said directly.

Ambiguity can also be used to mislead people. A politician might deliberately exploit an ambiguous sentence so that it is understood in different ways by different listeners. For example, 'I am opposed to taxes which damage incentives' could be taken to mean 'I am opposed to all taxes because they damage incentives' or 'I am opposed only to those taxes which damage incentives'.

EXPLORE 6.4

1   Each of the sentences a to k is ambiguous. Give two different meanings for each of them:

   a   Flying planes can be dangerous.

   b   They saw Mrs Gupta and the dog sitting under the table.

   c   Bob tickled the man with a feather duster.

   d   Refuse to be put in the basket.

   e   Neetha wanted to hear the pop star sing very badly.

   f   Visiting relatives can be boring.

   g   Javier ate the chicken on the sofa.

   h   As Imran came in to bowl, I saw her duck.

   i   Dogs must be carried on escalators.

   j   I went downstairs and found breakfast in my pyjamas.

   k   In this TV series, we will discuss debating with Dr Price.

2   To what extent can punctuation help to reduce the ambiguity of a sentence? Give some examples.

3   Many jokes are based on ambiguity. Research some examples and analyse them.

Context can help us to determine the meaning of an ambiguous sentence. In **b**, above the most reasonable interpretation of the sentence is 'They saw Mrs Gupta and the-dog-sitting-under-the-table' rather than 'They saw Mrs-Gupta-and-the-dog sitting under the table.' This is because people can, but do not usually, sit under tables with dogs.

Secondary meaning

Secondary meaning refers to the associations or connotations of a word. For example, to understand what the word 'chat' means, you also need to be aware of related words such as 'talk', 'gossip' and 'discuss', each of which has a different shade of meaning. While the denotation of a word is public, its connotations vary from person to person. Words such as 'love', 'death', 'school' and 'priest' may have different connotations for different people.

EXPLORE 6.5

1 Explain the different connotations of each of the sets of words a to i:

   a   slender, skinny, thin

   b   stubborn, steadfast, firm

   c   praise, flatter, commend

   d   energetic, spirited, frenzied

   e   stench, smell, fragrance

   f   euthanasia, manslaughter, murder

   g   gossip, chat, discuss

   h   obstinate, inflexible, fundamentalist

   i   passionate, addicted, fanatical

2 The philosopher Bertrand Russell (1872–1970) pointed out that we tend to interpret our own behaviour in the best possible light, and are less charitable when it comes to other people. To illustrate the point, he 'emotively conjugated' the following 'irregular verbs':

   'I am firm; you are obstinate; he is a pig-headed fool.'

   'I am righteously indignant; you are annoyed; he is making a fuss about nothing.'

   'I have reconsidered it; you have changed your mind; he has gone back on his word.'

Working in pairs, suggest how some of the verbs a to h might be 'emotively conjugated' in a similar way:

   a   'I speak my mind . . .'

   b   'I am lucky . . .'

   c   'I compromise . . .'

   d   'I take calculated risks . . .'

CONTINUED

   e   'I am realistic . . .'

   f   'I am idealistic . . .'

   g   'I am spontaneous . . .'

   h   'I am tolerant . . .'

Sometimes, we use **euphemisms** for harsh words because they have more acceptable connotations. Euphemisms, which substitute mild or neutral-sounding words, are a widely used form of emotive language – to replace negative-sounding words, or those not usually talked about in polite conversation. For example, 'passed away' is a euphemism for 'died'. Both expressions have the same denotation, but 'passed away' brings with it associations of peace and serenity that 'died' lacks. In Shakespeare's *The Tempest* (IV.1.147–8), Prospero says euphemistically, '*Our little life is rounded with a sleep*'.

> ### KEY WORD
>
> **euphemism:** a softer-sounding word or phrase used to disguise something unpleasant or not usually talked about in polite conversation

We sometimes resort to euphemisms in order to avoid taboo subjects, or to protect people's feelings. Therefore, we may speak of the 'rest room' rather than the toilet. There are also many euphemisms for sex. In addition to such benign uses, people sometimes use euphemisms to deliberately mislead people. For example, the timber industry no longer speaks of 'clear cutting' – an ugly-sounding expression – when it cuts down old-growth forest, but of 'landscape management'. This may serve to hide the reality of what is happening, and make an unacceptable practice sound acceptable.

DISCUSS 6.10

Think of as many different words or expressions for each of the following: 'vomit', 'drunk', 'stupid'.

1   What is the difference in their connotations?

2   How might this language shape your perspective?

Metaphor

DISCUSS 6.11

John Donne (1572–1631) said, '*No man is an island*'. Is this sentence true? If so, in what sense?

We use language not only literally, but also metaphorically. You might say that 'Sofia has got her head in the clouds', 'Francesco is a pillar of the community', or 'Ha Yoon has put her roots down in Canada'. Despite being literally false, each of these sentences might still be metaphorically true. Sofia does not have an unusually long neck, but she may walk around in a dreamlike state; Francesco is not made of stone, but he may be an important figure in his community; Ha Yoon has not grown roots, but she may have settled permanently in Canada.

When trying to decide whether a sentence is meant literally or metaphorically, we might get a hint from the context. Compare, for example, the following two sentences:

1   My brother is a butcher.

2   My dentist is a butcher.

Most people would interpret **1** literally and **2** metaphorically. For while your brother may well make his living as a butcher, there are probably not many people who divide their professional life between dentistry and butchery.

Metaphors can have explanatory power, and are sometimes used in the construction of knowledge. For example, you may have been taught that an atom is like a solar system, with a nucleus at the centre and electrons whizzing around like planets in orbit. However, metaphors that were once age appropriate in order to get across an idea can be replaced with much more sophisticated models that make the old metaphors redundant. Some systems might be too complex to model. In economics, the management of an economy has been compared with home economics or household management. However, some people might argue that a complex system such as the economy may be too complex for a metaphor like this to be meaningful. Moreover, some metaphors may be misleading or false, such as the comparison of human personality with a blank slate in psychology.

The challenge here is to find language that makes sense and contributes a simple idea, without compromising the accuracy of knowledge. In practice, it can be difficult to determine where literal meaning ends and metaphorical meaning begins, because ordinary language is riddled with *dead metaphors*. Consider, for example, the following expressions: 'night*fall*', '*sharp* tongue', '*brilliant* mind', 'chair *leg*' and '*in* love'. All of these phrases are – strictly speaking – metaphorical, but they are so familiar that we have forgotten their metaphorical origins.

EXPLORE 6.6

Take a paragraph from a newspaper or magazine, and identify as many metaphors in it as you can. Try to rewrite the piece without using any metaphors.

Self-assessment

How easy did you find this exercise? Did you feel you conveyed the sense and meaning of the paragraph as well as the original? How far is it possible to describe something or to explain something without metaphorical language? What does this suggest about the nature of language? What did it teach you about the use of metaphorical language to convey meaning?

DISCUSS 6.12

How far is metaphorical language an advantage or disadvantage for the knower?

Figure 6.6: *'No man is an island'* by John Donne (1572–1631) is an example of metaphorical language. How far is metaphorical language an advantage or disadvantage for the knower?

REAL-LIFE SITUATION 6.1

Using your IB Diploma Programme subjects, discuss examples of metaphors used in the construction of knowledge.

Irony

Irony – the saying of one thing in order to mean the opposite – shows just how problematic language in action can be. Despite the oddity of using a sentence that literally means *X* in order to suggest not-*X*, irony is something that is found in all cultures. If you turn up late to a class and your teacher says, 'Early again?' they have 'made light' of the fact that you are often late. If the weather forecast predicted sunshine and it is pouring with rain outside, you might look out of the window and say 'Nice weather, heh?' Irony means that we cannot necessarily take a statement at face value, and it adds another layer of ambiguity to language.

Context

Meaning is linked not just to the words themselves; it is also linked closely to the context in which they are spoken. Our use of language is influenced by who we are speaking to. We use language for self-expression, and it plays a role in our social and personal identity, as well as in the social groups that we belong to. Language can be used to identify who we are in relation to a group or within a group. You may use different language depending on the group you are with – the language used at a family party will not be the same as the language you use when you are in a group with your friends. There is such a thing as appropriate language use that depends on the

KEY WORD

irony: a figure of speech in which words are used to say one thing and mean the opposite

relationship. For example, it might be considered unethical to swear when speaking to children. On the other hand, the use of certain taboo words might be thought appropriate if spoken by a particular speaker and used in certain circumstances.

Language is closely linked with power and relationships. A lecture where only the lecturer speaks could be interpreted as a show of dominance or authority. Language can be used as propaganda, by an authoritarian regime to maintain power. What is considered appropriate language is determined by the nature of the relationship between the speakers.

Meaning and interpretation

We could perhaps summarise our discussion of problematic meaning in three words: *Language is ambiguous*. For vagueness, secondary meaning, metaphor and irony can all be seen as different kinds of ambiguity. The implication is that there is an element of *interpretation* built in to all communication. Although language is governed by rules, and you cannot make words mean anything you like, many of the rules are quite loose, and there is often more than one way of interpreting a sentence. As we have seen, *context* may help you to decide what someone 'really means'. If a friend says 'It was so funny that I nearly died laughing', you do not ask if they were rushed to hospital or think they had a near-death experience. But you cannot always rely on context. If someone says 'I am so angry I could kill him', you would probably not alert the police; but perhaps this time they really mean it!

Rather than think of meaning as an all-or-nothing concept – either you understand it or you do not – it might make better sense to think in terms of *levels* of meaning. For example, a physics professor is likely to have a much clearer idea of what the *theory of relativity* means than a non-physicist. And a 40 year old adult is likely to have a more sophisticated understanding of what 'love' means than a 6 year old child.

EXPLORE 6.7

What problems are there in trying to interpret the following sentences?

a   If Zhang Wei works hard, he should do himself justice in the final exam.

b   It is as difficult for a rich man to enter the kingdom of heaven as it is for a camel to pass through the eye of a needle.

c   After he had said this, he left her as on the previous evening.

d   What's up?

e $E = mc^2$

We have spent some time exploring the problem of meaning, but you may wonder why we should care about it. Does it really matter if we cannot pin down the meaning of a word? In some cases, it does. For an accused person, the difference between 'murder' and 'manslaughter' may be literally a matter of life and death; and if a government supports a war on terrorism, we need to be clear about what we mean by 'terrorist'.

Objective and subjective language

Words have a history, and etymology is the study of the origins and historical development of words and their meaning. This raises an important question for the knower, that while we may be innovative users of language in the formation of original sentences, our language is also inherited via our history and culture. To an extent, the languages we speak are part of a cultural inheritance and a product of history passed onto us. For example, the periodic table is largely a neutral list of elements, but some names of the elements have laden meaning, or indeed we develop meaning from them or ascribe certain values to them. For example, the noble gases were once known as the inert gases because it was believed they were inert and unable to form compounds. Labels, such as scientific Latin plant names, have deeper meanings and historical roots. Carl Linnaeus (1707–1778) developed a two-name system for classifying plants so that they could be identified individually. The genus is listed first, followed by the species – rather like a surname and first name to identify a person. For example, a maple tree is *Acer* in Latin, but there are many types, so the second word, *rubrum,* is an adjective which gives a more specific identification – a red maple, or *Acer rubrum*. These plant names are the product of a classification system from the 18th century, which relies on the ancient language of Latin.

Neutral questions

Einstein (1879–1955) claimed, 'The formulation of a problem is often more essential than its solution, which may be merely a matter of mathematical or experimental skill. To raise new questions, new possibilities, to regard old problems from a new angle requires creative imagination and marks real advances in science.'

This quote suggests that it is the creative imagination that makes possible any real advance in science. It follows that it is the formulation of questions for investigation that is essential in the development of knowledge and knowing. In a school curriculum, there is a scope and a limit to questions, whereas at university, the task of post-graduate researchers is to both formulate new questions for investigation and know what the current questions are.

However, the questions we ask might contain bias and lead us in a certain direction. A leading question contains a built-in assumption. The pursuit of knowledge and knowing may have a certain agenda. As knowers, we too need to formulate the right questions about knowledge and knowing, which raises a problem. Is there such a thing as a neutral or unbiased question that is genuinely open and objective?

DISCUSS 6.13

'It is not possible to ask a neutral or unbiased question.' Do you agree?

6.4 Language and translation

DISCUSS 6.14

Would it be an advantage or disadvantage if everyone in the world spoke a single common language?

It is thought that there are around 6,000 languages in the world, of which Chinese, Spanish, English and Hindi are spoken by the largest number of people. There is great language diversity, usually in populated areas. For example, in India, there are multiple languages and dialects. It is claimed that in Papua New Guinea, every three miles there is a new language.

Each of us has a privileged relation to our own native language, and we tend unthinkingly to assume that it fits reality like a glove. Some people will master many languages, but others will learn only one or two. As well as enabling you to communicate with other people, one of the benefits of learning a second language is that it gives you a fresh perspective on your own.

REAL-LIFE SITUATION 6.2

1   'Who does not know another language does not know his own', (Goethe, 1749–1832). What can you learn about your own language by studying a second language?

2   In what other ways does learning a second language contribute to, and expand, your knowledge of the world?

Some languages have developed naturally over time, and indeed Mark Pagel, an evolutionary biologist (1954–) argues that the evolution of language is a social process. There are also a number of constructed languages, also known as 'conlangs' whose vocabulary and grammar have been deliberately invented, such as Esperanto or Dothraki.

Just as species of animals are under threat or becoming extinct, so too, many of the smaller of the world's languages are vulnerable; we will see in Chapter 9 that it is estimated one indigenous language is lost every two weeks. Tofa, a language spoken in Russia, has fewer than 25 speakers remaining. The value of any language is that it is a product of a unique cultural perspective. The danger of these languages being lost is that along with the extinction of a language goes the identity of a community, and their shared knowledge and history, as well as their unique perspective on the world.

DISCUSS 6.15

If there was only one single language remaining in the world, what knowledge would we have lost?

Lost in translation

When you learn a second language, one of the things you discover is that different languages divide the world up in different ways. If words were simply labels we stuck on objects, and the only difference between languages was that they used different words to refer to these objects, then translation would be a relatively straightforward matter. But it does not work like that. If you make a word-for-word translation from one language to another, you will not get a workable translation, and will instead get nonsense. That is why translation is more of an art than a science.

The role of an interpreter is to ensure that meaning is not lost in translation. Here is a meaningful French expression used by Jean-Baptist Alphonse Karr (1808–1890) in his journal, 'The Wasps': 'Plus ça change, plus c'est la même chose'. This is translated literally as, 'The more it changes, the more it's the same thing'. However, Google Translate™ gives the modern idiom, 'What goes around comes around'. An interpreter might argue that this idiom is too broad and goes beyond the original meaning, which could be better translated as 'The more things change, the more they stay the same'. Moreover, some people might infer a broader meaning that 'history repeats itself' and some would argue that it points to a truth about human nature – that while a person's external circumstances or appearance can change, other aspects of their personality remain the same. Others would argue that the meaning can only be understood in the context of French history when it was written in 1849. This example shows that translation is closely connected with interpretation and context.

Perhaps not surprisingly, most linguists would say that there is no such thing as a perfect translation, and that something is always lost when we move from one language to another. As an Italian saying has it, *'Traduttore traditore'* – 'The translator is a traitor'. (Something is lost even in this translation!) So what makes one translation better than another? There are three commonly agreed criteria:

- *faithfulness* – the translation should be faithful to the original text
- *comprehensibility* – the translation should be comprehensible
- *back translation* – when we retranslate a translation back into its original language, it should approximate to the original

To take some simple examples, consider how one might translate the following sentences:

a   *'Guten tag.'* (German ⟶ English)

b   *'S'il vous plaît.'* (French ⟶ English)

c   'How do you do?' (English ⟶ any language)

The literal translation of *Guten tag* is 'Good day', but people in Britain do not usually say 'Good day' (although it is more common in Australia). So a better translation might be 'Good morning', 'Good afternoon', or 'Hello'. Similarly, we do not translate *'S'il vous plaît'* as 'If it pleases you', but as 'Please'. Finally, 'How do you do?' would sound absurd in German and French if translated literally – how do you do what? Perhaps it is best translated as *Sehr erfreut* and *Enchanté*.

These examples show in microcosm the tension between translating literally word-for-word versus translating using different words to retain the spirit of a text. The more faithful you are to the words – or literal meaning – of the text, the stranger the translation is likely to sound in the target language. The more natural the translation sounds in the target language, the more likely you are to have strayed from the literal meaning of the original text.

DISCUSS 6.16

How might different languages affect what we know, and shape our perspective?

We already have the technology of Google Translate™, which can assist with translating words, phrases and sentences. Artificial intelligence (AI) cannot yet translate perfectly between languages, although it manages better with some languages than others. When AI was used to translate the verse in the New Testament (Matthew 14.38 and 26.41) from English to Russian, 'The spirit is willing, but the flesh is weak', it came back as 'The vodka is agreeable, but the meat is rotten'. Nevertheless, AI is getting better and better, and may soon reach the point when it can translate as well as human translators. Indeed, neither can people translate perfectly, and arguably all translation is imperfect. There are problems that arise in translating something from one language to another that are particularly worth mentioning: *untranslatable words* and *idioms*.

Untranslatable words

Every language contains words that have no equivalent in other languages, and can only be translated by a lengthy and inelegant paraphrase. For example, the English word 'quaint' has no very precise equivalent in other languages. Here are some examples of untranslatable words from other languages:

- *Schlimmbesserung* (German): an 'improvement' that actually makes things worse

- *aware* (Japanese): the feeling engendered by ephemeral beauty

- *rojong* (Indonesian): the relationship among a group of people committed to accomplishing a task of mutual benefit

- *jayus* (Indonesian): a joke so unfunny that it becomes funny

- *puijilittatuq* (Inuktitut, Canadian Arctic): he does not know which way to turn because of the many seals he has seen come to the ice surface

- *mamihlapinatapai* (Terra del Fuegan): to look at each other, each hoping the other will offer to do something which both parties much desire done but which neither is willing to do (according to *The Guinness Book of Records*, this is the most succinct word in the world)

- *tatle* (Scottish): is the act of hesitating when introducing yourself to someone because you have forgotten their name

- *Torschlusspanik* (German): translated, literally it means 'gate closing panic', but refers to the concept of aging and therefore running out of opportunities

- *wabi-sabi* (Japanese): featured in Chapter 11, means beauty in imperfection and accepting peacefully that decay is inevitable.

Translation problems can even arise at a relatively simple level. For example, German and French – together with many other languages – have two forms of 'you' – *du* and *Sie*, and *tu* and *vous*. When both are translated into English as 'you', something is clearly lost.

Idioms

An idiom is a colloquial expression whose meaning cannot be worked out from the meanings of the words it contains: for example, 'I was over the moon'; 'Don't beat about the bush'; 'He was born with a silver spoon in his mouth'. Such idiomatic expressions are common – there are said to be more than 25,000 in English – and they are particularly difficult to translate from one language to another. According to one story, when the sentence 'Out of sight is out of mind' was translated into Russian, and then re-translated into English, it came back as 'invisible idiot'.

There are many amusing anecdotes about mistranslations. When Pepsi-Cola ran an advertising campaign in Taiwan, they translated the slogan 'Come Alive with Pepsi' into Chinese. The campaign was a flop. When the slogan was translated back into English, it read 'Pepsi brings your ancestors back from the dead!' – understandably a failure. And the Swedish company Electrolux were no more successful when they tried to advertise their vacuum cleaners in the United States with the slogan 'Nothing sucks like an Electrolux'.

EXPLORE 6.8

1   Give some examples of words in your own language, or any additional language, that have no precise English equivalent.

2   Give some examples of idiomatic expressions in other languages that are difficult to translate into English.

3   What kinds of text do you think are easiest to translate from one language to another, and what kinds of text do you think are most difficult to translate?

DISCUSS 6.17

Is it better to know many languages at a conversational level, or one language at a very deep level? How might your answer be influenced by the number of languages that you already speak or intend to learn?

Translation and knowledge

The difficulty of translating accurately from one language to another presents questions relating to knowledge and knowing. The art and science of interpretation and translation is partly a matter of know-how – there is great expertise in translating from one language to another. Equally, you may consider what impact your native language and the languages you have learnt have had on your perspective and shaping your identity as a knower. To some extent, the languages you speak influence what you know and how you think – a topic we turn to later in the chapter when we explore the Sapir–Whorf hypothesis and linguistic relativity.

Figure 6.7: How far is knowledge represented in different ways in different languages?

REFLECTION

Think about some of the texts that you only read in translation. These might include novels, poems, philosophical treatises, historical documents, scientific, political or economic articles and religious texts. To what degree do you allow for translation issues when you are analysing a text in translation?

6.5 The impact of language on the knower

REAL-LIFE SITUATION 6.3

How does the language world we inherit shape us as knowers?

Our discussions about language, meaning and translation in the previous sections have focused on the problematic nature of human communication, and shown that we cannot simply take the meanings of words or sentences for granted. We will now explore the way in which language affects the way we see and think about the world. In this section, we will focus on how language affects the kinds of value judgements that we make about things, including labels and stereotypes, and the inherent difficulty of articulating some experiences in language.

EXPLORE 6.9

Think of either an event in which you played a role, or a relationship or friendship.

Tell different stories about the same thing, as if you are either the protagonist or an on-looker. How does your perspective and your choice of language affect the way that you recall the past?

Peer-assessment

Tell your stories to a partner or a small group. Give each other feedback. What words did you find particularly striking and why? In what ways did each of you use language to express the perspective of the protagonist or an on-looker. How far does your perspective and viewpoint influence the language you use? Keep your discussion in mind as you read the remainder of this section.

KEY WORD

Protagonist: the main character in a story

DISCUSS 6.18

1 How does the language we choose to use frame our perspective and express what we know?

2 How does the language in which we communicate contribute to knowledge and knowing?

Language and labels

DISCUSS 6.19

According to a well-known children's rhyme, 'Sticks and stones may break my bones, but names will never hurt me.' Do you agree or disagree with this? Give your reasons.

One function of language is to describe the world we perceive. Describing the world can involve putting labels on things, which has advantages and disadvantages. On the plus side, using labels is efficient and economical, and makes the world intelligible to the knower. If, for example, there was no general word for 'sand', and we were standing on a beach and had to give each individual grain a proper name, communication would quickly become impossible. On the negative side, labelling creates the risk that the knower mislabels things, or imposes their own implicit bias or value judgement on the world.

Earlier in the chapter, we examined the periodic table and the Linnaeus system for classifying plants. The natural and human sciences use classification to describe everything from the species of plants and animals to human personality traits. Since it is always possible to find similarities or differences between things, there are in fact many different ways of labelling or classifying a group of objects. Since there are many different ways of classifying things, you might ask why we classify things the way we do. According to one view, the labels we use reflect natural classes of things that exist 'out there' – language describes and classifies the world that the knower pictures.

According to another, labels are essentially social constructions that we impose on the world – language describes and classifies the knower's picture of the world in their mind. While the first view says that labels are *natural* descriptions of the world, and there are objective similarities between things, the second says that labels are *cultural*, and that similarity is in the eye of the beholder or 'the mind of the knower'.

Since we classify things using words, what is at issue here is the role played by language in the *world* that the knower pictures and the role played by language in the *picture* of the world perceived by the knower. The idea that our labels reflect the natural order of things is supported by the fact that there really do seem to be elements out there that we can observe and classify corresponding to our categories – such as gold and silver, and species – such as dogs and cats. However, these labels – and especially those used to classify human beings – have both cultural and natural elements.

EXPLORE 6.10

Choose one of the following and prepare a short presentation to the class, exploring this question: How far can any classification system describe the world in a neutral and objective way?

a   the periodic table

b   the classification of plants or animals

c   any other classification system of the natural world

Social identity theory suggests that our identity is shaped in part by the groups we belong to – we may be perceived differently according to our membership of groups, and our belonging may in turn influence our own sense of identity and who we are.

EXPLORE 6.11

1   Organise a class survey about language and identity. Investigate the words and labels that you and your classmates do or do not identify with most.

2   Work together in pairs or small groups. Think of a list of 10–15 words that might define your identity; either your educational identity as an IB Diploma Programme student, or any of the following: your social, cultural, religious, political or gender identity.

3   Ask people to choose the three words that they identify with most.

DISCUSS 6.20

1   What are the main advantages and disadvantages of classifying people according to their nationality, age or gender identity? What other ways of classifying people are there? Are some more natural than others? Are some more useful than others?

2   How far do our labels and classifications influence the generalisations that we might make, and the conclusions that we can reach?

Language and stereotypes

One danger with putting labels on people is that our labels can easily harden into stereotypes. A stereotype arises when we make assumptions and hasty generalisations about a group of people purely on the basis of their membership of that group. The use of stereotypes is particularly apparent in the case of nationality, gender identity and racial identity.

What, then, distinguishes damaging stereotypes from generalisations? Typically, a stereotype is a caricature that exaggerates the features of a group, and assumes they are possessed by *all* members of the group. Furthermore, it is usually based on prejudice rather than fact, and is difficult to change in the light of contrary evidence.

What comes out of our discussion of labels and stereotypes is that we need to be aware of the disadvantages as well as the advantages of using general words to label things. Despite their obvious value, labels can trap us into one particular way of looking at things. It is difficult – if not impossible – to capture the uniqueness and individuality of things in words. Despite the power of language to describe and classify the world, it is also inherently limited – given that we cannot express everything we know in verbal language, and any description of a complex phenomenon such as personality will necessarily escape being pinned down in language.

Language and experience

If you try to describe one of your friends to someone who does not know them, you will see how hard it is to paint a verbal portrait of them. It is equally difficult to capture the taste of a strawberry, the colour of the sea or falling in love in the metaphorical butterfly net of language. Reality, it seems, always spills beyond any description that we are able to give of it. It is impossible to capture the knower's experience in language. For example, no words can convey the qualia or quality of my own subjective experience of the smell and taste of drinking a cup of coffee right now.

Moreover, the nature of some experiences is that they are difficult to articulate. For example, if you consider those who were first to circumnavigate the globe in a boat, or one of the 556 people who have been to space, you might consider how they would use language to describe and communicate their experience. When Italian astronaut Samantha Cristoforetti (1977–) saw Earth from space, this is how she articulated her new perspective: 'You've got this planet beneath you, and a lot of what you see, especially during the day, does not necessarily point to a human presence. If you look at it on a geologic timescale, it's almost like we are this flimsy presence, and we really have to stick together as a human family to make sure we are a permanent presence on this planet and not just this blink of an eye.'

Furthermore, some people would argue that some experiences cannot be articulated in any language, not even in metaphorical language. For example, according to the American philosopher and psychologist William James (1842–1910), the nature of a religious or mystical experience is that it is *ineffable*, that is 'No adequate report can be given in words', and it cannot be communicated to others via language. Interestingly, mystics in all the great world religions have held that the deepest truths cannot be expressed in language. The Taoist sage Lao Tzu (c 600 BCE) observes that 'Those who speak do not know; those who know do not speak'; the Buddhist *Lankaatara Sutra* tells us that 'Truth is beyond letters and words and books'; and in Judaism, the Talmud says that 'If silence be good for the wise, how much the better for fools.'

KEY WORD

stereotype: a fixed, oversimplified and often negative picture of an individual or group, based on their membership of that group

KEY WORD

qualia: the experience of a phenomenon arising from sense perception

Figure 6.8: How far can language convey qualia or experience?

EXPLORE 6.12

Investigate the words used to communicate their experience when a person or group of people have made a new discovery. Find two or three quotations from an extract of your choice, and contribute them to a class presentation or display board. Add a comment summarising the ways in which the language contributed to the power of the description. What does their language tell you about the significance of their experience and discovery?

You might explore one or more of the following, or a related example of your own choice:

- the words used by Sir Francis Drake, when he circumnavigated the globe in the *Golden Hind*

- the words used by Andrew Wiles, having proved Fermat's *Last Theorem*

- the words of any of the people who have walked on the moon

- the words of Carl Sagan, in response to seeing an image of the Earth from Space, known as *Pale Blue Dot*

REAL-LIFE SITUATION 6.4

Are some experiences beyond description? For example, does religious experience lie beyond language?

REFLECTION

In his publication *Personal Knowledge,* the polymath Michael Polanyi (1891–1976) said 'We remain ever unable to say all we know, so also … we can never quite know what is implied in what we say.'

CONTINUED

Can you think of an experience you have had that no matter how hard you tried, you could not fully express what you felt at the time? At the other end of the spectrum, can you think of words you have read or heard (in a poem, song or the words of someone special) that have meant far more to you than the literal meaning the words conveyed? What are the implications for the transmission of knowledge through language?

6.6 Language and thought

DISCUSS 6.21

How do we represent the world in language? How far can language either describe the world, or express our beliefs about the world?

In this section, we will consider the extent to which language influences the way we think about the world. Complex thinking seems to be closely connected to language, although language and thought are not the same thing. It is hard to see how someone could do calculus or trigonometry if they did not have the appropriate mathematical vocabulary. More generally, it might be hard to have various abstract ideas if you did not have the appropriate vocabulary. Admittedly, we sometimes think in images and then struggle to find the appropriate words, but we usually know what we think only after we have put it into language. Nevertheless, to come up with a new way of thinking usually requires the development of a new vocabulary – and this is one of the hallmarks of genius.

. . . As imagination bodies forth

The forms of things unknown, the poet's pen

Turns them to shapes, and gives to airy nothing

A local habitation and a name.

William Shakespeare, *A Midsummer Night's Dream*

REAL-LIFE SITUATION 6.5

If you speak more than one language, are there some things that are easier to think of in one language or the other?

The Sapir–Whorf hypothesis

According to the Sapir–Whorf hypothesis, language determines our experience of reality, and we can see and think only what our language allows us to see and think. There are two interpretations of this theory. Lingusitic determinism claims that our language determines our knowledge, whereas lingusitic relativity claims that language influences what you know.

> **KEY WORD**
>
> Sapir–Whorf hypothesis: the claim that the language you speak influences or determines the way you see the world

Benjamin Whorf (1879–1941), one of the proponents of the hypothesis, studied the difference between the language of the Hopi Indians of North America and European languages, and came to the surprising conclusion that the Hopi language contains no words, grammatical forms, constructions or expressions that refer directly to what we call 'time', or to past, present or future, or to enduring or lasting. Since the Hopi have no words for it, Whorf came to the conclusion that they have no concept of abstract time.

According to Edward Sapir (1884–1939), the other proponent of the hypothesis, 'The 'real world' is to a large extent unconsciously built upon the language habits of the group. No two languages are ever sufficiently similar to be considered as representing the same social reality. The worlds in which different societies live are distinct worlds, not merely the same world with different labels attached . . . We see and hear and otherwise experience very largely as we do because the language habits of our community predispose certain choices of interpretation.' For example, some people go to a forest and see trees, others see ash, birch, oak, larch, chestnut, etc. So even with the same language, the second group might see a much richer forest.

There are two interpretations of this hypothesis: **linguistic relativity** and **linguistic determinism**.

The implications of this hypothesis are significant for knowledge and knowing. If the hypothesis is correct, it follows that a culture can and does impose its own categories of thinking on the knower. Rather than the classifications and categories referring to the world, they are a product and an invention of culture. The stronger version of the hypothesis suggests that we are trapped in language, given that our thought patterns are already pre-determined by the language we inherit.

A more modern example has been put forward by the psychologist, Lera Bordisky (1976–). She claims that the gender of nouns shapes the way in which people think, specifically in relation to the qualities associated with them. For example, the German word for bridge 'die Brücke', which is feminine, leads German speakers to think of bridges with associations such as beautiful, slender and elegant; whereas the Spanish word for bridge 'el puente', which is masculine, results in Spanish speakers thinking of bridges in relation to strength and sturdiness. It is possible that this interpretation could be criticised for relying on gender stereotypes; however, it raises the key point about the effect that language has on the way we think.

> **KEY WORDS**
>
> **linguistic relativity:** the 'weaker' interpretation, that language shapes and influences the way we think and what we can know
>
> **linguistic determinism:** the 'stronger' interpretation, that our language and its structures limit and determine what and how we think, and what we can know

---

REAL-LIFE SITUATION 6.6

Are there some concepts that you cannot grasp? If so, is this a result of language? In what ways might language limit what it is possible for you to think?

Testing the hypothesis

Despite the above evidence, some people are not convinced by the Sapir–Whorf hypothesis. Our mental processes relate to, but are not necessarily the same as, language – we do not always think in words and sentences. Language and thought can be different from one another. For example, if you are asked to match similar shapes from a group of shapes, you may be able to picture them and then rotate them in your mind. When we think, we sometimes think beyond words and sentences. Further arguments against are explored below.

1 According to critics, although the Sapir–Whorf hypothesis says that language determines thought, there is in fact evidence to suggest that thought is possible without language. Psychologists have discovered that babies and animals are able

to think without the benefit of language. Some experiments have shown that babies as young as five months can do a simple form of mental arithmetic. And pigeons have been trained to identify general classes such as trees, human beings, bodies of water, dogs and fish. The key point here is that thinking is not necessarily the same as language – and it is wrong to assume that they are the same thing, or that language is essential to thought. It is also wrong to assume that all people think in the same ways.

2   Some creative people claim that language plays only a secondary role in their thinking, and that their ideas first come to them in images. Indeed, only some people think in sentences. Albert Einstein once observed: 'The words of a language as they are written and spoken do not seem to play any role in the mechanisms of my thought. The physical entities which seem to serve as elements in thought are certain signs and more or less clear images which can be voluntarily reproduced and combined. The above-mentioned elements are, in my case, of visual, and some of muscular type. Conventional words or other signs have to be sought for laboriously only in a secondary stage.'

3   We sometimes struggle to find the right words to express thoughts that feel as if they are already there. You have probably had the experience of saying something, and then adding in frustration 'No, that's not quite what I want to say', and then trying to express yourself with greater clarity. This suggests that our thoughts are there prior to language, and that we are simply trying to find the right words with which to express them.

4   If language determines thought, it is unclear how new words ever enter a language, or indeed, how language could have arisen in the first place. The most obvious explanation is that some kind of pre-linguistic thought is possible for which we later find words.

5   When we remember what we have heard or read, we often do not recall exact sentences, but instead we recollect the gist of what was heard or read. This suggests that the gist is a thought that relates to but is not the same as language, suggesting that thought does not always depend on language.

REFLECTION

Think about how you think. Not everyone processes thoughts in the same way. Are you a person who primarily thinks in words and sentences, or are you a person who primarily thinks in images, or do your thoughts take a different form?

EXPLORE 6.13

Plan and write a speech for a class debate: 'This house believes that language shapes and influences how we think and what we can know.'

In your speech, either for or against the motion, try and support your argument with good reasons, evidence and specific, concrete examples (from your own IB Diploma Programme studies). Then organise and deliver the debate. Vote on the motion before and after the debate.

Self-assessment

How well have you understood the arguments for and against whether language shapes what we know? Consider your response against these criteria:

CONTINUED

- Did you understand both sides of the argument?

- Did you think about how evidence and examples could support each side of the argument?

- Did you consider different perspectives and viewpoints?

- Did you arrive at a balanced conclusion?

6.7 Language and values

REAL-LIFE SITUATION 6.7

How does the language we use influence others, and shape their feelings and thoughts?

Earlier in the chapter, we explored meaning and language, and noted that meaning is dependent on multiple factors, including context, tone of voice and an understanding of the relationship between the people speaking. We use language not only to describe the world, but also to persuade and influence one another. It is possible that one person's criminal is another person's victim. Our choice of words do more than describe. Instead, our words convey our attitudes and express our values, something we will cover in Chapter 14, where we examine the difference between positive statements of fact and normative statements of value.

Using language to influence and persuade

To explore the connection between language and values further, consider ways in which language can be used to influence and persuade.

Figure 6.9: How far does language describe the world or express our feelings and beliefs?

Emotionally laden language

Some words have not only a descriptive meaning, but also an **emotive meaning**. Emotive meaning can be defined as 'the aura of favourable or unfavourable feeling that hovers about a word'. While some words such as 'hero', 'peace' and 'democracy' have positive connotations, others such as 'thief', 'liar' or 'pervert' have negative ones. That is why everyone claims to be in favour of peace, and no one likes to be labelled a liar. Language can be used not only to *reveal* certain aspects of reality, but also to conceal other aspects by diverting attention away from them.

> **KEY WORD**
>
> emotive meaning: the aura of favourable or unfavourable feeling that hovers about a word

> ### EXPLORE 6.14
>
> Analyse the way language is being used in each of the following pairs of expressions:
>
> a   terrorist / freedom fighter
>
> b   prolife / prochoice
>
> c   free speech / hate speech
>
> d   internet troll / online moderator
>
> e   public servant / career politician
>
> f   clique / microcosm
>
> g   make a decision / take a decision
>
> h   goodbye / farewell
>
> i   global warming / climate change

Although the influence of emotionally laden language is a matter of continuing debate, there is evidence to suggest that how people respond to survey questions depends on how they are phrased. In one US survey, when people were asked if more money should be spent on 'assistance to the poor', 68% replied 'yes'; but when they were asked if more money should be spent on 'welfare', the number dropped to 24%. In another survey, people were far more willing to spend money on 'national defence' than on the 'military'.

Modifier words

Modifier words are words such as 'many', 'should' and 'probably' which people slip into sentences to give themselves an escape route. For example, a manufacturer might say, 'Our product will work for you if you simply follow the instructions carefully.' You buy the product; it does not work; and when you phone up to complain, you are told that you clearly did not follow the instructions carefully enough. However, from another perspective, moderators make speech more accurate by avoiding sweeping generalisations.)

> **KEY WORD**
>
> modifier words: words that qualify a seemingly clear and precise statement, and make it vague or ambiguous

EXPLORE 6.15

Consider how modifier words are used in each of the following cases:

a   Our product can restore up to 25% of lost hair.

b   Probably the best lager in the world.

c   Dentifresh toothpaste helps fight tooth decay.

d   If Timothy works hard, he should do himself justice in the final exam.

What would be the implications for truth if the 'modifier words' were removed?

Grammar

Grammar can also affect the way people see things. For example, the passive voice may be used to cover up someone's responsibility for something. Compare the following two sentences:

a   Many villages were bombed.

b   We bombed many villages.

While the first sentence makes the bombing sound as if anyone might have been responsible, the second puts the spotlight on the perpetrators.

Language as an instrument of power and authority

While opinions differ about the relation between language and values, the fact that political parties and businesses invest so heavily in media consultants and **spin doctors** suggests that they think that it plays an important role in shaping our attitudes. At the limit, the seductive eloquence of demagogues such as Adolf Hitler reminds us that language can be used not only to educate and enlighten, but also to fuel the flames of hatred. So, we would be well-advised to take seriously the slogan that '*language is power*'. A more everyday example might be the power of your language in an essay, a presentation or a group discussion. For example, your ability to express yourself in written or spoken language gives you a capacity to share your thoughts with others, and the power to express your ideas.

KEY WORD

spin doctor: a person whose role it is to portray a political party in a favourable light, especially to present the media with a positive interpretation of a particular event

REFLECTION

Think about how words can convey power and authority. What sorts of things do you usually say or write in strong, powerful ways, and what do you say or write in a more tentative manner? What is it about your use of words in both cases that makes them seem powerful or not?

Language and politics

Political language lends itself to scrutiny and analysis. Language can be a vehicle for maintaining an existing power structure. For example, the CEO of a company, a headteacher or a religious leader might use language to establish and maintain a hierarchical organisation. A political narrative can be used to unite or divide people. A narrative that emphasises differences based on gender, ethnicity or class could be used to reinforce prejudice or maintain social and political divisions. Equally, language can be used to inspire revolutions, and to promote and encourage criticism and dissent. Written language, whether a religious sacred text or a political manifesto, might also function as a source of authority.

DISCUSS 6.22

1   To what extent does the language of politicians link to beliefs about national identity or a particular historical memory?

2   How far does the language of politics promote harmony or division?

There are particular challenges to understanding the historical context of political language. For example, in 1956, Mao Zedong (1893–1976) famously invited intellectuals to share their ideas about the communist state: 'Let a hundred flowers bloom, let a hundred schools of thought contend.' The Communist Party encouraged freedom of speech and freedom of thought in the Hundred Flowers Campaign. However, from 1957–1959, the Communist Party opposed those who spoke out, inflicting severe punishments from job loss and imprisonment to forced work in labour camps.

'There is huge debate among historians about how this language should be interpreted and some academics translate it to 'blossom' rather than 'bloom'. Moreover, Mao himself revised his interpretation for the published version of his speech in 1957. This is a historiographical problem – a theme that we explore in Chapter 10. Some believe that Mao was surprised and shocked by the level of criticism. For example, Lee Feigon (1945–), a Chinese American historian, takes a more favourable view of Mao as an intellectual who made a genuine move to encourage these ideas to come to the fore. By contrast, other historians think that the Hundred Flowers Campaign was a deliberate move to identify opponents. For example, Jung Chang (1952–) understands Mao's statement as a deliberate trick to entice enemies of communism. It is difficult to know for certain what Mao Zedong meant, and what he intended when he spoke. The Hundred Flowers Campaign is an example of the effects of inviting open criticism of the state, encouraging freedom of speech and of the consequences, and how a political regime punished those who were perceived as ideological opponents or enemies of the state.

EXPLORE 6.16

Choose a political leader from a particular country of your choice. Find a recent speech they have delivered, or their interpretation of a current event. Examine their use of language. Consider their language in relation to the following:

- How far do they present facts, interpretations and opinions?

- Do they appeal to emotions?

- Do they appeal to a person's identity based on nationality, gender or ethnicity?

- Do they reinforce similarities or differences between people?

Propaganda

Political organisations and governments can use language to create **propaganda** and spin. In politics, the role of a spin doctor is to present political events in a favourable light to the media, in order to influence public opinion. Spin is a form of propaganda, which might make use of so-called **alternative facts**. A fact can be either true or false, but an alternative fact – a term coined in 2017 – suggests that this distinction is not clear-cut in the context of politics.

George Orwell's novel, *1984*, shows an imaginary dystopian world in which language can be used to manipulate and control thought. Orwell imagines a totalitarian government called 'Ingsoc' which seeks to control not only how people behave but also what they think, by inventing a new language called Newspeak:

> 'The purpose of Newspeak was not only to provide a medium of expression for the world-view and mental habits proper to devotees of Ingsoc, but to make all other modes of thought impossible. It was intended that when Newspeak had been adopted once and for all and Oldspeak forgotten, a heretical thought – that is, a thought diverging from the principles of Ingsoc – should be literally unthinkable, at least so far as thought is dependent on words. The word "free" still existed in Newspeak, but it could only be used in such statements as "This dog is free from lice" or "This field is free from weeds". It could not be used in its old sense of "politically free" or "intellectually free", since political and intellectual freedom no longer existed even as concepts, and were therefore of necessity nameless. Newspeak was designed not to extend but to diminish the range of thought, and this purpose was indirectly assisted by cutting the choice of words down to a minimum.'

DISCUSS 6.23

When and how is language used for the purposes of propaganda?

How far do you think that the use of neutral language is possible or desirable?

Language at war

The fact that language is not innocent, and can be used to manipulate the way we see things, is particularly apparent in times of war. Military training camps have long been aware that to get their troops to kill, the enemy need to be dehumanised. Here are some more examples of 'warspeak', which is often used to cover up the reality on the ground.

Warspeak	Real meaning
security assistance	arms sales
neutralise	kill
no longer a factor	dead
take out	destroy
inoperative combat personnel	dead soldiers
pacification	bombing
service a target	drop bombs on a target

KEY WORDS

propaganda: the deliberate manipulation of information in order to influence what people think, usually for political purposes

alternative facts: in the context of post-truth politics, the view that alternative information might count as a fact

Warspeak	Real meaning
collateral damage	bombed cities
friendly fire	accidentally fire on your own troops
strategic redeployment	retreat
liberate	invade
reporting guidelines	censorship
pre-emptive	unprovoked
ethnic cleansing	genocide

EXPLORE 6.17

With a partner, discuss the two lists above, and explore the difference between the warspeak and the real meanings of these words.

Consider these questions below. Present your ideas to the class and contribute to a class discussion:

* How far is it possible to describe war using words with 'real meanings'?

* How far does language describe the world or communicate values and attitudes?

DISCUSS 6.24

1   How might our values influence the language we use, and the way that we represent the world using models and metaphors?

2   How does language impact on our feelings and thoughts? Are we ethically responsible for our choice of language?

6.8 Language and technology

Digital technology is changing the way that we think about language. There is a question arising about whether machines can understand language. In one way, they cannot. There are many situations in which information is communicated, but no one would describe it as language. For example, if you put a coin in a vending machine and press the button which says '*coffee white with sugar*', you get coffee white with sugar. Although information has clearly been communicated, you would not say the vending machine *understood* that you wanted a cup of coffee. Vending machines – and other mechanical devices – are simply not in the business of understanding things.

However, in another way, in the sense of **weak artificial intelligence**, they can. There are chatbots that can mimic speech and examples of weak AI, such as Alexa™ and Siri™, that can recognise and respond to limited instructions. Voice recognition is increasingly sophisticated to the extent that you can dictate and send an email using your voice, as a result of the technology of voice recognition.

KEY WORD

weak artificial intelligence: also known as applied AI or narrow AI, it is the use of software for a specific problem-solving or reasoning task

Benefits and drawbacks of technology for language

On the one hand, technology can contribute positively to the development of language.

New words and phrases are introduced as a result of technology – from *hashtag*, *Google it* and *emoji* to *podcast* and *comic sans font*. One new development is that we can see what 'real', unedited writing looks like. The internet makes language a rich source – from 'unedited' blog posts to facilitating group chats – increasing our sense of language that is not controlled, authorised nor filtered.

EXPLORE 6.18

Generate a list of further examples of words that have entered the English language as a result of the technological revolution.

Technology can also help people who are unable to speak. For example, Dawn Faizey-Webster (1972–) who has locked-in syndrome, communicates using the blink of her left eye. She has 'blinked out' a degree, and is the first person ever with locked-in syndrome to be studying for a PhD. She can blink out words at a rate of 50 words per hour, communicate her ideas and contribute to knowledge through her research. The theoretical physicist Stephen Hawking (1942–2018) was diagnosed with motor neurone disease in the early 1960s, and when he eventually lost his speech, he was still able to communicate with a speech-generating device. Living with this condition and using this technology for 50 years, he made an enormous contribution to science. In the mid-1980s, Hawking used an 'Equaliser' – a computer programme that enabled him to communicate by simulating his speech from the bank of 3,000 or so words and phrases he could pre-select. He used a hand-held device to select the words, and he could generate 15 words a minute. Stephen Hawking wrote lectures in advance, and delivered them using a speech synthesiser. The Equaliser spoke the words in an American accent, and Hawking later had the option to change it, but was keen to keep it the same, as he recognised it and others identified him by this voice, too. This example shows that technology can facilitate intended language – and Hawking was able to make an enormous contribution to knowledge within theoretical physics as Lucasian Professor of Mathematics at Cambridge University. These examples highlight how technology can support those with a disability, and that language is a capacity that we can have without speech, thanks to the power of technology to assist with communication.

However, technology can introduce new problems. Increasingly, the knower is becoming the source of language where AI can 'read' us – when we put down an, eReader a note can be made of the point where we became bored; and the traces of digital communication we leave on Instagram™, WhatsApp™ and Facebook™ can be read and used to build a picture of who we are. We are becoming the text and the language source for AI to interpret and use for purposes that we may not have given our consent to. In the same way that a laser could be used as a weapon to hurt, or used in eye surgery to help, so too words can be misused to harm or to benefit.

You might consider the effect of Twitter™ on language use and communication. On the one hand, it is a quick and efficient means of mass communication. However,

---

KEY WORD

Locked-in syndrome: A neurological condition where damage to part of the brain stem results in loss of voluntary muscle control and speech. A person with this condition usually retains their cognitive function, consciousness, and eye movements, and the capacity to communicate via blinking.

it also allows internet trolls to communicate hatred and ridicule, which can damage a person's mental health, reputation and livelihood. Jon Ronson (1967–), a documentary filmmaker and journalist, describes how an ill-judged tweet can ruin a career or a person's entire reputation. The language we use is coming under more scrutiny, exposing people to the judgement of internet trolls.

An Emoji is a picture on a keyboard that can be added to electronic messages and texts such as facial expressions, depictions of animals, places, objects and various symbols. In 2015, Oxford English Dictionary voted the '*face with tears as joy*' as their Word of the Year, suggesting that the genre of emojis have become part of modern western popular language. Emojis suggest the flexibility of language and an example of how technology is influencing how we communicate meaning.

REAL-LIFE SITUATION 6.8

1   Twitter limits users to only 280 characters per 'tweet'. What impact does this have on language? Does it help the knower, does it reduce or enhance what we know?

2   What might be the consequences of a tweet that many people find unethical?

REFLECTION

Do you find it easier or more difficult to express yourself by typing on a computer compared with writing with a pen and paper? Does it depend on what you want to write? How might using different media shape what you say and the way that you say it?

Figure 6.10: Stephen Hawking spoke via technology. How might technology help or hinder our use and communication of knowledge?

EXPLORE 6.19

How might you make use of linguistic objects in your TOK exhibition? For example, a tweet by a political leader could be an example of an object. Choose a tweet by a political leader, and consider how this specific digital object could be used in a TOK exhibition. Find some examples online of various tweets and compare them. Do they describe the world, or express the values of the speaker?

6.9 Language and ethics

DISCUSS 6.25

How far do ethical claims describe the world, or express feelings and emotions?

Our language can express our values and our choice of language is linked closely with ethics. Earlier in this chapter we have touched on ethical issues arising implicitly from language. For example, questions about right and wrong were involved in our discussion of language that may be interpreted as manipulative, misleading or rhetorical. Language conveys ethical values and attitudes such as respect or lack of respect. Furthermore, in certain contexts, language can be used to include or exclude others in a group. There are significant questions linking language and ethics such as freedom of speech, censorship of language and questions about whether we are free to use language that might cause offence?

In this final section, we explore the nature of ethical knowledge, and the language we use to express ethical claims. We all have beliefs about what is right and wrong, from what a government *should* do to protect democracy and how a driverless car *should* be programmed, to whether I *should* lie to my friend or be kind to them if I do not like their new haircut. If I express my view that something is right or wrong, I am making an ethical clam. Ethical language uses the imperative words *should* and *must*. Moreover, ethical language involves using words such as *good* and *bad*, and the words *right* and *wrong*. You might wonder whether these words refer to a property in the world we observe or whether they are simply expressions of personal like and dislike.

Emotivism is the view that ethical claims express emotions. If I describe something as 'good', 'virtuous' or 'right', I am expressing my pro-attitude or approval. Equally, if I describe something as 'bad' or 'wrong', I am expressing my feelings of disapproval. It follows that ethical claims do nothing more than express the personal attitudes and emotional feelings of the speaker, and they do not describe a property in the world. For example, if I say 'It is right to help others', it is similar to the claim that 'I like ice-cream'. **Prescriptivism** is the view that ethical claims are imperatives or instructions of what should be done; for example, 'Killing is wrong' means the same as 'Do not kill'. In contrast, other people would argue that there can be moral facts – they might say that the phrase 'Killing is wrong' is more than an imperative – it is a moral fact.

According to a group of thinkers known now as the *logical positivists*, ethical statements are meaningless. In the context of post-war Vienna in the 1920s, they challenged the meaning of language used by the political establishment and religious institutions. They argued that in order for a statement to be meaningful, it had to be verified. They argued

KEY WORDS

emotivism: the view that ethical claims are an expression of feeling and emotion

prescriptivism: the view that ethical claims are imperatives

that whereas scientific claims could be verified using an appeal to evidence, in contrast, religious, aesthetic and ethical claims could not be verified and were meaningless. The logical positivists had diverse views within their group, and many critiques of their views have been offered since. Verification and evidence, while important concepts, might not be necessary conditions of knowing something. Some people would argue that there are many knowledge claims we make that may be true even if they lack evidence to verify them – such as knowing 'this painting is beautiful', or that 'it is good to help others', or even the secular or religious belief that 'there is a meaning and purpose to life'.

EXPLORE 6.20

Choose an ethical issue where opinion is divided. Look at the arguments for and against, paying close attention to the language used. Do you think that ethical claims can describe a property in the world, or in our mind?

DISCUSS 6.26

1   What makes an ethical claim meaningful? What do we mean when we use ethical language and describe something as right or wrong?

2   In what ways is language in ethics the same or different compared to language used in history, natural and human sciences or the arts?

REFLECTION

Do you ever think about the ethical implications of the language you use? Can you think of ways in which the use of some language might be ethical in some circumstances but unethical in others?

6.10 Conclusion

Since much of our knowledge comes to us in words, our discussion of language in this chapter is clearly relevant to our quest for knowledge. Perhaps the key thing you will have discovered is that language is not as simple or straightforward as you first thought. We need to know what a statement means before we can decide whether it is true or false, but in practice, it is difficult to fix the meanings of words with complete precision.

REAL-LIFE SITUATION 6.9

Do you think it is possible to know something without the language to express it?

As a final point, brief mention should be made of two different views about the relationship between language and knowledge. On one side, some people claim that in order to know something, you must be able to put it into words, and that 'if you can't say it then you don't know it' (Hans Reichenbach, 1891–1953). Such a robust view suggests that the only way to demonstrate your understanding of something is to put it into words and share it with other people. Against this, other people insist that some of our knowledge is personal and lies beyond words; and that, as the Hungarian thinker Michael Polanyi (1891–1976) claimed, we know more than we can say. He also made the point that our words say more than we can know. Advocates of this view argue that our practical knowledge and knowledge of things we are acquainted with goes beyond our ability to describe them. This takes us back to the phrase mentioned in Chapter 3 – 'the map is not the territory' and in this sense language may not be able to perfectly describe the world around us.

There is a perceived gap here between the map and the territory. What is this fascinating gap – between what we know and what there really is? It would be wrong to assume that our knowledge perfectly maps the real world, and that our language expresses the real world. There are significant implications for us as knowers- consider the implications of the fact that language cannot perfectly map and describe the world. Is there a truth beyond language? Is it meaningful to speak of a reality beyond language? Our language may express our beliefs about the world and, as critical thinkers, we might strive towards holding beliefs that are justified – but we know that our knowledge of the world as it really is, is limited; and that language, while a remarkable aspect of human evolution, may be able to communicate what the knower believes they know, but it cannot describe the true nature of the world.

EXPLORE 6.21

TOK exhibition practice

Choose one of the knowledge prompts, prescribed by the IB for your TOK exhibition, which your teacher can give you.

1   Propose three or more suitable linguistic objects that link to the prompt.

2   Discuss the relationships between the objects and the prompt.

3   Justify your choice of object, in relation to the knowledge prompt.

Peer-assessment

Work in pairs and evaluate your partner's work.

1   How are the chosen objects suited to the knowledge prompt?

2   Can your partner offer a justification for their choice?

3   Suggest next steps for your partner. How compelling is their justification? What went well? What would be better?

KNOWLEDGE QUESTIONS

1   To what extent does language help or hinder us as knowers in two areas of knowledge?

2   To what extent is it possible to know something without language?

3   Considering two areas of knowledge, to what extent does language contribute to shallow, binary or polarised thinking?

6.11 Linking questions

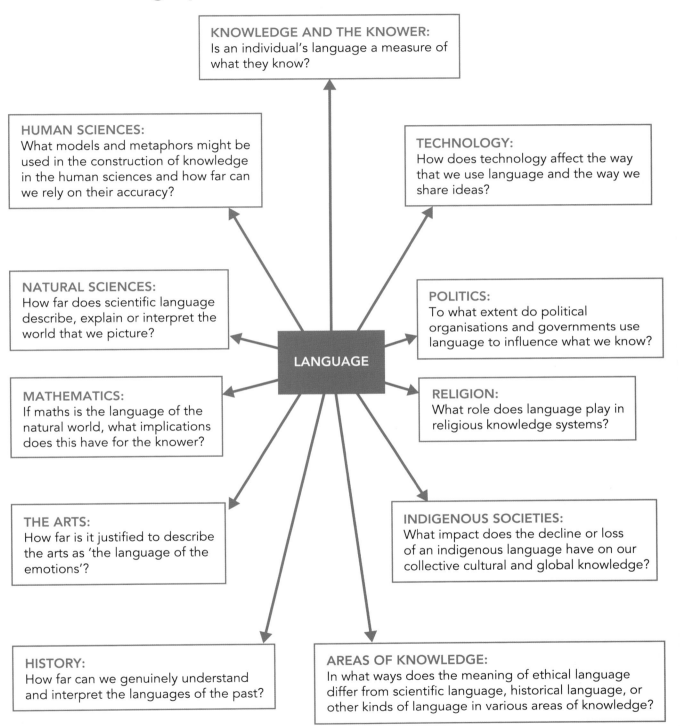

KNOWLEDGE AND THE KNOWER:
Is an individual's language a measure of what they know?

HUMAN SCIENCES:
What models and metaphors might be used in the construction of knowledge in the human sciences and how far can we rely on their accuracy?

TECHNOLOGY:
How does technology affect the way that we use language and the way we share ideas?

NATURAL SCIENCES:
How far does scientific language describe, explain or interpret the world that we picture?

POLITICS:
To what extent do political organisations and governments use language to influence what we know?

LANGUAGE

MATHEMATICS:
If maths is the language of the natural world, what implications does this have for the knower?

RELIGION:
What role does language play in religious knowledge systems?

THE ARTS:
How far is it justified to describe the arts as 'the language of the emotions'?

INDIGENOUS SOCIETIES:
What impact does the decline or loss of an indigenous language have on our collective cultural and global knowledge?

HISTORY:
How far can we genuinely understand and interpret the languages of the past?

AREAS OF KNOWLEDGE:
In what ways does the meaning of ethical language differ from scientific language, historical language, or other kinds of language in various areas of knowledge?

6.12 Check your progress

Reflect on what you have learned in this chapter and indicate your confidence level between 1 and 5 (where 5 is the highest score and 1 is the lowest). If you score below 3, re-visit that section. Come back to this list later in your course. Has your confidence grown?

	Confidence level	Re-visited?
Can I discuss how language and speech are characteristics that have emerged and evolved over time?		
Am I aware that animals and humans both use communication, but that spoken language is distinct in that it is a complex phenomenon made possible by multiple biological, anatomical, cognitive and neurological developments?		
Am I aware of the difference between speech and body language?		
Can I discuss the ways in which language is rule-governed, creative, innovative and intended?		
Am I aware that our capacity for language learning itself might be thought of as a skill or a matter of know-how?		
Can I describe different theories of meaning and their shortcomings – the definition, denotation and images theories of meaning?		
Can I discuss problematic and ambiguous meaning, and am I aware that interpretation is an aspect of all communication and language?		
Am I aware of the role language plays in our social and personal identity, and how the language we use is influenced by who we are speaking to?		
Can I discuss how different languages divide the world up in different ways and the problems of translating from one language to another?		
Am I aware that translation involves interpretation, and is more of an art than a science?		
Do I understand how, given that we use language to label and classify, this brings with it the danger that we misclassify or stereotype things?		
Do I appreciate that qualia (experience) can be difficult to communicate in language?		
Am I aware that we tend to think along the lines of our linguistic categories?		
Can I explain that although language may not *determine* our experience, as claimed by the Sapir–Whorf hypothesis, it is possible that it *influences* it?		
Can I distinguish between language that describes facts and language that expresses values?		
Am I aware of the ways in which language can be used to influence and persuade, and as a means to power and authority?		
Can I discuss how technology might help or hinder the use and communication of language?		
Can I understand ethical language and what it means?		
Am I aware of the responsibility of using and communicating language?		

6.13 Continue your journey

- To build on the knowledge that you have gained in this chapter, you could read some of the following articles.

- To extend your general understanding of the **science of language, psychology and the mind, read**: Steven Pinker, *The Language Instinct: The New Science of Language and Mind*, Penguin, 1995.

- For an exploration of the **science of language, with sections on what language is, the study of language and language and the brain**, read: P.H. Matthews, *Linguistics: A Very Short Introduction*, Oxford University Press, 2003.

- For a fascinating overview of the **origins and evolution of languages**, read: Guy Deutscher, *The Unfolding of Language: An Evolutionary Tour of Mankind's Greatest Invention*, Randon House 2005.

- For a short, accessible and entertaining book with chapters on **how we acquire language, whether animals have language, translation, and the relation between language and thought**, read: Donna Jo Napoli and Vera Lee-Schoenfeld, *Language Matters*, Oxford University Press, 2010.

- For an exploration of how **metaphors** pervade our language and often shape our thinking without our being aware of it, such metaphors as 'argument is war' and 'time is money', read: George Lakoff and Mark Johnson, *Metaphors We Live By*, University of Chicago Press, 1980.

> Chapter 7

Knowledge and politics

LEARNING INTENTIONS

This chapter will explore some of the traditional themes of politics as well as more contemporary debates, with a particular focus on the politics of knowledge.

You will:

- consider how knowledge is related to political power and authority

- examine how different perspectives lead to dissent and civil disobedience, and their roles in changing societies

- learn about some of the different political systems and the different methods they employ in making political decisions

- consider the advantages and disadvantages of political spectra as political models

- explore how different political frameworks can affect our beliefs about ownership and resource distribution

- learn about what we understand by *social justice*, *equality* and *equity*

- learn what a knowledge economy is, understand the political nature of knowledge hierarchies and appreciate the cost of knowledge production and its implications

- learn about the economic value and political power of intellectual capital

- study how political differences can affect the interpretation of global and international events

Analyse each of the following quotations and discuss the questions that follow.

1   'Politics determines who has the power, not who has the truth.' **Paul Krugman** (1953–)

2   'To me, consensus seems to be the process of abandoning all beliefs, principles, values and policies. So it is something in which no one believes and to which no one objects.' **Margaret Thatcher** (1925–2013)

3   'One of the penalties for refusing to participate in politics is that you end up being governed by your inferiors.' **Plato** (c 427–348 BCE)

4   'What difference does it make to the dead, the orphans and the homeless, whether the mad destruction is wrought under the name of totalitarianism or in the holy name of liberty or democracy?' **Mahatma Gandhi** (1869–1948)

5   'Politics is pointless if it does nothing to enhance the beauty of our lives.' **Howard Zinn** (1922–2010)

For each quotation, consider:

a   To what extent do you agree or disagree with the quotation?

b   How might you challenge the quotation?

c   What does the quotation tell you about the speaker's assumptions about politics?

d   Do you think the quotation could apply to all types of politics, everywhere?

7.1 Introduction

Politics is about how we make decisions for a group or as a group. A narrow view might regard politics as the exercise of power by politicians, whereas a broader view would be that politics occurs whenever power is exercised, and wherever society or some other human group organises itself. In other words, politics is often used to refer to activities associated with the governance of a country, state or region, but wherever there is an organised collection of people (for example a company, voluntary group or even a local sports club), political manoeuvring and political decisions arise.

It is sometimes said that there are two main political questions: 'Who gets what?' and 'Who decides?' However true this might be, these two foundational issues give rise to many more questions such as 'How do we choose who decides?' and countless answers are offered in response. The task for all of us is to deepen our knowledge and understanding so that we can discern the most appropriate answers for our context.

In the course of this chapter, we will see that knowledge and knowledge systems are inherently political. What is regarded as knowledge, how it is constructed, how it is shared and who it is shared with, are essentially all political issues. You will also look at some of the ideologies on **political spectra**, and consider the relationship between knowledge and politics. As you consider different political perspectives, you will be encouraged to examine your own political ideas and values, and reflect on where they might have come from.

> **KEY WORD**
>
> **political spectrum (plural spectra):** a system of classifying different political positions in relation to different political values

DISCUSS 7.1

If all knowledge is political, does this mean that all truth is political?

7.2 Political scope, power and authority

DISCUSS 7.2

Where does political authority come from?

Politics is about the ways in which decisions are made for or by groups of people, therefore almost nothing lies outside of the scope of politics. However, political scope is most often associated with power and authority.

Many people use **power** and **authority** interchangeably – we often speak of those in authority as being 'in power', because those in authority are usually the ones who wield power and exercise the rule of law. However, the words do have different meanings. Not all people who exercise power have the authority or legal backing to do so. Similarly, not every authority is able to exercise power, for example when a democratically elected government is overthrown by a military **coup**. In such circumstances, the elected government might be the theoretical authority, but it may have lost some or even all of its power to govern. When we consider the political scope of knowledge, we are thinking about the ways in which knowledge informs political views and systems, and the ways in which political perspective and systems can affect the production, distribution and use of knowledge.

DISCUSS 7.3

Do political leaders need to be knowledgeable?

Political authority

We may take it for granted that in most **states**, political authority is vested in a government; indeed, states have a government by definition, although established states can sometimes have extended periods without a government in place. Many of us grow up assuming that states naturally have authority over their citizens and territories, without ever really questioning the justification for it.

The idea that the authority of the state is granted through the tacit consent of its people is a proposal known as **social contract** theory. Many philosophers have argued that, historically, people consented (whether explicitly or implicitly) to state rule, and gave up some freedoms so as to be able to enjoy the protections of the state. They would say that each generation implicitly agrees to maintain the social contract by continuing to enjoy the state's protections. Although social contract theory is

> ### KEY WORDS
>
> **power:** the capacity to control and influence situations and people
>
> **authority:** a person or group that has a justified right to make decisions and exercise power
>
> **coup:** seizure of political power
>
> **state:** a legal entity that has one central government, which is sovereign over a defined territory and a permanent population
>
> **social contract:** an actual or implicit agreement between rulers and the people they rule, that defines the rights and responsibilities of each

predominantly associated with western philosophy, a version of the idea was first proposed by the ancient Chinese philosopher, Mo Tzu (470–391 BCE).

The Treaty of Waitangi is a rare example of an explicit social contract. It is a contract between Britain and the Maori people (the indigenous people of *Aotearoa* / New Zealand) which was signed in 1840 by representatives of the British Crown and more than 500 (but not all) Maori chiefs. The contract gave sovereignty of New Zealand to the British in exchange for certain rights, money and trade opportunities. Unfortunately, problems of translation led to the English version of the contract and the Maori version of the contract having different meanings, which in turn led to the two parties having different expectations of the terms of the treaty. The people of New Zealand have been trying to address these issues ever since.

LINKING QUESTION 7.1

Language: If different sides to an agreement sign documents in different languages, which version of the agreement is the 'true' agreement? How would you decide?

Figure 7.1: An artistic impression of a Maori chief signing the Treaty of Waitangi

Other theories for the authority of the state include the idea that we have a duty to the state because of the sacrifices made by fellow citizens, or that the state does not need our consent because we are products of the state, and we give our implicit consent when we benefit from the state and the services it provides. No matter how varied their reasons, most theorists believe that the authority of the state is morally justified. However, there are some **anarchists** who argue that instead of adhering to traditional structures of government, people should be able to create their own social organisations, and that power should not be vested in any one person or organisation. They also argue that when people do comply with an authority, it should not be as a matter of duty to that authority; rather it should be an **autonomous** decision because it is in the interest of the person to comply.

KEY WORDS

anarchist: a person who believes there should be no people or organisations who rule as a matter of right

autonomous: self-governing

Knowing what is expected of us by the society in which we live is important for each individual and that society. Membership of a society confers certain obligations upon us; our knowledge of and attitudes to those obligations define our place in society. Someone who does not know, endorse or respect the values of the society in which they live degrades that society.

DISCUSS 7.4

How do we come to know our responsibilities in the case of a social contract that we are not signatories to?

REFLECTION

To what extent do you obey the laws of your country because you have a duty to your country, family and fellow citizens, or because it is in your best interests to obey the laws?

Political power

We can think of political power as having three strands: power over, power to and power of. 'Power over' refers to dominion over territories, people and organisations that fall under an authority. 'Power to' refers to the rights of authorities, people and organisations. 'Power of' generally refers to the moral significance of rights, for example when people group together to claim their rights, they are demonstrating the power of unity.

Political power is vested in individuals according to the position of authority that they hold. Primarily it is bestowed upon authorities for the purpose of solving social problems. For many people, their motivation to enter politics is to help solve what they perceive to be problems in society; being granted political power enables them to make changes appropriate to the political position they hold.

Political power can take on different forms in different societies because of the different political structures that are in place. As political powers vary, so too do the political rights of the authorities and citizens. In some states, the government is extremely powerful and the citizens may have few rights, whereas in other states, the government's powers are more circumscribed and the government is more accountable to its citizens. The philosopher, Paul-Michel Foucault (1926–1984) argued, *'We are subjected to the production of truth through power and we cannot exercise power except through the production of truth.'* If he were correct, it would suggest that the more powerful governments are, the more 'truths' they produce, and/or the more powerful those 'truths' are.

EXPLORE 7.1

Think of a situation in which you feel powerful, and another in which you feel powerless. What is it about those situations that make you feel powerful or powerless? When you feel powerful, what sort of power do you have? When you feel powerless, who do you perceive to have the power and what sort of power do they have? To what extent is *feeling* powerful the same as *being* powerful, or *feeling* powerless the same as *being* powerless?

REAL-LIFE SITUATION 7.1

How might an imbalance of power between state and citizens affect an individual's access to knowledge, and even what is regarded as knowledge?

The relationships between authority, power and knowledge have been discussed by philosophers throughout the ages. Plato, for example, argued that we should be ruled by philosophers because philosophers hunger for knowledge rather than power, and would seek the greater good rather than primarily seek to benefit themselves. Others have observed that knowledge and power have a reciprocal nature in that they legitimise each other. Authorities use their power to legitimise certain knowledge, and that knowledge is used to legitimise the empowerment of authorities. This can be readily seen in historical and present-day theocracies, autocracies and other totalitarian states. There were just seven countries in the world with theocratic governments in 2019, although there have been many more throughout history, and there are an additional 30–40 governments that might be considered autocratic or totalitarian. Theocracies and totalitarian states decide what knowledge is legitimate, and what is not. The knowledge that they legitimise, in turn, legitimises the power that the leaders and their regimes wield.

DISCUSS 7.5

If authorities determine what counts as knowledge, and they validate knowledge that sustains their political power, how can those authorities be held to account?

It is important to note that this circularity is not only true for theocracies, autocracies and other totalitarian states; it is true of *all* authorities to some extent, albeit in more subtle ways. Every society has a politics of truth that provides a mechanism for deciding what counts as truth and what does not. Even in democratic countries, political authorities may deny knowledge that they regard as unfavourable by labelling it as 'fake', and promote 'truths' that support their own political agenda. However, many societies, particularly democratic societies, keep their authorities in check by allowing, and even encouraging, dissent. Dissent serves to foster discussion and debate, and to keep authorities accountable for their use of power.

REAL-LIFE SITUATION 7.2

To what extent is dissent encouraged or even allowed in your school, community or country? What structures are in place to facilitate dissent, and to deal with the divisions arising from dissent?

Authorities not only decide what counts as knowledge, but they also decide what knowledge needs to be shared through educational campaigns (such as campaigns to promote vaccination), what knowledge should not be shared (for example, what counts as an official secret) and what knowledge should be passed on to new and future generations through educational systems. They also determine, to a large extent, what knowledge is expanded through further research by, for example, controlling research budgets and monitoring intellectual property through such things as patent law.

REAL-LIFE SITUATION 7.3

Think about which episodes in history are on the school curriculum in your country and which are not. Which books are on your language reading list? To what extent were the books and episodes in history chosen to help mould students into citizens with the type of knowledge and beliefs that the state regards as desirable?

7.3 Political perspectives

DISCUSS 7.6

What kinds of knowledge shape our perspectives on politics?

Who we believe has the authority to rule, who we want to rule and how we want our rulers to be chosen are all political questions that invite multiple perspectives. The political parties we support, the issues we prioritise when deciding who to vote for and the degree to which we involve ourselves in political activism, all reflect our political perspectives.

DISCUSS 7.7

When different people are given the same information, why might there be disagreement between them about how to act or respond?

Civil disobedience

Even when people generally agree with the authority of the state, they sometimes question whether all laws should be followed. Plato writes about one very famous example in *Crito*. The philosopher Socrates had been sentenced to death by the state for being a destabilising influence on young people, and his friends tried to persuade him that he should escape from prison to avoid the unjust sentence. Socrates, however, argued that he should not try to escape his death sentence even though he had been falsely convicted, because to have an allegiance to the state means showing allegiance to its laws. He stressed the benefits that the law had brought to him over the years, and the fact that he had been free to leave if he objected to the law of the state, so if he were to evade the law to save himself just because he did not like the result of the law in this particular case, he would be breaking the implicit contract between citizen and state, and would therefore be guilty of the charges brought against him.

Henry David Thoreau (1817–1862), on the other hand, argued that we should obey our consciences rather than a government based on majority rule. He claimed that, '[u]nder a government which imprisons any unjustly, the true place for a just man is also a prison.' In the case of Socrates, the result would be the same, at least for Socrates, as a man unfairly sentenced. But Thoreau is arguing that, rather than continuing to obey the law, as Socrates would insist, Socrates's friends should disobey the law to demonstrate their displeasure with it, and be willing to undergo the same punishment as Socrates, which would include imprisonment and probably death.

There are many instances of when a duty to support governments that have been fairly and democratically elected is seen to conflict with our ethical responsibilities to the world. Slavery, apartheid, universal suffrage, animal rights and climate change are examples of issues that have caused some people to make a stand for ethical reasons against laws enacted and policies promoted by democratically elected governments. The rights and freedoms that many of us take for granted are only ours because of the political will of those who campaigned for them, often at great personal cost.

DISCUSS 7.8

How can we know whether laws are just or unjust? Are there occasions when we have a *moral duty* to disobey the law?

Gene Sharp (1928–2018), a political scientist, was one of the world's leading experts on non-violent revolutions. His work is thought to have been very influential in the overthrow of the Yugoslavian President, Slobodan Milošević (1941–2006) in 2000, and in bringing about the Arab Spring (2010–2012). Although the idea that governments only rule by the will and consent of the people has been discussed by philosophers through the ages, Sharp made the point that because the power of any state ultimately comes from the citizens of that state, the power structure could not be maintained without the continued obedience of the subjects. If the subjects do not obey and can develop ways of withholding their consent, the leaders will have no power and their regimes will collapse.

DISCUSS 7.9

What assumptions does Sharp make when he claims that withholding consent will lead to regime collapse? Do you think his assumptions are justified?

EXPLORE 7.2

1   In pairs or small groups, investigate an act of civil disobedience in history and present it to the class. (Well-known examples include: Gandhi's salt march, the Spanish Extremadura campaign, the non-payment of poll tax in the UK, the suffragette movement, Martin Luther King's civil rights movement and the Purple Rain protest in South Africa.)

Your presentation should include:

a   the issue underlying the example of civil disobedience you selected

b   what the protesters did to show their disobedience

c   the outcome of the acts of disobedience in the short- and long-term

Take part in a class discussion on whether civil disobedience was justified in the case you have chosen.

2   After listening to the different presentations, write a paragraph outlining what you think the criteria should be for deciding whether an act of civil disobedience is justified.

Self-assessment

Look closely at the criteria you have identified. Have you considered different perspectives? Would your criteria be useful in all of the cases your class has presented? What are the limitations of the criteria you have decided upon?

Hacktivism

A modern form of civil disobedience that is becoming increasingly common is **hacktivism**. Hacktivists are essentially computer hackers who use their hacking skills to disrupt traffic to particular websites and raise awareness of a political issue. Examples of their activities include providing citizens with access to government-censored websites, and making privacy-protected communications available to threatened groups. The methods hacktivists use are a form of cybercrime, but they are non-violent and do not put protesters at the risk of direct physical harm in the way that more traditional forms of civil disobedience can.

One of the earliest acts of hacktivism was the *Worm Against Nuclear Killers* developed by Australian hacktivists in 1989. The worm was sent to a computer network shared by the US Department of Energy and NASA, the day before the launch of Galileo (an unmanned spacecraft). Anti-NASA protestors were concerned that if Galileo broke apart in the same way that the space shuttle Challenger had in 1986, its plutonium-based modules would cause catastrophic destruction on Earth. The worm caused an image to appear on the screens of infected computers and tricked users into thinking files were being deleted, but actually did no physical damage.

In 2015, a group known as *Anonymous* began what was known as 'Operation ISIS', in which hacktivists tracked down ISIS sympathisers and operatives whom the NSA had claimed not to be able to find. They shut down more than 5,000 pro-ISIS Twitter accounts, and made multiple **Distributed Denial of Service** attacks against the terrorist organisation.

Many people regard hacktivists as digital **vigilantes**. Vigilantes are individuals or groups who take the law into their own hands, often because they perceive their governments and/or judicial systems to be inadequate. Vigilantes in the traditional sense (i.e. non-digital) sometimes form 'lynch mobs' who, often on the basis of rumours, misinformation and/or minimal information, measure out punishments to those they suspect of wrong-doing, without allowing a fair hearing. As a result, vigilantism frequently leads to injustice and the abuse, and sometimes death, of innocent people.

Others would argue that hacktivists are civil activists rather than vigilantes because they do not use physical force or intimidation. Any damage they do to their targets tends to be political, social and/or economic.

DISCUSS 7.12

We generally regard vigilantism as bad for society, yet most – if not all – fictional superheroes are vigilantes. How important is it to be consistent in our moral and ethical reasoning?

The French philosopher Paul-Michel Foucault (1926–1984) explored the relationship between power and knowledge, and noted how power is used to control and define knowledge. He argued that knowledge is always an exercise of power, and power is always a function of knowledge. It is important to note that Foucault understood the relationship between power and knowledge to be productive as well as constraining. The combination of power and knowledge not only limits what we can do, but can also open up new ways of acting and thinking about ourselves.

EXPLORE 7.3

1   Think about new knowledge you have learnt, whether in one of your IB Diploma Programme subjects or outside of school. How does that new knowledge empower you?

2   Think about who decides what counts as knowledge. Are the arbitrators and producers of knowledge people or organisations in authority?

3   Consider examination boards such as the International Baccalaureate Organisation (IBO). With a partner, brainstorm how power and knowledge reinforce each other in the context of examinations and examination boards.

4   Try to come up with another example of power and knowledge reinforcing each other.

REFLECTION

On what grounds might you call the 'naming and shaming' (and sharing) of alleged offenders on social media a form of vigilantism? To what extent is the practice of naming, shaming and sharing a way of exercising power over others?

Whistleblowing

Closely related to hacktivism is the practice of **whistleblowing**. Although whistleblowing generally relates to revealing misconduct that is occurring in a workplace, it can sometimes involve much wider issues on a national or global scale. In most cases of whistleblowing, the information revealed is usually obtained legally.

One example of this would be the leaking of highly confidential information belonging to the US National Security Agency (NSA) by Edward Snowden (1983–) in 2013.

KEY WORD

whistleblowing: when a person or group makes public or passes on information about wrongdoing usually by or within an organisation

Snowden was a former employee of the Central Intelligence Agency (CIA) and working as a contractor for the NSA at the time. He tried to raise ethical concerns about some of the NSA programmes through internal channels, but when his concerns were ignored, he copied thousands of classified NSA documents and sent them to journalists. The documents revealed the ways in which the NSA conducted wide-spread surveillance, including its access to citizens' phone records and personal text messages, and that it spied on foreign leaders, including those of allied countries.

REAL-LIFE SITUATION 7.5

Think about the NSA in terms of Foucault's analysis of power and knowledge. In what ways do those in power define different types of knowledge (thereby creating new knowledge), and how is this knowledge used to exercise power?

DISCUSS 7.13

To what extent are those in power justified in controlling access to knowledge?

The US Department of Justice charged Snowden with espionage and theft of government property, but he escaped to Russia where he was eventually given asylum. Some argue that Snowden is a traitor for putting American security at risk; however, in 2014, the UN Human Rights commissioner said that the US should not try to prosecute Snowden because his actions had been in the public interest. Later, a 2015 report by the United Nations found that Snowden's revelations were important for people everywhere by showing how government agencies were secretly wielding powers, and had made a lasting impact on law and politics because they led to new laws and legal frameworks governing surveillance powers and data protection.

KEY WORDS

espionage: the practice of spying to obtain political or military information

asylum: protection granted by a state to persons who are political refugees

DISCUSS 7.14

How might it be possible to know whether an action is ethical before we know the outcome of that action?

The ethics of whistleblowing is very difficult because it brings different ethical principles and loyalties into conflict. The issue is further complicated by the motivations of the whistleblower. Sometimes they will be motivated purely by a concern for the public good; at other times, they may have a personal grievance with the organisation or people they are exposing. Often there are elements of both.

DISCUSS 7.15

How does knowing the motivation behind an action affect our perception of the morality of that action? To what extent are actions ethical or unethical in themselves, and to what extent is their ethical nature dependent on the intent and motivation driving the actions?

7.4 Political systems, methods and tools

DISCUSS 7.16

How many different types of government are you aware of?

Political systems are the systems that states use to make decisions. The methods and tools that they use are the various processes and systems that allow the political systems to operate. These can include electoral and voting systems, party systems and administrative systems.

One of the big decisions facing states is what kind of political system they want to have. Although there were ancient Greek states that were democratic (provided you ignore the fact that women, slaves and non-citizens were denied a vote), democracy really only became a widespread, favoured form of government in the 20th century. Before the rise of democracies, **monarchies** were the most common form of government, and the role of monarch is passed on through family lines, usually (but not always) to the monarch's oldest son. Although monarchies still exist, there are very few states in which the monarch has absolute power. There are, however, numerous authoritarian states with a strong, centralised government and limited political freedoms; there are also states where the head of state – typically a president – is more a symbolic figure than someone who has real power. For example, Emperor Naruhito (1960–), who acceded to the Japanese throne in May 2019, has no political powers under Japan's constitution. His role is purely ceremonial, and he is bound to act on the advice of the government.

> **KEY WORD**
>
> **monarchy:** a form of government that has a monarch (king, queen or emperor) as the supreme authority

"I like it. It has authority."

Democracy

Democracies are traditionally understood as systems of government in which citizens and residents vote for representatives who then form a government. They provide a constitutional mechanism for making collective decisions and accommodating different points of view. Theoretically, every vote should carry equal weight and all people should be free to stand for election. If the voters are unhappy with their representatives, they can vote them out of office at the next election. Many democracies have legislation and procedures in place to help protect the rights of minority groups because, by definition, in any democracy there will always be a 'losing' minority who may need to be protected from the winning majority.

DISCUSS 7.17

How are language, emotion and reason used to persuade voters or sway their political views?

Popularly, in the West, there is a tendency to associate democracy with the freedom and equality of the people who live in the democracy. However, there are many different political and electoral systems that fall under the umbrella of democracy. Although people ideally have a free and equal vote in democratic elections, the type of electoral system in place significantly impacts the results of any election. Although the 'majority' rule in any democracy, the majority can be counted in many different ways, and it is far from the case that it always means 'more votes'. Different types of democracy, different electoral systems and different electoral boundaries often mean that some people's votes carry more weight than others.

EXPLORE 7.4

Singly or in pairs, find out how one electoral system works. Each person or pair in the class should try to choose a different electoral system. (Examples include the first-past-the-post, two-round, electoral college, mixed member proportional representation, party list proportional representation and preferential voting systems.) Each student or pair should then explain the system they have looked at to the rest of the class. As a class, try to decide which system you believe to be most 'fair', and why? Is 'fairness' or 'simplicity' more important in a political system?

REAL-LIFE SITUATION 7.6

What does 'fair' mean in politics? Are there any grounds on which you could say you *know* one system to be fairer, rather than to believe it?

An organisation called the Economist Intelligence Unit (EIU) has created a democracy index by which it ranks countries around the world each year according to how democratic they are. The index considers information such as whether elections are free and fair, and whether the civil service can implement government policies. According to the EIU, some countries have become increasingly democratic in recent years, but other have become less so. According to the EIU classification, full democracies are states in which civil liberties and political freedoms are respected, there is an independent **judiciary** and independent media.

KEY WORD

judiciary: the system of courts and collection of judges in a country

REAL-LIFE SITUATION 7.7

What issues might arise when trying to quantify abstract and subjective concepts such as freedom and independence?

In 2018, it was claimed that of the 167 countries rated, only 20 were full democracies. 55 countries (including the USA) were found to be flawed democracies, in which free and fair elections are held but they had significant problems through low participation in the political process and/or issues in the functioning of governance. 39 countries were determined to be democratic hybrids that had irregularities in their electoral systems making the elections unfair, and widespread corruption with a lack of independence in the judiciary and media. The final 53 countries were deemed to be authoritarian which may or may not have had some elements of democracy, but these elements were thought to be insignificant. In authoritarian regimes, both media and judiciary are controlled by the state, and civil liberties are abused, with people unable to voice any criticism of the government.

DISCUSS 7.18

How is it decided which elections are free and fair, and how much corruption there is in a country? When reading statistics like those above, how would you decide whether they are reliable?

In the EIU 2018 rankings, Norway was reported to be the most democratic nation in the world with a score of 9.87 (out of a possible 10), and North Korea was found to be the least democratic nation with a score of 1.08.

EXPLORE 7.5

Find out where your country has come in the EIU rankings and classifications. From your knowledge of your country, would you think this is a fair assessment?

> **REFLECTION**
>
> To what extent are you tempted to believe data and statistics that support your worldview, and dismiss those that challenge it?

> **REAL-LIFE SITUATION 7.8**
>
> What information might you need for you to decide whether the EIU rankings are valid? Assuming the methodology is valid, does this make the rankings true?

Non-democracies

Winston Churchill (1874–1965), Prime Minister of Great Britain from 1940 to 1945 and again from 1951 to 1955, famously said that democracy was the worst form of government except for all the other forms that had been tried. He was acknowledging the problems inherent in democracy while saying it is the best system we know. However, not everyone would agree.

Democratic political systems largely privilege individual freedoms over the welfare of the collective. In contrast, socialist and communist systems endeavour to prioritise the prosperity of the collective over the freedoms of individuals. After the Second World War, a number of communist states understood democracy to be a system of values that prioritise the collective over individuals, and so laid claim to the name 'democracy'. The problem with understanding democracy as a value system is that the values are regarded as so important that there is a tendency to believe that they need to be maintained at any cost. Hence some communist states become totalitarian in their efforts to preserve their communist values. With a values-based understanding of democracy, some communists would regard communism as true democracy, and see western democracy as a form of ochlocracy.

> **KEY WORD**
>
> ochlocracy: mob rule, majoritarianism

> **LINKING QUESTION 7.2**
>
> **Language:** What difficulties can arise through the use of language when discussing political issues?

Absolute monarchies and dictatorships, on the other hand, vary depending on the person at the head of state. While many monarchs and dictators have led repressive regimes, benevolent leaders have brought peace and prosperity to their people. A modern example of a benevolent monarch is King Abdullah II of Jordan. He has promoted economic and social reforms, and taken steps to improve the status of women. As a result of his reign, Jordan is regarded as an area of 'high human

> **KEY WORD**
>
> benevolent: kind, well-meaning

development' by the United Nations Development Programme (UNDP); it has a skilled work force and a well-developed health system. Despite having few natural resources and being surrounded by political turmoil in neighbouring countries, Jordan is regarded as a beacon of peace and stability in the region, despite not being a democracy.

REAL-LIFE SITUATION 7.9

To what extent are your political views a product of the political system you live in?

China

While we often read and hear horror stories about authoritarian states, the reality is not as polarised as we are sometimes led to believe. Over the past forty years, the People's Republic of China has risen to become the second largest economy in the world when measured by **Gross Domestic Product** (GDP), or the largest if you measure it in terms of **Purchasing Power Parity** (PPP). And it is now forecast to become the largest economy in the world (as measured by GDP) by 2030. During its rise, China has brought more than half of its population out of poverty; indeed, China accounted for more than 75% of the global reduction in global poverty between 1990 and 2005. No other country has been able to achieve nearly so much in the same period of time.

DISCUSS 7.19

To what extent does our judgement of different political systems depend on what we know about their economic performance? How might statistical evidence be used or misused to justify political systems?

> **KEY WORDS**
>
> **Gross Domestic Product:** a measure of the goods and services produced in a country to estimate the size and growth rate of the economy
>
> **Purchasing Power Parity:** a standard of measurement used to compare the economic productivity and standards of living of different countries

While it has nine registered political parties, China is effectively a one-party communist state with a highly-centralised government. Every decision has to be ratified by the Communist Party. While government leaders are expected to reach public consensus for new policies, they largely achieve that consensus by controlling information.

In recent years, China has made huge strides forward economically and environmentally in ways that benefit its population and the world. Now a world leader in clean energy, China invests more in renewable power than any other country, is the leading generator of solar power and has a thriving sharing economy in which people can scan QR codes using their smartphones to hire anything from an umbrella to a cement mixer. More than 6 million people hire bicycles every week. The city of Shenzhen has become the first in the world to have a fully electric bus system, with its fleet of over 16,350 electric buses. More than 60% of its taxis are also electric, and the city is well on track to have all taxis fully electric by 2020. But it has made this progress largely at the expense of individual freedoms.

Figure 7.2: Electric buses in Ning Xiang, China

By taking a **utilitarian approach**, China's authoritarian system has produced a modern and efficient infrastructure of highways and high-speed trains, while many democratic countries are struggling to maintain – let alone modernise – their infrastructures. Some people argue that efficiency is not an appropriate parameter on which to judge competing political systems; that systems should be compared according to the standards of living and levels of satisfaction their citizens enjoy.

> ### KEY WORD
>
> **utilitarian approach:** in this context, a perspective that values usefulness above all other considerations

DISCUSS 7.20

Does freedom always come at the cost of efficiency? How might it be possible to compare different political systems objectively?

REAL-LIFE SITUATION 7.10

According to the 2013 Pew Survey of Global Attitudes, 85% of Chinese people described themselves as 'very satisfied' with their country's direction, compared with only 31% of Americans. To what extent can we rely on quantified satisfaction levels as reported by the Pew Survey? On what basis might it be argued that prioritising the welfare of the collective over the rights of the individual is ethical progress?

EXPLORE 7.6

Create a mind-map to compare the political system in your country with a different political system operating in another country of your choice. What are the positives and negatives of each system? What would you need to know to decide if one system is better than the other?

DISCUSS 7.21

What role does our interpretation of history play when we make judgements about the political values of others?

7.5 The political spectrum

DISCUSS 7.22

What do you understand by the terms 'left wing' and 'right wing' in the context of politics?

The political spectrum is often spoken about as though it is a single entity, and western countries tend to talk about being left or right of the political divide. These terms originated in the late-18th century, and refer to the seating arrangements in the legislative bodies of France. On the left sat those who were largely in favour of civil liberties and republicanism, while on the right sat those who supported the authority of the French aristocracy and the church. Today, different countries use the terms in different ways. In most countries, the left is associated with a controlled economy and the redistribution of wealth such as in communism and socialism, and the right is associated with a free market, the right to private ownership and social hierarchies. However, in some countries (such as the USA) the political left is more often associated with liberalism and the political right with conservative views.

The way in which you view the society you live in will differ depending on the political views you subscribe to. For example, if you believe in socialist values, you may 'know' that the problems of the transport system in your country are due to the market economy, or if you believe in free enterprise, you may 'know' that a sluggish economy is because too many people are dependent on social welfare. What we 'know' may very much depend on the political lens that we look through, even if we are not aware that we have a political lens.

REAL-LIFE SITUATION 7.11

To what extent are we aware of the impact our political views have on what we believe or know?

KEY WORDS

communism: an ideology which advocates that all property is communally owned, and the government directs all economic production

socialism: a social system based on the common ownership of the means of production and distribution

liberalism: political views that regard protecting and enhancing individual freedoms to be a central issue for politics, and strive towards social changes that bring about mutual benefits for all

conservatism: political views that favour traditional values, authority and law and order, while often opposing change or innovation. It is often associated with a commitment to free enterprise and private ownership

There are multiple different political ideologies that might be placed on political spectra, and most political parties endorse more than one ideology.

DISCUSS 7.23

What are the benefits of creating a model that necessarily oversimplifies and misrepresents the subject of the model?

Matt Kibbe (1950–) has produced a single axis spectrum very similar to a left–right spectrum, except that it runs vertically from liberty to totalitarianism and places different types of political views along it accordingly. It is worth noting that the way a party names itself does not necessarily align with the way its political views fall on a spectrum. For example, a party that holds conservative values might nevertheless call itself the 'Liberal Party', just as a single-party communist state might name itself as a democracy. One example of this is the Lao People's Democratic Republic (more commonly known in English as Laos.) Laos has only one legal political party, and is often regarded as one of the world's few remaining communist states.

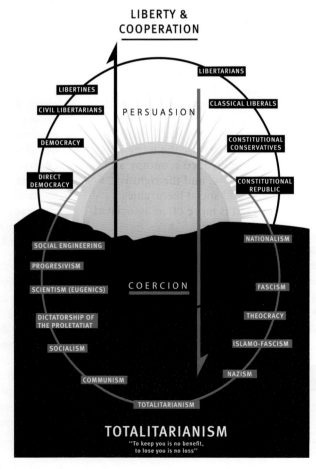

Figure 7.3: Kibbe's political spectrum

DISCUSS 7.24

Looking at Kibbe's spectrum (Figure 7.3), where do you think Kibbe's political views are likely to be situated? What leads you to think that? What does this suggest about the subjectivity of how we position different political positions on political spectra?

KEY WORDS

political values: abstract ideas about the needs of the people that drive political positions, for example, equality, freedom, tradition, progress, etc

radicalism: a political desire to change social structures in radical ways

While the left–right single-axis spectrum is commonly used, many people find it inadequate and opt for a model that has two or more axes. Double-axis spectra plot political positions according to their views on two different political values, for example one axis representing degrees of radicalism and the other representing authoritarianism, or axis for freedom and the other for equality. Some political scientists have proposed models with more than two axes. The more complex the model, the more accurate it may become, but it may also become less useful.

EXPLORE 7.7

If you could create your own political party, what importance would you give to equality, personal freedom, economic interests and environmental interests? Create a spectrum that would graphically illustrate where your party would position itself in relation to those issues.

Compare your spectrum with that of others in your class. Discuss the reasons for the way you have designed your spectrum and where you have placed your party.

DISCUSS 7.25

What are the limitations of different political spectra? What, if anything, can we know about a party from the way it is represented on a political spectrum?

REFLECTION

Does what you know about society affect your political views, or do your political views affect what you know about society? What factors have shaped your political beliefs?

7.6 Ethics, ownership and resource distribution

DISCUSS 7.26

Think about some of the things that you or your family own. Where does the right to own anything come from?

Ethics is an intrinsic element of politics in all of its aspects. Ethical thinking underlies the various methods and tools that politics relies on – from authority structures for electoral and voting systems to the ways in which political knowledge is produced and distributed. But perhaps ethical issues are most clearly seen in debates surrounding ownership and resource distribution.

You might believe that a person has a moral right to something that he or she has made, and that society has a duty to support this moral right, but that is largely a cultural assumption. While some philosophers have argued that we have natural property rights, others have pointed out that there is nothing natural about private property, and they may even regard it as unethical. Ownership is a human construction that is enabled by consensus, and every invention or new development, however original it may seem, owes an incalculable debt to the efforts of past generations.

One significant issue that every society needs to decide is whether its economy should be organised on the basis of private ownership and a free market, or on the basis of some form of centralised collective ownership and control. Many political parties are differentiated by where they sit along the private–social ownership spectrum. Generally speaking, parties to the left on a political spectrum advocate the nationalisation of many industries, particularly health services, education, transport networks and utilities. These industries are essential industries for any society and left-wing parties believe the government can and should prioritise social needs over profits by ensuring that the services of these industries are available to everybody. Parties on the right tend to favour private ownership because they believe the private sector is more efficient, and that market competition, which comes with privatisation, is an incentive for innovation and improvements.

These beliefs about the respective advantages of nationalisation and privatisation are considered by many to be political *truths*. While they might be argued, and stories may be spun, they are not merely opinions. Neither are they facts, yet people on both sides of the political divide can usually reach an agreement on them.

DISCUSS 7.27

How might you draw a distinction between a political opinion and a political truth?

Land ownership

The ethics of ownership is particularly unclear when it comes to land ownership. In most countries around the world, people with sufficient money are able to buy land 'freehold', which means permanent ownership with the right to dispose of it at will. However, there are some countries in which all land is owned by the state, and people can only purchase 'leaseholds' in which the land is leased from the state, usually for a limited period. In both freehold and leasehold, the land is legally owned – whether by individuals, corporations or the state.

REAL-LIFE SITUATION 7.12

The French philosopher Jean-Jacques Rousseau (1712–1778) argued that *'the fruits of the earth belong to all and the earth belongs to nobody'*, yet we *know* that individuals, corporations and states own most of the land on earth. Does this mean that Rousseau's claim is untrue? Is Rousseau's claim an ethical judgement? What might be a political truth in this context?

Private property laws generally allow people who own property to manage and use their property as they wish, regardless of whether others might have a greater need for it. The entitlement to private property is sometimes justified on the grounds that it is necessary for the development of individuals, and the creation of an environment in which people can thrive as free agents. A more popular justification is to argue that property (particularly land) ownership leads to a more efficient use of resources. The argument suggests that if land is held in common, no one has an incentive to make sure that the land is properly tended and not over-used. It suggests that it is only when land is assigned to individuals – so that whoever bears the costs of working and nurturing the land also reaps the benefits of doing so – that land is properly cared for and used efficiently.

DISCUSS 7.28

Political theories are often justified on the basis of assumptions about human nature. How reliable are those assumptions? How ethical is it to make political policies on the basis of efficiency?

Historically, there has been 'unowned' land where people have lived, hunted and farmed without there being any claim to ownership, and some of this land remains 'unowned'. However, as this land is increasingly being taken over and sometimes sold by states, the people who live on these lands are being displaced. One example is that of the Adivasis, who have had to apply to their Indian state governments to ask for titles to land they have lived on for generations. In many cases, their applications have been rejected because the land has been earmarked for other purposes (including the provision of conservation areas for endangered species such as tigers), and millions of Adivasis now face eviction. The ethical issues behind such political decisions are rarely straightforward. Governments must balance the needs of tribal peoples with the need for environmental conservation and the economic demands of the population majority.

REAL-LIFE SITUATION 7.13

When faced with knowledge about the global need for greater conservation efforts and a humanitarian requirement to protect indigenous peoples, is there a conflict between ethical and political responsibilities? To what extent do ethical truths conflict with political truths?

Figure 7.4: The Vedda are an indigenous people of Sri Lanka whose lives and culture are threatened by land acquisitions

EXPLORE 7.8

In small groups, imagine you are shipwrecked on a small, uninhabited island along with 250 other people of various ages, and assume that there is no hope of rescue. Try to reach an agreement on the following questions: Would you allow private ownership? How would you decide who gets to live where? Why might dividing the land equally not be fair? What provision would you make for future generations? How might you set up courts to decide between disputes, or governments to make laws?

Peer-assessment

Each group should present its ideas to the rest of the class. The class should ask questions to see if the ideas presented are coherent. The class can vote to decide which presentation offers the most acceptable, equitable, sustainable and coherent solutions.

DISCUSS 7.29

To what extent do ethical truths and political truths play a role in reaching a group decision?

REFLECTION

What would you regard as a political truth?

7.7 Social justice

How can you make fair decisions when making laws and structuring society?

Strongly related to issues of ownership are matters of social justice. Questions arise, such as whether some people can have too much or too little wealth, and people are – or perhaps should be – rewarded according to the effort that they make. Most people agree that social justice is a worthwhile goal, but political views differ widely on what it is, as well as how it could or should be achieved. Some look for the state to distribute wealth and other societal advantages fairly. Communism, socialism and liberal democracies all promote some form of redistribution of wealth in which more of societies' goods are given to the most disadvantaged groups, rather than giving all groups the same or allowing those who acquire wealth to retain all of it. Other people argue that it is more just to live with minimal or no state control, and to organise society in a way that engenders cooperation and brings benefits to all within it. Conservatism and anarchism would argue that inequalities in distribution are justified, providing people who have the most have achieved it legitimately, and we need to consider the choices that people have made before deciding whether uneven distribution is fair. Conservatives and those who support inequalities in wealth distribution would often advocate a trickle-down theory.

DISCUSS 7.31

How can political knowledge help us to know what social justice is, and what we need to do to achieve it?

Equality and equity

The idea of equality is frequently heard in discussions about justice. Many people believe that justice is about treating all people equally, but others argue that treating people equally can only be fair if all people are in the same place economically and socially. Equity, on the other hand, means that people are not treated equally, but that they are treated according to what they need to thrive.

REFLECTION

Can you think of some examples from your own experience when it has been important to treat (or be treated by) others differently in order to be fair to everybody?

KEY WORDS

social justice: the idea that all people should have equal access to – and opportunities for – wealth, education, health, and justice

trickle-down theory: the theory that lowering taxes for wealthy corporations and high-income earners will lead to greater investments, and will expand economic prosperity. The benefits of the expanded economy will then 'trickle down' to the workers

equality: the state of being equal in terms of status, rights and opportunities

equity: the quality of being fair and impartial

In the first image, it is assumed that everyone will benefit from the same supports. They are being treated equally.

In the second image, individuals are given different supports to make it possible for them to have equal access to the game. They are being treated equitably.

In the third image, all three can see the game without any supports or accommodations because the cause of the inequity was addressed. The systemic barrier has been removed.

Figure 7.5: Equality vs equity

Look carefully at Figure 7.5. The first two boxes depict clearly the difference between treating people equally and treating them equitably. However, this type of depiction has nevertheless been criticised because the disadvantage illustrated (shortness) is a disadvantage inherent in the people depicted, whereas most disadvantaged groups are not disadvantaged because of any inherent problems; rather they are disadvantaged because society obstructs some more than others from having access to opportunities. In other words, people from some races, religions or genders might be disadvantaged, not because they do not have the same abilities as others, but because the society they live in does not allow them full access to opportunities.

DISCUSS 7.32

1   In what ways might the knower's beliefs and biases affect the ways they perceive equality and equity?

2   To what extent are political leaders justified in making decisions about the needs and welfare of others?

EXPLORE 7.9

Discuss the advantages and disadvantages of the different approaches illustrated in Figure 7.5. Try to redraw the first two sketches in a way that shows how people who are inherently equal might still need different levels of support because they face greater or lesser obstacles.

Self-assessment

Does your diagram show that you understand the difference between equality and equity? Does the diagram show that injustice is caused by differing obstacles rather than a problem inherent in the people?

The veil of ignorance

John Rawls (1921–2002) was an American philosopher known for his work on the nature of justice. He believed that the first responsibility of social institutions should be justice, and he introduced a concept that he called the 'veil of ignorance', in which he proposed that lawmakers should make the kinds of laws they would want in place if they did not know where they would stand in society. He believed this would prevent laws that disadvantage people because of their gender, race, abilities, wealth, education, age, sexuality or religion. However, the veil of ignorance has been criticised on the grounds that it is only a thought experiment, and does not offer a practical way forward.

> **EXPLORE 7.10**
>
> In pairs, try to design a society from behind a *veil of ignorance*. How might your society differ from the one you live in?
>
> Discuss with your partner whether or not you found the *veil of ignorance* thought experiment useful in helping you to gain a fresh perspective on social justice.

> **DISCUSS 7.33**
>
> What are the advantages and limitations of thought experiments in helping us to develop new knowledge? (It may help you to compare the veil of ignorance thought experiment with a thought experiment from the natural sciences.)

Epistemic injustice

Epistemic injustice primarily relates to problems in the communication of knowledge. Although the term was first coined by Miranda Fricker (1966–) in 2007, the issues to which it refers go back centuries. Across all cultures, the voices of women have long been ignored, as have the voices of minority groups and indigenous peoples everywhere. Rajeev Bhargava (1954–) speaks of epistemic injustice in discussing the way colonial powers have negatively impacted on the concepts that colonised peoples have used to understand themselves and the world. Epistemic injustice is injustice at a very deep level because it wrongs people in their capacity as knowers.

> **KEY WORD**
>
> epistemic injustice: injustice that happens when knowledge is ignored, not believed or not understood

> **REFLECTION**
>
> Think about an occasion on which you felt as though you had not been listened to, not been believed or deliberately misunderstood. How did that experience affect you as a knower?

> **KEY WORD**
>
> epistemic power: the power to decide, produce, influence or authenticate knowledge

Epistemic injustice interacts with other forms of social injustice, such as social and political injustice. People who do not feel listened to lack epistemic power, and this readily translates to a lack of political and economic power. However, even people who are politically and/or economically empowered can still fall victim to epistemic injustice at times.

There are many different ways that people can be undermined as knowers. Sometimes this is done inadvertently; at other times, deliberately. To correct and to prevent epistemic injustice, it could be said that we have an ethical imperative to include all voices in a balanced way in any discussion.

LINKING QUESTION 7.3

Technology: How might technology, and particularly social media, impact epistemic injustice?

REAL-LIFE SITUATION 7.14

Think about a contentious political issue that might be **polarising** your nation or society. Do people with opposing views truly listen to each other, or do they try to shout the other down (literally or metaphorically)? What methods might be used in political discourses to convert disagreement into consensus, or at least develop thoughtful and respectful debate?

KEY WORD

polarising: in this context, dividing people into two main groups with opposite views

---

7.8 Knowledge economies

DISCUSS 7.34

Why is knowledge valuable?

A knowledge economy is one in which the national economy is largely dependent on the quantity and quality of the knowledge it uses and produces. Examples of some of the activities in knowledge economies include research, high-tech manufacturing and technical support and service sector industries like education and consultancy. Most countries have a mixture of agricultural, manufacturing and knowledge-based industries, but the economies of more developed countries tend to have a greater dependence on knowledge industries than the economies of developing countries.

Knowledge economies heavily rely upon **intellectual capital**, so they need their citizens to be well educated. Some of this education is the result of academic qualifications, but a significant proportion of the intellectual capital comes from learning in the workplace, and from the density of education in the general population.

KEY WORD

intellectual capital: the collective knowledge of people in an organisation or society

---

REAL-LIFE SITUATION 7.15

Why are countries with a predominantly knowledge economy likely to be most developed?

In what ways might having a knowledge economy inhibit the sharing of knowledge?

Knowledge hierarchies

Like authorities, knowledge tends to be structured into hierarchies in which different types of knowledge have a different status. In the western world, mathematics and the natural sciences tend to occupy the highest rungs, whereas in other societies, religious or political knowledge may take priority. These hierarchies of knowledge are historically and politically decided, and very much reflect the societies in which they arise.

Sometimes, there is an economic basis for the hierarchies, with those fields of knowledge that more directly contribute to the economy being most valued; sometimes, traditions or national identity might provide the basis for the hierarchy. What is taught in schools, what knowledge is required for public office and different careers, what kinds of research attract public funding and so on, are all political decisions made by the state in ways that legitimise some forms of knowledge over others.

EXPLORE 7.11

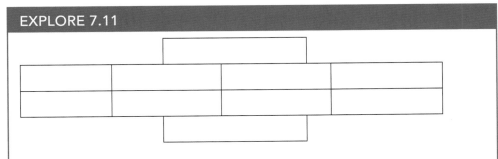

Figure 7.6: Does knowledge have a hierarchy?

Create a table like the one above and, in pairs, try to rank the subjects listed according to how you think your society regards them. Why do you think the subject at the top is most highly regarded in your society? Consider the subject at the bottom of your rankings, and try to come up with some arguments for why it should be at the top.

Subjects: art, computer science, economics, history, languages, mathematics, music, natural sciences, physical education, religion.

Are there any subjects you would prefer to include in this list so as to be able to place them in the top and/or bottom position?

REFLECTION

To what extent were you influenced by your own perceptions of a knowledge hierarchy when choosing your subjects for your IB Diploma Programme?

DISCUSS 7.36

1 How and why might different societies value subject areas differently?

2 To what extent are different knowledge hierarchies embedded into different cultures and/or different political structures? What may account for these differences?

The cost of knowledge

With the emergence of knowledge economies, there has been a growing commercialisation of knowledge production, partly driven by the increasing costs of knowledge production. In addition, the connections between knowledge production, production of goods and services and profitability are becoming more and more complex and intertwined. As a result, the cost of knowledge production needs to be factored in to the prices demanded for goods and services.

It cost an estimated $13.25 billion to find the Higgs boson particle, and it is estimated that it costs around $2.6 billion to bring a new prescription drug to market. Even knowledge produced without the extensive use of technology involves the costs of human resources, production overheads and publishing. This means that most producers of new knowledge are either very large profit-making organisations (such as pharmaceutical companies, energy companies and telecommunications companies), or large universities (public or private) that are heavily dependent on sponsors who often have their own political and/or economic agendas. For example, in 2019, a private equity billionaire gave the University of Oxford in the UK £150 million to research the ethics of artificial intelligence (AI). He had previously donated $350 million to MIT in the USA to establish a centre for computing and AI. By specifying what the donations are to be used for, the sponsor is able to focus research attention on areas that he has interests in, and thereby strongly influence the types of knowledge that is produced.

REAL-LIFE SITUATION 7.16

How might economics and politics affect not only what knowledge is produced and shared, but also what knowledge is sometimes dismissed or ignored?

EXPLORE 7.12

Just as tobacco executives were told in the 1960s by their own scientists that smoking is deadly, and fossil-fuel executives in the 1980s were told by their own scientists that burning oil, gas and coal would cause a 'catastrophic' temperature rise, so in the 1990s telecommunications executives were told by their own scientists that mobile phones could cause cancer and genetic damage. Do some research to find out what studies have since been conducted on the link between mobile phones and cancer, and where the funding has come from. Brainstorm reasons for both why it might be and might not be reasonable for phone companies to sponsor research into links between mobile phones and cancer. Organise a class debate to argue the issue.

DISCUSS 7.37

Why does it matter who funds the production of new knowledge?

7.9 Intellectual property

DISCUSS 7.38

What is intellectual property? How can you own knowledge?

The concept of intellectual property is particularly important in the context of a knowledge economy. It means that we own any creations and designs that we have come up with, providing we do not come up with them in the course of working for somebody else. Intellectual property does not include our ideas unless they have actually been created by us. In other words, if you have an idea that you want to write a book about, the idea for the book is not your intellectual property, but if you write the book, the words that you use are protected under copyright.

Intellectual property law says that no one else can copy or use the intellectual property of another without permission, and any intellectual property you have can be bought and sold in the same way as physical possessions. There are numerous types of protection for intellectual property including copyrights, design rights, trademarks, registered designs and patents. Typically, protection for intellectual property is given for a limited time period, after which others may use it.

REAL-LIFE SITUATION 7.17

The IB stresses the importance of academic honesty and citing sources when producing coursework. Why is academic honesty important? What are the ethical challenges related to using knowledge that is found on the internet?

REFLECTION

How might you feel if you created a wonderful piece of art and someone else wrote their name on it? How might your emotions inform or influence your knowledge and understanding of intellectual property?

Employee knowledge

In any organisation, one of the most valuable assets is its intellectual property. The intellectual property can include how products are made (formulae and processes), clients lists, business models and many other details that may not be public knowledge. Employees not only have explicit knowledge of the organisation such as the knowledge found in training manuals, but they also have tacit knowledge in the form of experience, insight and expertise. This knowledge gives them considerable political power within their organisation.

A serious challenge facing organisations is how to retain and protect that knowledge when an employee leaves. Equally important is the protection of confidential information that the employee knows. The law protects the organisation against the employee sharing trade secrets, but not any general employee knowledge or expertise gained while working for the organisation. In effect, this means that much of the intellectual property of an organisation is owned and/or controlled by the employees.

DISCUSS 7.39

1   What role might ethics play in the sharing and withholding of knowledge?

2   What is the role of political leaders in regulating the control and distribution of knowledge?

Traditional knowledge

In recent years, there has been a growing movement to extend intellectual property rights to **traditional knowledge**. There are two types of protections being sought: defensive protection and positive protection. Defensive protection is to stop people outside the community acquiring property rights over traditional knowledge and prevent traditional symbols becoming registered trademarks of commercial companies. Positive protection is the right of communities to promote their traditional knowledge and benefit from it economically.

In 1995, the US Patent and Trademark Office (PTO) granted a patent to two medical researchers for the use of turmeric (a spice native to south-east Asia) to heal surgical wounds and ulcers both through ingesting it and applying it to the wounds. In 1997, the Indian government was able to force the patent to be overturned on the grounds that Indians had been using turmeric as a wound healer for centuries. This was one of the earliest instances of a successful case of defensive protection for traditional knowledge.

> **KEY WORD**
>
> **traditional knowledge:** a body of knowledge that is developed, sustained and passed on over generations within a community

LINKING QUESTION 7.4

1   What makes traditional knowledge valuable?

2   When different cultures or nations have conflicting claims to the ownership of knowledge, how can we decide whose claim has priority?

7.10 International politics

REAL-LIFE SITUATION 7.18

Why do countries wage war?

International politics is as much about '*who gets what, and who decides*' as any other form of politics, but is arguably more difficult in that there is no overarching body elected and acknowledged by all nations to legislate and police matters of international justice. In addition, the difference in size and power of individual nations is far greater than the difference between individuals in any one state. The world's smallest states are Vatican

City with a population of just 800, and Tuvalu with a population of 11,400, whereas the largest states are China and India with populations of 1.42 billion and 1.37 billion people respectively (2019 figures). This makes it difficult to see how any kind of international democratic system could work. The idea of 'one country, one vote' hardly seems fair if the vote of Vatican City or Tuvalu counts as much as that of China or India, yet if votes were to be apportioned by population, smaller nations would have virtually no voice.

Figure 7.7: The chamber of the General Assembly at the United Nations

The United Nations

The United Nations (UN) is an organisation founded in 1945 to maintain peace and security, develop friendly relations between nations and achieve international cooperation in solving problems and promoting human rights. It was hoped that war would become obsolete if states could cooperate with each other. Since the UN began, it has been credited with saving millions of lives from sickness and starvation, and has helped to provide education in the poorest places. Debatably, the UN was also instrumental in helping to bring an end to a nuclear arms race. Yet the UN is not without its critics. The UN core budget for 2018–2019 was agreed at $5.4 billion but more than half of this goes into administrative costs, and many poorer nations are struggling to pay their share. Many countries see the UN as being heavily **bureaucratic** and ineffective; others see it as undemocratic and dominated by wealthier countries.

> **KEY WORD**
>
> bureaucratic:
> overly concerned
> with procedure and
> administration at the
> expense of efficiency

> **EXPLORE 7.13**
>
> With a partner or in a small group, imagine you are organising an international IB Diploma Programme student forum to promote international-mindedness. What structures would you want to put in place to ensure that all cultural perspectives are heard and respected? How might you resolve differences when incompatible beliefs and knowledge arise? How would the forum reach decisions?

REAL-LIFE SITUATION 7.19

In an organisation of 193 member states with widely differing perspectives on political and social issues, how can truth or justice be determined? Where does the UN's right to decide come from?

Since its formation, the UN Security Council has often been called on to help stop international disputes from escalating to war, or to help restore peace. When an issue arises that presents a threat to peace, the UN Security Council may investigate the issue and mediate between the different factions to try to reach a peaceful resolution. If fighting breaks out, the Security Council can request a ceasefire and deploy UN peacekeeping forces. The UN also engages in peace building by supporting justice and security, protecting human rights and promoting reconciliation. Despite its best efforts, there are still many armed conflicts occurring around the world.

DISCUSS 7.40

It is often said that 'truth is the first casualty of war'. What does this mean and why might it be? When faced with different cultural perspectives on truth, how can we decide where truth lies?

EXPLORE 7.14

Think about some of the conflicts going on in the world today. Alone or in pairs, choose one war that is happening in the world today and try to find two or more perspectives on the conflict. How might political differences affect how the events of conflicts are interpreted and understood?

EXPLORE 7.15

Choose an IA exhibition prompt and select an object referring to either the UN or an armed conflict. Write a short commentary (no more than 300 words) that identifies your object and its context in the world, and explain how it links to the IA exhibition prompt you have chosen.

Peer-assessment

Share your commentary with a classmate and give each other feedback. Are the object and its real-world context clearly identified? Are links between the object and the selected IA exhibition prompt explained well and made clearly? Are all points well supported with evidence and explicit references to the prompt?

Terrorism

When considering international armed conflict, it is important to consider **terrorism** not as a war between states, but as a violent expression of the disillusionment or dissatisfaction of dissenting minorities who often act across national borders. The term *terrorism* was originally used to describe the actions of a state against its domestic enemies, but although state-sponsored terrorism is still recognised as a type of terrorism, *terrorism* is now mostly used to describe violent actions taken against people by individuals and quasi-political organisations for ideological, political or religious reasons.

Terrorists generally try to destroy the public's sense of security by attacking places that attract large crowds and undermining people's confidence in the day-to-day use of places that are central to ordinary life. Schools, shopping centres, public transport stations, bridges, places of worship, hotels and restaurants are frequently targeted for greater destruction, increased shock value and greater publicity. Terrorism attacks many of the values at the heart of the UN Charter: human rights, the rule of law, tolerance among people and nations and the peaceful resolution of conflicts. One of its self-justifications for doing so is that it identifies the UN, many political systems and general civil society with the vested interests of political, economic and religious groups that it regards as oppressors. Terrorist groups can attract support not only from underprivileged and oppressed peoples and minorities, but also from the disaffected citizens of the very states they attack, who share their antipathy to the prevailing value-systems of their own societies. Terrorism is, as such, a malignant form of dissent.

It is important to recognise the significance of the *knowledge basis* of terrorism, and in particular the knowledge implications of worldviews built upon assumptions and accounts of the world that are both incompatible and irreconcilable with worldviews held by the majority. From outside, the worldview of terrorists may seem to be based upon hate, prejudice and ignorance, but terrorists may see their worldview as being built upon *alternative knowledge systems* that are principled, just and true.

KEY WORD

terrorism: the use of violence, especially against civilians, intended to create a climate of fear in the pursuit of political aims

---

DISCUSS 7.41

Under what circumstances does one person's terrorist become another person's freedom fighter? To what extent does our culture determine how we define and label different political groups?

One of the difficulties in countering terrorism has been a lack of international consensus on a definition of terrorism. There is argument over whether the use of state-controlled armed forces against civilians should be included in the definition. There is also a concern that people under foreign occupation should have a right to resistance without being labelled as terrorists.

LINKING QUESTION 7.5

Language: How might the lack of an internationally agreed definition of terrorism affect the ability of the UN to develop a clear counter-terrorism strategy?

International law

International law is a complex set of rules, principles and practices that provide normative guidelines for nations and international organisations. It is particularly focused on ethical issues such as human rights, the treatment of **aliens** and refugees and problems of nationality. It also addresses global issues such as world trade, global environmental issues, international waters and questions involving outer space.

There is a growing debate among academics, diplomats and politicians about the relationship between international law and national sovereignty. Some argue that international law should not interfere with how states govern themselves; others argue that all states should meet certain standards of conduct which would prohibit them from engaging in behaviours such as slavery, torture or genocide.

DISCUSS 7.42

To what extent should every country be allowed to determine its own laws and systems? Who should decide and how?

Figure 7.8: Slavery in Mauritania

In the Islamic Republic of Mauritania, it was legal to own slaves until 2007. Since then, only one person has been prosecuted for owning slaves even though 2% of the population were found to be still living in slavery in 2018. One of the reasons that slavery has not been abolished in Mauritania is that the majority of the population believe slavery is part of the natural order of their society.

To what extent are human rights and ethical knowledge global or culturally relative?

In pairs or small groups, brainstorm activities in your nation or society that are lawful and may seem 'natural', yet could conceivably be viewed differently by other cultures or even by your own culture in another era.

1   What role does knowledge play in shaping our understanding of ethical issues within politics?

2   What might it mean to make ethical progress?

Hegemony

Hegemony is a concept associated with international power and authority. In hegemony, a group or state is able to rule by consensus because others accept that the ideas supporting the ruling group are normal and even common sense. Because governments and large corporations are able to control information and technology, they are able to strongly influence the ways in which people think and the direction of any debates. In international politics, the USA is sometimes described as the global hegemon because of its military might and its economic power, which gives it significant influence over, and control of, how other nations interact and trade. In all cases of hegemony, the hegemon tends to have a vested interest in preserving the hegemonic system, and is often responsible for formulating the rules of the system. In many ways, hegemony might be seen as the antithesis of relativism because it promotes a set of standards that it believes everyone should adhere to.

hegemony: the dominance of one group supported by a set of ideas, or the dominance of a set of ideas that become the norm in a way that inhibits the circulation of alternative ideas

hegemon: the dominant group, class or state that exercises hegemonic power and promotes hegemonic ideas

To what extent is western belief in the superiority of democracy a hegemonic idea?

Do you live in a dominant culture? Consider the extent to which your life and political views are shaped or dominated by the culture you live in. To what extent are you aware of other cultural influences affecting your life and political views?

REAL-LIFE SITUATION 7.21

1   To what extent is the Americanisation of cultures around the world something that we take for granted as desirable and 'normal'?

2   How might your knowledge of what is 'normal' change if a non-western country were to become the global hegemon?

7.11 Conclusion

At the heart of politics lies the question of the relationship between the one and the many, between individual and collective good and the associated responsibilities and freedoms that relationship entails. Most of the world's political systems can be aligned either with a concern to protect and preserve the freedoms of individuals over or against the collective, or with a concern to protect and preserve the prosperity of the collective over or against individuals. Liberalism and capitalism fall clearly into the former category; communism and socialism at least make a pretence of falling into the second. All systems make assumptions about the amount of collateral damage they are ready to tolerate, whether at the expense of the collective or the individual, in pursuit of their goals.

In this chapter, we have seen how politics and knowledge are inextricably linked. Politics determines the authorities within our society and organisations, and those authorities ultimately decide what counts as knowledge, what knowledge needs to be shared, and what knowledge needs to be passed on to future generations.

The type of political system a state or society has will strongly influence the ways that individuals within the society think, the beliefs they hold, the knowledge they have ready access to and the knowledge they are denied access to. What we know, how we know it and the extent to which we can challenge that knowledge are all, to a large extent, the products of political decisions.

One of the tasks of the knower is to try to become more aware of how his or her own knowledge is shaped by politics, and endeavour to see knowledge issues from other political perspectives in an effort to somewhat disentangle the two. But just as politics shapes knowledge, so knowledge has the potential to shape politics. As knowers, we all carry a responsibility to engage with the politics of our society so that our knowledge can contribute to our relationship with our own society and the international community.

KNOWLEDGE QUESTIONS

1   To what extent do the perspectives fostered by a political system impact on our knowledge?

2   How does knowledge affect the political parties we support and the way we cast our votes?

7.12 Linking questions

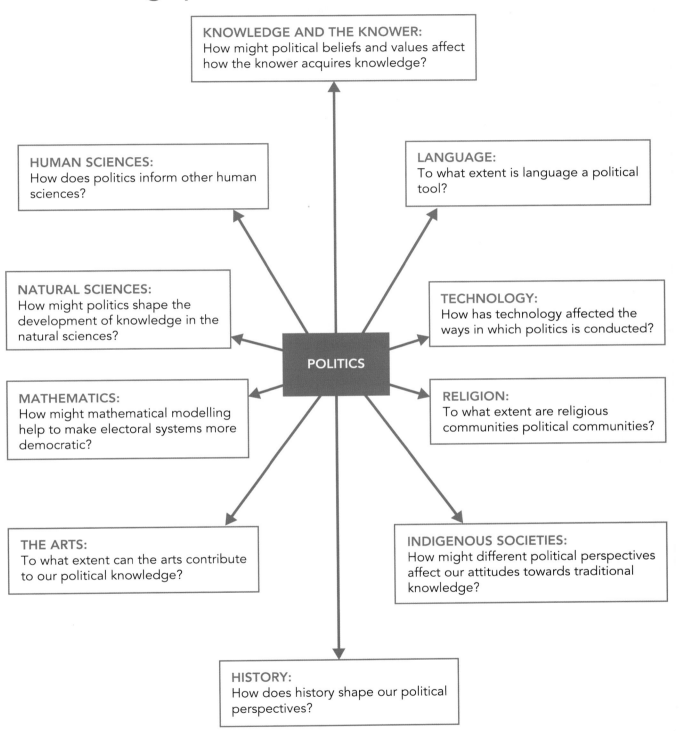

KNOWLEDGE AND THE KNOWER:
How might political beliefs and values affect how the knower acquires knowledge?

HUMAN SCIENCES:
How does politics inform other human sciences?

LANGUAGE:
To what extent is language a political tool?

NATURAL SCIENCES:
How might politics shape the development of knowledge in the natural sciences?

TECHNOLOGY:
How has technology affected the ways in which politics is conducted?

MATHEMATICS:
How might mathematical modelling help to make electoral systems more democratic?

POLITICS

RELIGION:
To what extent are religious communities political communities?

THE ARTS:
To what extent can the arts contribute to our political knowledge?

INDIGENOUS SOCIETIES:
How might different political perspectives affect our attitudes towards traditional knowledge?

HISTORY:
How does history shape our political perspectives?

7.13 Check your progress

Reflect on what you have learned in this chapter and indicate your confidence level between 1 and 5 (where 5 is the highest score and 1 is the lowest). If you score below 3, revisit that section. Come back to this list later in your course. Has your confidence grown?

	Confidence level	Revisited?
Do I understand how knowledge is related to political power and authority?		
Am I clear about how authorities are justified and what is meant by the social contract?		
Do I understand the distinctions between 'power to', 'power over' and 'power of'?		
Can I explain how fresh perspectives can lead us to interpret the same events differently?		
Do I appreciate the importance of dissent and civil disobedience in changing societies?		
Am I clear about the issues of knowledge control that arise through hacktivism?		
Do I appreciate that there are diverse perspectives on whistleblowing?		
Do I understand that different political systems employ different methods for decision making?		
Can I explain some of the methods used to assess majority opinions in democracies?		
Am I aware of a range of different non-democratic political systems and the various ways they might impact knowledge?		
Am I clear about the advantages and disadvantages of using political spectra to model the relationship between different political positions?		
Have I considered the ethical and political implications of ownership?		
Can I articulate what we understand by *social justice*, *equality* and *equity*?		
Do I understand what is meant by the veil of ignorance and how it might impact political beliefs?		
Can I articulate some of the ethical issues related to epistemic injustice?		
Do I know what a knowledge economy is?		
Can I explain the political nature of knowledge hierarchies?		
Am I able to discuss the cost of knowledge production and some of the implications of those costs?		
Do I understand what intellectual property is, and how it can impact businesses and indigenous societies?		
Am I able to discuss how political differences can affect the interpretation of global and international events?		

7.14 Continue your journey

- To build on the knowledge that you have gained in this chapter, you could read some of the following articles.

- To explore the **politics of knowledge** in greater detail, read: Hans N Weiler, 'Whose knowledge matters? Development and the politics of knowledge'. Search the *Stanford University* website for this article.

- To learn more about the **political use of scientific knowledge**, read: UNESCO, *Declaration on Science and the use of Scientific Knowledge*, 1st July 1999. Search the *Unesco* website for this article.

- To gain a greater insight into the **cost of producing pharmaceutical knowledge**, read: Thomas Sullivan, 'A Tough Road: Cost To Develop One New Drug Is $2.6 Billion; Approval Rate for Drugs Entering Clinical Development is Less Than 12%', *Policy and Medicine*, updated 21 March. Search the *Policy and Medicine* website for this article.

- To find out more about the **political issues of industries funding research**, read: 'The inconvenient truth about cancer and mobile phones', *The Guardian* 14 July 2018. Search the *Guardian* website for this article. Also, read 'How Big Wireless Made Us Think That Cell Phones Are Safe: A Special Investigation', Mark Hertsgaard and Mark Dowies, *The Nation* 23 April 2018. Search the *Nation* website for this article.

- To learn more about the **issues of knowledge in the workplace**, read: John Hagel III, John Seely Brown, and Lang Davison, 'Are all employees knowledge workers?' *Harvard Business Review*, 5 April 2010. Search the *Harvard Business Review* website for this article.

- To explore the **role of the UN** in further detail, read: 'Charter of the United Nations'. Search the *United Nations* website for this article.

- To find out some of the **criticisms of the UN** read: Chris McGreal, '70 years and half a trillion dollars later: what has the UN achieved?', *The Guardian,* 7 September 2015. Search the *Guardian* website for this article.

- If you wish to **explore epistemic injustice** in more detail, read: Miranda Fricker, *Epistemic Injustice: Power and the Ethics of Knowing*, Oxford University Press, 2007.

- To discover a **new perspective on China**, read: Ceri Parker and Oliver Cann, '10 astounding facts to help you understand China today', *World Economic Forum*, 24 June 2017. Search the World *Economic Forum* website for this article.

- If you want to know more about **challenges to democracy**, read: 'What's gone wrong with democracy?', *The Economist,* 27th February 2014. Search the *Economist* website for this article.

> ## Chapter 8
Knowledge and religion

LEARNING INTENTIONS

This chapter will explore some of the world's religious traditions, where they draw their religious knowledge from and how religious knowledge helps to inform the modern world.

You will:

*   examine different ways of thinking about religion and its scope; learn how rich and diverse the world's religions are and how classifying them can be both helpful and restrictive; and consider how differences in understanding of religious language can lead to misinterpretation of religious knowledge

*   look at some of the main sources of religious knowledge, and discuss different perspectives regarding the ways in which religious texts and narratives can be understood

*   examine some of the methods and tools that are used in the development of religious knowledge

*   explore different ways that individuals and communities develop religious understanding, and consider the role of religious ethics within a community

*   discover some of the initiatives for religions to work together using religious knowledge to overcome social problems and promote a more tolerant world

---

BEFORE YOU START

Analyse each of the following quotations and discuss the questions that follow.

1   'When I admire the wonders of a sunset or the beauty of the moon, my soul expands in the worship of the creator.' **Mahatma Gandhi** (1869–1948)

2   'Prayer does not change God, but it changes him who prays.' **Søren Kierkegaard** (1813–1855)

3   'I do not feel obliged to believe that the same God who has endowed us with sense, reason and intellect has intended us to forego their use.' **Galileo Galilei** (1564–1642)

4   'If one has the answers to all the questions – that is the proof that God is not with him. It means that he is a false prophet using religion for himself.' **Pope Francis** (1936–)

5   'Nature says women are human beings; men have made religions to deny it.' **Taslima Nasrin** (1962–)

For each quotation, consider:

a   To what extent do you agree or disagree with the quotation?

b   How might you challenge the quotation?

c   What does the quotation tell you about the speaker's assumptions about religion?

d   Do you think people from other religions or no religion could agree with the quotation?

8.1 Introduction

Throughout history, religion has played a significant role in all human societies – forming them, sustaining them and providing them with common values and a common vision. Often, religious organisations sustain communities in more practical ways by providing food, medical care and education. Literature, the natural sciences, the human sciences and philosophy all have roots in religious beliefs.

However, just as religion can bring people together, so it can divide them. Whenever we belong to a community, whether religious or not, it means there are some people who belong to the community and some who do not. We are divided into 'insiders' and 'outsiders': *us* and *them*. Some people believe that, because of this, religion is responsible for many of the wars between peoples, despite religious teachings about justice and compassion.

Very few knowledge themes incite human passions to the extent that religion does. Whether believers of a particular religion or believers in no religion, it is an area of knowledge that shapes people's worldviews perhaps more than any other.

In this chapter, we will explore what a religion is, how religions evolve and where religious knowledge comes from. We will also explore some key ideas and ways in which those ideas are interpreted.

8.2 What is religion and what is its scope?

DISCUSS 8.1

What are the features, events and activities that you associate with religion?

The word *religion* is thought to be derived from the Latin word *religare* which means to bind together, and the French sociologist Émile Durkheim (1858–1917) believed that this was exactly the role of religion: to bind communities together. He regarded religions as systems of beliefs and practices designed to unite people into single moral communities by providing a source of identity and solidarity, authority figures and a meaning for life. According to Durkheim, religions reinforce the moral and social norms of the societies they operate in, and therefore have a critical role in any society. Religious rituals provide a mode of communication in which people gather together to reaffirm their collective values, morals and beliefs. This is an essential element, because the public act of reaffirming beliefs helps to strengthen those beliefs while, at the same time, increasing a sense of community.

Of course, not everyone would agree with Durkheim about the nature of religion. Karl Marx (1818–1883), a philosopher, political and economic theorist and socialist revolutionary, saw religion as a tool of oppression. He referred to religion as the 'opium of the people', and regarded belief in a heavenly afterlife as a **panacea** to deter people from complaining about the injustices in their earthly life.

Sigmund Freud (1856–1939), a neurologist and the founder of psychoanalysis, believed that religion is an illusion which serves as an emotional crutch for people who need a powerful father figure to turn to. He thought religion was necessary in the development of civilisations to help humans restrain their violent impulses, but thought that, as we as a species became more knowledgeable and more rational, these would become motives for morality without the need for a father figure to make us behave. He strongly believed that science and reason would replace any need for a God or gods, and that religious beliefs would recede as people became better educated and more knowledgeable.

KEY WORD

panacea: a solution or remedy for all difficulties

REAL-LIFE SITUATION 8.1

How might developments in the human sciences influence the way we think about religion?

There are other people, of course, who believe that some religions are just what they claim to be – whether that be a set of narratives about one or more **divine** beings, a **covenant** between a god and that god's people, a spiritual tradition or a philosophy of how to live, which may or may not include supernatural beings. How you think about religion will at least partly determine your perspective on the scope of religion. If you are religious, you are likely to see everything as being within the scope of religion. Your religion will affect your political views, your opinions on ethical issues and can even influence the ways in which you interpret scientific evidence. However, if you have no religious beliefs or are a staunch **atheist**, you might think that religious beliefs are a personal matter, and religious perspectives have no place in the public sphere.

KEY WORDS

divine: something of a supernatural nature that is sacred or godlike

covenant: an agreement or promise of commitment

atheist: someone who believes there is no god

The world's religions

It is estimated that there are around 4,200 religions in the world, and many of these can be divided and subdivided into different sects, each with their own sets of beliefs and practices. The world's religions come in many forms. Some are focused on central beliefs and practices; others focus on community and culture. Some religions have supernatural dimensions; others are more rooted in this world. Some religions have multiple gods; some have just one, while others have no gods at all.

Based on 2015 figures, the five most influential religions are Christianity (with 2.3 billion followers), Islam (1.8 billion), Hinduism (1.15 billion), Buddhism (521 million) and Judaism (14.5 million). Together, they represent more than 70% of the world's population. However, if all of the non-affiliated people were grouped together in a single 'religion', it would be the third largest.

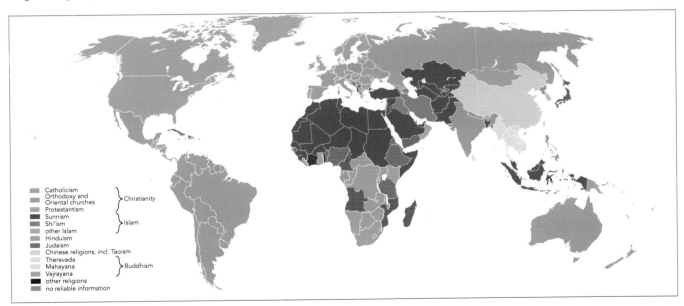

Figure 8.1: A map of the world's religions

REAL-LIFE SITUATION 8.2

1   Because religion is a significant aspect of life for most people, do we have an ethical responsibility to gain knowledge of different religions to develop a better understanding of people from around the world?

2   What can we learn from the knowledge claims of people whose views of the world we do not share?

Studies show that around the world, particularly in North America, Europe, Australasia and Latin America, young adults are less likely to have a religious affiliation than adults over 40. In the Middle East and much of Africa, young adults have the same degree of religious affiliation as older adults, and in just two countries – Chad and Ghana – young adults show a stronger religious affiliation than older adults.

DISCUSS 8.3

To what extent might people continue to have beliefs that could be classified as religious even if they do not belong to, nor are affiliated with, a particular faith?

EXPLORE 8.1

In small groups, brainstorm possible reasons why there has been a reduction in religious affiliation in younger people around the world. Try to form a hypothesis for why the reverse is true in Chad and Ghana. If you had sufficient resources, how might you test your hypothesis?

DISCUSS 8.4

To what extent can we apply scientific methodologies to understanding religion?

Changes in religious affiliation do not necessarily mean Freud was right about religion eventually going into decline. Although there is a tendency for people in more affluent countries to show less affiliation to organised religion, the same people will often still claim to be **theists** or adopt some form of **spirituality** as they wrestle with major questions like: 'Does life have meaning and/or purpose?', 'What is reality?', 'Why is there something rather than nothing?'.

DISCUSS 8.5

Does religion help to answer questions that other areas of knowledge are unable to answer?

KEY WORDS

theist: a person who believes in a God or gods who interact with people and the world

spirituality: a concern with the human spirit or soul, rather than with material or physical things

Some people claim that many countries are becoming increasingly secularised, in which case this trend is likely to increase, because children of secular parents are more likely to be secular themselves. In addition, modern secularisation tends to be correlated with internet access and usage, which suggests that secularisation will continue to grow. However, others claim that rather than religion declining, it is simply changing. People are holding on to their religious beliefs, but choose to keep them private rather than participating in any organised religion. Some have even claimed that religious beliefs are on the rise, citing 84% of people around the globe as identifying with a religious group without necessarily attending religious services.

KEY WORD

secular: not concerned with religion

DISCUSS 8.6

To what extent does knowledge of a particular god depend upon participation in religious services?

The global religious landscape in 2015

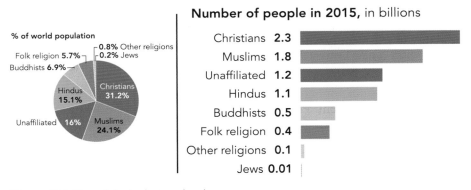

Figure 8.2: The global religious landscape

These differing views all cite the same 2015 statistics, but they interpret them very differently. One of the reasons behind this is that the group reported as 'unaffiliated' included a mix of people including atheists, agnostics and unaffiliated people who may nevertheless have some form of religious belief.

DISCUSS 8.7

What issues arise when using statistical methods to compare religious demographics?

KEY WORD

agnostic: a person who does not know or has not decided whether God exists; someone who believes that nothing can be known of the existence or nature of God

The classification of religions

Religions of the world can be classified in many ways. In the ancient world (and even among some people today), religions would be classified as a true religion (the religion that the classifier believed in); a partially true religion (one similar to the religion the classifier believed in); and false religions (all other religions). This kind of classification is not terribly helpful in a global society, so new ways were devised. One way is to divide religions into theistic (monotheistic, polytheistic) and non-theistic, but a problem with this is that it is not always clear which category many of the religions fit into. Depending on how it is defined and understood, Hinduism, for example, could be put into any one of these classes.

Sometimes, religions are classified according to where they originated or where they are now practised. This may be helpful in tracing historical contexts, but a more recent way to classify religions is in terms of assent and descent.

Religions of descent are the religions that people are born into and inherit. In these religious communities, individuals are considered members by virtue of having one or both parents of that background, and religion, culture and ethnicity are closely intertwined. Examples of religions of descent include Judaism, Hinduism and many indigenous religions. They tend to be pluralistic because membership does not depend on having any particular ideology; however, conversion to these religions is typically rare, and often difficult.

Religions of assent are those that openly invite and welcome people of all backgrounds to join them. Membership usually involves assenting to a set of beliefs that are regarded as essential to the religion. Examples of religions of assent include Christianity, Islam and Buddhism. These religions tend to be cross-cultural, and their key beliefs are often neatly packaged for purposes of proselytising. Because their identity is dependent on assent, these religious communities are often anti-pluralistic and intolerant of heretics. However, the ability to self-identify with a religion can be personally empowering, and allow a person to have a new history as well as a new community.

As with all classification systems, even these divisions are not hard and fast. Many religions of assent are gradually becoming religions of descent. For example, within Christianity, the modern-day Roman Catholic, Anglican, Russian Orthodox, Greek Orthodox and Armenian churches are intertwined with national identities, and many of them are now home to a plurality of ideas within a broadly Christian framework. In a similar way, some Islamic groups, such as the Ismailis, consider Islam to be a patrilineal religion, in other words you are Muslim if your father is Muslim, in much the same way that Judaism is a matrilineal religion. Equally, some religions of descent are more accepting of people entering their faiths than others. For example, it is generally easier to become a Reformed Jew than an Orthodox Jew.

DISCUSS 8.8

Consider the different knowledge claims of religions of assent and religions of descent. If someone makes a knowledge claim because of personal conviction, does that imply a different kind of knowledge from belief by practice or heredity?

Religions of descent tend to be primary religions, and religions of assent tend to be secondary religions. Primary religions are the ancient religions that are totally entwined with culture. They include tribal religions, and cannot be conceived of independently of the cultures that practise them. Secondary religions are those that were founded at

KEY WORDS

theistic: related to a Supreme being, god or gods

monotheistic: having one personal god

polytheistic: having many gods

non-theistic: having no personal god or no gods at all

assent: an expression of agreement

descent: dependent on parentage or ancestry

pluralistic: in this context, having many different beliefs and practices

proselytising: evangelising, persuading others to join a particular group or religion

heretic: a person within a group who has unconventional or unorthodox beliefs

patrilineal: passed down through the father

matrilineal: passed down through the mother

a particular time in history. They are associated with revelation, and usually represent a break from a primary religion; for example, Christianity began as a sect within Judaism, and Buddhism began as a breakaway group from Hindusim.

EXPLORE 8.2

In pairs, consider a major religion practised in your community or country. Is it a religion of assent, descent or something in between? Would you regard it as a primary or secondary religion?

Create a poster that illustrates some of what you perceive to be six key elements of the religion. (Your poster might include, but need not necessarily include, things like important texts and symbols, particular rituals and architecture, special people, plants and/or animals, certain clothing, and so on.)

Self-assessment

Compare your poster with others who may have featured the same religion. Have you identified the same key elements? Can you justify the elements you have included? If someone has created a poster on a different religion, what different elements have they featured? Do you understand how classifying religions could both help and hinder your understanding of them?

Theistic religions

For most of the world, being religious means belief in one or more gods. Judaism, Christianity, Islam, Sikhism, the Baha'i faith and Zoroastrianism are all monotheistic religions, meaning they believe in one god who reveals Godself to the world. They draw much of their evidence for their beliefs from special revelations made to individuals in history and passed on through authoritative texts, rituals and traditions, as well as reason applied to general revelations that reveal God or gods through the natural world.

REAL-LIFE SITUATION 8.3

Theistic religions rely heavily on personal testimony as evidence for their beliefs and knowledge. How can we know when there is enough evidence for a belief to become knowledge?

Polytheistic religions such as Taoism, Confucianism, Shinto and many tribal religions believe there is more than one god, and in most cases, these different gods represent different forces of nature and/or ancestral spirits. In some cases, the gods are organised in a pantheon that mirrors the organisation of the worshipping society: for example, the Chinese pantheon of gods tends to be organised as a bureaucracy.

KEY WORD

revelation: something that has been revealed or disclosed, usually by God or God's representatives or messengers

KEY WORDS

special revelation: knowledge of God that is not available through reason; knowledge of God that is revealed in a supernatural way

general revelation: knowledge of God that is discovered through natural ways, such as observing the natural world, observing patterns in history and applying reason

pantheon: an overview of a culture's gods and goddesses that reflects the culture's values

DISCUSS 8.9

It has often been suggested that pantheistic religions from those of the ancient Greeks onwards do not really 'believe' in the reality of their gods, but use them as metaphors for the human condition. Might religions contain important knowledge about the human condition even if their theistic or polytheistic claims are not literally true?

Although Hinduism is usually regarded as polytheistic, there are many different schools of thought within Hinduism that offer different perspectives. Some would say that Hinduism is essentially monotheistic because the pantheon of Hindu gods and goddesses are all different manifestations of the one God. However, Hinduism might even be regarded as nontheistic because many Hindus regard Brahman (the Ultimate Reality) as having no attributes (unlike theistic religions which usually, but not always, believe God has attributes such as goodness, wisdom and justice. Instead, Brahman is identical to the whole of reality rather than its cause or ruler. In a similar way, Jainism can be considered polytheistic, atheistic or even trans-theistic, depending on how you choose to define God.

Deism is a belief in a single God, however it can be theistic or non-theistic depending on how you understand theism. Deists believe in one God as creator of the world but, unlike theists, they regard God as impersonal. They believe that God upholds the natural order of the world, rather than intervening in it. Deists see God as evident through the natural laws of the world, and validated by human reason.

KEY WORDS

trans-theistic: beyond theism and atheism

deism: the belief in an impersonal creator god, who is evident through reason and the laws of nature, but does not intervene in human affairs

REAL-LIFE SITUATION 8.4

With so many different understandings of the word *god* across religions and even within religions, what are some of the difficulties that might arise when discussing religious knowledge claims?

Non-theistic religions

Although when we speak of religions, and particularly of faith, there is a tendency to think in terms of a god or gods, there are some religions and even some branches of theistic religion that are non-theistic by nature, although they are not necessarily atheistic.

The religion that generally comes to mind as not having a god is Buddhism. However, outside of the West, most schools of Buddhism acknowledge the existence of multiple deities (*devas*), although they reject the idea of a creator god. The Buddha, Siddhartha Gautama, acknowledged the existence of multiple gods, but saw them as trapped in the cycle of birth and rebirth just as human beings are. Buddhism teaches that the Buddha is a teacher of the gods, and is superior to them.

KEY WORD

deity: a god or supernatural being

Figure 8.3: Buddhist monks offer prayers as they go around a sacred Bodhi tree. To whom do you think the Buddhist monks are offering their prayers? Do they have to be offered to a specific personal being at all?

DISCUSS 8.10

Does personal experience play a different role in the production of religious knowledge than it does in the production of knowledge in other themes and areas of knowledge?

DISCUSS 8.11

1   What might be the implications of a god that is all knowing?

2   How might human beings with their limited knowledge understand a god who is omniscient?

KEY WORD

secular humanism: a system of belief that believes in human values, consequentialist ethics based on reason, and a commitment to science, democracy and freedom

Secular humanism rejects any form of theism, and many humanists would also reject the concept of religion as having been misleading and destructive. Yet there are many secular humanists who regard secular humanism as their religion. In March 1987, a US court declared that secular humanism is a religion, and is therefore entitled to all the protections and prohibitions extended to religions. Indeed, secular humanism offers many of the same rites of passage that more traditional religions offer: naming ceremonies, weddings and funerals, and some secular humanist groups offer weekly non-religious congregational models of community, complete with communal singing, which very much replicate a church service without reference to any kind of god.

REAL-LIFE SITUATION 8.5

Football is associated with numerous rituals and ceremonies, and has a congregational model of community and communal singing. Would you consider football to be a non-theistic religion?

It may be surprising to know that there are some Christian theologians who might also be regarded as non-theistic because, for example, they regard religious language as metaphorical. They describe God as 'the ground of all being', or that which 'concerns us ultimately' rather than as the personal, theistic God who is generally conceived as omnipotent, omniscient, omnipresent and personally involved in human lives and the world. Paul Tillich (1886–1965) was one of the most influential theologians of the 20th century. He suggested the notion of theism as an expression of our 'ultimate concern', and argued *God does not exist. He is being-itself beyond essence and existence. Therefore to argue that God exists is to deny him.'* By this, Tillich was not pronouncing himself an atheist; rather he was saying that God is not a being who exists in time and space like atoms or whales; God is beyond existence. According to Tillich, to argue that God *exists* is to deny God, because it is making God less than God is.

DISCUSS 8.12

Are there any logical contradictions in the notion of omniscience; for example, does an omniscient being know everything that is false as well as everything that is true, know all the uncountable infinite digits of every irrational number, every possible future or only everything that can be known?

The problem of language

Inextricably bound with religion, including the different types of religion, is the problem of language. The same words can mean very different things to different people, even if they share the same, culture and mother tongue, and this is particularly true in the context of religion. For example, *existence* is a word rather like the word *God* in that we all think we know what it means but often use it differently. The differences in usage vary not only between different people; all of us may sometimes mean different things depending on the context in which we use the word. Often, we mean the word in a material sense – things exist if they consist of matter and/or energy. But sometimes we use the word is an idealist sense. Idealists believe that the only reality that humans can know are mental constructions: thoughts and ideas. While the word *existence* may be very familiar to us, there is a whole branch of philosophy (ontology) devoted to trying to understand it. This further highlights some of the difficulties associated with religious language, because religious ideas and knowledge rely heavily on abstract words such as love, goodness and existence.

DISCUSS 8.13

How does language sometimes make it difficult to discuss religious claims?

KEY WORDS

theologian: a person who studies the nature of God and religious beliefs, usually within a particular religious tradition

omnipotent: being all-powerful

omnipresent: present everywhere and at all times

omniscient: being all-knowing; having an intuitive, immediate awareness of all truth

Figure 8.4: The problem of existence

EXPLORE 8.3

In pairs or small groups, try to decide what you think the word *exist* means. Then decide which, if any, of a to l exist:

a   elephants

b   time

c   dinosaurs

d   ideas

e   numbers

f $\sqrt{(-1)}$

g   unicorns

h   music

i   Harry Potter

j   love

k   justice

l   human rights

Reflect on your answers to the Explore activity. Do you think you use the word *exist* consistently?

Peer-assessment

Compare your answers with those of other groups. Which examples do you agree on? Do you understand why the other group decided the way it did on the examples you did not agree on? Can you see how our assumptions about another person's use of language (such as in the example of the word *exist*) can lead us to misinterpret what they mean?

DISCUSS 8.14

How does religious language shape our religious thoughts and knowledge?

What you understand by the word *God* will depend on whether you believe in a god or gods or not, whether you were raised in a particular religious community or not, the kind of education you have had and many other factors. Similarly, whether you believe in a god or gods will largely depend on what you understand by the word *God*, and even what you believe about the nature of reality. Often, people who argue over the existence of God are making assumptions about what each other means by the words *God* and *existence,* and those assumptions may not be correct. Even within the same religious traditions, people can have very different ideas about the concepts of *God* and *existence* without being aware of it.

REFLECTION

What do you understand by the word *God*? Where do your ideas about God come from? How do these ideas affect you as a knower when you think about different religions?

REAL-LIFE SITUATION 8.6

In the Explore 8.3 exercise, you may have decided that unicorns exist in the imagination but not in any physical reality. Is the distinction between imagination and the physical world adequate when we discuss the existence of God or gods?

8.3 Perspectives and sources of religious knowledge

DISCUSS 8.15

Do religious beliefs merit description as 'knowledge'? If so, where does religious knowledge come from?

KEY WORD

sacred: holy; entitled to reverence and respect; set apart for the worship of a god or gods

One way of learning more about a religion is to examine its sources of knowledge. Typically, the sources are claimed revelations, **sacred** texts and narratives, the teachings of a founding person or people, traditions, authority figures and personal experience. Of these, revelations and personal experience are the foundational sources, while sacred texts and narratives, traditions and authorities record initial revelations in order to communicate and pass down the knowledge that was revealed, along with testimonies of religious experiences and knowledge of the religious community's interpretations of events.

The status of all sources of religion can be contentious in some circumstances, not least for the members of the religious community they belong to. Different perspectives over who or what is more authoritative are usually behind divisions and the formation of new sects or denominations within religions. For example, the Sunni–Shia split in Islam occurred shortly after the death of the Prophet Muhammad in the year 632, as the result of different views about who should succeed Muhammad as leader of the Muslim community. Some (who became the Sunnis) wanted the community to choose Muhammad's successor, but others (who became the Shi'a) believed that his successor should be a member of the Prophet's family, and chose Ali, Muhammad's cousin and son-in-law. These different perspectives led to a schism that has persisted to current times.

Sacred texts can be a particular source of contention. There is often disagreement over which texts should be included in the canon, and which should be excluded. For example, Roman Catholics include books in their canon that Protestant churches do not, and Mahayana Buddhists and Theravada Buddhists have different views about which texts are to be included in the Triptika. Even when there is agreement over which texts are sacred and which are not, there are still different perspectives on how texts are to be interpreted, by whom, and in what contexts. On top of these concerns are issues surrounding translation.

KEY WORDS

schism: a split or a break

canon: in the context of religion, a body of authorised religious works accepted as authoritative within that religion

Triptika: a set of three texts that are said to record the words of the Buddha

REAL-LIFE SITUATION 8.7

1   As a knower, when looking for any answers, how do you decide which sources you might use are authoritative, and which are not?

2   What is the difference between a text regarded as authoritative by a believer and the status of that text for non-believers, considering the knowledge claims of a religion?

LINKING QUESTION 8.1

Politics: To what extent might political perspectives play a role in deciding who or what is authoritative in religion? Is this the same for other themes and areas of knowledge?

Revelation

Revelation is an important concept in religion, and is a foundational source of religious knowledge. It refers to knowledge that is said to be revealed by a god or divine agents to one or more human beings in a **religious experience**. The revealed knowledge is knowledge that would not be accessible by humans if it were not deliberately revealed to us. Examples of revelation include the revelation of the Ten Commandments to Moses on Mount Sinai in Judaism, and God's revelations to Guru Nanak during his three days in the river in Sikhism.

The psychologist and philosopher William James (1842–1910) believed that religious experience is at the heart of any religion, and that understanding religious experiences is more important to understanding religion than the study of religious teachings or practices.

KEY WORD

religious experience: a temporary experience that defies normal description, in which the person having the experience feels that a power from outside themself is acting to reveal a truth that could not be reached by reason alone

REAL-LIFE SITUATION 8.8

People are often more willing to accept religious knowledge claims made centuries ago than they are to accept claims of contemporary revelations.

1   Why might this be?

2   Is this difference in trustworthiness that is based on time similarly true in other themes and areas of knowledge?

There are two main types of revelation. The first is 'general revelation' (also known as natural revelation), which is a form of revelation readily accessible to anyone through everyday life if they choose to see it. For example, some might say that a star-filled night sky reveals the glory of God. People with a different perspective might marvel at the ability of human ingenuity, in that we are able to discover more and more about the universe; others might simply shrug and not experience any sense of awe or wonder. Reading a holy text and taking part in religious rituals can also provide general revelations by allowing us insights into the god or gods being worshipped.

General revelation includes the idea of providence: that God is directing everything that happens in the world, and that nothing happens by chance. If you take this view, the workings of God can be revealed through history. For example, *The Book of Judges*, which is believed to be one of the oldest books in the Hebrew Bible, dating to the 8th century BCE, interprets the history of Israel in terms of a cycle of Israel's rebellion against God, God's anger and punishment allowing their oppression by other nations, Israel crying out for a saviour, the repentance of Israel and God's forgiveness allowing Israel to prosper. This is known as the **Deuteronomic cycle**, and became a **paradigm** for explaining some of the troubles that befell early Israel.

KEY WORDS

Deuteronomic cycle: a cycle of rebellion, oppression and repentance as a way of interpreting historic events

paradigm: a pattern or model

DISCUSS 8.16

How might narratives that set human triumphs and disasters within a cosmic framework, perhaps controlled by a deity, help human beings to understand their lives and develop theories about their purpose?

REAL-LIFE SITUATION 8.9

Whether looking at a spectacular landscape, reading a religious text or participating in a religious ritual, some people might feel the presence of God while others might not, even if they are believers. Is this simply a matter of different perspectives?

The second type of revelation is 'special revelation'. Unlike general revelation, special revelation occurs in very specific ways to certain people. Examples of this would be the revelation of the Torah to Moses, the revelation of the Qur'an to the Prophet Muhammad and the revelation of God through the person of Jesus.

Special revelations usually involve a supernatural dimension, in that the revelations are made directly by God, or through one of God's messengers, such as an angel. Some people regard the whole of their **scriptures** as revealed or inspired by God and, as such, infallible.

KEY WORD

scriptures: sacred writings; religious texts

DISCUSS 8.17

What is the role of personal testimony in the production and understanding of religious knowledge?

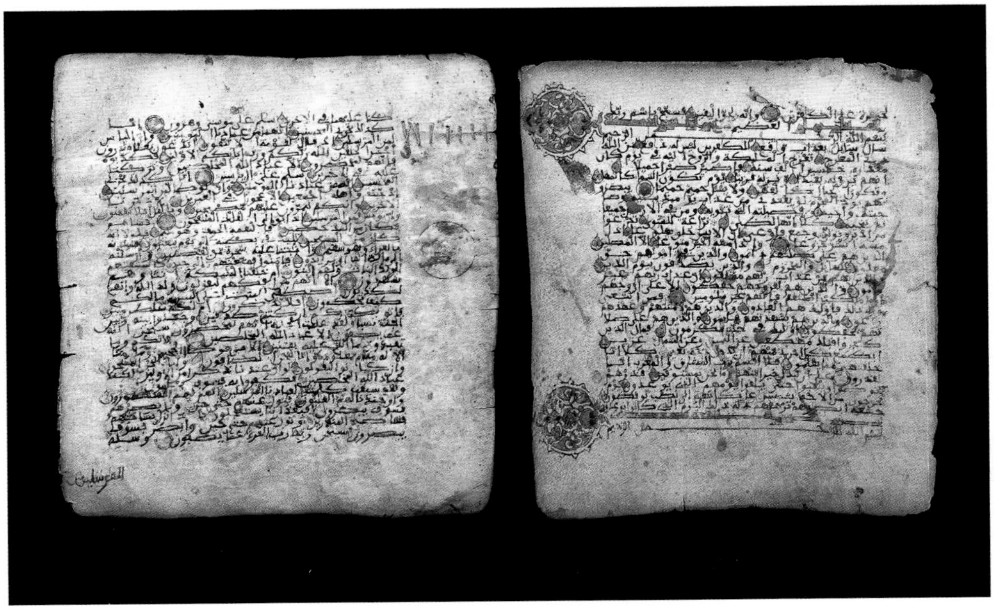

Figure 8.5: The revelation of the Qur'an is said to have begun in the month of Ramadan

In Hinduism, the most authoritative texts are called *Sruti,* meaning 'that which is heard', and central to the *Sruti* are four foundational Hindu texts known as the *Vedas.* The word *Veda* means knowledge, and the *Vedas* are regarded as direct revelations by Lord Brahma (the supreme creator god) to the ancient sages, known as *Rishis,* in much the same way as the angel Jibreel (Gabriel) is said to have revealed the Qur'an to the Prophet Muhammad. Indian tradition says that the *Rishis* saw or heard the truths contained in the *Vedas,* rather than composing those truths themselves.

KEY WORD
sage: a wise person

DISCUSS 8.18

1   To what extent can belief be regarded as knowledge?

2   Do we demand more or fewer justifications for accepting religious knowledge than we do for knowledge in other themes and areas of knowledge?

The concept of revelation is not restricted to theists. Buddhists believe that the four noble truths and the path to enlightenment are revealed and generally available to everyone through the teachings of the Buddha. It is important to note that in this case, the general revelation is not said to come from God. However, Buddhists will sometimes recognise special revelations from minor supernatural beings and deities, which can come in the form of dreams.

KEY WORD
enlightenment: a state of perfect knowledge about existence, perfect wisdom and infinite compassion

Religious texts

All sacred texts have their own histories, and they are usually regarded as direct revelations, or as telling the story of revelations received. Many of them were written and compiled over many years, and often not put into writing until long after the deaths of the religious founders and originators of the oral traditions.

The Buddha, Siddhartha Gautama, spent 45 years teaching in the Magadhi language. He did not write his ideas down and neither did his followers at the time, although they are said to have memorised his teachings. These memorised teachings were passed down by oral transmission. The remembered teachings were allegedly authenticated by the First Buddhist Council in approximately 400 BCE, shortly after the Buddha's death. Details of the council are recorded in the *Vinya Pitaka,* the first part of the Triptika, which was said to be transmitted orally until the teachings were written down in Sri Lanka in the Pali language, during the 1st century BCE. As well as the Pali canon, many Buddhists regard the *Mahayana sutras* as part of the Triptika, even though they were written in Sanskrit several centuries after the Buddha's death. It has been suggested by Buddhist scholars that the emergence of new scriptures and the reinterpretation of old ones is a sign of the vitality of a tradition.

DISCUSS 8.19

How might translating teachings from one language to another affect the teachings that are eventually recorded?

While Buddhists have welcomed additional scriptures, early Muslims had a different perspective. The Qur'an is said to have been revealed to the Prophet Muhammad over a period of 23 years, and it was only after Muhammad's death that his followers collected together his teachings and compiled them to create the book that is revered by Muslims today. According to orthodox Islam, many versions of the Qur'an existed at one time, but the third Caliph, Uthman, who reigned from 644–656, ordered all versions to be destroyed except for the one in the Quraishi dialect spoken by Muhammad. The purpose of this was to ensure that there would be only one Qur'an. However, when Uthman made his Qur'an, the Arabic script did not include vowel markings or dots to distinguish between certain letters. This ambiguity allowed words to be formed (vocalised or read) in different ways, and today there are ten different versions of the Qur'an, with the Qur'an according to Imam Hafs (706–796) being the most commonly used.

LINKING QUESTION 8.2

Language: Could ambiguity in language free you to intuitively discern meaning, or could it undermine your certainty?

REAL-LIFE SITUATION 8.10

In the case of all sacred texts, a decision was reached at some point to close the canon. This was sometimes to end disputes about its authenticity or scope, and sometimes to prevent spurious new texts from being added. As a result, almost all religious texts are regarded as 'closed' and 'finished'. What are the implications of these closures for the development of new religious knowledge, either inside or outside the religious traditions, whose sacred texts can no longer be revised or updated?

DISCUSS 8.20

How might knowing the historical origins of sacred texts and narratives affect any certainty that we might have about scriptures being the authentic records of the teachings of the founders?

EXPLORE 8.4

Think about your favourite teacher from one or two years ago. How much can you remember of what that teacher said or taught? What might help you to recall the teacher's words? How many of their actual words and phrases do you remember, and how much do you remember the gist of what was said?

Imagine you are tasked with recording the teachings of someone you admire and respect: perhaps a parent, grandparent, teacher, sports coach or friend. What would you choose to write down, and what would you leave out? To what extent would your answer depend on who wants you to record their teachings, and their reasons for wanting you to? How would you resolve disputes between different witnesses? How important would it be to record their teachings in exactly the words used by the person?

Consider how your perspectives on subjects and tasks impact on what you select to focus on and remember.

DISCUSS 8.21

How do we deal with historical experiences and evidence that contradict, or appear to contradict, our own perspectives or intentions?

One of the criticisms made of western scholars of religion is that they focus too much on the scriptural foundations of religions. Because scriptures are central to the Abrahamic religions – Judaism, Christianity and Islam, it is claimed that many religious scholars unconsciously assumed that scripture is central to all religions. In other words, because western scholars assumed scriptures would be central to all religions, they placed undue emphasis on any scriptures they thought to be sacred to the religions they were studying. There was a belief, for example, that to understand Buddhism, they needed to understand the Pali canon, whereas the practices of Buddhism are far more central to how Buddhists perceive their religion than the texts.

DISCUSS 8.22

1   How might our conscious and unconscious assumptions affect the construction of knowledge about religions other than our own?

2   How could being conscious of our assumptions help us to construct knowledge of other religions more reliably?

Religious symbols

Religious symbols can be significant features in religious knowledge and the declaration of faith. The symbols represent realities or truths, as well as being a means of identification for the initiated, and a passive means of outreach to the uninitiated. The symbols serve to convey religious concepts that might otherwise require a vast number of words, even if they could be expressed in words at all, and are seen to be important vehicles for knowing and expressing religious truths. As well as symbols that represent a religion as a whole, such as the Christian cross, the Buddhist *dharma* wheel, Taoist *Yin* and *Yang* and the Jewish Star of David, there are symbols that are more personal items of faith. For example, baptised Sikhs have five articles of faith that they carry with them to help keep them close to God. These symbols, called *Kakaars* (also known as the five Ks), are *kes* (uncut hair), *khangha* (a small comb), *kara* (a steel bracelet), *kirpan* (a small sword) and *kacchera* (a special undergarment). By carrying the five Ks, a Sikh is drawn into closer communion with the Sikh community past and present, and has an ever-present reminder of the tenets of Sikh faith.

As means of knowing, symbols can both reveal and veil truths, and are sometimes considered to provide ways of accessing spiritual truth.

Figure 8.6: A Sikh man leaving the water at the *Harmandir Sahib* or Golden Temple in Amritsar, India, wearing the five Ks; you can see his *kara* (bracelet), *kirpan* (dagger) and *kacchera* (a special undergarment); his *kes* (uncut hair) and *khangha* (comb) will be under his turban

---

REFLECTION

Do you carry any symbols (for example a friendship ring, a tattoo, a charm bracelet or a religious symbol) to help you remember special people, events or beliefs? In what ways does that symbol enhance your appreciation of who or what you want to remember? To what extent does it contribute to your sense of identity?

DISCUSS 8.23

1   How might symbols reinforce faith and/or religious knowledge?

2   How big a problem is the ambiguity of symbols in conveying religious knowledge?

EXPLORE 8.5

Religious objects are not the only form of religious symbols. Religious rituals are deeply symbolic, as are religious artworks. In pairs, choose an example of religious art and investigate some of the symbols found in it. Present your artwork and findings to the rest of the class.

How much similarity is there with respect to the concepts that are symbolised in the different works of art, and across different religions?

8.4 Methods and tools

Religions are diverse and complex, therefore religious scholars draw on a wide variety of methods, largely drawn from the disciplines of anthropology, archaeology, philosophy, sociology, psychology and history. As many of the more organised religions have strong textual bases, the tools of literature and linguistics are essential to the study of those religions, although less significant in the case of indigenous religions.

Many people consider faith as a major factor in the development of religious knowledge, but in many religions or branches of religions, reason is considered to be of even greater importance. Reason can be applied through philosophical approaches to religious questions, as well as through analysis of the various disciplinary approaches used to understand different aspects of religious traditions and practices.

Hermeneutics

Hermeneutics is the theory and methodology of interpretation. It can be used for all forms of communication and any style of text, but it is particularly important for the interpretation of philosophical texts, wisdom literature and scriptures. Hermeneutical methods include exegesis, which itself uses a range of tools from analytical and critical disciples, including textual analysis.

Exegesis involves trying to discover the purpose of a text and the context it was written in, who the authors were and who the intended readers were. It takes account of how the text is organised, as well as the style and genre in which the text is written. It is only when these answers are found that the exegete can decide what the text is about and what, if any, evidence is presented.

The opposite of exegesis is eisegesis. This is when meaning is read *into* a text. People who want to use a text to support their own beliefs and opinions will often do so by cherry-picking texts and reading into it whatever they want. One example of this is the biblical verse, 'an eye for an eye'. It is often used to argue for the right to retaliate on the grounds that the biblical verse appears to endorse such action. However, if the verse is read in the context of the wider Hebrew scriptures, scholars believe it was originally intended to curb excessive retaliation in what was a vengeful Babylonian society. In the Talmud, Rabbis interpreted the verse as mandating fair and reasonable (that is to say, not excessive) monetary compensation for harm done.

> ### REAL-LIFE SITUATION 8.11
>
> 1 How does reading a verse or story in its wider context result in a deeper understanding than reading a verse or story at face value?
>
> 2 How might you argue that one style of reading is more correct than another?
>
> 3 How important is translation in this process, since the meaning of a text can often change when it changes language?

KEY WORDS

hermeneutics: the science of interpreting texts

exegesis: drawing meaning from a text in a critical way

textual analysis: a data-gathering process that analyses choices of words and the ways in which they are used, to try to develop a greater understanding of the meaning of a text and the culture in which it was written

exegete: a person who engages in exegesis

eisegesis: reading meaning into a text

cherry-picking: picking out sections of a text that appear, at face value, to support a particular opinion, while ignoring the context and other sections of the text that might promote a different view

Talmud: the book of Jewish law and theology

The hermeneutical process is one that tries to see through a text in such a way that the reader can develop an understanding of the world in which the text was written, and can certainly lead the reader into a deeper understanding of a text than a literal or surface reading. However, it is important to realise that even hermeneutics cannot give a definitive answer to the meaning of a text. Different emphasis can be given to different methodologies, and there are multiple focal points that an exegete can apply. For example, a feminist hermeneutic will largely consider the text in relation to the experiences of women, both in the social setting in which the text was produced, and the social settings in which the text was received and passed on. A political hermeneutic will focus more on the political structures within the social settings. What is clear is that no single approach can give us the 'truth' about a culture, or the 'true meaning' of a text. Even if we approach a text as objectively as possible, how we read a text and what we look for in it will very much shape what we find.

DISCUSS 8.24

To what extent can we know with certainty what any ancient text means?

Languages evolve, and words do not always carry the same meanings today that they did centuries ago. The purpose that a text is written for can also have a profound effect on the way we should understand it. This raises serious questions when it comes to interpreting ancient scriptures.

Figure 8.7: Reading the Torah

There are almost as many ways to read and interpret any religious narrative as there are readers. At its very simplest, a narrative can be read as though it is a simple (perhaps literal) account of something that happened in a particular place and time. Many people who declare themselves to have a textually-based faith believe they are doing just that. However, not knowing something about the culture in which it was written and applying modern meanings to ancient words, combined with the vagaries of translation, can cause any originally *intended* meaning to be distorted. This includes an original meaning that was, rather than being intended, simply taken for granted, but is completely inaccessible to someone from another culture and time using a translation.

DISCUSS 8.25

To what extent can we know what any author *intended* when reading their work, and does it matter?

Some readers try to understand texts relative to the political and religious contexts in which they were written, but that does not mean they understand them literally as historical truth. Rather, the texts are thought to convey knowledge about the belief systems of the times in which they were written, and the political constraints of the period. Interpretation of scripture is an example of how modern knowers can attempt to link the past with the present, apply some degree of rational analysis of an ancient text and apply its perceived meaning in the world today.

Yet, other readers might look for **allegory** hidden in the text. One example of a text that is often interpreted allegorically is *The Song of Songs* found in the *Ketuvim* (writings) of the Hebrew Bible (also known as the Old Testament). The book is a series of poetic love songs, and does not mention God at all. At the time it was written, love poetry was a popular genre in Mesopotamia (modern day Iran and Iraq). *The Song of Songs* is now regularly read during the Jewish festival of Passover. While there has been a lot of debate over the book's inclusion in the Christian canon – and some people have wanted the book banned altogether as being too erotic – *The Song of Songs* has variously been interpreted as an allegory of God's love for the people of Israel, Christ's love for the Church and Christ's love for the human soul. Most modern scholars, however, regard the book as secular love poetry without any religious implications, yet Rabbi Akiba (50–135) argued that *The Song of Songs* is the apex of Jewish scripture, and the holiest of all holy texts.

> **KEY WORD**
>
> **allegory:** a text or artwork that can be interpreted to reveal a hidden meaning, usually moral or political in nature

DISCUSS 8.26

Any narrative can be open to various interpretations. Can just one interpretation be 'correct'? How would we know, and who decides?

One of the interesting aspects of Jewish tradition is that rather than trying to determine one 'true meaning' for Jewish scriptures, Jews usually read their scriptures in the *Mikra'ot Gedalot* (often translated as *Big Scriptures*) in which there is a biblical passage on each page, surrounded by several Rabbinic commentaries all offering different perspectives on what the biblical passage might mean, and no particular interpretation is given preferential status. The reader is entering a conversation that is being conducted over many centuries and across various cultures. In this way, religion is not only the subject of knowledge, but also a vehicle for the transmission of knowledge.

DISCUSS 8.27

How might a religion use history as a source of knowledge?

EXPLORE 8.6

In pairs or small groups, consider the following statement: 'She said she did not take his money'. How many different ways can you understand this statement? (Try reading it by stressing different words each time you read it.) Then see how many meanings can you find for, 'I saw a man on the hill with a telescope' by thinking about the structure of the sentence.

'Eating bananas is bad for you.' How might you interpret this if you read it in the contexts a to j?

a   a friend's Facebook™ status

b   a medical journal

c   a comic strip

d   a gardening magazine

e   a history textbook

f   a crime novel

g   a children's story book

h   a news broadcast from a reputable news service

i   a travel brochure

j   as 'clickbait' on a webpage

Self-assessment

Do you see why knowing the genre of a work is important to understand it?

DISCUSS 8.28

Do all written statements have some degree of ambiguity? Are some types of knowledge less open to variant interpretations than others?

Reason

DISCUSS 8.29

What is the relationship between faith and reason?

Faith and reason have both been considered to be sources of justification for religious belief throughout history. How the two are related has always been of interest to philosophers, theologians and (more recently) students of TOK.

Some people have argued that there should never be a conflict between reason and faith; that if reasoning is valid, and faith is properly understood, the two will never contradict each other. St Thomas Aquinas (1224–1274), one of the world's greatest mediaeval philosophers, believed that reason covers what we can know from experience and logic, without any special revelations. For Aquinas the knowledge provided by reason includes knowledge that there is a God. He famously came up with what is known as his five ways to God in his work *Summa Theologica*. These are five logical arguments for the existence of God.

St Thomas Aquinas' five ways to God

Aquinas believed that God is not self-evident to the human mind, and therefore needs to be demonstrated through the use of reason.

His arguments can be summarised as follows:

1 *The argument of the unmoved mover.* Everything in the world that moves or changes is moved by something else. But the chain cannot be infinitely long. There must have been something that caused change, without itself changing. This first unmoved mover is what we understand to be God.

2 *The argument of the first cause.* Everything in the world is created by something else. Nothing can create itself. The chain cannot be infinitely long, so there must be a first uncaused cause, and this is what we understand to be God.

3 *The argument from contingency.* Everything in the world is **contingent** and capable of not existing. But if everything is contingent and capable of coming into and going out of existence, at some point and thereafter, nothing would exist. As things clearly do exist, there must be something that is necessary. This necessary being is God.

> **KEY WORD**
>
> **contingent:** subject to chance, existing only under certain circumstances

4 *The argument from degree.* We see things in the world that vary in degrees of goodness, truth, and so on. For example, well-drawn circles are better and truer circles than poorly-drawn ones. But judging something as being 'more' or 'less' implies some standard against which it is being judged. Therefore, there must be something which is best and most true, and this we understand to be God.

5 *The argument from final cause.* Non-intelligent objects in the world behave in regular ways, so their behaviour must be set to reach a final cause. For example, an acorn behaves in regular ways to become an oak tree as its 'final cause'. Because objects are non-intelligent, they cannot set their own behaviour. Their behaviour must therefore be set by something else, and by implication, something that must be intelligent. This intelligent source of their behaviour is what we understand to be God.

Some people refer to Aquinas's five ways as five 'proofs', but Aquinas himself does not use that term.

DISCUSS 8.30

What is the role of reason in trying to reach religious truth?

Of course, there are multiple criticisms of Aquinas's five ways: even if there is an unmoved Mover or an uncaused Cause, there is nothing to say that this unmoved Mover or uncaused Cause must be a god, let alone the personal God of theistic religions. However, Aquinas's arguments are evidence of a philosophical interest throughout the Middle Ages to complement faith-based religion with reasoned arguments.

Aquinas was not alone in his efforts to demonstrate the existence of God using reason. Philosophers in many of the world's great religions made similar attempts throughout the Middle Ages. Some of the most well-known examples include two 'proofs' of God by Aviddhakarna (c 600), the Kalam cosmological argument traced back to Abu Yūsuf Ya'qūb ibn' Isḥāq aṣ-Ṣabbāḥ al-Kindī (c 801–873), St Anselm's (1033–1109) ontological argument, Moses ben Maimon's *Guide for the Perplexed* (1135–1204) and, in the 18th century, William Paley's watchmaker analogy (1743–1805).

DISCUSS 8.31

Why do you think medieval theologians and philosophers were not content to base their religious beliefs on faith alone?

EXPLORE 8.7

In pairs or small groups, try to find out what some of these other arguments are, and assess how successful you think they are.

DISCUSS 8.32

To what extent can reason be used to provide evidence for claims beyond our immediate experience? If we refused to believe anything at all, would reason have any 'raw material' to work with?

Faith

Faith is a state of confidence, fidelity and trust in a person, object, organisation or idea. Often, the word *faith* is used as a synonym for religion, for example when we refer to 'the Christian religion' as 'the Christian faith'. However, faith is not necessarily about religion; it is equally valid to talk about faith in science or faith in humanity.

The concept of faith is important in many religious traditions. For Buddhists, who do not believe in an omnipotent God, faith is a commitment to practise the Buddha's teachings, and to trust in – to have faith in the importance and value of – the teachings of the *bodhisattvas* and *buddhas* who have obtained enlightenment. In the Japanese form of Pure Land Buddhism, faith in Buddha Amithaba is the central **tenet**.

There are very many different views on the place of faith across religions and within religions. In the very early church, a Christian theologian named Tertullian (155–230) believed that reason should have nothing to do with faith. He is said to have claimed about a particular doctrine: 'I believe because it is impossible.' He believed that reason actually obstructed the discovery of truth, and therefore expected faith to be contrary to reason. Many other religious thinkers have posed the question of whether reason, being an activity of pure unaided human effort, is antithetical to belief in a god or gods.

KEY WORDS

bodhisattva: a Buddhist who has achieved enlightenment, but delays reaching nirvana out of compassion for those who are suffering

tenet: principle, important truth

Figure 8.8: A 36-metre high statue of Amithaba Buddha surrounded by 480 smaller statues in the Foguangshan monastery, Taiwan

DISCUSS 8.33

1   How confident are you that reason is the most effective way to know what is true?

2   What other methods might be more reliable?

Like Tertullian, there are still some people who regard faith as being independent of reason, and many even regard faith and reason as hostile to each other. The biologist Richard Dawkins (1941–) is well known for his criticism of religion, and asserts that religious faith is 'belief without evidence'. However, John Lennox (1943–), a mathematician and philosopher of science, argues that to reduce all faith to **blind faith** and then ridicule it is an anti-intellectual way of avoiding intelligent discussion. Lennox claims faith is a commitment based on reason and evidence, and not a leap in the dark.

KEY WORD

blind faith: faith without evidence, understanding or discrimination

DISCUSS 8.34

1   Is it possible to have faith without reason?

2   Is it possible to have reason without faith or belief?

There are some people who believe we should prioritise faith (particularly religious faith) over all other ways of knowing. This position is known as **fideism**. Fideism arose as an approach to knowledge in 19th-century Roman Catholicism, although the Roman Catholic Church has repeatedly refused to sanction the idea. Instead,

KEY WORD

fideism: reliance on faith for all knowledge; a belief that faith is superior to reason

the Church draws its position from Aquinas, who believed faith to be built upon reason and necessarily consistent with it. Aquinas believed that faith is what we can know from God's special revelation through the person of Jesus, the Bible and the Christian tradition, but that it must always be compatible with reason. If it appears incompatible, it must be because we have misinterpreted the revelation.

REFLECTION

Think about who or what you have faith in. (It could be your family, close friends, certain institutions, like the health service or the law, science as well as, or instead of, religious beliefs.) If your faith comes into conflict with reason, which do you prioritise?

DISCUSS 8.35

How can we know where our responsibilities lie when our reason conflicts with our faith? (This need not be religious faith.)

Some thinkers have suggested that faith and reason each function in different ways, and address different concerns. They would argue that in cases of apparent conflict between faith and reason, faith should take priority when it comes to religious or theological claims, but reason should take priority when it comes to empirical or logical claims.

REAL-LIFE SITUATION 8.12

1   Down the centuries, there have always been religious *charlatans* who have destroyed trust in religion. How do faith, trust and reason connect and interact?

2   As a knower, how do you decide which to rely upon if faith, trust and reason seem to disagree? Is it possible to eliminate faith *completely* from any knowledge system?

Religion and science

Although not a method or tool, the perceived debate between science and religion is significant because it is sometimes used to demonstrate an assumed incompatibility between the two knowledge systems, often with the intention of undermining religious beliefs. In such cases, people try to pit science and reason against religion and faith as though scientific knowledge is entirely based on [objective] reason supported by empirical evidence, and religious knowledge is entirely based on [blind] faith and evidenced by superstition.

Some people argue that science presents a different worldview to those presented by different religions, and that a scientific worldview is not compatible with any religious perspective. They would say that there are also conflicts in the methodologies, again associating reason primarily with science and faith primarily with religion, and so they have very different truths.

Other people, such as the palaeontologist and evolutionary biologist Stephen Jay Gould (1941–2002), try to reach a more amicable compromise by suggesting that science and religion are two different areas of knowledge that do not overlap; that they ask and answer very different questions. He believes science tries to document the factual character of the natural world, and to develop theories that explain these facts, while religion tries to document and understand the realm of human purposes, meanings and values. These, Gould claims, are areas that science might help to shed light on, but would never be able to resolve.

DISCUSS 8.36

To what extent do religion, the human sciences and the natural sciences try to answer different questions about the world?

However, not everyone sees science and religion as incompatible with, or indifferent to, each other. Saint Augustine of Hippo (354–430) believed that God has provided humanity with two forms of revelation: the *Book of Scripture* and the *Book of Nature*. He argues that because the two 'books' had the same divine author, they are both perfect and complementary. He insisted that the Bible is multi-layered, and not always intended to be read in a literal sense; rather, it had been written in a way to make it understandable for its original audience. St Augustine also taught that textual interpretations should not be held dogmatically; the *Book of Nature* should be the authority for revelations of truth about reality. When there appears to be a conflict between the *Book of Nature* and the *Book of Scripture*, we need to be prepared to accept that our interpretation of God's truth in the *Book of Scripture* is not correct. Interpretations of scripture must always be informed by science and other areas of knowledge.

Many Eastern religions also emphasise the synergy they see between science and spirituality, and they do not recognise any real divisions. They believe that all truths, whether scientific, religious or any other type of truth, are meant to teach us about the world and our place in it.

DISCUSS 8.37

How might scientific developments inform interpretations of scripture and help to shape religious thought?

Indeed, many eminent scientists have been (and are) devout religious observers. Johann Gregor Mendel (1822–1884), who discovered the fundamental laws of inheritance through his work on peas, was an Augustinian monk. Georges Lemaître (1894–1966), who proposed an expanding model for the universe (now known as the Big Bang theory of the origins of the universe), was a Roman Catholic priest. Abdus Salam (1926–1996), who was a joint winner of the 1979 Nobel Prize in physics, was a devout Muslim for all of his life, and he saw his religion as an integral part of his work. In a 1979 address to UNESCO, he said, 'The Holy Qur'an enjoins us to reflect on the verities of Allah's created laws of nature; however, that our generation has been privileged to glimpse a part of His design is a bounty and a grace for which I render thanks with a humble heart.' There are a number of associations for people who are interested in both religion and science, including the European Society for the Study of Science and Theology (ESSSAT), which attracts both scientists and religious scholars from different religious backgrounds.

Regardless of our personal stance on religion or science, most modern philosophers of science have demonstrated that all knowledge, including scientific knowledge, depends upon a complex mixture of belief in – and reasoning about – its subject, based upon social acceptance, historical experience and language. For example, our theories about the atom and the whole universe, quantum mechanics and Big Bang cosmology are dependent upon the collective affirmation of the common assumptions and empirical evidence by the accepted and respected community of scientists. A sophisticated and subtle balance between assumptions (beliefs) and deductions (reasoning) grounded in experimental evidence guides the whole of science.

REAL-LIFE SITUATION 8.13

There are many ways in which science can help in the development of religious knowledge. Can you think of ways in which religion might help the development of scientific knowledge?

EXPLORE 8.8

Choose an IA exhibition prompt from the TOK guide, and select an object referring to the science and religion debate. Examples could be something like a telescope as a symbol of astronomy, cosmology and Judeo–Christian ideas of creation; a pocket watch as a symbol of intelligent design; an image of the Hindu goddess, Namagiri, who is said to have inspired the mathematician Srinivasa Ramanujan (1887–1920); or a radio to represent the work of the theoretical physicist and biophysicist Jagadish Chandra Bose (1858–1937) who saw the Hindu concept of unity reflected in the study of nature. Write a short commentary (no more than 300 words) that identifies your object and its context in the world, and explain how it links to the IA prompt you have chosen.

Self-assessment

Read through your work carefully. Are the object and its real-world context clearly identified? Have you made sufficient links between the object and your chosen prompt?

Peer-assessment

Share your commentary with a classmate, and give each other feedback. Are links between the object and the selected IA prompt explained well, and made clearly? Are all points well supported with evidence and explicit references to the prompt?

8.5 Individuals, religious communities and ethics

REAL-LIFE SITUATION 8.14

To what extent is it necessary to participate in social worship to be a member of a religion?

There has been a tendency in recent years for academics interested in religions, including the psychology of religion, to focus on why individuals believe. These belief-centred approaches sometimes organise the study of religions into **intrinsic religiosity** and **extrinsic religiosity**, where intrinsic religiosity refers to the beliefs and practices of individuals, and extrinsic religiosity refers to social practices such as community rituals. Intrinsic religiosity is sometimes regarded as a spiritual quest in which an individual tries to reach an understanding of the divine, while extrinsic religiosity is often portrayed as a means to an end; even an act of hypocrisy.

This intrinsic–extrinsic divide is a particularly western-Protestant perspective, with its focus on individualism. It is part of a trend in the human sciences to understand social behaviour by the behaviours of individuals. However, it has been argued that social religious behaviours can only be understood by understanding ethical and moral concerns, and these can only be seen from a group perspective. Religious narratives and teachings often stress the obligations of members to the group and the need to show respect for authorities, rules and practices of the group. Together, these help to create a religious cohesion and moral harmony within the group.

KEY WORDS

intrinsic religiosity: where religion is the organising principle of an individual's life; a central and personal experience

extrinsic religiosity: participating in social worship to conform to a social norm or convention

DISCUSS 8.38

To what extent can group behaviour be explained as the collective behaviour of many individuals?

Religious ethics

Ethics is a crucial element of the relationship between individuals and communities. Most, if not all, religions have an ethical dimension. Religious communities tend to have a strong social order, often underpinned by ethical principles that are derived from religious sources. These sources can be traditional or contemporary interpretations of ethical principles found in religious texts and teachings.

Religious ethics try to address issues that are inherent in all human societies, such as 'What is a community?' and 'How can people live together harmoniously?' They consider which are the most important problems facing people living in societies, and promote solutions in keeping with religious principles. Often, the problems that are identified and solutions that are proposed in religious texts are specific to a particular culture and period in history. Religious scholars are then tasked with interpreting the lessons of the text for different cultures in the contemporary world.

Religious ethics have played a significant role in all societies, by constructing social norms and legal frameworks that are aimed at preserving moral codes. Even the moral laws and social conventions of modern secular societies are largely based on religious moral values.

DISCUSS 8.39

1   To what extent do you think the issues facing individuals living in communities have changed over the past 3,000 years?

2   If religious moral teachings have been found to be valuable to communities over hundreds – if not thousands – of years, is this enough to regard those teachings as being, in some sense, true?

REAL-LIFE SITUATION 8.15

Often religious leaders, even from the same religion, will have different opinions on moral questions in contemporary society. Issues such as abortion, euthanasia and gay rights draw passionate arguments from religious leaders on all sides of the debates. How do religions help to support social cohesion and moral rectitude, if they cannot provide definitive answers to contemporary moral questions?

Worship

Worship is an expression of reverence, adoration and commitment to a deity or deities, a Buddha or bodhisattvas or even, in some cases, to humanist ideals. Worship can take many forms, and can be both individual and communal. Individual worship is generally regarded as important, but many religions would say that it does not replace the need for communal worship, which enables all believers to come together in one spirit and one voice.

Almost all religions have some form of ancestor worship although it is particularly widespread in Asian countries, where many people have a shrine to their ancestors in their homes, regardless of their religious affiliations. The veneration of ancestors is incorporated into their religious practices. In some cultures, the veneration of ancestors is about helping ancestors to have a good afterlife, and is an important aspect of filial piety; it can also involve asking for blessings from the ancestors.

DISCUSS 8.40

If ancestor worship is practised by people of all religions in some places, is it a cultural practice rather than a religious practice?

An essential element of worship is the practice of religious rituals. Religious rituals are repetitive social practices that are encoded in myth. They are very powerful ways of communicating a complex set of ideas and emotions, and transmitting religious

KEY WORDS

veneration: the act of worship or showing great respect

filial piety: showing love, respect and support for one's parents

ritual: a prescribed ceremonial action or set of actions that have a symbolic meaning for the individual and the community

myth: an ancient, traditional story, usually concerning the history of a people or explaining a phenomenon. Myths often, but not always, involve supernatural beings

knowledge by symbolically expressing religious concepts in a series of words and actions. As well as varying across religions, religious rituals for the same religions can vary in different geographical regions and over time, yet even across different religions, religious rituals tend to symbolise similar themes.

REAL-LIFE SITUATION 8.16

Rituals are common in secular settings as well as religious worship.

1   Can you think of some secular rituals that are practised in the country you live in?

2   What do those rituals express?

3   To what extent can people outside of a particular community fully understand the practices of that community?

Pilgrimage

Pilgrimage is the act of taking a long, meaningful journey, often on foot, to a sacred place. Pilgrimages offer a break from ordinary life to think and reflect on the journey and/or to join in the company of others to build spiritual bonds. As well as being a physical journey, pilgrimage can also refer to an inner spiritual journey through prayer, meditation and mystical experience. Many people regard pilgrimages as life-changing and transformational experiences.

DISCUSS 8.41

1   How might visiting sacred places help the faithful to develop a link with history and shared memory?

2   What impact might visiting the reputed origins of a religion have on the knowledge claims or the convictions of believers?

One of the most well-known pilgrimages is the *Hajj*, which is one of the five pillars of Islam. All Muslims are expected to make this pilgrimage to Mecca at least once in their lifetime if they are physically and financially able to do so. Only Muslims are allowed in Mecca, and the idea of the *Hajj* is that all Muslims are dressed in the same shroud-like garment and participate in the same rituals, and hence are seen to be equal in front of God. As numbers attending the *Hajj* have increased, a number of the *Hajj* rituals have been modified for safety and convenience.

REAL-LIFE SITUATION 8.17

The modifying of important religious rituals is one way in which religions change and adapt to changing circumstances over time. To what extent does our understanding of religious knowledge also change?

Pilgrimage is particularly important in the practice of Hinduism, and one of the most sacred sites is the ancient city of Varanasi in Northern India. It is believed to be the home of Lord Shiva, a major Hindu god. Millions of Hindu pilgrims visit Varanasi each year, and purify themselves by bathing in the River Ganges at sunrise. The River Ganges is itself regarded as the goddess, Ganga. Her waters are considered to be spiritually very pure, and many people cast the ashes of cremated loved ones into the river. The *Kumbh Mela* is the world's largest congregation of religious pilgrims, and is held in four places across India on a rotational basis, with the festival being held only every 12 years in any one place. At the 2013 *Kumbh Mela*, an estimated 120 million people attended over a two-month period, and over 30 million on a single day.

Figure 8.9: Religious pilgrims taking a holy bath in the River Ganges at the 2013 Allahabad *Kumbh Mela*

It has been suggested by some Hindu scientists that the 'healing power' of the Ganges is due to **bacteriophages** and **non-putrifying bacteria** found in the water. However, other Hindu scientists claim the water in the Ganges poses a serious health risk due to an estimated 3 billion litres of untreated sewage being poured into the river every day. Some parts of the river have a faecal coliform count of more than 1.5 million per 100 ml, which is more than 3,000 times the recommended maximum level for safe swimming. Although some people who bathe in the River Ganges fall ill, this does not deter the millions of Hindus who joyfully bathe in the river, and drink its water in the hope of being 'purified' and perhaps cured of an illness.

> **KEY WORDS**
>
> **bacteriophage:** a virus that destroys bacteria
>
> **non-putrifying bacteria:** bacteria that do not help to decompose dead or decaying matter

LINKING QUESTION 8.3

Natural sciences

1   If two groups of Hindu scientists make conflicting scientific claims about the water of the Ganges, could both claims be equally valid?

2   To what extent might scientific knowledge be as susceptible to 'cherry-picking' as religious knowledge?

3   Should responsibility for warning pilgrims of the dangers of the water pollution primarily rest with scientists, religious leaders or politicians?

With an event as large and as popular as the *Khumbh Mela,* it is not always possible to know who is a pilgrim and who is a tourist. Often, visitors attend as both pilgrims and tourists. The same is true for many other pilgrimage sites, such as St Peter's Basilica in Vatican City, the Golden Temple in Amritsar and the Temple of the Tooth in Kandy, Sri Lanka.

EXPLORE 8.9

1   Have you or has anyone in your class visited a place that is popular with pilgrims? Describe the place and some of the activities you saw and heard, or perhaps participated in. What effect, if any, did the experience have? What knowledge and insights might the pilgrims have gained? What aspects of that knowledge would be objective, and what would be subjective?

2   Try to analyse a pilgrimage experience you know about – whether first hand or second hand. Do you think you could explain how pilgrimage might help to create religious knowledge?

REAL-LIFE SITUATION 8.18

1   How might the intentions behind a journey (for example whether you go as a tourist or a pilgrim) make a difference to the religious knowledge gained?

2   How might the knowledge found through introspection and reflection compare with knowledge found through a physical pilgrimage?

Sacrifice and fasting

The word *sacrifice* often brings to mind the act of slaughtering an animal, or even a person, to offer to a deity. It can also be the giving up of something of value, such as food, money or time. Fasting, similarly, is the giving up of certain foods and drink during certain times of the day and/or during certain times of a religious calendar. Most, if not all, religions endorse the principle that their members should be prepared to make some form of sacrifice, usually for the benefit of the wider community, but sometimes also to strengthen spiritual resolve.

Hindu scriptures detail rituals involving animal sacrifices, and some Hindu sects still slaughter animals for particular festivals, but most Hindus give priority to the concept of *ahimsa*, and their offerings to the gods tend to be food (especially sweets) and flowers. *Ahimsa* is an ethical principle that has clear benefits for creating a harmonious society.

KEY WORD

sacrifice: to give up something valuable to help others, or to appease a god or spirit

ahimsa: the principle of doing no harm

DISCUSS 8.42

To what extent might the concept of sacrifice contribute to an individual's and a community's identity?

Think about religious or secular sacrifices you may have made, or fasts you may have participated in. (Perhaps you have sacrificed a weekend of fun with your friends to fundraise for a charity, or maybe you have sacrificed your lunch to feed a hungry bird.) How might making a sacrifice or taking part in a fast give you new awareness, perspectives or knowledge?

In Chinese folk religion, often practised alongside Buddhism and/or Taoism, provision is made for the dead in the form of paper replicas of all the worldly goods they may desire. These replicas are burnt with the dead body, so that the deceased will want for nothing in the afterlife. Food and drink are also provided to sustain them on their journey to the next world. In the past, wealthy people had real valuables interred with them, and the Shang rulers (16th–11th century BCE) even had valued animals and human servants buried with them. Large tombs contained as many as 350 human bodies sacrificed to accompany the ruler. Later, clay figures were buried in place of human sacrifices. The famous Terracotta Army is an army of 6,000 life-sized pottery warriors buried with the first emperor of a unified China, Qin Shi Huang (259–210 BCE). In modern China, theoretically an atheist state, people buy token money with real money to send to their ancestors by burning it in ceremonial shrines.

DISCUSS 8.43

1   How has human understanding of religious knowledge changed over time?

2   Evidence of past religious practices provides us with historical knowledge, but to what extent can we really understand the key religious ideas behind those practices?

In the ancient world, many religions – such as Judaism and Shinto – included some animal sacrifices. Animal sacrifice is still a significant feature today in many indigenous religions, as well as in Islam during Eid and following the birth of a baby, although many Muslims no longer perform the sacrifice themselves. Instead, they pay for an animal to be slaughtered in an abattoir, and the meat is distributed to the poor. In many cases, animal sacrifices are a way of giving thanks to a deity, and honouring the life of the animals that the community will then eat in a celebration.

Christianity generally does not practise animal sacrifice because it teaches that Jesus's death was the perfect sacrifice and made any other sacrifices unnecessary. Instead, Christians remember Jesus's sacrifice through the sacrament of the Eucharist. However, in some remote, rural villages in Greece, Armenia and Ethiopia, lambs are sometimes sacrificed outside local churches at Easter and then consumed in a village feast.

DISCUSS 8.44

Is there an ethical difference between buying an animal slaughtered at an abattoir, and slaughtering an animal at a place of worship while giving thanks to a god or gods for its life?

Fasting is a form of self-sacrifice that is practised in many religions. It serves as a reminder to abstain from selfishness and physical desires, so as to focus on prayer and meditation at important times in the religious calendar. It can help to strengthen community bonds between those who are fasting, and may be seen as a way of showing empathy for, and solidarity with, the poor. Most religions also embrace the idea of sacrifice in terms of giving time and/or money to charities, to give service in honour of their God, gods or philosophical principles.

DISCUSS 8.45

There are many similarities in approaches to sacrifice and fasting in almost all religions. Are there any concepts that might be true for all religions? If so, could they be considered objective truths?

8.6 Ecumenism, inter-faith dialogue and religious fundamentalism

REAL-LIFE SITUATION 8.19

Why might it be beneficial for the world's religions to find common ground or common knowledge?

There will be no peace among the nations without peace among the religions. There will be no peace among the religions without dialogue among the religions.

Hans Kung (1928–)

Ecumenism is a movement in Christianity to build closer relationships and better understanding between the many and various Christian **denominations**. In addition to the movement to bring Christian churches together, there is a wider movement to promote cooperation and positive interaction between people of different religious traditions. This is generally referred to as interfaith dialogue. Some people prefer the term 'interpath dialogue' so as not to exclude people from non-theistic religions, atheists and any others who do not see themselves as belonging to a religion, but who have ethical and philosophical beliefs.

There are many different interfaith/interpath initiatives around the world. Some are local, some regional or national, and there are also international initiatives such as *Religions for Peace*. *Religions for Peace* is a network which runs a World Council of senior religious leaders from around the globe, and has six regional inter-religious organisations and over 90 national organisations. The organisation works to advance human development, bring an end to violent conflict and promote just and peaceful societies. A similar organisation is the *Parliament of the World's Religions*, which began in 1893 in an attempt to create a global dialogue between different religions. The *Parliament of the World's Religions* was reconvened 100 years later, and now meets every few years. Its programmes consider issues of religious, spiritual and cultural identity, approaches to interreligious dialogue and the role of religion in response to critical issues facing the world.

KEY WORDS

ecumenism: the principle of aim of promoting unit among the world's Christian Churches

denomination: a distinct religious group within Christianity (for example, the Anglican, Georgian Orthodox and Lutheran churches)

What implications does interfaith dialogue have for the knowledge claims of different religions? What roles do religions and religious authorities play in influencing ethical debates around the globe?

Figure 8.10: In November 2019, the Second Summit of World Religious Leaders took place in Baku, Azerbaijan

Religious fundamentalism

Two of the big issues that interfaith dialogue addresses are the problems of religious fundamentalism and extremism.

Almost every major belief system has fundamentalist adherents, who believe that their particular version of their religion is uniquely 'the one true religion' and beyond any criticism. Their lives are dictated by their religious beliefs, and they sometimes try to force their beliefs and practices on others. Even though they may not advocate violent conversion, many religions proselytise in an attempt to bring adherents of other religions to 'the one true faith'. Religious extremists go further, and will sometimes use violence to enforce their religious customs and practices, and even to eliminate dissenting voices.

REAL-LIFE SITUATION 8.21

To some extent, we all 'privilege our own tribe', and therefore our own systems of knowledge.

1   To what extent do you believe that there is only one true system of knowledge, and that those who have it should make every attempt to persuade others to accept it?

2   Does it matter whether this is a religious, scientific, philosophical or ethical system? Are some people entitled to believe in creation science rather than evolution if they want to, or should someone persuade them of the errors of their ways?

KEY WORDS

religious fundamentalism: a belief in the absolute authority of a particular sacred text, religious leader and/ or god

extremism: an ideology in which people are prepared to take extreme actions including the use of violence for their religious or political causes

---

REFLECTION

Have you ever tried to convince your friends to visit a new place, try a new food or avoid a particular situation? What are the underlying assumptions that motivate you to want to share your ideas, beliefs and knowledge with others? To what extent and in what contexts might your assumptions be reasonable?

Religious fundamentalists from all religious traditions tend to reject scientific principles and all forms of pluralism. There is a tendency for them to see everything as black or white with no shades of grey, and they are often not willing to listen to other perspectives, even from within their own religious traditions. Sometimes they have been taught to see other religious traditions as bad or even evil, and 'offences against God'. Religious extremism has brought violence and destruction to many parts of the globe, and caused the death of many innocent people. Often, extremists' violence is an attempt to protect their religious traditions as they understand them from being lost in the changes of the modern world.

Unfortunately, because religious extremists make the news more frequently than more moderate and mainstream religious adherents, many people come to associate mainstream religions with the actions of the extremist minorities.

DISCUSS 8.46

1   To what extent do religions try to promote the liberal value of tolerance?

2   Is tolerance always virtuous? How are we to decide on the limits to toleration, and what place do *religious* teachings and values have in deciding such matters?

8.7 Conclusion

When we consider the many thousands of religions in the world, and their various divisions and subdivisions with their diverse positions of the existence or not of God or gods, not to mention the pronounced differences in their many other teachings, it may seem difficult to see how there can be such a thing as religious knowledge.

However, human beings are even more numerous, diverse and contrary, and yet most of us have no difficulty in accepting that human beings can have knowledge.

Religion offers myths and narratives that can provide people with a sense of meaning and purpose, and religion continues to be relevant in the modern world. Nelson Mandela (1918–2013) spoke of a 'God-shaped space' in each of us; a religious non-theist might similarly recognise a craving for the teachings of the Buddha or the need to find meaning in human endeavour. The questions remain as to the social and cultural functions of religion and how far we create God or gods to be what we need, or shape philosophical traditions to suit our own worldviews.

When engaging with or studying any religion, whether as a believer or non-believer, it is important to do so with an open mind, a willingness to listen and a desire to understand. It is also important that we do not expect any one religion (or version of a religion) to uniquely hold all the truths and answers any more than we would expect one person to uniquely hold all knowledge. And it is also important to remember that we cannot approach any such questions with no presuppositions; everyone must make some assumptions before analysis or dialogue can begin. The question is, which assumptions should we make and how many of them derive their authority from a religious tradition?

All religions that have stood the test of time have done so because they offer their communities ways of understanding the world and our relationship to it, in ways that can hold very deep meanings for those who believe. Even those who do not believe may sometimes recognise underlying truths in religions that open their eyes to new perspectives on the world.

DISCUSS 8.47

Does all knowledge need to be consistent? If different people and different groups regard conflicting beliefs as 'knowledge', does that mean that at least some of the people must be wrong?

KNOWLEDGE QUESTIONS

1   Is certainty in religion any more or less attainable than it is in ethics or the arts?

2   How might thinking about questions to which there are no definite answers be of value to humankind?

3   Is an *insider* or an *outsider* best placed to objectively evaluate a religion or culture and its impact on knowledge?

8.8 Linking questions

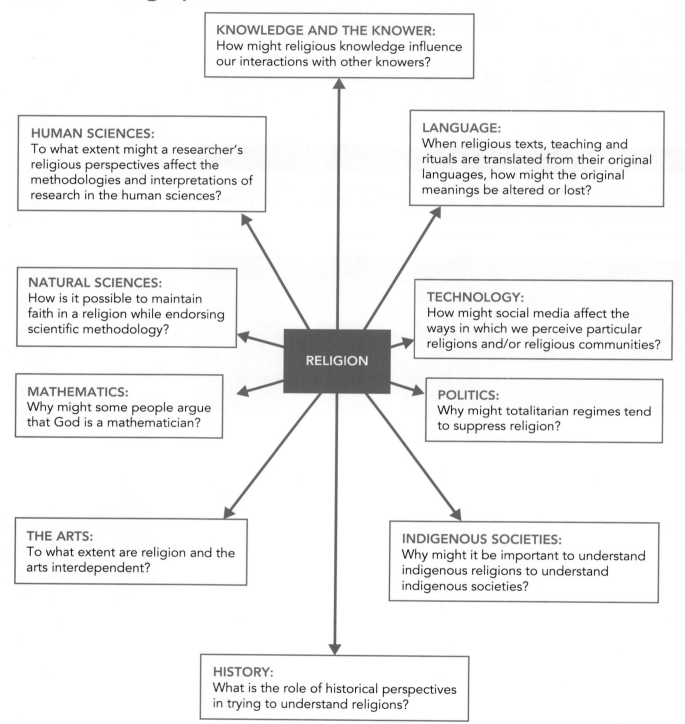

KNOWLEDGE AND THE KNOWER:
How might religious knowledge influence our interactions with other knowers?

HUMAN SCIENCES:
To what extent might a researcher's religious perspectives affect the methodologies and interpretations of research in the human sciences?

LANGUAGE:
When religious texts, teaching and rituals are translated from their original languages, how might the original meanings be altered or lost?

NATURAL SCIENCES:
How is it possible to maintain faith in a religion while endorsing scientific methodology?

TECHNOLOGY:
How might social media affect the ways in which we perceive particular religions and/or religious communities?

MATHEMATICS:
Why might some people argue that God is a mathematician?

RELIGION

POLITICS:
Why might totalitarian regimes tend to suppress religion?

THE ARTS:
To what extent are religion and the arts interdependent?

INDIGENOUS SOCIETIES:
Why might it be important to understand indigenous religions to understand indigenous societies?

HISTORY:
What is the role of historical perspectives in trying to understand religions?

8.9 Check your progress

Reflect on what you have learned in this chapter and indicate your confidence level between 1 and 5 (where 5 is the highest score and 1 is the lowest). If you score below 3, re-visit that section. Come back to this list later in your course. Has your confidence grown?

	Confidence level	Re-visited?
Can I discuss different ways of thinking about religion and its scope?		
Do I understand how rich and diverse the world's religions are, and how classifying them can be both helpful and restrictive?		
Am I aware of some of the different understandings of God that can be found in theistic religions?		
Do I appreciate that not all religions involve belief in a god or gods?		
Am I able to discuss some of the main sources of religious knowledge, including religious texts and the concept of revelation?		
Do I understand the different types of revelation?		
Am I familiar with different ways that religious texts and narratives can be understood?		
Do I appreciate how differences in understanding of religious language can lead to misinterpretation of religious knowledge?		
Do I understand the importance of hermeneutics in developing religious knowledge?		
Can I explain how faith and reason are used in the development of religious knowledge?		
Do I have a good understanding of different ways that individuals and communities develop religious understanding?		
Can I discuss some of the ways in which communities give rise to and communicate religious knowledge?		
Do I understand how religious practices and ethics can help to provide community identity and cohesion?		
Am I aware of some of the initiatives being taken to promote interfaith dialogue and understanding?		

8.10 Continue your journey

- To build on the knowledge that you have gained in this chapter, you could read some of the following articles.

- If you would like to know more about **religious demographics**, read: Conrad Hackett and David McClendon, 'Christians remain world's largest religious group, but they are declining in Europe', *Pew Research Centre*, 5 April 2017. Search the *Pew Research Center* website for this article.

- If you are interested in **changing trends in religion**, read: Harriet Sherwood, 'Religion: why faith is becoming more and more popular', in *The Guardian,* 27 August 2018. Search the *Guardian* website for this article.

- If you would like to further explore the **relationship between religion and science**, read: Anna Salleh, 'Are religion and science always at odds? Here are three scientists that don't think so', in *ABC Science,* 24 May 2018. Search the *ABC News Australia* website for this article.

- If you are curious about a **scientific perspective on why people believe in God**, read: Robert Winston, 'Why do we believe in God?', in *The Guardian*, 13 October 2005. Search the *Guardian* website for this article.

- If you are interested in the **relationship between individuals and communities**, read: Jesse Graham and Jonathan Haidt 'Beyond Beliefs: Religions Bind Individuals into Moral Communities', in *Personality and Social Psychology Review,* 2010, vol. 14, pp. 140–150. Search the *Personality and Social Psychology Review* on *the Sage Journals* website for this article.

Knowledge and indigenous societies

CONTINUED

- explore some of the ethical issues that arise when there are conflicts between indigenous societies and other communities, and conflicts with conservation endeavours

- understand why some people are concerned about drawing a distinction between indigenous knowledge and non-indigenous knowledge

BEFORE YOU START

Analyse each of the following quotations and discuss the questions that follow.

1   'I believe that when an elder dies, a library is burned: vast sums of wisdom and knowledge are lost. Throughout the world, libraries are ablaze with scant attention.' **Elizabeth Kapu'uwailani Lindsey** (1956–)

2   'I did have the longest hair, longer than of any of the boys . . . I braided it myself each morning, to keep it out of the way and to remind myself of things I couldn't quite remember but that, nevertheless, I knew to be true.' **Cherie Dimaline** (1975–)

3   'There is no concept of justice in Cree culture. The nearest word is 'kintohpatatin', which loosely translates to 'you've been listened to'. But 'kintohpatatin' is richer than justice – really it means you've been listened to by someone compassionate and fair, and your needs will be taken seriously.' **Edmund Metatawabin** (1948–)

4   'When the last tree is cut, the last fish is caught and the last river is polluted; when to breathe the air is sickening, you will realise, too late, that wealth is not in bank accounts and that you can't eat money.' **Alanis Obomsawin** (1932–)

5   'One thing to remember is to talk to the animals. If you do, they will talk back to you. But if you don't talk to the animals, they won't talk back to you, then you won't understand, and when you don't understand, you will fear, and when you fear, you will destroy the animals, and if you destroy the animals, you will destroy yourself.' **Chief Dan George** (1899–1981)

For each quotation, consider:

a   What do you think the quotation means?

b   To what extent do you agree or disagree with the quotation?

c   How might you challenge the quotation?

d   What does the quotation tell you about the speaker's assumptions about indigenous knowledge?

9.1 Introduction

According to UN figures, there are over 370 million **indigenous people** living in more than 70 countries around the world. According to the World Bank, although they make up only around 5% of the global population, they account for about 15% of the people who live in extreme poverty, and their life expectancy is up to 20 years lower than the average life expectancy of non-indigenous people worldwide.

Despite their political and economic marginalisation, indigenous societies have made significant contributions to the global wealth of knowledge. Indigenous knowledge tends to be deeply embedded in the culture and traditions of indigenous societies, which raises questions concerning how that knowledge can be shared more broadly, and what the ethical responsibilities are for those who benefit from that knowledge.

One of the major challenges facing our understanding of indigenous knowledge is the difficulty of defining what an indigenous society is. How indigenous societies are defined has implications for the scope of indigenous knowledge.

In this chapter, we will look at some examples of indigenous knowledge, and explore what kinds of indigenous knowledge are considered to be of value and worth preserving, and question who makes such decisions. In this discussion, we will address the importance of indigenous languages and the role they play in embodying indigenous perspectives, and consider some of the efforts to preserve them.

Finally, we will consider whether a distinction between indigenous and non-indigenous knowledge is sustainable or even desirable in an increasingly multicultural world.

> **KEY WORD**
>
> **indigenous people:** literally, 'people belonging to a place', the term is used to refer to people who inherit and practise unique cultures and ways of relating to people and their environment

9.2 What is an indigenous society?

> **DISCUSS 9.1**
>
> What do you think of when you hear the term 'indigenous society'?

Before we can discuss indigenous knowledge in any depth, it is important to understand what is meant by an indigenous society, because indigenous knowledge is defined by the society that produces, preserves and disseminates that knowledge. In a sense, the scope of indigenous knowledge is largely determined by what is understood by the term 'indigenous societies'. While the focus of indigenous knowledge tends to relate to ecological awareness and traditional practices, much of the debate surrounding indigenous knowledge involves 'Who are the indigenous societies?', 'What types of indigenous knowledge are valuable?', and 'Who decides?'.

Who indigenous people are and what counts as indigenous knowledge are deeply affected by historical **contingencies**. Questions around indigenous identity are serious, and challenging political and ethical concerns in a **post-colonial age**.

Indigenous societies tend to be broadly understood as communities of people who are descendants of those who occupied lands at a time when people of other ethnic origins and/or cultures arrived and became dominant through settlement, occupation or conquest. It is not necessary that a society is the original occupant of a land to be regarded indigenous; rather, that its people had a connection with the land when present state boundaries were established, which could be any time dating back to the 17th century.

> **KEY WORDS**
>
> **contingency:** something that is dependent upon chance
>
> **post-colonial age:** the period of time after colonial rule has ended

However, different countries largely create their own definitions of who is indigenous and who is not, based on a wide variety of factors that are often politically driven. There are some people who want to focus on hunter-gatherer communities as indigenous people, whereas others see indigenous people as being a much broader category.

The term *indigenous* is therefore complex and highly contextual, rather than carrying a definitive meaning. It usually includes peoples who are marginalised within a dominant society, and are living as minority communities in lands they have lived in for many generations. They have a culture and social structure that are distinct from the contemporary majority population, and they may also have linguistic differences. However, not all indigenous societies are minority groups in their homeland. In Greenland, for example, the Inuit make up over 80% of the total population. Papua New Guinea has hundreds of different indigenous peoples, and 82% of its population live in indigenous communities. In Peru, approximately 25% of the population are indigenous, and about 60% are *Mestidos* (mixed-race people of indigenous and Spanish descent).

REAL-LIFE SITUATION 9.1

Why might defining indigenous societies be a political issue rather than a biological issue? What might be the implications for indigenous knowledge if it depends on how indigenous societies are defined?

Indigenous self-identification

The question of who is indigenous is far from simple. In 1977, the World Council of Indigenous Peoples (WCIP) passed a resolution that stated only indigenous peoples can define indigenous peoples. Since then, there has been a growing trend by international organisations to promote the right to self-identification for indigenous peoples. Rather than defining an indigenous person as someone who has one or more grandparents or great grandparents belonging to an indigenous group, the suggestion is to accept self-identification. That is to say, a person belongs to an indigenous group if the person identifies as being part of that group and the group, in turn, accepts the person as a member of it.

"I'm already seeing an anthropologist."

In the Bolivian 2001 census, 62% of the adult population were recorded as indigenous based on their mother tongue, even though only just over 20% of the Bolivian population self-identified as indigenous. Of the people who did self-identify as indigenous, many did not have the **ethnolinguistic** markers of indigenous peoples. It was discovered that many people self-identified as indigenous or non-indigenous according to their politico-economic status, rather than because they identified with an indigenous culture or had a particular affinity with the land.

REAL-LIFE SITUATION 9.2

If non-indigenous people self-identify as indigenous, and indigenous people do not self-identify themselves, what are the implications for the concept of indigenous knowledge?

A number of **host states** have argued that if there are to be treaties and declarations to protect indigenous peoples, indigenous people need to be clearly defined. The WCIP, on the other hand, worries that any definition could exclude some indigenous groups from the protections they need, and the polarisation of indigenous and non-indigenous could mask the diversity of interests that indigenous peoples have.

Host states are also concerned that other ethnic groups could call themselves indigenous to have access to the international protection and legal status provided to indigenous peoples. This concern is shared by the WCIP. Indeed, there was shock and disbelief when Afrikaners in South Africa claimed to be indigenous. Nevertheless, without a clear definition, societies such as the Afrikaners could be seen to have a valid claim.

DISCUSS 9.2

To what extent is any discussion of indigenous knowledge dependent on having absolute distinctions between who is indigenous and who is not?

In the Scottish Highlands and Islands, the Scottish Crofting Foundation (SCF) is trying to achieve indigenous status for **crofters** based on self-identification. The SCF argues that indigenousness is an inclusive concept that should be regarded culturally rather than racially or genetically, therefore any person who adopts the traditional culture of crofting should be considered indigenous in accordance with Highland tradition. The UK government, on the other hand, claims that there are no indigenous peoples in the UK, although it does recognise several national groups of minority status under the European Framework Convention for the Protection of National Minorities. One example of a national minority group is the Cornish people: a Celtic group that has lived in Britain for over 2,000 years. Although Anglicised, the Cornish have maintained their own language, culture and identity.

DISCUSS 9.3

1 Without a clear definition of indigenous peoples, how might you decide if crofters and/or Afrikaners qualify as indigenous people?

2 How could such decisions impact on our perspectives on indigenous knowledge, and the scope of indigenous knowledge?

Figure 9.1: Traditional white-washed crofter's cottage in a Highland glen

The Indigenous Peoples of Africa Coordinating Committee (IPACC) recommends that indigenous peoples in Africa should be those who are marginalised economically and/or politically, and they particularly refer to hunter-gatherers and herders. However, other African groups argue that anyone who cannot trace their ancestry to outside of Africa should be regarded as indigenous, on the grounds that it is believed that all people originated in Africa, and they make the point that there are some Africans living in Africa who are even more marginalised than the hunter-gatherers and herders.

Every year, more and more young people leave their indigenous societies to live in urban settings in the pursuit of modern education and employment. The majority of the world's indigenous people now live in cities rather than on their traditional lands. This trend has implications for their lifestyles, culture and languages, and also for the survival of indigenous knowledge.

DISCUSS 9.4

Why might it be more difficult to pass on indigenous knowledge to new generations if they are living in an urban environment?

Indigenous diaspora

The concepts of indigenous societies and **diaspora** are closely related in many ways. Both groups share a deep connection with their ancestral lands. For many indigenous people and diaspora, land is a spiritual entity to be treasured and cared for, and their relationship with the land is an essential element of their collective identity.

Often, people of a diaspora hold on to myths and memories of their homeland, as well as the language and many of the customs and traditions. Typically, they identify more

KEY WORD

diaspora: people who have been dispersed from their homeland or have spread out from their homeland, while maintaining a close connection with it

strongly with their ancestral homeland than the place in which they live, even if it is the place of their birth.

Diasporas are often created as a result of forced migration, whether through oppression, human trafficking, war, famine or economic necessity. One example is the Armenian diaspora. While Armenians have established communities outside of Armenia throughout history, the modern Armenian diaspora was brought about largely as a result of the 1915 Armenian genocide, when, it is alleged, the Ottoman government systematically tried to exterminate the Armenian people. There are now approximately 3 million Armenians still living in Armenia, and a further 7 million Armenians living as diaspora in Armenian communities around the world, particularly in Russia, the USA, France, Argentina and Israel.

On a much smaller scale, the Warlpiri are an indigenous Australian Aboriginal tribe who have become an indigenous diaspora in their own country. There are approximately 6,000 Warlpiri people living in towns and cities, sometimes far away from their traditional homeland. Dispossession of lands, oppressive government policies and economic necessity forced them to give up their traditional hunter-gatherer lifestyles, but roughly half the people continue to speak the Warlpiri language and still abide by complex traditional kinship structures. The Warlpiri people feel a close affinity to their ancestral lands, even though they no longer live on them, and have adapted many aspects of their culture (particularly their arts and tribal dances) to urban living.

DISCUSS 9.5

Why might the arts and language be the primary areas of indigenous knowledge that people most value when living as a member of a diaspora?

Because the question of who is indigenous has become increasingly politicised, many organisations and host states have attempted to come up with their own definitions. Russia, for example, has an unusual policy of defining its indigenous peoples according to their population size. If an indigenous society within Russia has a population of fewer than 50,000 people they are regarded as indigenous people, but if their population exceeds 50,000, they are denied indigenous status. In New Zealand, the definition is biological. The indigenous people of New Zealand are the Māori, and a Māori is any person of the Māori race, including any descendants; if a person has a Māori ancestor, no matter how distant, they can choose to identify as Māori, regardless of how they identify socially or culturally. The Scottish crofters, as we have seen, want to define their society culturally; a crofter is anyone who adopts the crofter lifestyle and traditions.

EXPLORE 9.1

Do you know who your ancestors were and/or where they came from? Do you identify with any specific ethnic or cultural groups?

1   Create a starburst identity chart similar to the diagram in Figure 9.2, and put your name in the centre.

2   For each of the lines pointing out, write things that you regard as important to your identity. (You can add more lines if you wish to.) For each of the lines pointing in, write ways in which you believe other people see you.

CONTINUED

3   Choose three to five elements that you identify most strongly with, and make those lines bolder, or put them in a different colour.

Do you identify more with the place of your birth, where you currently live or where your ancestors may have come from? If you identify with any ethnic and/or cultural group and/or place, to what extent does it feature in your sense of identity as a knower? In other words, how is what you know influenced by your self-identification with a particular ethnic or cultural group, or place?

Figure 9.2: Starburst identity chart

REFLECTION

Think about the extent to which your identity enables you to have access to knowledge that others who identify differently cannot access. If each of us has a unique window to the world, and access to knowledge that no one else can know, how much more might that be the case for unique cultures and indigenous peoples?

DISCUSS 9.6

Does an indigenous person cease to be indigenous if they no longer live in an indigenous society? What about their children and grandchildren?

9.3 Indigenous knowledge

DISCUSS 9.7

How might our perspective of knowledge be shaped by belonging to a particular culture?

Indigenous knowledge is knowledge that is largely confined to a particular culture or society, and reflects that society's perspectives on a range of knowledge issues. This knowledge is transmitted from generation to generation, often through an oral tradition, including folklore, storytelling and cultural rituals. Indigenous knowledge often relates to the agro-ecological and socio-economic environments of the indigenous society, and passes on knowledge of agricultural practices, conservation, hunting and food preparation, health care and a wide range of other activities that help to sustain the society and its environment.

Indigenous knowledge has been largely ignored and often denigrated for centuries; indigenous societies were often depicted as communities of primitive, simple and non-progressive people, and their perspectives were regarded as irrelevant to 'civilised' societies. However, a growing number of states and organisations are now recognising the complexity and sophistication of many indigenous natural resource management systems, and are looking to indigenous knowledge to provide some foundations for cost-effective and environmentally-sustainable development.

REAL-LIFE SITUATION 9.3

1   If indigenous knowledge was once thought worthless but is now thought valuable because it can help to provide economic benefits, what does this say about how knowledge is valued?

2   To what extent is indigenous people's knowledge about gods and supernatural spirits as valuable as their knowledge about sustainable development, agriculture and traditional medicines?

3   Whose perspectives are taken into account, and by whom, when deciding what knowledge is to be valued?

Sustainable development

Indigenous societies around the world have much to teach the modern world about managing ecosystems and natural resources, by offering more **holistic** perspectives on them.

One example of how indigenous agricultural knowledge can be used and developed in ways to help other indigenous societies is that of rice-fish farming – a practice that has

> **KEY WORD**
>
> **holistic:** considering all factors of any situation, in the belief that all aspects are interconnected and can only be understood in relation to the whole

been in place in south China for more than 1,200 years. This practice involves keeping common carp (a type of fish native to China) in the rice paddies. The co-culture allows the establishment of a mutually beneficial relationship between fish and rice, in which the rice attracts insects which become food for the carp and, in turn, the fish reduce rice pests. The rice plants also help to lower water temperatures in the summer by providing shade, and reduce the amount of ammonia in the water, making a healthier environment for the fish.

A scientific trial of the method using loach (another species of fish) in fields that had previously only grown rice, demonstrated that with the right balance of rice being used as a refuge for fish, fish could be harvested without negatively impacting rice yields. In addition, rice grown alongside fish needed 68% less pesticide and 24% less fertiliser than ordinary mono-cultural rice crops. As fish have a higher market value than rice, the adaptation of the indigenous technique has lifted more than 10,000 people out of poverty in just two years. There is a project to extend the programme using different fish species in different regions. A local farming cooperative has been set up to share technical experience, deal collaboratively with external suppliers, set farming standards and help with marketing.

The UN Food and Agriculture Organisation has designated rice-fish co-culture a globally important agricultural heritage system.

REAL-LIFE SITUATION 9.4

If modern science is employed to develop indigenous knowledge, is the resulting knowledge still indigenous knowledge?

In 1992, Thailand declared 100-square miles of forest to be protected as Khun Jae National Park, and ordered indigenous people in the area to leave. After protests, the Hin Lad Nai community were granted permission to stay. The community practise a system of rotational farming, which had been outlawed by the Thai government in the belief that it caused too much forest destruction, but a study showed that their indigenous farming system is actually beneficial for biodiversity, and helps to prevent wildfires and soil erosion.

The Hin Lad Nai community now share their knowledge with other communities around the world, and are involved in cross-cultural dialogue to explore ways of collaborating across knowledge systems, in what is known as a Multiple Evidence Base (MEB). The MEB regards indigenous, local and scientific knowledge systems as complementary knowledge systems for sustainable use and the management of biodiversity.

DISCUSS 9.8

Does a holistic approach to knowledge provide a better understanding of reality than an approach that breaks knowledge into different disciplines?

Another example of indigenous knowledge complementing modern science to create a holistic approach can be seen in Arctic herd management. Sámi are indigenous people who have fished coastal waters, trapped animals and herded sheep and – more famously – reindeer for centuries in northern parts of Norway, Sweden, Finland

and Russia. Of the nomadic reindeer-herding Mountain Sámi, several families traditionally live and work together in reindeer herding groups, helping each other with reindeer husbandry and herd management. Now, alongside the use of satellite sensing, meteorology and computer modelling, indigenous herders are able to use their environmental knowledge to read complex changes in the Arctic environment, complementing quantitative measurements made by scientists. The holistic approach of combining indigenous and modern scientific knowledge promotes better environmental and herd monitoring. This is particularly important in the current conditions of climate change, in which the Arctic is warming twice as fast as the rest of the globe. However, the sharing of vital knowledge is not one way. As well as the Sámi benefiting from scientific advances, the ecological knowledge of the Sámi helps politicians and scientists to make more effective decisions to ensure regional green development initiatives are sustainable.

Figure 9.3: Two Mountain Sámi with their reindeer

DISCUSS 9.9

How can technology and indigenous knowledge complement each other in the production of new knowledge?

EXPLORE 9.2

Choose an IA exhibition prompt, and select an object referring to an indigenous knowledge system. You might like to choose a human skull collected by an Iban warrior to elevate his warrior status; ayahuasca – a hallucinogenic brew used by indigenous peoples of the Amazon Basin for medicinal and spiritual purposes; or a birch stick used by Hamar men to beat women during bull-jumping ceremonies as a way of helping the initiate decide upon a wife.

Write a short commentary (no more than 300 words) that identifies your object and its context in the world, and explain how it links to the IA prompt you have chosen.

Self-assessment

Have you clearly identified the object and its real-world context? Have you selected an IA prompt and linked it to your chosen object?

Peer-assessment

Share your commentary with a classmate and give each other feedback. Are the object and its real-world context clearly identified? Are links between the object and the selected IA prompt explained well and made clearly? Are all points well supported with evidence and explicit references to the prompt?

DISCUSS 9.10

Are there areas of human experience that cannot be transferred and translated from one culture or indigenous setting to another?

There is a tendency to generalise about, and even romanticise, indigenous peoples in ways that portray them as more spiritual than other people, and living lives that are fully sustainable and harmonious with nature. However, the lifestyles of indigenous societies are not always fully sustainable. The Ifugaos live in the Cordillera mountain ranges in the Philippines. They depend on rice, and use simple hand tools to manage their environment. Their main livelihoods are from farming, handicrafts and wood carving, which are highly dependent upon the sustainability of the natural resources. The Ifugaos use the natural shape of the valleys to create their rice terraces, but as they increasingly clear forests to expand their pasture and provide wood for carving and construction, the resulting deforestation leads to soil erosion and water shortages. While crop rotations and leaving ground fallow helps to replenish soil, some Ifugaos have abandoned their farms because they can no longer make enough to support their families.

REAL-LIFE SITUATION 9.5

If indigenous knowledge results in a lifestyle that is unsustainable, where does its value lie?

Traditional medicines

During the course of the 20th century and continuing into the 21st century, the natural sciences have made tremendous progress in the field of medicine. Mortality has declined, and many diseases that would have been fatal can now be managed, if not cured. However, it is estimated that over one-third of the world's population lack access to modern drugs, partly because they live in remote places, and also because modern drugs are not affordable for them. Traditional medicines, on the other hand, tend to be more widely available and affordable by most people. In India, it is thought that 70% of the population use traditional medicines. With so many people dependent on traditional medicines, one of the tasks challenging scientists is to investigate the efficacy of traditional medicines, to identify active ingredients and to try to eliminate the use of toxic plants and other contaminants in traditional mixtures.

Many herbal and traditional medicines are not well-researched, poorly regulated, sometimes contaminated and may produce adverse effects; however, there are some traditional medicines that are attracting the attention of modern science. For example, *Artemisia annua* (also known as Sweet Wormwood or *Qinghao*) has long been used in China as a traditional treatment for malaria. In 1972, scientists studying the effects of *Qinghao* were able to isolate artemisinine, and have since created several synthetic versions of it as effective malarial treatments.

KEY WORDS

traditional medicine: the indigenous knowledge, practices and skills used by indigenous peoples (and others) to diagnose and treat illnesses and injuries, and to maintain health

efficacy: effectiveness

REAL-LIFE SITUATION 9.6

Most indigenous societies do not regulate how traditional medicines are produced or used. Does the lack of rigour and controlled testing mean that traditional medical knowledge is unreliable?

Argemone mexicana, also known as the Mexican prickly poppy, is native to Mexico but now found wild in many parts of the world. Although poisonous to grazing animals and poultry, it has been used for various medicinal purposes by Mexicans, native Americans, Indians and the peoples of Mali. In Mexico, the plant is used to reduce kidney pain, treat snake bites and as a laxative; in Mali, prickly poppy tea has been used to treat malaria, and studies have shown it to be effective in non-complicated cases. In Tamil Nadu, India, the plant is known as *brahma thandu*, and is used for treating snake bites, improving eyesight, eliminating intestinal worms, easing toothaches as well as cleaning teeth and gums and helping with coughs, asthma and other respiratory problems. The seed extract has also been used to treat various skin disorders.

A scientific study in West Bengal has shown that the prickly poppy does have antibiotic properties against some bacteria, although scientists found it to be more effective when using methanol solutions rather than traditional water-based extracts.

DISCUSS 9.11

If a traditional medicine is tested in a laboratory in controlled conditions, and modified and produced in a way to make it more efficient and more reliable, who should own the resulting knowledge?

EXPLORE 9.3

The following plants are frequently used in herbal remedies. In pairs or small groups, research each of them to find out where they originated, what they are used to treat, if they have any contraindications and what the potential dangers are. Do you know where knowledge about contraindications and potential dangers comes from?

a   chamomile (flower)

b   echinacea (leaf, stalk, root)

c   feverfew (leaf)

d   garlic (cloves, root)

e   ginger (root)

f   gingko (leaf)

g   ginseng (root)

h   goldenseal (root, rhizome)

Select one of the examples, and discuss different perspectives of the medicinal value of the plant and how objective or subjective you think the different perspectives are. Each write a paragraph to conclude your discussion, stating why you believe the plant has medicinal value or why not.

Self-assessment

Does your paragraph sum up the different perspectives, and does it reach a clear conclusion?

Peer-assessment

Share your paragraph with a classmate and give each other feedback. Does the paragraph clearly summarise the main points of the discussion, and reach a conclusion that is consistent with the evaluations made during the discussion?

> **KEY WORD**
>
> contraindication: a situation when a particular remedy or procedure should not be used

DISCUSS 9.12

What is the relationship between unsystematic observation and controlled experiment when comparing indigenous and scientific approaches to medicine?

With scientific researchers taking a growing interest in traditional medicines, there is a growing concern to protect the **intellectual property** rights of indigenous peoples. Questions arise over how any financial benefits from the use of indigenous knowledge should be shared, and how intellectual property rights can be protected. Often, scientific researchers and industries from developed nations adapt and patent indigenous medicines without informed consent, and give little or no compensation to the indigenous societies from which the foundational knowledge came.

The issue is not a simple one. Indigenous medicines are frequently unpatentable in the way they are used in indigenous societies, because they tend to involve using crude parts of plants such as the leaves, seeds or flowers in simple ways, and therefore do not involve the discovery of a new chemical or an inventive step in processing. In addition, most indigenous societies do not have the financial or knowledge resources needed to patent a product or enforce patent rights.

KEY WORD

intellectual property: the ownership of knowledge or unique products that have been created

REAL-LIFE SITUATION 9.7

It might be possible to patent a new method of producing a drug, but it is not possible to patent the boiling (for example) of a plant from which a drug is derived, even if the brew is uniquely applied. Are there valid reasons for making such a distinction? How might this distinction disadvantage indigenous societies, and make them vulnerable to a loss of intellectual property?

The inappropriate use of traditional medicine and practices can often have negative, and even dangerous effects. Research is necessary to ensure the efficacy and safety of traditional medicines if they are to be used more widely; however, such research and testing is very expensive. If companies cannot at least recoup their costs and preferably profit from conducting the necessary studies and trials, they are less likely to conduct the necessary research.

Another problem facing indigenous medicines is the loss of biodiversity, partly produced by an expanding international market for herbal products. Commercially made herbal pharmaceuticals require large quantities of plants, and this has led to over collection. For example, the African wild potato (*Hypoxis hemerocallidea*), which was found to combat AIDS, is said to have disappeared from the Democratic Republic of the Congo within two years of its medicinal value being scientifically demonstrated.

DISCUSS 9.13

What is the impact of culture in the production and distribution of knowledge?

Indigenous approaches to health tend to be different from those of modern science, for example the National Aboriginal Health Strategy claims the Aboriginal view of health is to consider not just the physical health of the individual, but also to consider the social, emotional and cultural well-being of the entire community.

In general, Aboriginal people of Australia recognise two types of illness: natural and supernatural. Natural illnesses are treated with medicines made from plants and animal products; supernatural illnesses are treated with a spiritual cure. Aboriginal healers have special powers bestowed upon them by spiritual ancestors, and heal both mind and body.

DISCUSS 9.14

To what extent does our culture determine our understanding of what health and illness are?

Although many Aboriginal people still prefer to use traditional (bush) medicine, the use of bush medicine is declining because indigenous knowledge is being lost. Aboriginal knowledge is traditionally passed on through dance rituals and singing in **corroborees**, but corroborees are becoming far less common, causing the bush medicinal knowledge, as well as other types of indigenous knowledge possessed by the elders, to be lost.

KEY WORD

corroboree: an Australian Aboriginal dance ceremony

Figure 9.4: A corroboree is an important method of passing knowledge to the next generation for Australian Aboriginals

DISCUSS 9.15

If knowledge is communicated through dance, could dance be considered a form of language?

9.4 Indigenous languages

DISCUSS 9.16

Why are indigenous languages being lost?

There are approximately 6,700 languages in the world, but nearly 6,500 of them are spoken by only 3% of the population. Although fewer than 6% of the world's population are indigenous peoples, they speak more than 4,000 (about 60%) of the world's languages. It is estimated that one indigenous language is lost every two weeks, and that between 50% and 95% of the world's languages could be extinct by the end of this century.

DISCUSS 9.17

What are the implications for knowledge if the vocabularies of different languages create different sets of concepts?

Languages are more than just methods of communication. Languages are used to define our identities, preserve and express our history, traditions and culture, and provide us with ways of thinking. They are complex systems of knowledge that carry deep cultural understandings and insights, and are central to indigenous identity and the preservation of indigenous cultures. When indigenous languages are lost, so too are the history, traditions and cultural perspectives embodied in those languages.

EXPLORE 9.4

Watch the Ted Talk™, 'Dreams from endangered cultures' (2003) by the anthropologist and National Geographic photographer Wade Davis (1953–).

1   How objective do you think Davis is?

2   As a class, discuss: What does the loss of indigenous languages mean in terms of our knowledge and understanding of the world?

One example of the way in which a language can embody cultural perspectives is the Polynesian word *mana*. *Mana* is often translated as 'status', 'power' or even 'charisma', but no single word or simple phrase in English truly captures its true meaning. In Māori culture, a person with *mana* is one who has dignity and commands respect, partly because of their *whakapapa* (another untranslatable word that refers to ancestral, tribal and land connections) and also because of their charisma, and the spiritual power and authority that they embody. *Mana* is a spiritual concept that relates in many ways to life force and leadership, but not all people, and not even all leaders, have *mana*.

REFLECTION

As an IB Diploma Programme student, you may be able to speak more than one language, and even if you are not fluent in more than one language, you will at least be learning a language *ab initio* (from the beginning). How easily do the concepts of one language translate to another? When learning a new language, what new knowledge do you develop beyond the grammar and vocabulary of the new language?

DISCUSS 9.18

How are words empowered to do more than simply transfer knowledge from one person to another?

Globalisation has led to the rise of a few culturally-dominant languages, and indigenous societies have had to face policies of **assimilation,** the dispossession of their lands and discriminatory laws. Together, these have led to indigenous languages no longer being passed down to new generations.

In recent years, there has been a growing concern to record and preserve indigenous languages. Some indigenous people have been able to revive their languages by having them taught in schools as well as creating radio and television programmes that use indigenous languages. New technologies have also been harnessed to spread the use of indigenous languages via apps and online resources such as YouTube™; some work has also been done to use artificial intelligence to analyse and codify indigenous languages. Many governments have introduced policies, programmes and legislation to protect indigenous languages, and the UN declared 2019 as the International Year of Indigenous Languages, to draw attention to the urgent need to preserve, revitalise and promote them at both national and international levels.

Despite all the efforts being made, however, indigenous languages continue to be lost. This is partly due to a lack of resources. Most available funding goes in to recording, transcribing and translating indigenous languages before they disappear, but relatively little funding goes towards language revitalisation programmes.

KEY WORD
assimilation: integration

REAL-LIFE SITUATION 9.8

Is it possible to preserve an *entire* language by making recordings? To what extent does recording an indigenous language preserve the knowledge that is conveyed by and embodied in that language?

EXPLORE 9.5

Find out how many indigenous or minority languages can be found in the country you live in. What steps, if any, are being taken to preserve and promote those languages? How is it decided which languages are preserved, and which elements of a language are to be preserved? What would be the implications if those languages were lost?

REAL-LIFE SITUATION 9.9

Even when people speak the same language, those from different geographical regions often use language slightly differently, using words and expressions that are unique to their region. Why might that be, and how do the linguistic differences enrich our understanding of those different regions?

9.5 Protecting indigenous knowledge

DISCUSS 9.19

What does indigenous knowledge need protection from?

Since the United Nations Conference on Environment and Development in June 1992, there has been an increasing awareness of the importance of biodiversity, and the need for a diversity of perspectives might be seen as a parallel phenomenon. The world is waking up to the idea that indigenous knowledge needs to be saved and protected, and that indigenous knowledge can in turn help to protect biodiversity on the planet. In 2003, the World Health Organization (WHO) passed a resolution, urging member states to take measures to protect and preserve medicinal plants for sustainable development, and also to protect the intellectual property rights of practitioners of traditional medicine.

DISCUSS 9.20

To what extent is the protection and preservation of medicinal plants a way of protecting and preserving indigenous knowledge?

Very little indigenous knowledge has been recorded, yet it has the potential to provide humankind with immensely valuable insights on how widely diverse indigenous societies have interacted with their environments in mutually beneficial and sustainable ways.

One way that indigenous knowledge is being protected is through the development of national indigenous knowledge resource centres. These are organisational structures which record and store indigenous knowledge, as well as screen it for potential economic use, and disseminate it appropriately for use in education, sustainable development and preserving cultural heritage.

DISCUSS 9.21

Who decides which knowledge needs to be recorded and stored? In what ways can bias and selection make positive contributions to attaining knowledge?

The International Society of Ethnobiology

The International Society of Ethnobiology (ISE) is a global, collaborative network of individuals and organisations working to preserve links between human societies and the natural world. Many ISE members are affiliated with and support indigenous values and communities. Their expertise is cross-disciplinary and includes ethno-biology, intellectual property and resource rights, ecology, and applied ethics.

The ISE is concerned by the loss of traditional, local and indigenous knowledge, and the resulting effects of that loss on biological, cultural and linguistic diversity. The network is working towards creating a more harmonious existence between humans and the natural world by promoting dialogue on resources, knowledge, ethics and research methods across regions, cultures and worldviews. Central to this is the recognition of the valuable contributions to be made by traditional and indigenous societies if humankind is to conserve and protect biological, cultural and linguistic diversity.

> **REAL-LIFE SITUATION 9.10**
>
> Who decides which indigenous knowledge contributions are valuable? On what basis is that value assigned?

Intangible cultural heritage

There are many things from different cultures that are regarded as important to preserve for future generations, sometimes for their present or possible economic value, but also because they create a certain emotion or engender a sense of belonging. Often these things are buildings, art objects, tools and so forth; but the United Nations Educational, Scientific and Cultural Organisation (UNESCO) is also working to preserve the **intangible** elements of cultural heritage. These elements can include oral traditions, social organisation, performing arts and craftsmanship, social and religious practices and rituals, and traditional knowledge. These are the elements that bring a culture to life.

KEY WORD

intangible: non-material and unquantifiable

Intangible cultural heritage is an important factor in maintaining cultural diversity in an increasingly global world. Its importance lies in the wealth of knowledge and skills that are transmitted through the intangible elements of any culture. What is regarded as intangible cultural heritage is decided by the societies that create and transmit the practices; however, the heritage does not need to be specific to that society; rather, it is a body of knowledge that is practised within a community, and shared both within the community and passed on to other communities.

Like all aspects of culture, intangible cultural heritage is continually changing and evolving, but many aspects are in danger of being lost because of globalisation and cultural homogenisation if intangible cultural heritage is not properly understood and appreciated. For intangible aspects of cultural heritage to be kept alive, they need to remain relevant to the cultures they belong to, to be regularly practised and passed on within communities and between generations.

Sbekom (Cambodian shadow puppetry) is a method of storytelling that can be traced back to the 7th century. Originally, shadow puppetry was performed for **deities** on special occasions, and the puppetry ceremonies took place in rice fields and temples. In 2018, *Sbekom* was recognised by UNESCO as an intangible cultural heritage. The puppets are 2 metres tall and handcrafted from cow-hides, which must come from

KEY WORD

deity (plural deities): a god

cows that have died from natural causes. While many traditional aspects of *Sbekom* are maintained, the practice is evolving and modernising to keep it relevant, including allowing women to act as puppeteers.

DISCUSS 9.22

If you have indigenous knowledge that qualifies as intangible cultural heritage, do you have an ethical responsibility to practise and pass on that knowledge?

Just as Cambodian shadow puppetry was once performed for the gods to mark special occasions, but is now performed in a theatre to entertain locals and tourists alike, so many indigenous cultures have become a part of their national tourist industries. Tourists can visit 'traditional native villages' which may or may not be authentic, watch and photograph tribal dances that were once only permitted to be seen by those initiated into the tribe, and they can buy traditionally made objects as souvenirs. On one level, such tourism provides employment for indigenous peoples and helps to preserve some of their cultural heritage, but often what is seen and experienced at such events is far from traditional, and can be seen to reduce a complex and sophisticated social structure to little more than a variety show, and perhaps encourage stereotyping.

DISCUSS 9.23

To what extent is knowledge transmitted through intangible cultural activities different from knowledge that is transmitted orally or in writing?

Figure 9.5: Contemporary Cambodian shadow theatre has revolutionised the art by allowing women to operate the puppets

---

EXPLORE 9.6

1   Consider: Have you ever visited a 'traditional village' or watched a 'traditional dance' designed to attract and entertain tourists? How true to the cultural traditions do you think it was? How would you know? Did the event provide you with knowledge about the culture and a sense of respect for the tradition, or were you merely entertained?

2   Do some research on Bukchon Hanok Village, a traditional village in Seoul, Korea, that is popular with tourists. To what extent does tourism in this village help to preserve traditional knowledge and disseminate knowledge about traditional life, and how much does it exploit the people and destroy their way of life?

REFLECTION

Imagine your house was selected to be opened up to tourists to become an example of a 'typical home' in the place that you live, and you were paid to explain to the tourists what life is like living there. Would you feel exploited, or grateful for an opportunity to tell the story of your community? How might it affect the way that you live and the way that you present your home and your life to the curious visitors?

REAL-LIFE SITUATION 9.11

1   How ethical is it to promote tourism in traditional villages?

2   Is the commercialisation of indigenous societies justified by a wider distribution of knowledge?

Cultural evolution

The idea that Darwinian insights can be applied to changes in culture and that culture evolves is not new. Some people go even further and say that cultural inheritance is not just a process that runs in parallel to genetic evolution, but that the two are intertwined. They argue that cultural changes cause alterations to the environment, which in turn change genetic selection pressures.

The human species has survived and flourished because successful behaviours and technologies have been shared, adapted and built upon throughout the ages. Social learning has been an agent of adaptation.

There are different theories of how cultures have evolved, and a focus in modern anthropology is to try to determine how individual cultures have changed and developed over time. The evolutionary model is also applied to the growth of human knowledge, with **evolutionary epistemology** suggesting that knowledge itself can evolve through processes of selection. Theories become more or less acceptable as knowledge, according to how well they cohere with changes to the body of knowledge that give the theories their context.

KEY WORD

evolutionary epistemology: the theory that knowledge evolves by natural selection

The idea of cultural evolution is important in the context of indigenous knowledge because it draws attention to the constantly developing and changing nature of all knowledge, and supports the notion that knowledge systems, including indigenous knowledge systems, are not closed entities.

> **REAL-LIFE SITUATION 9.12**
>
> As indigenous people move into urban environments, their indigenous knowledge evolves to adapt to the new environment. At what point would you say their knowledge ceases to be indigenous?

9.6 Conflicts of interest

> **REAL-LIFE SITUATION 9.13**
>
> With the human population currently around 7.5 billion and expected to reach 10 billion by 2055, how can we find enough space to house and feed all the people, and at the same time conserve the flora, fauna and indigenous societies that share this planet?

The issue of diminishing lands and competition for resources is a serious one for all indigenous peoples. Chenchu are a Telugu-speaking society of hunter-gatherers, thought to be one of the oldest indigenous societies in South India. They have lived in the Nallamala hill ranges for centuries, where they hunt with bows and arrows and live on **forest produce**. They also harvest forest produce to sell to a cooperative which sells the produce on to urban peoples. This harvesting of forest produce brings them into direct conflict with nontribal but equally poor Indians from nearby villages, who also collect forest produce to eat or sell. Some Chenchu want non-Chenchu people to be prohibited from taking forest produce because there is not enough for everybody.

> **KEY WORD**
>
> **forest produce:** things other than timber that can be found in the forest, including wild honey, fruits, edible plants and firewood

> **REAL-LIFE SITUATION 9.14**
>
> How might it be possible to evaluate competing claims for resources from different communities in an objective way?

Conflicts with wildlife conservation

Aside from the potential conflicts of political interests and competition for limited resources among different peoples, significant potential conflicts of interest arise in the area of conservation.

In 2006, just over 2,000 Chenchu families were given rights to live in certain areas of the forests that had been their home. However, the Nallamala ranges are also home to the Nagarjunasagar Srisailam Tiger Reserve (NSTR), India's largest tiger reserve. Tigers are an endangered species, facing pressures from poaching, **retaliatory killings** and habitat loss. They need a large territory to thrive, but are increasingly forced to compete with growing human populations. In the core area of the Nallamala ranges,

> **KEY WORD**
>
> **retaliatory killings:** killings made in revenge for killing people or livestock

there are just 65 tigers and roughly 65,000 Chenchu people. In a bid to save the tigers from poaching and retaliatory killings, the NSTR wants an exclusive protection zone for the tigers, but those who want to protect tribal rights believe that the 65,000 people should have priority.

Currently there seems to be no serious conflict of interest between the people and the tigers; Chenchu are content to live alongside the tigers, and there are few reported fatalities. The tigers even provide employment, with 400 Chenchu being employed by the NSTR to watch out for poachers and wildfires. However, as tiger numbers recover and the human population continues to grow, an eventual conflict seems inevitable. Chenchu are now being offered a monetary incentive and options to relocate on a voluntary basis, but there are growing concerns that, in time, Chenchu will be forced to leave their forest home.

DISCUSS 9.24

How can we be confident of the ethical responsibilities we have when there are conflicting ethical issues?

Other ethical conflicts

In 1974, a group of scientists came into contact with a member of the Korowai people in Papua, Indonesia. This was allegedly the first contact between the Korowai people and the outside world. They had not had the advantages that come from cross-fertilisation of cultures, and knew nothing of the world beyond the forests in which they lived.

The Korowai live in treehouses and houses built on stilts 10–12 metres from the ground, keeping the homes safe from floods, and protecting women and children from being taken as slaves by rival clans.

When a member of the Korowai dies from illness, the tribe, who have no modern medical knowledge, believe the disease was caused by a *khakhua* magically eating the person's insides. The *khakhua* is a fellow tribesman (always a male) whose body has been inhabited by an evil spirit. The dying person is often persuaded to whisper the name of the *khakhua*, who may well be a friend or relative. The tribe then kill and eat the *khakhua* in retribution for the *khakhua* having 'eaten and killed' the deceased.

REAL-LIFE SITUATION 9.15

1   Is Korowai 'knowledge' about the cause of disease a form of indigenous 'knowledge' that should be preserved and protected?

2   On what basis can a decision be made, and by whom?

Paul Raffaele, an investigative journalist from Australia, who visited the Korowai in 2006, claims to have helped rescue a six year old Korowai boy whose parents had both died of illness. The boy had been named as a *khakhua,* and it is alleged that the tribe were waiting for the boy to turn 14 years old so that they could kill and eat him.

DISCUSS 9.25

Is there an ethical conflict between the supposedly objective reporting and recording of an indigenous society's practices, and interfering with that society's practices to save a life?

This practice of killing and eating *khakhua* has brought the Korowai fame as one of the last surviving cannibalistic peoples. However, some Papuans and anthropologists say that cannibalistic practices stopped 20 years ago. They claim that in recent years, the Korowai have perpetuated stories of cannibalism for the tourism trade which is now their main source of income. Others say that cannibalism still happens among the more remote clans who have less contact with Papuan society.

Figure 9.6: A Korowai tribesman with a skull he says is from a *khakhua*. The tribesman claims to have killed at least 30 *khakhua*

DISCUSS 9.26

To what extent is it possible to describe an indigenous society and its knowledge objectively?

EXPLORE 9.7

In pairs or small groups, find out about the Hamar tribe in Ethiopia. Imagine you are asked to investigate the Hamar to find out what knowledge their traditions are based on, without disturbing their way of life. Brainstorm how you would go about it. What methodologies would you use?

CONTINUED

Create a mind-map to illustrate what ethical conflicts might emerge while trying to understand Hamar knowledge and culture.

Self-assessment

Look at your mind-map carefully. Have you considered ethical conflicts that might be facing the indigenous people being studied, as well as the ethical conflicts that might emerge for you?

DISCUSS 9.27

Is it ethically responsible to reach out to remote peoples and try to understand them, knowing that doing so will inevitably bring about change?

REFLECTION

How would you decide what is the right course of action if you were faced with competing ethical issues?

9.7 Cultural appropriation

One of the issues facing people everywhere is the issue of **cultural appropriation**. Sometimes called 'cultural misappropriation', there are concerns when people from dominant cultures adopt elements from another, usually minority culture, without necessarily understanding the original culture and context.

Some people use the term *cultural appropriation* as a tool to promote social justice. It is frequently used to call out incidents in which people from a dominant culture dress in clothing or costumes of a minority culture in a way that, often unintentionally, perpetrates cultural stereotypes. The goal of using the term is usually to raise awareness of cultural imbalances, and the ways in which people from dominant cultures can inadvertently further a sense of oppression that can come from stereotyping and trivialising something which is an intangible cultural object and/or making something that is culturally valued an object of fun.

One widely known example of intangible indigenous culture that is frequently misappropriated is the Māori *haka*. The *haka* is a ceremonial dance in Māori culture. The dance is one that contains several postures, vigorous movements, facial gestures and rhythmic shouting.

Originally, war *haka* were performed by warriors before a battle as a way of proclaiming their strength and, at the same time, intimidating the enemy. Over time, different *haka* evolved to play other ceremonial roles, including to welcome visitors to a Māori meeting house (*marae*) and to open celebratory events, including Māori funerals. There are many different types of *haka*, and the performances express the emotions of the Māori people appropriate to the occasion. *Haka* can be used to express various concepts such as courage, friendship, joy, love and grief.

KEY WORD

cultural appropriation: the adoption of elements of one culture by members of another culture

In 1988, the New Zealand Native football team performed a *haka* during an international tour. This began a tradition, and the use of the *Ka Mate haka* by New Zealand's national rugby team (the All Blacks) has made the *haka* recognisable around the world.

Figure 9.7: The New Zealand All Blacks rugby team performing the *haka* in Rome just before the start of a match against Italy

In recent years, concerns were raised that the ceremonial significance of the *Ka Mate haka*, and its authorship by Te Rauparaha (1765–1849) from the Ngāti Toa tribe were being lost because of widespread misappropriation. In 2009, a legal challenge was settled between the New Zealand government, New Zealand Rugby Union and the Ngāti Toa tribe, giving the tribe authorship and ownership rights over the *Ka Mate haka*.

Some American football teams have begun to use a *haka* as part of a pre-game ritual; however this is regarded as highly inappropriate and disrespectful because the practice has been 'stolen' from a minority indigenous group (the Māori, or more specifically, the Ngāti Toa tribe) by a dominant western culture.

DISCUSS 9.28

How might we know when adopting some elements of another culture is respectful and when it is not?

Cultural appropriation does not mean that cultural exchange and cultural appreciation cannot happen. Goods, services and knowledge have been shared between cultures throughout history. But it is important that any exchange is not one-sided, and is done on a fair basis that improves the understanding of, and appreciation for, the other culture, rather than one culture simply taking from another.

An example of fair and respectful cultural exchange is when a Māori *kapa haka* group performed a version of the Gangnam Style dance (a dance that originated in South Korea) mixed with a traditional *haka* in Seoul in 2012, to help celebrate 50 years of diplomatic relations between New Zealand and South Korea.

True appreciation of other cultures must include a level of understanding and respect. Anything that reduces a race or indigenous group to a stereotype is not respectful.

However, it is not always easy to tell what is culturally acceptable and what is not. This is particularly true in the area of food. In 2019, the British food retail company, Marks and Spencer (M&S), was strongly criticised by an Indian chef for labelling a vegan wrap made with sweet potato, spiced basmati rice, buckwheat and roasted red pepper as a 'sweet potato *biryani*'. The chef argued that biryanis typically contain either meat or fish (although vegetarian *biryani* can be found in India) and are not wrapped in bread. M&S responded by saying that its developers are known for their food innovation and always use a fusion of flavours and ingredients to create a range of products that appeal to their customers' tastes.

REAL-LIFE SITUATION 9.16

People in urban areas often cook and eat foods from different cultures, and 'fusion foods', which blend tastes from different cultures, are increasingly popular. To what extent is this an appreciation of other cultures or cultural misappropriation?

EXPLORE 9.8

In pairs, consider the following activities. Which might you regard as cultural misappropriation and which might you see as a mark of respect?

1   wearing a *kimono* to a fancy-dress party

2   doing the *haka* at a family barbeque

3   serving *biriyani* at a dinner party

4   putting pineapple on pizza

5   wearing a turban as a fashion accessory

6   wearing dreadlocks

7   wearing a sari to a Sri Lankan event if you are not from a culture in which saris are traditionally worn

REFLECTION

Do you like to eat food from different cultures, wear clothing inspired by other cultures or decorate your room with items that reflect other cultures? How would you draw a line between respecting a culture, being inspired by a culture and exploiting a culture? Would your ideas change if someone else was cooking food, wearing clothes or decorating their room with items from your culture?

DISCUSS 9.29

How might cultural appropriation be seen as a violation of the intellectual property rights of an indigenous society?

9.8 A false dichotomy

DISCUSS 9.30

To what extent do think you would be able trace the origins of any knowledge you have?

Some scholars have raised concerns about what they perceive as a **false dichotomy** between indigenous and non-indigenous knowledge (which is often labelled as 'western' knowledge). There are two issues that they raise. The first is that to see indigenous knowledge as distinct from 'western knowledge' is to ignore the fact that a vast wealth of what is regarded as knowledge in the modern world was developed by non-western societies. The shared pool of modern, evidence-based knowledge has global origins. That humankind's shared knowledge is as rich as it is across all areas of knowledge, because of the contributions made from all parts of the globe throughout human history.

The second issue is that while a focus on indigenous knowledge has gained certain scholars a strong voice in the field of development, it also commits them to maintaining a dichotomy between indigenous and non-indigenous or 'western' knowledge. Many of the people working to preserve and promote indigenous knowledge are doing so using modern scientific methodology; any strong distinction between indigenous knowledge and non-indigenous knowledge would seem to be contrived.

In *Dismantling the Divide between Indigenous and Scientific Knowledge*, political scientist Arun Agarwal (1962–) argues that classifying knowledge into two distinct categories (indigenous and western/scientific) is bound to fail because of the **heterogeneous** nature of knowledge. He says that creating a distinction also involves trying to separate and fix knowledge in time and space, whereas knowledge is never static.

The separation of western and indigenous knowledge depends on there being significant differences between the two, in terms of both subject matter and characteristics. It also requires them to have different worldviews and use different methodologies to study the world, and there is an assumption that indigenous knowledge is more contextually embedded than western knowledge. However, all knowledge, whether indigenous or not, has a specific history and is born from a specific context. Similarly, not all western/scientific knowledge is guided by empirical studies and scientific methodology, and not all indigenous knowledge systems use the same methodologies. In other words, there is a great deal of variation in the methodologies of both indigenous and western knowledge, and they need not be mutually exclusive.

There is a great deal of evidence to show that what we regard as indigenous knowledge has influenced, and been influenced by, western knowledge over several centuries so neither is untouched by the other.

KEY WORDS

false dichotomy: when a situation is presented as having just two possible options, when other perspectives are not only possible, but highly likely

heterogeneous: mixed; composed of different parts

DISCUSS 9.31

What role do cultural assumptions play in the construction of knowledge?

EXPLORE 9.9

In pairs or small groups, consider the following items and decide to what extent they are the result of indigenous knowledge.

1   fireworks

2   quinine sulphate tablets

3   batteries

4   hexadecimal counting (as used for time and degrees of angles)

5   beer

Create a continuum with *Indigenous knowledge* at one end and *Nonindigenous knowledge* at the other, and place the items where you think they sit along the continuum. Can any of the items be placed at one of the extremes of your continuum? (That is to say, are any of them solely the result of indigenous knowledge or solely the result of non-indigenous knowledge?)

Compare your continuum with those of other groups. Can the class reach a collective agreement on where to place the items?

REFLECTION

Did anything in the Explore activity surprise you? How did the activity affect the way you think about knowledge? How realistic do you think it is to draw distinctions between western and indigenous knowledge?

Culturally safe research

One of the factors that led to a perceived dichotomy between indigenous and scientific knowledge is the culturally insensitive way in which some non-indigenous research programmes have been carried out. This has led to many indigenous peoples viewing non-indigenous research practices with distrust. Some scholars are calling for alternative approaches that are not only more culturally appropriate, but will also lead to more valid results.

One example is drawn from the idea that large, randomly selected population samples are usually representative for an **epidemiological** study. However, in many indigenous societies, some members of a population are difficult to reach by random sampling methods; they are a 'hidden population' who may be crucial to a full understanding of the subject of the research. In such instances, universal coverage would involve local expertise in defining the composition and distribution of the population, and this would improve the scientific validity and cultural safety of the sampling process.

KEY WORD

epidemiology: the study of the origins and spread of diseases

Figure 9.8: The Waorani people of the Ecuadorean Amazonia could be a hidden population in some studies

Scholars working towards culturally safe epidemiological research argue that scientific and indigenous knowledge are not mutually exclusive, and that research in indigenous societies can and should be both culturally safe and scientifically sound. They insist scientific validity often depends on indigenous knowledge, and it is at the interface in which neither indigenous nor scientific protocols are compromised that a culturally safe space can be achieved.

Culturally safe research would usually begin with a request from a community, and needs to respond to requests by designing research specifically for each particular group, rather than a generic approach for all indigenous studies. This would not only make the research more meaningful and relevant to the indigenous society that requested it; but it would also increase the scientific validity by ensuring the results more accurately reflect the realities of the target population.

DISCUSS 9.32

Should the researchers or the indigenous societies in which they work be responsible for exerting a greater influence on what is ethically acceptable in the search for new knowledge?

9.9 Conclusion

Knowledge that is developed in and transmitted by indigenous societies makes a valuable contribution to humanity's shared knowledge, but there is an imminent danger that much of it will be lost as indigenous societies dissipate and indigenous languages become extinct.

Moves are now underway to try to record and preserve knowledge that has been kept by indigenous societies, but these moves are hampered to some extent by a lack of clarity about what an indigenous community is. The lack of an agreed definition has allowed some host countries to limit the societies and people they will accept as indigenous to avoid having to extend special indigenous rights to them. Other host countries allow self-identification but this opens the door to potential abuse.

Indigenous knowledge is increasingly being used to complement scientific knowledge, particularly in areas of conservation, sustainable agriculture, land management and medicinal insights, but there is a need to ensure that indigenous intellectual property rights are honoured, and that indigenous societies reap the benefit when their knowledge becomes more widely available and is commercialised.

While there is little disagreement about the need to preserve knowledge held in indigenous societies, there is disagreement over whether it is helpful to draw a distinction between indigenous knowledge and knowledge from all other sources. It must be kept in mind that not all ideas that are regarded as knowledge in indigenous societies would be regarded as knowledge in a more evidence-based knowledge system, and some aspects of indigenous societies and indigenous knowledge can give rise to a number of serious ethical concerns.

KNOWLEDGE QUESTIONS

1   Could it ever be claimed that the natural sciences contribute more to the understanding of individuals and societies than the human sciences do?

2   To what extent must we look for a convergence of rational and empirical evidence to provide support for indigenous knowledge claims?

9.10 Linking questions

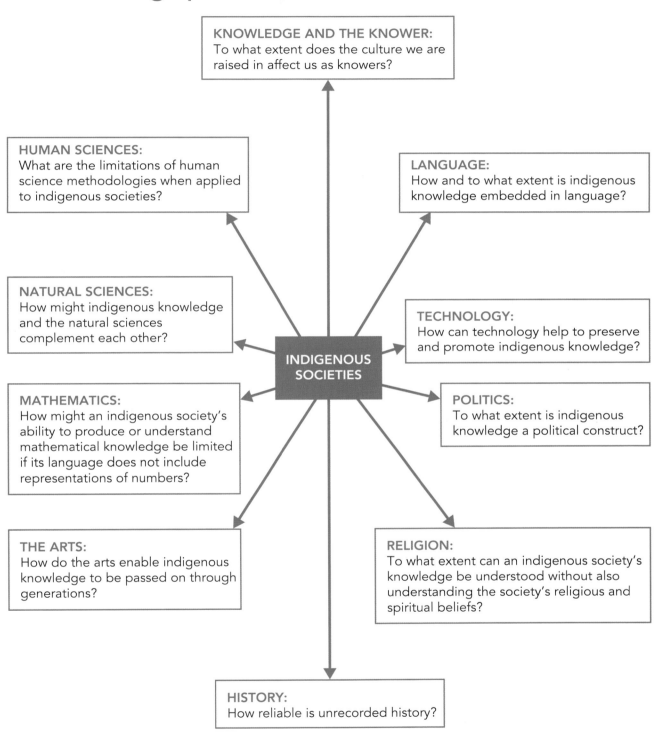

KNOWLEDGE AND THE KNOWER:
To what extent does the culture we are raised in affect us as knowers?

HUMAN SCIENCES:
What are the limitations of human science methodologies when applied to indigenous societies?

LANGUAGE:
How and to what extent is indigenous knowledge embedded in language?

NATURAL SCIENCES:
How might indigenous knowledge and the natural sciences complement each other?

TECHNOLOGY:
How can technology help to preserve and promote indigenous knowledge?

INDIGENOUS SOCIETIES

MATHEMATICS:
How might an indigenous society's ability to produce or understand mathematical knowledge be limited if its language does not include representations of numbers?

POLITICS:
To what extent is indigenous knowledge a political construct?

THE ARTS:
How do the arts enable indigenous knowledge to be passed on through generations?

RELIGION:
To what extent can an indigenous society's knowledge be understood without also understanding the society's religious and spiritual beliefs?

HISTORY:
How reliable is unrecorded history?

9.11 Check your progress

Reflect on what you have learned in this chapter and indicate your confidence level between 1 and 5 (where 5 is the highest score and 1 is the lowest). If you score below 3, re-visit that section. Come back to this list later in your course. Has your confidence grown?

	Confidence level	Re-visited?
Do I understand what is meant by an indigenous society?		
Am I clear about the significance of definitions, and the impact they can have on the scope of indigenous knowledge?		
Do I know what an indigenous diaspora is and how it can affect personal identity?		
Could I discuss different types of indigenous knowledge and how they can complement modern science?		
Am I able to articulate the importance of indigenous languages for the transmission and preservation of indigenous knowledge?		
Do I understand some of the ways in which indigenous knowledge is being protected?		
Do I understand what intangible cultural knowledge is?		
Can I discuss ways in which culture and cultural knowledge evolve?		
Am I aware of how the protection and preservation of indigenous cultures can set up a conflict of interest with other communities and conservation endeavours?		
Am I able to discuss the ethical dimension of adopting and adapting indigenous knowledge and practices?		
Do I understand why some people are concerned about drawing a distinction between indigenous knowledge and other knowledge?		
Am I able to articulate what is meant by culturally safe research?		

9.12 Continue your journey

- If you would like an overview of **how different countries and organisations approach questions of indigenous identity**, read: Jeff J Corntassel, 'Who is Indigenous? Peoplehood and Ethnonationalist Approaches to Rearticulating Indigenous Identity' in *Nationalism and Ethnic Politics*, vol. 9, no. 1, pp. 75–100, Spring 2003. Search the *Brown University* website for this article.

- If you would like to know more about some of the **issues self-identification as indigenous**, read: Andrew Canessa, 'Who Is Indigenous? Self-Identification, Indigeneity, And Claims to Justice in Contemporary Bolivia', in *URBAN ANTHROPOLOGY*, vol. 36, no. 3, 2007. Search the *Essex University* website for this article.

- If you would like to know more about some of the **issues concerning indigenous identity**, read: Bronwyn Carson 'The politics of identity and who gets to decide who is – and isn't – Indigenous' in *The Guardian*, 17 March 2016. Search the *Guardian* website for this article.

- If you would like to know more about **interactions between indigenous peoples and development**, read: Trevelyan Wing, 'Climate Change, Green Development, and the Indigenous Struggle for Cultural Preservation in Arctic Norway' in *Climate Institute*, 28 November 2017. Search the *Climate Institute* website for this article.

- If you want to explore the **relationship between indigenous knowledge, biodiversity and development**, read: Michael Warren,' Indigenous Knowledge, Biodiversity Conservation and Development' *Keynote address at the International Conference on Conservation of Biodiversity in Africa: Local Initiatives and Institutional Roles, 30 August – 3 September 1992, Nairobi, Kenya.* Search the *Indiana University* website for this article.

- If you would like to follow up on the **importance of indigenous languages**, read: *Rosalyn R LaPier,* 'Indigenous languages are disappearing – and it could impact our perception of the world' in *The Independent*, 11 October 2018. Search the *Independent* website for this article.

- If you are interested in the **UN's response to the demise of indigenous languages**, read: The United Nations Permanent Forum on Indigenous Issues 'Indigenous Languages', 2018. Search the *United Nations* website for this article.

- If you are interested in exploring the concept of **intangible cultural heritage**, read: UNESCO, 'What is Intangible Cultural Heritage?'. Search the *Unesco* website for this article.

- If you would like to further explore the problems of **dividing indigenous knowledge from other knowledge sources**, read: Arun Agrawal, 'Dismantling the Divide between Indigenous and Scientific Knowledge'. Search the *Indiana University* website for this article.

- If you want to know more about **culturally safe research**, read: Mary Cameron, Neil Andersson, Ian McDowell and Robert J Ledogar, 'Culturally Safe Epidemiology: Oxymoron or Scientific Imperative' in *Pimatisiwin,* vol. 8, no. 2, pp. 89–116., 2010. Search the *PubMed Central* website for this article.

Part 3

Areas of knowledge

Chapter 10

History

LEARNING INTENTIONS

This Chapter will consider how knowledge of the past is constructed, and how history connects with other areas of knowledge.

You will:

- explore the question 'What is history?', and the scope and nature of historical knowledge

- consider the reasons why we might pursue historical knowledge

- be able to identify what you think is central to the historical method; understand the role of selection and use of evidence, and the concept of significance; appreciate the problem of bias and selection in the construction of historical knowledge

- become familiar with the various knowledge tools, including language, imagination and empathy

- through an analysis of sources from the ancient historians and Herodotus and Thucydides, recognise the skills required to construct knowledge of the past and appreciate the standards and methods set by ancient historians

- consider the implications of hindsight and the concept of historiography

- examine various theories of history, and consider the nature of historical truth and different standards of proof

- consider the role of the arts, sciences and technology in representing the past and the impact this might have on historical knowledge

- appreciate the role of ethics in history, and be able to discuss ethical considerations that may shape a historian's interpretation and judgement

BEFORE YOU START

Analyse each of the following quotations and discuss the questions that follow.

1   'History is and should be a science. History is not the accumulation of events of every kind which happened in the past. It is the science of human societies.' **Numa Denis Fustel de Coulanges** (1830–1889)

2   'History is a pack of lies we play on the dead.' **Voltaire** (1694–1778)

3   'History is a continuous process of interaction between the historian and his facts, an unending dialogue between the present and the past.' **E.H. Carr** (1892–1982)

4   'The only thing we learn from history is that we learn nothing from history.' **G.W.F. Hegel** (1770–1831)

5   'Who controls the past controls the future, who controls the present controls the past.' **George Orwell** (1903–1950)

For each quotation, consider:

a   Do you agree or disagree with the quotation?

b   What do you think the quotation suggests about the nature and purpose of historical knowledge?

c   What is assumed or taken for granted about history in each quote?

d   Do you think the quotation could apply to other areas of knowledge? If so, in what ways?

10.1 Introduction

DISCUSS 10.1

1   What would you define as history, and how is this different from 'the past'?

2   Think of something you have learnt in history. Who decided what you learnt?

An understanding of the past is important for appreciating our place and context now, in time and space. The following cosmic calendar is a metaphor which explains the entire 13.8 billion years of cosmic time since the Big Bang to the present day as if it was just one year. If the universe were 1 year old, and the Big Bang took place on 1 January at midnight:

- 12 September The Earth is formed
- 21 September Life begins
- 25 December Dinosaurs emerge
- 31 December 23:54 *Homo Sapiens* evolve
- 31 December 23:58 Homo sapiens begin to create sculpture and painting

- 31 December 23:58:45 The invention of writing begins
- 31 December 23:59:32 Agriculture begins

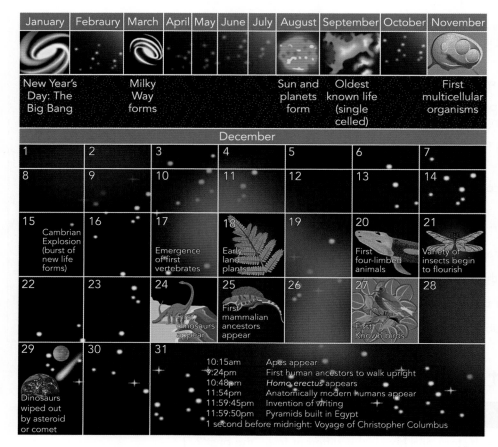

Figure 10.1: The history of the Earth condensed into a year

It is striking just how recent human life is in the context of time. Recorded human history is even more recent – the history of human civilisations during approximately the last 4,000 years or so. There are different scales that help us measure time:

- cosmic history can be considered to go back 13.8 billion years from the present day

- geological history (the Earth's history) goes back 4.54 billion years

- archaeological history goes back 3 million years

- *homo sapiens* go back 300,000 years

- the first cave paintings date to 40,000 years ago

- ancient history (recorded history) is normally considered as the period from 2000 BCE to 500 CE

- the years 500–1500 CE are usually classed as medieval history

- the years 1500 CE onwards are usually classified as modern history

10.2 What is history?

In answering the question 'What is history?', we might begin by saying that it is the study of the past. This may be a reasonable first approximation, but the answer is, in fact, more complicated than that. History once focused almost exclusively on telling the stories of kings and queens, great leaders, military campaigns, wars and politics. However, there has been a significant shift in focus in terms of topics, scope and modern methodology. Whereas some historians might specialise in a particular time period, such as the 18th century, or a particular event such as the French Revolution (1789) or the American War of Independence (1775), others may take a regional or national perspective, such as Uldis Ģērmanis (1915–1997) who wrote about modern Latvian history. Some historians will pursue even broader themes, analysing the broad sweep of continuity and change over time such as the global history of populations, gender and gender difference, power, medicine, commerce, religion or an intellectual history of ideas. Specialists in world history might focus on the history of entire continents. Moreover, history does not exist as a discipline in isolation. Historians might collaborate with experts from other areas of knowledge, and borrow from the methodologies of other disciplines in order to develop related subject areas, such as art history, economic history or archaeology.

CONTINUED

first three minutes of the lesson. Agree on your example. Take it in turns to describe what happened. Then discuss the following questions:

- How did your interpretations of the same event differ?

- What factors (such as memory, emotions, language and perspective) might have shaped your interpretation of the event? What effect does hindsight have on what you know?

- Can you still know what happened even if different accounts are given?

- How is knowledge of the past possible?

Self-assessment

How clearly were you able to describe your interpretation of the event? Were you able to identify a range of factors that shaped this interpretation? Could you explain in what ways your account differed from that of your partner's, and were you able to suggest reasons for these? In the light of this activity, how well do you now understand the difference between describing 'the past' and 'the study of history'?

A pluralistic approach

There is, of course, no easy way for us to gain certain knowledge of the past, nor escape from our own prejudices and achieve a god's-eye-view of history. Since history has often been used to promote the interests of dominant nations and powerful elites, it is not surprising that some people are suspicious of the 'official' version of the truth. And in an increasingly multi-cultural world, one might argue that textbooks should reflect the experiences not only of elites but also of groups such as women, the poor and ethnic minorities. Indeed, rather than thinking of *history* in the singular, it might be better to think in terms of *histories*. The ideal might then be a kind of pluralistic history. A pluralistic history explores the past from a variety of perspectives.

Such a pluralistic approach to history does not mean that we have to abandon the ideal of historical truth, or say that there is no certain knowledge. For within each approach to history, there are likely to be better and worse reconstructions of the past. For example, while some histories may be more propagandist and emotional, others are likely to be more accurate and objective. Therefore, we can embrace a pluralistic approach to history without succumbing to relativism. While there are many different perspectives in history, it is necessary to keep hold of some notion of historical truth. For on a basic level, it is surely the case that event X either did or did not happen. And although it is often difficult to discover the truth, this does not mean that there is no truth to discover. For example, we surely owe it to the victims of the genocides that have punctuated world history to bear witness to the fact that these things really happened.

KEY WORD

pluralistic history: accepting that there are various different perspectives that may be justified, and multiple possible accounts of the past

"It may seem dull to you now, Harry, but at one time, everything in that book was breaking news."

REAL-LIFE SITUATION 10.2

How far is it possible to gain certain knowledge of the past?

REFLECTION

What do you know about your personal history? Do you know where your parents, grandparents or perhaps great-grandparents were born, or what they did in their lives? How many generations can you go back?

How might knowing your personal history influence your sense of identity? To what extent do you think cultures and nations draw a sense of identity from their national or cultural histories?

10.3 Why pursue historical knowledge?

REAL-LIFE SITUATION 10.3

What do you think is the point of studying history?

There are many reasons for pursuing historical knowledge. We can justify history on various grounds, including that it gives us a shared memory, enriches our understanding of human nature, is a defence against propaganda and can provide a range of perspectives.

History gives us a shared memory

Just as you can know a person only if you know something about their history, so you can know a country only if you know something about *its* history and shared national memory. If you are to have informed opinions about current affairs, and your judgements about other countries are to go beyond mere prejudice, then a knowledge of history is indispensable. Education systems will take a particular approach to the teaching of history. For example, a school history textbook might shape a student's sense of identity and a shared national memory. Textbooks written about the same historical person or events may take differing approaches.

Sukarno (1901–1970) became the first President of Indonesia, having led his country to independence in 1949 from Dutch colonial rule. He governed using the principle of 'guided democracy' for 17 years, which was a euphemism for dictatorial control. General Suharto (1921–2008) became the second president of Indonesia, and he ruled with the support of the USA from 1967 until 1988. In the context of the Cold War, the USA had a policy of trying to stop the spread of communism. During his rule, Suharto exterminated up to 1 million Indonesian Communist Party supporters, but he was never put on trial for crimes against humanity. Indonesian, Dutch and American school history textbooks might offer different accounts of the history of Indonesia under the rule of Sukarno and Suharto.

The key issue is who interprets the shared national memory for today, and how it is represented. These issues have significant implications for knowledge and knowing.

> **KEY WORD**
>
> communism: a political and economic system in which there is no ownership of private property nor class divisions

> **REAL-LIFE SITUATION 10.4**
>
> Explain why some textbooks could offer different accounts of history.

History enriches our understanding of human nature

History enriches our understanding of human nature by showing us what human beings have thought and done in a wide variety of circumstances. History might remind us that human behaviour can never be fully explained in terms of neat and tidy models. If that is the case, then we might agree with historian R.G. Collingwood (1889–1943), who suggested that if you want to know yourself and other people better, you might want to pursue historical knowledge: 'My answer is that history is *for* human self-knowledge … Knowing yourself means knowing what you can do; and since nobody knows what he can do until he tries, the only clue to what man can do is what man has done. The value of history, then, is that it teaches us what man has done and thus what man is.'

History is a defence against propaganda

Arguably, the value of studying history is that it could be an antidote to propaganda or a commonly held narrative written by the victors. The study of history promotes critical thinking skills to help us to distinguish between bias, propaganda and fact. For example, analysis and weighing up of sources, in addition to understanding and evaluating different interpretations of the past (which we explore later in the chapter), both guard against taking historical accounts at face value. The study of history encourages these skills of analysis, so that it is possible to discern between multiple perspectives. A historian's method allows them to tell the difference between historical fact, and a historical opinion, and to come to a justified interpretation based on the evidence.

The counter-argument suggests that history can play a significant role in propaganda. While history has the potential to be a defence against propaganda, it is open to manipulation, and a particular version of events can be used to promote a particular perspective. It can be convenient and sometimes too easy for governments to see history through the political lens of their own nationality, and to impose their own judgements on the re-telling of history. The historical narrative told by governments may or may not be based on reliable knowledge. Propaganda is the misuse of information to suit the agenda of either an individual, a group, an organisation or a government, A government's selection can be very biased if national pride dictates a one-sided interpretation of the past which highlights a country's achievements and overlooks its mistakes. At worst, history can be exploited by a corrupt regime to legitimise its rule, justify territorial expansion and whitewash past crimes. Later in the chapter, we will explore one of the best-known examples of the abuse of history, from the Stalinist era in the former Soviet Union. As well as liquidating his political opponents, Stalin (1879–1953) also sought to erase them from the historical record.

Figure 10.2: The photograph on the left, taken in 1937, shows Joseph Stalin with a senior member of the Soviet secret police, Nikolai Yezhov (1895–1940). The photo was later manipulated to remove the image of Yezhov following his trial and execution. The study of history can reveal examples that show how the past can be mis-used as propaganda, to misrepresent the facts

History can provide a range of perspectives

You may have heard it said that history is written by the victors; a historical narrative can reflect the language and power of those who have conquered. However, the counter-argument might be that history can and should be told from alternative viewpoints. Historians are interested in understanding the same event from all viewpoints – 'from the cook to the captain'. For many years, the history of the Spanish conquest of Mexico and the defeat of the indigenous Aztecs was told in the language of and from the colonial perspective of the Spanish who conquered them. However, in his classic book *The Broken Spears* (1959), Miguel León-Portilla (1926–2019) offers a different perspective, focusing on the view of the indigenous peoples to show the continuity of the Aztec oral tradition. It poses a particular challenge for the historian to go beyond commonly accepted accounts of the past to take multiple perspectives and voices into consideration.

The historian sets out to know the difference between fact and interpretation, in addition to the difference between truth and propaganda – to look at history not only from the rulers or leaders 'from above' but also 'from below' – the perspective of ordinary people.

REFLECTION

Think about what you know about the history of your own country. Do you think that it was 'written by the victors' or does your country's history speak from many different perspectives? Can you think of any perspectives that might be missing?

REAL-LIFE SITUATION 10.5

1   Of the four reasons suggested in the red subheadings above for pursuing historical knowledge, which do you think is most important and why?

2   At what price should we pursue historical knowledge?

EXPLORE 10.2

1   As a class, discuss:

   a   How important do you think it is for our political leaders to have a good knowledge of history?

   b   Do you think some countries are more concerned with their history than others? What dangers, if any, are there in ignoring the past, or being obsessed with the past?

2   Read the following quotation from the German philosopher Immanuel Kant (1724–1804): 'One cannot avoid a certain feeling of disgust, when one observes the actions of man displayed on the great stage of the world. Wisdom is manifested by individuals here and there; but the web of human history as a whole appears to be woven from folly and childish vanity, often, too, from puerile wickedness and love of destruction: with the result that at the end one is puzzled to know what idea to form of our species which prides itself so much on its advantages.'

From your own knowledge of history, to what extent do you think Kant's assessment of humans is justified? Are there any grounds for taking a more optimistic view?

10.4 The historical method

1   In order to gain reliable knowledge of the past, what methods do historians use?

2   How does the historical method compare with other methods used to gain knowledge in different areas?

Given that we are unable to directly observe the past, and are dependent on often incomplete and sometimes contradictory source material, historians have developed a method of study to overcome these problems and lead to reliable knowledge. In this section, we explore some features of the historians' method for understanding the past, including the examination of and selection of evidence, the assessment of significance and the explanation of actions and events.

Understanding the past

The historian is not just interested in a recall of information, nor an accumulation of facts and dates; they are interested in understanding patterns. The same event or the same person can have different legitimate interpretations, and the task of the historian is to understand this complexity. The study of history involves an understanding of historical context and skill in interpretation. For example, the figure of Mohandas Karamchand Gandhi (1868–1948) might be studied by historians, political scientists or even economists. It is well known that Gandhi achieved independence for India in August 1947; however, his contribution might be understood in diverse ways. Historians might understand him not simply as the political leader of an independence movement. They might also evaluate his place more globally in relation to the history of civil disobedience movements, non-violent protests, Hindu–Muslim unity or even his contribution to writing (he was a prolific writer). Gandhi campaigned for the rights of the so-called 'untouchables', who at the time made up around 20% of Indian society. He wanted to elevate their place so they could enjoy an equal status with others in Indian society, and he accordingly renamed them *harijans* or 'children of God'. When Gandhi lived, he divided opinion – Albert Einstein and Lord Wilmington reached very different conclusions about him.

Source 1: Einstein

Albert Einstein, writing about Gandhi in 1944:

> A leader of his People, unsupported by any outward authority, a politician whose success rests not upon craft nor the mastery of technical devices, but simply on the convincing power of his personality; a victorious fighter who has always scorned the use of force; a man of wisdom and humility, armed with resolve and inflexible consistency, who has devoted all his strength to the uplifting of his people and the betterment of their lot; a man who has confronted the brutality of Europe with the dignity of the simple human being, and thus at all times rises superior.

> Generations to come, it may be, will scarce believe that such a one as this ever in flesh and blood walked upon this earth.

Source 2: Lord Wilmington

Lord Willingdon, Viceroy of India, writing about Gandhi in 1933:

> It's a beautiful world if it wasn't for Gandhi who is really a perfect nuisance . . .
> At the bottom of every move he makes, which he always says is inspired by God,
> one discovers the political manoeuvre . . . I see the American Press is saying
> what a wonderful man he is in that if he threatens to starve, there is a terrible
> hullaballoo over here. It's true, but the fact is that we live in the midst of very
> unpractical, mystical and superstitious folk who look upon Gandhi as something
> holy, whereas I look upon him as the biggest humbug alive.

Today, Gandhi continues to divide opinion. The key point is that the same person and
the same events can be understood in very different ways. Historical knowledge is still
possible, but the construction of knowledge is highly situated – it is a method that
takes place in relation to the interest and selection of a person living today who looks
back and tries to understand the past with the benefit of hindsight. As we will see later
in the chapter, hindsight can be both a strength and a weakness for the historian.

Figure 10.3: M.K. Gandhi (1869–1947) who led the Indian Independence movement. What
would be a justified interpretation of a historical figure?

DISCUSS 10.5

1   Describe the different views of Gandhi expressed by Lord Wilmington
    (Source 2) and Albert Einstein (Source 1).

2   How might historical knowledge still be possible despite disagreement
    between sources?

The historical method selects the relevant sources available in order to make sense of and interpret the past. Primary and secondary sources are used to explain the causes of events, or understand the patterns of continuity and change over time. Roughly speaking, a primary source is from the time being studied, while a secondary source is a later, second-hand account of what happened. For example, Julius Caesar's (100–44 BCE) *The Conquest of Gaul* is a primary source because it is Caesar's own account of the wars he fought. Primary sources may also include physical evidence, such as archaeological evidence or objects from a historical period. By contrast, Edward Gibbon's (1737–1794) *The Decline and Fall of the Roman Empire* is a secondary source because it is a much later reconstruction of the fate of the Roman Empire. While inference, imagination and language also play a role in the historical method, evidence is always the fixed point. A historian's narrative only makes sense in relation to the evidence. Indeed, R.G. Collingwood (1889–1943) recognised the role of both imagination and evidence in the construction of historical knowledge: 'The historian's picture stands in a peculiar relation to something called evidence. What we mean by asking whether an historical statement is true is whether it can be justified by an appeal to the evidence; for a truth unable to be so justified is to the historian a thing of no interest.' To use an analogy, if the evidence is like the fixed poles of a tent, the historical narrative is like the tent fabric stretched between those fixed points.

The best historians are capable of a first-rate selection and synthesis of evidence. You might consider the skills required to produce a high-quality construction of the past. It is worth noting that whereas in school history textbooks, there will be a pre-packaged evidence neatly labelled source a, source b and c, etc., the reality for the historian consulting archives is somewhat different. Simply put, there is no pre-existing file called 'the evidence'.

Arguably, there are connections between the historical and the scientific methods, given that both areas of knowledge share similar concepts, such as hypothesis, evidence, pattern and interpretation. On the other hand, the scope and aim of the subject and the nature of knowledge in each is very different, with history enquiring into the past and science investigating natural phenomena.

> ### KEY WORDS
>
> **primary source:** Any object or written source from the time or based on the time being studied, for example the eyewitness account of a soldier fighting in the Second World War would be a primary source even if it was written fifty years after the event
>
> **secondary source:** a second-hand account of a historical event, such as a history textbook
>
> **synthesis:** the placing together of different parts or elements (evidence) to form a connected whole

DISCUSS 10.6

What factors might influence your understanding of the past and your examination of evidence?

LINKING QUESTIONS 10.1

Science: What are the similarities and differences between the historical method and the methods used in the natural and human sciences?

Selecting evidence

The evidence available to a historian is necessarily limited. There are obvious reasons for this. Firstly, the primary sources of evidence, both archaeological and written, will be limited to what has survived from the time, meaning that the selection of evidence available is already restricted to what has survived. Primary sources might include, for example, the remains of a Roman villa – including archaeological findings such as the underfloor heating (hypocaust), the wall paintings and frescos or jewellery, but many objects will not have survived. There is an additional level of selectivity. Historians only need to select the *relevant* evidence – the evidence that is pertinent to the scope of their enquiry. If the scope of a historical investigation is phrased as, 'What was it like to live as a Roman?', we might select all of the evidence that is relevant to asking that question – and here the heating system, artwork and personal adornments will be relevant. However, if the question is 'Why did the Roman Empire end?' it is unlikely that any of this particular evidence will be relevant to the selection – unless the evidence contains any relevant clues. This process of selection is essential to the craft of the historian; it is an integral part of the historian's method.

Figure 10.4: Ancient remains. Why is the selection of evidence important?

One problem related to selection is the historians' choice of the range of source material. When we select evidence, we might make a judgement about the provenance of the source – in the case of a written source, who wrote it and why it was written. Bias can influence the evidence we select. For example, if you are studying the Cold War, you would end up with a one-sided view if you only selected evidence from an American perspective and left out the communist perspectives or the perspectives of the indigenous people in other countries such as Vietnam, Korea or Indonesia.

Examining evidence

Since we can know the past only to the extent that we have evidence for it, it would be more accurate to say that history is not so much the study of the past as of the *present traces* of the past. Historians commonly draw on both primary sources and secondary sources. Moreover, there is an appetite for additional modern secondary sources, with historians today re-visiting traditional areas. For example, Mary Beard (1955–) has written a popular history of Rome that takes into account new sources and methods (which were unavailable to Gibbon) and offers a fresh look at Rome from the viewpoint of the ordinary people.

Some accounts of what happened in the past are based only on secondary sources. For example, if you write an essay about the causes of the French Revolution towards the end of the eighteenth century, your bibliography may list a range of history books but no original documents. But it is obvious that if such sources are to have any authority, they must ultimately be grounded in primary sources – the first-hand accounts of individuals who witnessed the events in question. For this reason, primary sources are often described as the 'bedrock of history'.

Assessing significance

This brings us to another qualification we need to make about the nature of history. History is not a record of *everything* that happened in the past, but is concerned with only the *significant* events in the past. For example, while the assassination of John F. Kennedy on 22 November 1963 is a historically significant event, your exact choice of title for your 4,000-word IB Extended Essay is probably not. Once we start talking about 'significant events', we run into the problem of how to decide whether or not an event is significant. While you might think that significance – like beauty – is in the eye of the beholder, there are various *criteria* we might appeal to in order to decide whether or not an event is historically significant. For example, you can look at how many people are affected by the event, and the extent to which they are affected. Historians might identify significant events as turning points if they have far-reaching consequences, such as the origin and rise of Islam or Christianity. Moreover, technology can affect significance, such as the spread of ideas made possible by Chinese mechanical woodblock printing in the 8th century, or moveable type in the late-1300s in Korea.

DISCUSS 10.7

When and why might we disagree about the significance of people, places or events?

Of course, assessing historical significance is closely related to selection, which can be problematic. For example, a school history syllabus or a school history textbook will contain a selection from history. This can create the impression that history encourages a particular perspective or viewpoint, such as a focus on military or political history. If some time periods and themes are not considered significant, they may be neglected. Increasingly, historians recognise the significance of the perspectives of minority communities or the perspectives of women. Historical significance is a product of society, culture and education, and what is considered significant will change through time.

REAL-LIFE SITUATION 10.7

What do you think are the time periods and historical themes that are most significant? What factors have influenced your selection? How did you decide and why?

EXPLORE 10.4

Consider the list, a to l. Begin on your own. Order the list into a hierarchy that puts the event that is most historically significant at the top, and the least at the bottom. Share your list with a partner. Compare the top three items and bottom three items on both of your lists. Evaluate and discuss your lists together. Decide on the criteria for your ordering.

CONTINUED

a   the French Revolution in 1789

b   the publication of Charles Darwin's *The Origin of Species* in 1859

c   women in New Zealand gain the right to vote in parliamentary elections in 1893

d   the First World War in 1914

e   the Second World War in 1939

f   the assassination of Mohandas K. Gandhi in 1948

g   the birth of Bill Gates in 1955

h   the Cuban Missile Crisis in 1962

i   the release of Nelson Mandela from prison in 1990

j   the publication of *Harry Potter and The Goblet of Fire* by J.K. Rowling in 2000

k   the terrorist attacks on the World Trade Centre and the Pentagon in the USA in 2001

l   the inauguration of Barack Obama as 44th President of the United States of America in 2009

Peer-assessment

Which of the items on your list did your partner think were most significant and why? Which of your criteria did your partner think were most valid, and which did they think were most or least useful? From your discussion, did you

LINKING QUESTIONS 10.2

The arts and science: Compare historical significance with artistic, ethical and scientific significance. How far are they similar? How do we know what is historically significant? What is the nature of this knowledge?

Explaining the past

History is concerned not simply with describing the past, but also with *explaining* it, and trying to understand *why* events happened. Historians might typically be trying to understand such things as the collapse of the Roman Empire, the causes of the First World War or the origins of communism or fascism. The historian E.H. Carr (1892–1982) distinguished between three types of causes: long-term, intermediate and short-term causes. E.H. Carr used the example of a car accident to illustrate his point about an event having short-term, medium-term and long-term causes, raising the question about how far back we need to go in order to meaningfully explain the causes of an event.

Tyche was the Greek goddess of fortune or destiny (*Fortuna* in Latin), who was believed to be the reason for the fate of men. If an unlikely event occurs, it might be explained in terms of luck or chance. Some Greek historians such as Polybius (200–118 BCE) considered the role played by fortune. In contrast, some historians might take for granted the materialist view that historical explanations are like a scientific explanation, as if there were universal laws that determined and explained the outcome of events, as in the laws of nature. Other historians might disagree, and suggest that there is nothing that determines events; they are neither random nor pre-determined. Hence, the historian offers reasons or causes that constitute an explanation of what happened.

Taking seriously the idea that events have no one single predetermined outcome, modern historians have developed 'virtual history', also known as 'counter-factual' history. This approach asks the question 'What if…?' and speculates about why other plausible options, which were seriously considered at the time, were in fact not pursued.

LINKING QUESTIONS 10.3

Natural science: In what ways is a historical explanation similar to or different from a scientific explanation?

The problem of bias

DISCUSS 10.8

What do we mean by bias in the context of studying history?

We should now consider the problem of bias, and address the widespread perception that the historical method is more prone to bias than the natural sciences. There are at least four reasons (or arguments) why someone might think this is the case. Although we should not underestimate the danger of bias in history, something can be said in response to each of these points (counter-arguments).

Argument	Counter-argument
Topic choice bias Topic choice bias is when a historian picks something related to their society. This bias is at the level of their selection. A historian's choice of topic may be influenced by current preoccupations; and the questions that they ask – or fail to ask – are likely to influence the answers that they find.	Although a historian's choice of topic may be influenced by the society they grow up in, this does not necessarily mean that the topic, once chosen, cannot be studied objectively. While there may be an element of bias in a historian's *choice* of topic, this will not necessarily affect their *treatment* of it.
Bias identified in evidence A primary source may be biased if it implicitly or explicitly favours one particular viewpoint or person.	Despite the identification of bias in primary and secondary sources, it is still possible to develop reliable historical knowledge. Rather than dismiss biased evidence, the historian is interested in understanding and offering an explanation. The identification of bias in sources does not mean that no historical knowledge is possible.

Argument	Counter-argument
Confirmation bias A historian might be tempted to appeal only to evidence that supports their own case, and to ignore any counter-evidence. As we have seen, this can also be a problem in the natural and human sciences. Historians are interested in understanding continuity and change over time, and identifying essential patterns. They select relevant source material and put forward arguments based on that source material, with the benefit of hindsight.	In order to understand continuity and change, historians identify patterns in history – however they are not in the business of imposing patterns that they believe must be justified against the available evidence. Although history is selective, and a bad historian may be tempted to simply find the facts they are looking for, a good historian is likely to do the opposite and actively seek out evidence that goes against their hypothesis. As a matter of fact, the historian Keith Windschuttle (1942–) has observed that it is a common experience among historians to find the evidence *'forces them, often reluctantly, to change the position they originally intended to take'*.
National bias Since people come to history with a range of pre-existing cultural and political prejudices, they may find it difficult to deal objectively with sensitive issues that touch on things like national pride. Questions such as 'To what extent were ordinary Germans aware of the Holocaust?', 'Was the British bombing of Dresden a war crime?' or 'Why did the USA drop the atomic bomb on Hiroshima?' may be hard to answer without strong emotions colouring our interpretation of the facts. Faced with such questions, the danger is that we begin with our prejudices and then search for the evidence to support them. At worst, history may then become little more than the finding of bad reasons for what we believe through prejudice.	There is a serious danger of national bias infecting history. However, if rival historians of different nationalities, and with different background assumptions and prejudices, are able to critique one another's work, then at least the more obvious errors and biases should be rooted out.

Essential to the historical method is the identification and evaluation of bias. Arguably, historical knowledge is still possible despite the problem of bias.

> ## EXPLORE 10.5
>
> Using the Argument and Counter-argument table, evaluate the arguments and counter-arguments put forward. Discuss any specific concrete examples, and where they might fit in the table.
>
> Rate the four types of bias – which is the most and least problematic for historians, and why? Is historical knowledge possible despite the problem of bias?

Figure 10.5: How does an individual's national background influence their perspective on history?

DISCUSS 10.9

To what extent do you think there could be a single historical narrative of the world on which all nations could agree? Explain why this might or might not be possible.

10.5 Knowledge tools

DISCUSS 10.10

If we are to gain knowledge of the past, what roles should be played by language, imagination and empathy?

The study of history uses a range of knowledge tools including language, imagination and empathy. History can encourage empathy and an insight into how people in the past have lived and what they have valued. The study of history also invites us to consider how far neutral language can be used to describe the past.

Language

In this section, we explore history and language in its written and spoken forms, and more broadly, the relationship between knowledge and language. There is a distinction between communication, language and speech. Arguably, speech is a human characteristic, and a facility that is distinctive of *homo sapiens* since the emergence of our species some 300,000 years ago. At the start of the chapter, we noted that humans began to create art around 40,000 years ago; however, written and recorded history has only occurred for the last 4,000 years.

Language is necessary for recorded history, and is a key tool. The average adult knows around 20,000 to 35,000 words. We make records, write sources, leave written accounts, produce spoken evidence and take part in or contribute to oral traditions. Languages express our values, and in turn, the language world we inherit gives us the linguistic tools that might define us and even shape our knowledge. There's a broader question about the relationship between language and knowledge, specifically the power of language to determine our thinking and our knowledge. With language, we tell stories to 'make sense' of the world, and we express values. Language is an expression of what we know. Furthermore, language shapes who we become and in some sense, influences what we know.

Language presents particular issues for historical knowledge. It is an essential tool for the construction of knowledge. Language is necessary for the production of sources; for writing eye-witness or primary accounts of those who lived at the time. Language is also essential for historians to interpret sources and articulate a new narrative for an audience today, which can also be passed down through time. There are multiple levels of meaning in any one given event – the language of the sources from the time and the interpretation of subsequent historians after the event. There are also gaps in language and evidence – the lost words of the people who lived through an era, but who left no records. Language is a necessary, if imperfect tool for the historian. Let us examine some of problems involved.

The past is a foreign language we cannot translate nor understand

> ### LINKING QUESTIONS 10.4
>
> **Language:** To what extent is it justified to describe the past with words that express present day opinions such as 'evil', 'villain', 'victor' or 'conqueror'?

This argument suggests that the language of the past is lost to us. We can only operate within the language of the time that we live in. This is the only language that we can claim to make sense of. It could be argued that eras and their languages are lost. The false assumption that there is *one* language that belongs to a country is highly misleading. For example, in India, there are 22 official languages such as Hindi, Gujarati and Bengali, and several hundred unofficial tribal languages spoken; and within the English-speaking world, there is diversity with American English, Australian English and many other variants. In order to understand ancient Indian history or Jewish history, it is generally thought necessary to understand Sanskrit or Hebrew respectively. If you live in the West, you may find it difficult to understand the Manchu dynasty that spanned the era of Chinese history from 1644 to 1911/12.

This is problematic if we are relying on translations of sources, which themselves express unfamiliar paradigms and cultural values. Furthermore, it may be difficult for us to understand the nature of the German Reformation and the disagreement that emerged between Martin Luther (1483–1546) and Pope Leo X (1475–1521) because the languages are lost to us and the interpretation of religious concepts that divided people then have lost some of their resonance and meaning.

In any attempt to understand and shed light on the past, we might fail to understand the language of the past and increase obscurity. This poses a particular problem for the historian when they try to construct knowledge using objective and neutral language.

Modern readers need simple and clear language

Historians face a further problem. Even if a historian succeeds in interpreting a lost language from the past, they might still neglect to communicate the complexity and accuracy of that history because of the need to write with simplicity and clarity. When a historian writes history, their interpretation needs to appeal to a modern audience. The language of communication could risk being too simple.

REFLECTION

If historical truth is complex, how much accuracy might be lost in the requirement for simplicity and clarity in language? Do you think it is better for a historical account to be more accurate but complicated, or less accurate but clear? Do you think the historian has a responsibility to let the audience know the extent to which accuracy has been sacrificed for clarity?

The language of sources may have no essential or fixed meaning

This argument suggests there are some concepts that may have no essential or fixed meaning, such as communism. When we consider the October 1917 Russian Revolution you may have assumed that Lenin, inspired by Karl Marx (1818–1883), implemented communist ideas in Russia. However, here the language used gives rise to a deeper problem of interpretation. Our assumption that Marxism means essentially the same as communism may not be the case. Marxism could be interpreted to mean any of the following: Karl Marx's teachings, Lenin's interpretation of those teachings or Lenin and Stalin's application of these ideas in the Soviet Union. Historians make this distinction clear by referring to Marxist-Leninism, meaning the doctrines of Marx that were built upon by Lenin and adapted to the Russian context. Some would argue that all historical attempts to apply communism have failed to live up to the ideals set out by Marx himself. This is a point about the problem of language – because the label 'Communist' or 'Marxist' may have so many meanings and interpretations that it could have no essential meaning. This poses a particular problem for the historian when they try to use language that is clear, accurate and meaningful.

Language expresses values

This argument suggests that it is difficult for any description of the past to be described in neutral language, given that language is value-laden. Since each generation interprets the past in the light of its own experience, we might agree with E.H. Carr's characterisation of history as 'an unending dialogue between the present and the past'.

This suggests that when you read *The History of the French Revolution* by Jules Michelet (1798–1894), you may learn as much about the values and prejudices of 19th-century France as about the events that Michelet describes. It is well known that the same historical person might be described as a liberator or a dictator, and the description might reflect the views of the speaker more than it might refer accurately to the past.

DISCUSS 10.11

To what extent can we use neutral and objective language to describe the past?

KEY WORD

censorship: the suppression or limitation of any material or views and beliefs that are considered to be unsuitable or inappropriate

History is an emotive subject that divides nations, and raises ethical issues relating to truth, responsibility and censorship. Korean girls and women who were forced into sexual slavery in Japanese military brothels in the 1930s and 1940s, have been euphemistically described using the term 'comfort women'. This is an offensive term which obscures the suffering that they underwent. However, there is disagreement about the number of women and the involvement of the Japanese government. The Japanese perspective argues that these incidents were isolated acts of individuals, and were not done on the order of the Japanese military or the government. Nevertheless, some historians disagree with the Japanese interpretation, and believe that this is an example of censorship where a government seeks to distance itself from a past atrocity. This raises ethical questions about national bias, and whether any historical language that describes an atrocity could ever be conveyed in neutral language. This poses a particular problem for the historian when they try to recount the past in a way that is respectful to the memory of people who have suffered. You might consider the responsibility of historians to tell the truth about the past.

REAL-LIFE SITUATION 10.8

1　Can and should history tell the truth? Why? Why not?

2　Should history ever be censored? Why? Why not?

3　How might our national or political bias shape what we claim to know about the past?

Imagination and empathy

If the focus of historical research is on individuals, then we need to get beyond the outside of events, and think ourselves into the minds of the agents. The historian R.G. Collingwood (1889–1943), with whom this idea is particularly associated, commented: 'When a historian asks "Why did Brutus stab Caesar?" he means "What did Brutus think which made him decide to stab Caesar?" The cause of the event, for him, means the thought in the mind of the person by whose agency the event came about: and this is not something other than the event, it is the inside of the event itself . . . All history is the history of thought.'

What Collingwood meant by his observation that 'all history is the history of thought' is that we can understand people's actions only by delving into their minds and trying to make sense of their motives. Collingwood drew particular attention to the importance of empathy in trying to understand a situation in the same way that a historical agent would have understood it. Some people have gone further, and used ideas from psychoanalysis to shed light on the motivations of historical characters.

For Collingwood, imagination plays a crucial role in reconstructing the past.

'I described constructive history as **interpolating**, between the statements borrowed from our authorities, other statements implied by them. Thus our authorities tell us that on one day Caesar was in Rome and on a later day in Gaul; they tell us nothing about his journey from one place to the other, but we interpolate this with a perfectly good conscience. . . As works of imagination, the historian's work and the novelist's do not differ. Where they do differ is that the historian's picture is meant to be true . . . This further necessity imposes upon him obedience to three rules of method, from which the novelist or artist in general is free.'

However, G.R. Elton (1921–1994) disagreed with Collingwood's approach. For Elton, facts are important, and a historical narrative could only be based on the facts. Furthermore, historical facts might be dependent on a number of factors. We will find the facts that we go looking for, which suggests that the historical era and topic that we choose to select might determine the facts that become significant. E.H. Carr suggested that:

'The facts are really not at all like fish on the fishmonger's slab. They are like fish swimming about in a vast and sometimes inaccessible ocean; and what the historian catches will depend, partly on chance, but mainly on what part of the ocean he chooses to fish in and what tackle he chooses to use – these two factors being, of course, determined by the kind of fish he wants to catch. By and large, the historian will get the kind of facts he wants. History means interpretation.'

KEY WORD
interpolate: to insert something of a different nature into something else

DISCUSS 10.12

1   What is the nature of historical knowledge? What is the difference between 'the past' and 'our knowledge of the past'?

2   What can we know? What do we want to know from history?

Despite its merits, a number of criticisms can be made of Collingwood's approach to history. To start with, although the ability to empathise may be a useful tool of the historian's trade, it clearly has its limits. Most people would find it difficult to empathise with some of the monsters of history, such as Genghis Khan, Ivan the Terrible or Adolf Hitler. Furthermore, in trying to explain historical events, it is not clear why we should limit ourselves to the agent's perception of the situation. As we saw earlier, one of the advantages that a historian has over the people they study is hindsight, and their retrospective vantage point may enable them to find a significance in events that was not apparent to people at the time.

DISCUSS 10.13

What role should imagination and empathy play in a historian's work?

10.6 How can the past be known?
Herodotus and Thucydides

The ancient Greeks enjoyed a flourishing of rational thought, literature, poetry, art, music, politics and history. Their focus was on understanding man and nature, and applying a logical framework of thought in order to understand the natural world. Whereas Homer, commonly known as the author of the epic poems *Iliad* and *Odyssey*, had already begun a literary tradition, the ancient Greek historians Herodotus (484–425 BCE) and Thucydides (460–400 BCE) are both regarded as the founders of history. Indeed, Herodotus' *Histories* was the first work of non-fiction in the western world, and the first ever history book known to be written. Herodotus came from Halicarnassus in Asia Minor (today, Bodrum in Turkey). He spent many years recording the wars between Greece and Persia from 500 to 449 BCE, and his *Histories*, published around 426 and 415 BCE, are the only source for our knowledge of these wars. For Herodotus, explanation and interpretation are included in that recording of the past; he is explicit about wanting to explain why the two sides fought and why, against the odds, the Greek armies defeated the Persians.

Figure 10.6: The Greek historian Herodotus (484–425 BCE) was one of the founders of history. What can we learn from the approach he took?

Histories literally means 'enquiries' in Greek; the Greek word is *historiai* (singular, *historie*). Herodotus began a new and highly innovative method of enquiry – for around one-quarter of a century, he consulted sources, gathered and selected evidence. He travelled to Egypt and interviewed diverse people, including priests and war veterans; he was interested to know how others think and behave, and to record the past. It is highly significant that he considers both viewpoints – the Greek and Persian perspectives (source A); he had contact with both sides. He represents the Persians – who had conquered his own hometown and waged war against Greece – as having dignity and courage, and is explicit about his intention to record their achievements in battle. In this sense, he takes for granted that there is an integrity to the writing of history (source B) – a responsibility to consider sources from both sides.

The following primary sources are extracts taken from Herodotus' *Histories*, and the activity that follows invites you to read the extracts carefully and try to answer the questions that follow using evidence from the source. This is an opportunity to develop the skills of a historian, interpreting sources in order to construct knowledge of the past.

By contrast, Thucydides of Athens wrote the history of the war fought between Athens and Sparta (a state in the south Peloponnese, Greece). Thucydides wrote mainly about contemporary history and politics, which gave him the opportunity to gather and evaluate evidence, but he also recognised the difficultly of remembering and recording speeches with accuracy (source C). He takes for granted that a record of the past is also an attempt to interpret and explain it. Thucydides, is clear about the need for causes and explanations in terms of human actions (source D) rather than fate or religion.

Herodotus and Thucydides both move away from explanations in relation to the gods, the oracle, or good or bad fortune. For Herodotus, the cause of the war between Greece and Persia is not due to a series of mythical abductions of women, as the Persians thought. Instead, he understands that actions have motives – and knowing why someone did something is to know the cause.

Primary Source A – Herodotus – the proem

'This is the display of the inquiry of Herodotus of Halicarnassus, so that things done by man not be forgotten in time, and that great and marvellous deeds, some displayed by the Greeks, some by the barbarians, not lose their glory, including among others what was the cause of their waging war on each other.'

Primary Source B – Herodotus – Book 1.5

'So much for what the Persians and Phoenicians say; and I have no intention of passing judgement on its truth or falsity. I prefer to rely on my own knowledge, and to point out who it was in actual fact that first injured the Greeks ...'

Primary Source C – Thucydides 1.22.1–2

'In this history I have made use of set speeches some of which were delivered just before and others during the war. I have found it difficult to remember the precise words used in the speeches which I listened to myself and my various informants have expressed the same difficulty; so my method has been, while keeping as closely as possible to the general sense of the words that were actually used, to make the speakers say what, in my opinion, was called for by each situation.'

KEY WORD

barbarian: Herodotus refers to the Persians as barbarians. For Herodotus 'barbarians' denoted all non-Greeks, and the word originally meant a speaker of an incomprehensible language. The word did not have the same negative connotations that people might associate it with today

Primary source D – Thucydides 1.23.6–7

But the real reason for the war is, in my opinion, likely to be disguised by such an argument. What made war inevitable was the growth of Athenian power and the fear which this caused in Sparta. As for the reasons for breaking the truce and declaring war which were openly expressed by each side, they were as follows …

EXPLORE 10.6

1   What do sources A to D tell us about the historical method?

2   Using sources A to D, discuss the roles of perspective, causation, memory and language.

DISCUSS 10.14

1   What can we say about Herodotus' and Thucydides' standards and integrity as historians?

2   If a rigorous method is followed, do you think that it is possible to gain historical knowledge? Why? Why not?

So what are we to say about the value of primary sources? Despite their limitations, if they are properly used, we should not be overly sceptical about their value. From the previous activity, it is possible to gain an insight into the methods and standards set by two ancient historians. When you encounter primary sources, analysis and interpretation is possible. There are, after all, ways of distinguishing a more reliable from a less reliable source. To start with, we can ask questions such as:

•   Who wrote it?

•   What was their motive in writing?

•   How long after the event was it written?

In addition, we can compare different primary sources to see how far they agree with one another. For example, if Israeli and Palestinian eye-witnesses agree about something, then it is likely to be true. Finally, we can look at documents of a legal and administrative nature, which are less likely to be biased than such things as letters and diaries. So although it would be naive to accept primary sources at face value, some of them are reliable, and in the end, they are all that we have to distinguish truth from fiction. The fact that historians frequently disagree with one another should not blind us to the truth that there are a vast number of basic historical facts that everyone agrees about. No one seriously doubts that Julius Caesar crossed the Rubicon in 49 BCE, the atomic bomb was dropped on Hiroshima in 1945, or Nelson Mandela was released from prison in 1990. There is, however, far less agreement about the meaning and significance of such facts. Moreover, there are justifiable reasons why historians disagree. One reason is the different perspectives of historians – which leads us to our next section on historiography.

REFLECTION

If you were to construct an account of a historical event from a variety of sources, how much do you think you would need to rely on imagination to weave the different accounts together? To what extent do you think imagination and certainty are mutually exclusive?

10.7 Hindsight and historiography

It is a common fault of men not to reckon on storms in fair weather.

Niccolò Machiavelli (1469–1527)

DISCUSS 10.15

What are the advantages and disadvantages of hindsight for the knower?

Hindsight

One of the advantages historians have over the people whose behaviour they describe is *hindsight*. Unlike them, historians know how things turned out. An event which seemed insignificant at the time might later turn out to be of great importance, and *vice versa*. Certain ways of describing events may not be available to people at the time, but only retrospectively. For example, we can talk about the First World War, but since people in the 1920s did not know there would be another world war, they called it the Great War. Sadly, their description of the First World War as 'the war to end all wars' now sounds very hollow.

The division of history into various periods is similarly influenced by hindsight. In European history, we commonly speak of eras such as the Stone Age or pre-history, followed by ancient history, medieval history and modern history; but for the people at the time, they had no way of knowing how future generations would pre-package their era. Terms such as 'the Renaissance' and 'the Enlightenment' are retrospective ways of trying to capture the spirit of a particular historical era.

REAL-LIFE SITUATION 10.9

1   What description do you think future historians will use to sum up the age in which we are living?

2   According to the historian G.M. Trevelyan (1876–1962), 'Unlike dates, periods are not facts. They are retrospective conceptions that we form about past events, useful to focus discussion, but very often leading historical thought astray.' How can dividing history into periods be useful, and how can it be misleading?

The disadvantages of hindsight

Despite the advantages of hindsight in helping us to determine the significance of things, it can also distort our understanding of the past. When you are living through events, they seem genuinely open and you are not sure how they will turn out; but when you look back on them, it is hard to avoid the feeling that they were inevitable and could not have happened any other way. This can easily lead to hindsight bias. After a catastrophe, it is easy to believe that any fool could have seen what would happen, and that if you had been in the situation in question, you would not have made the same mistake.

The fact is that we are all good at being wise after the event. Many commentators now see the collapse of communism in Eastern Europe as inevitable, but almost no one was predicting its fall in the 1970s. If we are to get into the minds of historical actors and see situations as they themselves saw them, then we must try to avoid such hindsight bias.

Our discussion suggests that hindsight can be both a benefit and a drawback to the historian. On the plus side, it enables us to see the significance of events in the light of their consequences; on the minus side, it may lead to our being wise after the event, and failing to appreciate how open and uncertain the past was to the people living through it.

Hindsight and perspective

History is a subject that lends itself to various perspectives. This is partly a result of hindsight, where historians look back and interpret the past in different ways. There are justifiable reasons why their interpretations of past events may vary, and as knowers, we need to be able to assess and make sense of these disagreements.

Using hindsight, historians can look back at events that happened long before Marx lived, and interpret them through a Marxist lens. For example, Georges Lefebvre (1874–1959) interpreted the French Revolution (1789) from a Marxist viewpoint. He looked at 'history from below', and focused on the role of the peasantry and their level of participation in revolutionary events and the effects of the Revolution on these ordinary people. As a Marxist, he understood the French Revolution as an example of class struggle between the old aristocracy and the rising bourgeoisie, and a step from feudalism in the direction of capitalism: 'The ultimate cause of the French Revolution of 1789 goes deep into the history of France and of the western world. At the end of the 18th century the social structure of France was aristocratic. It showed traces of having originated at a time when land was almost the only form of wealth

KEY WORDS

hindsight bias: mistakenly thinking, after something has happened, that you had known it would happen

bourgeoisie: the middle class – Marx thought that they benefited most from a capitalist economic system

capitalism: an economic system where there is limited government intervention, and the production and distribution of resources depend on the investment of private capital

… Meanwhile, the growth of commerce and industry had created, step by step, a new form of wealth and a new class, called the bourgeoisie.'

REAL-LIFE SITUATION 10.10

How far might our nationality, language or emotions impact on our understanding of the past? How far is it desirable or possible to transcend one's own bias?

Historiography

The writing of history is also influenced by the era in which it is written. The passage of time is constantly adding new pages to the book of history, and this means that what has gone before will be reassessed by each new generation in the light of subsequent experience. Since we judge events partly in the light of their consequences, this suggests that we may be too close to recent events to understand their significance.

History involves **historiography** – the study of historical perspectives. In historiography, the focus is not on the historical event itself but on the key thinkers who have studied it. Historians will understand the same historical event differently – each from the unique viewpoint of the time when they lived. Historians themselves are influenced by the social, political and military context of their own time. The main question is how far we can gain objective knowledge, despite these factors that impact on what we think we know?

KEY WORD

historiography: the study of historical perspectives

DISCUSS 10.16

1   It has been said that you can learn more from a history textbook about the author writing it than about the period in question. Do you agree?

2   Does the fact that historians disagree mean that historical knowledge is still possible?

The historiography of a national revolution illustrates the role of hindsight. Historians recognise many concepts, including trends, patterns, causes, turning points and false dawns. A turning point is such a change, characterised as a point of no return, when there is a significant change or irreversible shift that takes place. A revolution is usually, but not always, an example of a turning point. Taking a comparative view, historians might compare and contrast the English Civil War in the 1640s with the French Revolution in 1793, the American Civil War of 1861–1865 or the Russian Revolution of 1917. A comparison of the role, intentions and actions of Oliver Cromwell during and after the English Civil War with those of Robespierre in the French Revolution or Lenin in the Russian Revolution might illuminate these events.

Figure 10.7: Jean-Baptiste Belley (c 1746–1805) depicted wearing the uniform of the National Convention, France, of which he was a member during the period of the French Revolution. Why are there different interpretations of the same historical events?

In the rest of this section, we consider historical interpretations. Some people might assume that historical facts are more reliable than historical interpretations. However, we explore how different interpretations of the same event may be justified.

Historiography: Example 1 – The Russian Revolution

Historical topic: the Russian Revolution

Historical knowledge claim: Lenin ruled Soviet Russia from 1917 to 1924, and the Soviet Union from 1922 to 1924

Historiography: historians take different views of the event when he took power – known as the October Revolution

Karl Marx argued that history was a series of progressive steps towards communism. He thought that historical development was based on a pattern of class conflict between the 'ruling classes' who controlled society's resources, and an exploited 'under-class' of workers. Marx argued that only a revolution of the working class in an industrialised country could challenge and overthrow the ruling classes, and

Note that the dates given in this book for the Russian Revolution are based on the old-style calendar used in Russia at the time of the events, whereas some other accounts use the Gregorian calendar used in Europe.

bring about socialism and then communism. Lenin followed Marx's ideas and he led a political party – the Bolsheviks – who would seize power during the revolution. In February 1917, the Russian middle-class or bourgeoisie sought to overthrow the autocratic rule of Tsar Nicholas II. They did not actively seek to overthrow the Tsar, but the provisional government accepted his abdication, and the actions of both bourgeoise and the people led to the collapse of the Romanov dynasty.

Lenin and Stalin

In October 1917, Lenin and the Bolsheviks hijacked this revolution to set up communism in a revolution 'from below'. Following Lenin's death in 1924, Joseph Stalin became the communist leader in Russia, and planned the 'revolution from above', whereby he forced policies of rapid economic social development. This revolution resulted in a huge amount of suffering, including the suffering and deaths of millions of people, including leaders in the Bolshevik party.

Communism continued in Russia, which was known as the Soviet Union from 1922 until 1991. It spread globally to central and eastern Europe, China, North Korea and later, Cuba. Historians are interested to explain the role of individuals, and how and why Lenin and Stalin were able to have such a deep and widespread impact on Russia and beyond. However, historians are also interested to understand the origins and the broader social, economic, technological and cultural causes of these global developments. The Cold War which followed for decades was characterised by a global and mutual distrust between communist and capitalist countries.

> **KEY WORD**
>
> **capitalist:** employing an economic system where there is limited government intervention, and the production and distribution of resources depend on the investment of private capital

The October Revolution

Historians disagree about the nature of the October 1917 Revolution, and the extent to which it was a 'popular' uprising. The differences in historical interpretation could be explained by the fact that it is difficult to know the level of support for the Bolsheviks from the sources. There are a number of issues that make it complicated. It is difficult to establish who and what the Russian people were supporting – and therefore the nature of the popular element. The historian Beryl Williams (1987–) pointed out that people who supported the October 1917 Revolution and voted for the Bolsheviks in elections did not necessarily agree with all Bolshevik policies once they were known, nor the idea of one-party rule.

The following secondary sources are extracts taken from historians writing after the Russian Revolution and the activity that follows invites you to read the extracts carefully, and try to answer the questions that follow, using evidence from the sources.

Source 1

> The Russian Revolution of October 1917 is arguably the most important event in the 20th century, since it led to the creation of the world's first Communist state, which lasted over 70 years and had a huge impact on world affairs for the greater part of the 20th century … The Communist model was exported to Eastern Europe, China, south-east Asia, parts of Africa and the Caribbean.
>
> **Chris Corin and Terry Fiehn**, 2002

Source 2

> The working class led the struggle of the whole people against the autocracy and against the dictatorship of the bourgeoisie.
>
> **B.N. Pomomarev**, 1960

> **KEY WORD**
>
> **autocracy:** a government based on one person with supreme authority and power

Source 3

> October was not a revolution but a classic *coup d'etat* … Eyewitnesses, including the best chronicler of 1917, the Menshevik Nicholas Sukhanov, are virtually unanimous in depicting October as a *coup d'état*; so too are such historians as S.P. Melgunov, who had lived through it.
>
> **R. Pipes**, 1992

KEY WORD

coup d'état: when a small group of people seizes power by force

Perspective: The Soviet view (1917–1991) – it was a popular revolution

This perspective views the October 1917 Revolution as a popular uprising of the people, led and carried out by the working class (Source 2). The communist regime grew out of this popular revolution. This view makes sense in relation to a narrative of the birth of communism. The October 1917 Revolution is the turning point which puts Lenin as communist leader centre stage.

This was the prescribed view of the Soviet leadership and under communism, writers were not allowed to challenge this view. Social and economic reasons are the agents of change. This is the Marxist or communist view, which makes a value judgement in support of communism.

Perspective: The main western view after 1945 – it was a coup d'état

This perspective views the October 1917 Revolution as the action as a *coup d'état*, where a minority of people seized power for their own purposes. The communist government that grew out of this event was an autocratic and tyrannical regime which imposed its will against the Russian people. With hindsight, the October Revolution can be interpreted as the turning point that led to Bolshevism, the rise of communism, Stalin's totalitarian government and the global spread of communism. Lenin also appears as the unchallenged dictator who is the agent of change. This is the western school of thought, or so-called orthodox view, which makes a value judgement that opposes communism.

Perspective: The revisionists – 1970s

The Cold War was an era when the USA and Russia understood each other as having conflicting ideologies and interests – under capitalism and communism respectively.

This school of thought recognised that a negative view of communism informed the traditional western view. While Stalin was in power and communism was the form of government in Russia, historians could identify the October Revolution as a decisive event that led eventually to the rise of communism. This view looks at both 'history from above' and 'history from below', and recognises that according to the latter, the ordinary people played a significant part in the October Revolution. Sheila Fitzpatrick (1941–) argued that the people created the conditions in which Lenin and the Bolsheviks could act. This view questions the assumption that Lenin was a dictator in total control of the Bolsheviks; instead, this may be a misunderstanding of hindsight bias.

KEY WORDS

history from above: also known as 'top-down' history, this focuses on the perspectives of the leaders, rulers and those in power, and the social and cultural elites of the time

history from below: also known as 'bottom-up' history, this focuses on the perspectives of the ordinary people, such as the working class, women, ethnic minorities or any other voices that may have been neglected by a 'top-down' approach

DISCUSS 10.17

What are the merits of these interpretations of the October Revolution? Is one interpretation more convincing or more justified than the others, and if so, in what ways?

EXPLORE 10.8

Consider the following ten knowledge claims.

1   Karl Marx (1818–1883) with the assistance of Friedrich Engles (1820–1895) published *The Communist Manifesto* in 1848, which encouraged workers to seize power.

2   In 1903, Lenin (1870–1924) and his followers founded the Bolshevik party.

3   The 1905 Revolution failed to overthrow the autocratic rule of Tsar Nicholas II.

4   Communism is a form of government which sets out to eliminate social and economic class divisions and private ownership of property.

5   The course of history is shaped by individuals whose actions have a profound impact, such as those of Lenin and Stalin.

6   The real agents of change are not individuals but long-term social and economic trends.

7   The first Russian revolution of 1917 (23 February) destroyed the government of the Tsars.

8   In the second revolution of 1917 (25 October), the Bolsheviks led by Lenin seized power.

9   Lenin led a popular revolt supported by the people.

10   Lenin imposed the will of the Bolsheviks on an unwilling people.

Classify those that are facts and those that are interpretations. Select the most interesting claim, and the most certain claim.

Peer-assessment

Share your classifications with a partner.

1   Did you come up with the same answers? Where your answers differ, justify your arguments.

2   What reasons did each of you give for your choice of the most interesting claim and the most certain claim? Explain these reasons to each other.

From the justification that you have given, how well did your partner feel that you have understood the reasons why historians might interpret the same event in different ways?

Historiography: Example 2 – The Cold War

Historical topic: the Cold War

Historical knowledge claim: the Cold War is the period between 1945 and 1991 which is characterised by heightened tension between communist and capitalist countries

Historiography: historians explain this period differently, and take different views of the causes, consequences and significance of the Cold War

Figure 10.8: Consider how and why historians might disagree in their interpretation of historical events and the actions of individuals. The meeting of three leaders at the Yalta Conference in 1945: The UK Prime Minister, Sir Winston Churchill (1874–1965), the US President, Franklin Roosevelt (1882–1945) and the Soviet leader Joseph Stalin (1879–1953). The meeting was followed by a period of over 40 years of political tension after the Second World War between the Soviet Union and its satellite states (the Eastern bloc), and the US and its allies (the western bloc). This period was known as the Cold War

The *orthodox* or *traditional* view claims that the Soviet Union was responsible for the Cold War. However, *revisionist* historians of the 1970s claimed that the USA was responsible. This revisionist perspective considered the role that the USA played in causing and developing tension, and questioned US foreign policy which was linked to the Vietnam war from 1955 to 1975. The USA, along with South Korea, the Philippines, Australia, Thailand and other anti-communist allies, supported South Vietnam. The Soviet Union, China and other communist allies supported North Vietnam. The events and politics of the present day can and do impact our interpretation of the past. In this example, the 1970s view – that the USA was responsible for the Cold War – was possibly influenced by the fact that the USA was currently fighting the war in Vietnam against the perceived threat of communism.

EXPLORE 10.9

1 Research different perspectives of a person, e.g. Lenin, Trotsky, Stalin or another historical figure. You might want to explore this person from different perspectives. For example, find out about Stalin from a German, Russian and American viewpoint. How do we know which perspective is justified?

2 Work on your own to produce a brief version of your own history of an event in your own life. Consider how reliable your reconstruction is. Present your ideas to the class.

3 Choose two historians such as G. Elton (1921–1994) and R.G. Collingwood (1889–1943) or Thomas Carlyle (1795–1881) and Herbert Spencer (1820–1903). Find out why they disagree.

4 'Historiography tells us a great deal about the constant development of historical knowledge, its transient nature and power of bias.' Using the example of the different interpretations of the October Revolution of 1917, explain how you think this could be justified, and whether you agree.

REFLECTION

Think about an event in your life, it could be a family holiday, a school trip or even a memorable class. If you wanted to write about it for future generations, how would you go about it? What would you include and what would you leave out? How would you portray each of the people involved? To what extent is it possible to write an objective account even if you wanted to?

10.8 Theories of history

REAL-LIFE SITUATION 10.11

1 What do you think causes change? How do you know?

2 In what ways can historians explain the past, and how far are these explanations justified?

Few individuals in history have had a real impact. However, in the context of Russian history that we looked at in the previous section, Lenin and Stalin arguably had a huge influence. On the other hand, some might argue that the social and economic conditions and circumstances that they lived through allowed them to take and wield power. This introduces an important debate about the relative importance of individuals as agents of change and, more broadly, the nature of causation in history. When we construct historical knowledge, we should appreciate that there may be multiple histories interpreted from different viewpoints. For example, feminist history, Marxist history or indigenous history might articulate the perspective of women, ordinary working people or oral traditions that may have been neglected in the past.

The 'great man' theory of history

As the name suggests, the **'great man' theory of history** holds that the course of history is mainly determined by great individuals. Thomas Carlyle (1795–1881) put forward this theory by claiming that the actions of great individuals are the cause of change. However, Herbert Spencer (1820–1903) argued against Carlyle's theory, putting forward the counter-argument that historical events cannot be explained in terms of the actions of great individuals who are products of a society and culture.

> You must admit that the genesis of a great man depends on the long series of complex influences which has produced the race in which he appears, and the social state into which that race has slowly grown. . . . Before he can remake his society, his society must make him.
>
> **Herbert Spencer**

The historian A.J.P. Taylor (1906–1990) continued Carlyle's theory, claiming that 'The history of modern Europe can be written in terms of three titans: Napoleon, Bismarck and Lenin.' What this theory implies is that if one or other great individual had not existed, then the course of history would have been different.

Further critiques of 'the great man' theory have been made, pointing out that the history told from the viewpoint of ordinary people is as important as the view of political leaders. Aparna Basu (1913–2018), a Professor of History at the University of Delhi, India, claimed that, 'History is no longer just a chronicle of kings and statesmen, of people who wielded power, but of ordinary women and men engaged in manifold tasks. Women's history is an assertion that women have a history.'

KEY WORD

'great man' theory of history: the belief that history is driven by great individuals

---

EXPLORE 10.10

1   If you could travel back in time and interview one character from history, who would it be and why?

2   Why do you think that this person is significant?

3   How much evidence do we already have about them and the era in which they lived?

4   What would you like to know, and what questions would you want to ask them?

5   What new knowledge would you like to discover and why?

6   Does our pursuit of historical knowledge tell us more about the present day or the past?

Hegel

Georg Hegel (1770–1831) understood history as a trend towards greater freedom and rationality. He understood the past as a series of different stages in relation to the pursuit of human freedom. He saw the Reformation (1517–1648) as a turning point in history because it was an expression of freedom. Hegel believed that once humans have become aware of their freedom, they will eventually achieve it. In his introduction to his *Lectures on the Philosophy of History*, Hegel argued that, 'The History of the world is none other than the progress of the consciousness of freedom.'

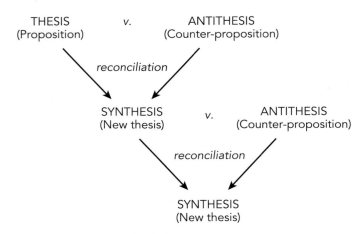

Figure 10.9: The Hegelian dialectical method

Economic determinism

The theory of **economic determinism** claims that history is shaped by economic factors, and its most famous exponent was Karl Marx. Whereas Hegel focused on ideas, Marx focused on material conditions. Marx claimed to have discovered the laws of historical change which operate with *'iron necessity'*, and from which the future course of history can be predicted; and he claimed to have done for history what Isaac Newton (1642–1727) did for physics almost two centuries earlier. According to Marx, it is not great individuals but rather technological and economic factors that are the engines of historical change. For changes in technology determine how society is organised, and this in turn determines how individuals think. An industrial economy, for example, will need to be organised in a very different way from a peasant economy, and this will affect how people think about such things as time, work and money. So rather than focusing on the actions of great men, we might do better to study the effects of key inventions such as the printing press, the steam engine and the computer.

Marx's emphasis on economics as the engine of historical change has been very influential, but most people now reject his deterministic approach to history. The idea that one can predict the future from a study of history seems intuitively implausible, and Marx's own predictions about where revolutions would occur have not in fact come true.

The philosopher Karl Popper (1902–1994) provided a counter-argument to Marx, saying that the belief in the predictability of the future is not merely implausible, but *incoherent*. The essence of Popper's argument is that if you could perfectly predict the future, then you would be able to predict such things as future scientific discoveries;

> KEY WORD
>
> **economic determinism:** the theory that history is determined by economic factors

but if you could predict the details of such discoveries, you would then have discovered them now and not in the future – and that contradicts the original supposition.

Although Marxist truth claims have been discredited, Marxism offers a model for understanding – a lens for understanding – the past in terms of long-term social and economic causes, such as technology, beyond the actions of individuals.

REAL-LIFE SITUATION 10.12

Do you agree or disagree with Marx's claim that technology plays a bigger role than the actions of individuals in shaping the future?

LINKING QUESTIONS 10.5

Natural sciences: In the natural sciences, we can predict the behaviour of a gas with a great deal of accuracy, even though the behaviour of an individual molecule is unpredictable. Do you think that, in a similar way, we can make accurate predictions about society even though individual behaviour is unpredictable? Why? Why not?

EXPLORE 10.11

If it is the case that technology is a major cause of change, which inventions do you think have had the most decisive impact on history, and why?

Rank the following ten inventions in order of importance:

1   the world wide web

2   the iPhone

3   the atom bomb

4   the printing press

5   the wheel

6   the computer

7   the gun

8   electricity

9   penicillin

10   the airplane

Peer-assessment

Which of the items did your partner think has had the most decisive impact on history and why? What changes, if any, would you make following your discussion and why? From your discussion, did you feel you had a good understanding of how technology can be a cause of change?

Historical truth

DISCUSS 10.19

What part does truth play in the construction of historical knowledge?

One obvious problem with trying to know the past is that it no longer exists. Like fleeting shadows, things that happened long ago sometimes have an air of unreality about them, and we may find it hard to believe they really happened. **Post-modern** thinkers made the criticism that history cannot escape from the problem of limited evidence and the interpretation required to fill in the gaps. Moreover, according to post-modern thinkers, the language of the past may be lost to us; and it would follow from this that we cannot fully understand the language of the past.

A counter-argument has been put forward by Quentin Skinner (1940–) who argues that despite these problems, the pursuit of history can still be credible and coherent. By understanding the context of the time, a historian can at least approach an understanding of the meaning of language from the past. At the opposite extreme from post-modern scepticism, it could be argued that, since the past no longer exists, it cannot be changed, and is therefore completely objective. In this vein, the historian G.R. Elton (1921–94) provocatively argued that:

> In a very real sense, the study of history is concerned with a subject matter more objective and independent than that of the natural sciences. Just because historical matter is in the past, is gone . . . its objective reality is guaranteed; it is beyond being altered for any purpose whatsoever.

While you would probably agree that the past cannot be changed, when it comes to the question of whether or not history is objective, we should make a distinction between the past and our *knowledge* of the past. Elton's argument may show that the past is objective, but it says nothing about our knowledge of the past. Such knowledge is problematic because we can know the past only by reconstructing it on the basis of evidence that exists in the present. Since memory is fallible, evidence is ambiguous and prejudice is common, we might have serious doubts about the claim that historical knowledge is more objective than scientific knowledge. At the start of the chapter, we mentioned that the past is not the same as history. History is the academic study that uses the historical method to interpret evidence and construct knowledge. History is arguably rigorous in its method, but this does not mean that historical knowledge claims are objective.

However, the counter-argument might be that objectivity surely remains an important ideal in history. For if we abandon it, we have no way of distinguishing between history on the one hand, and propaganda and fiction on the other. Moreover, historical knowledge claims can be tested and scrutinised against the evidence. The work of a historian is plausible if it is consistent and coherent with the evidence and other known facts. History therefore has a standard of proof, and can at least approach truth.

This raises a question about a historian's standard of proof. Some would argue that the historian's standard of proof is 'on the balance of probabilities', and others would argue for a still higher standard, 'beyond reasonable doubt'. In an English criminal court of law, the jury need to decide whether the person on trial (defendant) is innocent or guilty. Based on the evidence put before them during the trial, they need to make a judgement that is the most probable; i.e. 'beyond reasonable doubt' (BRD).

KEY WORD

post-modern: a movement of 20th-century thinkers who thought that knowledge, reason, ethics and truth are a social, cultural and political construction

It is generally agreed that 'BRD' would be interpreted as 0.91 probability. That means that the evidence needs to satisfy a high standard of 'proof'. Another question is to what extent a trained historian can approach the ideal of objectivity, and this requires that we look in more detail at the nature of historical evidence.

DISCUSS 10.20

1   Compare Elton's claim that history is objective with Samuel Butler's (1835–1902) wry comment: 'Though God cannot alter the past, historians can.' Which of these views do you think is closer to the truth?

2   What should be a historian's standard of proof? Should it be on the balance of probabilities, beyond reasonable doubt or another standard? Justify and explain your choice.

REFLECTION

Think about the way in which 'proof' is used in relation to history. How is it different to mathematical proofs? The natural sciences tend to avoid the word 'proof' altogether. Why do you think some historians want to talk about proof rather than evidence?

10.9 History and the arts, science and technology

History and the arts

> Truth is stranger than fiction, but it is because Fiction is obliged to stick to possibilities; Truth isn't.

Samuel Langhorne Clemens (1835–1910), better known by his pen name – Mark Twain

---

LINKING QUESTIONS 10.6

The arts: How far might the arts contribute to or detract from historical knowledge?

The literary, visual and performing arts have an important connection with history. Novelists, painters and film-makers may be inspired by people and events from the past, to re-tell for a modern audience. There's an ethical question about artistic licence – can the arts depict any representation of the past, or should there be limits? Arguably, creators' art might be accused of 'appropriating' the past for their own creative purposes.

The historian Anthony Beevor (1946–) has argued that some Hollywood films distort history in a manner that he thinks is shameless and irresponsible. For example, the film *Saving Private Ryan* (1998), which is based on the Normandy landings in the Second World War, makes no explicit mention of British troops or the Soviet role in the event, and presents the story from an American national angle. There may be an explanation – that there is a mismatch between historical accuracy and the needs of Hollywood directors to engineer a pacey story, craft compelling narrative arcs and manufacture happy endings that are unlikely to fulfil an academic historian's standards of integrity.

> ### REAL-LIFE SITUATION 10.13
>
> 1   Why do some stories from the past continue to speak to a modern audience?
>
> 2   In their depiction of the past, what are the ethical responsibilities of historical novelists, painters and film-makers?

In contrast to Beevor's opinion, there is an argument that the arts can contribute to historical knowledge by offering a fresh perspective. For example, Hilary Mantel (1952–) and Robert Harris (1957–) have written historical novels set in Tudor and Roman times respectively, and arguably they bring history alive for a modern audience. Moreover, the arts can move an audience. *Schindler's List* (1993) is a film that depicts the Holocaust. The course of the story tracks the plight of a child in a red coat, and invites the audience to empathise with the individual. Arguably the arts have an ethical responsibility, and films should encourage an audience to feel emotion, compassion and empathy. Furthermore, the arts can challenge our sense of time and history, and contribute a fresh perspective. Kurt Vonnegut (1922–2007) in the book *Slaughterhouse-Five* (1969) explores what war would be like if it was fought backwards. *Groundhog Day* (1993) is a film that explores the idea of recurrence, and of history repeating itself every day when a person lives the same day repeatedly.

> ### REAL-LIFE SITUATION 10.14
>
> 1   What is more important – telling a story for a modern audience or integrity to the past?
>
> 2   When might the use of emotion and imagination be justified in order to move an audience?

The arts can convey emotion and horror more than a historian is able. Picasso's painting *Guernica* depicts the horror of the 1937 bombing of the Spanish city of Guernica by German and Italian warplanes during the Spanish Civil War. Arguably, the painting depicts the suffering and horror of this event more immediately and effectively than an academic history work could. This is an example of the arts contributing a legitimate perspective on the re-telling of history, and impacting on our recollection of the Spanish Civil War as well as shared knowledge and 'image' of the past.

The arts can also be a vehicle for propaganda. The playwright William Shakespeare (1564–1616) wrote history plays in addition to his comedies and tragedies. His plays *Henry VI Parts I and II* were so successful that he then wrote *Part III*, an early example of a blockbuster trilogy. Following this, he wrote his play *Richard III*. You might wonder how far his history plays were true to the known facts about these English kings. Some people would argue that Shakespeare, writing about Richard III during the reign of Elizabeth I, offered a predictably negative portrait of Richard as an unethical, evil king. Some would say his play is an example of Tudor propaganda, and this was justified by the politics of the day; to portray Richard III in a negative light.

Figure 10.10: Cleopatra (69–30 BCE), the ruler of the Ptolemaic Kingdom of Egypt, as depicted by the actress Theda Bara in 1917

The arts might also contribute to history and mythology. Theophile Gautier (1811–1872) described Cleopatra (69–30 BCE) as 'the most complete woman ever to have existed'. However, if we ask how we know what she was really like, the answer lies in the mythology. Cleopatra was a queen of Egypt, and 200 years after her reign, the Roman historian Plutarch depicted two very different interpretations of her. One was that of a scholar, linguist, effective ruler, mother, and even a goddess on Earth. The other record was from the Roman perspective – the negative representation of a superficial and manipulative woman who had seduced and brought about the downfall of the Roman leader Mark Anthony. What is significant is that Cleopatra's character and qualities defy one monolithic description. Language cannot contain her.

In his play, *Anthony and Cleopatra*, Shakespeare represents Cleopatra's 'infinite variety'. The history of Cleopatra is also the history of her mythology. Her myth has a meaning which has been re-told for multiple audiences throughout time. However, the many layers of interpretation are impossible to unpick. While Shakespeare crafted his own narrative for his own dramatic purposes, he relied and depended heavily on Plutarch for his source material. This shows that history involves multiple perspectives – there are multiple levels of interpretation involved. All we have is the sources – the interpretation of Plutarch, Shakespeare's interpretation of Plutarch and our interpretation of Shakespeare. Even if we want to know the historical truth, it may be impossible to know the unvarnished history. Here there is a mismatch between the history of the mythology that we can have and the true history of Cleopatra that we might want. The more significant question is why are we interested? Why does a modern audience find her history interesting or otherwise?

EXPLORE 10.12

1   Choose a historical painting, for example *Guernica* by Picasso, and find out more about how far it represents a historical event or person.

2   Can you think of ways in which representations of the past in literature, paintings, novels or films have shaped the way you think about people and events from the past?

Often, artists find inspiration by creatively retelling or re-enacting the past for modern audiences. For example, George Orwell's (1903–1950) novel *1984* and Aldous Huxley's (1894–1963) *Brave New World* were written in response to Stalin's totalitarian rule in Russia. Their dystopian worlds reflect a fictional perspective on an imaginary society that operates under authoritarian rule. In summary, the arts recognise our appetite for and interest in the past. The arts may offer a fresh perspective, but it could be argued that they sometimes appropriate the past for their own creative purposes.

KEY WORD

authoritarian: relating to a government that imposes its authority over people and limits their freedom

EXPLORE 10.13

The primary source material for the battle of Thermopylae (480 BCE) was written by Herodotus (484–425 BCE). It inspired the 2006 film *300*, directed by Zack Snyder (1966–). It depicts the 300 men from Sparta who fought at Thermopylae against the Persians. It speaks to a modern audience, and is the story of the few fighting against the many, the cause of freedom against tyranny, the defence of a country against invasion and the price of fighting for that freedom.

Choose a historical film of your own choice or one from the following list.

Braveheart, Schindler's List, Saving Private Ryan, 19, Gladiator, Gone with the Wind, I Claudius, The Favourite, Mary Queen of Scots, Dunkirk, Bohemian Rhapsody, Lincoln, Troy, 300, Gandhi, The Bridge on the River Kwai.

You might consider the extent to which it is reliable, offers a particular perspective, tells a compelling story and depicts historical events or people with factual accuracy. Watch the film, read some reviews of it and write your own review exploring how far it contributes to or detracts from our knowledge of the past.

Self-assessment

Did you manage to reach a well-argued judgement as to how far the film contributes to detracts from our knowledge of the past? How well does your review demonstrate the relationship between history and the arts? Did you manage to incorporate some TOK analysis into your review? How far did you consider reliability, the perspective and factual accuracy?

DISCUSS 10.21

In what ways does creativity relate to knowledge and knowing?

History and science

The historian and scientist share a number of concepts relating to their method for producing knowledge: hypothesis, evidence, discovery and data collection. Although some scientific claims are based on theories, most knowledge claims in science can be tested or falsified. The scientific method sets out to falsify a hypothesis so that if you find contrary evidence, you can modify your hypothesis. History has a lower standard of proof than science, but can at least approach truth if it meets the criteria of plausibility such as consistency and coherence.

> Every historian would agree, I think, that history is a kind of research or inquiry . . . Science is finding things out: and in that sense history is a science.
>
> **R.G. Collingwood**, *The Idea of History,* 1946

LINKING QUESTIONS 10.7

Science and the arts

1   Is history closer to literature or science?

2   Is the relationship between history and historical fiction the same as the relationship between science and science fiction? How far can fiction contribute to knowledge?

EXPLORE 10.14

Which of the scenarios, a to e, can be best compared with the task of the historian? Which, if any, describe the work of a historian?

a   a barrister in court arguing a case 'beyond reasonable doubt'

b   a detective uncovering the scene of a crime; establishing what happened: the chronology, the motives and causes of the events in question

c   a novelist retelling a story based on evidence from the past

CONTINUED

> **d** a scientist testing a theory or hypothesis, and looking to falsify their theory
>
> **e** an economist who can predict the likely future development of a financial market
>
> Compare your ideas with a partner. Then discuss with your partner how each of you came to decide on your answers. How far might your prior knowledge of history and other factors shape your judgement here?

REFLECTION

> Think about the phrase, 'beyond reasonable doubt'. What might count as 'reasonable doubt' when constructing an account of history? To what extent do you think 'beyond reasonable doubt' is the same as 'proof' or 'certainty'?

History and technology

The history of technology describes the invention and development of tools over time. Often, technology has driven change and new knowledge – such as the first instruments and compasses used for navigation. Technology also supports the historian's methods. To an extent, technology allows us to perceive the past in new ways, or obtain a new perspective. The age of an object that contains organic material can be dated using carbon dating. New evidence which gives clues about the past climate can be studied by drilling down through layers of ice or sedimentary layers of rock.

LINKING QUESTIONS 10.8

Technology: In what ways does technology help us study the past?

Historical archives are collections of documents and records from the past. The internet democratises information. For example, the *Domesday Book* – a medieval record from around 1070 – is now on the internet for everyone to access. Technology raises important questions about how these historical sources are conserved and kept for future generations. For example, documents that may need special preservation can be kept in an anoxic or oxygen-free zone.

One question arising from the development of technology is who controls access to these documents. Historical archives can be restricted, or private collections that have private owners may only be accessible to a limited number of people. In this way, access to some historical documents can be linked to power and privilege. For justifiable reasons, some sensitive information is not released for a certain time. For example, in some countries, political documents may not be made public until 50 years or so after the events, making new perspectives possible at a later date. This was also the case before digital technology; access to original hard-copy documents could be restricted, raising questions about who controls access and who owns archives.

On the other hand, there may be sources that have limited access and the digital era that we live in today raises new issues about the availability and ownership of digital data and source material. For example, in 2013, Edward Snowden (1983–) who worked for the Central Intelligence Agency in the USA became known as a whistle-blower when he leaked information from the National Security Agency and exposed the government's uses of digital data. Governments may have access to digital sources, such as social media, and the implication for historians is that there is a huge volume of digital data and information which may not be available nor accessible, but which could be potential primary sources for future historical enquiry.

Furthermore, technology also poses the problem for historians of too much information. Given how much data and information is being produced, there may be too much information to make sense of, and the task of selection of relevant information is becoming an increasingly difficult, if impossible, task.

LINKING QUESTIONS 10.9

Technology: What opportunities and problems might technology (and historical archives) pose for the pursuit of historical knowledge?

Knowing the future

We are living through a so-called 'fourth revolution', following the agricultural, industrial and digital revolution, characterised by advances in big data, robotics, artificial intelligence, quantum computing and developments in biotechnology. *Homo Deus: A Brief History of Tomorrow* by Yuval Noah Harari (1976–) speculates about the impact of digital technology for the future of knowledge and knowing, and for the future existence of humanity.

REAL-LIFE SITUATION 10.16

1   How far should a historian make predictions about the future?

Figure 10.11: Professor Yuval Noah Harari is an Israeli historian and best-selling author of various history books including *Sapiens: A Brief History of Humankind* and *Homo Deus: A Brief History of Tomorrow*. What do you think historians can tell us about the future?

DISCUSS 10.22

1   Why do you think the past is irreversible? Can the same be said of the future? What implications does this have for historical knowledge claims?

2   Based on patterns identified in history, how far can we predict the future with any accuracy?

10.10 History and ethics

REAL-LIFE SITUATION 10.17

To what extent should historians make ethical judgements about the past?

There are multiple questions about history and ethics. For example, issues like the return of the Elgin marbles from the ancient Parthenon to Greece; whether the preservation of historical sites should take precedence over the need for development; whether we are right to condemn people who were products of their own time (like Cecil Rhodes, 1853–1902) and try to eliminate them from our history; the extent to which people today are responsible for the 'misdeeds' of people of the past, and the extent to which we still benefit or suffer from the legacy of the past. For example, in 2008, the Australian prime minister Kevin Rudd apologised for the systematic dispossession and mistreatment of the indigenous population of Australia. Moreover, there are examples of political regimes who have appropriated the past, and woven a narrative of national history in line with their own interests.

Ethical issues might arise if a country plays down or even tries to forget their past. For example, following the collapse of the Soviet Union in 1991, thousands of statues of the once powerful leaders Lenin and Stalin were torn down. There are ethical questions associated with the way that the past is represented and remembered.

Furthermore, some governments might be understood as appropriating not just the past but also the present. For example, governments might have an interest in limiting access to sources and information that might compromise national security. WikiLeaks™, which publishes leaked material, raises important questions about information, power, ownership, access and freedom, which also have implications for historians today. When considering organisations like WikiLeaks™, how do we decide what is in the national interest, and how far the interests of the government and the interests of the people are necessarily the same?

In conclusion, a historians' access to information and the way in which history is remembered and represented occurs in a present-day context. National identity often rides on national history, and therefore nations have a vested interest in promoting their versions of the past; they also tend to control the educational systems that determine what histories are taught.

REAL-LIFE SITUATION 10.18

Should historians have any moral standards?

REFLECTION

Have you ever deliberately misled others about an event that happened, either to avoid getting yourself into trouble or to protect a friend? Sometimes, such misrepresentations are found out, but at other times, they are accepted as 'truth', and can become so familiar that you end up believing the misrepresentation yourself. Sometimes you can hear this happening when politicians from different parties discuss an event or political era: while they may agree on core aspects, each can have a very different version of what happened, and each can genuinely believe their version to be true. Given that there is no 'view from nowhere', how can you be confident that the history you learn is a 'fair' representation of the past?

In George Orwell's novel *1984*, the past is not just forgotten, it is deliberately rewritten. The character Winston Smith notes that, 'The past was erased, the erasure was forgotten, the lie became the truth.' This suggests that remembering the past comes with a responsibility. It implies that there is integrity and honesty involved – to re-tell the past in a way that is in line with the truth and reality of that past.

A study of the past reveals how rich and varied moral standards have been. From the marriage markets of ancient Babylon to the slaughter of people and animals for entertainment (once thought acceptable in ancient Rome) or the buying and selling of people into slavery, history suggests that there are no universal moral standards.

The past might remind us of significant ethical questions. In 63 BCE, Cicero uncovered a terrorist plot led by Catiline against the Roman government. In the name of national security, Cicero executed the conspirators with no trial, and afterwards he was declared a hero of the state for defending and protecting it against an immediate threat. However, he was then accused of acting illegally and sent into exile. Ever since, it has been debated whether Cicero was right to act in this way. The enduring question illuminated by this event remains: which should take priority – the interests and rights of the individual or the security of the state? The debate about the Guantanamo Bay detention camp raised the same discussion for our own time. On Cicero's house, a statue to liberty was erected. The concept of liberty or freedom has been the key idea behind the US Civil War, the French Revolution and M.K. Gandhi's Indian Independence movement.

REAL-LIFE SITUATION 10.19

1   To what extent should the writing of history be limited by any ethical considerations?

2   Should the only rule be 'anything goes'?

Figure 10.12: The Statue of Liberty, in New York Harbour, by the French sculptor Bartholdi (1834–1904), depicting the Roman goddess 'Libertas' was dedicated in 1886. What does this statue represent and mean to you?

REAL-LIFE SITUATION 10.20

1   In school curriculums, what criteria should be used for selecting the topics and periods studied? Do you think that there are any essential historical topics that have such a global and moral significance that everyone should study them, regardless of their cultural and social background?

2   What might be the cost of forgetting the past?

10.11 Conclusion

We began this chapter with the whole history of time compared with one year. History – the study of human civilisations recorded by humans during the last 4,000 years – is something very recent in the context of cosmic time. One feature of *homo sapiens* is our ability to be aware of our past, to record it and to communicate it for the next generation.

What the study of history can perhaps give us is knowledge of our human nature. History enriches our understanding of human nature by showing us what human beings have thought and done in a wide variety of circumstances. Arguably, history can help us to gain knowledge of the present day. In this chapter, we have explored the concepts of perspective, selection, significance and bias, and examined various knowledge tools, including imagination and language. While language poses a particular problem at the level of interpreting and translating sources – and there are many different interpretations of the past which require some interpretation and imagination – knowledge is still possible. Our interpretation of history and historiography is a matter of judgement, but there may nevertheless be a requirement for a justified interpretation.

History is an academic subject in its own right. However, there is also significant crossover between history and other academic subjects – such as the arts, natural and human sciences and technology.

Despite the fact that the past no longer exists, history seeks to reconstruct it on the basis of evidence that can be found in the present. However, we might disagree about the implications of ethics for history, and the extent to which a historian has a responsibility towards the past. If history is not to collapse into fiction or propaganda, we must take seriously the idea that there is some kind of truth about the past, and that a good historian can at least help us to get closer to this truth.

EXPLORE 10.15

What can be achieved by a historian?

1   Choose one of the works written by historians in section 10.13, the 'Continue your journey' further reading section, at the end of the chapter. Find one of their books, and consider what can be accomplished by a top-level thinker making an expert selection of the evidence. Also consider the factors that might shape their perspective – such as their age, gender, political persuasion, social and educational background.

2   Reflect on your work. Did you make a judgement about their choice of historical period, theme and quality of writing? If so, how did you gain those insights into their work? What other questions about them and their writing arise for you as a knower?

DISCUSS 10.23

1   How much history (ancient, medieval and/or modern) do we need to know about if we want to be informed, educated and responsible?

2   How exactly might history enable us to understand our place and role in the world today?

3   If you were to write a world history of ideas or a global intellectual history, where would you begin and what approach would you take? What problems and challenges would you expect to encounter? Consider how it might be possible to construct a narrative that makes sense and tells this history in a way that is accurate, justified and truthful.

4   Discuss the nature of historical knowledge using the four aspects of the knowledge framework: scope, perspectives, tools and methods, and ethics.

KNOWLEDGE QUESTIONS

1   Explain why historians might disagree. How far might their disagreements be similar or different to the disagreements of scientists, artists or mathematicians?

2   To what extent do you think there is a historical truth? In what ways might this compare with truth in the sciences or the arts?

3   Should there be any limits to a historian's rights to free interpretation of evidence? Discuss the ethical responsibilities of historians, and compare these with the responsibilities of those pursuing knowledge in one other area of knowledge.

10.12 Linking questions

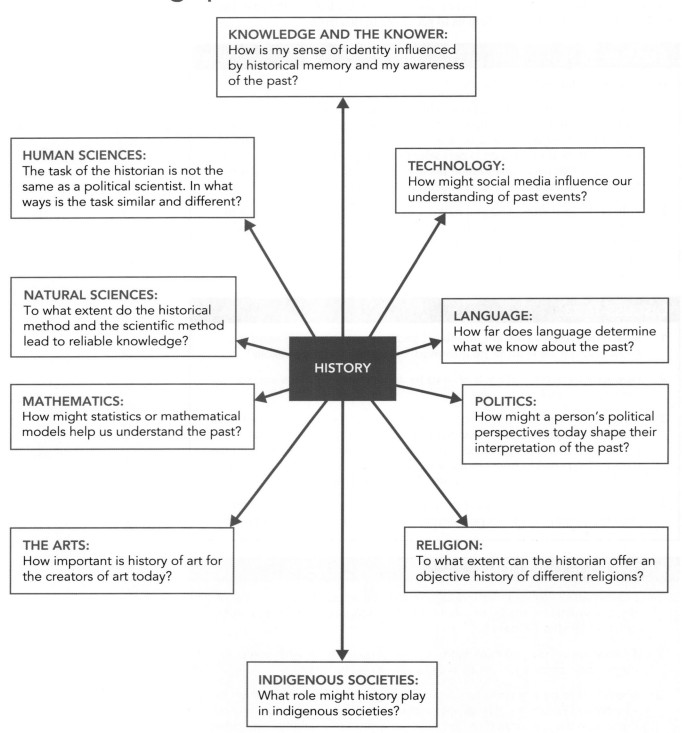

KNOWLEDGE AND THE KNOWER:
How is my sense of identity influenced by historical memory and my awareness of the past?

HUMAN SCIENCES:
The task of the historian is not the same as a political scientist. In what ways is the task similar and different?

TECHNOLOGY:
How might social media influence our understanding of past events?

NATURAL SCIENCES:
To what extent do the historical method and the scientific method lead to reliable knowledge?

LANGUAGE:
How far does language determine what we know about the past?

HISTORY

MATHEMATICS:
How might statistics or mathematical models help us understand the past?

POLITICS:
How might a person's political perspectives today shape their interpretation of the past?

THE ARTS:
How important is history of art for the creators of art today?

RELIGION:
To what extent can the historian offer an objective history of different religions?

INDIGENOUS SOCIETIES:
What role might history play in indigenous societies?

10.13 Check your progress

Reflect on what you have learned in this chapter and indicate your confidence level
between 1 and 5 (where 5 is the highest score and 1 is the lowest). If you score below 3,
re-visit that section. Come back to this list later in your course. Has your confidence grown?

	Confidence level	Re-visited?
Do I understand the scope and nature of historical knowledge?		
Am I able to explain the reasons why we might pursue historical knowledge?		
Do I have a firm understanding of what is central to the historical method, in particular the concepts of evidence, analysis and interpretation?		
Am I familiar with the role that selection plays in the construction of historical knowledge?		
Do I appreciate the issues encountered in interpreting and using evidence, including the analysis of primary and secondary sources?		
Am I able to appreciate the concept of significance in constructing historical knowledge?		
Do I understand the problem of bias in relation to historical knowledge, and how this might be overcome?		
Can I discuss the various knowledge tools available for the study of history, including language, imagination and empathy?		
Am I aware of the skills required in source analysis in order to construct knowledge of the past?		
Can I appreciate the standards and methods set by ancient historians such as Herodotus and Thucydides?		
Am I aware of the advantages and disadvantages arising from hindsight and the concept of hindsight bias?		
Do I understand the significance of historiography and the ways in which different interpretations can help us get closer to historical truth?		
Do I have a good understanding of various theories of history, such as the 'great man' theory of history, and the ideas of Hegel and Marx?		
Can I discuss the different standards of proof required in history as opposed to the natural sciences, and the implications for the nature of historical truth?		
Do I understand the role that the arts, sciences and technology might play in representing the past, and the impact this might have on historical knowledge?		
Do I appreciate the role of ethics in history, and am I able to discuss ethical considerations that may shape the historian's interpretation and judgement?		

10.14 Continue your journey

- To build on the knowledge that you have gained in this chapter, you could read some of the following articles.

- For overviews of **different approaches to the study of history** and a variety of themes including world history, the status of historical knowledge, causation, science and religion, read: *A Concise Companion to History*, edited by Ulinka Rublack, Oxford University Press, 2012.

- In order to develop your understanding of the **study of history** including specific examples of the concepts of causation, interpretation, read: John Arnold, *History: A Very Short Introduction,* Oxford University Press, 2000.

- For a series of insightful essays on the **nature and value of history**, read: Barbara Tuchman, 'When does history happen?' or 'The historian as artist', in *Practising History*, Papermac, 1989.

- To explore questions about **what might have happened if historical episodes had turned out differently**, such as 'What if Germany had invaded Britain in May 1940?' and 'What if communism had not collapsed?' read: *Virtual History,* edited by NIall Ferguson, Penguin, 2011. Read any one of these nine speculative essays, and it will soon have you thinking about the nature of historical explanations.

- For a book which addresses the **nature of historical knowledge** including what constitutes a justified historical interpretation, and the concepts of evidence, objectivity, and memory, and key thinkers since Herodotus and Thucydides, read: A. Megill, *Historical Knowledge, Historical Error: A Contemporary Guide to Practice* (new edition), University of Chicago Press, 2007.

- For a podcast that explores **the study of history from various national perspectives including Japan, Lebanon and India**, and takes a critical looks at school history textbooks, listen to the BBC podcast by historian, Priya Atwal, 'Lies My Teacher Told Me.'

- For an exploration of the nature and scope of history in general and the history of art in particular, see the BBC TV series, and App, 'Civilisations' by Mary Beard, Simon Sharma and David Olusoga.

> Chapter 11
The arts

LEARNING INTENTIONS

This chapter will consider what art is and what functions it serves, how it is interpreted, how it relates to knowledge and knowing and how it helps to shape each of us as knowers.

You will:

- consider the scope and limits of the arts, and think about some of the different ways the arts can be classified, along with some of the difficulties of trying to define and classify art

- explore how the arts affect you as a knower, and consider the factors that might shape your own judgement of the arts

- examine the purpose of art, considering: the intention of the artist, the functions of the arts, the power of the arts and the notion of beauty

- think about how art can be interpreted, and how we might look for symbolism and allegory in the arts, and question whether it is possible to be too analytical

- consider how we might try to achieve some kind of objectivity in judging the arts, and the subjectivity of different perspectives

- explore some of the roles that the arts play in communities, and be able to discuss examples of how the arts are involved in community identity

- consider the roles of language, reason and emotion in relation to the arts

- explore the connections between the arts and sciences, and the concepts of creation, creativity and discovery

- consider the ethics of using art to promote products, ideas and ideologies, and think about the ethical responsibilities of artists

BEFORE YOU START

Analyse each of the following quotations and discuss the questions that follow.

1   'To create one must first question everything.' **Eileen Gray** (1878–1976)

2   'I found I could say things with colour and shape that I couldn't say any other way – things I had no words for.' **Georgia O'Keeffe** (1887–1986)

3   'Every work of art is the child of its age and, in many cases, the mother of our emotions. It follows that each period of culture produces an art of its own which can never be repeated.' **Wassily Kandinsky** (1866–1944)

4   'Literature adds to reality, it does not simply describe it.' **C. S. Lewis** (1898–1963)

5   'I don't think art is elite or mysterious. I don't think anybody can separate art from politics. The intention to separate art from politics is itself a very political intention.' **Ai Weiwei** (1957–)

For each quotation, consider:

a   Do you agree or disagree with the quotation?

b   What do you think the quotation suggests about the nature and purpose of the art it refers to?

c   Can you identify any implicit or explicit assumptions that the speaker makes about the arts?

d   Do you think the quotation could apply to other areas of knowledge? If so, in what ways?

11.1 Introduction

It took around 2 million years of biological history for *homo sapiens* to evolve. It is much more recently, in the last 10,000 years, that humans have developed civilisation and cultural history. Our instinct to survive has been mirrored by our instinct to make and create. It is perhaps no coincidence that at the same time *homo sapiens* discovered and developed the use of tools to manipulate the material world, we also started making what we now call art or images.

On the Indonesian island of Sulawesi are cave paintings that are among the oldest artworks in the world. Some cave paintings depict human hand prints that date back 39,000 years. It is possible that some are even older – the cave painting that resembles a bull in Borneo dates back at least 40,000 years. Another ancient example is the sculpture of *The Lion Man*, a product of the human imagination which was carved from ivory around 4,000 years ago. At this time, hunting to survive was perhaps the most important human activity, yet archaeologists believe that someone spent around 400 hours carving this sculpture: something which could only exist in the imagination – a human body with a lion's head. The object survives and many questions remain: why was it carved, why was it thought to be worth the effort required, what was it used for, did it tell a shared story?

Art can be considered a tool for understanding the world. Art is the means by which the internal world is placed into a shared space so that it becomes collective knowledge. It may even help to build a consensus around which a community can gather, and from which the community can gain a sense of identity. As examples of the earliest forms of art, they have an important connection with the history of human knowledge and knowing, the value we place on the arts and the human impulse to make images.

The arts are a diverse area of knowledge. Together they show us new ways to understand the world, and new ways of interpreting the world in terms of meaning – whether it is through literature, architecture, music, theatre, dance or the fine arts. They appear to be fundamental to what it is to be human, yet each of us has different understandings of what 'good art' is, and our tastes change throughout our lives. Many people regard aesthetics as an important aspect of art – that is, they think that great art and beauty coincide – but others will argue that great art needs to be challenging, engaging and original.

KEY WORD

aesthetics: the branch of philosophy that studies beauty and the arts

In general, there are three main categories of the arts: visual arts, performing arts and literary arts. The visual arts include print-making, textile arts, drawing, painting, photography, film-making, architecture, ceramics and sculpture. The performing arts include music, singing, dancing, opera, mime, puppetry and theatre. The literary arts include play-writing, poetry and creative writing.

Although many of the examples in this chapter come from the visual arts, you should keep in mind that the arts include not only painting and sculpture, but also the literary and performing arts. You will therefore need to decide whether points made about a particular art form apply to the arts in general.

REAL-LIFE SITUATION 11.1

Can you think of ways in which artistic representations (especially paintings, literature or films) have shaped the way you think about particular people, events or issues?

11.2 What is the scope of art?

REAL-LIFE SITUATION 11.2

Give a specific example of a work of art that you like from each of the three main categories: the literary arts, the visual arts and performing arts. Say what it is that appeals to you for each of your chosen examples.

Since the arts have traditionally claimed a right to our thoughtful attention, we need to spend some time exploring their nature and value. Hence the question: 'What is art?'. Most people would agree that for something to be a 'work of art', it must be human-made. A sunset may be beautiful and Mount Everest awe-inspiring, but neither would be called a work of art.

Many people use the word 'art' to refer to the fine arts of drawing, painting, photography and sculpture, and when they talk about 'the arts', the meaning broadens to include music, dance, theatre, film, poetry and literature. But how can we define the scope of art? What are the limits to what we would define as art? Can we regard all drawings as art? If you draw a pie chart in a mathematics class, is it art? What might make the video you take on your smartphone worthy of exhibition in a gallery or worthy of a prize for visual arts? In 2018, none of the artists nominated for the Turner Prize entered paintings or sculptures. All the artists used film and digital imagery, and the winner was Charlotte Prodger, with her half-hour, single-screen video shot on her smartphone.

REAL-LIFE SITUATION 11.3

Why might something be regarded as art if it looks or sounds like 'anyone' could do it? Should the scope of art be extended to include things like fashion, design, cake decorating and food presentation?

Some would argue that art is what sells. Some critics regard Mark Rothko's (1903–1970) *Orange, Red, Yellow* an example of fine art at its best, and it was sold for $86.9 million dollars in 2012. At the time, this was the highest price ever paid for a work of contemporary art. Although it is aesthetically pleasing, other people struggle to see its artistic merit because, when compared to other highly technical pieces of art, it might be judged to display a less *obvious* degree of technical skill. Similarly, Cy Twombly's (1928–2011) *Untitled* (New York City), which depicts background scribble on an old-fashioned school blackboard is another example of a valuable piece of art (it sold for over $70 million in 2015) that exhibits no obvious technical skill.

Figure 11.1: A painting by Cy Twombly at Tate Modern, London, UK, in 2010

DISCUSS 11.1

To what extent do the technical skills required to create a work of art dictate the work's aesthetic or financial value?

Look at Figure 11.2. How might Tracey Emin's (1963–) *My Bed* fit a dictionary definition of art?

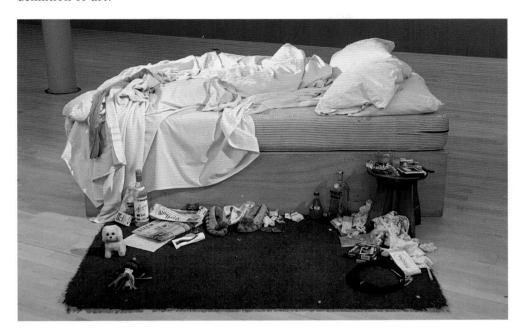

Figure 11.2: *My Bed* (1998) by Tracey Emin

One dictionary definition of art is, 'The expression or application of human creative skill and imagination, producing works to be appreciated primarily for their beauty or emotional power.' But are beauty and emotional power qualities that we can all agree on? Some critics would argue that Tracey Emin's *My Bed* is in the tradition of Dutch still life paintings, as it depicts a representation from real-life, an idea which we explore later in this chapter. Knowledge of where Emin's work fits into its historical art context may affect your appreciation for her imagination in this piece. However, others might believe that putting a bed in a gallery, or a pile of bricks – as some people referred to Carl Andre's (1935–) *Equivalent VIII* (1966) – in an art exhibition, is beyond the proper scope of art. People might also disagree about how far expert opinion is relevant in relation to judging the arts. Many factors shape our understanding of what constitutes art.

To understand the artistic significance of Tracey Emin's *My Bed*, we need to consider it in the context of the pieces that came before it and inspired it.

The symbol of a bed is a significant image in the history of European painting, representing the place of conception, birth, dreams and death. Emin's bed is not any bed; it is entitled *My Bed,* based on her personal experience of a 'mini nervous breakdown' in which she stayed in bed for four days. The piece turned her personal experience as a knower into art.

DISCUSS 11.2

1   To what extent is the creation of new art the same as the creation of new knowledge in the arts?

2   What is the relationship between art and knowledge?

Emin was specifically influenced by the Norwegian expressionist painter Edvard Munch (1863–1944), in particular *The Sick Child*: a series of six paintings plus various lithographs and etchings depicting his dying sister in a bed. However, Emin's focus on the everyday can also be traced back to the 17th-century Dutch Protestant still life painters, who painted the ordinary objects of their lives (a move away from the Catholic tradition of paintings of the great religious **narratives**). For example, Willem Claesz Heda's (1593–1680) *Breakfast Table with Blackberry Pie* (1631) represents the ordinary experience associated with the turmoil of a finished meal. This perspective replaced religious images of saints and biblical scenes, and elevated scenes from ordinary life to the status of high art so that meaning and symbolism could be found in the everyday world.

> **KEY WORD**
>
> **narrative:** a story that tells about a series of events. It can be factual, fictitious or a blend of both

Figure 11.3: *Breakfast Table with Blackberry Pie* (1631) by Willem Claesz Heda

Figure 11.4: *The Sick Child* (1907) by Edvard Munch

Moreover, the focus of art on the ordinary and everyday further inspired an Italian tradition of the 1960s and 1970s known as the **Arte Povera** movement. Emin continues these precedents – *My Bed* shows the raw details of her everyday life, depicting pills and condoms.

While the ingredients for the piece have precedents, Emin's combination of these elements arguably makes her work highly original. It reflects her authentic knower's perspective. In this way, an expertise in interpreting and 'decoding' art historical images is like learning a language. Seeing how Emin's work fits into the bigger story of art history is only possible with reference to artists and traditions of the past.

> **KEY WORD**
>
> **Arte povera:** An Italian art movement that used ordinary but unconventional materials to create art works

EXPLORE 11.1

Tracey Emin's *My Bed* makes real-life into art. With a partner, come up with a list of ideas about what you think should be the main focus of art. Choose one idea and come up with three arguments to support your idea. Then consider and evaluate some counter-arguments.

DISCUSS 11.3

To what extent do we need to know about art history in order to appreciate or understand contemporary art?

Art or craft?

If you decide that not everything is art, the scope of art may be thought to have limits. Some people regard pottery as a craft rather than an art. The same is true of textile arts, which are often denied a place in galleries. Indeed, the boundaries between arts and crafts have long been disputed. Some would say the difference is in the materials used; others might say that art lies in the artist's intentions. Others still would describe art as communicating an idea, and crafts as the physical manipulation of materials. But, of course, crafts can also communicate ideas, and sculpture (a fine art) involves the manipulation of materials. Even painting could be viewed as the manipulation of materials.

Giorgio Vasari (1511–1174) was an Italian artist, and one of the first art historians. In his work *Lives of the Artists*, he depicts Michelangelo and Leonardo da Vinci not so much as artists as we might think of them today, but as artisans or craftsmen. At the time, they were considered craftsmen working for wealthy patrons.

In 2003, however, Grayson Perry (1960–) won the prestigious Turner Prize for art with his ceramics (typically regarded as a craft), demonstrating how indistinct the boundaries between arts and crafts are.

DISCUSS 11.4

1   Does it matter whether we distinguish artistic activity from craftsmanship? If so, why?

2   What are the criteria for deciding what is art?

The French artist and sculptor, Jean Dubuffet (1901–1985) began a movement known as 'art brut' meaning 'raw art', which recognised the value of art made by children, prisoners and people with mental health problems. His movement recognised the value of the 'low' art of outsiders, in contrast to 'cultural art' which he saw as the product of an elite academic tradition of fine art. He thought that 'primitive art', 'graffiti art' and 'naïve art' were raw expressions of emotions and visions, often overlooked by conventional artists. He tried to include these features in his own art, which is displayed today in La Collection de l'Art Brut in Lausanne, Switzerland. This is a good example of where consensus and disagreement about what constitutes art is relevant.

When considering the arts, a common approach is to believe, among other things, that not all novels are literature, not all paintings are art and not all sounds are music, but many people have challenged these ideas. In the early-20th century, the French artist Marcel Duchamp (1887–1968) began exhibiting what he called 'readymades'. As the name suggests, these were simply objects taken out of their everyday context, renamed and put in an art gallery. Perhaps the most famous of Duchamp's readymades was his work called *The Fountain*, which was a white porcelain urinal with the pseudonym 'R Mutt', the name of the industrialist that manufactured the object daubed on it. By suggesting that everyday objects might have aesthetic value, Duchamp can be seen as raising the question of authorship, authenticity and where art ends and non-art begins.

DISCUSS 11.5

1   If anything can be art, does this imply that everything *is* art?

2   To what extent does popular opinion affect what we think of as art?

Even if we accept the idea that not all novels are literature, not all paintings are art and not all sounds are music, who decides whether a book is literature or just an entertaining read? And why might it matter? One answer is to base the decision on popularity or consensus. If enough people find a work emotionally moving or thought provoking to buy it, or pay to see or hear it, then we can call it art, literature or music. A counter-argument might be that there are criteria for judging art, and that art critics have a particular expertise that makes their judgements of art worth recognition, even authoritative. But both of these positions overlook the issue of artists who were not recognised in their own lifetimes by art critics or popular consensus, but who were subsequently acknowledged as great masters.

EXPLORE 11.2

Consider the list below. In pairs, order the list of items and activities below into a hierarchy of 5 groups: definitely art, probably art, undecided, probably not art, definitely not art.

1   pottery

2   manufactured pots and pans

3   gymnastics

4   football

5   Mount Everest

6   a holiday snap-shot of Mount Everest

7   a painting of Mount Everest

8   a beautiful face

9   a rock that happens to resemble a face

10   a child's drawing of a face

11   an artist's drawing of a face done in the naive style of a child

12   opera

13   rap music

14   a piece of music generated by a computer

15   the *Mona Lisa*

16   a perfectly-detailed accurate copy of the *Mona Lisa*

17   a print of the *Mona Lisa*

CONTINUED

18 a copy of the *Mona Lisa* with a moustache and beard added

19 a person dripping paint randomly on a canvas

20 a monkey dripping paint randomly on a canvas

21 Jackson Pollock dripping paint apparently randomly on a canvas

22 a bucket and mop left in an art gallery by a cleaner

23 a bucket and mop exhibited in an art gallery by an artist

24 tattoos

25 video games

DISCUSS 11.6

Can anything be art? Who decides? What roles are played by culture and authorities in deciding?

'Real art' or kitsch?

Even if the scope of art is difficult to define, many people would agree that there is a difference between real art and **kitsch**. Kitsch is often characterised by sentimentality, and may be thought of by some people as pseudo-art, or art that pretends to be real art. Although we will discuss it here in relation to the visual arts, kitsch can also apply to music and literature. It is a term generally given to art that is regarded as being purely for ornamental or decorative use, rather than having any 'real' artistic merit. There are plenty of competent but unoriginal artists turning out pictures for calendars and greeting cards. We also find many 'original' paintings painted quickly and sold as souvenirs in tourist markets. Such art is known as **kitsch**. Kitsch is basically any form of clichéd art that is generally designed to soothe and reassure people rather than challenge them. Some people argue that the 'real job' of art is to question traditional ways of looking at things, and give us new ways of experiencing the world, and therefore suggest that kitsch art is not 'real' art.

However, a kitsch movement began in the late-20th century, when the Swedish-Norwegian painter, Odd Nerdrum (1944–) declared himself a kitsch painter at an exhibition of his paintings at the Astrup Fearnley Museum in Oslo. By wearing the kitsch label with pride, he opened the way for a new acceptance of kitsch art. In his book *On Kitsch* (2000), Nerdrum argued that kitsch is about eternal human questions, and appeals to our senses – to our human nature.

To be classed as great kitsch art, a work must display technical skills, emotion and the ability to tell a story. Composition and beauty are important factors in Kitsch art, and it is generally understood on an emotional rather than an intellectual level, making it accessible to all people, including those uneducated in art.

Andrew Wyeth (1917–2009) is one of the USA's most popular and well-known artists of the 20th century, yet his work has been widely disparaged by some critics, who regard his art as kitsch.

KEY WORD

kitsch: derivative, clichéd art

Avant-garde

Henri de Saint-Simon (1760–1825) coined the term *avant-garde*, which, in English, means the 'advanced guard'. Just as the *avant-garde* in an army would go ahead of the rest of the troops, Saint-Simon believed that artists, like industrialists and scientists, should forge ahead as pioneers of a new society. He wrote: 'We artists will serve you as an avant-garde, the power of the arts is most immediate: when we want to spread new ideas we inscribe them on marble or canvas. What a magnificent destiny for the arts is that of exercising a positive power over society, a true priestly function and of marching in the van [i.e. vanguard] of all the intellectual faculties!'

When art is classified as *avant-garde*, it therefore means that it is cutting-edge and innovative in the context of the time when it is produced, and again it can apply to any of the arts. *Avant-garde* movements include: futurism, which captured the energy of the modern world, surrealism, which explored the subconscious and irrational, and cubism, which represented reality in an innovative way.

> ### REAL-LIFE SITUATION 11.4
>
> Something that is *avant-garde* today may become a *cliché* tomorrow. To what extent are such classifications helpful?

Problems with classifying art

Edgar Degas' (1834–1917) sculpture *Little Dancer aged Fourteen* was originally exhibited as a wax model, and later cast in bronze. Degas shocked his audience because his sculpture depicted the pain and stress of an adolescent ballerina. It was considered *avant-garde* at the time because it drew attention to the difficult life of a young dancer.

By contrast, William Baxter Collier Fyfe (1836–1882) depicted a somewhat kitsch view of a girl selling flowers. His painting *The Flower Girl* (1869) represents a happy and healthy girl selling her flowers. Critics say that it is sentimental and misrepresents the life of poor girls who were obliged to sell flowers for a living in 19th-century Britain.

However, not all art is so easily classified. While new movements in the arts may sometimes challenge our understanding of reality, they can in time lose their shock value, and simply become part of the way in which a culture sees the world. On the other

Figure 11.5: Degas' sculpture *Little Dancer aged Fourteen*

hand, more traditional, realistic works that touch our emotions can sometimes cause us to see our world afresh in new generations. One example of this is *The Broken Pitcher* by William-Adolphe Bouguereau (1825–1905), which was inspired by a painting with the same title by Jean-Baptiste Greuze (1725–1805).

KEY WORDS

avant-garde: innovative ideas considered to be at the forefront of new developments and techniques in the arts

futurism: an artistic movement that began in Italy and emphasised speed, technology, youth, violence and objects such as the car, the airplane and the industrial city

surrealism: an artistic movement that tried to release the creative potential of the unconscious mind by expressing imaginative dreams and visions

cubism: an artistic movement in which objects were analysed, broken up and reassembled in an abstracted form

The broken pitcher in Bouguereau's painting is an example of sexual symbolism, and used to denote to the viewer that the young girl portrayed in the painting has been raped; a suggestion made more explicit by the girl's plaintive expression. While Bouguereau's painting is seen by many as sentimental kitsch that serves to arouse pathos while softening the harsh realities of life for the peasant girl, the haunting understatement of the violence she has suffered could also be said to speak volumes to the generations that cry 'me too'.

Figure 11.6: Look closely at *The Broken Pitcher* (1891) by Bouguereau. Is it just a 'pretty picture' or does it communicate something more profound about the world?

EXPLORE 11.3

The ancient Greeks had a myth about a young girl, Amymone, who went to the well for water and was raped. During the attack, her water pitcher was dropped and broken. This story later inspired French playwrights and artists, who adopted the broken pitcher as a symbol of 'broken' virginity and rape. Look again at Figure 11.6, *The Broken Pitcher*. How does knowing about the symbolism in the painting change the way you would otherwise interpret it?

To what extent can we understand the arts if we do not have a cultural understanding that allows us to recognise, appreciate and interpret the symbolism that is inherent in the art form?

Perhaps the philosopher David Novitz (1945–2001) was right when he argued that disagreements about the definition and classifications of art are more often disputes about our values and where we are trying to go with our society, rather than being about any theory of art.

DISCUSS 11.7

Do you prefer to look at or listen to art that is beautiful and soothing, or do you like art that challenges you and makes you think? To what extent are the two mutually exclusive?

Should art be 'permanent'?

Art defies any single definition, but we might agree that it has definitional elements. It may be impossible to define the scope of art with any precision, but it is at least possible to identify some of the common features of artistic expression. Perhaps the distinguishing feature of a great work of art is that it is *inexhaustible*, in the sense that every time you come back to it, you discover new things in it. A related idea is that great works of art stand the test of time, and speak across generations and cultures. There is, for example, something extraordinary about the fact that Sophocles' (c 497–406 BCE) play *Oedipus Rex* appears to move us with the same power and intensity that it moved Athenian audiences two-and-a-half thousand years ago. Indeed, it could be argued that the sorting effects of time act to help us distinguish enduring art from art that is merely fashionable. Art can be tested and verified over time.

But this presupposes that art is permanent. Performance art cannot be returned to over and over again. Even if a performance is repeated, it can never be exactly the same from one performance to the next.

In 1974, Marina Abramović (1946–) a Serbian performance artist, 'performed' by remaining completely physically passive for six hours in a Belgrade art gallery. In the gallery with her were 72 items on a table. These items included a feather boa and a pair of scissors, olive oil, a bullet and a gun. Visitors to the gallery could interact with the items in any way that they chose. Although Abramović remained totally passive throughout the 'performance', at one point the gallery manager had to wrestle the loaded gun away from a viewer and throw him out of the gallery. By the end of the six hours, Abramović was almost naked and bleeding. She claimed that viewers who were still present when the six hours were over 'ran away' because they were unable to face the return of a person to what they have previously seen as merely a physical body.

Abramović's work is said to explore body art, endurance art and feminist art, the relationship between performer and audience, the limits of the body and the possibilities of the mind. Her performances can only be returned to by recollection, and they are inaccessible to new audiences except through accounts by those who participated in or witnessed her performances.

DISCUSS 11.8

Are there any features that are common to all art? If art cannot be returned to and verified over time, what other criteria might we use to assess it?

EXPLORE 11.4

1   In pairs, consider whether you think Marina Abramović's 1974 performance or a similar example should be regarded as art. One partner should write a paragraph on why the performance could be regarded as art and the other partner should write a paragraph on why it should not qualify as art.

Peer-assessment

Assess each other's arguments, using the assessment criteria below.

•   Are specific and relevant reasons used to support and justify the argument?

•   Does the argument show an awareness of other perspectives?

What is the overall quality of the argument, in terms of how compelling and convincing it is?

2   As a class, discuss: What new knowledge might Abramović's performance give us about human nature? What is the relationship between performance art and the human sciences?

REFLECTION

Consider how you decide if a work is an art form or not. Do you use criteria that you have learnt from others, or have you developed your own criteria, based on your intuition and reflecting on your emotional responses to the work?

11.3 The arts and the knower

DISCUSS 11.9

1   What is your favourite book, poem, piece of music, painting and film?

2   What do your preferences in art say about who you are?

3   In what ways might your nationality, age, religion or other factors shape your choices?

Given that we have our own tastes and preferences in music, film, theatre and literature, the arts appear to be simply a matter of a person's like or dislike. Many people have favourite images displayed on their walls at home, and listen to their favourite music on various players. Many of us say 'we know what we like', but equally we can be said to 'like what we know'.

"I like his earlier work better, particularly the ones I said I didn't like at the time."

When we create our own art, we are communicating our values, knowledge and ideas; so on one level, art is an individual expression. However, on another level, we are aware that the art we create might have the power to shape *us*, and influence what we know and how we think.

The arts appear to benefit us on an individual level in many ways. It is said that they can shape our minds by improving connectivity in our brains: learning to play music (particularly classical music) is said to improve our ability to collaborate, as well as to increase our **creativity** and self-discipline; reading literature can increase our ability to empathise and improve our social awareness; and dance has been found to improve our mental health by reducing stress and helping us to feel more socially connected.

However, there is also a strong argument that the arts connect with knowledge that can benefit us as a society. The existence of art galleries and concert halls suggest that arts are a shared expression or a celebration of what a community values, and can serve to increase community bonds. For example, it is thought that the earliest arts served religious purposes as part of a community's religious rituals, and arts today continue to express and interpret religious ideas in all societies.

> **KEY WORD**
>
> **creativity:** the ability to bring something into being through the imagination

REAL-LIFE SITUATION 11.5

Consider an occasion when you may have watched a movie or been to a concert with your friends. How did the shared experience contribute to increasing your social bonding compared with attending a lecture or assembly together? How can knowledge of the arts contribute to personal identity?

Throughout history, the arts have been used to commemorate important events, make social commentaries, and help to spread propaganda.

Sometimes the intention of the use of arts in public events can appear obvious, such as when music is played at a celebration, or when artworks are displayed in a gallery to invite us to observe and think about the works displayed. In such circumstances, we tend to be conscious of whether the art is intended to entertain us, unite us or perhaps challenge us in some way.

At other times, the use of the arts may be **subliminal**. Advertising and propaganda can use the arts in this way, causing us to associate beautiful images and bright or catchy music with a particular product, or they can be used more perniciously to create negative associations with a particular group, leading to stereotyping. This can have important implications for knowledge and knowing, because we can sometimes end up thinking that we 'know' something as a result of it being 'planted' in our minds. This is particularly true if we do not think critically about what we *know* or take to be *knowledge*.

> **KEY WORD**
>
> subliminal: subconscious

REAL-LIFE SITUATION 11.6

Can you think of ways in which artistic representations have helped to shape the way you think about particular people, events, products or issues?

The interaction of the arts and the knower is two-way. Every original creation, whether in fine arts, literature, theatre or music, plays a role in shaping the history of that art. We can all name influential composers, artists, poets, playwrights, novelists and musicians, but others too have made a great contribution to the arts; you may never have heard of John Lydon, but, as Johnny Rotten, he headed up one of the most influential bands in the history of popular music. And while you yourself may never be a Van Gogh or Kahlo, what you offer to the arts will be unique. You can never know what changes your work will bring about until you create the work, and even then, you may never know how your work might affect or inspire others to go on and create unique works. The point is that not only can the arts change you, you also have the potential to change the arts.

EXPLORE 11.5

1   Consider: Do you like to write poetry, prose or plays? Do you like to compose music, dance, act, draw, paint or sculpt? Think about your own involvement in the arts and their importance in your life. To what extent do the arts affect your sense of identity?

2   Think about an art gallery you have visited, a music concert, dance production or a theatre performance you have attended, a novel you have read or even a film you have watched. Think about how it affected you as a knower. Did it change your perspective in any way? Did it give you new insights?

3   Choose some examples, and write about 300 words on the extent to which your ideas, beliefs and perspectives have been shaped by the arts.

CONTINUED

Self-assessment

Consider your written work. Ask yourself the following questions:

- What did I do well? Did I give a clear and convincing account of the ways in which my examples shaped my ideas, beliefs and perspectives? Did I provide firm evidence or reasons to support my points? Did I raise any counter-arguments?

- What do I need to improve on?

- What have I learnt from this activity?

REFLECTION

Consider how the arts may have affected you as a knower, and contributed to your sense of identity. If you had *never* been exposed to the arts, how different a person do you think you would be today?

11.4 The purpose of art

DISCUSS 11.10

To what extent do you think art should serve a purpose?

The intention of the artist

Figure 11.7: Summertime: Number 9A (1948) by Jackson Pollock

> When I am in my painting, I'm not aware of what I'm doing.

> **Jackson Pollock**, 1912–1956

Art needs both individual creativity and a collective culture for it to be produced. Arguably, an artwork is not solely the product of the artist, because the artist's understanding of the world is determined by their cultural and historical context. The intention of the artist is therefore not completely located within the artist's imagination, but arises from an interaction between the artist and the world.

If you ask a painter, musician or novelist about the function and purpose of their work, they may have a specific intention in mind. On the other hand, it may be difficult to articulate or offer an explanation for artwork, as creativity can take unexpected directions. Moreover, art may not always be directly intentional. In the act of making art, the unknown can be accessed and made known through the expression of sounds and images in ways that the artist may not have envisaged before creating the artwork. For example, in the surrealist movement, there is an assumption that the subconscious plays a role in the production of images, suggesting that surrealist art is not always deliberately or intentionally crafted in a straightforward way.

The intention of the artist can often be tied closely to the intention and values of the culture the artist lives in. Some societies have elevated the role of the individual artist and give recognition to individual artistic achievements, but this is a fairly recent and predominantly western idea. It was during the early Renaissance that the role of the artist was elevated from an artisan (like a craftsman or stonemason) to that of a uniquely creative individual with free agency to determine his or her own works. Some cultures continue to promote the collective over the individual. For example, the Bushmen of the Kalahari have painted stories of their **shamans** for 40,000 years, and not a single artist has ever been identified.

In the Russian Orthodox Church, the **icon** painters are nearly always anonymous, and repeat certain images over and over again. Individual creativity is actively discouraged because the icons are regarded as communicating the **Gospel** in paint, and it is therefore considered important that the Gospel is faithfully and accurately conveyed. Nevertheless, there has been a slight widening of subjects, along with changes to the acceptable styles of icons over the centuries.

KEY WORDS

shaman: a priest or priestess who uses magic to cure the sick, divine the hidden and control events

icon: a symbol or representation often uncritically venerated. In Eastern churches, these figures usually represent Christ, the Virgin Mary, or a saint.

Gospel: the teachings or revelations of Jesus, meaning 'good news', originally set out in the four gospel accounts of his ministry, crucifixion and Resurrection in the New Testament books: Matthew, Mark, Luke and John

---

DISCUSS 11.11

To what extent is knowledge in the arts attributable to the intentions of the artist, the expression of a culture, the art work itself or the views of those who engage with the art?

Art as imitation

Perhaps the best-known theory of art is the imitation or copy theory, which says that the purpose of art is to copy reality. (This is also known as the **mimetic** theory of art.)

The theory was developed by the Greek philosopher, Plato (c 428–348 BCE), who said that all art is an imitation of life, and mimetic by nature. Plato believed that ideas are the ultimate reality, and argued that as the physical world imitates ideas, so art is an imitation of the physical world. He gave the example of a carpenter and a chair. Plato believed that the idea of a chair must first have come in the mind of a carpenter, who then gave physical shape to the idea by making the chair out of wood. If an artist then paints an image of the chair, the artist's chair is twice removed from reality. For Plato, this meant that all art is twice removed from truth, and therefore something to be avoided.

KEY WORD

mimetic: from *mimesis*, the Greek word for 'imitation', associated with the idea that art copies reality

While Plato's student, Aristotle (384–322 BCE), agreed that art (particularly poetry) is mimetic, he argued that the arts do much more than purely reflect what is real, and they cannot be slavish imitations. Rather, he claimed, artists represent selected events and characters, then exalt and idealise them to imaginatively recreate new worlds with their own meaning and beauty. By creating something *less than reality*, Aristotle felt that the artist can create *more than reality* through intuition and perception. It is this 'more' that Aristotle believed to be the aim of the artist.

DISCUSS 11.12

1   To what extent can abstract images show us more about a subject than a photograph, or a poem say more than a lengthy description?

2   How can the arts allow us to discover truths about reality that we might not otherwise see?

Realism, which is related to the idea of mimesis, is a movement that developed in France in the 1840s. The protagonist of realism, Gustave Courbet (1819–1877), sought to portray real people and real situations with accuracy, rather than as ideal representations, as had been the practice. The popularity of realism grew with the advent of photography, when movements such as pop art and photorealism emerged.

DISCUSS 11.13

How true is it to say that what constitutes art is dependent on the time and place?

The functions of art

Imagine there are some chickens that need feeding. You watch someone throw them seeds, which the chickens eat. To your surprise, you notice that the seed is mixed with diamonds. You watch the chickens peck at the seed and ignore the diamonds. For the chickens, the diamonds are useless, and yet for humans, they are considered priceless. Like precious stones, works of art have a value that only humans decide upon. Since, arguably, many works of art do not have any clear practical function like most other objects made by humans, you might think that their only purpose is to decorate, entertain or give pleasure. Doubtless, works of art *do* frequently give us pleasure, but many people would say that they also have a social and cultural purpose, and that they contribute to our knowledge of the world and our sense of human identity. As societies change, so the function of art changes within it. Art can sometimes be seen as a close-fitting garment wrapped around a society or community. When that group eventually disappears, it leaves these artistic signs and symbols behind as evidence (like a piece of clothing that survives) for future generations to interpret.

Communication

One possible function of the arts is to represent and communicate the culture, society and values of the time. We have noted that an artist's intentions are difficult to define, but one consequence of art is to leave behind a trail of evidence from the era in which it was created. An artist's creative expressions may or may not be typical of their era but they can give us clues about the past. One example of how artistic expressions can give us insight into the past comes from the 19th-century architect, artist and art collector, Sir John Soane (1753–1837) who requested that his house and art collection in London should be left untouched. An Act of Parliament passed in 1833 ensured that it would be preserved and open for future generations, and today, over 100,000 people visit each year. Every room in Soane's house is an art treasure trove; the collection includes items as diverse as the sarcophagus of the Egyptian king, Seti I and paintings by William Hogarth (1697–1764). The legacy of Soane's house offers a fascinating window on the role that art played in the life of one highly creative individual, and provides an example of how art can function as a time capsule that can be opened to transfer knowledge across time. This house enables us to gain a new insight into one particular 19th-century viewpoint. Art historians might take a special interest in this example because here, art can preserve a moment in time. History of art is an academic discipline and subject in its own right, distinct from history which we explore in Chapter 10. By studying the history of art, we are able to increase our awareness of the ways in which art has changed over time, and learn more about the perspectives of the societies that create, collect and preserve that art.

DISCUSS 11.14

Does the fact that art can provide us with evidence about past cultures and events imply that one of the purposes of art is to communicate knowledge, and provide evidence about cultures and events for future generations?

EXPLORE 11.6

The *Voyager* and *Pioneer* space probes were launched into space in the 1970s, as part of NASA's scientific programme. The spacecraft, which continue to travel through interstellar space, include a golden record with pictures and sounds from Earth, representing the variety of visual images and music from Beethoven to Chuck Berry. The record was intended as a time-capsule.

Consider: why did NASA send examples from the auditory and visual arts rather than examples from the literary arts?

If the space probes were sent today, what would you include in terms of music, paintings, and films to represent the world today? Choose a range of artistic items that you think would represent your society and culture, and the wider world to aliens and/or generations in the future.

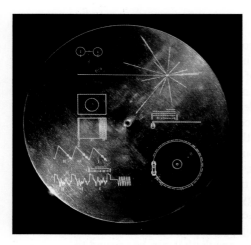

Figure 11.8: The golden record, launched into space in the 1970s

REFLECTION

If you were to create a time capsule for your potential grandchildren, great grandchildren or great-great grandchildren, to let them know who you were, what would you choose to represent you? Can you think of one or more artworks (possibly a song, or a film) that best represents who you are today? Try to articulate what it is about the artwork that you identify with. To what extent do the arts contribute to your identity, compared with other areas of knowledge?

At various points in history, artists have been agents of propaganda to illustrate the politics and ideology of their dominant culture. Sometimes, the arts reveal the individuality and personal obsessions of the individual; at other times, they mirror the consciousness of society. Open or closed, centralised or dissipated, authoritarian or democratic, art can express the values that a society collectively embodies. The key point here is that art is a way of communicating the values of society, and art can either endorse those values or speak out against them.

Ai Weiwei (1957–), a Chinese artist and activist based in Beijing, has long criticised the Chinese government for its stance on human rights and democracy. He uses his art as a vehicle for protest and dissent. One of his works, *Sunflower Seeds,* was a 2010 installation at Tate Modern in London. The work was made up of what appeared to be millions of apparently identical sunflower seeds, but each one was hand crafted out of porcelain, hand painted and actually unique. Hundreds of skilled artisans in the Chinese city of Jingdezhen worked to create the collection. The porcelain seeds were poured into the vast industrial space that is the interior of the Tate Gallery's Turbine Hall, where visitors could walk all over them. The precious nature of the material, the effort of production and the narrative and personal content made the work a powerful commentary on the human condition, and the relationship of individuals to the collective. They also reference the sunflower seeds that the Chinese communist leader, Mao Zedong (1893– 1976) put in his pocket to share on the Long March 1934-1935. The installation was said to raise questions such as: 'What does it mean to be an individual in today's society? Are we insignificant or powerless unless we act together?' and 'What do our increasing desires, materialism and number mean for the future?' Some people interpreted visitors walking over the sunflower seeds and examining individual seeds as analogous to the Chinese Communist Party 'walking over' the Chinese population and being able to 'examine' any individual it chooses to. Others saw the installation as a suggestion that together, the Chinese people could rise up against the ruling party.

Figure 11.9: A view of the 53-metre high cave in the Bamiyan Valley, where a Bamiyan Buddha stood for more than 2000 years until it was blown up by the Taliban in 2001

REAL-LIFE SITUATION 11.7

To what extent is one of the purposes of art to critique society?

EXPLORE 11.7

Working on your own, place a to l in order of importance – what do you think are the purposes of art? For each one, think of an example of artwork to illustrate the idea. You can choose examples from the visual arts, music, dance, poetry, theatre or literature.

a   art as a representation or imitation of real-life

b   art as an expression of emotions

c   art as a tool to transform and question the way we see the world

d   art as a therapy – to restore, heal or keep us hopeful

e   art as an affirmation or critique of moral values

f   art as an expression of religious or political ideas

g   art as harmony, balance, rhythm and beauty

CONTINUED

h   art as transcendence, epiphany or revelation

i   art as a symbol and/or ritual

j   art as protest, shock and revolution

k   art as entertainment and stimulation

l   art as commerce and sales

Peer-assessment

Compare your ideas with a partner. Ask your partner to tell you why they might agree with your order, or why they might choose to change it. What criteria did each of you use, and how did they differ? What might you agree on as the result of your discussion?

The power of the arts

Many of us enjoy looking at art, but perhaps some of us may not believe that it holds any real power over us. It might have great financial value but no magical effect over our own lives. However, the power of images and music in advertising can affect our every choices – from the shampoo we use to the holidays we take.

Political extremists sometimes actively destroy art they do not agree with. So threatened are they by its latent power that they feel they have to deface and obliterate the arts of the cultural heritage they reject. In Afghanistan in 2001, the largest standing statues of the Buddha in the Bamiyan Valley were destroyed by the Taliban. Since 2015, Islamic State militants have destroyed various antiquities in Syria, These works of art dated back 2,000 years, and included the Temple of Bel, part of a Roman theatre in Palmyra along with many other priceless items of cultural and architectural heritage.

In December 2018, the Russian President, Vladimir Putin, announced to a group of cultural leaders that they must come up with a way to lead and direct rap music to prevent it leading to the degradation of Russian society. His comments followed the arrest of a popular rapper Dmitry Kuznetsov (1993–), known as *Husky*, who raps about poverty, corruption and police brutality.

The actions of the Islamic State militants and President Putin are tacit acknowledgements that the arts have the power to subvert social order. The Russian example also illustrates the power of certain genres, such as rap, to challenge a nation's political establishment. Moreover, the arts have the ability to change our perspective on truth; in the words of Pablo Picasso (1881–1973) 'Art is a lie that makes us realise the truth – at least the truth that is given us to understand.'

DISCUSS 11.15

To what extent would you agree that the arts can be dangerous if not controlled?

The Picture of Dorian Gray, a novel by Oscar Wilde (1854–1900), depicts a character who sells his soul in order that he will forever stay young and beautiful.

The character, Dorian Gray, indulges in every pleasure, and lives a wild and abandoned life, never showing any sign of aging; only his **portrait** ages and becomes disfigured as a means of recording Gray's every wrongdoing. Gray comes to fear and hate the portrait, and moves it to the attic as it shows the increasing corruption of his soul. At the end of the novel, in a fit of rage, Gray plunges a knife into the picture, causing his own death. As he dies, his beautiful face becomes the aged and ugly face that had been seen in the picture, and the painting is restored to depict his lost youth. As well as having philosophical significance about the personal identity and the nature of self, the story of Dorian Gray can remind us of the power of images to embody concepts such as beauty, despair and corruption.

There are some cultures that regard an image of a person as being in some way a part of that person. Taking a photograph of someone in such a culture can be regarded as a form of 'soul theft'. The superstition about breaking a mirror causing bad luck is related to the same idea: that anything that damages a person's image can somehow cause damage to the person.

> **KEY WORD**
>
> portrait: a painting, photograph, or other artistic representation of a person which tries to show the personality of the person portrayed

EXPLORE 11.8

1   Take a photo of yourself or your friend. How would you feel if it were ripped in half? A slight shiver may remind you that the link between the real and the image is not altogether lost.

2   In the Buddhist tradition, a *mandala* is a spiritual symbol. Tibetan Buddhists make *mandalas* from coloured sand, working in groups and working outwards from the centre of the picture. Once completed, they are destroyed. From the Tibetan perspective, the process of creating the art is more important than the final product, and as a reminder of the truth of impermanence. Discuss whether you think the value of art is the creative process, the final product or both. How does this relate to other areas of knowledge – can you think of examples of where the process is as or more important than the product?

3   Take this one step further. Is the process of knowing as important as the knowledge produced?

The notion of beauty

To describe a work of art as ugly is usually interpreted as an insult. It follows that the condition of beauty is one that holds great aspirational power over our imagination. Beauty, however, is a shifting enigma. It has been used to describe all forms of the arts from architecture to poetry, and even to describe a mathematical formula and a game of football.

DISCUSS 11.16

Can anything be beautiful, or is beauty only applicable to particular categories of things?

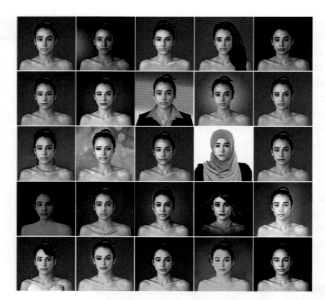

Figure 11.10: These images of Esther Honig demonstrate that the notion of beauty is dependent on cultural expectations

Many of us have a strong sense of what is beautiful, but the idea may vary across cultures. Journalist Esther Honig (1990–) sent an image of her face to various Photoshop editors from different countries, with the request that they make her look beautiful according to the standards of their culture. The various images show a variety of makeup and hair styles to achieve various different looks, suggesting that the notion of beauty is highly situational and dependent on cultural expectations. However, it is also the case that beauty may have a universal basis. For example, some studies have shown that across cultures, faces that are regarded as beautiful usually fit the **golden ratio**. This suggests that while hairstyles and makeup preferences may vary, there may be a commonality in terms of facial structure. See Chapter 12 for more on the golden ratio.

The beautiful can simply be defined as being fit for purpose. The Greek word for beautiful, *horaios*, is literally translated as 'being of one's hour', e.g., a perfectly ripe fruit in its prime. A yacht, perfectly designed to sail through the ocean waves, might be seen as beautiful because of its function as much as its aesthetics.

The ancient Greeks were particularly interested in beauty, and described it as a moral condition or virtue as much as what something looks like. We still have a similar idea when we refer to a person as being 'beautiful inside and out'. Aristotle believed the main features of beauty are order, symmetry and definiteness, which he argued, mathematics demonstrates to the highest degree. In Chapter 12, you will find further discussion on the relationship between the golden ratio and aesthetics.

True beauty, for Plato and many of the ancient Greeks, was a perfect ideal that reality could never reach; reality could only try to get closer to the ideal. This idea has gone in and out of fashion for the past 2,000 years, but has never really gone away. For many, beauty is still an ideal that we hold up as a standard for the real to aspire to.

Contrasted with the Greek notion of beauty found in perfection is the Japanese philosophy of *wabi-sabi*, which finds beauty in the imperfect and transient nature of life. The idea is rooted in Buddhism, and arose from tea ceremonies in which

KEY WORDS

golden ratio: if you divide a finite line into two parts so that the longer part divided by the smaller part is also equal to the whole length divided by the longer part, the ratio between the two parts is $\frac{1+\sqrt{5}}{2}$ which is roughly equivalent to 1.618. This is called the Golden Ratio and given the Greek symbol φ (*phi*)

wabi-sabi (侘寂): finding beauty in the imperfect, impermanent and incomplete

prized utensils were handmade, irregular and imperfect. *Wabi-sabi* is a very popular theme in photography. You have probably seen beautiful photographs of old people who often have wrinkly faces and missing teeth. These people may not fit the classic ideal of beauty, but in their photographs, an inner beauty shines forth. Similarly, beautiful photographs may be taken of ruins and dilapidated buildings, decaying leaves, etc. Buddhism sees our craving for new things and perfection as the main reason for suffering in the world. *Wabi-sabi* is an antidote to this, in that it teaches us to appreciate the worn and the imperfect. Perhaps, above all, *Wabi-sabi* values authenticity.

Figure 11.11: Can you see beauty in this portrait? To what extent is our concept of beauty a social construction that we learn?

EXPLORE 11.9

Find ten images of objects or scenes. They can be images of buildings, landscapes, mathematical formulae or even works of art, but *not* of people or animals. In pairs, try to arrange the images in a diamond diagram according to how beautiful you think they are.

CONTINUED

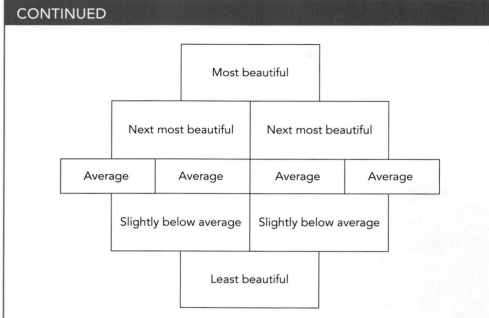

Figure 11.12

Each pair should justify their hierarchy.

Self-assessment

How well do your arguments show that you understand the concept of beauty, and the different perspectives that can be taken? Have you considered aspects of beauty such as symmetry, the golden ratio and *wabi-sabi*? After hearing other pairs' justifications, did you change your views? If you were to repeat the activity, are there additional factors that you would consider next time?

DISCUSS 11.17

How do cultures decide what is beautiful? To what extent do we find the most beauty in things or places (or animals and people) that we have most affection for?

LINKING QUESTIONS 11.1

How might beauty be interpreted differently in different areas of knowledge? What can we know about the idea of beauty from maths, the natural sciences, the human sciences and history?

11.5 The interpretation of art

Roland Barthes (1915–1980) argued that the text (or work of art) and the author (or artist) are dead once the work is complete because the only thing that brings it alive is the reader or spectator. If he is right, it follows that the transmission of art is essential to the survival of that art, and suggests that an artwork somehow has a 'life beyond' its creator. It also follows that interpretation of art plays a key role after the creation of the artwork.

From musicians busking on the street, to video games and music online, we occupy a rich musical, visual and literary world, but it is not always clear whether there is meaning in the arts that surround us. There are many different theories of interpretation that apply to the arts, and all works of art can be subject to multiple interpretations. Some people would argue for some kind of relativism that says all interpretations are equally valid; others would insist there can only be one 'true' interpretation, even if they may disagree as to what that interpretation is.

The interpretation of music is sometimes seen to be a combination of interpreting the intent of the composer, interpreting the intent of the performer and filtering both through our own emotional responses to what we hear. The composer's intent might be discerned by observing the tempo and dynamic markings of the score, along with its structural or harmonic context. The performer's interpretation of the composition might be discerned by the emphasis given at certain points during the performance. It could be argued that all musical interpretation requires some familiarity with the style of the composer and the musical conventions at the time of composition.

The interpretation of other arts also requires a degree of knowledge for the interpretation to be more than an emotional response to the aesthetics of the work. The American literary critic E. D. Hirsch (1928–) argues that the interpretation of a work can only be determined by knowing the author's intention. Others will look for symbolism in the work, whether placed there intentionally or not.

DISCUSS 11.18

If a feature of an artwork is unintentionally symbolic, why might it still be relevant to how the artwork is interpreted?

Symbols and their interpretation are part of our everyday lives. Throughout history, art has been full of religious symbolism, some of which you may be familiar with. The halo, for example is a ring of light above the head of a person in a painting, to indicate to the viewer that the person is considered divine. While this tradition largely died out in the 15th century (although it is still a major feature of Eastern religious icons), Leonardo da Vinci (1452–1519) used natural sunlight to highlight the head of Jesus in *The Last Supper*. This effect is to subconsciously remind the viewer that Jesus is divine. Other common symbols in Christian artworks include a lamb to symbolise Jesus, a fig tree to symbolise the virgin birth and a red rose, which usually signifies Mary, but can also suggest the crucifixion of Christ.

In Buddhist and Hindu traditions, *mudra* are hand gestures which can convey many meanings. While the Buddha is usually portrayed in one of four basic postures: reclining, walking, sitting and standing, different *mudras* can appear in any of the postures to provide different meanings. In Hindu classical dancing, all movement in the arms and shoulders, as well as in the hands and fingers, can express complex meanings to help tell a story. There are hundreds of mudras described in technical manuals, but in practice, performers usually limit their gestures to those familiar and meaningful to their audiences, and the selection of *mudras* used in a dance may differ depending on the region where the dance is to be performed.

Figure 11.13: In Indian dance, every hand gesture communicates a meaning that needs to be interpreted

We briefly explored the use of allegory in Chapter 8. Allegory has long been a feature of literature and the visual arts. The subject of the artwork, and various elements within the composition, can be used to symbolise deeper moral or spiritual meanings such as life, death, love, virtue and justice. By using allegory, the artist can give a single subject multiple meanings. One famous example is the epic poem *Faerie Queene* by Edmund Spenser (1553–1599). The poem is a moral allegory in which each character in the poem represents a particular virtue or a vice, and the poem can be read on several different levels.

Against interpretation

In 1966, the American writer Susan Sontag (1933–2004) argued that the spiritual importance of art was being lost and replaced by an emphasis on intellectual interpretations. She believed that art critics were taking the transcendental power of art for granted, preferring to focus on their own intellectually constructed abstractions such as 'form' and 'content'.

Sontag was particularly disturbed by allegorical interpretations and complex hermeneutics that she regarded as sometimes forced upon works of art; she thought that over-intellectual analysis could actually destroy art's true content. She advocated returning to a more sensual appreciation of the arts.

KEY WORDS

transcendental power: supernatural power; in this case, the power of art to take us anywhere, show us anything including past lives and let us see into the minds of others

hermeneutics: the science of interpretation

DISCUSS 11.19

To what extent do you think it is possible to 'overthink' a work of art? How can we find a balance between developing a sufficient knowledge of the symbolism and allegory within a work of art so as to understand it, and appreciating the artwork in a sensual or emotional way?

REFLECTION

Do you like to reflect on a work of art that moves you (whether it is a piece of music, a novel, a play or a painting) to develop a deeper understanding of it, or do you prefer to stay with your emotional response? How might your preference affect your interpretation of the work?

11.6 Subjectivity and objectivity in the arts

REAL-LIFE SITUATION 11.9

How would you explain the difference between subjectivity and objectivity in relation to the appreciation of art?

From art galleries, concert halls and literary festivals to creative writing courses, the arts occupy a prominent place in society. It could be said that we have a voracious appetite for the arts. On one level, art is about enjoyment and entertainment: a story we like, a song that moves us or a picture we find beautiful. However, there is an interesting shift that happens when we make the claim, 'I like that painting,' to 'that work of art is beautiful,' or even, 'that is an example of great art'. The first claim is a subjective claim of personal preference; the second and third are aesthetic judgements that allude to objectivity.

When we describe art as great or beautiful, we are expressing more than our preferences. We are making a significant type of knowledge claim about the quality or value of the art, assuming there are criteria for judging it. This is an aesthetic knowledge claim. The justification for such a claim might be based on any number of criteria for judging the art work, such as:

• the artwork might display technical skill

• it might be popular or fashionable

• it might have an art-historical significance

• it might have a financial value

According to the philosopher Immanuel Kant (1724–1804), there is a big difference between judgements of taste and aesthetic judgements. For, unlike judgements of taste, aesthetic judgements make a universal claim, and have a sense of 'ought' built into them. This sense of 'ought' is a claim for objectivity.

Compare the following two knowledge claims:

1   I like this painting.

2   This painting is beautiful.

If one person says 'I like the painting' and another says they *do not* like it, these two statements can happily coexist with one another. But if one says that the painting is beautiful and the other says that it is *not* beautiful, then they are contradicting one another. To say that something *is* beautiful implies that other people *ought* to find it beautiful.

According to Kant, what distinguishes aesthetic judgements from personal tastes is that they are **disinterested**. Kant's point is that if we are going to judge a work of art on its merits, we should not bring our personal life-stories with us. When Kant says that we should look at a work of art disinterestedly, he does not mean that we should be *uninterested* in it, but rather that we should try to go beyond our individual tastes and preferences so that we can appreciate it from a more universal or objective standpoint.

KEY WORD

disinterested: free from bias and self-interest, which may help us to make objective aesthetic judgements

REFLECTION

Have you ever found yourself looking at or listening to something that is considered a masterpiece and wondering why anyone would admire it, or being really taken by a work of art that is generally regarded as having no great merit? Where do your artistic tastes come from?

DISCUSS 11.20

To what extent is it possible to leave our personal story behind when making aesthetic judgements? What are the implications of this for objectivity in the arts?

When it comes to deciding on what good art is in contrast with mediocre or poor art, there is a validation process which often leads to a degree of consensus. For example, many people would agree that Shakespeare (1564–1616) was a great writer and Beethoven (1770–1827) was a great musician. Even if their works are not to your personal taste, you might still appreciate the quality of the work they produced. You may or may not like Italian renaissance art, but most people would agree that this time and place produced great artists. For example, you may not choose to put a painting by Michelangelo (1475–1564) on your wall at home, but you could nevertheless acknowledge the mastery needed to produce work of that standard. Benvenuto Cellini's (1500-1571) 'Perseus with the Head of Medusa' is a technically impressive and remarkable artwork regardless of whether or not you happen to like it. The key point is that a work of art may not be to your taste but it can still be judged as 'good art'.

If consensus can be reached about what good art is, it suggests that there may be some criteria involved in judging the arts. For many, however, contemporary arts practices are a confusing cacophony of competing and clashing propositions. How then are we meant to know what is good or bad art? Some would argue that the arts were once completely accessible, but are now the province of the expert whose expertise is a form of 'inside knowledge'. If this perspective is justified, you could no longer know the quality of what you are looking at or listening to unless you were told, which would arguably put the arts alongside other contemporary disciplines such as physics, maths and biochemistry.

The art world has 'gatekeepers', including the art dealers who buy and sell art, the art critics who judge it, the galleries which display the artwork, the media and ultimately, the public who visit galleries. There is a significant question about how a consensus could be achieved when each of these groups has very different levels of expertise. There is also an interesting ethical issue about the extent to which the 'gatekeepers of the arts' have a vested interest in elevating the monetary values of some artworks as a means of establishing and maintaining an elitist market.

Should the arts be for everyone and not just the few? Is an elitist club of the initiated the opposite of what art should be for a community? You might wonder how much (if any) training in the arts is needed in order to develop the expertise either to create or interpret art. Perhaps one way to understand the arts is to trust your own instincts, try and make sound judgements and say what you like.

DISCUSS 11.21

What expertise might you need to appreciate or interpret visual, literary and performing arts? If an art gallery is paid for by taxes, should experts or public opinion be called upon to decide on the contents of the gallery and how much the gallery should be willing to pay for each work that it purchases?

KEY WORD

canon: a collection of works considered by scholars to be the most important and influential

It is well known that some artists do not achieve recognition in their lifetime. The artworks of the English printmaker, painter and poet William Blake (1757–1827) were misunderstood during his lifetime, and the Dutch painter, Vincent van Gogh (1853–1890) sold no paintings when he was alive. However, both of the them are now recognised among the canon of great artists.

REAL-LIFE SITUATION 11.10

If some art is not considered great during the life of the artist, but may be 'discovered' later, what might this say about objectivity and the validation process for artistic merit? Could there ever be a situation of mediocre art being considered great, or great art never being acknowledged?

EXPLORE 11.10

Work in pairs or a small group to discuss the following checklist.

a   Can any interpretation of an artwork be justified?

b   What are some of the criteria for judging different genres of art?

c   To what extent is consensus about art desirable?

d   Why might people disagree about the role of experts and expertise in the arts?

Perspectives

The knower's perspective appears to be central to the judgement of arts. In contrast, however, there is some evidence for the idea that some aesthetic judgements are universal. Two Russian artists living in New York – Vitaly Komar (1943–) and Alexander Melamid (1945–), set out to discover what kinds of painting people find most attractive, for the purpose of creating their own artistic series, *People's Choice*. Perhaps surprisingly, they found a striking similarity in the most popular paintings across a wide range of cultures. What these paintings had in common was that they depicted landscapes in which the viewer can see without being seen. Some people have argued that our preference for such landscapes is rooted in our biological past, and it is not hard to see why they might appeal to a human animal struggling to survive in a hostile world. Other research by Komar and Melamid indicates that there is a similar universality in people's musical tastes. We might speculate that the metronome of the human pulse is the biological basis for our sense of rhythm in music.

LINKING QUESTIONS 11.2

In Chapter 12, you will find discussion on loaded and leading questions, and hidden populations. What would you need to know about the surveys conducted for *People's Choice* before reaching any decision about the validity of the research by Komar and Melamid?

Rather than attribute the similarity of people's aesthetic tastes to biology, some commentators argue that the similarity derives from the fact that we live in a world that is dominated by American culture. Since we are increasingly exposed to the same kind of image on posters, the same kind of music in shopping malls and the same kind of movie in cinemas, it is perhaps not surprising that, despite our cultural differences, we end up with broadly similar tastes.

Cultural differences

At this point, we might ask how similar the aesthetic tastes of different cultures really are. To some extent, it is simply a matter of perspective – some people are more inclined to see the similarities between things, and others are more inclined to see the differences between them. We may decide that there are universal elements running through all cultures; but this should not blind us to the differences between them. You can get an idea of such differences by looking at two paintings of Derwentwater in England (Figure 11.14), the first done by an English painter, the second by a Chinese painter. Although they show the same scene, they are very different in style.

Figure 11.14: Two paintings of Derwentwater

The difference between Chinese opera and European opera is even more striking, and those accustomed to one tradition may – initially at least – find it very difficult to make sense of what is going on in the other. In the same way, someone raised on baseball may find it difficult to make sense of cricket. However, in the case of both sports and the arts, we may be able to learn a new vocabulary, and gradually come to appreciate the subtleties of a sporting or artistic tradition that is different from our own.

11.7 The role of the arts in communities

REAL-LIFE SITUATION 11.12

Can you think of a work of art (it could be a story, song, play or film) that helps to create a bond within your family or a group of friends?

The arts have the capacity to bring people together in many ways. We may come together physically to play in a band, listen to a concert, attend an art exhibition or visit the theatre, and the shared experience can create a sense of community. There are communities of artists: creative people who share an interest in particular art forms or genres. The arts can also tell a community's story. Such stories can help to build social connections and social identity within that community, and can sometimes become part of a sacred tradition.

A national anthem is a patriotic song recognised by the government of a country as the country's official song. It serves to help unite the nation. A football team's anthem similarly helps to unite a team's supporters. In Sri Lanka, many schools have a 'school song', which is sung proudly at school events, and serves to unite alumni long after they have left school. There may be multiple meanings behind singing together. The singing of shared songs could be interpreted from various perspectives; they might play a part in a knower's identity connecting them with a community, or they might be interpreted as 'manipulating emotions' or suppressing tensions within a community or a nation. It is possible that people will disagree about the role, purposes and significance of shared songs.

> **KEY WORD**
>
> **genre:** an artistic style or type; it can apply to any of the arts

DISCUSS 11.23

1   If you hear your national anthem, how does it make you feel? From your perspective as a knower, what emotions are involved? If you hear another country's anthem, is the effect on your emotions similar or different to hearing your own?

2   When we interpret the role of the arts in a community, which perspective is more useful – that of the individual knower 'from within' that community, or that of the knower observing 'from outside' that community? To what extent can we identify and evaluate the bias inherent in each perspective?

Sometimes societies, families or groups tell their own stories. These narratives may not always be written down in a definitive form, but they can help to identify those who belong to the group and influence the arts that the groups' members produce. For example, the story of the Armenian genocide is as fundamental to Armenian identity as the story of the Holocaust is to modern Jewish identity, and both stories have given rise to multiple artworks in the form of novels, poetry, paintings, films, music, etc. Artworks arising from these community narratives include *The Book Thief*, a novel by Markus Zusak, the song *P.L.U.C.K.* by heavy-metal band 'System of a Down', and *Gassing*, a painting by David Olère.

If we think about the arts produced by different cultures, they frequently have their own style. Aboriginal art often reflects the Dreamtime narratives of the Aboriginal people; traditional Chinese painting uses meticulous brush strokes of the kind associated with Chinese calligraphy, and some Ethiopian paintings are distinctive, colourful works, mostly illustrating Christian themes, reflecting a strong Christian cultural identity. These shared stories communicated via the arts can play a role in shaping our identities and perspectives. It is through the expression of the arts that a knower, a local community, a nation or an international community can make sense of and remember its past.

Figure 11.15: A corroboree is an Aboriginal dance ritual. Each Aboriginal clan group has its own style of dancing and body painting. The dancing, music and body art are used to pass down Aboriginal cultural knowledge, celebrate rites of passage and interact with the Dreaming. They also help to strengthen bonds within the clan group

DISCUSS 11.24

To what extent can the arts reflect or represent society with any degree of accuracy or truth?

REFLECTION

Do you have any stories or shared memories that are part of your identity? How do these stories or shared memories help to shape your identity?

In 2017, ceramicist Grayson Perry (1960–) made two vases called *Matching Pair* to communicate ideas about Brexit, the very contentious withdrawal of the United Kingdom from the European Union. One vase represents those who voted to remain in the EU and the other, those who voted to leave. In an interview, Perry said, 'I asked people to send in their ideas for what should be included, what represented the whole thing to them, even what colour they should be, and they've come out surprisingly similar … which is a good result, for we all have much more in common than that which separates us.' This example suggests that the role of the arts is to express, reflect or represent society. Moreover, the arts might capture different emotions or express and articulate different perspectives on the same topic.

Figure 11.16: *Matching Pair* (2017) by Grayson Perry

One of the world's most significant art prizes is the Leonore Annenberg Prize for Art and Social Change, which was granted between 2009 and 2014. Its goal was to commission and present ground-breaking, historically important artwork to foster a culture of experimentation and change in society. The 2014 recipient, filmmaker Amar Kamwar (1964–), creates complex narratives which cover topics such as **indigenous rights**, gender, religious fundamentalism and ecology. That a prize such as the Leonore Annenberg Prize exists, and that multiple other art awards have been granted to Amar Kamwar, are an indication of how important a role the arts are seen to play in the changing of society.

KEY WORD

indigenous rights: the rights of native people who originate from a particular place

11.8 Knowledge tools: language, reason and emotion

If a picture paints a thousand words

Then why can't I paint you?

The words will never show

The you I've come to know

David Gates of *Bread*

Language

The lyrics of the song *If* by David Gates (1940–) make use of a common idiom which suggests that a picture can convey far more than words. Poetry, on the other hand, is said to paint pictures with words. Music is said to convey emotions, intentions and even meanings, and dance has been used in many cultures to tell stories.

The arts have the power to move us, and to make us feel emotions. It is significant how the performing arts can convey emotion even when no verbal language is used. For example, if you went to a ballet production (rather than a play or film) of Shakespeare's *Romeo and Juliet*, you could feel moved by the story even though no words are spoken. The performing arts can communicate insights with their own non-verbal language.

We sometimes speak about 'the language of art'; but it is, of course, quite different from ordinary language. If you try to explain a poem in prose, the meaning or depth of the poem may be lost. Similarly, the sense of triumphant joy in the last movement of Beethoven's Ninth Symphony goes beyond anything that can be expressed in words. The analogy between art and language suggests that, just as we need to understand the grammar and vocabulary of a language to know what a native speaker means, so we need to understand the grammar and vocabulary of art in order to know what an artist means. Perhaps before dismissing, say, classical music or modern art, we need to make an effort to learn the language. We might then be in a better position to decide what is being communicated and whether it is worthwhile.

Reason

The role of rationality and reasoning is significant in the arts. From the perspective of creating and interpreting an artwork, there is arguably a degree of convention and rationality involved. If you consider the task of criticism of poetry or prose, there is an expertise involved in analysing the use of language, unpacking the literary devices and commenting on the effect that they create. In this way, the arts can be rationally analysed.

When we interpret the visual arts, we use our reason to analyse the symbols and analogies we recognise, and we weave a narrative around them to create a coherent interpretation that helps us to decide on the meaning of the work.

The existence of prizes in the literary arts and the visual arts, such as the Nobel Prize for Literature or the Edvard Munch Art Award, suggests that we can and do make rational judgements about the arts. Arguably, there is a degree of consensus regarding the canon of artists and authors from Rothko (1903–1970) to Rabindranath Tagore (1861–1941), and the interpretation of the arts is not simply the subjective opinion of an individual knower. Communities are expected to justify, to some extent, how they judge, rationalise, recognise and give awards for art, particularly if the money for purchasing art and awarding prizes comes from the public purse.

Emotion

Our emotional responses to stimuli are perhaps the earliest responses each of us experience. Emotions can grab our attention and direct our behaviour in very primal ways. Fear will tend to make us run or lash out defensively, whereas love might make us feel safe and secure. Often, we rely on visual and auditory clues to stimulate our emotions, and this may be why the visual arts and music can affect us so profoundly.

Many people would say that however much we might use reason to justify our interpretations of art, our primary responses are emotional. If you look at *The Third of May 1808* by Francisco Goya (1746–1828), your first response is likely to be an emotional one. The painting is a stark illustration of the martyrdom of Spanish troops attempting to protect the city of Medina del Rio Seco from Napoleon's invasion. Only after your initial emotional reaction are you likely to turn your mind to analysing the technical details and features, and analysing the work in a rational way. Many of us will not go beyond the emotional response; we might appreciate the power and the greatness of the art, yet may not necessarily 'like' it, perhaps because of its power and greatness, and the emotional response it evokes.

REAL-LIFE SITUATION 11.14

Think about your musical tastes and those of your parents or grandparents. What might be full of emotional power for you may be just 'noise' to them. Similarly, music that moves them deeply may leave you cold. How do you define 'emotional power'?

REFLECTION

How does emotion inform, enhance, weaken, motivate or otherwise influence your knowledge in the arts?

11.9 Art and science

Despite the obvious differences between the arts and the sciences, there are some interesting similarities between them. At the deepest level, we might say that both are trying to make sense of the world by looking for patterns in things. *The difference is that in science, the patterns are usually expressed in mathematics and logic, and in the arts, they are expressed in more allusive and intuitive forms.*

Although some people would argue that science appeals more to reason, and the arts more to imagination, both reason and imagination play an important role in each area of knowledge. On the one hand, artists need to impose some kind of rational control on their creative insights if they are to be of lasting value. On the other hand, scientists need to have good imaginations if they are to come up with new ways of looking at things, ask new questions, formulate new hypotheses and develop new theories.

Interestingly, many great scientists have appealed to the beauty of their ideas in order to justify them. For example, Albert Einstein (1879–1955) once observed that the *theory of relativity* was too beautiful to be false. Such a reference to beauty is, at first sight, puzzling; but it makes sense once we realise that beauty and order are closely related concepts, and that a scientist's appeal to beauty is usually a reflection of his or her conviction that the universe is orderly. Einstein demonstrated that aesthetic considerations play a role in convincing scientists of the truth of their theories. However, beauty is no guarantee of truth. If Einstein's theory of relativity had been repeatedly contradicted by experimental results, he would eventually have had to abandon it and think again. For it is always possible that the universe operates with an aesthetic that is quite different from our own.

LINKING QUESTIONS 11.3

Natural sciences: How is knowledge in the arts similar to knowledge in the natural sciences?

Discovered or created?

One important difference between science and art would seem to be that while scientific laws are *discovered*, works of art are *created*. But, as usual, things are not quite as simple as they appear. Many great artists have felt that their work is as much one of discovery as of creation – that the form is somehow already out there waiting to be unpacked. *'The pages are still blank'*, said the novelist Vladimir Nabokov (1899–1977), *'but there is a miraculous feeling of the words being there, written in invisible ink and clamouring to become visible.'* This idea is nicely illustrated by Michelangelo's (1475–1564) famous unfinished sculptures known as *The Prisoners*. When we look at these figures, it is hard to avoid the feeling that they are already in the marble, and are simply waiting to be released with the help of the sculptor's chisel.

Figure 11.17: Michelangelo, *The Prisoners* (early-16th century)

Just as some people have argued that art is as much discovery as creation, so others have argued that science is as much creation as discovery. To support this idea, they point out that even if a scientific law is useful and illuminating, it may eventually turn out to be false. That, after all, was the fate of Newtonian physics. So rather than think of scientific laws as eternal truths, we should perhaps see them as *useful fictions* which help us to make sense of reality.

Nevertheless, it may still make sense to say that science is more discovered than created, and that art is more created than discovered. To see why, imagine the following situation.

A building is on fire, and the last surviving copy of Darwin's *The Origin of Species* is in one room and the last surviving copy of Shakespeare's *Hamlet* is in the other room. Ignoring the danger to yourself, you leap into the building, but you only have time to rescue one of the books. Which should you rescue?

There is an argument for saying that you should go for *Hamlet* rather than *The Origin of Species*. Why? Because if Darwin's manuscript goes up in smoke, then sooner or later someone else will probably come up with the theory of natural selection. In fact, Alfred Russel Wallace, (1823–1913), came up with the theory around the same time as Darwin. But if Shakespeare's manuscript meets a similar fate, it is unlikely that anyone else is going to write *Hamlet*. The play as we know it could be lost forever.

What this example suggests is not that works of art are more precious than works of science, but that there is an impersonal aspect to scientific discoveries that is lacking in the case of the arts. It is this which justifies our using the word 'discovery' more in the case of the natural sciences than the arts.

REFLECTION

The question, 'Discovered or created?' can be asked in all areas of knowledge. We will consider it in relation to mathematics in Chapter 12, but it could equally be asked of history, religion and so on. What does this imply about the nature of knowledge?

Science and art as complements

These two areas of knowledge were once much closer. For example, Leonardo da Vinci was both an engineer and an artist, at home with both science and art. Another way of thinking about the relation between the sciences and the arts is to say that today they are still complementary ways of making sense of the world, and that for a balanced outlook, we need both. Following this line of thought, it could be argued that while science looks at things from the outside, art looks at them from the inside. Einstein once said that science does not give the taste of the soup. What he meant by this is that while science can tell us what soup is made of and why it is good for us, it has nothing to say about what it feels like to drink soup on a cold day. Admittedly, soup is not a major theme in the arts, but the arts do deal with other complex experiences. Think of an emotion such as love. While science may be able to tell us what happens to our hormones and heartbeat when we fall in love, it is to the arts that many people instinctively turn to make sense of the *experience* of love.

EXPLORE 11.11

What would you say are the main similarities and differences between the arts and the sciences? Create a mind-map to illustrate your ideas. Use the four strands of the knowledge framework as a tool for your comparison. The following words may help to stimulate your thinking:

- beauty

- creativity

- discovery

- emotion

- reason

- symmetry

- description

REAL-LIFE SITUATION 11.15

What can science tell us about the nature of love that the arts cannot; and what can the arts tell us about the nature of love that science cannot?

If the arts did not exist, are there aspects of human nature that would remain unknown to us? In other words, what knowledge and insights are uniquely offered by the arts?

11.10 Ethics, censorship and the arts

REAL-LIFE SITUATION 11.16

Can you think of examples of the arts that try to raise awareness of issues such as racism, poverty, war, domestic violence or environmental destruction?

The arts tend to have a more direct emotional effect on individuals and communities than other areas of knowledge. Because of this, artists have often used their art to support political campaigns and movements. In 1751, the artist William Hogarth (1697–1764) produced two prints in support of the Gin Act – an act of parliament designed to reduce the drinking of spirits. Hogarth's prints were *Beer Street* and *Gin Lane*. In *Beer Street*, people are depicted as prosperous, happy and healthy, whereas in *Gin Lane*, the people are shown as poor, and surrounded by death and decay. The message is clear: it is OK to drink beer, but drinking spirits is the way to ruin.

Figure 11.18: Hogarth's *Beer Street*

Figure 11.19: Hogarth's *Gin Lane*

Street art is an interesting phenomenon. The British artist Banksy began his career as a graffiti artist, and started developing stencils after nearly being caught by the police for vandalising public spaces. His work often contains a message of anti-war or anti-establishment. Many people see graffiti as vandalism and a sign of lawlessness. The cost of removing graffiti can run into millions of pounds each year, and those caught can face tough penalties, including prison. On the other hand, some graffiti artists are lauded by art galleries. Indeed, some of Banksy's works are now valued at more than £1,000,000. This is an interesting example of how art street art, which might have originated as something anti-establishment, can become part of the canon of art that is sought after and attracts a high price.

The French street photographer and street artist known as JR (1983–) creates large black and white photographic images which he puts up in public spaces, rather like those a graffiti artist uses. Identifying himself as an 'urban activist', JR's work offers a new artistic perspective on multiple political, social and economic issues. He likes to exhibit his work in the streets to reach an audience that never visits galleries, and has exhibited his large-scale public images in many different international locations, from the *favelas* of Brazil and the separation barrier between Israel and Palestine, to the border between Mexico and the USA.

Figure 11.20: Art by the French artist JR on the US–Mexico border in 2017

A related example is the production of artistic street signs. The French artist Clet Abraham (1966–) creates sticker graffiti which he has placed on public signs in Florence in Italy and Edinburgh in the UK. It could be interpreted as a humorous way of changing our perspective on something familiar; arguably, it could be a playful way of questioning our tendency to follow signs and instructions. However, it could also be regarded as public disruption, given that the actual public signs are obscured by the 'graffiti art'. There is disagreement about the value and purpose of this art.

EXPLORE 11.12

1   Think about ways in which an artist can take something familiar, such as a road sign, and transform it so we can think about it in new ways. What ethical responsibilities does the artist have in making such a transformation?

2   How would you feel if you discovered graffiti or street art on the wall of your house or on your car? Would it make a difference to how you felt if you later discovered the work was by a famous graffiti artist (and potentially worth a lot of money)? What criteria would you use to decide whether the graffiti is art or vandalism?

REAL-LIFE SITUATION 11.17

Do artists or the societies in which they operate exert a greater influence on what is ethically acceptable in the arts?

Because of their influence, well-known artists, actors and musicians are often recruited to promote humanitarian and political causes. However, they are also called upon to endorse products such as chocolate bars, toiletries, perfumes and groceries. This appeal to celebrity is in many cases fallacious, but it is a fallacy that most of us are vulnerable to. This power of influence has led some people to argue that people with celebrity status have a greater responsibility to behave ethically.

In 2016, actor Pierce Brosnan, most known for his role as James Bond, featured in a *Pan Bahar* advertising campaign in India. (*Pan Bahar* is a tobacco product.) After being heavily criticised on social media for his endorsement of a product that is carcinogenic, Brosnan apologised and claimed that he did not know the product carried health risks. The Indian government is planning to amend the Consumers Protection Act to make it possible to prosecute stars who appear in fraudulent advertisements. The stars could find themselves with a five-year jail sentence or an INR 50 lakh fine (approximately $US 70,000).

Jahseh Dwayne Onfroy (1998–2018), who was known as XXXTentacion, was an American rapper and songwriter whose music expressed a disconnect with society, focusing on themes such as mental illness, suicide and misogyny. During his short life, he was accused of numerous violent crimes including the battery of his pregnant girlfriend, and spent time in prison. Nevertheless, his experience of drugs and crime enabled him to reach out to young fans who were similarly disconnected. He is said to have brought solace to the distressed while, at the same time, validating violence. One critic said that Onfroy's music shows how hate-filled songs might normalise such feelings in people, and saw him as contributing to society's paranoia about the hatred that might be in the minds of others.

REAL-LIFE SITUATION 11.18

To what extent can we or should we avoid imposing our own ethical values when we judge the arts?

The Italian artist, and painter Caravaggio (1571–1610) was forced to move from Milan to exile in Malta following his involvement in a brawl and murder. More recently, a number of well-known artists have faced criminal charges. It is said that the value of Rolf Harris's paintings has plummeted since he was found guilty of 12 counts of indecent assault on young girls. Similarly, actor Kevin Spacey has been cut from scenes and replaced in a number of projects following numerous accusations of sexual harassment and sexual assault. He has also been dropped by his publicist and talent agency. Yet some music labels have used criminal charges as marketing tools for promoting music, and musicians such as Gucci Mane and Boosie Badazz achieved their highest-selling albums upon release from prison. Furthermore artist and rapper, Digga D, known for his contribution to the drill / grime genre in the UK, is on a rapid rise to fame despite being in and out of prison in the last two years.

REAL-LIFE SITUATION 11.19

If artists act unethically or are found guilty of committing serious crimes, are we still justified in valuing their work?

Censorship

When we think of censorship, we tend to think about movie censorship when some films are age restricted, usually because of 'bad language', graphic violence or sex scenes. This form of censorship is justified on the grounds of protecting children. But censorship goes much further than this, and different societies and different ages have very different ideas about what is acceptable.

Most people believe that we should have censorship in some circumstances. In conservative societies, censors might prohibit any works that are thought to undermine the authority of the rulers, or ban works that seem to promote what they consider to be 'immoral lifestyles'.

An international literary festival is held each year in Kuwait. Between 2013 and 2018, more than 4,000 books were blacklisted by the Kuwaiti authorities. The list of banned books included Victor Hugo's *The Hunchback of Notre Dame*, Dostoevsky's *The Brothers Karamazov* and *One Hundred Years of Solitude* by Gabriel García Márquez – all books that would be prescribed reading in many literature courses. This is an example of a country placing limits on what it considers appropriate and acceptable content. Even in more liberal societies, there are people who would want to censor works that are seen to promote violence or ideologies such as racism, misogyny, antisemitism or Islamophobia.

DISCUSS 11.26

How can we decide whether censorship in the arts is justified? If you decide that some censorship is justified, what criteria should be applied?

In 2018, many people in Kansas, USA, were outraged by a collage. The untitled image by Josephine Meckseper was part of a year-long exhibition ending in July 2018, and featured a collage composed of a graphic design of the American flag, a painting of a black and white striped sock, and a painting that depicts the contours of the USA in dripped black paint. The State Governor and the Kansas Secretary of State put pressure on the University of Kansas to take down the offending work, and wanted the work destroyed on the grounds that desecrating the American flag is offensive. Others described the work as 'immoral', and 'disgusting'. Words like 'immoral' and 'disgusting' suggest powerful emotions were triggered in those who opposed the flag collage, but doubtless there are many more people who would look at the work and shrug, wondering what all the fuss is about.

Figure 11.21: Untitled image by Josephine Meckseper. Why does it evoke outrage?

As knowers, our perspective on the tastefulness of a work of art is very much shaped by our beliefs and values, which are in turn shaped by our family, friends, religion and culture, our personal and collective memories, and by the discussions that are being held in our communities.

The arts have the ability to reflect our morality as well as to challenge it. No cultural values remain static, and often it is the arts that push the boundaries and open us up to new ways of thinking.

REAL-LIFE SITUATION 11.20

Should the arts ever be censored? If yes, on what grounds and according to what criteria? If no, justify why you think there should be no censorship or limits. Do your arguments also apply to other areas of knowledge, such as the sciences or history?

REFLECTION

Are you more conservative or more liberal than others in your community? Where do your values come from?

The arts as a political tool

DISCUSS 11.27

'All art is propaganda . . . not all propaganda is art.' George Orwell

Why do you think Orwell regarded all art as propaganda?

The arts sometimes have a significant link with cultural, national or political beliefs. In some countries, taxes pay for publicly-funded galleries, and some governments may try to limit or control the production of art, even to the extent of sponsoring and organising the mass production of art to express a narrative of national identity or shared values. One example of this is in North Korea. The Mansudae Art Studio is one of the largest artistic production lines in the world, with around 4,000 people manufacturing art works on behalf of Kim Jong Un's government. The monumental sculptures of the Kim family serve as a powerful reminder of the power of political leaders in Korean society.

In Cuba, the government is planning to implement Decree 349, a new law that will require artists, film-makers, writers and musicians to have a government licence. Creators of artworks who are perceived to violate national symbols or damage national values could face imprisonment. Tania Bruguera and other Cuban artists have gone on hunger-strike to protest against this proposed law and to defend their freedom of artistic expression.

REAL-LIFE SITUATION 11.21

To what extent can governments wanting to protect the national image through censorship be ethically justified?

Figure 11.22: How does a nation use the arts to remember its heritage and affirm its identity? In this context, what is the ethical justification for this use of images?

Piracy and plagiarism

One of the most significant issues facing the world of the arts in the contemporary world is artistic piracy, in which unauthorised copies of artworks are mass-produced and sold. This practice is most frequently associated with music and film, but can also affect books, fashion and design.

Some of this happens on a small scale, such as if you photocopy a friend's book or copy a friend's DVD. Although this seems to be a minor infringement of the artist's rights, multiplied millions of times across the world, it can make a significant impact on the relevant industries. When this happens on an industrial scale as it does in some countries, it can lead to significant financial losses. Intellectual and artistic property rights are increasingly important areas of law in different areas of knowledge, and particularly so in the arts.

REAL-LIFE SITUATION 11.22

While there is no doubt that illegal downloading costs production companies and artists many millions in lost revenues, some libertarians argue that all artistic creations should be held in common, and freely accessible to all. What are your thoughts? How might we use reason to evaluate two competing ethical systems?

Related to piracy is the practice of plagiarism. As an IB Diploma Programme student, you have probably been warned about the consequences of plagiarism many times, but what constitutes plagiarism is perhaps more difficult to grasp in the visual and performing arts.

While it is easy to understand that it is important to acknowledge when you use somebody else's words or ideas when you write, and the written form makes it simple to make acknowledgements in the form of footnotes or endnotes, it is not so simple to know when you are using somebody else's ideas when it comes to music or the visual arts. There is no rigorous and precise distinction between practices like imitation, stylistic plagiarism, replica and forgery.

Vincent van Gogh (1853–1890) was a great admirer of Japanese art and made three paintings based on Japanese prints that he had collected as a way of exploring Japanese style and use of colour. One of his paintings was a copy of Utagawa Hiroshige's (1797–1858) *Plum Garden in Kameido*. The composition of van Gogh's painting was a direct copy, but he changed some of the colours and made them much more intense. While this practice was acceptable in 1888, and indeed copying has long played an important role in the arts, it might not be so well regarded if he were to have done it today.

Figure 11.23: Comparison of a woodblock print by Hiroshige (left) to its copy painted by van Gogh

The Broken Pitcher by Bouguereau (1825–1905) – which we have looked at a couple of times in this chapter – was a new interpretation of *The Broken Pitcher* by Jean-Baptiste Greuze (1725–1805), painted about 100 years earlier. In this case, the idea of the paintings and the symbolism they employ are very similar, but the paintings themselves are very different to look at. Bouguereau's painting reproduces the same theme as Greuze's but in a different style for a different audience, so might be considered a new and original creation that pays homage to Greuze.

In 2019, the singer Katy Perry (1984–), her co-songwriters and music label, Capitol Records, were ordered to pay $2.78 million for copyright infringement on the grounds that her song *Dark Horse* was a copy of the catchy electronic beat of the 2009 Christian song *Joyful Noise* by the artist Flame whose real name is Marcus Gray (1981–). While copyright law allows *fair use* to limit infringement claims, and permit artists to 'borrow' parts of existing works in the process of creating new, transformative works, there is a very fine line between fair use and plagiarising a work. This is particularly true when an artwork has great commercial appeal, and large sums of money are involved.

EXPLORE 11.13

In all areas of knowledge, wherever we live in the world, we are surrounded by a culture or cultures that undoubtedly influence our own creativity, sometimes without us being aware of their influence.

CONTINUED

1   Create a mind-map to think about how copying the style and/or composition of a work might affect any creative work we produce, and how it might affect the work that we copy.

2   With a partner, think of ways that you could avoid plagiarism in the arts.

DISCUSS 11.28

How can we know the difference between being inspired by another work of art, and plagiarising it?

11.11 Conclusion

We have drawn attention to the fact that the arts can help make sense of our experience of the world. Yet the kind of truth we find in them does seem to be different in some ways from that found in the sciences. If two scientific theories contradict one another and one of them is true, we can conclude that the other one is false. But when it comes to the arts, we may feel that two quite different works can be equally revealing of the truth. This suggests that when we look at a work of art, it may be more illuminating to ask, not 'Is it true?' but 'What has the artist seen?'. Understood in this way, the arts might be said to contribute richness and depth to our experience of the world. We might speak of the *paradox of fiction* – the fact that fiction is sometimes able to reveal deep truths about the human condition.

For human beings, a life without the arts is difficult to imagine and it would surely be a cold, grey, drab affair. (A single day without music would be more than some people could bear!) Since we derive great pleasure from the arts, that in itself is enough to justify them. But, as we have seen in this chapter, they can also be said to contribute to our knowledge of the world. Typically, great works of art are able to make the familiar strange or make the strange familiar. At their best, they can perhaps help us to recognise truths we were previously unaware of and reignite our sense of wonder at the world. While it may seem strange that we human beings often turn to fiction in search of the truth, it also seems to be true!

Kurt Vonnegut (1922–2007), an American writer, speaking to students at a graduation ceremony said, 'The arts . . . are a very human way of making life more bearable. Practising an art, no matter how well or badly, is a way to make your soul grow, for heaven's sake. Sing in the shower. Dance to the radio. Tell stories. Write a poem to a friend, even a lousy poem. Do it as well as you possibly can. You will get an enormous reward. You will have created something.'

KNOWLEDGE QUESTIONS

1   How important is the knower's perspective for interpreting art?

2   Does knowledge creation in the arts rely more heavily on imagination than the creation of knowledge in other areas of knowledge?

3   To what extent do the arts reflect or change the ways we view the world?

11.12 Linking questions

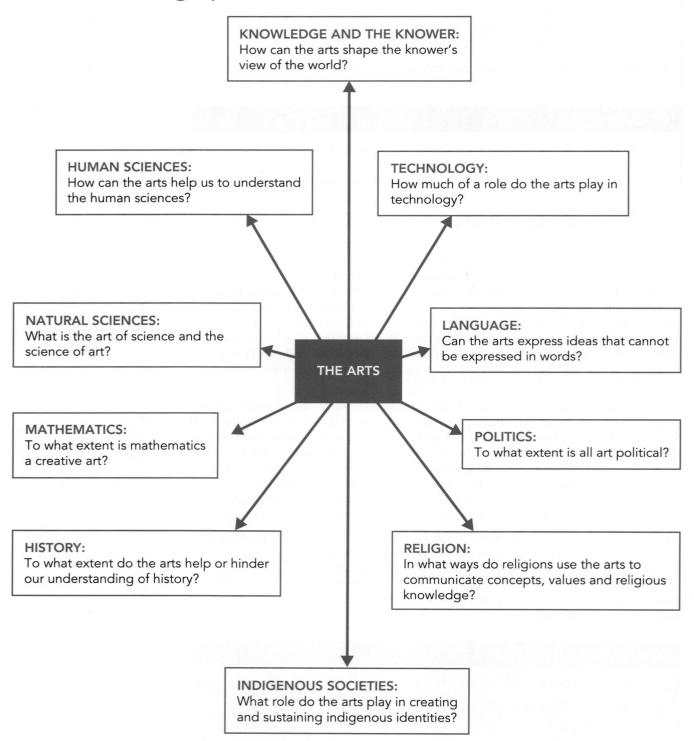

KNOWLEDGE AND THE KNOWER: How can the arts shape the knower's view of the world?

HUMAN SCIENCES: How can the arts help us to understand the human sciences?

TECHNOLOGY: How much of a role do the arts play in technology?

NATURAL SCIENCES: What is the art of science and the science of art?

THE ARTS

LANGUAGE: Can the arts express ideas that cannot be expressed in words?

MATHEMATICS: To what extent is mathematics a creative art?

POLITICS: To what extent is all art political?

HISTORY: To what extent do the arts help or hinder our understanding of history?

RELIGION: In what ways do religions use the arts to communicate concepts, values and religious knowledge?

INDIGENOUS SOCIETIES: What role do the arts play in creating and sustaining indigenous identities?

11.13 Check your progress

Reflect on what you have learned in this chapter and indicate your confidence level between 1 and 5 (where 5 is the highest score and 1 is the lowest). If you score below 3, re-visit that section. Come back to this list later in your course. Has your confidence grown?

	Confidence level	Re-visited?
Can I discuss the scope and limits of the arts, including some of the different ways the arts can be classified, along with some of the difficulties of trying to define and classify art?		
Am I able to articulate my own thoughts as to what art is? Could I discuss different works and why they might or might not be classed as art?		
Can I discuss the purpose of the arts, including the significance of the intentions of the artist?		
Am I familiar with some of the functions of art: the power of images and the notion of beauty?		
Can I discuss ways in which art might be interpreted and give examples of symbolism and allegory in the arts?		
Am I able to articulate a criticism of an analytical approach to interpretation of the arts?		
Am I able to discuss how we might try to achieve some kind of objectivity in judging the arts? Can I counter the discussion with examples of subjectivity and different perspectives?		
Do I understand the roles of the arts in communities and can I discuss examples of how the arts are involved in community identity?		
Can I explain the importance of language, reason and emotion in relation to the arts?		
Am I familiar with the connections between the arts and sciences and the concepts of creation, creativity, and discovery?		
Do I understand different perspectives related to the ethical responsibilities of artists?		
Can I discuss the ethics of using art to promote products, ideas and ideologies?		
Do I understand the issue of plagiarism in the arts?		

11.14 Continue your journey

- To build on the knowledge that you have gained in this chapter, you could read some of the following articles.

- For an interesting article on **what counts as literature**, read: Jonathan Gibbs, 'What counts as literature?', in *The Times Literary Supplement*, 1 March 2017. Search the *Times Literary Supplement* website for this article.

- For a fascinating account of some of the **issues in art**, read: Michael Glover, 'The Big Question: How many of the paintings in our public museums are fakes?', in *The Independent*, 16 April 2010. Search the *Independent* website for this article.

- If you are interested in following up on the **history of aesthetics** from ancient Greece to today, read: Umberto Eco, *The history of beauty* and *On ugliness*, Rizzoli, 2004 and 2007, respectively.

- If you would like to explore **how we look at art** more deeply, read: John Berger, *Ways of Seeing*, Penguin, 2008.

- For examples of some **iconic paintings and the themes they addressed**, read: Klaus Reichold, *Paintings That Changed the World*, Prestel, 1998.

- For a fascinating look into the **lives of great artists who changed the world of art**, read: Simon Schama, *The Power of Art*, BBC Books, 2006.

- If you would like an **insight into modern art**, read: Grayson Perry, *Playing to the Gallery*, Penguin, 2016.

- For a classic introduction to the **history of art**, read: E.H. Gombrich, *The Story of Art*, Phaidon, 2007

- If you would like to explore some of the **women who have been influential in art**, read: Linda Nochlin, *Women, Art, And Power*, Routledge, 2018.

> Chapter 12
Mathematics

LEARNING INTENTIONS

This chapter will consider what mathematical knowledge is, how mathematical knowledge is developed, how it connects with other areas of knowledge and its importance to us as knowers.

You will:

- consider what mathematics is, and how mathematical knowledge has been constructed and developed over time

- understand what mathematical objects are, and consider their relationship to the world

- develop an understanding of axioms and theorems, and their roles in mathematical certainty

- explore the use of deductive and inductive reasoning in mathematics, and the notion of 'certainty'

- understand some of the issues that arise in the creation of statistical knowledge

- explore the role of mathematical intuition

- be able to discuss the relationship between mathematics and aesthetics

- consider some of the ethical issues that arise in mathematics

---

BEFORE YOU START

Analyse each of the following quotations and discuss the questions that follow.

1   'Mathematics is the most beautiful and most powerful creation of the human spirit.' **Stefan Banach** (1892–1945)

2   'In mathematics, the art of proposing a question must be held of higher value than solving it.' **Georg Cantor** (1845–1918)

3   'In reality, however, [mathematics] is a science which requires a great amount of imagination.' **Sofia Kovalevskaya** (1850–1891)

4   '[Mathematics] is the blueprint of the universe.' **Stephen Hawking** (1942–2018)

5   'The definition of a good mathematical problem is the mathematics it generates rather than the problem itself.' **Andrew Wiles** (1953–)

For each quotation, consider:

a   To what extent do you agree or disagree with the quotation?

b   What does the quotation tell you about the speaker's perspective on mathematics?

c   Does the quotation challenge or affirm your own perspective on mathematics?

d   Do you think the quotation could apply to other areas of knowledge? If so, in what ways?

12.1 Introduction

DISCUSS 12.1

Do you believe mathematics is *invented* or *discovered*?

Mathematics is the discipline that deals with shape, quantity and arrangement, and the relationships between them. It is a formal system used to recognise, classify and exploit the patterns and properties of the world around us. As such, it is concerned with everyday **phenomena**, as well as more profound questions about the nature of the universe and the laws that govern it. Most people recognise mathematics as the subject that deals primarily with numbers.

Every human society in history – from the most primitive tribes to sophisticated civilisations – has needed mathematics, and the more complex the society, the more complex the mathematics that it has needed and developed. The relationship between societies and mathematics tends to be self-reinforcing and self-amplifying: more advanced mathematics prompts the development of more advanced societies; those more advanced societies in turn develop even more advanced mathematics.

The mathematics that we learn today is derived from the work of many civilisations from far-flung places, including China, India, Egypt, Greece, Central America and the Middle East. In addition to the contributions from Europe and North America, they have all contributed to what is a truly international language.

KEY WORD

phenomenon (plural phenomena): an event, experience or occurrence

If you are fluent in a language, it can be difficult to imagine that there was a time when some of the words you commonly use had not been created; so too, in mathematics, it is difficult to comprehend that there was a time when key concepts, such as the number zero, had not been invented, thought about or discovered.

DISCUSS 12.2

In what ways might mathematics be regarded as a creative art, a science or a language?

12.2 The universality of mathematics

DISCUSS 12.3

To what extent must mathematics be the same everywhere in the universe?

It has been argued that just as humans have an innate ability for language, so they have an innate ability for mathematics, and that thinking mathematically is a specialised form of our linguistic ability. Indeed, mathematics is generally regarded as a uniquely human activity, but many animal species have a sense of number. Species that have so far been tested and found to have a sense of number include several species of fish, a few different bird species, rats, dogs, monkeys and chimpanzees. It is not just a matter of being able to count – some fish can 'count' to four – but also the ability to perform simple addition and subtraction, as has been demonstrated in dogs and wolves.

The ability to do simple **arithmetic** is useful for many species. For example, a she-wolf might use it to check that all of her cubs are safely in the den when she returns from hunting. A simple calculation will let her know if any cubs have strayed. This knowledge would give her the opportunity to search for any missing cubs, and to know when all missing cubs have been found.

KEY WORD

arithmetic: the process of counting and calculating in numbers

Figure 12.1: A wolf needs to be able to keep count of her cubs

It has been suggested that where mathematics is very simple and has real-world consequences, it is likely that most intelligent species will exhibit some inherent ability in mathematics similar to that of humans.

Chimpanzees have been shown not only to do simple addition and subtraction, but also to be capable of doing them using Arabic numerals, and to use these skills for tasks beyond those that have been trained. Their ability to perform new arithmetic tasks at the first opportunity is similar to that of young children. Some chimpanzees have even shown an ability to add simple fractions.

If we were to meet with intelligent aliens from another planet, they might also share our simple mathematics, because 2 + 2 = 4 must be true everywhere for every kind of civilisation or intelligence using the **natural number** system, but for more abstract fields of mathematics, their mathematics is likely to be different to that of human mathematics.

One reason for believing that the natural numbers (1, 2, 3, …) are universal is that they can be derived from a purely logical definition. The German mathematician Gottlob Frege (1848–1925) asked the purely logical question "How many things are there that are not identical to themselves?" and from the answer derived the concept "zero" because there are none. He then asked how many elements are there in the set of numbers of things that are not identical to themselves (i.e. the set {0})? The answer is 1; there is just one element in it, namely "0". Once we have 0 and 1 we can produce all the natural numbers by a simple extension of the same process, namely that the set {0, 1} has **cardinality** 2; the set {0, 1, 2} has cardinality 3, and so on for ever.

Since the natural numbers plus zero are pure logical concepts, it seems likely that they are universal.

> ### KEY WORDS
>
> **natural number:** often called the counting numbers, they go from 1, 2, 3 … infinity (∞)
>
> **cardinality:** the number of elements in a set; for example, the set {0, 1, 2} has three elements and so has cardinality 3

DISCUSS 12.4

Why might aliens share our simple mathematics but not our more complex mathematics, even if they were to be at least as intelligent as humans?

The early history of mathematics

The history of mathematics is a long and fascinating journey that reaches across the globe. It can be difficult for us today to envisage a world without a zero, or a world in which numbers are calculated to base 60, although we still use it to some extent. (There are 60 seconds in a minute; 60 minutes in an hour; 6 times 60 degrees in a full circle, and 60 minutes in a degree.) It is useful to glimpse even a little of that journey to understand how mathematical knowledge has developed and grown through human history.

The discovery in Africa of notched bones dating back to around 30,000 years ago suggest that humans have long thought about numbers, at least for counting or what we might call *tallying*. However, mathematics was largely developed in response to needs that arose as civilisations developed agriculture, trade and taxation. Evidence has been found of early mathematical developments emanating from ancient Egypt and Mesopotamia (roughly where Iraq is today).

The Sumerians and Babylonians were perhaps the first peoples to assign symbols to groups of objects to indicate larger numbers in the 4th millennium BCE. Their

> ### KEY WORD
>
> **tally:** to keep count (of things or events)

numbers were developed on a base 60 system. The Egyptians are believed to have introduced the first fully developed base 10 system as early as 2700 BCE, and possibly much earlier; however they had no **place value**, which made representing large numbers difficult. Although 1,000,000 could be represented with a single symbol, 999,999 needed 54 different symbols (nine for each power of ten). Papyruses exist from the 2nd millennium BCE that indicate the Egyptians had an understanding of prime numbers, arithmetic, geometry linear equations and quadratic equations.

KEY WORD

place-value system: a numerical system in which the position of a digit indicates its value as well as the digit itself; therefore in '9', the digit 9 denotes only 'nine'; in '90' because its place has shifted left, it denotes 'ninety' in a decimal system

EXPLORE 12.1

The Babylonians are said to have been able to count to 60 on their hands, using twelve knuckles on one hand and five fingers on the other. Can you work out how they did it? The number 10 has the factors 5 and 2; what are the factors of the number 60? What advantages might there be in having a number system based on 60?

REAL-LIFE SITUATION 12.1

The choice of a number system to the base 10 is completely arbitrary, yet many cultures chose it. Why might that be? To what extent could a culture be shaped by the number system it adopts?

The ancient Chinese had two different numbering systems to the base 10, one of which dates back to at least the 2nd millennium BCE. The second system was developed around the 4th century BCE, when counting boards (a precursor to the Chinese abacus) started to be used. This system used a decimal place value system not unlike what we use today, but still had no symbol for zero.

As early as the 8th century BCE, long before the philosopher Pythagoras (570–495 BCE) was born, the *Shulba Sutras* in India contained several simple Pythagorean triples, and a simplified *Pythagorean theorem*. They also had geometric solutions to linear and quadratic equations, and knew $\sqrt{2}$ to an accuracy of five decimal places. This geometry related to the construction of fire altars, and so linked mathematical research to their religious world-view.

KEY WORD

Shulba Sutras: a body of Hindu writings regarded as appendices to the *Vedas*; they are arguably Hinduism's most authoritative scriptures

REAL-LIFE SITUATION 12.2

As well as having administrative purposes, much of ancient mathematics was developed to support religious purposes as well. How might faith and reason work compatibly together in mathematics and other areas of knowledge?

The philosopher and mathematician Thales of Mileus, in the 6th century BCE, is thought to have been the first person to develop guidelines for abstract geometry. Although Pythagoras is most known for the *Pythagorean theorem*, it was in use by the Babylonians and Indians many centuries earlier. However, Pythagoras may have been the first to identify five regular solids. He is also credited with being the person to coin the term *mathematics*. The Pythagoreans, who were students and followers of Pythagoras, mistakenly believed that all numbers were either whole or could be expressed as a ratio of whole numbers (fractions), and based their view of the whole universe on numbers.

REFLECTION

How might you perceive the world differently if you were to use a different number system?

During the late-4th and early-3rd centuries BCE, the Greek mathematician Euclid (c 325–265 BCE) deduced the **theorems** of geometry on a flat plane from a small number of **axioms**, creating Euclidean geometry as we know it today. His **treatise**, *Elements,* is one of the most influential works in the history of mathematics. Also, in the 3rd century BCE, another Greek mathematician, Archimedes (287–212 BCE) developed the antecedents to modern calculus. He also proved a range of geometric theorems, including the area of a circle, the surface area and volume of a sphere, and the area under a parabola. Many regard Archimedes as one of the greatest mathematicians of all time.

One of the most significant inventions in the history of mathematics was the creation of a symbol for zero. There is some dispute as to who first invented the idea, and when. In the 2nd millennium BCE, the Sumerians had a symbol that denoted a vacant place in a number, and the Mayans developed something similar independently. Around 130 CE in Alexandria, the Roman mathematician Ptolemy used a zero in his work on mathematical astronomy, but it was not used as part of a number, and really referred to *none* rather than a zero as we think of it today. In 690 CE in China, Empress Wu promoted a small circle to represent a vacant position, but this zero was not treated as a number. The modern decimal place-value notation is believed to have originated with the Indian mathematician Aryabhata (476–550), but it was not until the 7th century that Brahmagupta (598–668) wrote the *Brahmasputha Siddhanta,* which was the first text to treat zero as a number in its own right, and give rules for its use.

KEY WORDS

theorem: a principle or statement that can be demonstrated or proved using axioms (or other established theorems) and a particular logic, but is not self-evident

axiom: a starting assumption, often regarded as a self-evident truth or, more loosely, something we choose to be true, assume to be true or insist is true

treatise: a detailed written account

DISCUSS 12.5

Can you imagine a world without a zero? To what extent can the history of mathematics provide us with a window into the past?

Mathematics as a language

Many people, mathematicians included, have long argued about whether mathematics is a language. Some would argue that it is a truly international language; others that it is not a language at all.

Because *language* is a vague concept, there are many different definitions of it, but most definitions involve language having certain components: words or symbols with meanings, a defined grammar and syntax. Under such definitions, mathematics qualifies as a language, and it can be regarded as an international language used by mathematicians, scientists and others around the world to communicate a wide variety of concepts.

Taking this perspective, the nouns of mathematics are the various numbers and variables, as well as the different shapes and diagrams that are described by mathematics. The verbs are the various operations that can be performed, as well as the equalities and inequalities. Syntax is the set of rules that directs the order in which the mathematical symbols must be written and read for clarity and avoiding ambiguity. We can build complex mathematical ideas using simple mathematical symbols and rules of syntax in much the same way that we can build complex sentences using appropriate words and syntax.

However, not all people agree that mathematics is a language. Some would argue that whereas languages like English, Swahili or Vietnamese can refer to things that exist in the natural world, mathematics can only refer to concepts. Others make the point that even mathematics papers involve the use of conventional human languages because there are many things that cannot be expressed mathematically. Even in the solving of a mathematical problem, we find words such as *let, define, if* and so on.

One solution is to distinguish between ordinary languages – the languages we might learn as a mother tongue – and formal languages. Ordinary languages have usually evolved over many thousands of years, and are generally shared by the majority of people in our communities, although they vary immensely across the world. Formal languages, on the other hand, are usually developed over a shorter period of time, are deliberately designed for a specific purpose and are usually shared by smaller groups of people.

Figure 12.2: To what extent is mathematics a language?

EXPLORE 12.2

1   Translate the following into mathematical language:

   a   seven and five is the same as twelve

   b   fifty-two is bigger than nineteen

   c   three of these things do not give us nine

   d   if we have two of these things but lose four of those, we are left with nothing

   e   'I wandered lonely as a cloud'

   In a–d, which is clearer – the statement written in English or the mathematical statement? Are any of the statements that are written in English ambiguous? In what way? Can you translate the fifth statement into mathematical language? If not, why not?

2   Write a short paragraph to argue why mathematics is or is not a language.

Peer-assessment

Pair with a classmate and assess each other's work. Have they given a clear answer? Have they defined what they mean by 'language' for the purpose of this exercise? Have they provided evidence to support their opinion?

Self-assessment

Listen to your feedback. What have you done well? What could you have done better?

DISCUSS 12.6

Does the question of whether mathematics is or is not a language matter? What hangs on it? How might calling (or not calling) mathematics a language influence our perception of it?

12.3 Mathematical reality

DISCUSS 12.7

What kind of knowledge is mathematical knowledge? Is it knowledge of the real world, derived from the real world? Or is it knowledge of an abstract system invented by human beings, which just happens to have applications to the real world?

KEY WORDS

abstract: conceptual, nonrepresentational, independent of concrete specific physical existence

proof: generally refers to conclusive evidence, leaving little place for doubt; however, a mathematical proof is more than just a general proof – it is a conclusive deduction from axioms that leaves no room for doubt or argument

Mathematical objects are **abstract** objects that can be formally defined, and can be used in deductive reasoning and mathematical **proofs**. Common mathematical objects include numbers, sets, functions and geometrical objects like lines, points and various shapes, as well as structures that combine other objects such as complex numbers, vectors, matrices, tensors and differential equations. The reason they are regarded as abstract is that they do not refer to anything that exists in physical reality.

If you talk about apples, the word 'apple' represents a fruit that you can hold, pass around and eat. Although there are different types of apple, and different individual apples of each type, the word 'apple' still refers to something in the 'real world'. You could say, 'I saw an apple on the table' and you would be understood. However, were you to talk about the number *two*, people would want to know *two what*? To say 'I saw two on the table' only makes sense in a wider context, such as if you were looking for a cup, in which case the response, 'I saw two on the table' would be taken to refer to two cups. We cannot see, touch or taste *two* without it being two *of something*, or made of something, such as a symbol of 2 cut out from paper or a drawing of the symbol 2. In other words, the number 2 (like all numbers) is an abstract concept.

Of course, when we speak of two things, the things do not have to be physical entities like apples. We can speak of two centimetres, two unicorns or two ideas. The point is that the number two is not a property of whatever it is we have two of. If we have two dogs, two apples, two moons and two smartphones, it would be absurd to say that the dogs, apples, moons and smartphones all share the property 'two-ness' in the way that they might share the property 'yellow'.

There is an old riddle which asks the question, *'What was the largest island on Earth before Australia was discovered?'*. The answer is, of course, Australia. Just because we did not know that Australia was there does not mean that it did not exist. But is that true of numbers? Could zero have existed independently of human thinking of, and knowing about, it? Do numbers only exist in the minds of **sentient** beings? Or to put it another way, if there were no sentient beings in the universe, would there be no numbers? Would Frege's derivation of the numbers {0, 1, 2, …} remain legitimate even if no one had ever performed such a logical **inference**?

KEY WORDS

sentient: conscious, capable of feeling

inference: a conclusion based on evidence and reasoning

EXPLORE 12.3

In your classroom, you probably have rectangular doors and windows. When we look at the world around us, we often see an assortment of shapes. With a partner, try to come up with an example from objects in the world around you of a circle, square, rectangle, triangle, sphere, cone and cube. How close do you think your examples are to the shape you have identified?

REAL-LIFE SITUATION 12.3

You can draw a circle freehand or, more accurately, with a compass. But however accurate you are, you cannot draw a *perfect* circle. Why is there no such thing as a perfect circle (or any other geometrically-defined shape) in the 'real world'? Does the impossibility of perfect circles in the real world mean that circles do not *exist*? If circles, squares, spheres and so forth do not exist in the real world, are there limits to what we can learn about the world through perception?

The number π (*pi*) is a mathematical constant, which is to say that its numerical value does not change, much like any of the ordinal (or ordinary) numbers. It is also an **irrational number**, which means that it *cannot* be precisely expressed as a common fraction (although it is often approximated in elementary mathematics as $\frac{22}{7}$). When written as a decimal, its number of decimal places is infinite and never becomes a pattern in which the same sequence of digits repeats forever.

All **rational numbers** have decimal expansions which consist of expansions that are finite (e.g. $\frac{1}{4} = 0.25$) or sequences that repeat forever (e.g. $\frac{22}{7} = 3.142857142857142857\ldots$). But π is not of this form: its expansion consists of an endless sequence of digits where no pattern ever arises that then repeats. Here are the first 2,000 digits of that expansion (courtesy of Wolfram *Mathematica*™):

3.14159265358979323846264338327950288419716939937510582097494459230781640
6286208998628034825342117067982148086513282306647093844609550582231725359
4081284811174502841027019385211055596446229489549303819644288109756659334
4612847564823378678316527120190914564856692346034861045432664821339360726
0249141273724587006606315588174881520920962829254091715364367892590360011
3305305488204665213841469519415116094330572703657595919530921861173819326
1179310511854807446237996274956735188575272489122793818301194912983367336
2440656643086021394946395224737190702179860943702770539217176293176752384
6748184676694051320005681271452635608277857713427577896091736371787214684
4090122495343014654958537105079227968925892354201995611212902196086403441
8159813629774771309960518707211349999998372978049951059731732816096318595
0244594553469083026425223082533446850352619311881710100031378387528865875
3320838142061717766914730359825349042875546873115956286388235378759375195
7781857780532171226806613001927876611195909216420198938095257201065485863
2788659361533818279682303019520353018529689957736225994138912497217752834
7913151557485724245415069595082953311686172785588907509838175463746493931
9255060400927701671139009848824012858361603563707660104710181942955596198
9467678374494482553797747268471040475346462080466842590694912933136770289
8915210475216205696602405803815019351125338243003558764024749647326391419
9272604269922796782354781636009341721641219924586315030286182974555706749
8385054945885869269956909272107975093029553211653449872027559602364806654
9911988183479775566369807426542527862551818417574672890977772793800081647
0600161452491921732172147723501414419735685481613611573525521334757418494
6843852332390739414333454477624168625189835694855620992192221842725502542
5688767179049460165346680498862723279178608578438382796797668145410095388
3786360950680064225125205117392984896084128488626945604241965285022210661
1863067442786220391949450471237137869609563643719172874677646575739624138
9086583264599581339047802759901

π has been an important number in many civilisations throughout history, and each civilisation has developed ways of calculating its approximate value to several decimal

KEY WORDS

irrational number: any number that cannot be written as a fraction with one integer over another (e.g. $\sqrt{2}$, π)

rational number: any number that can be written as a fraction, that is, a ratio of integers

places, but it was not until the 14th century that Indian mathematicians discovered that the exact formula for π is based on an infinite series. π cannot exist physically, that is, it cannot be written down in its entirety, because the decimal value of π goes on forever; it cannot be stored in a finite universe because it would need infinitely many **bits**; yet we can write it down with a single symbol.

In 2010, Nicholas Sze made world headlines when he calculated the two-quadrillionth (2×10^{15} or 2,000,000,000,000,000th) digit of π, plus a few digits either side using 1,000 Yahoo computers for 23 days. It is estimated that to run the same calculation on a standard desktop would have taken 500 years.

REAL-LIFE SITUATION 12.4

The 10^{23}th digit of π has not yet been calculated, so nobody knows what it is, and we may never know what it is. Does it nevertheless already exist in some metaphysical world in which the perfect expansion of π exists, just waiting to be discovered, or will it be a human creation if and when it is ever calculated?

EXPLORE 12.5

Most calculations using π rely on a rough approximation of its value. What does this suggest about the accuracy of our answers? Does it matter? With a partner, brainstorm situations in which greater accuracy might be crucial. Think about what safeguards you might need to put in place to overcome inaccuracies in those situations.

DISCUSS 12.8

What is the relationship between accuracy and certainty?

Figure 12.3: How accurate do we need to be with regards to knowing the tensile strengths of ropes and chains?

Over the centuries, many great thinkers have tried to understand what mathematical objects are, and a number of philosophical theories have emerged. Perhaps the most commonly held position is the **Platonist** position (also known as mathematical realism), which says that mathematical objects are real, and that they exist in a perfect form (such as the perfect circle) in some **metaphysical** world, but the mathematical objects we work with are just poor approximations of those ideal objects, imperfect **instantiations** of their perfect form in an imperfect physical world. If you believe that perfect numbers (or squares or triangles) exist, or that the digits of π are determined and exist whether they are known or not, then you are, in essence, a Platonist. A Platonist regards mathematical objects as existing, albeit metaphysically, ready to be discovered.

DISCUSS 12.9

What roles do metaphysical objects play in other areas of knowledge or knowledge themes?

Imaginary numbers

When you square any **real number**, the answer is always positive. For example, $2^2 = 4$, and $(-2)^2 = 4$. This means that we are unable to get the square root of a negative number using real numbers alone. To resolve this problem, which emerged from the discovery that third-order (cubic) equations sometimes only had one real solution, mathematicians proposed the concept of what came to be called 'imaginary' numbers. The fundamental imaginary number is called I, and it is defined by the equation $i^2 = -1$. This means $i = \sqrt{(-1)}$.

DISCUSS 12.10

Do you think imaginary numbers 'existed' before they were conceived by Gerolamo Cardano in the 16th century? Do you think they 'exist' even now?

We can use i to find the square root of any negative number. For example:

$$\sqrt{(-16)} = \sqrt{(16 \times -1)}$$
$$= \sqrt{16} \times \sqrt{(-1)}$$
$$= 4 \times i$$
$$= 4i$$

This result can be generalised to the form $\sqrt{(-x)} = i\sqrt{(x)}$. When an imaginary number is combined with a real number, the result is called a **complex number**.

The number i cannot be represented on any real number line; however, complex numbers can be represented in the two-dimensional **Argand diagram** by using the 'vertical' axis as the imaginary axis.

Although imaginary numbers are not like real numbers, they have very real applications in the world. For example, complex numbers are used to create visual displays when you

KEY WORDS

Platonist: relating to the ideas of the Greek philosopher, Plato (c 427–348 BCE)

metaphysical: abstract, beyond physical, supernatural, independent of physical reality

instantiation: the representation of an abstraction by an example of the abstraction; for example, 'apple' is an abstract idea; this particular apple is an instantiation of the idea

real number: any number that can represent a position on a number line; real numbers include all rational and irrational numbers

complex number: a combination of a real number and an imaginary number, for example $3 + 4i$

Argand diagram: a geometric representation of complex numbers that uses the x axis to represent the 'real' part of the complex number, and the y axis to represent the 'imaginary' part of the complex number (the Argand diagram is also called the complex plane or z-plane)

play music through electronic equipment with spectrum analysers. They are also used for work with AC current, radar and wireless technologies, and they are fundamental to Maxwell's electromagnetic equations and quantum mechanics in physics.

12.4 Mathematical formalism

Besides mathematical realism, one of the most popular ways of understanding mathematical objects is the formalist view. This is to say that mathematicians work with axioms and theorems in **formal systems**, but their meanings are irrelevant; the systems need only be **consistent**. This makes mathematics more like a game. Formalists would argue that mathematical objects are really just the symbols themselves and the relations between them as determined by arbitrary rules. The symbols can be manipulated according to a system of well-defined rules, but they have no intrinsic meaning outside the system. In this way, we could liken mathematics to a game of chess: the moves a piece can make in a chess game are well-defined, and how you move the pieces is of great significance in the game, but it has no meaning in the world beyond the game. (Some modern versions of chess try to avoid the book-learning of historical moves by altering the rules or the starting positions of the pieces to try to make the game more unpredictable and original; this is very much like altering the axioms of a mathematical system to produce different theorems that would not be true of the original system.)

You might ask why *any* purely invented system should have application to reality. A possible response is that some of the formal systems we invent are originally suggested to us by reality and that we have, as one might say, unwittingly intuited them only later to 'discover' them in a different form and context. For example, since geometry first arose in response to practical problems, and was then formalised (reduced to axiomatic/propositional form) by Euclid, it is perhaps not surprising that **Euclidean geometry** turned out to be a useful way of describing reality, despite the fact that it is, in objective terms, completely false since there is no part of the universe that is exactly Euclidean or 'flat'.

> ### DISCUSS 12.13
>
> If mathematics is an abstract game that means nothing beyond itself, like chess, how might you explain its apparent ability to describe everything in the universe?

> **KEY WORD**
>
> **Euclidean geometry:** a system of mathematics attributed to the Greek mathematician, Euclid, based on five axioms

Axioms

It may appear that the axioms of a system are its starting points or basic assumptions, but in reality, the formalised axioms of a system are generally derived long after the system has been studied. Think of it like chess: for many centuries, the rules were varied, and pieces could move in different ways; only when what was agreed to be the 'best', 'most fruitful' or 'most enjoyable' set of rules was arrived at did the modern form of the game emerge as if set in stone. Much the same is true of mathematical axioms: they are what are considered to be the best way to formulate the fundamentals of a system in a particularly economic and simple way. As such, they are not really the 'starting point' of the system at all. For example, geometry had been studied for many years before Euclid formulated his *Elements*.

Nevertheless, at least until the 19th century, the axioms of mathematics were considered to be self-evident truths which provided firm foundations for mathematical knowledge.

There are four traditional requirements for a set of axioms. They should be consistent, independent, simple and fruitful.

1   *Consistent.* If you can deduce both p and non-p (a theorem and its contradiction) from the same set of axioms, then they are not consistent. For example, if you can correctly deduce, using the *same* axioms, both that the sum of the angles inside a triangle add up to 180 *and* that the sum of the angles inside a triangle *do not* add up to 180, your system is inconsistent. Inconsistency is considered to be problematic because once a system is found to be inconsistent, it can prevent you from solving anything. For example, if you are given $a+b=7$ and $a+b=9$, you cannot solve the equations for a or b because the equations are not consistent.

2   *Independent.* For the sake of elegance, you should begin with the smallest possible number of axioms, and they should be independent of each other. Which is to say, you should not be able to deduce any one of the axioms from any combination of the others.

3   *Simple.* Since axioms are accepted without further proof, they should be as clear and simple as possible.

4   *Fruitful.* A good formal system should enable you to prove many theorems using a few axioms.

DISCUSS 12.14

Do you think faith is required for the adoption of a system of axioms? To what extent does the arbitrariness of a set of axioms mean that all the knowledge or theorems based upon the axioms will also be arbitrary?

Starting with a few basic definitions – such as 'a line has length but no breadth' – the Greek mathematician Euclid, around 300 BCE, claimed the following five axioms (also known as **postulates**) to be true:

1 a straight-line segment can be drawn joining any two points

2 any line segment can be extended infinitely in a straight line

3 given any straight-line segment, a circle can be drawn having the segment as its radius and one endpoint as the centre

4 any two right-angles are equal to one another

5 if two lines are drawn which intersect a third in such a way that the sum of the inner angles on one side is less than two right-angles, then the two lines must inevitably intersect each other on that side, if extended far enough

Figure 12.4: Euclid's fifth postulate

DISCUSS 12.15

The axioms that Euclid started with were believed to be 'self evident'. Can you think of any self-evident 'truths' in other areas of knowledge? What happens if axioms (or self-evident truths) are later found to be false or, if not false, arbitrary?

You may notice that Euclid's fifth postulate is more complex than the first four, so it is often written in a more concise way as: '*Given a line (L) and a point (P) not on line (L), there is just one line that can be drawn through P that is parallel to L.*'

The additional complexity of the fifth postulate led many mathematicians to try to prove it as a theorem using the first four axioms. Such a proof was never achieved, and it is now known that it cannot be achieved, but in the process of attempting it, mathematicians discovered a new field of geometry. They did this by trying to show that the fifth postulate would be logically inconsistent with the first four postulates if it were to be changed. In other words, they assumed that 'Given a line (L) and a point (P) not on line (L), there is *not* just one line that can be drawn through P that is parallel to L.' Rather than finding this logically inconsistent as they expected, they were able to create multiple consistent geometries different from that of Euclid. These became known as non-Euclidean geometries which describe geometry on surfaces other than Euclidean (flat) **planes** and in spaces other than Euclidean space. It subsequently turned out that these non-Euclidean geometries are universal, and absolutely fundamental to everything in modern physics.

> KEY WORD
>
> **plane:** a flat surface that extends forever in two dimensions but has no thickness

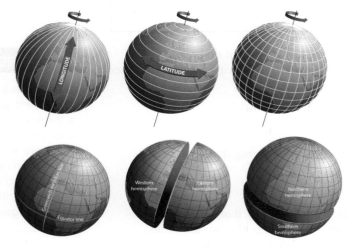

Figure 12.5: Lines of longitude are parallel at the equator and run straight in both directions, but eventually merge

EXPLORE 12.7

One of the things you will have learnt in (Euclidean) geometry is that parallel lines can never meet. Draw two parallel lines on a sheet of paper. It may seem obvious to you that, providing they are straight, the two lines cannot meet, no matter how far you were to extend them. Now look at a two-dimensional map of the world at the equator. You will see that although the lines of longitude are parallel at the equator and *remain straight* as they extend north and south, they nevertheless get closer together until they eventually meet at the poles. That is because the geometry of the Earth is non-Euclidean. Indeed, the essential difference between Euclidean and most non-Euclidean geometries is the nature of parallel lines.

Using a marker pen, draw a triangle on a round balloon that is lying deflated on a flat surface. What do you notice about the sum of the angles inside the triangle while the balloon is deflated and lying flat? Now blow into the balloon. What happens to the angles inside the triangle when you inflate the balloon? Can you explain why?

DISCUSS 12.16

Consider each of Euclid's axioms/postulates in terms of the surface of a sphere: which of them remain true? Why do some fail? How does the human need for simple models and easily understood explanations manifest itself in mathematics?

DISCUSS 12.17

If Kant's *certain knowledge that could never be disputed* was soon superseded, what does this say about certainty in mathematics and other areas of knowledge?

The German philosopher Immanuel Kant (1724–1804) regarded all the propositions of mathematics as examples of *a priori* knowledge: 'knowledge absolutely independent of all experience'; knowledge that could not under any circumstances be mistaken or doubted. He held that it follows necessarily from the definition of a triangle as a figure with three straight sides where the sum of its interior angles is two right-angles, and that we can deduce this without any reference to experience (empirical evidence) at all. However, the emergence of non-Euclidean geometry a few decades later overturned this '*absolute and indisputable knowledge*'.

REAL-LIFE SITUATION 12.5

Human beings live on an approximate sphere, and although we dig and fly, we are mostly not very far from the surface, yet in most circumstances, we rely on Euclidean geometry to go about our daily lives. Why is that? When we construct a mathematical model, how can we decide which aspects of the world to include and which to ignore?

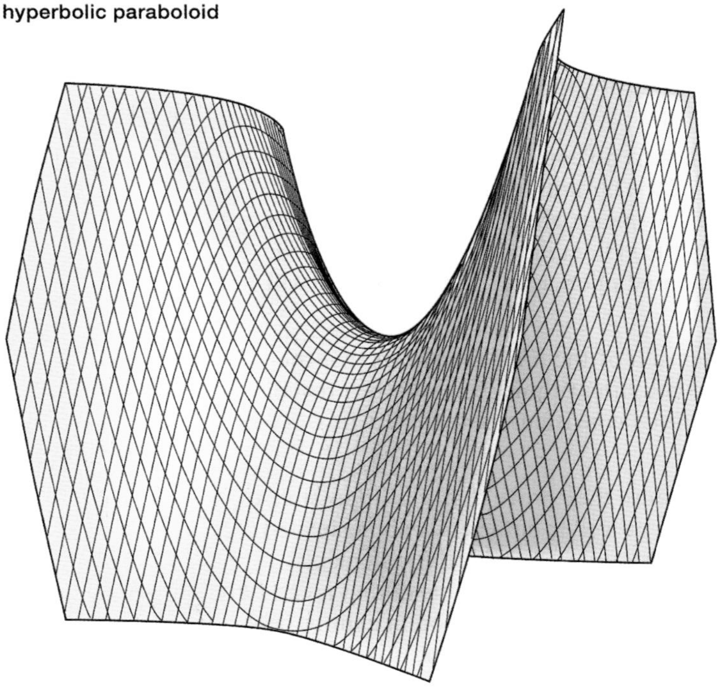

hyperbolic paraboloid

Figure 12.6: How are straight lines in curved space (as seen in Figure 12.6) different to straight lines on a plane?

Theorems

Theorems are the assertions or logical conclusions that can be derived by using axioms and deductive reasoning. Using his five axioms and deductive reasoning, Euclid derived various simple theorems, such as:

1   if two lines intersect, then they intersect in exactly one point

2   two straight lines cannot enclose an area

3   the sum of the angles inside a triangle is 180 degrees

4   the angles on a straight line add up to 180 degrees

Such simple theorems were then used to construct more complex proofs.

The formalist approach to understanding mathematics tried to establish a firm foundation by proving that consistently following logical reasoning in mathematics cannot lead to a contradiction. Unfortunately the endeavour failed because, in 1931, Kurt Gödel (1906–1978) famously showed both that there are well-formed formulae in some systems that cannot be proved within those systems, and that it cannot be proved with certainty that such sufficiently rich mathematical axiomatic systems do not lead to contradictions.

Gödel's incompleteness theorems

It was once believed that everything that is true in mathematics would necessarily have a mathematical proof (that every true theorem could be proved), and that mathematical systems could be proved to be consistent. That means that they could not prove any theorem and its opposite/converse true in the same system at the same time. However, Gödel showed that no non-trivial (interesting; rich enough to contain arithmetic) formal system can be proved to be complete or consistent, by proving two theorems:

The first incompleteness theorem states that there is no consistent system of axioms that can prove all truths about the arithmetic of the natural numbers. For any such consistent formal system, there will always be statements about the natural numbers that are true, but that cannot be proved within the system in which they are framed. In other words, in any sufficiently rich system based upon a set of axioms, there will always be true theorems that cannot be proved.

The second incompleteness theorem is an extension of the first, and shows that the consistency of a formal system rich enough to contain arithmetic cannot be proved. Note that this is *not* the same as saying that it is *not* consistent, only that, if it is consistent, that consistency cannot be proved.

The incompleteness theorems are important because they prove that it is impossible to create a set of axioms that allow everything to be proved in sufficiently sophisticated mathematics. To use a simple non-mathematical example, consider the statement: '*This statement cannot be proved.*' If the statement is false, it would mean that it can be proved. To prove the statement would be a contradiction, and therefore it cannot be the case that the statement is false. If, on the other hand, the statement is true, it means there are statements that are true but cannot be proven to be true. Most 'Gödelian sentences' involve self-reference of a similar kind.

DISCUSS 12.18

Gödel has shown us that not everything that is true can be proved, and we cannot prove that every mathematical system is consistent. What does this mean for certainty in mathematics and other areas of knowledge?

Besides realism and formalism, there are many other philosophical approaches to understanding mathematical objects, including **mathematicism**, **mathematical empiricism**, **constructivism**, **logicism** and **intuitionism**. These all tend to be variations of realist and non-realist positions. We will not go into them here, but it is important to realise that not even mathematicians agree about the foundations of mathematics, or what the relationship is between mathematics and the 'real world'. Neither do they agree about what constitutes the 'real world'.

B. Smaller

"Maybe it's not a wrong answer—maybe it's just a different answer."

REAL-LIFE SITUATION 12.6

The question about whether mathematics is invented or discovered has been asked in several ways so far, and how you answer reflects whether at heart you are a Platonist (mathematical realist), a formalist or perhaps believe one of the multiple variations of these two positions. How might the philosophical view you have of mathematics and mathematical objects affect the way you think about mathematics and mathematical knowledge? To what extent might your philosophical view of mathematics affect the way you think about the world?

12.5 Mathematics and certainty

> As far as the laws of mathematics refer to reality, they are not certain; and as far as they are certain, they do not refer to reality.
>
> **Albert Einstein** (1879–1955)

Mathematics is the area of knowledge in which most people expect to find certainty. If something has been proven mathematically, it is expected to be true with complete certainty. We rely on mathematical deductive reasoning to help us construct things like bridges and skyscrapers, send rockets into space and predict phenomena such as eclipses; and our experience tells us mathematics works. However, a number of mathematical developments in the recent past have somewhat shaken (or at least shifted) belief in mathematical certainty. These developments include:

- the work by Gödel that we have already looked at

- a computer-generated proof of the four colour theorem – this is the theorem that any plane broken into different regions like a map needs no more than four colours to colour it in so that no two adjoining regions have the same colour. Although long believed, the four colour theorem was eventually proved using a computer in 1976, using a method of exhaustive search that is so long and complex that it is not possible for a human to check it manually. Questions are raised about the nature of certainty when no human can be certain of the proof being offered

- the discovery of 'super sensitive' systems that are so sensitive to their initial conditions – the values we put into the equations at the 'start' – that *any* change in those initial conditions, no matter how tiny, will send the systems along a completely different trajectory (this is sometimes known as the butterfly effect)

- the emergence of new geometries with fractional dimensions – fractal geometries

- the development of the mathematics necessary to do the physics of quantum mechanics, which is based upon probability and statistics rather than precise predictable mathematical theories and which, among other things, appears to require a different kind of logic in which classical logical rules do not apply

- the very recent emergence of viable artificial intelligence (AI) systems based upon neural networks whose operation is so complex that no human being can understand it: we can see *that* the AI does what we want it to do, but we have no idea *how* it does so in any deep, comprehensive sense

In 2004, the mathematician Brian Davies (1944–) argued, '**Pure mathematics** will remain more reliable than most other forms of knowledge, but its claim to a unique status will no longer be sustainable. It will be seen as the creation of finite human beings, liable to error in the same way as all other activities in which we indulge. Just as in engineering, mathematicians will have to declare their degree of confidence that certain results are reliable, rather than being able to declare flatly that the proofs are correct.'

KEY WORD

pure mathematics: the study of mathematical ideas independently of any possible applications

DISCUSS 12.21

Why might pure mathematics be more reliable than most other areas of knowledge, even if not completely certain?

We have spoken at some length about Euclid and Euclidian geometry but, as we have seen, Euclid's theorems are not valid on the surface of a sphere or any non-planar surface. Further, geometric planes do not exist in 'real-life', nor do sections of planes. Therefore, we can say with reasonable confidence that there is nowhere in the universe where Euclid's geometry is true. It is a beautiful, **elegant**, useful system, but it bears only a superficial resemblance to reality.

KEY WORD

elegant: concise; stylish and graceful

DISCUSS 12.22

Euclid's geometry has been rigorously proved from his five postulates, but it is not true except in imaginary circumstances that do not exist in the real word. What does this say about the relationship between proof and truth?

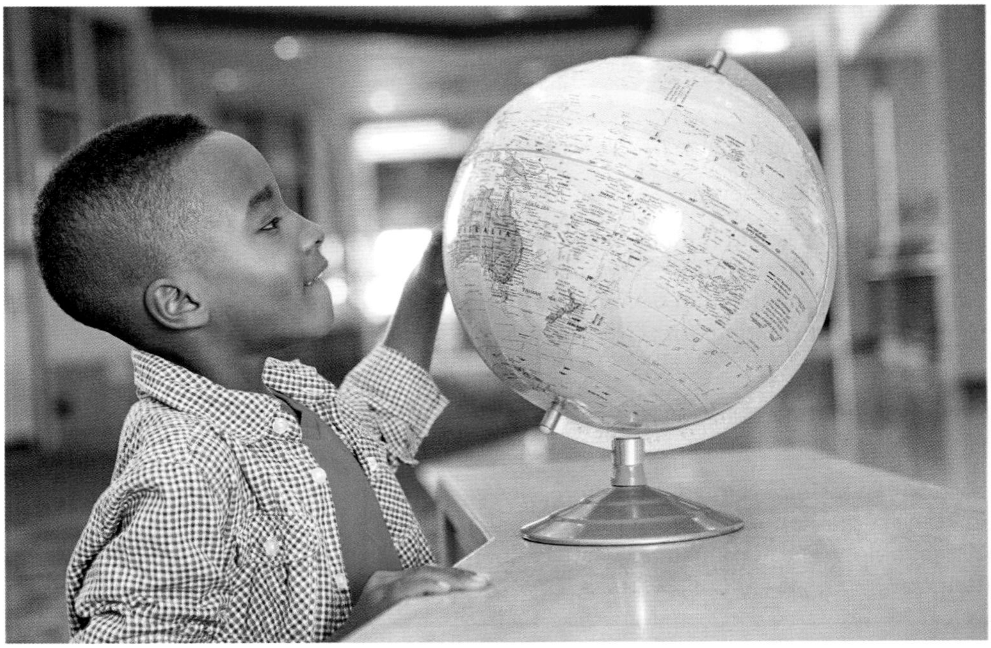

Figure 12.7: Using lines of latitude and longitude on a globe

---

EXPLORE 12.8

1   If you start at Stjørdal in Norway and travel due east along the line at 64 degrees latitude until you get to Anadyr in Russia, the distance is 5,717 km. If you then travel due south along the line at 178 degrees longitude until you arrive in Funafuti, Tuvalu, you will travel an additional 8,145 km.

2   Draw this as a right-angled triangle, then calculate the distance you would need to travel if you go directly from Stjørdal to Funafuti using Pythagoras's theorem: $a^2 + b^2 = c^2$

3   Did you calculate a distance close to 9,951 km? The actual distance directly from Stjørdal to Funafuti is 13,832 km.

4   Discuss in class: Why was the result of your calculation so far from the actual distance? What does this mean for the truth of *Pythagoras's theorem*?

Deductive reasoning

We have discussed deductive reasoning in Chapter 3, and will return to it again in more detail in Chapter 13, but it is also an essential tool in mathematics, where deductive reasoning is used to create mathematical proofs using mathematical axioms as premises. For example, you may want to prove that the sum of any two even numbers (let's call them x and y) is even. That is to say, $x + y = 2n$ for **integer** n.

Because you know x is even and y is even, you can say $x = 2a$ for some a, where a is half of ($\frac{x}{2}$), and $y = 2b$ for some b, where b is half of $\frac{y}{2}$.

Therefore: $x + y = 2a + 2b$

$x + y = 2(a + b)$

You know $2(a + b)$ is divisible by 2, so $x + y$ is divisible by 2.

Therefore, the sum of any two even numbers must be even.

The advantage of a mathematical proof like this is that it holds true for any value of x and y, providing x and y are even. There is no need to test every combination of even numbers to see if the theorem holds true (and it would be impossible to do so). Conclusions reached by deductive reasoning are *always* correct, *providing* the axioms are true and the reasoning used is valid.

> **KEY WORD**
>
> **integer:** a whole number

REFLECTION

Consider a mathematical proof you have studied in your mathematics class. How does being able to understand a mathematical proof (or being able to create a proof from first principles) help you to understand what mathematical knowledge is and how it is attained?

Why does mathematics work?

The idea that mathematics might not be 100% certain could be unsettling, yet it is clear from the great advances that humans have made in physics and engineering that mathematics works. The world seems to obey our equations, but it does not obey them in the way that we might assume. Rather, our equations have been designed to model the world around us. As we have already seen, the models that we create are far from perfect, but we are very good at choosing the right models and the right equations for each situation that we use mathematics for. If we lived in a different universe, perhaps even in a different part of this universe, say close to a black hole, our models and equations would no doubt be different too.

REAL-LIFE SITUATION 12.7

What is the role of selection (in terms of the models and equations we choose to use when solving problems) in the production of mathematical knowledge?

When we do mathematics, we tend to think that the mathematics we know when we have finished is more than we knew when we started. However, most of the mathematics we do does not result in new knowledge, even if we discover something that is new to us. Rather, mathematics is largely a **tautology** in that what we 'discover' is already implicit in the axioms the mathematics is founded on, providing we apply the rules consistently. This means that whatever we 'discover' by doing mathematics is already determined by the axioms, even if it is unknown to us. All Euclid's theorems are implicit in his postulates; we just cannot always see them from the postulates alone.

> **KEY WORD**
>
> **tautology:** saying the same thing in two different but completely equivalent ways; repeating something already implied

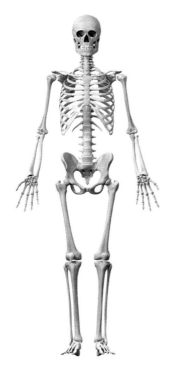

Figure 12.8: A tautology: the usual human body has enough bones to create an entire human skeleton

A good example is the so-far-unproved Goldbach's conjecture, which states that every even number greater than 2 can be expressed as the sum of two prime numbers $(4 = 2 + 2; 6 = 3 + 3; 8 = 5 + 3$, etc). All mathematicians seem to believe intuitively that the conjecture is true, but nobody has so far been able to prove it; whether it is true must – so most Platonist mathematicians believe – nevertheless be embedded (buried) in the axioms of arithmetic; we just cannot 'see it'.

DISCUSS 12.23

To what extent does belief play a role in mathematics?

Inductive reasoning

Although formal systems rely on deductive reasoning, inductive reasoning also has a place in mathematics. As we will discover in Chapter 13, inductive reasoning is the form of reasoning that reaches general, often universalised conclusions based on a finite number of observed results or patterns.

EXPLORE 12.9

Give the next term in the sequence: 1, 3, 5, 7, … .

Compare your answer with that of a classmate. Do you agree on the answer? How certain are you that your answer is correct?

If you were given options a to f as possible next terms in the sequence, would your answer change?

a   526

b $-\dfrac{7}{8}$

c $\sqrt{2}$

d   9

e   all of the above

f   none of the above

Among the options above, most people would say the answer is **d** 9. But this is not correct. The correct answer is actually **e** all of the above. The only incorrect answer is **f**.

The answer is only 9 if you assume that the intended sequence is the sequence of odd numbers in which the terms can be written as $x_n = a(2n-1)$ with a being the first term (x_1). In this arithmetic sequence, $x_5 = 1(2 \times 5 - 1) = 9$, so *in this case*, you would be correct to give the answer as 9.

But there are an infinite number of functions that could generate a sequence 1, 3, 5, 7… . In fact, it is possible for the next term to be any rational number.

The same is true even for a seemingly simple sequence of {1, 2, 3, …, 5, 6} in which you are asked to 'fill in the gap'. Unless the sequence is defined (for example as $a_n = 1 + a_{n-1}$), *any rational number* can legitimately be used to full in the gap.

To illustrate the point, look at the following formulae:

$$a_n = \left\{ \frac{1}{3}\left(-2n^5 + 34n^4 - 214n^3 + 614n^2 - 789n + 360\right) \right\}$$ generates the sequence 1, 2, 3, **–4**, 5, 6 for n = 1, 2, 3, 4, 5, 6.

$$a_n = \left\{ \frac{1}{6}\left(19n^5 - 323n^4 + 2033n^3 - 5833n^2 + 7530n - 3420\right) \right\}$$ generates the sequence 1, 2, 3, **42**, 5, 6, for n = 1, 2, 3, 4, 5, 6.

$$a_n = \left\{ \frac{1}{12}\left(913n^5 - 15521n^4 + 97691n^3 - 280291n^2 + 361560n - 164340\right) \right\}$$ generates the sequence 1, 2, 3, **917**, 5, 6, for n = 1, 2, 3, 4, 5, 6.

Indeed, if you have access to sophisticated mathematical software such as *Mathematica™*, a formula can be created that will generate any sequence you want, so if you are asked to 'fill in the gap' for the sequence {1, 2, 3, …, 5, 6} you can fill in *any integer at all* (and, again, infinitely many – but not all – non-integers) with full mathematical justification. This creates a paradox – the more mathematics you know, the less certain you are to give the expected or '*supposedly* right' answer.

EXPLORE 12.10

If you were given the sequence: 10, 30, 90, 270, 810, … and asked for the 6th term, you might be well advised to answer 2430 even though the answer could be almost anything at all. Why? What does this say about social expectations and perceptions of 'correctness'?

Create a mind-map to plan an answer to the question: To what extent is mathematical truth determined by social conventions?

Peer-assessment

Swap your mind-map with that of a classmate, and give each other feedback on the plan. What did your partner do well? What could be improved? Does the mind-map consider the question from different perspectives?

Self-assessment

Think about the feedback you have received. What did you do well? What might you choose to do differently if you were asked to write an essay on this question?

REAL-LIFE SITUATION 12.8

If any integer can be put into an undefined sequence, what does this say about IQ questions that ask participants to fill in the 'next' or nth term? What are those kinds of questions really measuring? To what extent might we say: *There is no such thing as a neutral question*?

12.6 Probability and statistics

I can prove anything by statistics except the truth.

George Canning (1770–1827)

DISCUSS 12.24

What do we mean by probability, and what is its relationship to statistics?

Although probability is widely recognised as a field of mathematics, there is some disagreement about whether statistics is a branch of mathematics or a separate science. This may be because they had separate origins. Statistics arose in the 17th century and primarily related to demographics rather than the abstract problems that mathematics traditionally tackled. However, in the early-19th century, mathematicians turned their attentions to statistical theory, and statistics has been largely brought under the mathematical umbrella. Those who like to maintain a distinction between mathematics and statistics argue that mathematics is about certainty and exactness, whereas statistics deals with the inexact.

> **KEY WORD**
>
> **demographics:** the characteristics of human populations

DISCUSS 12.25

To what extent is mathematics about certainty and exactness?

Some kinds of mathematical models, for example in physics, make very precise predictions about the behaviour of a system under ideal theoretical circumstances, but most systems in the 'real world' lack the purity of ideal models and are less easy to predict. Nevertheless, we still seek to understand systems despite the uncertainties created by the differences between ideal and real systems. For that reason, mathematics has developed two disciplines dealing with uncertainty and variation: probability and statistics. These are important in mathematics as an area of knowledge because they attempt to deal with predictions in, and knowledge of, systems where there is uncertainty.

One way to think of the relationship between probability and statistics is to think about probability as a theoretical approach to obtaining knowledge about things that are intrinsically uncertain – 'If the coin is fair, then …' – whereas statistics is a way to test whether our probability assumptions are legitimate – 'Given that it came up heads 37 times and tails 63 times, what is the likelihood that the coin is fair?' Both probability and statistics therefore attempt to furnish us with knowledge of an uncertain world.

> **KEY WORD**
>
> **population:** in the context of mathematics, the entire group of objects, measurements or events from which a sample is drawn

DISCUSS 12.26

How can we be sure that patterns we discern in the world are genuine features of reality, and provide a sound basis for mathematical knowledge?

This kind of statistics is often called 'inferential' statistics because it tries to infer something about the world from observed behaviour or data. Inferential statistics is based on probability theory; it uses random samples of data from a population to describe and make inferences about that population as a whole, usually because it is impossible to analyse the entire population. As only a sample is being analysed, it is important that the sample is an accurate representation of the whole population if the inferences are to be valid.

Another type of statistics – one we are possibly more familiar with in everyday life – is descriptive statistics, which deals with the gathering, analysis and interpretation of data from groups of things that we call populations. Descriptive statistics describe, show or summarise data from a population in a way that draws out some important and interesting features, and show up patterns that appear. Typically, they measure frequency, measures of central tendency (mean, median and mode), the size of variation and ranking. Descriptive statistics are used to provide useful information about a population.

Statistics are used for all kinds of purposes including weather forecasting, scientific research, setting insurance premiums, testing products, determining causes of disease, predicting elections and planning for schools. Almost all businesses, organisations academic disciplines and government departments rely heavily on statistics in one way or another, so it is important that statistics are trustworthy. However, they are notoriously difficult to collect fairly, and are famous for being misused and manipulated.

LINKING QUESTIONS 12.1

Indigenous societies: In Chapter 9, you will find reference to 'hidden populations'. These are usually people who live in remote places and are hard to contact, so they are frequently missed when sampling the human population of the geographical area they live in. How might their omission from statistical data affect the reliability of knowledge based on statistical methodologies?

Although we cannot predict the outcome of a single event reliably, we can predict the behaviour of large groups of events much better. Insurance companies have historical data that show the probability that a house will burn down, a driver will have an accident, a person will be taken seriously ill or when someone will die. They can analyse these data by age, gender and all sorts of other measures to produce insurance policies that reflect their exposure to risk. They know that, while the future of one particular person is impossible to predict reliably, the collective fortunes of 10,000, 100,000 or 1,000,000 people are very stable under normal conditions.

DISCUSS 12.27

Why is a group of people more stable than a single person when faced with uncertainty?

REAL-LIFE SITUATION 12.9

Suppose historic data showed that people from certain ethnic groups were more or less likely to have motoring accidents or die young; would it be ethical to surcharge their premiums accordingly? Is there some knowledge that cannot be ethically used?

Modern technology helps us to deal with large datasets more easily, and we can now ask more ambitious questions and look for less obvious patterns in all sorts of data sets that used to be too large to manage, especially in areas like health. Big data, as it is generally called, can also be used by computers to detect patterns in data that human beings did not even suspect to be there, and so did not look for. You may have already read about big data in Chapter 5. This kind of analysis, often using artificial intelligence (AI), is starting to disclose hidden and sometimes profound connections in data we have until now thought either empty or benign, using techniques that are based on applied statistics.

The misuse of statistics is unfortunately very common, and can be misguided, accidental or deliberate. The most common types of misuse include:

- faulty sampling: typically taking either too small a sample and/or a non-representative sample

- faulty polling: asking leading or loaded questions

- drawing false conclusions from **correlations**, such as inferring causal connections on the basis of mere correlation

- creating misleading graphs in which the scales are not clear, are foreshortened to exaggerate variation or are non-existent

- selection bias: choosing a sample population that has a special interest in the subject being studied (this is a specific type of faulty sampling)

> **KEY WORD**
>
> **correlation:** relationship; all sets of data exhibit correlation: some are positive; some are negative; some are neutral or negligible; correlation in itself never justifies an inference of causal connection, although it may suggest it

Leading and loaded questions

The use of leading and loaded questions is a common problem when polling for people's preferences or opinions, and you will come across them again in Chapter 14. Leading questions are questions that suggest the way you are expected to answer, and loaded questions are questions that contain an assumption within them. Both types of question put the person who is answering in a difficult situation, and often cause the person to answer in a way that they otherwise would not. For example, when people were asked, 'Do you get headaches often?' they went on to report a higher incidence of headaches than the number they reported if they were asked, 'Do you get headaches occasionally?'

REAL-LIFE SITUATION 12.10

Loaded questions are usually fairly obvious, but leading questions can often be very subtle. On what basis can we decide whether a question is neutral or not?

Descriptive statistics can be used to show the percentage of people in different countries who participate in organ donation schemes. If you look at the statistics, some countries have a far greater participation rate than others. What sets the countries with high participation rates apart from countries with low participation rates is not primarily religious or social values as might be expected; rather, it appears to be the way in which people are asked to participate.

Figure 12.9: The questions we ask will affect the data we collect

The countries that have fewer organ donors have an opt-in system which usually involves them filling in a form that says something along the lines of 'Check the box below if you want to participate in the organ donor programme.' The majority of people do not check the box, and as a result, most people do not join the programme. Countries that have a higher number of organ donors have an opt-out system which involves a form that says something like, 'Check the box below if you don't want to participate in the organ donor programme.' Again, most people do not check the box, and therefore join the organ donor programme.

EXPLORE 12.11

1   Look at a to f. There are three loaded questions and three leading questions. Which questions are leading and which are loaded? What are the assumptions contained in each of the loaded questions? What are you being led to say in each of the leading questions?

    a   What makes Ms Fernando such a good teacher?

    b   Do you have any problems with your boss?

    c   Do you think house prices will rise this year?

    d   Do you think we should convict the criminal?

    e   Are you naïve enough to believe mainstream media?

    f   How large was the dog that you saw?

2   Rewrite the questions in a way that is neither loaded nor leading.

Peer-assessment

Share your rewritten questions with a partner and give feedback on whether you think the questions your partner has written are now fair.

Self-assessment

How many of the questions were you able to write in a fair way? What was the main difficulty in the task? If you were to do a statistical assignment, do you think you could create a fair set of questions which would give you non-biased data to analyse?

DISCUSS 12.28

How can the features of ordinary languages help or frustrate the production of knowledge even when using statistical mathematics as a tool? To what extent are mathematics, the human sciences and language interdependent?

REFLECTION

How often do you take statistics at face value without really thinking about them? What do you need to be aware of when considering knowledge claims generated by statistical information?

12.7 Mathematical intuition

DISCUSS 12.29

What does intuition mean to you?

Many mathematicians regard intuition as an essential part of mathematics, but it is far from clear what intuition is, where it comes from, why it is important and whether it is reliable.

Our brains continually process information without us being conscious of them doing so, and we rely on this unconscious processing to go about our daily lives. For example, once you know your way, you might walk from one class to another, or walk home without having to consciously think about the route you are taking. Intuition is believed to emerge from this unconscious processing, and is generally regarded as the emergence of spontaneous feelings (sometimes called gut feelings) we sometimes experience when faced with a problem to solve, or a choice or decision to make.

Raymond Wilder (1896–1982) claimed that intuition is necessary in the evolution of mathematical concepts, mathematical research and for creativity within mathematics, but also acknowledged that mathematical intuition is reliant upon mathematical knowledge for its growth. **Fields medallist** Terrence Tao (1975–) also wrote about the importance of intuition as a way of knowing the truth of something before there is an airtight proof. So intuition involves 'feeling our way' in literal or metaphorical spaces where we do not know how to go on.

KEY WORD

Fields medal: an award made every four years by the International Congress of Mathematics to recognise outstanding mathematical achievements; it is sometimes described as the equivalent of a Nobel Prize for mathematics

It has been claimed that intuition allows mathematicians to have a conceptual bird's-eye-view, which allows them to draw inferences from high-level abstractions without having to systematically trace out each step. It is as if their prior experience somehow 'programmes' their unconscious minds in ways that enable them to generate hypotheses and suggestions about how to go on when their conscious minds are 'lost'.

But the human ability to bypass computational, conscious steps can also cause us to see patterns where none exist, or fail to see them where they do; and this can introduce error. For example, many people find it surprising to find two people in a school class sharing the same birthday. With 365 days in a year, and perhaps around 20–30 people in a class, most of us intuit that each person will have a different birthday, but the probability is that in any group of 23 people, there is a greater than 50% chance (in fact a 50.73% chance ignoring leap years) that two of them will share a birthday. This is often called the birthday paradox.

EXPLORE 12.12

Every student in the class should collect the birthdays of 23 or more randomly grouped people. You could do this by each going to different classes and getting the birthdays of the children in them, or finding the birthdays of 23 or more celebrities online. (If you find the birthdays of a group of 40 people, there is an 89.12% chance that two will share a birthday.)

Once you have your list of people and their birthdays, look to see how many matching birthdays are in your group.

CONTINUED

Compare your results with those of your classmates. If you have 12 or more students in the class who have done this exercise with different groups, you would expect half of the groups to have a matching birthday within them.

REAL-LIFE SITUATION 12.11

Why do you think most of us do not find the birthday paradox intuitive?

There seems to be a correlation between the amount of mathematics we know and understand, and our ability to rely on mathematical intuition. If, for example, you were asked to intuit a **ballpark** answer for 112×296 without working it out, you would probably expect the answer to be in the vicinity of just over 30,000, rather than guessing the answer to be in the millions or under 1,000, because you have a solid understanding of multiplying in a number system to the base 10.

When you are working on mathematical problems in your maths classes, if you come across a problem that is slightly different from problems you have done before, you may be able to use your intuition to help you go on and solve it, and you can often check your answer in the back of your mathematics text book to see if your method was correct. If your intuition is wrong or cannot help you, your teacher can usually give you some guidance. The same is true if you were to study mathematics at undergraduate level at university. However, if you were developing new mathematics or solving problems that have never been solved before, there would be no people who could tell you how to go about it, and no answers to check in the back of a book to make sure you are on the right track, so a mathematical intuition based on a deep understanding could be crucial to finding a way through.

KEY WORD

ballpark: estimated, rough, imprecise

EXPLORE 12.13

Imagine a piece of string wrapped around the Earth's equator – that is about 40,000 km. Roughly how much *more* string do you think you would you need for it to sit 15 cm above the ground, all the way around?

a   1 metre

b   1 kilometre

c   1,000 kilometres

First use your intuition to decide your answer. Now stop and think about how you would calculate it. Try to calculate the correct answer (or look it up on the internet). Did your intuition give you the correct answer? Did your intuition help you to work out how to calculate the correct answer?

You could try the same thought experiment by imagining a string around the moon's equator (about 11,000 km). If you then imagine the string sitting 15 cm above the surface of the moon, how would the extra string needed compare with the extra string needed for the problem about the Earth? What about the same problem applied to a tennis ball? Or the sun? What does your intuition tell you? Find out if your intuition is correct.

DISCUSS 12.30

Do you think that your intuition might be more reliable in some fields of mathematics than in others? Why might that be?

Bertrand's box paradox

Bertrand's box paradox is a paradox of probability theory described by a French mathematician, Joseph Bertrand (1822–1900), in 1889.

Imagine you have three boxes, each with two drawers. In each drawer is one coin. In the first box (GG), each drawer has a gold coin; in the second box (SS), the two coins are silver; and the third box (GS) contains one gold coin and one silver coin. Assume you choose a box at random and open one of its drawers, in which you find a gold coin. What is the probability that there will be a gold coin in the second drawer? What does your intuition tell you?

If you say the probability of a second gold coin is 0.5 (one in two chance), you probably reasoned that because the coin was gold, you must have selected either the box with GG or the box with GS, therefore there is a one in two chance that the second coin will be gold. It sounds very reasonable, however it is incorrect.

Although it is true that you must have selected either the box with GG or the box with GS, the coin could have come from either the G drawer of GS or *either* of the two drawers of the box with GG. In other the words, the second drawer to be opened could either be the S drawer of GS or either of the two GG drawers, so there is a two in three chance that the second coin will also be gold.

EXPLORE 12.14

The Jones family was selected at random from families that have two children, and you are told their older child is a girl.

The De Zoyza family has two children, and was selected at random from all two-child families where at least one of the children is a boy.

Assuming that the chances of having a girl or a boy are both one in two, with a partner try to decide, first using your intuition, and then trying to work it out mathematically: What is the probability that both of the Jones' children are girls? What is the probability that both of the De Zoyza's children are boys?

Did your intuition give you the same answer in both cases? What about after you tried to work it out? The probability for the Jones family having two girls given that the first child is a girl is one in two. However, the probability that the De Zoyza family have two boys is one in three. Can you work out why? (If you cannot work out the reason, you can look up the 'Two children problem'.)

Infinity

Infinity (∞) is a mathematical concept that can be very counter-intuitive; it may even leave us incapable of thinking at all, and so be, in a sense, beyond understanding. You might like to think of infinity as the 'final' number of the set of natural numbers {1, 2, 3, 4, . . ., ∞} in which the *n*th term in this sequence obviously has no 'greatest' number because whatever number *n* we thought to be greatest there would always be *n* + 1 and so on, forever.

Mathematicians have been troubled by infinity since ancient times, and one of the ways they have attempted to come to terms with it uses the concept of **countability**.

One way of thinking of this was suggested by David Hilbert (1862–1943): imagine a cloakroom in a hotel with capacity for an infinite number of guests in an infinite number of rooms. Suppose the hotel has an infinitely large cloakroom. The cloakroom has coat-hooks labelled {1, 2, 3, ...}. If we can hang the elements of a set onto these hooks, one to each hook, then the set is countable; if not, we cannot. It does not matter if the set is *infinite* because we have infinitely many coat-hooks in our imaginary hotel. We might think/intuit that necessarily *all sets* are countable in this sense, perhaps because we imagine taking one element and hanging it on hook #1, then another and hanging it on hook #2, and so on; but we would be wrong.

The set of integers {... –3, –2, –1, 0, 1, 2, 3, ...} is countable, and has ∞ terms even though it appears to contain 'twice as many' terms as the set of natural numbers. A seemingly even larger infinite set of numbers is the set of rational numbers. There is an infinite set of rational numbers between 0 and 1, and between any other integers on the number line. This means that there are infinitely more rational numbers than integers, yet even the set of rational numbers can be proved to be countable, and so contains the same ∞ terms as the set of natural numbers. Similarly, it seems *obvious* that there are half as many *even* whole numbers as there are whole numbers, but since we can 'hang' the even numbers on our coat-hooks very easily (2 goes on #1; 4 goes on #2; 6 goes on #3; etc.), there are in fact 'just as many' even numbers as numbers. The same goes for odd numbers and rational numbers. We seem to be coming to the conclusion that any set of any kind of number has the same 'size' (albeit an infinite size). But that proves to be a mistake, too.

Infinite sets can get bigger than simple infinity because there are an infinite number of infinite sets. We have seen that the set of rational numbers between 0 and 1 is infinite, yet countable. However, if we look at the set of real numbers between 0 and 1, there are infinitely many, which, unlike rational numbers, are *uncountable* and so the set of real numbers is an infinitely larger set than the set of rational numbers. And we can go bigger still with the infinite set of all infinite sets.

Georg Cantor (1845–1918) showed using his **diagonalisation argument** that there are *more* real numbers than there are natural, odd, even or rational numbers; as a result, we have to acknowledge that there is *more than one kind of infinity*. This ushered in an entirely new mathematics: the mathematics of transfinite arithmetic in which our intuitions (unless we are as clever as Georg Cantor) completely fail us.

KEY WORDS

infinity: something without bounds, often treated as an unreal number

countability: a set is *countable* if it can be put into a one-to-one relationship with the natural numbers {1, 2, 3, ...}

diagonalisation argument: a mathematical proof published by Cantor in 1891 which demonstrated that there are infinite sets which cannot be put into one-to-one correspondence with the infinite set of natural numbers

EXPLORE 12.15

Hilbert's Grand Hotel is the largest hotel in the universe, with an infinite number of rooms. One night, an infinite number of guests were staying, so every room was full. An unexpected traveller arrived in the lobby and asked for a room. The concierge was able to accommodate her by asking each guest to move to the room numbered one higher than the room they were in. By doing this, Room 1 became empty and the traveller was able to stay there.

Assume you are the manager of Hilbert's Grand Hotel, and on a night when the hotel is full, an infinite number of unexpected travellers arrive, all needing accommodation. How might you make room for them?

Figure 12.10: Infinity poses many problems for our intuition

DISCUSS 12.32

How important is imagination in mathematics?

Compound interest

Mathematics has important applications in finance and economics, where calculations to do with shares and insurance, loans and accounts are essential to good management. Yet one area of mathematics that often defies our intuition is **compound interest**. Even if compound interest is not a part of your mathematics syllabus, it is important that you are aware of its counter-intuitive nature, because it is very likely that you will one day require a student loan or a mortgage, or you may consider opening a savings account.

Assuming interest is compounded annually, compound interest is calculated with the formula $A = P(1 + i)^n$ where A is the total amount owed (or received), P is the amount borrowed, i is the interest payable, and n is the number of years over which the loan operates. If the interest is compounded monthly, the formula would be

$$A = P\left(1 + \frac{i}{12}\right)^{12n}$$

KEY WORD

compound interest: the addition of interest to the principal sum of a loan or deposit to make that sum larger, and therefore make subsequent interest greater; or in other words, interest on interest

To find how much interest you will owe on £100 at 7% compound interest at the end of 1, 2, 3, … years if you do not pay anything off, you first calculate $100 + 100 \times \dfrac{7}{100} = 107$ for the first year. This is the same as $100 \times (1.07)$. So at the beginning of the second year, you owe £107, not £100, and interest is charged on all of that including the interest added to the original loan. After two years, you then owe $£100 \times 1.07 = £114.49$, so the interest on the second year is a little bit more (just £0.49 more) than it was in the first year. This may seem very reasonable, but how much do you owe after 10 years on this basis? What does your intuition tell you?

The answer is £196.72 or almost *double* the original loan, and if the interest were to be compounded daily rather than yearly, you would owe £201.36. After 20 years, you would owe £386.97 (or £405.47 if compounding occurred on a daily basis) roughly *four times* as much as the original loan.

And our intuition does not deal well with the effect of, say, doubling the rate of interest to 14%. What does your intuition tell you the outstanding loan would be after 10 years then? The answer is £370.70, but since £100 of this is what you borrowed, the interest is now £270.70 rather than £96.72, so almost *three times as much*, despite the fact that the interest rate only doubled.

EXPLORE 12.16

Suppose instead of borrowing at 7%, you borrow £100 at 1,000% as is the case with some loans being advertised: what do you owe after one, two, three, four or ten years on your loan if you do not pay anything off? Since most people tempted to borrow money at these rates think they only need the money for 'a few days', how much do you think you will need to pay back on your £100 loan after just one week or one month? What about after a year, two years or ten years? How long will it take before you owe over £1,000,000? Make your guesses before you read further.

The answer to the previous activity is something like £119.23 after just one week, so you are paying £19.23 interest per week, over 19% interest *per week*. After one month, you will owe something like £183.33, almost double what you borrowed. After one year at an interest rate of 1,000% your £100 loan has grown to $100 + 100 \times \dfrac{1000}{100} = £1,100$, eleven times the loan you took out. After two years, it grows to $100 \times 11 \times 11 = £12,100$; after three years to £133,100 and after four years to well over one million, in fact £1,464,100; and after ten years, if you are unfortunate enough to be unable to pay off the loan because it has grown so quickly even after one year, you will owe £2,593,742,460,100 …, over two-and-a-half *trillion* pounds!

Most of us have almost no reliable intuition about the workings of compound interest!

REAL-LIFE SITUATION 12.12

What are the ethical implications of lending money at high interest rates if those borrowing lack the intuition or the mathematical skills to understand what they are contracting into? What might the relationship be between mathematics and ethical knowledge?

EXPLORE 12.17

Suppose you were fortunate enough to have £1,000,000 in a plastic bag under your bed. Assume that you do not invest the money; instead, you take out £25 per day every day for living expenses. How long would it be before the bag was empty? Do not calculate; what is your intuition?

People often guess 3 to 10 years, but the actual answer is 40,000 days or over 100 years. Actually 109 years and about 7 months.

Although many great mathematicians throughout history have stressed the important role that intuition has played in helping them to solve problems and create new ways of doing mathematics, it is important to bear in mind that their mathematical intuitions are born of deep familiarity with, and understanding of, the patterns relating to the mathematics they are working with. Without that deep knowledge, we do better to rely on actual calculations.

REFLECTION

Although mathematicians claim to rely heavily on their intuitions when approaching problems, mathematical intuition is generally not a method that most non-mathematicians can rely upon. Do you think your intuition would be more reliable in other themes or areas of knowledge? Why might your intuition be more reliable in some areas of knowledge than others?

12.8 Aesthetics

DISCUSS 12.33

What is beauty? Why might some people equate mathematics with beauty?

Mathematics, rightly viewed, possesses not only truth, but supreme beauty – a beauty cold and austere, like that of sculpture, without appeal to any part of our weaker nature, without the gorgeous trappings of painting or music, yet sublimely pure, and capable of a stern perfection such as only the greatest art can show. The true spirit of delight, the exaltation, the sense of being more than Man, which is the touchstone of the highest excellence, is to be found in mathematics as surely as poetry.

Bertrand Russell (1872–1970)

Some of the world's greatest mathematicians have regarded **aesthetics** as being of central importance to their work. They gain enormous pleasure from mathematical research, and demonstrating the beauty and elegance of particular theorems, proofs and theories. The French mathematician and theoretical physicist Henri Poincaré (1854–1912) regarded mathematical beauty as an aesthetic feeling that all true mathematicians recognise. Others have gone further, recognising mathematical beauty not only as a well-known phenomenon, but also as one of the key motivations behind the formulation of mathematical proofs, and as a criterion for choosing one mathematical theorem over another. Therefore, the German mathematician and

KEY WORD

aesthetics: the study and appreciation of beauty

theoretical physicist Hermann Weyl (1885–1955) famously declared: 'My work always tried to unite the true with the beautiful, but when I had to choose one or the other, I usually chose the beautiful.'

It has been argued that there is an aesthetic way of understanding reality, and this aesthetic sense is as important as any other method for knowing, and not just in the arts. To suppress or ignore aesthetics is to restrict how we can experience and interpret the world.

Mathematicians rely heavily on aesthetic modes of knowing. Producing mathematics requires engaging in the creation process, and the aesthetic nature of the activities of a mathematician helps to provide coherence to mathematical knowledge.

Plato considered mathematical beauty as the highest form of beauty, and scientists through the ages have noted, often with some astonishment, not only the remarkable success of mathematics in describing the natural world, but also that the best mathematical formulations are usually the most beautiful. Almost all research mathematicians pepper their description of important mathematical work with terms like *elegance*, *simplicity* and *beauty*. Some have argued that mathematical principles are experienced as *beautiful* because they point directly to the fundamental structure of the universe.

In February 2014, a team of British researchers, including two neurobiologists, a physicist and a mathematician, published a ground-breaking study, 'The experience of mathematical beauty and its neural correlates', on the human experience of mathematical beauty. Their research showed that those who appreciate the beauty of mathematics activate the same parts of their brain when they look at a beautiful mathematical formula as others do when appreciating the visual arts or music. This suggests that there is a neurobiological basis to mathematical beauty.

Educationalist Paul Betts (1965–) suggests that recognising the importance of a connection between aesthetics and mathematics would help to make mathematics more accessible to students, and to bridge the gap between mathematicians and every citizen, perhaps removing some of the mystery associated with mathematics and the activity of mathematicians.

REAL-LIFE SITUATION 12.13

We have spoken of mathematics as a system of recognising and classifying patterns. Are all patterns beautiful? What features best contribute to a pattern's beauty?

Fractals

Fractals are never-ending patterns made of geometric shapes which repeat their structure on an ever-smaller scale. Fractal-like behaviours are often found in nature in things such as clouds, snowflakes, Romanesco cauliflowers (also called brocciflowers) and even the physiological processes in our bodies. Technically, these are called quasi-fractals because the fractal-like behaviour cannot continue infinitely in nature like it can in mathematics.

In the field of aesthetics, researchers are trying to discover what makes works of art and natural scenes visually appealing. One important factor they have identified is the presence of fractals. If you look closely at Jackson Pollock's *Number 1* on the internet it has a fractal-like nature. Computer pattern analysis has shown that the fractal nature of Pollock's art is similar to the fractal patterns in nature.

In 2004, an interdisciplinary group of psychologists, neuroscientists, physicists and mathematicians measured people's responses to fractals in nature, art and mathematics. They discovered that fractals induce particular eye movements that activate the brain in a way that people enjoy an aesthetic experience, and their stress is reduced.

DISCUSS 12.34

How can imaginative processes that are used in the visual arts and mathematics lead to knowledge about the world?

Figure 12.11: The beautiful fractal nature of the Romanesco cauliflower

The Fibonacci series

The Fibonacci series (also called the Fibonacci sequence) is named after a famous 13th-century Italian mathematician, but had been developed long before by a 6th-century Indian mathematician called Virahanka (विरहाङ्क). The series begins with 0 and 1, and then each subsequent term is the sum of the two terms before it. So the sequence is 0, 1, 1, 2, 3, 5, 8, 13, 21, 34, 55, ... The rule of this series can be written $x_n = x_{n-1} + x_{n-2}$. This series has many interesting properties. If you make a square of each of the numbers in the Fibonacci sequence, you can create the Fibonacci spiral.

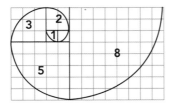

Figure 12.12: The Fibonacci spiral is constructed from the squares of the Fibonacci sequence

If you take the ratio of any two successive numbers in the sequence, the ratio gets closer and closer to a number that is called the golden ratio (also known as the golden mean) which is exactly $\dfrac{(1+\sqrt{5})}{2}$. This ratio is given the Greek symbol φ (phi), and is roughly equivalent to 1.618.

$$\frac{2}{1} = 2$$

$$\frac{3}{2} = 1.5$$

$$\frac{5}{3} = 1.6666\ldots$$

$$\frac{8}{5} = 1.6$$

$$\frac{13}{8} = 1.625$$

EXPLORE 12.18

144, 233 and 377 are three consecutive numbers from the Fibonacci sequence. Find the ratios of $\dfrac{233}{144}$ and $\dfrac{377}{233}$. The higher the numbers you use from the sequence, the closer their ratio will be to φ.

If you apply the Fibonacci sequence rule to two random numbers (instead of 0 and 1), the ratios that this sequence generates will also approximate the golden ratio, although it may take a little longer to get such close values. For example, if you start with 58 and 6, using the Fibonacci rule, you will generate a sequence:

58, 6, 64, 70, 134, 204, 338, 542, 880, 1422, 2302, 3724, 6026, 9750 …

Using the sequence generated above, find the ratios to see for yourself how the ratios converge to φ. Generate your own sequence by choosing two random numbers and applying the Fibonacci rule.

Fibonacci numbers have been described as 'nature's favourite numbers', and patterns connected with them can be found in such things as the petals of flowers, the branching pattern in trees and the arrangement of seeds on the head of a sunflower. Such arrangements ensure that things fit together in an efficient way so that, for example, each petal on a flower gets maximum exposure to sunlight and moisture.

There are many claims made about the golden ratio. and it can be hard to distinguish fact from fiction. One common assertion is that rectangular and spiral patterns based on it are particularly beautiful. Some people claim that the Parthenon was built according to the golden ratio, perhaps not intentionally, but because the proportions it creates are aesthetically pleasing.

EXPLORE 12.19

1   Visit the Interactive Mathematics website to explore its 'beauty mask'. Search for 'the maths behind the beauty'. Find some URLs of photographs of people you find attractive and paste the URLs into the box available, one at a time. You can use the facial mask to compare with the photographs you have chosen.

Do the photos you have chosen as attractive fit the golden ratio? Whether your chosen photographs fit the golden ratio or not, how scientific is this 'experiment'? What are the reasons for your answer?

2   With a partner, look at some photographs of a building you find attractive. (Examples might include the Taj Mahal in India, St Basil's Cathedral in Moscow, the Potala Palace in Tibet or Al Khazneh in Petra.) Take some measurements of different features of the building. Are any of the measurements proportional to others in the ratio of φ (1.618:1)?

Figure 12.13: Martha, a Neapolitan Mastiff, who won the 2017 World's Ugliest Dog competition

REAL-LIFE SITUATION 12.14

In 2017, Martha, a Neapolitan Mastiff, won the World's Ugliest Dog competition, but many animal enthusiasts, especially lovers of Neapolitan Mastiffs, would find her beautiful. Her face is symmetrical and partially fits the 'beauty mask' based on the golden ratio.

Do you agree with the competition judges that Martha is ugly, or do you think she is beautiful? What does this say about our ideas of beauty?

12.9 Mathematics and ethics

DISCUSS 12.35

Why is it important to learn mathematics?

Mathematics is the most widely taught of all subjects. Once regarded as the queen of the sciences, it is perhaps the only subject that is compulsory for most students from the earliest childhood years until their tenth year of schooling, or even beyond. The assumption is that mathematics is an essential element of preparing children for the world, and that they can only benefit from learning mathematics. But is this true?

Is mathematics harmful?

Mathematician and educationalist Paul Ernest (1944–) argues that school mathematics has sometimes left students feeling inhibited, belittled or rejected. Those students who are labelled as 'mathematical failures' can have their life choices reduced. He also argues that students who are successful in mathematics are often trained to think in ethics-free, **amoral** ways. In other words, they learn to think only about the abstract nature of the mathematical problems they solve, and do not concern themselves with the ways in which humans, industries and governments exploit the mathematics that is developed. He believes that by approaching mathematics as an amoral discipline, we implicitly support ethics-free governance.

KEY WORD

amoral: outside the scope of morality; lacking any moral framework

Ernest's solution is not to abandon the teaching of mathematics, but to pay more attention to the causes of success and failure and their impacts on learners, and to teach the social responsibility of mathematics alongside the teaching of mathematics. He believes all students and mathematicians need to be able to critically evaluate the uses and applications of mathematics.

In his paper, *The Struggle is Pedagogical: Learning to Teach Critical Mathematics*, Eric Gutstein (1952–) wrote that teaching critical mathematics, and in particular, mathematics for social justice, should not be merely an 'option' for mathematics teachers, but a requirement because it involves a responsibility to the future. Do you agree?

REAL-LIFE SITUATION 12.15

Can any subject be morally neutral? If you were to design a course called *Mathematics for Social Justice*, what would you include in it?

Ethics in statistics

Ethical issues abound in the use of statistics. It can be relatively simple for unscrupulous people to manipulate and hide data, using data that supports a particular view rather than using all data. We have already considered how data collection can be biased simply by the way questions are asked. This can be done inadvertently, but it can also be done deliberately, which is one reason why statistical research is best carried out by independent researchers rather than interested parties.

As well as collecting data in an ethical way, and using all data collected, including outliers, it is important that the data is properly represented and interpreted. Graphs need to be properly labelled and drawn to stated scales covering suitable ranges.

KEY WORD

outlier: a value or datum very different from others

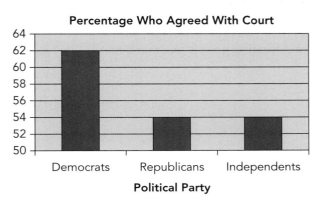

Figure 12.14: It is important that graphs fairly represent the data

In 2005, a young woman in a persistent vegetative state, Terri Schiavo, was removed from life support machines following a much publicised and long legal battle. Figure 12.14 is a graphic representation that was used by one media outlet to compare the political views of people who agreed with the court's decision to allow Terri Schiavo to be removed from life support.

At first glance, it looks as if there were three times as many Democrats who supported the decision than Republicans or Independents. (That is 300% more Democrats.) However, this is very misleading. If you look at the vertical scale (the y axis), it only begins at 50%. In fact, the number of Democrats who supported the court's decision was only slightly more than the number of Republicans and Independents who supported it. (62% vs 54%, which means just under 15% more Democrats than Republicans supported the decision.)

Graphs should show a baseline (preferably 0 on the vertical scale) to accurately represent data. When an arbitrary starting point is used, the graph can be very misleading, so the arbitrary starting point should be stated explicitly and emphasised.

DISCUSS 12.36

Can you think of some examples in which it might be reasonable to start a scale somewhere other than the baseline at zero?

Unfortunately, the misuse of statistics has made people increasingly distrustful of statistical information. This has led to statistics and statisticians having a declining authority, and opened the door to 'post-truth' and populist politics. However, it is a *false inference* to argue that because *some* statistics are misleading, biased or unreliable that means that *all* statistics are similarly tarnished.

To avoid flawed or biased questions, you need to be honest with yourself about whether you expect or desire a particular answer. You need to make sure that your questions do not expect responders to confirm your own beliefs or opinions, and that you remove any biased language. You also need to look at whether you are asking responders to give an answer that might not completely represent the way they would want to answer.

REFLECTION

'I am not a number; I am not a statistic; I am a human being.' How might you use mathematics and statistics in ways that avoid treating people like numbers or impersonal objects?

12.10 Conclusion

Mathematics is the area of knowledge most frequently associated with certainty, and its methodology, which relies primarily on deductive reasoning to provide rigorous mathematical proofs, is somewhat comforting even for those who perhaps do not regard themselves as 'mathematically minded'. There is something immensely appealing about the idea of demonstrating something in such a way that any rational person will come to the same conclusion, and it is not surprising that mathematics has often served as a model for knowledge.

Nevertheless, we have seen that mathematics is not just about deductive reasoning. Creativity, intuition and aesthetics all play significant roles in mathematics, particularly in its higher levels and in the development of new mathematical knowledge.

Mathematics provides us with a certainty that is rarely, if ever, found in any other area of knowledge, but even this most rigorous of subjects has limits to its certainty. At an abstract level, Gödel showed that we can never prove that mathematics is consistent in some circumstances. At a more practical level, we have seen that when mathematics is applied to the real world, we usually have a choice of axioms, and we can only decide which are the most useful by testing them against what we perceive in the world.

Mathematics can be regarded as an art, a science and a language. It plays a key role in a wide variety of subjects from all areas of knowledge. Although mathematics cannot give us absolute certainty in every instance, there is something surprising, captivating and mysterious about its extraordinary usefulness and effectiveness.

KNOWLEDGE QUESTIONS

1   'Film is one of the three universal languages, the other two: mathematics and music.' To what extent do you agree?

2   What room is there for personal interpretation or cultural differences in mathematical knowledge?

12.11 Linking questions

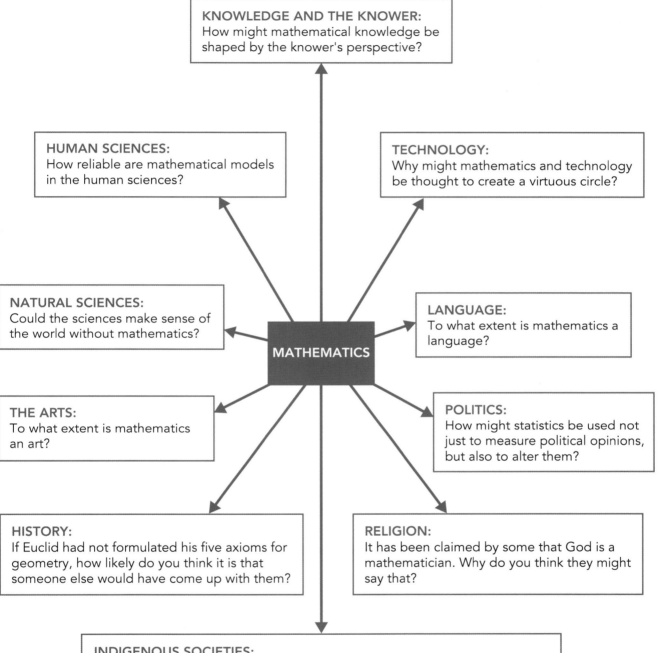

KNOWLEDGE AND THE KNOWER:
How might mathematical knowledge be shaped by the knower's perspective?

HUMAN SCIENCES:
How reliable are mathematical models in the human sciences?

TECHNOLOGY:
Why might mathematics and technology be thought to create a virtuous circle?

NATURAL SCIENCES:
Could the sciences make sense of the world without mathematics?

MATHEMATICS

LANGUAGE:
To what extent is mathematics a language?

THE ARTS:
To what extent is mathematics an art?

POLITICS:
How might statistics be used not just to measure political opinions, but also to alter them?

HISTORY:
If Euclid had not formulated his five axioms for geometry, how likely do you think it is that someone else would have come up with them?

RELIGION:
It has been claimed by some that God is a mathematician. Why do you think they might say that?

INDIGENOUS SOCIETIES:
A few indigenous communities do not have a language that enables them to count, only to talk about *a few* or *many*. In what ways might you expect their communities to be different from societies that can count?

12.12 Check your progress

Reflect on what you have learned in this chapter and indicate your confidence level between 1 and 5 (where 5 is the highest score and 1 is the lowest). If you score below 3, re-visit that section. Come back to this list later in your course. Has your confidence grown?

	Confidence level	Re-visited?
Do I understand what mathematics is and its relationship with other areas of knowledge?		
Can I describe some of the ways in which mathematical knowledge has been constructed and developed over time?		
Am I clear about the concept of mathematics as a language?		
Do I understand what mathematical objects are and what is meant by mathematical realism?		
Can I articulate what is meant by an imaginary number?		
Am I clear about what is meant by mathematical formalism, axioms and theorems?		
Do I appreciate the importance of Gödel's theorems in terms of the relationship between mathematical proofs and truth?		
Do I understand the difference between deductive and inductive reasoning, and how they are used in mathematics?		
Can I explain some of the issues that arise in the creation of statistical knowledge?		
Do I know how to critically assess questions that are used for gathering statistical data?		
Do I understand what is meant by mathematical intuition, and why many mathematicians regard it as an essential tool for developing new mathematical knowledge?		
Am I aware of the dangers for a non-mathematician trying to rely on intuition to solve mathematical problems?		
Can I discuss the relationship between mathematics and aesthetics?		
Am I familiar with some of the ethical issues that arise in mathematics?		

12.13 Continue your journey

- To find out more about the study of how the brain expeiences mathematical beauty, read: S Zeki, J.P.Romaya, D.M.T Benincasa, and M. F Atiyah "The experience of mathematical beauty and its neural correlates" in *Frontiers of Human Neuroscience* 13 Feb 2014 https://www.frontiersin.org/articles/10.3389/fnhum.2014.00068/full

- To build on the knowledge that you have gained in this chapter, you could read some of the following articles.

- If you would like to know more about **ethical approaches to mathematical education**, read: Paul Ernest 'The Ethics of Mathematics: Is Mathematics Harmful' in *The Philosophy of Mathematics Education Today*, 2018. Search the *Research Gate* website for the artible.

- For a general understanding of **mathematics and its relationship to deductive reasoning**, read: Liaqat Ali Khan, 'What is mathematics – an overview' in *The International Journal of Mathematics and Computational Science,* vol. 1, no 3, pp 98–101, 2015. Search the *Research Gate* website for the article.

- If you would like to know more about the **counting abilities displayed by some animals**, read: Michael Tenneson, 'More Animals Seem to Have Some Ability to Count', in *Scientific American,* 2009. Search the *Scientific American* website for the article.

- To explore **philosophical understandings of mathematics** further, particularly alternative approaches to realism and formalism, read: Stephen Ferguson, 'What is the philosophy of mathematics?' *Philosophy Now,* Winter 1997/1898. Search the *Philosophy Now* website for the article.

- If you would like to develop your understanding some of the **real-world challenges to the use of statistics**, read: William Davies, 'How statistics lost their power – and why we should fear what comes next' in *The Guardian*, 19 January 2017. Search the *Guardian* website for the article.

- If you are interested in knowing more about **connections between aesthetics and mathematics**, and the possibilities this creates for mathematical education, read: Paul Betts, 'Adding an Aesthetic Image to Mathematics Education'. Search the *Centre for Innovation in Mathematics Teaching* website for the article.

- For a deeper understanding of **fractals and their aesthetic appeal**, read: Richard Taylor, 'Fractal patterns in nature and art are aesthetically pleasing and stress-reducing' 31 March 2017 in *The conversation*. Search the *The Conversation* website for the article.

- To explore the **mathematics of beauty**, read: Mina Teicher, 'The Mathematics of Beauty', 2012. Search the *Institute for Advanced Study* website for the article.

- For a closer look at **how the golden ratio can be applied to architecture**, read: Gary Meisner, 'The Parthenon and Phi, the Golden Ratio', 20 January 2013. Search the *Golden Number* website for the article.

- For a fun exploration of **fractals**, read: Dr Dilts, 'Fractal dimensions', 15 September 2018. Search the *Infinity plus one - Math is awesome* website for the article.

- If you are interested in learning more about some of the **challenges to mathematical knowledge**, read: E B Davies, 'Whither Mathematics?' 2005, Whither Mathematics?' *Journal- American Mathematical Society*, vol 52, no 11, pp. 1350–1356. Search the *CiteSeerX* website for the article.

- If you are interested in learning about the **human experience of mathematical beauty** read: S Zeki, J.P.Romaya, D.M.T Benincasa, and M. F Atiyah 'The experience of mathematical beauty and its neural correlates' in *Frontiers of Human Neuroscience*, 13 Feb 2014. Search the *Frontiers of Human Neuroscience* website for the article.

> Chapter 13
The natural sciences

LEARNING INTENTIONS

This chapter will consider what the natural sciences are, how knowledge is developed within the natural sciences and how the scientific method influences the acquisition of knowledge in other areas of knowledge.

You will:

- understand what is meant by the scientific method, and appreciate the use of scientific equipment and models

- be aware of some of the limitations inherent in the scientific method

- develop an understanding of issues concerning objectivity, and learn about scientific paradigms

- recognise the role of inductive reasoning in developing scientific knowledge, and understand the principle of falsification

- be able to compare and contrast theoretical science with experimental science

- develop an appreciation of the scientific community and the many roles that it plays in developing scientific knowledge

- recognise the importance of communication in the natural sciences

- learn to discuss some of the ethical issues that are found in the natural sciences, and some of the knowledge issues that arise

Analyse each of the following quotations and discuss the questions that follow:

1   'Science is not only a disciple of reason but, also, one of romance and passion.' **Stephen Hawking** (1942–2018)

2   'Science knows no country, because knowledge belongs to humanity, and is the torch which illuminates the world.' **Louis Pasteur** (1822–1895)

3   'One of the things I love about science is that you always end up with new questions.' **Andrea M. Ghez** (1965–)

4   'Science is not a heartless pursuit of objective information. It is a creative human activity, its geniuses acting more as artists than as information processors.' **Stephen Jay Gould** (1941–2002)

5   'Einstein's results again turned the tables and now very few philosophers or scientists still think that scientific knowledge is, or can be, proven knowledge.' **Imre Lakatos** (1922–1974)

For each quotation, consider:

a   Do you agree or disagree with the quotation?

b   What does the quotation tell you about the speaker's perspective on science?

c   Does the quotation challenge or affirm your own perspective on science?

d   Do you think the quotation could apply to other areas of knowledge? If so, in what ways?

13.1 Introduction

DISCUSS 13.1

What do we mean by the 'natural world'? What might fall outside of the scope of the natural world?

Science is both a body of knowledge and a process of discovery. It explores the natural world from subatomic particles through to the galaxies that make up our universe, and everything that falls in between.

The natural sciences explore and try to understand the natural world around us. In essence, this is the physical world and the forces that act upon it. Under the umbrella of the natural sciences come the life sciences, which are comprised of the various branches of biology, and the physical sciences, which include disciplines such as physics, chemistry and the earth sciences.

The natural sciences provide us with knowledge that can enhance human lives, extending them quantitatively and qualitatively through better nutrition and hygiene as well as improved medical interventions; improving standards of living through the invention of labour-saving devices; and better infrastructures, which give us greater access to products that benefit us. The natural sciences also help us to explore the world we live in, and have the potential to help us solve problems facing the world, including those of our own making.

Perhaps because of the power that scientific knowledge can wield, there is a tendency for many people to want to declare a range of knowledge claims as 'scientific' when, in reality, they fall short of the criteria required to be regarded as knowledge claims within the natural sciences. One of the tasks facing us when we assess scientific knowledge claims is to distinguish genuine scientific knowledge claims from **pseudoscience** and propaganda.

KEY WORD

pseudoscience: a system of beliefs and practices that are claimed to be scientific but which are incompatible with the scientific method

13.2 The scientific method

REAL-LIFE SITUATION 13.1

Think about the general steps involved when you do an experiment in science. To what extent might those steps change depending on the experiment you are conducting?

The natural sciences have a long history reaching back into antiquity, when early philosophers tried to understand the world around them. People of all ages and across all cultures have been fascinated by the night sky, and some of the earliest scientific observations were made of the sky. Records of solar and lunar eclipses were kept in Mesopotamia from 747 BCE, while detailed records of observations of comets and other astronomical phenomena were made by unnamed astronomers in China going back as far back as 613 BCE, and possibly earlier.

We have accounts of **empirical** studies that were undertaken by natural philosophers such as Thales of Miletus (624–528 BCE) and Aristotle (384–322 BCE). Later, **polymaths** such as Abu Ali al-Hasan ibn al-Hasan ibn al-Haytham (965–1040), Abu Rayhan al-Biruni (973–1050), Roger Bacon (1219–1292) and Galileo Galilei (1564–1642) all made significant contributions to the ways in which science is done, and helped prepare the way for what we now call the **scientific method**.

The gradual move to base scientific knowledge on observations and experimentation, along with the formulation of **hypotheses**, has led to remarkable progress in our understanding of the world, because it involves analysing evidence and drawing conclusions which advance our understanding. Sometimes, these conclusions help to form the basis of new theories that may even go against mainstream beliefs and doctrines of the time. Sometimes scientists, however, will devise new theories before they have clear evidence for them, and then design experiments to test the theories.

While we often refer to the scientific method as if it were a single way of correctly doing science or acquiring reliable knowledge, there is no set of fixed steps that scientists always follow. Instead, there are many different ways of doing science. What they share is an empirical approach that involves numerous practices including, among others: asking questions or defining problems, planning and carrying out investigations, designing and creating models, analysing and interpreting data, looking for patterns, constructing possible explanations, making generalisations, evaluating results and theories and communicating information. Because there is no universal step-by-step methodology, practising science requires creativity and imagination, as well as a solid grounding in scientific knowledge to develop hypotheses and design appropriate experiments.

KEY WORDS

empirical: based on and verified by observation and experience

polymath: a person with expertise in several different fields of knowledge

scientific method: a method of procedure for the way scientific investigations are conducted

hypothesis (plural hypotheses): a provisional explanation based on limited evidence that provides a starting point for further investigation

REFLECTION

Think about the different ways you acquire or develop new knowledge. Why is there not a single way to follow scientific methodology?

These practices do not occur in a predefined order, and not all practices will be used in every experimental study. They will vary according to what is being investigated, and the field of investigation. With that caveat in place, perhaps what is most commonly described as *the* scientific method is **inductivism**, which is based on a method developed by Francis Bacon in the early-17th century. Inductivism starts with observations about the natural world which might lead the observers to ask a question. The more specific the question is, the more useful it is for developing a testable hypothesis.

KEY WORD

inductivism: the use of and preference for inductive methods of reasoning to develop natural laws

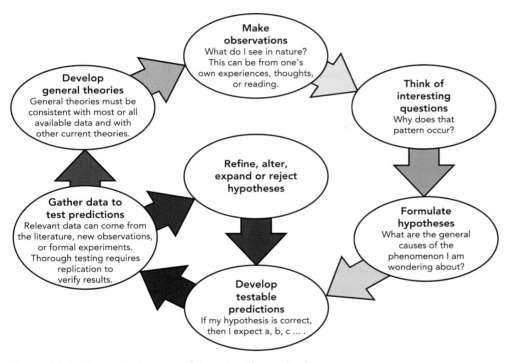

Figure 13.1: The cyclical nature of the scientific method

KEY WORDS

controlled experiments: experiments that are performed with carefully regulated variables to provide a standard of comparison for similar experiments with just one differing variable

law: a generalised description of observations about a relationship between two or more things in the natural world; often the description is mathematical

theory: an interconnected system of ideas intended to explain something in depth

Once a question is formulated, the question then leads the observers to develop one or more hypotheses to explain the observations. A good hypothesis will provide predictions which can be tested.

The testing of each hypothesis is done through carefully **controlled experiments**, the results of which are painstakingly recorded and analysed. The analysis of the results may then lead the scientists to refine the hypothesis, expand it or even to reject it. The process is continuous, with an approximately successful hypothesis being further and further refined, until its predictive powers are so good that the hypothesis may lead to a scientific **law** or **theory**.

DISCUSS 13.2

Consider why we ask questions at all; what is it about human inquisitiveness that makes a contribution to human nature and to continued human growth and development?

It is important to understand that laws and theories are quite distinct, and one does not necessarily lead to the other. Scientific laws simply describe what has been observed, often in a mathematical way, but they do not describe *how* or *why* they work. For example, Newton's *Law of Universal Gravitation* states that every particle in the universe attracts every other particle with a force that is directly proportional to the product of their masses and inversely proportional to the square of the distance between their centres (mathematically this is written $F = G\dfrac{m_1 m_2}{r^2}$) but this does not explain *why* the law holds universally.

Scientific theories, on the other hand, are detailed explanations of phenomena that explain how and why the phenomena occur. For anything to be accepted as a scientific theory, it must have been rigorously scrutinised and, where possible, undergone extensive experimental testing.

REAL-LIFE SITUATION 13.2

Can you think of any scientific theories that cannot be experimentally tested? How might evidence be gathered in such cases?

Because inductivism is based primarily on observations, whether they be initial observations or observations made when collecting experimental data, it relies very heavily on **inference** and **generalisation**. For example, when studies on a group of moles showed that the moles accurately found food in a tunnel within five seconds of sniffing the air, it was *inferred* that moles rely on their sense of smell for locating food. Although only a small number of moles were tested, the results were generalised to suggest that *all* moles locate their food using their sense of smell.

EXPLORE 13.1

Assume that the study on moles was conducted in a fair and controlled way. Do you think that the inference that moles rely on their sense of smell to find food was reasonable? Do you think it was reasonable to generalise the results to all moles? Do you think the conclusion that moles rely on their sense of smell for locating food qualifies as a scientific law or scientific theory? How might you test the conclusion?

LINKING QUESTION 13.1

Can you think of examples from other areas of knowledge in which practitioners might make inferences and generalisations?

KEY WORDS

inference: reaching conclusions based on evidence and reason

generalisation: making statements that apply to all cases, on the basis of some specific cases

As well as making careful observations and performing controlled experiments, another requirement of the scientific method is that any experiments repeated under the same conditions should produce the same results. This is called *repeatability* or **replication**. The method of testing and the subsequent results are then written up in a report for the purpose of **peer review**.

KEY WORDS

replication: the process of repeating

peer review: the evaluation of work by experts working in the same field

REAL-LIFE SITUATION 13.3

Consider what conditions must exist for an experiment to be repeated 'under the same conditions'. How easily can such repetition be achieved? Does the 'real world' often (or ever) repeat conditions in this way?

Figure 13.2: The sheep are grazing on just one part of the field

EXPLORE 13.2

Look closely at Figure 13.2. You may observe that the sheep are grazing more on one part of the land than the other. You may also notice that some parts of the land are rockier, some parts are steeper, and the type of grass appears different in different areas. The sheep also seem to be focused on a particular spot which possibly has water.

Working in pairs, try to brainstorm several possible reasons for your observations, and identify the variables.

Together, develop a specific question and list some possible hypotheses. Evaluate your hypotheses and select one that you could test. Together, plan an experiment that would test your hypothesis.

Peer-assessment

Swap your plan with that belonging to another pair of students and critique their plan while they critique yours. Do they have a specific question and testable hypothesis? Is their plan for an experiment likely to provide useful data? Would their experiment be repeatable?

Scientific equipment

Integral to the scientific method is the use of increasingly sophisticated technology and highly engineered scientific instruments. These allow scientists to make more detailed studies of the natural world, and test predictions made by theoretical research. The size and scope of scientific equipment varies enormously, from giant **radio telescopes** and particle colliders to molecular 3D printers that can synthesise molecules using **nanotechnology**.

Scientific equipment and their integrated technologies help to overcome many human deficiencies by enabling scientists to see further and deeper, measure more accurately, generate more and better data and analyse that data more effectively.

The careful use of scientific equipment in the scientific endeavour allows scientists to investigate and conduct controlled experiments on unprecedented scales. This contributes significantly to the validity and reliability of scientific knowledge emerging from engaging in the scientific method.

> ### DISCUSS 13.3
>
> To what extent could technical advances in scientific equipment in themselves be regarded as scientific progress?

Models

Scientific models are central to the process of developing scientific theories. They can be used to help explain data or phenomena and make predictions. As knowledge increases, so the models improve. Some models can be physical representations, such as a globe which is a model that represents Earth. Perhaps in your school laboratories, you have coloured plastic spheres which can be linked together to create models of molecules. Other models are mathematical, and are run on computers. An example might be a model of Earth's climate, used to help predict climate change. Model building can take time. It took around 2,000 years to develop an accurate globe of the world, so we should not be surprised if our models for climate change are not totally accurate yet. However, the continually increasing sophistication of human technology and the vast amount of data we are able to draw on, enable us to develop and update useful models at a much faster rate than ever before.

Figure 13.3: A model of the DNA molecule with its distinctive double helix shape

EXPLORE 13.3

1   List some models that are used in biology, chemistry and physics. Do you use models more in some areas of science than others? Why might that be? Are the models you have used necessarily over-simplified?

2   As a class, discuss: Is there a relationship between simplification and accuracy? Is there a relationship between simplification and usefulness or intelligibility?

3   Now think about some of the models you have used. Examples might be a model of a human showing the relationship between our internal organs, a model of a molecule or even a model train set.

Focus on one of the models you have used, and consider some of the ways in which it was like the reality it was modelling, and some of the ways in which it differed. Can you think of ways in which models are used in areas of knowledge other than the natural sciences? Write a short paragraph on how models help us to understand the world.

Self-assessment

Review your paragraph. What do you like about it? How might you have explained your ideas better? Have you included different perspectives, including an instance in which the use of a model may have limited our understanding?

DISCUSS 13.4

'All models are wrong but some are useful.' George Box (1919–2013)

What do you think Box meant by this? Why do you think he says all models are wrong?

13.3 Limitations of the scientific method

REAL-LIFE SITUATION 13.4

Think about some of the practical work you do in your science subject. How are errors most likely to arise?

While the scientific method has enabled human knowledge to progress in leaps and bounds, and allows us more certainty than we might otherwise have, the scientific method is not fool-proof. Any method that requires human participation is, to some extent, subject to human error and human limitations. The natural sciences try to overcome these with their requirement for replication of results using the scientific method and their system of peer review, which we will explore in more detail later in the chapter.

Observer expectations

In Chapter 5, we considered how the use of scientific equipment, such as microscopes and telescopes to make observations, has opened up the world by enabling us to see things that we would not be able to see with the human eye, and allowing us to make more accurate measurements. The degree of accuracy we can achieve in every field of measurement is continually increasing as our technology improves. But whatever level of equipment we might have, a person is often needed at some point to make an observation or form a judgement.

In 1609, Galileo (1564–1642) built one of the earliest telescopes, and used it to discover the phases of Venus and the moons of Jupiter. Although it allowed Galileo to see the planets more clearly, his home-made telescope was a fairly crude instrument. Given that it can be fairly difficult to see Jupiter's four largest moons even using modern telescopes, it raises the question of how much of Galileo's observation was real and how much was the result of imagination. It is perhaps not surprising that some of Galileo's drawings of the Earth's moon are quite inaccurate, and include some craters and mountains that do not exist.

From your own experience in the science laboratory, you are probably aware that it takes quite a lot of practice to learn how to see through a microscope. Often, shapes seem indistinguishable to untrained eyes, and you may find yourself using your expectations and imagination to augment your vision.

When we make observations, *our expectations can influence what we see*. For example, when the planet Mercury was found to be deviating from the orbit predicted by Newton's laws, a phenomenon known as its **precession**, some 19th-century astronomers suggested that the anomaly was caused by an undiscovered planet they called Vulcan. So confident were they in their belief that several astronomers then claimed that they had observed Vulcan. But it turned out that Vulcan does not exist. The correct explanation for the precession of Mercury's orbit had to wait for Einstein's *general theory of relativity*.

Our expectations and focus can also affect what we do not see, sometimes in very surprising ways. In Chapter 14, when we return to the topic of observation, we will explore the concept of 'change blindness', which causes people to fail to notice changes in a visual stimulus. Change blindness raises serious questions about human powers of observation for eyewitness accounts. It also has implications for **ethology** and other branches of the natural sciences. Change blindness suggests that more intentional monitoring of changes is necessary when undertaking field studies, particularly when observing complex scenes.

However, while the fallibility of human perception can be significant, it is important not to exaggerate the problem. The great strength of science is that it is a communal and largely self-correcting enterprise. Sooner or later, the errors of one individual or team are likely to be corrected by someone else.

In 1989, Martin Fleishmann (1927–2012), a leading electrochemist, and Stanley Pons (1943-) reported that they had achieved cold fusion – a nuclear reaction at room temperature – and they claimed to have measured small amounts of nuclear reaction by-products. Initially, their reported findings drew a lot of media attention because they raised hopes of cheap energy. However, other scientists were unable to replicate their results, and it was soon found that the experiment by Fleishmann and Pons had been flawed. Further, it was discovered that there had been no nuclear by-products. Funding into cold fusion was subsequently cut, and cold fusion is no longer seen as a serious possibility.

KEY WORDS

precession: a slow and continuous change in the orientation of the axis of a rotating body

ethology: the study of animal behaviour

In 2011, some Italian scientists led by Professor Antonio Ereditato (1955–) claimed to have measured **neutrinos** travelling faster than light. The claim rocked the scientific world because it appeared to overturn Einstein's *special theory of relativity*, but repeats of the experiment showed that the neutrinos travelled at the speed of light, not faster than light as had been claimed. It later emerged that a loose fibre-optic cable had been responsible for the initial false finding.

DISCUSS 13.5

How does replication help to counter errors caused by observational errors and/or equipment failure? To what extent can we be certain that an initial set of results were wrong just because they cannot be repeated?

The observer effect

Limitations of the scientific method are not restricted to human fallibility and technical weaknesses. There are some limitations that are inherent in any physical system. One limitation is due to what we know as the **observer effect**.

To take some simple examples, having your blood pressure taken could cause your blood pressure to go up, particularly if you were feeling anxious about it, and this could affect the clinical picture your doctor sees. If you want to measure the air pressure of your bicycle tyre, you need to release some air to be able to make the measurement. Similarly, when measuring the temperature of a substance with a standard thermometer, the thermometer will either lose heat or absorb heat to record a temperature, and so change the temperature of the substance it is measuring.

Figure 13.4: What we see will be influenced by what we expect to see, and our presence as observers may affect what is there to be seen

A perhaps more significant example was demonstrated by researchers at the Weizmann Institute who, in 1998, conducted a series of highly controlled experiments to see how a beam of electrons is affected by being observed. Electrons are particles that can also act as waves under certain conditions. Researchers found that a beam of electrons being 'observed' by an electronic detector (not by a person) resulted in the electrons behaving as particles rather than waves, even though the detector had no effect on the current. When the levels of observation were raised by increasing the detector's capacity to detect electrons, the particle behaviour increased, and when the observation levels dropped by decreasing the detector's capacity, wave-like behaviour increased. This experiment confirmed the prediction made by *quantum theory* – that the act of observation will affect experimental results.

The observer effect is so small that it is negligible in most situations, however it can play a significant role in particle physics, electronics and **quantum mechanics**.

quantum theory: a theory in physics which explains the behaviour of subatomic particles

quantum mechanics: a branch of mechanics describing the motion and interaction of subatomic particles

---

REAL-LIFE SITUATION 13.5

Given that is it not possible to make observations without affecting whatever is being observed, what are the implications for objective knowledge about the world 'as it is'?

Related to the observer effect is the *Heisenberg uncertainty principle*, which was first articulated by the German physicist and pioneer of quantum mechanics, Werner Heisenberg (1901–1976) in 1927. He stated that the position and the velocity of an object cannot both be measured exactly, at the same time, even in theory.

According to the uncertainty principle, the more precisely the position of a particle is determined, the less precisely its momentum can be known, and *vice versa*. The uncertainty principle is inherent in the properties of all wave-like systems, and it arises in quantum mechanics because of the wave-like nature of all quantum objects. Therefore, the uncertainty principle actually refers to a fundamental property of quantum systems, and is not a statement about the observer effect with which it is often confused.

scientism: an exaggerated trust in the efficacy of the methods of the natural sciences applied to any and all areas of investigation

positivism: the belief that the only authentic knowledge is that which can be scientifically verified or proven through experiment, logic or mathematics

---

REFLECTION

Although most scientific knowledge is not and cannot be *proven*, we can and do place great confidence in it. To what extent is this true for all human knowledge?

Scientism

Scientism is the belief that scientific methodology offers the only valid way of seeking knowledge in any field, even those that are outside the scope of the natural sciences. It is closely linked with **positivism**, **logical positivism** and **logical empiricism**. Together, they form the view that knowledge must be based on experimental verification rather than personal experience, and that unanswerable philosophical questions about things like causality or freedom are meaningless.

The most famous principle of logical empiricism is that any statement that is not inherently verifiable is meaningless and can be safely ignored. The irony is that the principle is itself inherently unverifiable, and can therefore be safely ignored.

Those who believe in scientism believe that the scientific method should be used to solve most, if not all, of the problems facing society, and they are very critical of knowledge claims they regard as non-scientific. However, it has been argued that scientism is more like a religion than a scientific position, because it claims that only science can resolve any of our questions. The great danger of scientism is that it promises that science can do more than it really can, and this could serve to increase

logical positivism: the belief that all knowledge comes from logical inferences based on observable facts, and that a statement can only be meaningful if it can be determined to be true or false

logical empiricism: the belief that all human knowledge should be reduced to logical and scientific foundations (it is often regarded as synonymous with logical positivism)

scepticism about science: people might start to question the ability of science to address even the questions that involve the natural world.

REAL-LIFE SITUATION 13.6

Although the vast majority of scientists accept that climate change is happening at least partly as a result of human activity on the planet, many people in the world are sceptical and there is reported to be a growing distrust of experts. To what extent might this be a populist backlash against the tendency of media and some scientists to overstate the ability of science to give us truth and certainty?

13.4 Objectivity

DISCUSS 13.6

What do you mean when you say something is an objective truth? Can you think of some examples of objective truths?

One of the frequently stated goals of science is objectivity. An objective truth is one that is totally unbiased, which is to say that it would be confirmed by anyone approaching its verification with sufficient open-mindedness, skill and fairness. One reason for the success of the scientific method is that it helps to eliminate the personal bias of the researchers, and to reach conclusions that are independent of the beliefs of the researchers.

Of course, objectivity may be an admirable goal, but it is one that can never be *fully* achieved. The observations you make, the questions you ask, the variables you identify, the hypotheses you formulate, the experiments you design and the conclusions you reach can all be susceptible to influence by your deepest-held beliefs without you realising it, and by the prevailing accepted theories of the scientific community.

KEY WORDS

objectivity: judgement that is not influenced by personal feelings or opinions

verification: the process of establishing the validity or accuracy of something

---

DISCUSS 13.7

Could something be considered objective in one culture but subjective in another?

Beliefs and objectivity

One belief very deeply held by many scientists is that only humans, and perhaps a few other species such as chimpanzees and orangutans, are self-aware. A mirror test, invented by Gordon Gallup (1941–), an evolutionary psychologist, has been widely used to test self-awareness and demonstrate the lack of it in other species. The test has been criticised by some scientists who argue that the mirror test discriminates against species that are less visually dependent than humans. Dogs routinely fail the mirror test; however, when subjected to a sniff test of self-recognition – a test very similar to the mirror test but based on the sense of smell rather than vision – they were found to have self-awareness. The results of these studies have largely gone unheeded because the results of the visual mirror test uphold the prevailing view.

Figure 13.5: A cleaner wrasse

In 2018, however, the visual mirror test was conducted on a few cleaner wrasses. (The cleaner wrasse is a small fish that feeds on parasites and the dead skin cells of other fish.) By the parameters of the mirror test, some of the fish demonstrated self-awareness. That a fish has passed the test has led some scientists, including Gallup, to doubt the validity of the test rather than overturn their beliefs that only humans and perhaps a few other species can be self-aware. Others argue that the test was very thorough, and we must be willing to open our minds to the thought that at least some fish might be more self-aware than we have so far given them credit for.

If you are willing to accept the results of the mirror test on the cleaner wrasses because you believe that most, if not all, animals have self-awareness, you are demonstrating confirmation bias. Confirmation bias refers to the fact that people tend to look for evidence that confirms their beliefs, and overlook evidence that goes against them. If you refuse to accept the results of the mirror test on cleaner wrasses and say the experiment must have been flawed because you believe that fish cannot be self-aware, you are also demonstrating confirmation bias, which we discussed in Chapter 2. A common form of confirmation bias is for a scientist to dismiss results they do not expect as 'experimental error'.

EXPLORE 13.4

Consider the list of topics, a to f, that are the subjects of scientific debate.

a   genetically modified (GM) foods

b   climate change

c   fracking

d   vaccination

e   human cloning

f   artificial intelligence (AI)

Think about your attitude to each of the topics. Which issues are you more interested in, or even passionate about? Are you truly open-minded? Would you be more *willing* to be persuaded by some arguments than by others?

Attaining *total* objectivity is not only impossible, but sometimes undesirable. To begin any scientific investigation, we have to make choices about what to observe. Even if we could observe every element of a situation, we would not want to because we would soon become overloaded with information.

EXPLORE 13.5

1   Imagine that you are interested in finding out why some students catch a cold in the winter term and other students do not. Which of the variables, a to f, might you look at in comparing the two groups, and which would you consider irrelevant?

   a   diet

   b   colour of underwear

   c   amount of physical exercise

   d   middle name

   e   domestic heating

   f   movies watched

2   Partner with a classmate and compare your answers. Did you agree on which variables are relevant? Can you think of *any* situations in which the colour of your underwear, your middle name or the movies you have watched might be relevant to whether or not you catch a cold?

3   Only six possible variables are listed in this Explore activity. Individually, try to create a list of 20 variables, and then compare your list with your partner's. How many do you have in common? How many possible variables do you think there *could* be?

In the Explore activity, it is possible to imagine a chain of events in which any one of these variables could, in theory, be relevant, but the probability of some of those chains of events occurring is so small that it would be a waste of time and money running scientific experiments to eliminate them, unless all more likely options had already been ruled out. When you decide to run a series of experiments, it is important to try to isolate the most likely candidates to test.

The point of the preceding activities is to demonstrate that we always begin with some idea of what is and what is not relevant to any problem, and our brains filter the information available to us accordingly. Without this, we could drown in a flood of observations. Experimentally eliminating the infinite possibilities would be impossible, and the cost of even trying would be incalculable, therefore it is essential that we make choices based upon our beliefs. However, the selective nature of perception means it is always possible we have overlooked a factor that later turns out to be relevant, and cultural bias can systematically eliminate certain features even though they are relevant. For example, when you do an experiment in chemistry, you do not normally count how many people are in the room, or where in the room you are conducting your experiment. However, in a particularly sensitive experiment, both of these variables could, in theory, affect the results.

Figure 13.6: Controlled experiments are an essential feature of the scientific method

REAL-LIFE SITUATION 13.7

How might the number of people in a room or where in a room you set up your experiment have an effect on the results? What are the implications for the repetition of experiments, particularly by scientists in other laboratories?

Pseudoscience

One of the goals of objectivity is to be able to distinguish science from pseudoscience. Often, our beliefs cause us to think that something we regard as true has scientific validity, when it does not. There are many examples of pseudoscience, some of which were at one time inextricably linked with legitimate science. **Astrology** would be an example of this.

Early astronomers made valuable, detailed observations of the night sky that were of great scientific merit, and beginning around the 4th century BCE, these studies were regarded as the basis for astrology. Chinese astrology is thought to have arisen in the 5th century BCE but many believe it to be much older. It was not until the 17th century that western astronomy and astrology began to gradually separate.

Other examples of pseudoscience include phrenology, mental telepathy, numerology, extrasensory perception (ESP) and channelling.

> **KEY WORD**
>
> **astrology:** a belief that the movement of the planets affects human behaviour in predictable ways

EXPLORE 13.6

Research an example of pseudoscience. It can be one from the list or another one of your choosing. Why is it a pseudoscience and not a legitimate science?

DISCUSS 13.8

If you believe in something (such as fortune-telling with Tarot cards) why might it be difficult to accept that it is a pseudoscience? How can we be objective about determining what is a science and what is a pseudoscience?

Scientific paradigms

In 1962, Thomas Kuhn (1922–1996) published *The Structure of Scientific Revolutions,* which became one of the most influential books of the 20th century, and one of the most cited books of all time. Before the publication of the book, people tended to think of science as a linear process in which researchers and theorists follow the scientific method to move ever closer to a greater understanding of the natural world.

Kuhn, however, argued that within fields of science, discontinuities happen which throw the field into disarray and uncertainty. He regarded these as revolutionary periods, which come with great conceptual breakthroughs. These ideas were revolutionary at the time, because they challenged the contemporary philosophical assumptions about how science works. What Kuhn realised was that to understand scientific development, it is important to understand the intellectual and social contexts that scientists work in. These intellectual frameworks were what he referred to as scientific paradigms.

A paradigm shift happens when there is a dramatic change of world view. The Copernican Revolution is often cited as a classic example of a paradigm shift. It refers to the change from a Ptolemaic worldview in which it was believed that the Earth is at the centre of the universe, to the Copernican model which puts the sun at the centre of the solar system.

A rather tragic example of the power of an established paradigm is the case of the Hungarian, Dr Ignaz Semmelweis. In 1847, after a friend cut his finger during an autopsy and contracted puerperal fever, Sammelweis noted that 13% of women in his hospital died of puerperal fever after giving birth. Sammelweis had observed that medical students moved between the autopsy room and the delivery room without washing their hands, and developed a hypothesis that this was the reason for the high death rate in the maternity wing. When he insisted that students wash their hands in a chlorine solution before entering the maternity wing, mortality rates from puerperal fever among new mothers promptly dropped to 2%.

Sadly, the medical establishment rejected Semmelweis's ideas because they saw them as a criticism of the established practices of the prevailing medical paradigm, and the disillusioned Dr Semmelweis died in a mental institution after being severely beaten by guards. It was another 16 years before the British surgeon Joseph Lister (1827–1912) began using carbolic acid as a disinfectant, and championed sterile surgery. Even Lister's arguments about the spread of infections were widely criticised, with the prestigious medical journal *The Lancet* warning the medical profession against such ideas in 1873.

The 'Semmelweis effect' is now a name given to cases in which new research based upon bold hypotheses is swiftly rejected because it threatens established paradigms. The example shows how paradigms can sometimes block or inhibit scientific progress, but we often only become aware of the paradigms we operate in if they are challenged, or after they have been overturned.

> **KEY WORD**
>
> scientific paradigm: a worldview that underlies the theories and methodology in a particular field of science

---

REFLECTION

To what extent do your culture, beliefs and/or political views influence your attitudes to contemporary issues?

REAL-LIFE SITUATION 13.8

Can you think of ways in which scientific paradigms might benefit the production of scientific knowledge?

A more recent example of a paradigm shift might be the change in thinking that accompanied the development of radio telescopes. Development of radio telescopes began around 1930, and enabled astronomers to observe radio waves and microwaves which are outside the visible spectrum. Using radio telescopes in conjunction with **optical telescopes**, astronomers are now able to develop a richer understanding of the universe. In 1965, a radio telescope facilitated the discovery of cosmic microwave background (CMB) radiation coming from all directions in space by Arno Penzias (1933–) and Robert Wilson (1936–), earning them the 1978 Nobel Prize for physics. This background radiation was a major finding because it was the first direct evidence in support of the **Big Bang** theory, and it changed the way scientists thought about the universe.

Figure 13.7: The VIa Radio Telescope in New Mexico and the Hale-Bopp Comet. Radio telescopes have allowed astronomers to make new discoveries that cannot be seen with optical telescopes

KEY WORDS

optical telescope: a telescope that gathers and focuses light, mostly from the visible light spectrum, to create a magnified image that can be viewed directly

Big Bang: the theory that the universe began with an infinitely dense singularity 'exploding' in a rapid expansion 13.8 billion years ago

The idea of a paradigm shift in science certainly struck a chord in many people both within and outside the scientific community, and Kuhn's model has since been applied to many other areas of knowledge. However, Kuhn's approach is not without its critics. Aside from ignoring the way competing models can emerge within paradigms, Kuhn assumes that new paradigms fully replace old paradigms, but in reality, two paradigms can operate side by side for many years. For example, it took quantum physics at least 30 years to emerge and achieve full acceptance through the slow accumulation of collecting experimental data and developing theories, and scientists still use non-quantum physics where its limitations do not apply.

There is no doubt that the idea of paradigm shift is still very significant in popular thought, and perhaps primarily in the human sciences. It is a valuable model to help us appreciate how much our thinking is shaped by the intellectual frameworks of our time and place. However, even Kuhn argued that one of the great strengths of the natural sciences is that they are dogmatic and conservative; their reliability is largely because a vast amount of evidence is needed to overturn accepted theories.

13.5 Reasoning and falsification

All creatures rely on the world being stable and predictable, so we tend to reason by induction and assume that if something has happened repeatedly in the past, it will continue to do so in the future. You will have learnt about inductive reasoning in Chapter 3, and know that it is a form of generalisation which allows us to navigate our way in the world. If we could not rely on the world being stable and predictable, science as we know it would not be possible.

Scientific knowledge is heavily dependent on inductive reasoning, and this is one of the reasons why the replication of scientific experiments is so important. However, as we know from inductive reasoning, no matter how many times a result is repeated, there is always an element of doubt, even if it is very, very tiny.

Sir Karl Popper (1902–1994) argued that instead of developing a hypothesis and then running experiments to confirm the hypothesis by means of inductive reasoning, we should come up with a **conjecture** and then look for evidence to **refute** it, on the grounds that no amount of evidence can prove a hypothesis true, but a single piece of evidence can **falsify** it. For example, if we consider a simple knowledge claim such as *all ravens are black*, however many black ravens we might see in support of our claim, we cannot possibly claim to have seen every raven that ever has, does or will exist. It would only take one non-black raven to refute the hypothesis and prove that not all ravens are black. Indeed, a few ravens have been discovered with a condition called leucism, similar to albinism.

KEY WORDS

conjecture: a guess or imaginative hypothesis

refute: to prove a statement or theory wrong

falsify: in this context to prove something to be false

Popper claimed that the best hypotheses are ones that are easily refutable and testable. If a hypothesis is tested many times without being refuted, we could then regard it as well-**corroborated**. The more the falsifiable hypothesis has been tested without being successfully refuted, the more confident we can be in its validity.

For two-and-a-half centuries, experiment after experiment seemed to confirm the truth of Newtonian physics. Nevertheless, Einstein showed that there is a deep sense in which Newton's laws are not the best description of physical reality. What this appears to show is that even very well-confirmed hypotheses can sometimes turn out to be inaccurate or wrong.

KEY WORD

corroborate: to confirm or support a statement or theory

> ### REAL-LIFE SITUATION 13.9
>
> We claim to have discovered laws of physics that apply to *all* times and *all* places, including those billions of years ago and billions of light-years away, yet we have observed only a minute fraction of the universe.
>
> Is the claim that the laws of physics are universal and unchanging *falsifiable*? What would it take to falsify the claim?

Figure 13.8: White ravens falsify the claim that all ravens are black

Some people would argue that the difference between science and non-science is that scientific statements are falsifiable whereas non-scientific statements are not. If you were to make a claim such as 'Willow trees need water to survive', to attempt to falsify this claim, you could try to grow a willow tree without watering it. If you succeed, you will show the claim to be false; if not, your experimental data would *corroborate* the claim, but it would not *prove* the claim, since there could be many other reasons why your trees failed to grow. According to the principle of falsification, the claim that Willow trees need water to survive could be considered scientific because it is falsifiable. However, if you were to make a claim such as 'An alien space craft landed in the Sahara Desert', this is not falsifiable. You cannot prove it never happened. You may be able to come up with lots of evidence, such as there being no recorded sightings or that no evidence of its landing was found, but a believer in the landing could argue that records were destroyed, people's memories were erased, evidence was covered up, etc. So, the claim that 'An alien space craft landed in the Sahara Desert' could possibly be true, but it is not a scientific claim. However, while the claim cannot be falsified, it could be verified by, for example, finding the alien ship beneath a sand dune.

It is important to understand that a claim that is *falsifiable* can be true, whereas a claim that has been *falsified* is known to be false. A claim that is unfalsifiable could be true or it could be false, but it is not possible to find evidence that would *prove* it to be false.

EXPLORE 13.8

Which of the claims, a to g, are falsifiable and which are not?

a   All elephants are grey.

b   A giant reptile lives in Loch Ness.

c   No spaceships have ever landed in New Mexico.

d   Ancient alchemists could turn lead into gold.

e   The moon is made of green cheese.

f   There is a planet in the universe made of green cheese.

g   There are no planets in the universe made of green cheese.

For the statements that you have identified as falsifiable, say what evidence you would need to falsify them. Have any of them already been falsified?

Although Popper's principle of falsification is widely used in the experimental sciences, it is not without some problems. There are statements that can be made which are verifiable empirically, but which cannot be falsified. These generally have to do with existence. For example, we can claim that *penguins exist* and we can verify it empirically by observing and counting penguins, but we cannot falsify the claim.

It is also the case that some aspects of physics cannot be falsified through observation. For example, it is highly unlikely that we will be able to experimentally falsify all knowledge claims about dark matter or black holes because our knowledge about them is largely based on theory. Most of our knowledge claims about dark matter and black holes are only likely to be overturned if the theories that support our knowledge claims are superseded. This suggests that, for all its value, falsification is limited in scope.

DISCUSS 13.11

Would it be right to argue that the claim the *Higgs bosun exists* is non-scientific in the same way that the claim *fairies exist* is non-scientific?

Principle of simplicity

A scientific theory is based on a body of knowledge that has been repeatedly confirmed through observation and experiments. It must also be capable of making accurate predictions. The strength of a scientific theory is related to the range of phenomena it can explain, and, perhaps surprisingly, its simplicity. A good theory is expected to be elegant. In fact, scientists usually appeal to a *principle of simplicity* which says that, given two competing theories that make exactly the same predictions, the simpler theory is to be preferred. The principle reflects a deep belief in the orderliness and comprehensibility of nature, but no further justification can be given for it. Since simplicity is also related to concepts such as 'beauty' and 'elegance', we can say that in practice, aesthetic considerations are likely to play a role in a scientist's choice of hypothesis.

DISCUSS 13.12

Why do you think elegance is an important quality for a scientific theory to have? Could the universe in fact be too complicated for our human understanding, and our requirement of simplicity is a reflection of our limited intelligence?

Occam's Razor (sometimes known as Ockham's Razor) is a philosophical principle made popular by William of Ockham (1285–1347) which says that when there are two or more possible explanations, you should select the simplest one – the one with the least assumptions, unless a more complex explanation does a better job of explaining.

EXPLORE 13.9

Look at the events 1 to 3 and their two possible explanations below. Which explanation is the simplest? Which is most likely to be correct?

1   You find a strange football in your garden.

  a   One of the children who live next door accidently kicked it over the garden fence.

  b   An eagle picked it up thinking it was a rabbit, then dropped it while flying over your garden.

2   You arrive home as usual but find your study notes scattered on the floor.

  a   Vandals broke into your house and ransacked your desk, but were disturbed before they could do any further damage.

  b   Your cat jumped onto your desk and accidently knocked down your pile of notes.

3   Your friend did not call when she said she would.

  a   She forgot.

  b   She accidently dropped her phone and broke it.

Of course, it is always possible that the simplest answer is not the correct one, but Occam's Razor remains a useful guide for scientists, and for all of us in daily life.

REFLECTION

Consider the extent to which you apply the principle of simplicity in your own life. How reliable is it? How does it affect what you choose to believe?

13.6 Theoretical science

Ever since human beings began to ask questions about the nature of the world and universe in which they found themselves, ever since they ceased to be merely victims of life's events and started to seek to control them, they found that they wanted and needed to invent theories about life, the world and the stars.

We might think of the emergence of this theorising – itself a reflection of a developed language and an enhanced capacity to think – as the beginning of 'civilisation' as we know it. The ancient Chinese, Indian, Egyptian, Babylonian and Mayan civilisations, among others, were interested in **cosmogony** and **cosmology**. Their theories were reflected in their ancient temples, monuments and architecture. Their attempts at astronomy and astrology also demonstrate an increasing interest in trying to understand, and to some extent, control and predict the world around them.

DISCUSS 13.13

What is the difference between astronomy and astrology? Do you think the difference would have been evident or important in ancient times?

So far in this chapter, we have mostly thought about experimental science, but there are some branches of science, most notably in physics, that use mathematical models to explain and predict events in the universe. We might consider theoretical science to be the modern equivalent of the speculations and hypotheses of ancient civilisations.

Although theoretical scientists do take note of experimental studies at times, they often regard mathematical rigour as more important than observations. They tend to work in areas where experimentation cannot be done, or can only be done in limited ways, often at great expense.

The search for the Higgs boson is an example of how theoretical physics can provide a direction for experimental physics, and lead the way in making scientific progress long before there are experimental data to support it.

Figure 13.9: A worker rides his bicycle in a tunnel of the European Organisation for Nuclear Research (CERN) Large Hadron Collider

In 1964, a group of six theoretical physicists suggested the existence of a new particle to try to overcome a problem with the *standard theory* of particle physics, but it was not until the late 1990s that a real search for the particle began. The Large Hadron Collider (LHC) was designed and built specifically to be able to either confirm or exclude the existence of the Higgs boson. Building the LHC started in 1998. It took ten years, and involved the collaboration of over 10,000 scientists from more than 100 countries. The LHC consists of a 27-kilometre ring of superconducting magnets with a number of accelerating structures to boost the energy of the particles along the way.

It was 2010 before the LHC eventually started to collect data, and because the possibility of producing a Higgs boson in a particle collision was likely to be very rare (1 in 10 billion), hundreds of trillions of collisions needed to be analysed. Evidence for the particle first emerged in 2012, and further corroborating evidence was found in 2013, but it was 2017 before the existence of the Higgs boson was officially confirmed.

"Always the last place you look!"

EXPLORE 13.10

1   Draw a flow diagram of the scientific method as you understand it. To what extent does the discovery of the Higgs boson fit the basic scientific method? How far do the processes match? What steps are missing?

2   Try to find some examples in which a theory provides a direction for research in other areas of knowledge. Can you draw any parallels between science and one other subject area in the way that theories are used to develop new knowledge?

REAL-LIFE SITUATION 13.11

CERN relied heavily on the cooperation of scientists from around the world. Do you think a more competitive approach would have brought faster results? Does competition or collaboration provide the best route to the production of new knowledge in the natural sciences?

The history of theoretical science goes back to ancient times, and theoretical scientists often build on the theories of those who have gone before by tweaking – or completely overthrowing and reinventing – older theories as new information is discovered, or new ways of measuring are invented.

One example of this comes from the history of our understanding of atoms. It was around 440 BCE that Leucippus first came up with the idea of atoms as invisible and indivisible building blocks for all matter. (A similar theory arose independently around the same time in India.) Over the years, Leucippus and his pupil Democritus refined the concept, and regarded atoms as solid structures surrounded by empty space. They believed atoms were homogeneous in nature, although they did think there were different kinds of atoms, differing in size and shape.

There were many disagreements about atoms in the ancient world. Epicurus (341–270 BCE) and Hero of Alexandria (c 100–70 BCE) were atomists, but Aristotle (384–322 BCE) and Cicero (106–43 BCE) spoke out against them. Debates continued into the Middle Ages, with people like William of Conches (1080–1154) teaching the ideas of Democritus (c 460–370 BCE); however, the Catholic Church was more influenced by the teachings of Aristotle, and came out against the existence of atoms.

During the Renaissance, Daniel Sennert (1572–1637) taught that atoms joined together to form composites, but that they keep their essential form. Shortly after, Pierre Gassendi (1592–1655) made the idea of atoms more socially acceptable by claiming that they were a gift from God. He also developed the idea of molecules, as a group of atoms held together, he imagined, by structures hooked on to each other.

Robert Boyle (1627–1691) is often considered the first modern chemist, and published *The Sceptical Chymist* in 1661, in which he made a distinction between mixtures and compounds.

Although he came a long time after the originators of the idea of atoms, the father of chemical atomic theory is generally regarded to be John Dalton (1766–1844), who worked on ways to determine atomic weights. It was Dalton who first proposed that elements are made up of identical atoms with identical masses, and that atoms of different elements have different masses.

In this brief overview of the early history of atomic theory, many contributors have been omitted, and the account stops a long way short of our contemporary understanding of atoms. Work continues on atomic theories to this day. But it is important to note that much of the development of atomic theory happened in times when microscopes and so much of the technical apparatus scientists use today were either non-existent or very rudimentary, so the theories were not based only upon empirical evidence.

KEY WORD

homogeneous: consistent; of uniform structure throughout

REAL-LIFE SITUATION 13.12

To what extent do you think natural philosophers and early scientists relied on imagination and creativity to develop their atomic theories? Do you think theoretical scientists rely on imagination and creativity to the same extent today?

We have noted that atomic theory started independently in ancient Greece and India, but not in Egyptian, Chinese or Mayan civilisations. It is interesting that the writing of Greeks and Indians involved alphabets, whereas the writings of other civilisations used pictograms which represented entire words or concepts. One hypothesis offered for the rise of atomic theory in civilisations with an alphabet is that there is an analogy between making words from letters and making matter from atoms.

EXPLORE 13.11

1   With a partner, begin by brainstorming the analogy. How might the way in which letters make up words be similar to the way in which atoms make up matter? How are they different? Do you think familiarity with the concept of letters would make it easier to think about atoms?

2   This hypothesis is the result of observing the historical and cultural patterns of atomic theory. With your partner, try to come up with reasons why this hypothesis is being considered under theoretical science rather than experimental science.

As you saw in Chapter 12, correlation is not the same as causation. Just because there is a correlation between the nature of a civilisation's written language and its belief in atomic theory, this does not necessarily mean that one causes the other.

Today, theoretical physicists work on ideas as diverse as how the universe began, the nature of time, the structure of atoms, the nature of gravity, black holes and dark matter. Some are working on the *theory of everything* – a theory which reconciles Einstein's theory of gravity within the *general theory of relativity* with quantum physics.

For any scientific theory or law to be accepted by the scientific community, it must be repeatable, and it must be falsifiable, but it need not be *true* in any absolute sense.

One famous example of it being more important to be useful than to be exact is Isaac Newton's *law of universal gravitation*, which describes gravity as a force of attraction between two bodies, with the force proportional to the product of their masses, and inversely proportional to the distance between them squared. Newton's laws work extremely well in most cases, but they are inaccurate at cosmic levels and do not work at sub-atomic levels. At cosmic levels, Einstein's *general theory of relativity* can more accurately predict what Newton's laws cannot, such as the precession of the orbit of Mercury, but even Einstein's theory is thought to be incomplete because it is incompatible with quantum mechanics.

REFLECTION

The idea that something can be both scientific and useful without being true is one that may seem counter-intuitive. Can you think of some everyday examples of things that are very useful without necessarily being accurate? What are the implications for the importance of truth and certainty?

13.7 The scientific community

REAL-LIFE SITUATION 13.13

What does the term 'scientific community' mean to you? To what extent are you a part of it?

Often, when we study the history of science, we learn about a single scientist who made a new discovery or invented a new tool, but nowadays scientists rarely, if ever, work in isolation from the scientific community. The scientific community is made up of all the people and organisations that contribute to our scientific knowledge. These are the people and organisations that generate new ideas, provide the resources to test those ideas and check the **rigour** of those ideas through tests. The scientific community is also responsible for scrutinising and publishing ideas and test results in scientific journals, which in turn open up the published ideas and test results to further scrutiny.

> **KEY WORD**
>
> **rigour:** strictness; the quality of being extremely thorough and careful

Peer review

Professional peer review provides a way of self-regulation within scientific fields, and can be an excellent way to maintain high standards, particularly if the reviews are anonymous.

When a scientific paper is sent to a publisher for publication, editors, along with scientific experts from the same field as the work being reviewed, check the research being reported to ensure that the methods used are valid, that data has been correctly gathered, organised and analysed and that any interpretations of data are justified. They have to decide whether the research is worthy of being published or whether it should be rejected. The peer review system helps to hold scientists accountable and ensure that only the most reliable research is published. If the work is accepted for publication, it is then open to further scrutiny from all who read the journal or book. Sometimes, a paper may be accepted into a journal, only to have readers discover flaws in it at a later date.

The process of peer review is not without its critics. Several studies have shown that peer review has an **inherent** bias against research done by women, by scientists from poorer nations and even in favour of established results over innovative and sometimes controversial results that subsequently prove to be true. Some reviewers are reluctant to speak out against work by scientists who are considered high ranking in their field, so the process can disproportionately disadvantage researchers who are in the early stages of their careers. In addition, because journals often take months or even years to publish some reports, a great deal of research time can be wasted and funding lost by the time-consuming and painstaking process of peer review.

> **KEY WORD**
>
> **inherent:** existing in something as a permanent characteristic

However, despite its difficulties, the peer review system remains an important one for maintaining scientific rigour and improving the overall reliability of scientific knowledge.

REAL-LIFE SITUATION 13.14

1   Why is it important that scientists are reviewed by their peers, rather than publishing editors alone?

2   Suppose an authoritarian political regime held a particular scientist or theory in the highest regard. Could you objectively review a theory or a hypothesis put forward by such a scientist in that climate? Discuss the factors that may or may not be relevant.

Collaboration

For science to progress, it needs interactions within the scientific community, and it mostly progresses by developing ideas, techniques and tools that originated with others. Furthermore, most scientific research is **collaborative**. Even though single scientists might work alone for years within laboratories, or doing field studies in remote areas, they collaborate with others when attending conferences, reading or writing journal articles and communicating with other interested parties, whether by letter, email, telephone, or even chatting over lunch. This collaboration is necessary to help collect ideas and/or evidence, to receive **critical** feedback, to help build theories and ultimately, to help build the body of scientific knowledge that is used to serve the world.

It is the scientific community that evaluates the work of individual scientists and scientific teams. It can also help to interpret data, generate new questions, provide financial, intellectual and moral support and watch out for **inadvertent** bias or even deliberate fraud.

> **KEY WORDS**
>
> **collaborative:** produced by two or more people working together
>
> **critical:** involving objective analysis and evaluation
>
> **inadvertent:** not deliberate, happening without design or intention

---

DISCUSS 13.14

'If I have seen further, it is by standing on the shoulders of giants.'
Sir Isaac Newton (1643–1727)

What do you think Newton meant when he said this? What implication does this have for science and for knowledge? To what extent might it apply to other areas of knowledge?

Figure 13.10: In scientific research, collaboration is necessary at almost all levels

Scientific sub-communities

Within the scientific community are countless sub-communities. These tend to be based on different scientific fields, fields within fields and within particular institutions. These sub-communities can be anything from informal groups of interested people to highly specialised organisations, such as the International Permafrost Association or the World Climate Research Programme. These organisations arrange conferences, support international collaboration, propose areas of future research and help to develop international standards in their particular fields.

The Royal Society in the UK is the world's oldest national scientific institution. Its role is to promote science, recognise scientific excellence, give scientific advice to policy makers and foster international cooperation throughout the global scientific community.

REAL-LIFE SITUATION 13.15

Why might smaller, more specialised scientific sub-communities be beneficial? What drawbacks could there be in having highly specialised sub-communities?

EXPLORE 13.12

Create spider diagrams to compare and contrast the roles of scientific sub-communities with the roles of sub-communities related to another area of knowledge. Compare your spider diagrams with those of a classmate who has chosen the same area of knowledge as you.

Peer-assessment

Did your classmate come up with the same ideas that you did? What have they done differently? Was there anything significant you or your classmate left out? What could you have done better? Tell each other which ideas in your spider diagrams you find most helpful for comparing and contrasting the role of sub-communities in different areas of knowledge.

Scientific authority

Because the natural sciences have become so very specialised, it is often difficult for even scientists working in similar fields to be aware of, or even to fully understand, breakthroughs in fields of science outside their own. Non-scientists need to be able to turn to a scientific authority for guidance or verification. Typically, this authority comes from specialised scientific sub-communities and scientists who have the endorsement of the scientific communities to which they belong.

Sometimes we do not need to turn to a specialist organisation; someone who is endorsed by them would be more appropriate. For example, if you are ill in the UK, you would not consult the British Medical Association, but you might consult a medical doctor. Similarly, if you wanted to ask a specific question about the properties of light, you might ask your physics teacher, or if it were a particularly specialised question, you might contact someone from the Optical Society of Japan; if you had a question about genomes, you could ask your biology teacher, or you might consult the International Mammalian Genome Society.

EXPLORE 13.13

In the table, link the problem with the most appropriate authority. (You may need to look up some of the words.)

Problem		Authority	
1	You have a bad toothache.	a	Ornithologist
2	You have an unexplained rash on your hand.	b	Cardiologist
3	There is an unusual bird in your garden.	c	Horticulturist
4	You want to know whether there is life on Mars.	d	Dentist
5	Your tomato plants appear to be diseased.	e	Pharmacist
6	You want to know if your medication has any side effects.	f	NASA
7	You have a heart murmur.	g	Dermatologist

Scientific authorities are those deemed to be experts in their field; they are the people or organisations who can most reliably give up-to-date information about knowledge in their field. This does not mean they are infallible, but they can give the best available advice relating to their specialism.

This activity is somewhat artificial in that you would most likely see a General Practitioner (family doctor) before visiting a specialist, and you would possibly approach others long before trying to contact NASA or an ornithologist. But the point is we would not consult a horticulturist, no matter how well qualified, for a toothache.

One of the difficulties facing the world today is that many people have become distrustful of authorities, including scientific authorities. Almost anyone can set themselves up as an 'authority' on the internet and social media, and not all internet users are diligent in checking the credentials of those who profess to be experts. As we saw in Chapter 2, fake news and disinformation is widespread. Whenever we see a new scientific claim, we need to try to verify its **authenticity**, and its authenticity is largely contingent on the authority of the person or group who first makes the new claim.

KEY WORD

authenticity: validity, genuineness

EXPLORE 13.14

There are many competing voices talking about the issue of climate change. One such voice is The Lancet Countdown on Health and Climate Change. With a partner, look at the organisation's website.

Would you regard the organisation as authoritative? Why? Why not? Make a list of further information you might want to know before deciding.

Draw a line with 'blind faith' at one end and 'total scepticism' at the other. Where on the line would you want to put The Lancet Countdown?

CONTINUED

Self-assessment

Compare your scale with others in your class. Do you agree? Did you have good reasons for your decisions? Are your classmates' reasons more compelling than your own? Try to reach a class consensus, then consider how you would change your answer (if at all).

In 2005, John Ioannidis (1965–), a professor of Medicine and of Health Research and Policy at Stanford University School of Medicine and a professor of Statistics at Stanford University School of Humanities and Sciences, famously argued that, statistically, most published medical research conclusions are false, largely because of sloppy research, competitiveness, prejudice and financial or other interests. His studies have also been extended to some non-medical scientific research conclusions and these showed a high falsity rate similar to that of medical research.

You might see Ioannidis's studies as a reason to distrust scientific research, but it is more an illustration of reflection and self-regulation at work within the scientific community. Indeed, Ioannidis's statistical research has been very important in identifying solutions on how to optimise research practices, and to improve the number of validated and useful scientific findings.

REAL-LIFE SITUATION 13.16

Looking to improve the ways in which science is done might be regarded as an ethical imperative by the scientific community. To what extent does the imperative to improve scientific methodology help to justify scientific authority?

Disagreements in science

There is an old joke: If you ask ten doctors a question you will get eleven different answers. The same appears to be true when it comes to some of the more contentious issues in the natural sciences.

Some laypeople are unsettled by the lack of certainty they experience when scientists disagree, and it may lead them to 'lose faith' in the scientific process. However, far from undermining science, disagreements within the scientific community actually contribute to scientific progress. Disagreements happen for good reasons. For example, one theory might be simpler; another might yield more accurate predictions. This could lead to disagreements about which theory is better, but in this case, neither theory might be objectively or absolutely better: each could be better for different purposes. The great advantage of disagreements in science is that the disagreements usually lead to more rigorous testing of the contentious issues, and more stringent scrutiny of all evidence by peers. As a general rule, scientific debates will continue until there is sufficient evidence to help a consensus to be reached.

A scientific controversy occurs when there is significant disagreement among scientists. Disagreements could be about the fundamentals of a theory; for example, physicists may disagree on whether multiple universes exist. This is not something that can be directly answered by experimentation but theoretical physicists involved in the field will continue to develop their theory until such time as the theory sufficiently explains the phenomena observed, or another theory provides a better explanation.

Disagreements can also occur when scientists agree about main points but disagree on details. One example of this is that while there is widespread agreement on what constitutes good human nutrition, there are disagreements over particular details such as whether drinking limited quantities of red wine can be good for us. Scientists on all sides of the debate will continue to experiment and accumulate data until the evidence, one way or the other, is regarded as conclusive – although it is perfectly possible that drinking red wine proves good for people with some metabolisms and bad for others, so a single statement cannot be expected to encompass every circumstance.

DISCUSS 13.15

To what extent is disagreement a vital part of the scientific endeavour?

REFLECTION

Some people regard disagreement as damaging and divisive; others believe it is both healthy and necessary. Where do you stand, and would your position change for other areas of knowledge?

Figure 13.11: Is chocolate a health food?

In China, there is an on-going debate about the efficacy of traditional Chinese medicine in which people take up forceful positions both ways. Similar debates surround **homeopathic** and traditional remedies, and these debates also attract passionate arguments.

KEY WORD

homeopathy: a system of alternative medicine that believes in treating ailments with minute concentrations of substances that in larger amounts would case the same symptoms of the ailment; it is based on the principle that like cures like

REAL-LIFE SITUATION 13.17

How is our scientific knowledge susceptible to cultural influences?

13.8 Communication and popular science

Every science subject in which you do experiments will involve the writing of a scientific report, in which you have to describe how you conducted the experiment. The IB Diploma Programme produces guides for how to write scientific reports for each of the Diploma Programme sciences. Sometimes these reports might seem a chore compared to the enjoyment of doing practical work. But writing reports is an essential element of the scientific endeavour.

A good science report not only shows your teachers and examiners that you understand what you have done, but it also gives you the opportunity to reflect on the process, and helps to develop your understanding of the scientific method and the scientific concepts behind the subject of your research. This is how real learning happens, and how scientific knowledge is shared and evaluated. All scientists – from those at the top of their fields to the humblest science student – write reports on their research.

Many scientists also write academic articles about their reports. These articles can be for scientific journals, books or presentations at scientific conferences. While the principle of simplicity might apply to scientific theories, not all scientific theories are easy for the **layperson** to understand. If you start to read an academic article, you might easily become lost in the scientific jargon of the field and the complex mathematics that often accompany the science. Even scientists who work in one field can struggle to understand the complexities of science in a field outside their own. Richard Feynman (1918–1988), a recipient of the Nobel Prize for Physics in 1965, once famously said, 'If you think you understand quantum mechanics, you don't understand quantum mechanics.'

Despite the difficulties of communicating some aspects of science, today's world is heavily reliant on scientific knowledge, and if we are to express any views on issues in science, or the ethical questions that emerge, we have to have some understanding of what is happening in the many fields of science. To this end, many of us are reliant on the large numbers of popular science books that are published each year.

> KEY WORD
>
> layperson: a person not from the profession

Popular science books are often written with much more certainty than specialist scientists actually hold, but they are there to engage the public in a conversation. Scientists do not always write popular science books just for the love of sharing their passion for their research, although that undoubtedly plays a part. Rather, they are increasingly expected to engage with the public, because scientific policies – and with them, scientific funding – tend to be strongly influenced by public opinion. If the general public is engaging with scientific ideas and keen to hear about new developments, it is easier for research centres to attract the funding they need to work in those fields.

REAL-LIFE SITUATION 13.20

'Popular' books about other areas of knowledge are also published, although possibly not to the same extent as in science. Can you think of examples of 'popular' books about mathematics, history, the human sciences or the arts? Why might there be more in some fields than others? What implications does popularisation, with its implicit simplification, have for scientific *knowledge*?

Scientific language

One of the issues facing people reading scientific books or articles is the use of specialised language. As well as encountering words that you may not be familiar with because they are specific to a particular field of science, you may also come across familiar words that carry a different meaning. For example, some students will think of *gas* as referring to natural gas used for heating, or students in the USA will think of it as fuel for a car, whereas in the natural sciences, *gas* refers to a particular state of matter.

Good scientific writing requires precise writing that explicitly defines its terms. Changes in the use of words can affect the way we think about the world around us. If people use scientific terms in different ways, it can become very confusing for readers.

As IB Diploma Programme students, when writing scientific reports, or writing about the natural sciences in TOK, it is important that you are clear, and that you use technical words appropriately and accurately. If in doubt, explicitly say how you are defining a word.

EXPLORE 13.15

Below are a number of familiar words that also have specific scientific meanings in certain fields of science. Find out what the scientific meanings are.

a   family (in taxonomy)

b   mole (in chemistry)

c   patch (in computer science)

d   shear (in physics)

e   belt (in astronomy)

f   alien (in ecology)

DISCUSS 13.16

Does all knowledge rely on clear definitions of terms?

To what extent could the languages we speak affect how we understand scientific ideas?

Scientific censorship

In recent years, there has been increasing debate in some countries about the need to censor some scientific communications in the interests of national security. While deleting methods from a scientific publication might prevent terrorists from being able to exploit the information, it would compromise the effectiveness of the peer review process, and could potentially increase the risks faced by the general public. For example, if hospitals and health services do not have direct access to updated medical information, misdiagnoses and wrongful treatments are more likely.

Scientists argue that the best protection against the possibility of bioterrorism is the ability of the scientific community to collaborate fully to develop products that will benefit human health.

Politics can play a significant role in scientific censorship. One example comes from the Trump presidency in the USA. The White House allegedly removed most references to climate change in governmental websites, and risks from extreme weather conditions and rising sea levels were removed from its National Security Strategy. This is an example of the politicisation of science: the manipulation of science for political purposes.

Public opinion can also lead to censorship of science. An example of this also comes from the USA where, in the 1920s, Tennessee, Arkansas and Mississippi passed laws that banned the teaching of human evolution in schools. Although the last ban was lifted in 1970, many American citizens are still fighting to have evolution challenged in schools and 'creation science' taught as a viable alternative. Even today, Saudi Arabia and the Sudan ban the teaching of evolution in schools, and in 2017, Turkey announced plans to end the teaching of evolution.

KEY WORD

creation science: treating the theory that God created the universe as recorded in the Book of Genesis as a scientific theory

REFLECTION

If scientific knowledge claims clash with widely held public beliefs and practices, (and perhaps even what you want to believe), where do your responsibilities lie?

13.9 Science and ethics

REAL-LIFE SITUATION 13.21

Which issues spring to mind when you think about ethics in relation to science? Are they mostly to do with the way science is done, or the applications of science in the world?

Science requires honesty and integrity at every step of the scientific process. If observations are fabricated, or inconvenient findings are overlooked, the process can become distorted and false conclusions could be reached. As we have already seen, many elements of the scientific method, including collaboration, the publication of data, peer review and replication, help not only to identify errors, but also to maintain integrity. There is little point claiming a discovery if no one else is able to verify it. Even so, occasional cases of fraud do happen, and sometimes people make mistakes, so the scientific community has to remain vigilant.

However, honesty in reporting of scientific data and being scrupulous when recording and analysing data to avoid errors are just two aspects of ethics in science.

Deeper issues arise when we think about who does science, and why. Often, scientists rely on funding from universities and governments for their research, or they work for large companies who expect a product to be developed. In some cases, large sums of money can be involved, and this can put pressure on scientists or scientific companies to analyse, interpret and promote their results in a particular light.

One well-documented example is when GlaxoSmithKline™, a large pharmaceutical company, suppressed the results of some clinical trials of an anti-anxiety medication it had developed. The results of the suppressed trials showed that the drug was often ineffective in children and teenagers, and possibly increased the risk of suicidal tendencies in this age group. The issue came to light when a memo outlining ways to 'effectively manage the dissemination of these data in order to minimise any potential negative commercial impact' was leaked. GlaxoSmithKline™ was eventually sued by the US Department of Justice for spreading false and fraudulent claims. The company pleaded guilty and had to pay a three-billion dollar fine.

KEY WORDS

fabricate: manufacture, make up

pharmaceutical: related to drugs

REAL-LIFE SITUATION 13.22

We tend to be quick to criticise research into sugar funded by sugar companies, or research into the effects of tobacco funded by tobacco companies. Should we have more faith in research into drugs funded by pharmaceutical companies? Why? Why not?

Academic honesty

An important ethical issue in science, as well as many other disciplines, is the proper acknowledgement of sources of information, ideas and data. Unfortunately, this is not always observed as well as it should be.

There is a long history, particularly in physics, of women going unrecognised for their achievements and contributions. Often their advisors or collaborators – almost always more senior men in the field – take credit for any achievements. One example is that of Jocelyn Bell Burnell (1943–), the British astrophysicist who discovered pulsars. When she reported her finding to her PhD supervisor, Antony Hewish, he dismissed the pulsating signals as radio interference. However, Bell Burnell was convinced the signals were coming from deep space. She continued to gather observations until there was no doubt. The discovery was awarded the Nobel Prize in 1974, but it was awarded to Hewish rather than to Bell Burnell.

Fortunately, the issue of gender inequality in science is starting to be acknowledged, and women in science are beginning to be recognised for their accomplishments. In

KEY WORD

pulsar: a small, dense, spinning neutron star

2018, Donna Strickland became just the third woman in history to be awarded a Nobel Prize in physics, and Bell Burnell was awarded a $3,000,000 *Breakthrough Prize* for her many valuable contributions to science over the past 50 years.

Bell Burnell intends to use her prize money to promote diversity in science by providing doctoral studentships for people in under-represented groups, including women, minority ethnic groups and refugees, to help them become researchers in physics.

In January 2019, Oxford University abolished a women-only junior research fellowship, claiming that it was discriminatory on the grounds of gender, and breached equality laws. Other universities may follow suit. Some people agree that women should have to compete for fellowships on their own merits; others have argued that because the history of universities has been almost exclusively male and there is still a lack of women in academia, initiatives such as women-only fellowships are still needed to redress the imbalance.

REAL-LIFE SITUATION 13.23

Ethical decisions are rarely easy. How would you decide whether it is more ethical to promote diversity in science through positive discrimination or to offer equal opportunities?

Why might diversity in science be important in the quest to further scientific knowledge?

Ethical conduct

During the Second World War, Nazi scientists conducted many experiments on concentration camp prisoners. Although the knowledge that the Nazis developed has sometimes proved useful, some of their experiments were horrific. One of these experiments was designed to investigate the effects of hypothermia on humans. The experiments involved making prisoners sit in ice water and being left naked in freezing temperatures for hours. Many prisoners were left to freeze to death; others were rewarmed but left with permanent injuries from their treatment.

REAL-LIFE SITUATION 13.24

If the knowledge gained from an experiment proves useful for helping people, does it justify cruelty to the experimental subjects? Would your answer change if the experimental subjects were non-human animals? How would you justify your response?

> **KEY WORDS**
>
> hypothermia: unusually low body temperature
>
> experimental subjects: the individuals who are experimented on
>
> informed consent: permission given in full knowledge of the known possible consequences

After the war, the Nuremberg Code was published in 1949, following the Nuremberg trials. The Nuremberg Code is a fundamental document for the guidance of ethical behaviour when researching on human subjects. It features ten main points, including that subjects need to be volunteers who give informed consent; that the experiment should avoid any unnecessary suffering; the risks must be proportionate to the expected benefits; and the experiments should be stopped at any time if they are found to be dangerous. Most countries around the world adopted the Nuremberg Code and supplement it with their own additional guidelines and standards.

The Helsinki Declaration was a later development, and was first adopted in 1964. It has gone through several revisions since, and is now the cornerstone of most national policies on the ethical use of human subjects in scientific experiments, including the testing of drugs on volunteers.

One of the most contentious areas of scientific ethics lies around the concept of informed consent. Some drug companies pay 'volunteers' to participate in experiments, including in developing countries. Sometimes information given out about the possible consequences is not available in the language of the paid participants. Even in cases when the information is in the language of the volunteers, there is a question of how much a volunteer can truly understand possible consequences; many patients who agree to participate in a trial may have physical and emotional issues that cloud their ability to give clear, informed consent. Even those who have developed a drug cannot know all the possible consequences of taking it.

In 2006, eight healthy young men volunteered to participate in a routine drugs trial in a British hospital. They would be the first humans to take a drug, known as TGN1412, which had previously been tested on monkeys. The men were each paid £2,000 for their participation. The men believed it was 'easy money', and that their participation would help cancer research. They understood that possible consequences would be headaches and/or nausea that could last several hours.

Within an hour of taking the drug, six of the eight men had severe reactions to the drug, including a high temperature and multiple organ failure. Their bodies swelled up so much that news reports referred to them as 'elephant men'. The men's lives were saved, but one man lost some of his fingertips and had to have parts of his feet amputated. The long-term effects of the trial on their bodies remain unknown. The two men who had no reaction had been given a placebo.

REAL-LIFE SITUATION 13.25

If people receive money to participate in a drugs trial, are they really volunteers? Is it possible to give informed consent if the consequences of taking a drug are unknown? Can all the consequences of taking a drug ever be known?

KEY WORD

bioavailability: the measure of drug absorption over time

It could be said that in prescribing any drug to any patient, doctors generally cannot be certain what effects the drug will have because the **bioavailability** of drugs can vary dramatically from patient to patient. If you have read a fact sheet accompanying any medication, you will often see a frightening range of possible side effects listed.

In the case of the drug TGN1412 described, testing the drug on monkeys had shown no serious side effects, and the drug was deemed safe to test on human subjects. But we know different animals react differently to different substances. Some foods that we enjoy can be poisonous to our pets. This raises the issue of using animals in scientific research.

REAL-LIFE SITUATION 13.26

Experiments on animals can be helpful, but they are not always reliable. How might the uncertainty of reliable results in any research project affect our ethical responsibilities?

Animal testing

Hundreds of millions of animals are said to be used in science experiments every year. These include frogs, fish, mice and guinea pigs, sheep, pigs, dogs and primates. Some studies are behavioural, and the animals may live reasonably comfortable lives, but others involve injecting animals with **pathogens** or toxic drugs, performing unnecessary surgeries, strict confinement and other procedures that may cause psychological and/or physical suffering. Many of the subjects are later killed.

Testing on animals is generally regarded as more ethical than experimenting on people, and it is certainly true that some scientific breakthroughs have occurred as a result of animal experimentation. Some people would argue that it is acceptable for animals to suffer and die if there is a chance that their suffering could save or improve human lives. Other people argue that testing on animals is acceptable if, and only if, suffering is minimised, and the potential benefits to humans could not be achieved any other way.

> **KEY WORD**
>
> **pathogen:** a virus, bacterium or other micro-organism that can cause disease

Figure 13.12: Hundreds of millions of animals are used in scientific experiments each year

Those against animal testing argue that to cause any suffering is too much, and even more so because the number of animals affected is so high. They also argue that testing drugs on some animals is not a reliable indicator of how other animals or human beings will react to the same drugs, and therefore animals suffer needlessly.

These days, scientists are generally asked to reduce the number of experimental animals they use, refine their experiments to reduce any suffering, and replace animal testing with other methods such as using cell cultures or computer modelling. Even so, supplying animals and the accompanying equipment for animal testing is a thriving industry, and many people have an economic stake in the continuation of animal testing.

Jeremy Bentham (1748–1832) was an English philosopher and social reformer who, among other things argued for social welfare, the equality of women, the abolition of slavery, corporal and capital punishment. He was one of the founders of utilitarian ethics, and had a significant influence on the reform of schools, prisons and the court system. He was also one of the first people to talk about animal rights.

DISCUSS 13.17

'The question is not, can they reason? Nor, can they talk. But can they suffer?'
Jeremy Bentham (1748–1832)

What do you think Bentham meant by this? To what extent do our life experiences and cultural backgrounds affect our ethical values?

Taking a TOK perspective on ethical issues

One of the difficulties many students have in TOK is that they tend to examine issues in terms of arguments for and against an issue, rather than looking at the knowledge issues that arise. This is particularly true when it comes to issues they are passionate about. You need to be able to take a step back from an issue to examine the knowledge issues.

Examples of knowledge questions that could be applied to the issue of animal testing and other ethical issues include:

- To what extent can we distinguish between reason and emotion when making an ethical decision?

- Can emotions play a positive role in helping us to develop effective methods for the production and acquisition of knowledge?

- Can knowledge be independent of ethical responsibilities?

- To what extent do ethical judgements about methods in the natural sciences vary over time and across cultures?

- Are there circumstances in which the value of the knowledge produced is more important than concerns as to how the knowledge was produced?

EXPLORE 13.16

Choose one of the knowledge questions above, and create a mind-map to plan an essay, drawing examples from an ethical issue in science that is important to you. (It could be animal testing, abortion, euthanasia, drug testing on humans, etc.)

Self-assessment

Critically evaluate your plan. Have you used your chosen issue to provide examples to discuss your knowledge question, or have you fallen back into arguments for and against the issue you selected? How can you improve your plan to make sure you stay focused on the knowledge issue?

> **CONTINUED**
>
> **Peer-assessment**
>
> Exchange mind-maps with a classmate who has chosen a different question and/or issue. What do you like about your classmate's plan? How could it be made even better?

Ethics and social benefits

Scientific progress is generally equated with the progress of the human race. Certainly, advances in science have brought better nutrition and health care, which allow us to lead longer, healthier lives. We tend to enjoy better standards of living than people of the past, and many menial and dangerous tasks have become mechanised, giving us more free time than our ancestors enjoyed. But some people have asked the question, 'Is scientific progress good for humanity?'

Some would argue that for all the technical and economic advantages brought by the Industrial Revolution, we have lost the ability to live happily and sustainably on the Earth. Our scientific advances have brought upon us the *Age of Pollution*, and with our ever-increasing population and our desire for technology, we have put a strain on global resources to the detriment of our planet. Human activity has led to a loss of biodiversity.

The field of ethics is struggling to keep up with the rate of scientific advancement. Advances in science have made possible genetic modification, cloning, increasingly sophisticated weapons, greater surveillance technologies, etc, and most recently advances in AI. The question is not whether these advances are good or bad in themselves, as all things have the potential for both depending on how they are used or misused. But they throw up ethical issues that are yet to be fully addressed.

For example, we might believe it is perfectly reasonable to genetically modify an embryo to prevent it from suffering from cystic fibrosis, sickle cell anaemia, muscular dystrophy or some other life-limiting single gene disorder. But what about disorders such as achondroplasia? Achondroplasia is a genetic disorder that causes short limbs (sometimes referred to as *dwarfism*). The life expectancy of people with this disorder is not significantly lower, and most people with the disorder lead normal and productive lives. Some people would argue that if we say that we modify the gene that causes achondroplasia, we are effectively implying that people with achondroplasia are of less value.

> **REAL-LIFE SITUATION 13.27**
>
> If we accept genetically modifying embryos, or selecting embryos for implantation based on specific traits, where, if anywhere, should we draw the line?
>
> How can we decide?

When couples use *in vitro* fertilisation (IVF), embryos are often screened for genetic traits and selected accordingly. Some are screened to avoid implanting embryos with genetic diseases, but they have also been screened so that couples can specify the sex of the child they want. Genetic science is not far away from being able to select embryos on the basis of eye colour, muscle strength, etc. It raises the spectre of *designer babies*. Currently, designer babies only exist in the realms of science fiction, but the possibility is very real.

REAL-LIFE SITUATION 13.28

Biochemist Jennifer Doudna (1964–) once asked: 'Is it more ethical to edit embryos or to screen a lot of embryos and throw [unselected embryos] away?' How would you answer her?

Whenever we destroy natural habitats to put in roads and build more houses for people, and whenever we kill natural predators such as wolves or leopards because they sometimes kill our livestock or pose a threat to human life, ethical questions are raised.

EXPLORE 13.17

In *The Hitchhiker's Guide to the Galaxy*, a novel by Douglas Adams (1952–2001), the planet Earth, with everything on it, is destroyed by a fictitious Vogon Constructor Fleet to make way for an intergalactic super highway. If you suspend disbelief, would it be any more ethical for us to destroy a forest with all the animal, insect and microscopic life it supports for the construction of a motorway, or to destroy a remote island for the purpose of nuclear testing, than it would be for the Vogons to destroy Earth to enhance their infrastructure?

Have a class debate with one side representing the Vogons who want to create an intergalactic super highway, and the other side representing the planet Earth.

DISCUSS 13.18

How can we decide what *sacrifices* are acceptable in our quest for knowledge?

It is not only the biological and ecological sciences that throw up deep ethical issues. Some people argue that instead of spending billions of dollars on space exploration, the money would be better spent on helping the poor, improving food production, cleaning the oceans, battling climate change or any other need that they perceive to be greater. The construction of the LHC mentioned earlier was similarly controversial.

KEY WORDS

in vitro fertilisation: a laboratory procedure in which an egg is fertilised outside the body; the term *in vitro* means 'in glass'. In the past, IVF babies have been called 'test-tube babies'.

designer baby: a baby genetically engineered *in vitro* with specially selected traits, which can vary from lowered disease-risk to gender selection

Artificial intelligence (AI) is developing at a rapid rate, and some scientists are becoming increasingly concerned about the effects it could have on human life. In 2014, Stephen Hawking claimed that 'The development of full artificial intelligence could spell the end of the human race.' Not everyone is so pessimistic, but how can we know? Is it a reasonable risk to take, and who should decide?

REFLECTION

The question of *who decides* is very much a political one, and, for some people, it may be a religious question too. Think about the ways in which your political or religious views might affect your ethical position on some scientific issues, and how your ethical position on some scientific issues might affect your politics.

13.10 Conclusion

The natural sciences have been largely responsible for the enormous growth of knowledge over the last three centuries, and science is widely seen as one of humanity's great success stories. However, our pride in science needs to be tempered by a degree of humility. Overstating scientific certainty and objectivity opens the way to the undermining of the scientific endeavour. That said, scientific methodology, in conjunction with the system of peer review, is widely regarded as the 'gold standard' for knowledge production, and offers a degree of certainty and objectivity that is difficult to match in other areas of knowledge.

This respect for scientific methodology too often leads to science and the scientific method being fraudulently invoked to give credibility to ideas and products that do not necessarily warrant such confidence. We need to be aware that not everything that purports to be science is really science.

Within the natural sciences, knowledge is growing at an ever-increasing rate, and as a result, ethical issues are arising faster than scientific ethicists, regulatory bodies or wider society can cope with. These ethical issues give rise to many complex and interesting knowledge questions that need to be addressed if we are to satisfactorily resolve the underlying ethical issues.

KNOWLEDGE QUESTIONS

1   To what extent do our expectations affect how we perceive the world?

2   What is the role of creativity and imagination in the natural sciences?

3   What impact do specialized vocabularies have on the shaping of knowledge in the natural sciences?

13.11 Linking questions

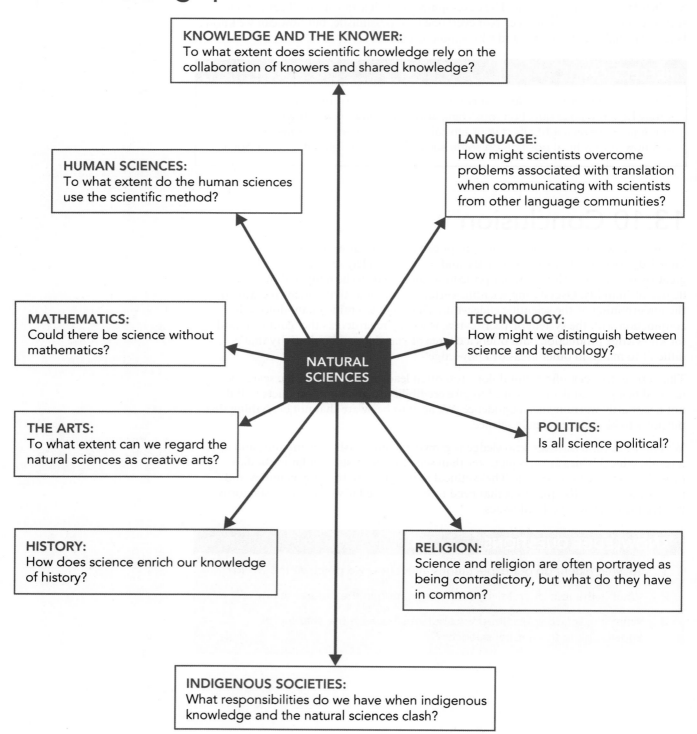

KNOWLEDGE AND THE KNOWER:
To what extent does scientific knowledge rely on the collaboration of knowers and shared knowledge?

LANGUAGE:
How might scientists overcome problems associated with translation when communicating with scientists from other language communities?

HUMAN SCIENCES:
To what extent do the human sciences use the scientific method?

MATHEMATICS:
Could there be science without mathematics?

NATURAL SCIENCES

TECHNOLOGY:
How might we distinguish between science and technology?

THE ARTS:
To what extent can we regard the natural sciences as creative arts?

POLITICS:
Is all science political?

HISTORY:
How does science enrich our knowledge of history?

RELIGION:
Science and religion are often portrayed as being contradictory, but what do they have in common?

INDIGENOUS SOCIETIES:
What responsibilities do we have when indigenous knowledge and the natural sciences clash?

13.12 Check your progress

Reflect on what you have learned in this chapter and indicate your confidence level between 1 and 5 (where 5 is the highest score and 1 is the lowest). If you score below 3, re-visit that section. Come back to this list later in your course. Has your confidence grown?

	Confidence level	Re-visited?
Do I understand what is meant by the scientific method and appreciate there is no one definitive scientific method?		
Am I aware of the importance of scientific equipment and models?		
Do I recognise some of the limits of scientific methodology, and could I discuss the implications of the observer effect?		
Do I understand why total objectivity is an unachievable goal?		
Am I able to discuss paradigms, and the concept of a paradigm shift?		
Am I comfortable explaining what is meant by inductive reasoning, and do I understand the principle of falsification?		
Can I articulate what Occam's Razor is, and why it is important?		
Can I compare and contrast theoretical science with experimental science?		
Do I have a sound understanding of the scientific community, and the roles that it plays in developing scientific knowledge?		
Do I recognise the importance of communication in the natural sciences, including the significance of scientific language and the implications of scientific censorship?		
Am I able to discuss some of the ethical issues that are found in the natural sciences and some of the knowledge issues that arise?		

13.13 Continue your journey

- To build on the knowledge that you have gained in this chapter, you could read some of the following articles.

- If you are interested in how we can **fail to see things we are not expecting**, search for the invisible gorilla video online and read: Christopher Chabris and Daniel Simons, *The Invisible Gorilla*, HarperCollins, 2010. Search the *Invisible Gorilla* website to watch the video.

- If you would like to follow up on **self-awareness tests**, read: Alexandra Horowitz, 'Smelling themselves: Dogs investigate their own odours longer when modified in an "olfactory mirror" test' in *Science Daily*. 27 February 1998. Search the *PubMed Central* website for the article.

- For another account of studies on the **self-awareness of dogs**, read: National Research Tomsk State University 'STSR tests confirm that dogs have self-awareness'. Search the *Phys* website for the article.

- For a fascinating look at the **interplay between history, culture and science**, read: Ryszard Sosnowski, 'The scientific and cultural role of atomists' in *Nukleonika*, 2005;50 (Supplement): S5-S10. Search the *Institute of Nuclear Chemistry and Technology (Warsaw, Poland)* website for the article.

- For an in-depth account of some of the **issues with scientific research** read: John P Ioannidis 'Why most published research findings are false.' *PLoS Med.* 2005, vol. 2, no. 8, page 124. Search the *AMA Journal of Ethics* website for the article.

- For a closer look at how **observation affects what is being observed**, read: Weizmann Institute of Science. 'Quantum Theory Demonstrated: Observation Affects Reality' in *Science Daily*. 27 February 1998. Search the *Science Daily* website for the article.

- For a discussion on **gender discrimination in science**, read: Ethan Siegel, 'These 5 Women Deserved, And Were Unjustly Denied, A Nobel Prize In Physics', *Forbes*, 11 October 2018. Search the *Forbes* website for the article.

> # Chapter 14
> # The human sciences

LEARNING INTENTIONS

This chapter will explore the scope and range of subjects included within the human sciences, the tools and methods for constructing knowledge, the impact of technology on the study of humans, the ways in which the disciplines within the human sciences connect with the natural sciences and the ethical considerations involved.

You will:

- consider the place of observation within the human sciences, and the difficulties that arise when using observation to study human behaviour

- understand the other methods for constructing knowledge in the human sciences, including qualitative and quantitative measurements and the use of statistics, modelling and questionnaires, and appreciate the problems inherent in these

- explore the concepts of patterns, predictions, correlation and causation

- consider the impact of big data and technological developments on the study of human phenomena

- appreciate some of the criticisms that may be applied to the human sciences, including the problems of bias, reliability of data and errors in reasoning

- compare the similarities, differences and connections between the human sciences and natural sciences

- consider the role of ethical considerations within the context of the human sciences

Analyse each of the following quotations and discuss the questions that follow.

1   'It has been said that man is a rational animal. All my life I have been searching for evidence which could support this.' **Bertrand Russell** (1872–1970)

2   'It is quite possible – overwhelmingly probable, one might guess – that we will always learn more about human life and human personality from novels than from scientific psychology.' **Noam Chomsky** (1928–)

3   'Human behaviour makes most sense when it is explained in terms of beliefs and desires, not in terms of volts and grams.' **Steven Pinker** (1954–)

4   'You never change things by fighting against the existing reality. To change something, build a new model that makes the old model obsolete.' **Richard Buckminster Fuller** (1895–1983)

5   'I want to make sure that the future we're creating is one that is the best it can be for people around the world, and also one that includes the full range of our talent and our skills – and, you know, gender and ethnicity, geography – to solving the world's problems.' **Mae Jemison** (1956–)

For each quotation, consider:

a   Do you agree or disagree with the quotation?

b   What do you think the quotation suggests about the nature and purpose of the human sciences?

c   What is assumed or taken for granted about the human sciences in each quote?

d   Do any of the quotations suggest disagreements about the human sciences?

e   Do you think the quotation could apply to other areas of knowledge? If so, in what ways?

14.1 Introduction

REAL-LIFE SITUATION 14.1

1   Can you predict a person's behaviour at home and at school? If there is a difference between their behaviour in the two situations, can you explain why?

2   It may be easier to measure a person's height than it is to quantify their happiness, intelligence, personality and moral values. Why might you want to understand, measure and predict these human characteristics? In what ways might the pursuit of this knowledge be problematic?

KEY WORDS

sociology: the study of the structure and function of society

anthropology (cultural and social): the study of the development of culture and society

psychology: the scientific study of the human mind and behaviour

Since human beings have been able to reflect about themselves and their place in the scheme of things, they have been struck by their own complex and mysterious nature. The human sciences are an attempt to reduce the mystery by studying human behaviour in a systematic way. The human sciences include a range of subjects including geography, economics, sociology, anthropology and psychology. Despite the obvious differences between these subjects, they are all based on observation and experimentation, and seek to understand humans.

However, there is a significant question arising here regarding the scope and limits of the human sciences. For example, arguments could be put forward for human sciences to include religious knowledge systems, political science and history. For the purposes of organising this book and in order to deal with each in sufficient depth, these areas are covered in separate chapters.

KEY WORD

political science: the scientific study of the state, governments, power and political activity

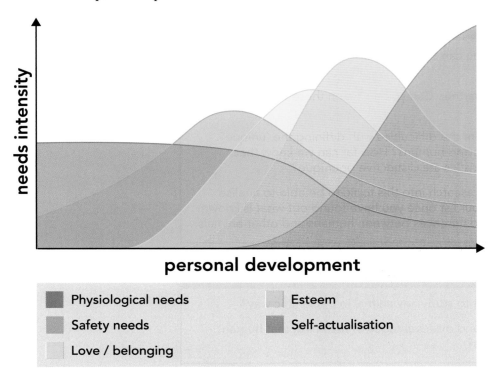

Figure 14.1: Maslow's hierarchy of human needs

Maslow's hierarchy of needs sets out that we are aware of our human potential beyond simply survival – once we have basic material needs met such as food, water and shelter, we can aspire to be creative and have intellectual pursuits, implying that human aspiration is more than just having our material needs met. We have a conscience, we follow ethical norms, we laugh, we cry, we have the capacity for self-reflection and for language. Moreover, we record knowledge and pass it on, we are creative, we have opposable thumbs, we are aware of the past and future and we develop technology. We might think that we are more than just a body and a mind – some people believe that they have a soul which cannot be explained in terms of material processes. Whatever your opinion about this, there are likely to be special challenges in studying human beings in a scientific way.

In Chapter 13, we investigated the scope of the natural sciences, which is to investigate the chemical, biological and physical properties of our natural world and discover the laws that govern them using a rigorous method. The natural sciences can describe the forces affecting a falling object or the structure of a cell, or calculate how reactive a metal is. By contrast, the human sciences set out to understand, explain and predict human behaviour. The fact that humans are the subject of the human sciences makes the human sciences different to the natural sciences. The human sciences are called sciences because, to some extent, they use a scientific method, including use of data in order to establish models, principles or laws. They identify general trends of human behaviour using hypotheses and tests, falsification and inductive reasoning. In this way, human sciences claim to produce reliable knowledge that is logical, as objective as possible, and accepted. In this chapter, we will look at various key concepts in the human sciences – observation, measurement, patterns and experiments. We will also compare the human sciences with the natural sciences.

EXPLORE 14.1

1 List as many features as you can that distinguish human beings from other animals.

2 Compare your list with a partner. Can you agree on these features? Why? Why not?

3 As a class, discuss: What are the difficulties with defining the 'unique' features of various animals and humans? How far can we know that particular human characteristics are distinctive or unique?

4 Do you need to do some research into this topic to be able to finalise your list? If so complete your list once you have found out what is known about the similarities and differences between humans and other animals.

DISCUSS 14.1

1 To what extent is it difficult to study any animal in a scientific way?

2 What are the advantages and disadvantages of assuming that human beings are rational animals?

14.2 Observation

REAL-LIFE SITUATION 14.2

What problems do we face when trying to observe and describe what we see?

Perhaps the most important characteristic of science is that it is based on observation. One problem in the human sciences is that, although you can observe other people's behaviour, you cannot directly observe their minds. You may be able to make an educated guess about what they are thinking, but you can never be entirely sure that you are right. In Chapter 3 we explored empiricism, the school of thought that claims that all knowledge is ultimately based on our sense perception. Our observations are closely linked to our senses; our brain interprets and 'makes sense' of the sense data it receives, via sight, sound, taste, touch, smell and our other senses. There are important questions here to evaluate, regarding the reliability of our senses and the scope and accuracy of our observations.

The observer effect

In the human sciences, as in the natural sciences, there are a number of factors that affect us when we are making observations, and when we are being observed. In

KEY WORD

Sense perception: our brain interprets the data via our various senses including sight, hearing, sound, taste, touch and other senses such as our awareness of where our body is in space

Chapter 13, we discussed the so-called observer effect (the principle that the act of observing a phenomenon changes the phenomenon being observed) as it applies to the natural sciences. The observer effect is also a problem for the human sciences where it refers more generally to the tendency of people to behave differently when they are being observed. If a psychologist is observing people, they may become nervous or embarrassed by the attention, and this may lead them to change their behaviour.

REAL-LIFE SITUATION 14.3

1　Think of examples of when your observations have been accurate and when they have let you down. When can we trust our observations?

2　To what extent can we ever know how people behave and think when they are not being watched or observed?

There are at least two ways in which a human scientist can try to get round the observer effect. The first is *habituation*. If a television crew came and filmed your TOK class for a whole term, you would probably get used to the presence of the cameras, and eventually ignore them.

Anthropologists use a similar strategy when they **go native** and live with a tribe for an extended period of time. The hope is that the people they are studying will eventually get used to them and behave normally in their presence.

Another solution to the observer effect is to use hidden cameras. If you do not know that you are being observed, then it will not affect your behaviour. But this raises ethical questions about whether or not it is acceptable to film people without their knowledge.

KEY WORD

go native: adopting the attitudes and behaviour of a foreign group with whom one has lived for an extended period

---

EXPLORE 14.2

Imagine that a television crew were coming to your school tomorrow to film a typical TOK class for a documentary to be shown on national television. How would this affect your behaviour, the behaviour of the class and your teacher? Make a list of things that might be similar and different.

Then consider the question 'When observed, people will behave differently.' Discuss how far you agree, and why.

REAL-LIFE SITUATION 14.4

Is living as a member of a gang the same as *being* a member of a gang? How might the observer effect manifest itself?

REFLECTION

If you have someone come and stay with you for a year or two (perhaps a grandparent, an aunt or even an older sibling who moves back home) how would this affect your family dynamics? What about if the new person in your house was a stranger from a different culture? Are there things that you would do or would not do if another person was staying with your family?

Change blindness

When we make observations, we have a tendency to miss certain things. If our attention is focused on one thing, we might fail to observe what is really there. This is the phenomenon known to psychologists as *change blindness*, which you first read about in Chapter 13. Change blindness is an important phenomenon in the human sciences as well as in the natural sciences. Christopher Chabris (1966–) and Daniel Simons (1969–) developed a short film where viewers were invited to count the number of basketball passes made between players in white T-shirts, ignoring those in black T-shirts. However, while pre-occupied by the counting task, many people failed to notice a gorilla that walked in-between the players. Search for the 'invisible gorilla' website online and watch the clip of film. After watching the film, those who did not observe the 'invisible gorilla' were very surprised, and convinced that there was no such gorilla. We may fail to observe changes when our attention is focused elsewhere because our cognitive load is limited; in other words, our brain has a finite capacity to process cognitive tasks.

REAL-LIFE SITUATION 14.5

1   In what ways does your IB Diploma Programme Group 3 subject (human science) rely on observation?

2   To what extent do our observations enable us to produce reliable knowledge?

Figure 14.2: How far might our sense perception be affected by various factors?

The effect of language on observation

Our observation may also be affected by the language used to describe human behaviour. The distinction between positive and normative is relevant here. When we make observations, we might use language to describe facts – such statements would be known as *positive statements*. Alternatively, our observations might use language in a prescriptive way, to express values – these statements are known as *normative statements*. Here are some examples of knowledge claims:

Positive statements describing facts – based on observations

1   There are 50 states that make up the United States of America.

2   IB Diploma Programme students are encouraged to develop the attributes of the learner profile so that they become learners who are inquirers, knowledgeable, thinkers, communicators, principled, open-minded, caring, risk-takers, balanced and reflective.

3   Economics is the study of a society's material resources and work force.

4   SAT or ACT tests are required for admission to many US universities.

Normative statements expressing values about those observations

1   The USA ought to have a strong and stable government that upholds the constitution.

2   IB Diploma Programme students should apply the 10 attributes of the learner profile in everyday life.

3   Economists should have a responsibility to use their theories to promote a more even distribution of wealth and resources in practice, to make a fairer world.

4   US universities should consider all the aspects of a university application, and not place too much emphasis on the just the SAT or ACT scores.

Positive statements usually contain the words 'are' and 'is', whereas normative statements contain words such as 'should', 'must' or 'ought'. In this way, normative statements express an opinion, our ethical values or cultural norms. What we observe via our sense perception relates to the language we use to describe it. When we use language, we might be simply expressing and reinforcing the values that belong to our culture, or challenging the norms and values of that culture.

However, moving from an 'is' to an 'ought' is an error in reasoning known as the naturalistic fallacy (or error of reasoning). The Scottish philosopher David Hume (1711–1776) identified this mistake of moving from an 'is' statement to an 'ought' statement, or assuming that ethical terms such as 'good' and 'right' are natural properties. This is problematic, given that statements of value and ethical knowledge claims do not describe the world in a straightforward way. We explored the relationship between knowledge, ethics and language in Chapter 3.

EXPLORE 14.3

1   Play positive and normative ping pong! Work as a pair. One of you begins with an example of a positive statement. The other has to come up with a related normative statement.

2   Taking it in turns, together develop your list of examples of positive and normative statements. (You could draw on examples from IB Diploma Programme subjects.)

3   Was it easier to generate the positive or normative statements? What do you notice about your examples? What factors affected your choice of examples and language? Did you come up with different types of facts, and different types of value judgements? How far is it possible to establish facts?

DISCUSS 14.2

1   Might some statements of value have a basis in fact? How might we establish the facts about human values?

2   To what extent can we make observations in a way that is objective and **neutral**? Can we make neutral observations about human values? Why? Why not?

KEY WORD

neutral: unbiased, impartial, not supporting either side of an argument

14.3 Methods

DISCUSS 14.3

1   In the study of humans, what would be appropriate methods to gain knowledge?

2   How far do particular methods used in the human sciences produce reliable knowledge?

3   How do we decide if methods in the human sciences are ethical?

The methods that are suitable for studying humans will depend on a number of factors. Sometimes measurement can be used; for example, for population, income and the rate of inflation. On the other hand, there may be things that are difficult to quantify or measure, such as intelligence, personality or happiness.

Why can we not just ask people?

REAL-LIFE SITUATION 14.6

How far might questionnaires or surveys offer a reliable method in the human sciences?

One way to find out what people think is, of course, to ask them. Since most people are reasonably honest, we can learn a lot from questionnaires, surveys, opinion polls and interviews. At the same time, since people generally want to be seen in a good light, we cannot always take what they say at face value. There is evidence from psychology to suggest that we tend to overestimate our strengths and underestimate our weaknesses. For example, in one well-known survey of a million US high school seniors, *all of them* ranked themselves as above average in terms of their ability to get on with other people! Since people care about what others think of them, they may also be unwilling to admit holding unpopular opinions. This may explain why in some countries, extreme political parties often do better in general elections than in opinion polls.

An understanding of the human science behind a particular topic might determine the questions we ask. Consider the questionnaire on happiness in Explore 14.4. As you do so, bear in mind that the psychologist Daniel Kahneman (1934–) describes two types of happiness. Firstly, 'the experiencing self' finds joy and happiness in ordinary day-to-day moments. Secondly, 'the remembering self' recalls our memory of those experiences. Kahneman claims that being happy in the moment is very different from remembering those experiences. Inevitably, what we claim to know will impact on the questions we might ask in a survey, hence the different questions about happiness in the last three questions of the questionnaire.

EXPLORE 14.4

1   Complete a copy of the following short questionnaire as honestly as possible.

		Below average	Average	Above average
a	How much do you worry about what other people think of you?			
b	To what extent do you see yourself as a considerate person?			
c	Do you have a good sense of humour?			
d	How open are you to new ideas?			
e	How worried are you about environmental problems?			
f	Do you experience happiness in day-to-day moments?			
g	Do you have happy memories of your experiences?			
h	Are you happy and satisfied with the general direction of your life?			

2   Now collate the results for the class as a whole. How would you interpret the results, and what conclusions would you draw from them?

REAL-LIFE SITUATION 14.7

1   What are the factors that might shape the questions asked in a survey?

2   How might different factors affect your response to the questions in a questionnaire? How might people's expectations of you impact on the answers you give?

3   Would your answers be different if you had to put your name on the sheet?

There are various techniques for sampling such as systematic sampling (a form of random sampling) and stratified sampling which classifies the population into subgroups before sampling. You will find more information about questionnaires, sampling and survey data by looking back to Chapter 12.

Loaded questions

Another problem with asking people what they think is that it is not easy to frame questions in an unbiased way. You will have come across loaded questions and leading questions in Chapter 12, where you will have discovered that any statistical analysis is only as good as the data it is based on, and that data is dependent on the way it is collected. A loaded question, which contains a hidden assumption, may encourage people to answer one way rather than another. For example, if someone asks 'Do you always cheat in exams?', then if you answer 'yes', you are admitting that you always cheat, and if you answer 'no' you are implying that you *sometimes* cheat. What you have to do is challenge the assumption built into the question and say 'I *never* cheat in exams.'

Statements may also contain built-in assumptions. A sentence such as 'The headteacher was not drunk today' may in a narrow sense be true. But it carries with it the implication that this is unusual, and that they are often drunk – and, in most schools at least, this is likely to be false!

LINKING QUESTION 14.1

Language: To what extent can questionnaires be written in neutral language?

When governments hold referenda, or when social scientists or polling organisations seek to gather data of various kinds, they should try to avoid loaded questions. But in practice, it may be difficult to decide whether a question is biased or not given, that it is difficult to express anything in a completely neutral way.

In the 2016 UK referendum, the original question proposed was, 'Should the United Kingdom remain a member of the European Union?' This phrasing invited a response, 'yes' or 'no'. However, this question was perceived to contain a built-in or implicit bias because it only referred to the 'remain' option, and the choice to vote 'yes' favoured the status quo. Therefore, the Electoral Commission recommended that the question be changed to the following:

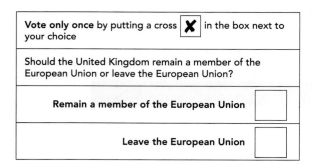

Figure 14.3: Ballot paper for the 2016 election in the UK

The new phrasing of the question was thought to be more open-ended because it implied two equally legitimate options. However, despite this, critics argued that the question was arguably misleading because it gave the impression that leaving the EU was a straightforward option with no sense of the conditions of the deal. This example illustrates the difficulty of phrasing neutral questions so that they avoid bias in favour of a particular response.

Consider, too, the following 1980 US poll in which a similar question was worded in two different ways:

	In favour	Opposed
Do you think there should be an amendment to the Constitution prohibiting abortions, or shouldn't there be such an amendment?	29%	67%
Do you believe there should be an amendment to the Constitution protecting the life of the unborn child, or shouldn't there be such an amendment?	50%	34%

REAL-LIFE SITUATION 14.8

Which of the questions in the 1980 US poll do you think is loaded? Give reasons.

EXPLORE 14.5

1   In pairs, take a topic that interests you – such as abortion, euthanasia or capital punishment. Once you have agreed on your topic, develop two biased questionnaires (about five or more questions per questionnaire) each designed to elicit different responses, one in favour and one against your topic. For example, if you choose abortion, one questionnaire should invite pro-abortion responses and the other pro-life responses.

2   Exchange your questionnaires with a partner and answer each other's questions. Now consider the results. Compare and assess each other's questions.

   • Which questions produced the intended answers?

   • What words or phrases did you find were influential in triggering the desired response?

   • What else might you have said to encourage a particular answer?

   • How might you have phrased your questions to elicit a different answer?

3   Now, working together, design an unbiased questionnaire to discover people's opinions about it. This time, be sure to avoid loaded or biased questions. Present your surveys to your classmates.

Self-assessment

Now step back and consider how you designed these two questionnaires. What was the process you used for phrasing questions so that they are either biased and loaded or unbiased, open and neutral? How did you decide on the different types of questions used in each questionnaire? What would you keep in mind if designing such a questionnaire in the future?

REAL-LIFE SITUATION 14.9

1   What are the problems and challenges with finding out what people really think?

2   Does posing questions to people qualify as a scientific method? What assumptions are made about questionnaires and surveys?

3   What special challenges arise in applying the scientific method to the human sciences?

KEY WORD

response bias: the tendency to try and please a person interviewing us or a person carrying out a questionnaire, by choosing the answer we feel will please them

The example of the referendum questions suggests that if you ask questions with sufficient skill and cunning, you may be able to get people to give you the answer you want. Moreover, even the act of asking may elicit a particular response. Psychologists have identified **response bias**, which is the tendency we might have to please the person asking an interview question or the person carrying out a questionnaire. A final point we can make about questionnaires is that there is often a difference between what people say they would do in a hypothetical situation, and what they *actually* do in reality.

"How would you like me to answer that question? As a member of my ethnic group, educational class, income group, or religious category?"

Have you ever answered a questionnaire or filled in a survey? How accurate do you try to be in your responses? Have you ever found questions with a range of responses where none of the responses accurately corresponds with what you want to answer, or questions that are ambiguous so your selected answer will very much depend on the interpretation you make? What are the implications for any knowledge that such a survey produces?

Quantitative and qualitative research and analysis

Research techniques are based on either quantitative or qualitative methods, and there is value to both types of research. Quantitative research tests a hypothesis using numerical data and statistical analysis. For example, a study might use a data set to produce a theory that there is a correlation between reading levels and examination results. The numerical data provides the evidence for the theory or hypothesis. However, some aspects of human society might lend themselves to a different methodology and approach. For instance, an ethnographer uses a type of qualitative research that is suited to studying cultures and groups of people from a unique perspective. For example, an ethnographer might live as a member of a gang in Chicago. The researcher becomes an observer who studies the culture, group or situation by immersing themselves within it. Based on their observations and contact with the group being studied, they can write a full description.

Quantitative and qualitative methods of research may complement each other, Imagine that a school governing body is monitoring the academic performance and the level of student satisfaction among IB Diploma Programme students. The governors might use both quantitative data (such as grades on reports and previous exam scores) in addition to qualitative data (such as responses to questionnaires and interviews with students and staff). Both types of data might help their investigation. If only one type of data was used, something would be missed.

KEY WORDS

quantitative: relating to, measuring or measured by the quantity of something, rather than its quality

qualitative: relating to, measuring or measured by the quality of something, rather than its quantity; qualitative studies use a method to give a detailed narrative about a human phenomenon that describes a culture or shares a story

EXPLORE 14.6

Collect qualitative and quantitative data on a topic of your choice.

Work on your own at first. Identify some topics of interest for your research, and some methods you could use. [For example, you could interview members of your class, construct a survey or use other appropriate methods to find out about their uses of social media or their views on freedom of speech.]

Then work with a partner. Decide which topic you will research together, and select from your proposed methods so that you have a comprehensive plan for acquiring the data you are seeking. When you choose your methods you might consider the following:

- Do they include quantitative and qualitative research?

- What is the role of observation in your methods?

CONTINUED

- Will you gain reliable data using these methods?

- What assumptions underlie the methods you have chosen?

- Are there ethical considerations you need to take into account?

- How might your data lead to new knowledge?

Then go ahead and conduct your research together.

Self-assessment

After you have conducted your research, evaluate and critique it. Consider:

- Are you clear about which data is quantitative and which is qualitative?

- How far did your methods enable you to acquire reliable data?

- Were your expectations and assumptions justified?

- Which methods worked well, and which proved less successful?

- Do you have enough evidence to reach any conclusions that are justified?

- If you were to undertake a similar exercise on another topic, what would you do differently?

REAL-LIFE SITUATION 14.10

What do you think might be the strengths and weaknesses of qualitative and quantitative research for constructing knowledge? Discuss, using examples from your IB Diploma Programme studies, in particular Group 3 (human science).

Measurement and statistics

The human sciences develop and use numerical data, but the interpretation and use of data is complex. Take war, for example. Stephen Pinker (1954–) argues that we are living in the most peaceful era of history. Statistics show that the percentage of people who die in war has decreased as populations increase. However, anthropologists Dean Falk (1944–) and Charles Hildebolt have arrived at a different conclusion. This raises issues about the various ways of selecting and interpreting the relevant data.

REAL-LIFE SITUATION 14.11

Find out more about Stephen Pinker's work on violence, and the reviews that it generated. Consider why experts here might disagree.

EXPLORE 14.7

1   Begin on your own and make two lists. Which of the following are *easy* to measure, and which are more *difficult*?

   a   weight

   b   brand loyalty

   c   temperature

   d   social class

   e   inflation

   f   intelligence

   g   happiness

   h   reading ability

   i   progress

   j   age

   k   population

   l   height

2   Compare your list with a partner. How far do you agree? Discuss how you would go about trying to measure each item on the list. Can you agree on suitable methods you might use for each?

3   Share your findings with the class. What factors determined the methods that each of you came up with?

LINKING QUESTION 14.2

Mathematics and language: To what extent can human phenomena be expressed in mathematical language?

Figure 14.4: How far can intelligence be measured?

In Chapter 5, we examined the increasing use of big data, which means that more can be known about our behaviour and attitudes from the traces of our online activity. Big data has significant implications in the human sciences, and we will explore these later in this chapter.

Difficulties in using statistics

When we apply numbers to things, it sometimes creates a spurious sense of objectivity. After the 2016 Olympic Games in Rio de Janeiro, Bloomberg™, a data and media company, produced an article entitled, *'Who Won in Rio: Bloomberg's Olympic Medal Tracker'*. You might think that we can find the answer simply by consulting the official rankings. The table below shows some of the results, ranking the countries in terms of the total number of medals won.

Rank	Country	Medals total
1	USA	121
2	China	70
3	Great Britain	67
4	Russia	42
5	France	42

From this table, it seems clear that the USA came first with 121 medals. However, there are a number of factors that could be taken into account.

Firstly, some people argue that the total number of medals is more important than the total number of gold medals won but this is contestable. For example, in the 2016 Rio games, China won a total number of 70 medals including 26 gold medals whereas Great Britain won a total of 67 medals including 27 golds. China is ranked second overall if the total number of medals is measured, whereas Great Britain is in second place according to the total number of gold medals won. If we return to the distinction between positive and normative statements (earlier in the chapter), we can see that our normative assumptions about values might shape our understanding of the facts. If we value a gold medal, we might think it is worth three bronzes. On the other hand, we might argue that it is fairer to count the total number of medals. Legitimate arguments can be put forward for prioritising the total number of medals or the total number of golds.

REAL-LIFE SITUATION 14.12

Should we value total gold medals over total medals? Why? Why not?

What other information might we need before making a decision?

We now have to decide how to *interpret* these figures. Consider Germany and Russia – Germany won two more medals in *total* than Russia, but Russia won six more *gold* medals than Germany. So who did the best? Well, the standard Olympic convention is to award 3 points for a gold, 2 for a silver and 1 for a bronze. Following this convention, the only change at the top is that China and Great Britain change places.

But what if we now take into account the *population* of each country? After all, the USA has a much larger population base than Germany from which to choose its athletes. This dramatically changes the picture. If we now look at medals per million, we get the following result:

Rank	Country	Medals per million population
1	Grenada	9.03
2	Bahamas	6.16
3	New Zealand	4.06
25	Jamaica	3.73
37	Denmark	2.69

If we look at the results in this way, some nations rise to the top of the table, with Grenada ranking first. But we do not have to stop there. We might think of more ways of refining the ranking.

- Since children and seniors do not form part of the pool of potential athletes, we should perhaps take into account age distribution, and look not at points per million population, but points per million people of eligible age – say between the ages of 16 and 60.

- We might consider comparative wealth, on the grounds that athletes from wealthy countries have better training facilities than their poorer counterparts.

We now risk getting lost in a welter of rankings established in accordance with different criteria. It is beginning to look as if there is no clear answer to the question

'Who won the Olympics?' Perhaps we should simply abandon the obsession with ranking countries. That, however, is easier said than done.

REAL-LIFE SITUATION 14.13

1 How far might our values influence the way we think about facts?

2 How might our values impact on the measurements and methods used to gain knowledge in the human sciences?

How do we measure quality?

There are over 50 universities that claim to be in the top 10!

How do you measure a university? Some things are relatively easy to measure – the cost of a course, exam grades and test scores. You might want to find out how many people graduate with a first-class degree, and that data is available. However, you might also want to know whether people enjoy their course, and gauge the levels of student satisfaction as well as the levels of graduate employment following a degree course, and data is available for each of these elements. Most people want to visit a university, and speak to other students already enrolled.

The discussion in the preceding section has shown that we run into problems when we try to measure the quality of different things – such as gold, silver and bronze medals – on a common scale. Moreover, with universities, there are different metrics that could have different levels of importance – student satisfaction, teaching excellence, research excellence, graduate employment rates, etc. People are often accused of 'comparing apples and oranges' when they try to do this. However, an economist might argue that we can in fact compare different things on a common scale by looking at how much people are willing to pay for them. Whether or not it is in practice possible to put a price on everything, is something for you to decide.

REAL-LIFE SITUATION 14.14

1 To what extent can we measure human phenomena accurately?

2 How do we know if our measurements in the human sciences are justified?

EXPLORE 14.8

1 What use, in general, is there in ranking things such as a university? Have you ever looked at university rankings? How seriously do you take them? How seriously should you take them? What do you think is a good university, and why? What factors should shape your judgement? Find out more about university league tables such as:

- QS World Rankings

- The Times Higher Education University Rankings

- The Complete University Guide

CONTINUED

2   Do some research into the Bhutanese model for measuring Gross National Happiness. Find out more about the nine domains of happiness, and how happiness is measured in Bhutan. Consider the extent to which the Bhutanese GNH can produce reliable knowledge.

Modelling

If we want to observe and measure human interaction within a complex system, we will require an appropriately complex method. Agent based modelling (ABM) is an example of a computational tool that models complex systems. These models have been used by economists to represent parts of an economy, or by town planners to simulate the way pedestrians might move through an urban environment. These models can offer an insight into the behaviours of humans when they obey simple rules, while also factoring in some inevitable randomness. Moreover, the model can take into account different human traits and behaviours.

One example of the use of modelling is the attempt to measure the number of people who live in a country, or predict how the population will develop. The demographic transition model (DTM) represents the birth rate and death rate of a country (see Figure 14.5) by showing the annual number of births and deaths per thousand people. The model assumes that as its economy develops, a country goes through various stages.

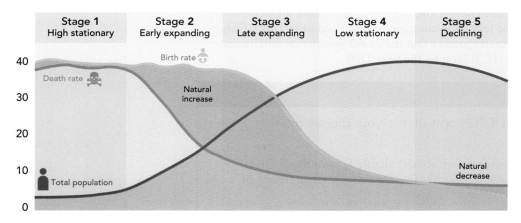

Figure 14.5: How far can a model of population trends be accurate?

According to the model, at Stage 1, before industrialisation, countries have both high birth and death rates, but their overall population begins to increase slowly. Stage 2 models what happens when a country begins to develop; improving social and economic conditions as well as modern medicine lead to longer life expectancy and a decline in death rates, while birth rates remain high. This results in an overall increase in population. Stage 3 shows what happens in less developed countries where population growth becomes slower as birth rates decline due to the result of various factors such as access to contraception and better economic conditions. Stage 4 shows a more developed country where the population stabilises as a result of access to healthcare, education, changes in female expectations and economic prosperity. Stage 5 typically sees the population stabilise, characterised by an aging population and zero population growth.

REAL-LIFE SITUATION 14.15

1   How do we know what factors affect a country's population?

2   How reliable is the DTM as a measure of a country's population? Why?

Problems with modelling

The DTM attempts to model the relationship between birth and death within a country. However, as with any model, it does not take into account complexity such as outliers, exceptions or other factors beyond birth and death rates that affect a country's population, such as immigration or emigration. There are multiple questions arising from this model in terms of its accuracy as a measure of population trends, its reliability and its predictive power.

Moreover, the model does not fit with population predictions being made about particular countries. For example, there are 11 countries where the population is predicted to decline: Lithuania, Japan, Latvia, Hungary, Croatia, Serbia, Ukraine, Romania, Bosnia, Bulgaria and Republic of Moldova. The population of Bulgaria is known to be decreasing, and could be just 3.4 million people by the end of the century. The reasons for this include emigration, low birth rates and a high death rate. By contrast, the population in the following countries is predicted to increase: Qatar, Oman, Lebanon and Kuwait. Experts predict that the world population will increase from 7.6 billion people today to 11.2 billion by the year 2100.

EXPLORE 14.9

Do some research to find out if the population in your country growing. How do you know?

What method would you develop to establish reliable knowledge? What factors do you need to take into account? How far can a measurement of population be accurate?

REAL-LIFE SITUATION 14.16

1   Is it possible for a model to be both simple and accurate?

2   How far can knowledge be reliably represented using a model?

DISCUSS 14.4

How far do particular methods used in the human sciences produce reliable knowledge?

Experiments

As in the natural sciences, human scientists frequently use experiments as part of their method. Psychologists are an obvious example of this. However, one of the problems with research in the human sciences, in particular psychological experiments, is that of sample sizes. Even if a sample of 100 experiments are considered, it will be difficult to generalise from these due to individual differences. With **meta-analyses**, the sample sizes can be in the tens of thousands, but then there is the problem that not all experiments are being carried out in the same way.

Psychologists therefore identify trends, and can generally only make knowledge claims about likelihoods that individuals will behave in a certain way, in a particular situation and under certain circumstances. Alternatively, psychologists can predict that a certain percentage of a group will be likely to behave in a certain way, rather than being able to make accurate predictions about specific individuals. Psychological experiments tend to reveal the complexity of human behaviour, which we explore later in the chapter on ethics, when we consider two famous specific examples, the Milgram experiment and the Stanford Prison experiment.

KEY WORD
meta-analysis: analysis of data to establish trends based on various different studies

14.4 Patterns and predictions

DISCUSS 14.5
If natural sciences can identify the laws of the natural world, can the human sciences identify patterns of human behaviour?

The human sciences can identify patterns of behaviour in individuals and groups, in addition to the complex interactions that take place within groups. Psychologists, economists and social scientists are interested in identifying trends that occur. Although individual behaviour may be unpredictable, we can make surprisingly accurate short-term predictions about such things as the number of births, marriages and deaths in a country. The explanation for this derives from the **law of large numbers**, which says that in a large population *random variations tend to cancel out*.

Since the law of large numbers enables us to predict group rather than individual behaviour, many laws in the human sciences are *probabilistic* in nature. Although we cannot predict with any certainty whether or not John Smith will get married this year, we may be able to predict the *probability* of this happening.

You might think that such probabilistic laws are inferior to the universal laws that are typically associated with the natural sciences. But in fact, the laws governing the behaviour of atoms and genes are also of a probabilistic kind, and a physicist can no more predict the behaviour of one individual gas molecule than a human scientist can predict the behaviour of one person in a crowd.

KEY WORD
law of large numbers: a statistical principle which says that random variations tend to cancel out when a population is large enough

DISCUSS 14.6
Is the goal of the human sciences' primarily to predict human behaviour, or to understand it?

Figure 14.6: How far can we make accurate predictions about populations and food supply?

Predictions: Malthus vs Boserup

The human sciences have predictive power. For example, we can predict:

- the increase in world population

- climate change: how fast the globe is warming up

- technology will have an impact on how we think about knowledge and knowing

- cryptocurrencies such as Bitcoin™ will transform the way that we think about money

Consider the relationship between world population and food production, a question which has interested economists, natural scientists, and other human scientists for hundreds of years. In 2011, the world population reached 7 billion. If the human sciences predict an increase in population, we might also want to know if food production will keep pace. There are multiple theories.

Thomas Malthus (1766–1834) came up with the theory that population growth is exponential (1, 2, 4, 8, 16) but food production is linear (1, 2, 3, 4, 5). His prediction was that population would outstrip food production, resulting in catastrophe and starvation unless the population was contained. He assumed that farming would be limited, and that there was therefore a limit to food production; living in the 18th century, Malthus could not have anticipated modern farming methods nor the role of technology, pesticides and fertilisers in food production.

Ester Boserup (1910–1999) agreed that population growth is exponential, but predicted that this will cause agriculture to develop to feed the population. The disagreement here is effectively around whether humans will have the capacity to develop new techniques to feed the world population, and Boserup was more optimistic.

> ### REAL-LIFE SITUATION 14.17
>
> 1 Food is one of the resources that we need to survive. Can you think of other resources that humans compete for? How far can we make accurate predictions?
>
> 2 What are the variables we can and cannot control? How does this impact on the knowledge we can gain?

Correlation and cause

It is more difficult to establish a causal relationship than to identify a correlation. The fallacy of *post hoc ergo propter hoc* (literally, 'after this, therefore because of this') consists of assuming that because one thing, *B*, follows another thing, *A*, then *A* must be the cause of *B*. For example, just because the murder rate in a country goes up after the abolition of capital punishment, it does not necessarily follow that capital punishment is an effective deterrent. The increase in the murder rate could be explained by other factors – such as a rise in poverty or a greater availability of guns. Notice that we said 'it does not *necessarily* follow that capital punishment is an effective deterrent'. The point is that while it *could be* the case, we cannot jump to this conclusion simply from the fact that the murder rate has gone up, because we need more evidence.

> ### KEY WORD
>
> *post hoc ergo propter hoc:* the fallacy of confusing a correlation with a causal connection

> ### REAL-LIFE SITUATION 14.18
>
> 'Students' IB Diploma Programme Grades Improve at School since New Headteacher Took Over.' What does this headline *imply* about the cause of the improving academic achievement? How reasonable is it to draw this conclusion? What other factors might have caused the improvement? What information might you need to decide?

Phillips curve

In the 1960s, an economist called A. W. Phillips (1914–1975) gathered data on the relationship between inflation and unemployment in the UK from 1861 until 1967. The data appeared to suggest a stable relationship between the two, as illustrated in Figure 14.7.

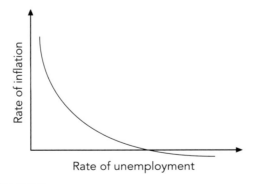

Figure 14.7: The Phillips curve

Many governments understood the curve to show that there was a trade-off between inflation and unemployment, and that lower unemployment could be bought at the cost of higher inflation, and *vice versa*. Unfortunately, when they tried to reduce unemployment by allowing inflation to rise, the Phillips curve broke down, and for much of the 1970s, many countries experienced both rising inflation *and* rising unemployment.

What this example shows is that just because two things are *correlated* it does not follow that the first is the cause of the second. To think that it does is to commit the fallacy of *post hoc ergo propter hoc*. A correlation between two variables, *A* and *B*, could mean that *A* causes *B*, or that *B* causes *A*, or that *A* and *B* are both caused by some other factor, *C*.

EXPLORE 14.10

1   Work with a partner and discuss the question: How might you explain each of the following correlations?

   a   as a country develops economically, birth rates tend to go down

   b   children brought up by talkative parents tend to be talkative themselves

   c   married people tend to be happier than unmarried people

How do you decide the difference between a correlation and a cause? What would you need to do to find out if there is causation underlying the correlation?

2   Make a table for your IB Diploma Programme subjects. For each of your six subjects, try to think of a specific example of a correlation. Rate each of the subjects out of 10 (where 10 is the highest score and 1 is the lowest), according to the ability of that subject to establish correlations. Correlation never implies causation in any area of knowledge. It's something that a lot of students struggle to understand so it's important that we do not suggest that they can in some circumstances.

Are there some subjects where there are many, few or no examples? What does this show about the subject? How easy or difficult is it to establish a correlation?

The effects of predictions on human behaviour

The insurance and pensions industries can correlate your life chances to your gender, address, lifestyle and other factors. Using large data sets, we can calculate life expectancy. In 2016, the average life expectancy across the global population was 72 years. How long you are likely to live depends on many factors and variables – for example, your gender, nationality and lifestyle. Certain habits will affect the likelihood of your decreasing or increasing your life expectancy – for example, if you smoke two cigarettes every day, you are likely to live half an hour less, whereas if you run for half an hour each day, you are likely to live for half an hour longer. Human scientists can identify and calculate risk factors such as the impact of smoking on a person's lifespan. This data can be used to calculate chances and probability. In this way, human scientists are not gazing into a crystal ball to predict the future. Instead, they are calculating probabilities and likelihoods based on the data available. 'If I study river profiles and predict what will happen in the future, it will not affect the course of the river. However, predictions might affect behaviour.' Moreover, the effects of predictions on human behaviour can have serious consequences.

Psychology

In a well-known psychology experiment, Robert Rosenthal (1933–) and Leonor F Jacobson (1922–) researched into the 'expectancy effect' of teachers. School children were randomly allocated to one of two groups labelled 'bright' and 'less bright'. Teachers were informed of the high-performing students in an intelligence test but in reality, this 'bright' group had been randomly allocated.

Although there was no initial difference between the two groups, the children labelled 'bright' made greater academic progress in the following year than the students labelled 'less bright'. This suggests the power of labelling, and that teachers' expectations affected how well the students did and helped to produce the differences between the two groups. Furthermore, psychologists recognise that the expectations people have of you as an individual and the groups you belong to will affect your behaviour. You will either react against or live up to those expectations.

DISCUSS 14.7

1 How far might language and labelling affect our expectation and judgement?

2 Is it justified to infer patterns and reach conclusions based on what we expect? How far do our expectations shape our knowledge?

REFLECTION

Why do you think there is a human tendency to try to do more for people who 'believe in you' than you do for people who expect little from you? Think about how this idea can be harnessed by believing in yourself. How and why do beliefs and expectations become self-fulfilling prophecies?

EXPLORE 14.11

According to a phenomenon known as psychological **reactance**, if a person is inclined to do X, and you then tell them to do X, they become more likely not to do X. This may explain why some teenage anti-smoking campaigns have the perverse effect of encouraging teenagers to smoke. With this in mind,

KEY WORD

reactance: the tendency of people to react against advice, rules and regulations perceived as a threat to their freedom

CONTINUED

hold a class discussion on how you would communicate the concept of anti-smoking in an effective anti-smoking campaign. How far do you think it would be possible to make sure that the campaign does not promote smoking?

LINKING QUESTION 14.3

The arts: Do we learn more about human nature from psychology or from literature?

Economics

If you follow the stock market, you are probably aware that people's expectations can affect share prices. In a *bull market*, when most people expect prices to rise, a rational investor will buy stocks now, hoping to sell them later at a higher price and thereby making a profit. If everyone behaves like that, the demand for stocks will increase, and cause prices to rise. Conversely, in a *bear market*, when most people expect prices to fall, a rational investor will sell stocks now, hoping to buy them back later at a lower price. But if everyone does that, the increased supply of stocks will push prices down. So if everyone expects prices to rise, they will rise, and if everyone expects prices to fall, they will fall. Similarly if someone is hoping to buy a cryptocurrency such as bitcoin™, they might wait until the price is low. If everyone buys when the price is low, the effect will be that the price will increase.

REAL-LIFE SITUATION 14.20

1   Do you think that it is possible to predict with accuracy where the stock market will be in 12 months' time? Give reasons.

2   If economic markets rely on feelings of confidence, how far is it possible to quantify that confidence?

EXPLORE 14.12

How far can the human sciences make accurate predictions? Using reasons, examples or evidence from your own experience and IB Diploma Programme studies, consider both sides of the question, and aim to write around 200 words.

Peer-assessment

Compare your response with a partner and read each other's work. How well have they responded to and understood the question? Have they used reasons, examples or evidence to support their points? Which reasons, examples or evidence did you find most convincing and why? Ask your partner the same questions about your work. Which points did they think you had supported with evidence and argued most clearly, and which did they feel could have been improved?

14.5 Big data and the impact of technological development in human sciences

Figure 14.8: What impact is big data having on the way knowledge is perceived in the human sciences?

We are living through a digital age where technology is transforming what we can know. Developments in technology are creating many opportunities for understanding humans from new perspectives. New disciplines are made possible from 'computational statistics' to 'behavioural analytics'. The use of biometric data can predict biological processes and human behaviour.

It is claimed that in the last two years, more data has been produced by humans than throughout the entirety of human history. The technology to gather, manage and use this data has implications for what we can know and understand about humans, and far-reaching consequences for the future of knowledge and knowing.

> ## LINKING QUESTION 14.4
>
> **Technology:** How might technology influence and change our perspective about humans?

Data science uses tools and methods to collect and analyse data sets about humans, thereby enabling us to better understand human behaviour. There is an important difference between large data and big data, both of which can influence the methods used in the human sciences. A large data set is a huge quantity of information; for example, an enormous number of brain scans, a vast record of standardised test scores or a multi-national business' sales patterns over the last year.

Big data combines multiple large data sets. For example, in the context of medical science, if you wanted to investigate if there is a link between human health and the weather, big data could combine data showing patterns of disease with information about postcodes and another data set relating to weather patterns. In this way, big data has many dimensions, and has the potential for us to know more through combining different data sets in new ways.

Big data is driving and contributing to the development of artificial intelligence (AI), creating the possibility of new insights into human behaviour. For example, in China, where a population of 700 million people no longer use cash nor credit cards and instead use Mobile Payment, there is a huge amount of data generated. In 2017, the mobile internet in China dealt with the equivalent of 18.8 trillion US dollars. This vast set of information gathers data about the sales and purchases of a huge market, as well as the behaviour of the consumers, enabling AI developers to further advance technology to provide even deeper analyses.

REAL-LIFE SITUATION 14.21

1   What are the potential uses for big data in the human sciences?

2   To what extent is big data a reliable tool in the human sciences?

KEY WORD

deep learning: a technology at the centre of artificial intelligence that uses big data to predict or decide

There is an important connection between big data and artificial intelligence. **Deep learning**, also known as machine learning, was discovered by American scientists around ten years ago. For example, if you give the deep learning network a vast number of pictures of flowers, it can identify and recognise other flowers and tell if a new picture is of a flower or not. It can also learn to identify the flower in the new photograph. This technology is now being used in diagnostic medicine, and AI is able to diagnose some illnesses more accurately than medical doctors.

Moreover, the network can be given speeches made by a person and then invent a speech given in the voice and style of that person. Furthermore, if the network is shown pictures, videos and data relating to a human driving a car on the road, it can learn to drive a car. Big data supplies and feeds developments in AI. The branches of AI discovery include computer speech recognition and speech synthesis, computer vision and facial recognition, machine translation, drones and others. The impact that each of these has for the human sciences is significant – the collection and use of this data will be of interest to multiple groups, including entrepreneurs and governments.

REFLECTION

With the advent of deep learning and the technology it can give rise to, it is predicted that humans will no longer be required to fill many of the occupations and professions on which we currently rely. Think about what skills, knowledge and attributes you need to develop to be prepared for an ever-changing world.

LINKING QUESTION 14.5

Technology: What are the benefits of technological developments (such as big data) for the human sciences?

There are multiple positive ways that technology can be used in order to understand human behaviour. For example, the use of big data and AI to model the movement of a large group of people through a transport system – such as an underground train network – may be very useful for passenger safety. Technology such as facial recognition can help with identifying missing persons, and voice recognition can help with human–AI interfaces such as Alexa™ and Siri™. Eye tracking technology can enable us to understand human attention and observation. This technology can be used to benefit humans – for example, robotics and prosthetic limbs can contribute to healthcare.

Algorithms and big data can also be used for informing decisions behind sentencing in criminal justice systems. In criminal trials, judges need to assess the risk of a person re-offending when deciding whether to temporarily release them while awaiting trial, and deciding on the punishment or sentence if they are found guilty. Algorithms based on a person's past can be used to assist with this.

However, as we explored in Chapter 5, algorithms can contribute to bias, and may not always make accurate predictions. Moreover, while big data opens up new methods which can increase our ability to understand the behaviour of individuals and communities, it also raises questions about the effect that this knowledge will have on the way we behave, in addition to issues about consent, freedom and privacy. Moreover, the collection, ownership and use of big data raise wider ethical and political questions. As social and cultural interactions take place online, it is possible to use that data to scientifically investigate the history and evolution of cultures and societies. Human data is automatically generated and stored, through the online traces that we leave. For example, it is possible to analyse data about the dynamics of social networks, such as Facebook™ and Twitter™ or the Chinese networks, WeChat™ and Weibo™, in order to understand how people interact online. From searching the web to using an app to wearable technology, our use of digital technology automatically makes us the generators of data. We are becoming the subject of data analysis.

EXPLORE 14.13

Find out more about the Data Science Institute at Imperial College London, and the Multidisciplinary Labs, which research into big data, machine learning and analysis.

Prepare a presentation based on your findings, and give your own ideas on the following:

1   To what extent are methods in the human sciences influenced by developments in technology?

2   What responsibilities do data scientists have?

The implications of AI are really interesting and significant for knowledge. Some people might argue that the use of big data by deep learning and AI means that humans are largely subservient to the output it produces. In many respects, we have no human means of even checking the methodology of the deep learning network. As we increasingly use and rely on AI, we are arguably not far away from losing control of knowledge. It does not follow that AI is taking over however, but it may mean that we have no certainty – or alternatively misplaced certainty – as a result of trust in AI.

EXPLORE 14.14

Watch or listen to Kai-Fu Lee's 2018 TED Talk, which sets out the impact of AI on human values. He argues that the loss of jobs through automation, and with it, the loss of meaning, is an opportunity for humans to reflect on what makes them unique. As AI replaces routine jobs, there will be a need for human creativity and compassion, which AI cannot do.

Apply some TOK thinking as you watch. Consider:

- Lee's argument and perspective

- the justification, evidence or reasons he uses in support of his points

- what the counter-arguments are

What do you think about the impact of technology on human values and human meaning?

DISCUSS 14.8

1   How might big data make the human sciences more scientific in their methods, perspectives and uses?

2   How might technological developments (such as big data and AI) influence how we might understand human knowledge and the future of knowledge?

14.6 Why are the human sciences contestable?

DISCUSS 14.9

How might the different human sciences interpret the word 'science', and in what ways are they scientific?

The problem of bias

The human sciences set out to identify and understand the nature of bias and **heuristics**. Psychology examines the relationship between physiology, emotions and cognition. Our cognitive ability may be prone to certain errors, either conscious or unconscious. Human scientists recognise **cognitive bias** and fallacies that might skew our judgements and decisions, as well as impair our ability to think rationally.

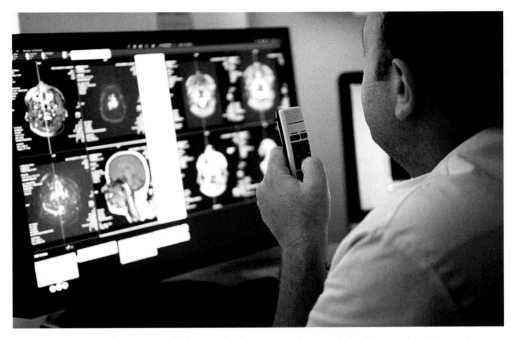

Figure 14.9: How far can psychologists help us to understand the factors that determine our knowledge?

However, one common accusation against the human sciences is that they are more prone to bias – and therefore less scientific – than their natural science cousins. We are, arguably, more likely to begin with prejudices about the nature of individuals and societies than we are about the nature of bacteria and cells. This means that we may find it difficult to be genuinely open-minded about controversial topics such as gender differences or taxation policy. In this situation, the danger is that we simply look for evidence that confirms our pre-existing prejudices while overlooking evidence that contradicts them.

Moreover, the assumptions we make about human nature might influence the models and the patterns of human behaviour that we perceive. For example, economics models in the past have been built on the idea of *homo economicus*, the idea of a 'rational' person who acts competitively and in their own self-interest to achieve goals at the least possible cost. This assumption has been challenged on the grounds that altruism and reciprocation might better characterise human behaviour. The risk here is that models intended to simplify can make false assumptions. Furthermore, models with built-in assumptions can become misinterpreted as containing a truth about human nature.

There are a number of types of bias to which human scientists might be prone, as follows:

Confirmation bias

As we saw in Chapter 2, confirmation bias is the tendency we have to notice only evidence that supports our beliefs. For example, if you believe that human nature is essentially generous, you might interpret people's actions in a positive light. Equally, if you assume that humans are self-interested and egotistical, you might place more emphasis on the occasions when people act uncharitably – to confirm the belief that you were correct in the first place.

At this point, it is worth recalling that bias can also be a serious problem in the natural as well as the human sciences. A physicist, for example, may be so committed to their own favourite theory that they obstinately refuse to abandon it in the light of contrary evidence. Or their research into the safety of nuclear energy may be tainted by the fact that it is funded by big commercial businesses. Since natural scientists are only human, they will sometimes be swayed by bias.

Availability heuristic

Another example of bias is known as the **availability heuristic**, a term invented by psychologists Daniel Kahneman (1934–) and Amos Tversky (1937–1996), and defined as 'the process of judging frequency by the ease with which instances come to mind.' The ease with which instances come to mind affects our ability to estimate the size of a category or the frequency of an event. They give the following example. If we consider whether there are more words that begin with the letter T or the letter K, we might quickly assume that it is T because more words beginning with T come to mind, and here the availability heuristic helps us arrive at the correct answer. However, it can lead to errors in judgement. Dramatic, scandalous and vivid events can easily be remembered, and the ease with which we can recall them might skew our ability to make a judgement. We assume that if we can think of it, it must be significant, which leads us to assume that an event is more frequent than it actually is. If you can think of several examples of aeroplane accidents, you might overestimate the likelihood of plane crashes, and believe they are more likely to happen because that information is available to you. When you have listened to a news story about a plane crash, you are more likely to think it could happen, and you give the information more credit than it deserves – and ignore the contrary evidence which is less memorable.

> **KEY WORD**
>
> **availability heuristic:** a bias where recent or easily remembered examples affect our judgement

REAL-LIFE SITUATION 14.22

Discuss some specific examples of bias that you have come across in the natural sciences and human sciences that you have studied.

Language and bias

There is a significant link between language and bias. The way in which a knowledge claim or a question is framed or presented might affect the conclusions drawn. Compare the two statements:

Chocolate bar, 90% sugar free

Chocolate bar, 10% sugar

The sugar-free item seems like the healthier option, even though they are describing exactly the same chocolate bar. This is a bias known as **anchoring bias**, which can have a priming effect. Daniel Kahneman constructed the following experiment to find out about the effects of anchoring using a roulette wheel. Participants believed that the roulette wheel randomly allocated them a number between 1 and 100. In fact, the wheel was designed to allocate them either the number 10 or 65. The participants were then asked the same question: how many African countries are part of the United

> **KEY WORD**
>
> **anchoring bias:** where a particular concept or idea is mentioned before a question is asked – this has a 'priming effect' which may affect the response given

Nations? The researchers found that those who had been given the low number gave a lower answer than those with the high number, who gave a high answer. In summary, the randomly allocated numbers had a priming effect, which affected the response of the participants to the question. This anchoring effect has also been identified in many other contexts, and our beliefs can be easily changed by information that we have just received, even if it is irrelevant.

> **LINKING QUESTION 14.6**
>
> **Language:** In any investigation of human phenomena, how might our own assumptions and bias influence the language we use, the method we select and the conclusions we reach?

Overcoming bias

We might find ways to avoid or overcome our biases. In the first place, we should look not only for evidence in favour of our beliefs, but also for evidence that would count against them. Whatever the subject matter, a good antidote to bias is to make it a matter of principle to actively look for evidence that counts *against* your hypothesis. For example, if you think that younger siblings are more rebellious than older ones, you should not only trawl for evidence that confirms your hypothesis, but also look for examples of rebellious older siblings and conformist younger ones.

Another way to overcome the problem of the availability heuristic is to look at probabilities based on statistical evidence. There are in fact six small aeroplane fatal accidents per week in the USA; however, commercial planes are much safer. Moreover, your statistical chance of dying in a commercial plane crash is remarkably low compared with other modes of transport. This example shows that there is sometimes a mismatch between our own intuitive sense of risk and the statistical likelihood of that risk. Here, the human sciences can enable us to calculate and become more aware of the actual probability of an event. According to Professor David Spiegelhalter (1953–), a 'micromort' is a 1 in a million chance of sudden death – a unit of acute risk. For each of these activities, we expose ourselves to a 1 in a million chance of dying:

- 11.27 kilometres on a motorbike
- 24.14 kilometres in a small aeroplane
- 32.19 kilometres of walking
- 41.84 kilometres by cycling
- 482.8 kilometres in a car
- 12,070 kilometres on a commercial aeroplane
- 12,070 kilometres on a train

> **REAL-LIFE SITUATION 14.23**
>
> 1 How can we reduce the danger of bias in scientific research?
>
> 2 Is knowledge in the human sciences still possible despite the problem of bias?

Problems of errors in reasoning

We will now consider some other errors in reasoning, known as fallacies, that crop up frequently in arguments and discussions about human phenomena.

Ad hominem fallacy

The *ad hominem* fallacy (literally, 'against the man') consists of attacking or supporting the person rather than the argument. If, for example, you make an argument for world government, and are told that you are too young and idealistic to know what you are talking about, that is *ad hominem*. Although the *ad hominem* fallacy is usually committed by *criticising* someone, it can also be committed by *supporting* them. For example, if you say 'Einstein was in favour of world government, so it must be a good thing', you are again focusing on the speaker rather than the argument. A similar mistake arises when we appeal to what 'most people' or the 'vast majority' believe, in order to justify something. As we saw in our discussion of truth and consensus in Chapter 3, just because the vast majority of people believe something does not make it true. If you say, 'It must be true because Einstein said so', this carries more weight if we are discussing relativity theory than if we are discussing politics, society or religion – areas in which Einstein had no particular authority. The human sciences recognise that this fallacy occurs when a value judgement is made about the speaker before consideration of the content of their knowledge claims or arguments.

Special pleading

The fallacy of 'special pleading' involves the use of double standards – making an exception in your own case that you would not find acceptable if it came from someone else. For example, if your neighbour says 'I know there is a drought and we need to save water, but I am putting my prize flowers in a competition next week and I need to give them plenty of water', this is an example of special pleading. They are giving a justification for their behaviour that they would not accept if it were given by somebody else. Human beings tend to be rather good at special pleading – perhaps because there are many situations in which it would be convenient if everyone followed the rules *except me*.

DISCUSS 14.10

Imagine that you accuse your neighbour of special pleading in the example given here, and they say, 'No, I'm not. Despite the drought, I think that everyone with prize flowers should be allowed to water them.' Are they still engaging in special pleading?

Equivocation

Equivocation is a fallacy that occurs when a word is used in two different senses in an argument. Consider the following syllogism:

A hamburger is better than nothing.

Nothing is better than good health.

Therefore a hamburger is better than good health.

Although this argument is formally valid, in the sense that the conclusion follows from the premises, there is clearly something wrong with it. The problem lies with the word 'nothing' because it has a different meaning in each of the premises. In the first premise, it means 'not having anything'; in the second, it means 'there is not anything'. The second premise is clearly not intended to mean that 'not having anything' is better than having good health. In practice, it is not always easy to tell if someone is using a word consistently or not. This may be why so many arguments end up being about the meanings of words.

Argument *ad ignorantiam*

You commit the fallacy of argument *ad ignorantiam* if you claim that something is true on the grounds that there is no evidence to disprove it. During the 'witch hunt' against communists in the USA in the early 1950s, Senator Joe McCarthy's case against one alleged communist was that *'there is nothing in the files to disprove his communist connections'*. The point is, of course, that to show that someone is a communist – which is, in any case, no crime – we need *positive* evidence of their political affiliation. The key feature of this fallacy is that it assumes that a knowledge claim can be justified if there is no evidence available. For example I can claim that 'I believe that little green men exist on Mars' on the basis that there is no evidence to disprove their existence. The particular relevance of this fallacy to TOK is nicely expressed by the biologist Richard Dawkins (1941–): 'There is an infinity of possible things that one might believe – unicorns, fairies, millions of things – and just because you cannot disprove them it does not mean there is anything plausible about them.' In Chapter 3, we explored how evidence is often used to justify a knowledge claim, and justification is one of the conditions of knowledge. The human sciences offer various types of evidence in support of their knowledge claims using both quantitative and qualitative data.

REAL-LIFE SITUATION 14.24

1   Can you think of examples from your IB Diploma Programme study of Group 3 (human science) where there has been limited or contestable evidence?

2   You may know things that have limited or no evidence. How far is this an error in reasoning?

3   In many legal systems, someone who is accused of a crime is considered to be innocent until proved guilty. Is this an example of argument *ad ignorantiam*? If so, does this mean that we should abandon the assumption that someone is innocent until proved guilty?

False analogy

In trying to persuade people of something, you might use various analogies to support your argument, and this can be an effective rhetorical device. A false analogy arises when you assume that because two things are similar in some respects, they must also be similar in some further respect. Consider the following example: 'Just as in time the gentle rain can wear down the tallest mountains, so, in human life, all problems can be solved by patience and quiet persistence.' Well, maybe and maybe not. The point is that there is not much of a similarity between the action of rain on mountains and that of patience on problems. For one thing, it takes millions of years for mountains to be worn down by the action of rain, and when it comes to solving problems, we do not have that kind of time.

False dilemma

This is the fallacy of assuming that only two alternatives exist when there is in fact a wider range of options. If, for example, someone says, *'Do those who advocate an increase in military expenditure really want to see our schools and hospitals close?'*, they are implying that we have only two choices: *either* we increase military expenditure *or* we keep our schools and hospitals open. Since you are probably in favour of keeping schools and hospitals open, you seem forced to conclude that we should not support an increase in military expenditure. But there may in fact be more than two choices. For example, if we raise taxes, we might be able to increase military expenditure *and* keep our schools and hospitals open. Of course, if there really are only two choices, then this kind of reasoning is perfectly valid. One reason that false dilemma is a common fallacy is that we tend to see the world in black and white terms. Such *binary thinking* does not take into account the reality that many ethical and social issues are not black and white, but various shades of grey.

Hasty generalisations

A final alleged weakness of the human sciences is that they are prone to the fallacy of hasty generalisation – jumping to conclusions on the basis of a small, unrepresentative sample. Researchers have drawn attention to the fact that the vast majority of experiments in the behavioural sciences are conducted on so-called 'WEIRD' people – where WEIRD is an acronym for 'western, educated, industrialised, rich and democratic'. This is relevant because there is a growing body of evidence that WEIRD people are not representative of humanity as a whole. Indeed, cross-cultural studies suggest that there are significant cultural differences in the way people see and think about the world.

REFLECTION

In addition to the issue of WEIRD people is the issue of gender. Most studies in both the human and medical sciences have been predominantly done on men, yet women and men have physiological differences that mean they may respond differently in many situations, as well as to some drugs. Given that all studies in human behaviour invariably involve generalisations when making knowledge claims, how reliable do you think the knowledge they produce can be? To what extent is it possible to get a fully representational sample of human beings?

Consider, for example, 'the ultimatum game' – much loved by psychology and economics researchers. The game involves two players, one of whom is randomly designated as 'deal-maker' and the other as 'responder', and a sum of money, say $100. The deal-maker proposes how the money should be divided between them, and the responder can either accept or reject the offer. If the responder accepts the offer, the money is divided according to the proposal; if he rejects the offer, neither player gets anything. When this game is played in Western societies, the deal-maker typically proposes a 50–50 split and the responder typically accepts it. If the deal-maker proposes a split which is perceived as unfair – say 85–15 – the responder usually 'punishes' the deal-maker by refusing the offer, and neither player gets anything. This might be taken to show that we have a deep and innate sense of unfairness. However, it turns out that different cultures behave quite differently in the ultimatum game. For example, when Machiguenga people from the Amazon basin play the game, responders almost always accept an offer, no matter how low, on the grounds that it is crazy to reject free money.

By contrast, in cultures with a strong gift-giving tradition, such as the Gnau of highland Papua New Guinea, responders sometimes reject generous offers of over 60%. This is because they do not like the idea of being under an obligation to the deal-maker. As this example shows, we should be cautious before concluding that a particular form of behaviour is universal. The responses vary according to various factors including moral values and social cultural norms and expectations. As individuals, it is important that we think and act as free agents, not just reinforcing our social, cultural, and moral norms, but also making our own judgements and decisions based on our critical thinking.

Figure 14.10: The ultimatum game

Fallacies: a summary

As we have seen, it requires an element of judgement to determine whether or not a fallacy has been committed. Throughout the chapter we have considered the 'deadly fallacies' of informal reasoning, which are summarised in the table.

Fallacy	Definition
post hoc ergo propter hoc	confusing a correlation with a causal connection
ad hominem	attacking/supporting the person rather than the argument
special pleading	using double standards to excuse an individual or group
equivocation	using language ambiguously
argument *ad ignorantiam*	claiming something is true because it cannot be proved to be false
false analogy	assuming that because two things are alike in some respects, they are alike in other respects
false dilemma	assuming that only two black and white alternatives exist
hasty generalisation	generalising from insufficient evidence

EXPLORE 14.15

In each of the following cases, 1 to 17, state which of the following, a to k, best applies to the argument:

a   valid argument

b   invalid syllogism

c   hasty generalisation

d   *post hoc ergo propter hoc*

e   *ad hominem* fallacy

f   special pleading

g   argument *ad ignorantiam*

h   false dilemma

i   false analogy

j   equivocation

k   loaded question

1   Arisa said she trusted me, and she must be telling the truth because she would not lie to someone that she trusted.

2   The ends justify the means. After all, if you want to make omelettes, you have to break eggs.

3   Since the English always talk about the weather, if you meet someone who talks about the weather you can be sure they are from England.

4   That cannot be right. None of my friends would believe it.

5   Since many great scientists have believed in God, there must be some truth in religion.

6   We got on very well on both of our dates together. We are clearly well suited. Let's get married!

7   I agree that everyone should pay their taxes. But since I'm short of money this year and want to take my family on a much-needed holiday, it is OK if I do not declare my full income.

8   The average UK family has 2.5 children. The Smiths are very average people. Therefore, they must have 2.5 children.

9   Since no one has been able to prove that we are alone in the universe, we must conclude that alien life-forms exist.

10   Many great artists were not recognised in their own lifetimes. Since my work has not been recognised, I must be a great artist.

11   Since there are two candidates for student president – Boris and Bertha – and I know he did not vote for Boris, he must have voted for Bertha.

CONTINUED

12 As no one succeeds without hard work, the fact that you failed your exams shows how idle you have been.

13 No breath of scandal has ever touched the senator. So he must be an honest man.

14 Just as you are more likely to take care of a car that you own than one that you rent, so a slave owner is more likely to take care of their slave than an employer is of their worker.

15 To ignore the possibility that America was discovered by Africans simply because these explorers are unknown is irresponsible and arrogant. If we are unaware of an event, it does not mean it never happened.

16 In the fight against terrorism, you are either with us or against us.

17 The English cannot cook. If he really is English, then obviously he will not be able to cook.

Evaluating the methods in human sciences

DISCUSS 14.11

What distinguishes human science from pseudo-science (fake science)?

Our consideration of the reasons why the human sciences can be contested brings us back to the methods by which human scientists construct knowledge, and their reliability. Earlier, we explored various methods in the human sciences, including observation, measurement, experiments and patterns. The problems associated with each can be summarised as follows:

Human sciences: summary of problems	
Observation	We cannot directly observe other people's minds.
	Questionnaires may be misleading or biased.
	Observing people may affect the way they behave.
Measurement	Social phenomena are difficult to measure.
Experiments	Human sciences study complex social situations in which it is difficult to run controlled experiments.
	Ethical considerations limit the types of experiment that are appropriate in the human sciences.
Patterns	Patterns and trends can be identified but accurate predictions are limited.
	The act of making a prediction may affect the behaviour predicted.
	Human sciences can calculate probabilities and likelihoods.
	Human sciences can produce data using quantitative and quantitative methods.
	Human sciences usually uncover trends rather than laws.

EXPLORE 14.16

Look at the table titled 'Human sciences: summary of problems'. Work with a partner and discuss the following question: In seeking to defend the human sciences, how would you respond to each of the problems mentioned?

It is clear that psychologists, economists, political scientists, anthropologists and other human scientists each use methods that attempt to offer accurate and reliable conclusions about human nature and human behaviour; but what counts as a reliable or appropriate method might be slightly different in each of these human sciences. We have considered the strengths and weaknesses of approaches which involve asking people, using statistical data, qualitative and quantitative research and big data. It seems that if we are to evaluate the conclusions made about human nature and human behaviour, we also need to be able to understand and assess the reliability of the methods used to produce the conclusions reached. Indeed, in order to evaluate the certainty of a knowledge claim in the human sciences, we need to know and understand something about how that conclusion was reached.

Figure 14.11: How do we evaluate the methods and the uses of knowledge in the human sciences?

We have also explored how technology is influencing the methods used in the human sciences. The collection and use of data, including big data, has the potential to make human sciences more scientific, but we should avoid the assumption that quantitative methods that use data are accurate and reliable. The use of digital technology raises new questions. Big data and improvements in information technology and biotechnology might change the methods used in the human sciences. With sophisticated enough biometric data, we might believe that big data algorithms could end up knowing us better than we can know ourselves. We might imagine that technology promises the possibility of making far more accurate predictions than we can. Some people might argue that the future task of understanding humans is best done by machines. The counter-argument is that if we should not put too much trust in quantitative methods, neither should we reduce an understanding of humans to numerical data. In the future, we may struggle to evaluate the reliability of big data if we do not understand how it is being produced.

Find out more about the impact of data on methods used in the human sciences. For example, search Duke University's website for data and digital humanities.

The methods used in the human sciences, despite their problems and limits, need to be robust if they are to succeed in making any scientific claim about humans. We can conclude by suggesting that if we are to understand humans even better and reach reliable conclusions, we will also need to know what a sound method looks like, and evaluate the methods used.

Using examples from this chapter and others from your own knowledge or research, prepare a presentation that describes the methods for constructing knowledge in the human sciences.

You might consider some of the following concepts and ideas: observation, classification, reasoning, identification, theory, experimentation, hypothesis building, association, language, patterns, problem solving, the creation of models and any other relevant tools or methods.

Are the methods used in the human sciences as reliable as those used in the natural sciences? Work with a partner and, as a pair, present your ideas to the class.

Self-assessment

Evaluate your presentation. How well did it demonstrate that you have understood the concepts used in the human sciences, and the methods used for constructing knowledge in this discipline? Which aspects were you able to articulate most clearly? Which caused you most difficulty? Make a list of any areas that you feel you need to re-visit, and prioritise these.

14.7 The relation with natural sciences

Natural sciences: Can we study human beings in the same way that we study other natural phenomena?

Reductionism

Some thinkers hold out the hope that, as our knowledge in areas such as neuroscience and genetics grows, it will eventually be possible to establish the human sciences on firmer foundations. Since it seeks to explain some subjects in terms of other – more fundamental – ones, such a position is known as **reductionism**. A reductionist might, for example, argue that one day we will be able to understand economics in terms of psychology, and psychology in terms of neuroscience. At the limit, a reductionist might argue that everything is ultimately a matter of atoms whizzing around in space in accordance with the laws of physics.

Since science is supposed to explain complex phenomena in terms of simpler underlying principles, reductionism might seem to be an attractive position. A subject such as physics has, after all, been amazingly successful in explaining a wide variety of phenomena in terms of a small number of underlying laws. A good example of the success of this approach was the reduction of thermodynamics to mechanics, which enabled scientists to explain heat in terms of the motion of molecules. We can observe changes in the brain following cognitive behavioural therapy, and some would claim that they are similar to the effects of taking anti-depressants. Therefore, we can explain mental phenomena in terms of underlying physical ones.

> ### KEY WORD
>
> reductionism: the belief that some subjects can be explained in terms of other more fundamental ones

EXPLORE 14.19

Look at the following sciences:

- physics
- biology
- chemistry
- economics
- geography
- psychology

Do you think there is a hierarchy of sciences? If so, try to order the various sciences on the list (and any others you can think of) according to any criteria of your choice. If you cannot, explain why not.

The reductive fallacy

When we try to explain complex things in terms of simpler underlying ones, there is, however, a danger that we commit the **reductive fallacy**. This is the fallacy of saying that just because *A* is composed of *B* it follows that *A* is *nothing but B*. Here are some examples of such 'nothing-but-ism':

A cathedral is nothing but a heap of stones.

A violin sonata is nothing but a sequence of vibrating strings.

A human being is nothing but a bunch of chemicals.

> ### KEY WORD
>
> reductive fallacy: the fallacy of saying that just because *A* is composed of *B*, it follows that *A* is nothing but *B*

REAL-LIFE SITUATION 14.25

Do you agree with any of the 'reductionist' claims above?

At one level, it is true that we are 'just a bunch of chemicals'; and it is humbling to discover that there is no secret ingredient in the recipe for a human being – we are made of the same basic stuff as cats, cucumbers and chrysanthemums. Nevertheless, there is all the difference in the world between so much hydrogen, oxygen and carbon measured out in a chemistry laboratory and a living human being. We may know the ingredients that make up a human being, but we are still very far from understanding the recipe!

There are, in fact, good reasons for doubting that the reductionist programme can succeed. Since we cannot even reduce chemistry to physics, it seems unlikely that we will ever be able to explain the human sciences in terms of physics. In any case, the resulting knowledge would probably not be very useful. Trying to understand the laws of supply and demand at the level of atoms and molecules would be like trying to learn a computer program by analysing the flow of electrons through the electrical circuits.

A reductionist perspective assumes a value judgement about the human sciences. There are problems with judging one area of knowledge (human sciences) by the standards of another (the natural sciences). It would be unjustified to assume that the methods and tools which are characteristic of the natural sciences *should* be used in the human sciences. Moreover, the production of knowledge in the human sciences is arguably robust, and uses its own methods, tools and concepts to construct knowledge. Furthermore, it has its own practical applications and uses, and produces knowledge in distinctive ways. A counter-argument to reductionism is the unique and highly situated way in which each area of knowledge in the human sciences produces knowledge. Geographers, economists, political scientists, sociologists, anthropologists and psychologists can each reach conclusions that are justified, by using methods appropriate to their subject area.

DISCUSS 14.12

To what extent should the human sciences be judged according to the standards of the natural sciences?

Holism

The reductionist idea that the best way to understand something is to break it up into parts seems particularly inappropriate when it comes to the study of living things. For, as the writer Douglas Adams (1952–2001) observed, 'If you try to take a cat apart to see how it works, the first thing you have on your hands is a non-working cat.' This might suggest that we can only make sense of some things by looking at them as a whole. Such a view is known as **holism**, and its central claim is that *the whole is greater than the sum of the parts* – that the whole contains properties that cannot in principle be discovered through an analysis of the parts.

When applied to the human sciences, holism means that you cannot understand a group only in terms of the individuals that make it up, or an action independent of the context in which it takes place. Therefore, economists distinguish between macro-economics – which studies the economy as a whole – and micro-economics – which studies the behaviour of individual economic agents – on the grounds that you cannot understand a complex economy simply by analysing the behaviour of individual economic agents. Anthropologists insist that you should immerse yourself in a culture before trying to make sense of its individual practices.

KEY WORD

holism: the belief that the best way to understand some things is by looking at them as a whole rather than by analysing them into separate parts

DISCUSS 14.13

Do you think that a group can have a general 'character' that is distinct from the individuals that make it up?

At the heart of the argument between holism and reductionism is the question of the relation between wholes and parts. Rather than make an *either–or* choice between these two positions and say that you must understand the whole in terms of its parts, or the parts in terms of the whole, perhaps it would be better to think in terms of there being two-way traffic between parts and wholes. Consider the relation between individuals and society. Although society is influenced by the individuals that make it up, it is also true that individuals are affected by the society they live in. For example, the American cultural anthropologist, Richard Schweder (1945–) identified sociocentric and egocentric cultures. Whereas a sociocentric society prioritises the institutions and rules of the community over the individual, an egocentric society emphasises the rights and freedoms of the individual over that society.

An awareness of our perspective as knowers is important here. Societies might be characterised in the human sciences according to the emphasis they place on individual civil liberties in relation to community rules, however there may be different perspectives on this. For example, an outside observer of a North Korean Military Parade might arrive at a very different conclusion about that society from someone living within that society – something which Michael Palin (1943–) explored in a TV travelogue documentary series on North Korea. When it comes to studying something as complicated as a human being, there is no reason why we should limit ourselves to a single approach – and both perspectives might have a valuable role to play in the construction of knowledge.

Figure 14.12: To what extent is it possible for an anthropologist to understand how other people see the world?

The *Verstehen* position

One reason for doubting that we will ever be able to reduce the human sciences to the natural sciences is that human sciences typically explain things in terms of *meanings* and *purposes* rather than mechanical causes and effects. According to what is known as the *Verstehen* position – *Verstehen* is German for 'understanding' – the main aim of the human sciences is to understand the meaning of various social practices *from the inside* as they are understood by the agents themselves. The common sense of this is that if you want to figure out what a group of people are up to, you cannot simply observe their physical movements, but must try to get 'inside their heads' and understand how *they* see the situation. If you are unable to do this, then you are likely to misunderstand what is happening.

Since many explanations in the human sciences are in terms of meaning rather than mechanism, it is perhaps not surprising that the human sciences have few universal laws to their credit. For the meaning of an action depends on the *context* in which it takes place, and it is therefore difficult to generalise. For example, if a man is writing his name on a piece of paper, he could be writing a cheque, giving an autograph or signing a death warrant. Since the consequences of the same physical action are completely different in each case, you cannot make a universal law of the form, 'If a person writes his name, then ...'

While the *Verstehen* approach to making sense of human behaviour is illuminating, we should not get carried away with it. Just because a lot of human behaviour can only be understood in context, we should not, for example, conclude that there are *no* universals in the human sciences. On the contrary, anthropologists have found many traits that seem to be common to all cultures – including gossiping, joking and taking an interest in sex.

KEY WORD

Verstehen position: the belief that the main aim of the human sciences is to understand the meaning of various social practices as they are understood by the agents themselves

CONTINUED

f   a person eats at a McDonald's™ restaurant

g   a student takes an IB Diploma Programme exam

h   a person attends a birthday party

i   a person checks in at an airport

j   someone works out in a gym

REFLECTION

If you want to understand why a person behaves in a particular way, what sort of explanation are you usually looking for? To what extent does the explanation you seek vary according to who the person is, and the context in which the behaviour occurs?

14.8 Ethical considerations

REAL-LIFE SITUATION 14.26

Should we pursue knowledge in the human sciences at any cost? Why? Why not? How do we know?

The link between the human sciences and ethics is important. Firstly, we might want to explore morality through the lens of the human sciences. Ethics is a topic to study. For example, an anthropologist might be interested in the values as well as ethical and social norms that operate within a gang culture. Psychologists and economists might also be interested to know how and why we possess a sense of right and wrong, and how those values affect our attitudes and behaviours. Secondly, the human sciences have a particular responsibility towards the people that they study. For example, as we saw in Chapter 13, if you are conducting research that involves people, there are various standards that need to be followed; a minimum requirement might include informed consent if you are asking people to take part in a survey.

DISCUSS 14.15

What values and responsibilities should influence the inquiry of geographers, economists, political scientists, sociologists, anthropologists and psychologists?

The Milgram experiment

One of the best-known experiments in the history of psychology took place at Yale University (USA) in 1963. Stanley Milgram (1933–1984) was interested in the extent to which people are willing to obey orders. He advertised for volunteers to participate in an experiment allegedly to 'test the effects of punishment on learning'. When a volunteer arrived, he was told that he was to play the role of 'teacher', and another 'volunteer' – in reality an actor – was to play the role of 'learner'. The learner was strapped to a chair and electrodes were put on his wrists. The teacher was then taken to an adjoining room and asked to give the learner a simple memory test. Every time the learner answered incorrectly, the teacher was to give the learner a successively higher electric shock by flicking a switch on a generator. Each switch was clearly labelled with voltage levels ranging from 15 to 450 volts, and verbal descriptions such as 'slight shock', 'strong shock', 'intense shock', 'danger', and finally 'XXX'. Although the teacher could not see the learner, he was able to hear his responses. Once the voltage reached 120V, the learner began to complain; at 150 volts he demanded that the experiment be stopped; at 270V he started screaming; and after 330V there was an ominous silence. Whenever the teacher hesitated to administer a shock, a scientist standing behind him insisted that it was very important that he continue with the experiment. In reality, of course, the learner did not receive any shocks, but the 'teacher' was not aware of this at the time.

REAL-LIFE SITUATION 14.27

1   Given your knowledge of human nature, what percentage of 100 volunteers do you think would continue administering electric shocks up to 450 volts?

2   If you had been a volunteer in this experiment, what do you think you would have done?

The result of the experiment was that almost two-thirds of the volunteers continued to give electric shocks up to 450 volts. Many expressed concern about what they were doing, and had to be reassured that they would not be held responsible for the fate of the learner; but it did not seem to occur to them to refuse to comply. Only one-third of the volunteers refused to continue to the end. The Milgram experiment raises some disturbing questions about human nature. Why were so many of the volunteers willing to obey white-coated authority figures, and give what they thought were lethal shocks to complete strangers? One crumb of comfort was that if, instead of working alone, the volunteer was paired with two other teachers (who were again actors), and the other teachers rebelled, then only 10% of the volunteers were willing to continue giving shocks up to 450 volts.

We might question the ethics, not of the participants, but of the experiment. After all, the volunteers were misled about what they were getting involved in, were made to feel uncomfortable during the experiment and may have suffered a loss of self-esteem once the experiment was over. The consent of the participants was not obtained, and they are probably not going to feel great about themselves if they discovered that they are the kind of person willing to administer a lethal electric shock to a stranger! This experiment did not meet the standards that would be expected today, and some would argue that the experiment itself was deeply unethical.

DISCUSS 14.16

1   How has our understanding of human nature and human behaviour changed over time?

2   Can a scientific framework be applied to *everything* about humans? Can and should *anything* be measured?

REFLECTION

Do you think there should be *informed* consent for all behavioural research on humans? If you answer *yes*, what would the impact be on any human behavioural studies? How might informing participants ahead of any experiment alter the results?

The Stanford prison experiment

A second famous experiment designed by psychologist Philip Zimbardo (1933–) took place at Stanford University in 1971. The aim of the experiment was to see how 'the power of the situation' can influence the behaviour of ordinary people. The basement of the psychology department was made to look like a prison, and 24 student volunteers were recruited and divided randomly into guards and prisoners. The guards were given complete control over the prisoners. The experiment was supposed to last two weeks, but it had to be abandoned after six days because some of the guards were behaving sadistically, and the prisoners were becoming psychologically traumatised. Zimbardo took the experiment to show that the situation is more important than character traits in determining how people behave. When news emerged of prisoner abuse by American guards in Abu Ghraib prison in Iraq in 2004, Zimbardo said he was horrified but not surprised. As he memorably put it, 'You can't be a sweet cucumber in a vinegar barrel.' Zimbardo's work can be seen as an extension of Milgram's, in that it suggests people can do terrible things not only when they are told to by authority figures but also when they find themselves in a toxic environment.

Together with the Milgram experiment, the Stanford prison experiment is often cited as an example of unethical research. Whatever your thoughts about the ethics of the experiment, one might also question the alleged findings of the experiment on the following grounds.

1   *Selection bias*. To find participants for his study, Zimbardo made an advertisement which explicitly mentioned an experiment about 'prison life'. Such an experiment may have appealed to atypical – and possibly aggressive – individuals who were not representative of the general population.

2   *Experimenter expectations*. At the start of the experiment, Zimbardo briefed the guards on how to behave, and it could be argued that the guards were simply doing what he encouraged them to do.

3   *Ambiguous results*. Although some guards did engage in sadistic behaviour, others did not; so it could be argued that the overall results of the experiment suggest that a bad situation does not turn everyone into a sadist.

Arguments about the significance of the Stanford prison experiment, together with the question of whether behaviour is influenced more by character traits or the situation, continue to this day. As this brief discussion suggests, experiments in the human sciences are sometimes inconclusive and open to a variety of different interpretations. Both of these experiments aimed to discover how people would respond and interact in different circumstances, and what they both revealed was the complexity of human behaviour.

REAL-LIFE SITUATION 14.28

1   Do you think that the Milgram and Stanford Prison experiments were unethical? Why? Why not?

2   How have ethical considerations over time shaped the methods used in human sciences?

3   Can we still accept, value and use knowledge that has been produced by unethical means? Why? Why not?

EXPLORE 14.21

There are ethical reasons for not conducting experiments that have a negative effect on the people who participate in them.

Write an answer to the following question: In what ways might ethical considerations influence the methods used to study humans in the human sciences?

You might consider examples of experiments conducted in the human sciences, the methods used, the ethical considerations that were or were not taken into account and the extent to which accurate conclusions can be reached.

If you want to research further examples to include in your answer, you could find out more about the following: Solomon Asch's 1950s experiment or the Tuskegee experiment from the 1930s.

When you have completed your answer, consider the following:

- What factors shaped your answer?

- How far might your own perspective – age, gender and ethical values – impact on your response to the question and why?

- How do we decide if a method is appropriate or ethical?

- What would you say in response to people who do not agree with you?

- What is the process we use for knowing values? Should our own ethical values coincide with those shared within our society?

Figure 14.13: What role do you think ethical considerations should play in the human sciences?

14.9 Conclusion

The human sciences have made a significant contribution to knowledge in multiple and diverse disciplines – from economics and psychology to anthropology and sociology. This chapter has explored what we can achieve if we apply a scientific framework to the study of humans. However, the human sciences are far from straightforward, and they demonstrate the rigour and sophistication needed to successfully study human phenomena. Since the human sciences deal with complex phenomena, we can learn a great deal more about human beings by studying subjects such as psychology, economics and anthropology than we can by relying on uninformed common sense. We have examined the methods and processes for constructing this knowledge. Any discussion about the human sciences inevitably raises some big questions about our place in evolutionary history. We began with the idea that human sciences could help us understand people better, and we have explored the role that they might play if we want to better understand human behaviour and interaction, and their societies and cultures.

We might conclude with a forward-looking view, and consider questions arising such as the nature of human consciousness, the relationship between mind, brain and body, or the extent to which we have freewill, or the relationship between genetics, environment and identity. Perhaps scientific research will cast light on these questions, but the challenge of the human sciences remains – to acquire knowledge of human phenomena.

KNOWLEDGE QUESTIONS

1   Can the human sciences identify trends and patterns in human behaviour? If so, what are the similarities and differences compared to the laws of natural sciences?

2   How far are humans predictable? Will there one day be a science of human behaviour that is as precise about us as physics is about the world? Justify your answer carefully, considering possible objections to your position.

3   Sometimes, human sciences are described as 'soft' and natural sciences as 'hard'. Is there really a difference, and if so, is it adequately characterised by these terms?

14.10 Linking questions

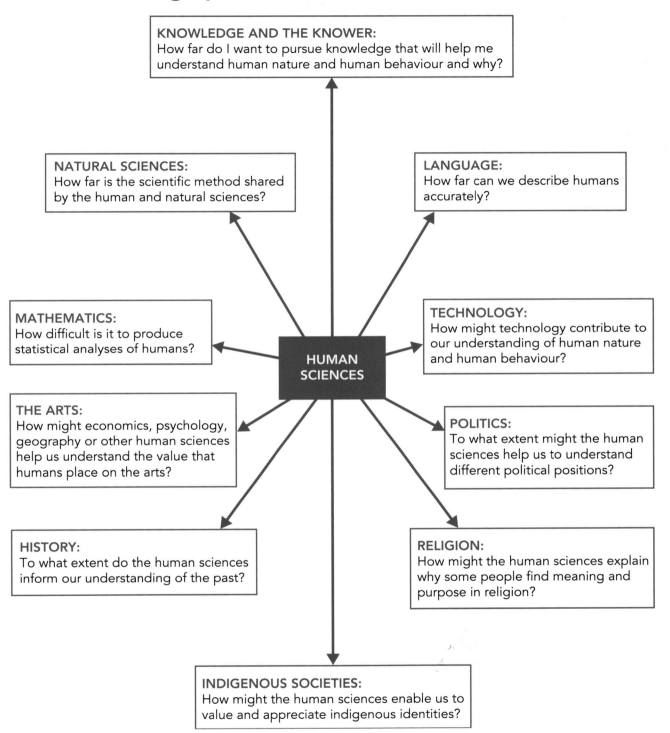

KNOWLEDGE AND THE KNOWER:
How far do I want to pursue knowledge that will help me understand human nature and human behaviour and why?

NATURAL SCIENCES:
How far is the scientific method shared by the human and natural sciences?

LANGUAGE:
How far can we describe humans accurately?

MATHEMATICS:
How difficult is it to produce statistical analyses of humans?

HUMAN SCIENCES

TECHNOLOGY:
How might technology contribute to our understanding of human nature and human behaviour?

THE ARTS:
How might economics, psychology, geography or other human sciences help us understand the value that humans place on the arts?

POLITICS:
To what extent might the human sciences help us to understand different political positions?

HISTORY:
To what extent do the human sciences inform our understanding of the past?

RELIGION:
How might the human sciences explain why some people find meaning and purpose in religion?

INDIGENOUS SOCIETIES:
How might the human sciences enable us to value and appreciate indigenous identities?

14.11 Check your progress

Reflect on what you have learned in this chapter and indicate your confidence level between 1 and 5 (where 5 is the highest score and 1 is the lowest). If you score below 3, r-visit that section. Come back to this list later in your course. Has your confidence grown?

	Confidence level	Re-visited?
Do I understand the place of observation within the human sciences, and the difficulties that arise when using observation to study human behaviour?		
Am I familiar with the methods for constructing knowledge in the human sciences including: • asking people via questionnaires and polls • qualitative and quantitative research • measurement and statistics • modelling?		
Can I discuss the use of statistics, measurement and modelling in the human sciences, and appreciate the problems that arise when studying and measuring human behaviour?		
Do I have a sound understanding of the concepts of patterns and predictions, and the implications of using these to model human behaviour?		
Do I understand the difference between correlation and causation, and the challenges of establishing causal relationships?		
Have I considered the impact of big data and technological developments on the study of human phenomena?		
Can I explain the criticisms which may be applied to the human sciences, for example the various types of bias and the different kinds of fallacy, or errors in reasoning?		
Am I able to provide counter-arguments against such criticisms, and suggest ways in which they can be overcome?		
Am I familiar with the similarities, differences and connections between the human sciences and natural sciences?		
Do I understand the role of ethics within the context of the human sciences, for example the ways in which ethical considerations limit our ability to conduct experiments on human beings?		

14.12 Continue your journey

- For an outstanding exploration of our **fast-intuitive thinking and our slow rational thinking**, with a focus on bias and heuristics, containing insights from psychology and economics, read: Daniel Kahneman, *Thinking Fast and Slow*, Penguin, 2011

- For a critique of the **concept of measurement** and a highly engaging challenge to the popular belief that measuring human performance and sharing the results leads to accountability and reliable knowledge, read: Jerry Muller, *Tyranny of Metrics,* Princeton University Press, 2018. He explores the uses and misuses of data in the context of healthcare, governments, business, education and other areas, examining the benefits and threats of metrics and measurement and mismeasurement.

- For a highly engaging understanding of the insights of **psychology into human behaviour and decisions**, written from the perspective of an international lawyer and bestselling author and UK Judge, read: Dexter Dias QC, *Ten Types of Human*, Penguin, 2018.

- For a perspective on what **skills, capacities and attributes humans will need in the future** drawing on the insights of psychology, read: Howard Gardner, *Five Minds for the Future*, Harvard Business School Press, 2011. This book puts forward the case for the need to learn at least one specialism or subject area (the disciplined mind), the ability to organise and make sense of large amounts of information (the synthesising mind), the ability to come up with answers to new questions (the creating mind), the need to understand differences between people (the respectful mind) and the ability to be responsible (the ethical mind).

- For a good introductory account of the **social sciences** read: Reuben Abel, *Man is the Measure*. Chapter 11: 'The Social Sciences', Simon & Schuster, 1997, where there is an excellent discussion of the *Verstehen* position.

- For a chapter on **big data**, read: Yuval Noah Harari, *21 lessons for the 21st century*, Penguin, 2019

- For an argument that many **human traits, such as violence, are more the result of genetic inheritance than environmental conditioning** read: Steven Pinker, *The Blank Slate*, Penguin, 2002. He writes with such verve and style that, whatever your own beliefs, Chapter 17: 'Violence' should engage your interest.

Part 4

Assessment

Introduction

The TOK assessment consists of two elements:

- the TOK exhibition

- the TOK essay

The assessed tasks are an intellectual challenge that we hope you will enjoy. Unlike your six IB Diploma Programme academic subjects, there is no external examination to sit for TOK. Instead, there are two pieces of assessed coursework – the TOK exhibition and the TOK essay. You need to complete both of them to be eligible for the IB Diploma Programme. The exhibition and the essay are each marked out of ten, but your TOK essay grade will be weighted to account for 65% of your overall TOK grade, and your TOK exhibition grade will make up the remaining 35%. The final grade for TOK can range from A (excellent) to E (elementary). Your TOK grade will be combined with the grade you get for your IB Extended Essay, and together these will determine the number of *core points* you receive as part of your total IB Diploma Programme score. There are a maximum of three core points available.

Although there are some obvious differences between curating and justifying objects for an exhibition and writing a TOK essay, there is considerable overlap in the skills you need to demonstrate in the exhibition and those you need to write the essay. In both cases, a response to a knowledge question is required, and the focus should be on TOK *analysis and evaluation of that question* rather than general description. However, a significant difference between the two assessment tasks is that they move in opposite directions. The exhibition moves from concrete objects, and relates them to an abstract knowledge prompt. The essay, by contrast, moves from the abstract – a prescribed title – to concrete examples in the world around us.

The aim of this final part of the book is to give you some practical tips to help you do your best on the assessment tasks. While advice and guidance are useful, you need to be aware that there is no infallible formula for creating a successful exhibition or writing a strong essay. The points made in these assessment chapters cannot guarantee you success, but they should provide you with some of the knowledge and resources to help you to develop and refine your TOK skills.

Some students take the view that as TOK only contributes to a maximum of three possible core points, they will not put too much effort into their TOK assessments, but this would be a mistake. The critical thinking skills you develop through doing your TOK assessments (along with your IB Extended Essay) will enhance the work you do in your other IB Diploma Programme subjects, and will serve you well at university and the rest of your life. If you can fine-tune your higher-order thinking skills in TOK, you will benefit greatly in your six IB Diploma Programme subjects. In short, if you want to know how to get sevens, pay attention in TOK!

While traditional education has often emphasised remembering information, this alone is not enough for success. Information is readily available on the internet, so the most valuable skills that people have include creativity, critical thinking and communication. For example, 'The Future of Jobs Report' produced by the World Economic Forum in 2018 suggested that, as automation increases, by 2022 there will be a demand for skills including analytical thinking, active learning, creativity, originality and initiative-taking. These skills lie at the heart of both TOK assessments.

You will find it helpful if you maintain a good set of notes during your TOK classes. By writing notes in your own words, you will develop a better grasp of TOK concepts.

If you record some of the different ideas and points of view that are raised in class discussions, this will help you to think about different perspectives that might be taken on your exhibition or essay topic. And if you include real-life examples, whether from your own IB Diploma Programme experience, the media or the six subjects you study, you may find that some of these examples will be useful when you prepare your exhibition and write your essay.

Your TOK toolkit

As you have gone through the TOK course, you will have acquired several new skills and TOK 'tools', in the form of questions you can ask of different knowledge claims. As you prepare for your TOK assessments, you should think about these 'tools', and which ones might apply to the essay title you have chosen and/or the exhibition you are planning. You do not need to use all the tools at once; choose the tools that seem most relevant to the points you are trying to make.

Things that you can ask of knowledge questions include:

1   *What does it mean?* Check to see if any of the language in the knowledge question is ambiguous, or has multiple definitions. Is the meaning literal? Does the knowledge question make use of similes or metaphors? Is it open to interpretation in any other way?

2   *What counts as evidence for and against?* You can apply this question to any evidence that you offer in support of your arguments. Consider the methodologies that have been employed, and the possible use of models. What are the underlying principles and assumptions that ground the evidence? How might they be challenged? How might evidence vary from one area of knowledge to another or depend on context? What makes evidence strong or weak, compelling or otherwise? Would it be justified for an argument to have a truth value, even if there is weak or limited evidence for it?

3   *Where does it come from?* What is the source of evidence that could be presented for or against the question? Is the source reliable, and if so, why? Does it have authority? If so, which knowledge authority? What are the implications of this for the question you are exploring?

4   *How certain is it?* This question can be applied to the arguments you construct for or against the question. You might consider the evidence presented, assumptions made and underlying principles, depending on the context in which you wish to use it. You might wish to evaluate the quality as well as quantity of any evidence, and consider whether assumptions are reasonable or not, whether there have been generalisations made and whether any exceptions are possible or probable.

5   *What other perspectives could be taken?* This question encourages you to see issues from other points of view. Would the knowledge question look the same from a man's or a woman's perspective, from the perspective of an indigenous society or from an atheist's standpoint? How far can we generalise about this perspective? What about at different moments in history? Considering different perspectives can help you to develop arguments and counter-arguments.

Figure 1: How different would the world be from a dog's perspective?

1   *What are the limitations?* Are there some areas that the knowledge questions do not apply to? Are the constraints physical, political, economic, ethical, personal or something else?

2   *Are there ethical considerations?* Many knowledge questions give rise to ethical considerations. Was the knowledge constructed in an ethical way? Was evidence sourced ethically? Are there ethical constraints upon exploring an issue further?

3   *Is it valuable?* When considering any knowledge question, you need to give some thought to its value or significance. What are the implications? What practical value does the pursuit of a knowledge question have, and what implications might it have for knowledge and knowing?

4   *How does it link and connect to other areas?* How does a knowledge question in one area of knowledge compare with knowledge questions in other areas of knowledge? Do they have a similar scope? Are methodologies comparable? Do they offer unique perspectives, and are ethical issues similar?

5   *What TOK concepts are involved?* Think about which TOK concepts that you have learnt about might be useful in your analysis of a knowledge question. In the Introduction to this book, we explore 12 of the main TOK concepts, and it may help to refer back to these pages when you are working on your assessed tasks. TOK concepts include, but are not limited to: abstraction, allegory, ambiguity, assumption, authority, axiom, belief, bias, causation, certainty, cognitive bias, coherence, context, correlation, creativity, cultural appropriation, deduction, definition, doubt, empiricism, epistemology, evidence, experience,

experimentation, expertise, explanation, fact, faith, falsification, generalisation, hypothesis, ideology, imagination, implicit bias, induction, interpretation, judgement, justification, knowledge, logic, memory, metaphor, metaphysics, methodology, model, narrative, objectivity, opinion, paradigm, perspective, power, prejudice, principles, probability, proof, reason, reflection, relativism, stereotype, subjectivity, technology, theology, tool, translation, trend, trust, truth, understanding, value and wisdom.

Last but not least, when thinking about which TOK tools to employ, consider the position of the knower. Think about how personal, cultural, educational and psychological factors (among others) might influence the position of the knower or questioner, your personal interpretation of any knowledge claim or knowledge question and the possible interpretations that others may make.

> Chapter 15
The TOK exhibition

"Now we're leaving the hall of stuff we stole from other cultures and entering the hall of stuff we paid too much for."

C. Cass

Figure 15.1: Your exhibition needs to show 'how TOK manifests itself in the world around us'. Think of ways in which you can successfully do this by exploring the link between your internal assessment (IA) prompt and the real world

---

BEFORE YOU START

1   'The biggest problem with communication is the illusion that it has occurred.' **George Bernard Shaw** (1856–1950)

2   'The privilege I've had as a curator is not just the discovery of new works . . . but what I've discovered about myself and what I can offer in the space of an exhibition – to talk about beauty, to talk about power, to talk about ourselves, and to talk and speak to each other.' **Thelma Golden** (1965–)

3   'I see a curator as a catalyst, generator and motivator – a sparring partner, accompanying the artist while they build a show, and a bridge builder, creating a bridge to the public.' **Hans-Ulrich Obrist** (1968–)

4   'I must emphasise, no matter how obvious it sounds, that good curating depends upon a bottomless passion and curiosity for looking and questioning; and the desire to communicate that excitement.' **Donna De Salvo** (1960–)

5   'Enlighten yourself and you will enlighten the viewer.' **Jean-Christophe Ammann** (1939–2015)

15.1 Introduction

The TOK exhibition is an internal assessment (IA) that gives you the opportunity to explore how TOK relates to the world around you.

You will curate and produce an exhibition that demonstrates how theory of knowledge is relevant in the real world. Your exhibition will be assessed and graded by your TOK teacher, internally moderated by your school and then externally moderated by the IB.

The TOK exhibition is one that you will create as an individual. The IB Diploma Programme provides 35 questions, called 'IA prompts', of which you must select just one. The IA prompt is a knowledge question that cannot be changed in any way. You will then need to decide on three objects that you can connect to your chosen prompt, and all three objects must be linked to the same prompt.

It is intended that your exhibition is based on either the core theme ('the knower') or one of the optional themes (technology, language, religion, politics or indigenous societies). Your exhibition needs to demonstrate the link between a knowledge question relating to one of these areas and the real world. The main requirement specified by the IB Diploma Programme is: 'Does the exhibition successfully show how TOK manifests in the world around us?'

> **KEY WORD**
>
> **manifest:** to become clear, obvious, visible, evident or noticeable

15.2 The IB Diploma Programme requirements

> **REAL-LIFE SITUATION 15.1**
>
> 1 What different types of exhibitions have you seen? What do they have in common?
>
> 2 What might an exhibition in an art gallery have in common with an exhibition in a museum?
>
> 3 What do you think makes a successful exhibition?

Given that every student must create an individual exhibition, you cannot work in a group. You are allowed to choose the same IA prompt as other students in your class, but if you do, you cannot choose any of the same objects.

Once you have chosen your theme, your prompt and your three objects that show how your IA prompt question is manifested in the world, you need to type a commentary on each object. In the commentary, you must identify the object and its specific real-world context. You must also justify why you have included it in your exhibition, and show how it links to your chosen IA prompt. Your three commentaries must be placed in a single file which also contains images of the objects you have chosen. Your file must have a title that clearly identifies the IA prompt you have chosen.

As with all IB Diploma Programme work, it is important to include any citations and references along with your commentaries. You can only write a maximum of 950 words for your exhibition, so you should ideally aim for 300–315 words for each commentary. The 950-word limit does not include anything that may be written on your objects, nor does it include any acknowledgements, references or bibliography.

15.3 The role of your TOK teacher

The TOK exhibition is designed to be completed in the first year of your Diploma Programme to avoid it having to compete with the internal assessments for your other Diploma Programme subjects. Your TOK teacher will explain the task to you, and support you through the planning process, as well as monitor your progress, so as to be able to authenticate your work. You will be given approximately eight hours of TOK class time to plan and work on your exhibition, and you can approach your teacher for any advice or clarification needed.

Your TOK teacher can read and give you feedback on one draft of your exhibition file, including written or oral advice on how to make improvements, but your teacher cannot edit your work.

After you have had feedback on your first draft, the next exhibition file you submit will be the final version. When you submit your final version, you will need to confirm that the work is your own, and you will not be able to retract your work. Once complete, your file is submitted. Your TOK teacher will mark it, and it may be submitted to the IB Diploma Programme for moderation.

As well as marking your work, your teacher will also create an opportunity for all completed exhibitions to be displayed to an audience. This is not a part of the formal assessment task, so the exhibition can be quite flexible. There are many opportunities here, and different ways of displaying your TOK exhibition work – including a digital or physical display. Your audience could either be your own class, another TOK class or a wider group such as parents or visitors to your school.

15.4 Practical suggestions for exhibition practice

It is worth finding out if your school offers the opportunity to display a practice exhibition. Some schools will offer one opportunity, usually in the first year of your IB Diploma Programme course. As you explore the core and optional themes, you may want to practise by doing some or all of the following:

1 select an IA prompt from the list of 35 questions

2 choose one or more objects with a real-world context that relate to the question

3 justify your choice in around 300 words

15.5 What objects can I use in my TOK exhibition?

Your exhibition needs to include three objects. An object can be either physical or digital – but it must have a tangible physical presence in your exhibition – such as photos or a printed tweet. It must be a concrete, specific object with a real-world context, and have a clear connection with your chosen IA prompt.

Each of the three objects you choose needs to have a clear connection with your chosen IA prompt. Look closely at the IA prompt to identify and unpack the relevant TOK concepts, and ensure you have understood what the question is asking.

Having selected your objects, you need to be able to explain and justify why each of your three objects relates to your IA prompt. Your written justification needs to include evidence and/or reasons to support how it links to the IA prompt, as well as why you have selected and included it in your exhibition.

Objects can be either physical objects or digital objects. For example, if your exhibition is on the optional theme of 'language', you could select the physical object of an actual poem written by a specific author – which you could justify by making a point about the use of metaphor as a means to communicate knowledge. However, you could also use a copy of a digital tweet™ to justify a similar point about language; the key idea is that it does not matter whether the object is physical or digital – a print-out of a tweet™, a printed photograph or a screen shot is enough to constitute an object in your exhibition.

How to select an object

In the first instance, it may be worth doing some research before you decide on the objects that are most relevant to your IA prompt. For example, if your exhibition is on the optional theme of 'technology', artificial intelligence could be a useful starting point for your research into possible objects – a specific, real-life object with an actual context could be Alpha Go™ or a specific robot with an actual real-world context, whether a specific humanoid robot, a particular aerial, an underwater robot, etc. The main consideration here is to choose objects whose specific real-world context is clearly relevant to your chosen IA prompt.

Figure 15.2: A review of the moves played by Ke Jie and AlphaGo™, the AI software that plays the game Go™ (shown here). AlphaGo™ could be an appropriate object, if linked to a relevant IA prompt

15.6 Relating objects to IA prompts
Technology

Possible prompt: How important are material tools in the production or acquisition of knowledge?

Possible objects and avenues to explore:

1   a photo of the telescope used by Galileo to observe space

2   a photo of one of the first pendulum clocks from the 17th century

3   a sextant – a traditional tool used for navigation before the invention of a compass

> The possible knowledge prompts used in this chapter have been used as a guide – you *must* choose your knowledge prompt from the list publishing by the IB

Each of these objects gives you opportunities to explore how a physical object can be used to make our observations more precise, make measurements and produce knowledge.

Figure 15.3: A sextant, a tool used for navigation

Language

Possible prompt: How does the way that we organise or classify knowledge affect what we know?

Possible objects and avenues to explore:

1   a photo or a copy of *Chambers Encyclopaedia* dating from the 1890s, which makes scientific classifications that we may no longer recognise or agree with

2   your IB Extended Essay on 'The Cold War', a classification for a period in 20th century history

3   a photo of a medieval map which classifies countries according to their proximity to Rome, Italy

Each of these objects gives you opportunities to explore the extent to which the labels and language we use to group and classify, shape and influence what we know.

Politics

Possible prompt: Can new knowledge change established values or beliefs?

Possible objects and avenues to explore:

1   a photo of the monuments of Korean leaders in Pyongyang, including the bronze statues of Kim Il-Sung and Kin Jong-Il

2   a hangman's noose once used for capital punishment

3   a Phillips curve, a once-held economic theory

Each of these objects gives you opportunities to explore what the new knowledge is or was, and how it has changed established political beliefs and values.

Religion

Possible prompt: What is the relationship between knowledge and culture?

Possible objects and avenues to explore:

1   a photo of the font in a local Christian church where new members of the community are baptised

2   a photo of the goddess Kali, worshipped in specific regions in India, taken at the Kali Temple in Varkala, Kerala, India

3   a photo of a vulture as a link to the Tibetan Buddhist tradition of sky burials

Each of these objects gives you opportunities to explore the extent to which religious knowledge is culturally based.

Figure 15.4: The link between religion, culture, art and architecture, shown in an image of the goddess Kali in a temple, Varkala, Kerala, India

Indigenous societies

Possible prompt: Does some knowledge belong only to particular communities of knowers?

Possible objects and avenues to explore:

1   a photo of traditional rice cultivation used in indigenous rice farming techniques

2   a photo of a witchetty grub, an example of Australian Aboriginal bush tucker

3   a model or photo of a kayak representing the traditional one-person boat invented by Inuit

Each of these objects gives you opportunities to explore what counts as knowledge and whether it is unique to particular communities.

Key features of objects for your exhibition – a summary

- they should relate to either the core theme or one of the optional themes that you have chosen

- they can be physical or digital

- they must have a specific, concrete context in the real world

- they need to have a clear link to your chosen IA prompt

- in writing, you need to be able to explain and justify the link between the object and the IA prompt

- each of your objects needs to be referenced so that someone could check the source or origin of the object

PRACTICAL TIP

The suggested objects listed above are to give you an idea of the diverse range of possibilities, but when you choose objects for your exhibition, you should try to choose objects that are of personal interest to you. It is very important that you identify a real-world context for each object, and one that is personal to you has a much stronger real-life context than a generic image or idea taken from the internet.

15.7 What is meant by 'justification'? How can I justify how my chosen objects relate to my chosen IA prompt?

In this context, 'justification' means an explanation or a reason why. A justification is a *good reason or reasons* given in support of your choice of object. In other words, your justification should provide the grounds for, or the explanation of, your choice in relation to the IA prompt. In your justification, it is advisable to offer analytical points over description. In fact, highly descriptive justifications that include unsupported claims and points will only receive low scores. As with all strong TOK writing, your written justification for your exhibition needs to make points that are well-supported by suitable and appropriate evidence. It is worth checking the descriptors in the IB Diploma Programme TOK assessment instrument, so that you are familiar with the requirements, and fully understand the way that your exhibition will be assessed.

Frequently asked questions about the exhibition	
How does a TOK exhibition differ from a general exhibition?	A TOK exhibition differs from a general exhibition in that it is focused on a IA prompt which relates to knowledge and knowing.
Can anything be an object in a TOK exhibition?	An object can be either physical or digital. It must: • have a tangible physical presence in your exhibition – such as photos or a print-out • be a concrete, specific object with a real-world context • have a clear connection with your chosen IA prompt
How much research should I do for my objects?	You only have about 300 words for each of your commentaries, so you will need to keep it succinct. The more personal the object, the less research you are likely to have to do, but you may need to do some research to find some counter-arguments.
How much can I rely on textbooks or websites as sources?	You can use textbooks to help stimulate your own ideas, but you should not be using textbooks as a primary source for your ideas. If your ideas do not come from your own reflections and personal experiences, your exhibition may lack originality, and your personal voice will be lost.
Must an exhibition include citations and references?	Although there is no formal requirement to include references, there is a requirement to reference any sources that you use.
What should I reference?	You should reference all quotations and any paragraphs in which you paraphrase or closely follow someone else's ideas. If you use any photos taken by somebody else, you should acknowledge the photographer; similarly, if you use ideas or information from other sources, these must be cited.

Frequently asked questions about the exhibition	
What is included in the word count?	The word count includes everything in the main body of the written justification, but it does not include footnotes or the bibliography. (Note that extensive footnotes are not considered appropriate, and may not be read.)
What is the minimum I can write?	There is no minimum word count, but 950 words is not very many for three commentaries. Ideally, you should write at least 300 words for each commentary but no more than 320 for any one commentary, because you will need to keep all commentaries approximately the same length without going over the word count.
Is allowance made for non-native speakers?	Although you are not assessed on your language as such, if an examiner cannot understand what you are saying, you cannot be credited for what you have written.

15.8 Continue your journey

- To investigate further **how exhibitions can be used to explore and represent ideas**, you could read some of the following articles.

- Neil Macgregor, *A History of the World in 100 Objects,* Penguin, 2011.

- Ian Hislop, *I object: Ian Hislop's search for dissent,* Thames and Hudson, 2018.

- Neil Macgregor: Shakespeare's Restless World. Search the *BBC Radio 4* website to listen.

> Chapter 16
The TOK essay

16.1 Introduction

The word 'essay' comes from the French verb *essayer* meaning 'to try' or 'to attempt'. The French philosopher Michel de Montaigne (1533–92) was the first to use the word in its modern sense. The origin of the word *essay* is of interest here, because TOK is concerned with questions that usually do not have definite answers. However, the lack of a definite answer does not make such questions redundant. On the contrary, many of the most important questions in life do not have definite answers. Writing a TOK essay is not so much about answering questions; rather it is about shedding light on a knowledge question. That is what you are *trying* to do. A certain amount of humility is needed because you are unlikely to come up with a definitive solution.

Because the TOK essay deals with open-ended and contestable questions, there is an important personal element to it. While you may be able to learn from similar explorations made by others, it is important that your essay voices *your* opinions and arguments, and that you acknowledge your own perspective and assumptions as a knower.

To explore a knowledge question, you need to dip in to your TOK toolkit and use it in an attempt to:

- explain what the problem in the essay title is and why it matters
- clarify the meaning of any key words or key terms in the essay title
- uncover hidden assumptions that are taken for granted
- offer a thesis statement that answers the knowledge question
- argue your case for your thesis with a clear argument or a coherent sequence of ideas
- consider different ways of thinking about the problem
- investigate and evaluate different perspectives
- identify, construct and evaluate both arguments and counter-arguments
- use specific examples or evidence to make a point or support a discussion
- assess and evaluate supporting evidence

- make relevant connections, explore links and comparisons between areas of knowledge where relevant

- apply the 12 TOK concepts and ideas as you see fit (see the Introduction at the beginning of this book)

- think through the implications of an argument or conclusion, and what follows

16.2 The IB Diploma Programme requirements

REAL-LIFE SITUATION 16.1

How does an externally assessed essay differ from one assessed internally?

The TOK essay involves students writing an essay to be marked by IB Diploma Programme examiners. For your TOK essay, you will need to choose one of six titles that will prescribed by the IB Diploma Programme for your examination session. Each title will be in the form of a knowledge question, and each knowledge question will focus on areas of knowledge.

Essay titles – key points

- six prescribed titles are published six months before the submission deadline

- you have time to think about each of the questions before you start planning and writing

- you choose only one essay title from the list of six

- your essay needs to answer the exact prescribed essay title set, and you cannot change the wording

Formal requirements – key points

- the maximum word count is 1,600 words in the body of the essay, including any quotations used

- the word count does not include additional material such as acknowledgements, references or bibliography; nor does it include any notations on maps, charts, diagrams or tables that you have included in your essay

- the essay is submitted to the IB Diploma Programme in a standard size 12 font, such as Times New Roman, Ariel, Calibri or Cambria, and the text should be double spaced

- you would normally be expected to use some source material, and anything you use must be acknowledged using some form of footnotes, endnotes or parenthetical citations and a bibliography

- your essay should not have any discussions in footnotes or endnotes
- the total number of words you have used should be clearly typed on the title page of your essay, as this number will need to be indicated when the essay is submitted to the IB Diploma Programme
- your school will set internal deadlines well before the IB Diploma Programme published deadlines

16.3 The role of your TOK teacher

It is expected that you will spend about ten hours of TOK class time on your TOK essay, and your teacher will help to support you in the planning and writing of your essay, by helping to clarify any queries. However, the TOK essay must be your own work.

During the planning and writing of your TOK essay, you will have three formal meetings with your TOK teacher. These meetings (or interactions) need to be recorded on the TOK essay planning and progress form (PPF) for submission to the IB Diploma Programme along with your essay.

Although the PPF does not contribute to your essay mark, it helps to ensure that all TOK students receive an appropriate level of support when writing their TOK essay. The PPF also provides important evidence that your teacher has taken appropriate steps to ensure the authenticity of your work. Your TOK teacher has a responsibility to ensure that your work is your own, and that you have properly acknowledged any sources you have used in accordance with your school's Academic Honesty Policy. You will also be asked to confirm that the final submitted work is entirely your own.

Although you can still seek advice from your TOK teacher after your third formal meeting, your teacher is not able to read or give feedback on further drafts. The next time you submit your TOK essay to your teacher, it must be the final version, ready to submit to the IB.

16.4 Assessment criteria

The TOK essay is marked holistically according to an assessment instrument, which is focused on the question of whether your TOK essay provides a clear, coherent and critical exploration of the prescribed title that you chose.

There are six main descriptors in the assessment instrument. You should be aiming to produce a TOK essay that:

- discusses the prescribed title in a sustained way that links effectively to different areas of knowledge
- presents arguments that are clear and coherent
- uses specific concrete examples to support your arguments
- identifies and evaluates other perspectives or viewpoints
- shows that you understand the implications of your arguments

"Your essay was grammatically correct but politically incorrect, Arnold."

16.5 Planning your essay – top tips

Once you have selected your essay title from the list of six prescribed titles, make a start with planning your ideas. Make sure that:

- you understand it properly – you cannot do justice to an essay question if you do not fully understand it

- you are interested in it – although not impossible, it is more difficult to do justice to an essay question if the question does not interest you

- you have something to say about it – think about some of the different perspectives you can bring to the question, and examples that you can raise from news items, your own experience or the subjects you study

- you have a thesis statement – this is your direct answer to the question in two or three sentences

- you have an argument in support of your thesis – some students find it helpful to brainstorm ideas on the prescribed title; once you have a number of ideas written down, you can go through and evaluate them to decide which ideas are the strongest to support your thesis and are likely to be the most clear and convincing

- you can organise your ideas – you might find a spider diagram or mind-map to be helpful for this. For your essay, you may want about six main ideas where each has two or three sub-points. It is important to think about your own response to the question before trying to find out what other people have said. The points you make need to develop and justify your thesis so that each point follows logically to the next one

---

PRACTICAL TIP

SAMPLE TOK ESSAY PLAN

1 Identify key terms: **key concepts** and **command words**.

2 Clarify and explain what you think the knowledge question is asking – in your own words.

3 Develop a thesis statement.

4 Identify the assumptions behind and implications beyond your thesis.

5 Come up with a sequence of points to support the thesis (aim for up to six points).

6 Come up with ideas for using examples and counter-examples (base these on your own subject-specific IB Diploma Programme learning, experience and any specific real-life situations).

7 Investigate different perspectives (explore an approach to the question from a different intellectual, social, geographical, historical or cultural or gender point of view).

8 Identify and evaluate the counter-arguments.

KEY WORDS

key concept: the central TOK idea specified in the essay title, for example 'certainty', 'justification', 'interpretation' etc.

command word: the instruction that the essay requires you to do, for example, 'Discuss …' or 'To what extent …' etc.

16.6 Writing your essay

During your TOK course, you will hopefully have written some practice essays. It also helps to look at some example essays to see what a good TOK essay looks like. You should familiarise yourself with the assessment criteria, and refer back to it frequently during the writing process.

Structure

It is important that you give some attention to your essay's structure. Make sure that your points flow naturally in a way that will help your reader (the IB Diploma Programme examiner) to follow your argument. Your essay will need an introduction, several paragraphs through the body of the essay and a conclusion.

Figure 16.1: A good essay needs structure

Introduction

The introduction should set out why the question is interesting, and what you are going to argue during the course of your essay. The introduction should also set out what you understand by the question, identify any key terms and, where applicable, say what you mean by them. You should also state what your parameters for the essay will be. This is called 'signposting' – where you set out the direction of the essay from the start.

Remember that the introduction of your TOK essay is the first thing your reader (the IB Diploma Programme examiner) will read, and will create the important first impression. Equally, the conclusion is the last thing that your reader will read, and this tends to leave a lasting impression. It is therefore important that both your introduction and conclusion are clear and well written.

Introduction

Knowledge question: How far is the production of knowledge a result of the work of individuals or group collaboration in two areas of knowledge?

Example

Collaboration can be described as something that requires one or more people working together to complete the task. This could mean that there would be several individuals working together to produce knowledge, or one individual referring to another's work to create their own. I will first look into the practice of collaboration in psychology from the human sciences, and compare it with collaboration in the natural sciences. Then I will investigate the role of individual knowledge producers in both areas of knowledge.

Main body of the essay

The paragraphs in the main body of your essay should each raise a major new point. The best way to start each new paragraph is with a topic sentence that introduces the new idea for analysis. If someone else read your essay but only had time to read the opening topic sentence at the start of each paragraph, would they follow your argument? It makes sense to begin each paragraph with your next point or idea that moves your argument forward. Typically, each paragraph will contain a number of arguments and appropriate evidence related to the main point of the paragraph. You might also check that the final sentence at the end of each paragraph make some link back to either the question, or to your thesis or answer to the question.

When writing your paragraphs, try to focus on the most important points, and do those well. Try not to be side-tracked by minor or irrelevant details. When you move from one paragraph to another, try to ensure that you maintain a smooth flow so that the reader can follow your train of thought easily. Sometimes, it helps to explicitly tell the reader where you are up to in the course of your response. For example, *I have shown that the evidence is inconclusive and I will now demonstrate the implications of this in the field of …*

Topic sentences at the start of paragraphs which each introduce a new point in the sequence of your argument

Example

1   *Considering psychology as a human science, the human sciences follow similar but not identical approaches and methods to producing knowledge as the natural sciences.*

2   *It is important that we distinguish direct collaboration and indirect collaboration.*

3   *Similarly, direct collaboration is often required to progress with the development of new or existing theories in the natural sciences.*

4   *While we have seen that direct collaboration between groups is a key aspect in the production of knowledge, it is important that the role of the individual should also be recognised.*

5   *Having seen that both direct collaboration and individual inspiration are important, we need to ask whether individual work comes before direct collaboration.*

Examples

Your personal perspective will come through in the points you raise, the comparisons you make and your choice of examples. You can use a range of examples from different sources, whether from books you have read, the media or your own IB Diploma Programme studies. By using examples from your personal experience and personal interests, your essay will be much more distinctive and original, and your personal voice will shine through. Examples should always be used to support the analytical points in your essay – so that they add weight to your argument. You should also use counter-examples. You can evaluate examples to demonstrate the quality of your evaluation.

Using an example to make a TOK point

Example

The human sciences are varied and use many different methods; however, the common features include empirical observation, the formation of a hypothesis, the gathering of quantitative or qualitative data, and an interpretation and evaluation of these results. These distinct characteristics were also present when I did my Psychology IA. I chose to replicate a 1975 study by Craik and Tulving about whether the depths of processing can affect how well we remember information. The 1975 study was based on the levels of processing theory Craik and Lockhart had proposed in 1972, indicating Craik and Lockhart had collaborated with each other over a number of years.

Analysis and evaluation

The central question in TOK is: *How do you know that?* It would be useful to bear this in mind when thinking about your prescribed essay title. TOK is not so interested in first-order questions within areas of knowledge; rather it focuses on second-order questions that ask about knowledge, quality of evidence, degrees of certainty and so on. TOK questions are open questions, so answers cannot be memorised; rather, they need careful thought and analysis, and personal judgements. Analysis and evaluation are essential elements of your essay.

Conclusion

Your conclusion is a very important feature of a TOK essay. The central question in TOK is: *How do you know that?* and in some way your essay will be related to that broader question. It should clearly summarise and evaluate your arguments, and bring your essay to a close. A conclusion can also point to the bigger picture in relation to knowledge and knowing. Your conclusion should address the deeper, wider and more insightful TOK points. You might choose to end with a forward-looking view. You may also use your conclusion to mention unresolved issues that might need further investigation, and for a brief discussion of some of the implications of your findings. You might also reflect on the central question in the specification – how far have you offered a clear, coherent and critical exploration of the essay title?

Conclusion

Example

To conclude, while it may be possible to find knowledge that has been produced by an individual, the production of knowledge is nearly always collaborative. In both the human and natural sciences I have shown that even when not directly collaborating with others, the producers of new knowledge are always building upon the knowledge of others within their field of study, which is in an act of indirect collaboration. I have also shown that the level of collaboration may be even more extensive if new knowledge is produced by creating or developing links with other fields of study, because the producer of that new knowledge must collaborate directly and indirectly with producers of knowledge in those other fields. These findings suggest that knowing is a collaborative enterprise, and that human beings are very reliant on others for all that we know.

Content

Top tips – do!

- Offer arguments in support of your thesis. Remember that any arguments you make will only be as good as the evidence you offer.

- Evidence is needed if you are making a central claim or a controversial claim.

- Be careful about the evidence you give. Make sure it comes from reliable sources, and approach all sources critically.

- Ask questions such as: Who says this? Do they have the relevant expertise? Do they have a vested interest? What's the evidence and how plausible is it? Do other experts agree?

- Your TOK essay should not only consist of arguments backed up by evidence; you must also consider counter-arguments. Because controversial issues are a key element of TOK, you should be able to find at least two sides to every question. Once you have given a counter-argument, you can either refute it or qualify your original argument to take account of it.

- Prepare to be **subtle**. Bring out the **nuance** and subtle distinctions in your points. It is possible that a claim about an area of knowledge may be true in some instances but not in others. If you can show that you are aware of such differences, your essay will show more depth. For example, if you are talking about reason as a tool or method, it might be appropriate to show that you know the difference between inductive and deductive reasoning.

- Making connections across different areas of knowledge will help to give your essay more analysis and breadth.

- Demonstrate personal reflection and independent thinking, along with an awareness of your personal perspective and assumptions as a knower.

> **KEY WORDS**
>
> **nuance:** subtle differences or shades of meaning
>
> **subtle:** precise and delicate distinctions

Figure 16.2: Not everything on the internet is reliable

Top tips

- Avoid superficial generalisations about any subject, culture or group of people, and stay away from clichéd examples which are unoriginal at best, and often false.

- Try to avoid too much descriptive writing. A little bit of description may be necessary, but you should soon move towards analysis.

- Do not confuse critical thinking with destructive thinking. Avoid the kind of scepticism that mindlessly questions everything. Your goal is not to reduce the edifice of knowledge to rubble, but to engage in the difficult task of distinguishing between more and less reasonable claims to knowledge.

Writing in general terms about an area of knowledge without losing subtlety and nuance

Example

An alternative area of knowledge that is subject to change is history. Unlike scientific knowledge, we could argue that historical facts cannot change as they are based on the events and actions that have happened in the past. Historical knowledge is produced using these facts. However, changes in historical knowledge can arise as a result of different interpretations of the past; either from historians' differing historiographical perspectives over time, or from the discovery of new sources or evidence that allow a new perspective on a historical topic. It follows that historical knowledge can never be truly certain, as the past cannot speak for itself and it requires interpretation in the present. The historical method relies on the historian's ability to interpret evidence together, without allowing their bias, cultural experience and national identity to influence their assumptions, which is virtually impossible to do. As R. G. Collingwood suggested, historical events consist of both 'inside' motives and 'outside' actions and behaviours. The inside motives are invisible and inaccessible to historian's so it follows that we cannot ever be certain that our historical knowledge today reflects the past accurately. However, if historians are able to come to a consensus after being objective in their examination of the same sources, with no ulterior motives or hidden agenda, then that is the closest to historical truth we can get, and we must be confident in that. My thesis is that historical knowledge, while it may not be entirely certain, is still possible despite these problems discussed.

16.7 After writing your essay – practical tips

Once your essay is written, it is important that you read through it carefully and ask yourself the following questions:

1   *Is it clear? Have you expressed yourself succinctly? Is anything written in your draft essay irrelevant, gratuitous, or meaningless?* It is very hard for an examiner to give you marks if your essay cannot be understood. If you waste too many words on tangential issues, 'padding' or repeating points, you will not have used enough of your 1,600 words on careful analysis. If something is in your essay but does not enhance your essay in any way, remove it.

2 *Are there words that could be removed or changed to something more accurate and possibly simpler?* Sometimes, in an effort to get words down on paper it is possible to use the wrong words, which may be close in meaning to what you intend, but often you can think of more accurate words when you read through your draft essay and reflect on it. Subtle differences in the meanings of words can create a significant difference in what you say.

3 *Do you have a thesis statement or a direct answer to the question?* Ensure that you have answered the question directly at some point in the essay. A thesis statement is an answer to the question in a few sentences – and it can appear anywhere in the essay, but is usually in the introduction or the conclusion and often in both.

4 *Do your paragraphs develop a sequence of ideas to support an argument?* You might take another look at your first sentence at the start of every paragraph to check that each of these moves your argument on.

5 *Have you overstated your case or made any sweeping generalisations?* All too often, students use words like *proven* when they mean *supported*, or *proof* when they mean *evidence.* Similarly, they may make claims like *no one believes …* or *we all know …* when usually this is not the case. Words like *few, many, some,* or *most* can help to moderate your response, and give you greater credibility as well as accuracy.

6 *Have you checked your evidence?* If you refer to 'facts' that are not correct, you will undermine the credibility of your essay. Do not refer to things that you really know nothing about. You may have read on the internet the cliché that Inuit have 16, 52 or even 112 words for snow, but do not be tempted to use this information unless you speak Inuit and have some solid ground for making such a claim. If you want to raise issues with language, use languages you are familiar with; perhaps languages you are studying for your diploma. That does not mean you need to be an expert on everything you mention, but you should at least double check your information using reputable sources.

16.8 Final checklist – practical tips for completing the essay writing process

☐ Your essay will probably have to go through several drafts before it is finished so it is important not to leave it to the last minute.

☐ Start the writing process long before the deadline.

☐ When you have a good draft, leave it aside for a day or two, then read it afresh. This should help you to spot any remaining weaknesses in your work.

☐ *Have you acknowledged your sources?* There is nothing wrong with using ideas and information that you have found, as long as you say where the ideas and information have come from. If you are quoting somebody, you should put the quotes in quotation marks and reference it according to your school's guidelines. If you are paraphrasing somebody, you should not use quotation marks, but you should still reference what you have written. Your footnotes or endnotes and bibliography do not count in your word limit, so you will not be in danger of exceeding your 1,600 words by referencing.

☐ *Can your information be traced?* As well as acknowledging where ideas have come from, references offer the reader the opportunity to follow up ideas in your essay, and to check the accuracy of your information. So it is important that whatever referencing system you use, you are consistent in the way that you use it, and accurate in the details you give. If you refer to a website, include the date you accessed, it because websites are often updated.

☐ *Have you used what is in your bibliography?* The bibliography for your essay should not be a list of books, articles and websites that vaguely relate to your topic; it must be a list of works that you have referred to in your essay, A rule of thumb is that if a work is listed in your bibliography, there should be at least one footnote, endnote or parenthetical reference to it in the body of your essay.

Frequently asked questions about the essay	
How does a TOK essay differ from a general essay?	The central requirement in a TOK essay is to write an answer to the question that offers a 'clear, coherent and critical exploration'. A TOK essay differs from a general essay in that it is focused on the question 'How do you know?', and answers the question using appropriate TOK tools and TOK language.
How does a TOK essay differ from a philosophy essay?	While there is some overlap between the questions asked in TOK and those asked in philosophy, your essay should not consist of lengthy explanation of 'what the philosophers said'. The point is rather to apply TOK tools to *your* academic experience and the real world.
How much research should I do for my essay?	A TOK essay is not a research essay. The essay should express your own personal voice and reflections on your IB Diploma Programme experience.
How much can I rely on textbooks?	You can use textbooks to help stimulate your own ideas, but you should not be using textbooks as a primary source for your arguments. If you simply paraphrase ideas that are in your TOK textbooks, your essay will lack originality, and your personal voice will be lost.
Must an essay include references?	You are likely to use sources of information, and there is a requirement that these are referenced. You must acknowledge and cite sources using a recognised convention, such as footnotes. It is a very rare TOK essay that does not reference sources.
What should I reference?	You should reference all quotations, and any paragraphs in which you paraphrase or closely follow someone else's ideas. You should also reference specific knowledge claims given as evidence.
What is included in the word count?	The word count includes everything in the main body of the essay, but it does not include acknowledgements, footnotes or the bibliography. (Note that extensive footnotes are not considered appropriate, and may not be read.)
What is the minimum I can write?	There is no minimum word count, but unless you are close to 1,600 words, you will not be able to do your topic justice. You are strongly advised to write no fewer than 1,500 and no more than the prescribed maximum 1,600 words.
Is allowance made for non-native speakers?	Although you are not assessed on your language as such, if an examiner cannot understand what you are saying you cannot be credited for what you have written.

16.9 Continue your journey

- To further develop your **skills in essay writing**, you could read some of the following articles.

- 'Writing an essay' QUT. Search the *Queensland University of Technology* website for the article.

- 'QUT Cite'. Search the *Queensland University of Technology* website for the article.

- 'Citing references' University of Reading. Search the *Reading University* website for the article.

> Glossary

ahimsa: the principle of doing no harm

abductive reasoning: reasoning that infers the best explanation based on the evidence available

absent-mindedness: inattentiveness that leads to lack of memory

absolutism: belief in absolute truth and absolute cultural, religious, political and moral standards against which all other views can be judged

abstract: conceptual, nonrepresentational, independent of concrete specific physical existence

aesthetics: the branch of philosophy that studies beauty and the arts; principles concerned with beauty and artistic taste

affiliation: having a connection with a specific group or organisation

agnostic: a person who believes that nothing can be known of the existence or nature of God

alien: a person who is a not a citizen of the country that they live in or a species that is not native to the environment it is found in

allegory: a text or artwork that can be interpreted to reveal a hidden meaning, usually moral or political in nature

AlphaZero: a computer that can play the game Go and beat human world champions

alternative facts: in the context of post-truth politics, alternative views to more widely-accepted and verified beliefs

ambiguity: when a word, statement, image or situation can have more than one meaning or interpretation

amoral: outside the scope of morality; lacking any moral framework

anarchist: a person who believes there should be no people or organisations who rule as a matter of right

anchoring bias: where a particular concept or idea is mentioned before a question is asked – this has a 'priming effect' which may affect the response given

anthropology (cultural and social): the study of the development of culture and society

antithesis: the negation of a thesis

applied artificial intelligence: also known as weak AI or narrow AI, the use of software for a specific problem solving or reasoning task

Argand diagram: a geometric representation of complex numbers that uses a real x axis to represent the'real' part of the complex number, and the real y axis to represent the'imaginary'part of the complex number (the Argand diagram is also called the complex plane or z-plane)

arithmetic: the process of counting and calculating in numbers

art brut: the 'raw art' movement began by Jean Dubuffet (1901–1985), which recognised the value of primitive or low art that belonged outside the conventional tradition of fine art

Arte povera: An Italian art movement that used ordinary but unconventional materials to create art works

artificial general intelligence (AGI): also known as strong AI or full AI, the capacity of a machine to perform the same intellectual task that a human, can including the full range of human cognition

artisan, craftsman: a worker skilled in a particular trade or craft

assent: an expression of agreement

assimilation: integration

astrology: a belief that the movement of the planets affects human behaviour in predictable ways

asylum: shelter and protection; in a political context, protection granted by a state to persons who are political refugees

augmented reality: the technology that overlays a computer simulation onto the real world

authenticity: validity, genuineness

authoritarian: relating to a government that imposes its authority over people and limits their freedom

authority: the moral or legal right to make decisions in, and take responsibility for, and exercise power within a particular field of knowledge or activity; the word can also be used to denote a person or group who has that authority

autocracy: a government based on one person with supreme authority and power

automation: the use of robots and machine systems to replace human work

autonomous: self-governing

availability heuristic: a bias where recent or easily remembered examples affect our judgement

avant-garde: innovative ideas considered to be at the forefront of new developments and techniques in the arts

axiom: a starting assumption, often regarded as a self-evident truth or, more loosely, something we assume to be true or accept as true within a particular system

bacteriophage: a virus that destroys bacteria

ballpark: estimated, rough, imprecise

barbarian: Herodotus refers to the Persians as barbarians. For Herodotus 'barbarians' denoted all non-Greeks, and the word originally meant a speaker of an incomprehensible language. The word did not have the same negative connotations that people might associate it with today

belief: a confident opinion; something thought to be true

benevolent: kind, well-meaning

benign: harmless, non-threatening, innocent

bias: prejudice, unfairness, favouritism, one-sided preference

bioavailability: the measure of drug absorption over time

Big Bang: the theory that the universe began with an infinitely dense singularity 'exploding' in a rapid expansion 13.8 billion years ago

big data: the vast amount of varied digital data sets, which can be analysed to identify patterns, associations and trends

bit: a binary unit of information in a computer

bitcoin and Ethereum: types of cryptocurrency

blind faith: faith without evidence, understanding or discrimination; faith that is not open to evaluation or critical thought

block chain: a decentralised distributed ledger of transactions which is permanent

blocking: when there is an obstruction to your ability to recall information

bodhisattva: a Buddhist who has achieved enlightenment, but delays reaching nirvana out of compassion for those who are suffering

body language: conscious or unconscious body movements and positions that communicate our attitudes and feelings

bot: an automated computer programme

bourgeoisie: the middle class – Marx thought that they benefited most from a capitalist economic system

breadth of knowledge: a span of knowledge covering many aspects of a subject

bureaucratic: overly concerned with procedure and administration at the expense of efficiency

canon: a collection of works considered by scholars to be the most important and influential; in the context of religion, a body of authorised religious works accepted as authoritative within that religion

capitalist: employing an economic system where there is limited government intervention, and the production and distribution of resources depend on the investment of private capital

cardinality: the number of elements in a set; for example, the set {0, 1, 2} has three elements and so has cardinality 3

caricature: comic exaggeration

censorship: the suppression or limitation of any material or views and beliefs that are considered to be unsuitable or inappropriate

centipede effect: over-consciousness of your performance in a way that interferes with what you are doing

certain knowledge: a state of affairs when we can be definite that something is the case

certainty: the quality of having no doubt

chatbot: a computer that simulates human conversation

cherry-picking: picking out sections of a text that appear, at face value, to support a particular opinion, while ignoring the context and other sections of the text that might promote a different view

circular reasoning: the fallacy of assuming the truth of what you are supposed to be proving

clickbait: content deliberately designed to encourage you to click on the link, which will take you to another web page; for example a visual image or an attention-grabbing headline

cognitive (knowledge) tool: the mental process of acquiring knowledge, for example via the senses, memory, imagination, experience and rational thought

cognitive bias: when bias affects the process of acquiring knowledge and understanding

cognitive science: the study of the mind and its processes through an interdisciplinary approach that involves philosophy, psychology, linguistics and the natural sciences

coherence theory (of truth): the theory that a proposition is true if it fits in with our overall set of beliefs

collaborative: produced by two or more people working together

communism: a social, political and economic ideology in which there are no class divisions, all property is communally owned, and the government directs all economic production

competency: capability; the possession of sufficient knowledge or skills

complex: complicated, multifaceted

complex number: in mathematics, a combination of a real number and an imaginary number, for example $3 + 4i$

compound interest: the addition of interest to the principal sum of a loan or deposit to make that sum larger, and therefore make subsequent interest greater; or in other words, interest on interest

concept: an abstract idea or something conceived

conceptual: relating to abstract ideas

confirmation bias: the tendency to believe evidence that supports your opinions, and ignore or discount evidence that goes against what you believe

conjecture: a guess or imaginative hypothesis

connotation: the ideas and associations a word evokes in addition to its literal meaning

consensus theory (of truth): the theory that truth is based on a set of beliefs that the majority of people agree on

consistent: noncontradictory, not permitting the proof of two statements that contradict one another

conspiracy theory: either a denial that an event took place, or the belief in an explanation for an event based on the idea that there was a deliberate and secret agency of people or organisations

constructivism: the theory that mathematical truth and proofs should be positively constructed

contestable: where there are different possible answers, opinions or views on the same question or topic; a contestable knowledge claim or question is one that can be argued about, where there is more than one possible interpretation or answer

contingency: something that is dependent upon chance

contraindication: a situation when a particular remedy or procedure should not be used

controlled experiments: experiments that are performed with carefully regulated variables to provide a standard of comparison for similar experiments with just one differing variable

conviction: a firmly held belief

correspondence theory (of truth): the theory that a statement is true if it corresponds to a fact

corroborate: to confirm or support a statement or theory

corroboree: an Australian Aboriginal dance ceremony

cosmogony: the study of the origins of the universe

cosmology: the study of the universe

countability: in mathematics, a set is *countable* if it can be put into a one-to-one relationship with the natural numbers $\{1, 2, 3, \ldots\}$

coup d'état: when a small group of people seizes power by force

covenant: an agreement or promise of commitment

creation science: treating the theory that God created the universe as recorded in the Book of Genesis as a scientific theory

creativity: the ability to bring something into being through the imagination; the ability to generate ideas or produce objects that are original, surprising and valuable

critical: involving objective analysis and evaluation

crofter: traditionally, a tenant farmer of a small agricultural land holding in the Scottish Highlands and islands, although since 1976, it has been possible for crofters to purchase their crofts to become owner occupiers

cryptocurrency: a medium of exchange and store of value which can be used like money

cubism: an artistic movement in which objects were analysed, broken up and reassembled in an abstracted form

cultural appropriation: the adoption of elements of one culture by members of another culture

culture: the shared ideas, beliefs, customs and practices of a community or society

cyborg: a cybernetic organism, which combines organic and mechanical parts

datum (plural data): in the context of technology, 'something given' – usually any facts and statistics gathered together for investigation; an unstructured collection of facts and figures

decode: decrypt, decipher, translate

deductive reasoning: reasoning from the general to the particular

deep learning: a technology at the centre of artificial intelligence that uses big data to predict or decide

deepfake: the use of artificial intelligence (AI) to create fake videos creating the false impression of authenticity

deism: the belief in an impersonal creator god, who is evident through reason and the laws of nature, but does not intervene in human affairs

deity (plural deities): a god or supernatural being

dematerialisation: when technology loses its physical substance

demographics: the characteristics of human populations

denomination: a distinct religious group within Christianity (for example, the Anglican, Georgian Orthodox and Lutheran churches)

denotation: the literal meaning of a word

deontological ethics: the belief that ethics is fundamentally a matter of doing your duty and fulfilling your obligations

depth of knowledge: knowledge that focuses on, amplifies and explores specific topics

descent: as an adjective, dependent on parentage or ancestry

designer baby: a baby genetically engineered *in vitro* with specially selected traits, which can vary from lowered disease-risk to gender selection

Deuteronomic cycle: a cycle of rebellion, oppression and repentance as a way of interpreting historic events

diagonalisation argument: a mathematical proof published by Cantor in 1891 which demonstrated that there are infinite sets which cannot be put into one-to-one correspondence with the infinite set of natural numbers

dialectics: a method of argument that involves a disagreement between opposing sides

diaspora: people who have been dispersed from their homeland or have spread out from their homeland, while maintaining a close connection with it

discernment: the ability to use sharp perceptions to judge well

disinformation: intentionally false or inaccurate information spread as an act of deception

disinterested: free from bias and self-interest, which may help us to make objective judgements

dissent: disagreement; nonconformity

Distributed Denial of Service: flooding the bandwidth of a target (usually a web server) to prevent it from conducting normal business; this is an illegal practice in many countries

divine: something of a supernatural nature that is sacred or godlike; as a verb, it can also mean 'to discover something in a supernatural way'

dogmatism: a tendency to lay down principles as undeniably true without consideration of evidence or the opinions of others

Dunning–Kruger effect: a cognitive bias where we find it difficult to know the limit of our knowledge and expertise. If we have a little knowledge in a particular area, we may overestimate our level of knowledge and competence in that area. In this way, a little knowledge may lead to an unjustified illusion of greater knowledge

echo chamber: a space in which sound reverberates, so any sounds made are repeated over and over as they bounce from the walls; an environment in which people only encounter beliefs or opinions like their own, so they don't consider alternative ideas and their own ideas are reinforced; in the context of technology, the effect created by social media and news whereby people only encounter ideas that are the same as their own, reinforcing their existing perspective

economic determinism: the theory that history is determined by economic factors

efficacy: effectiveness

eisegesis: reading meaning into a text

elegant: concise; stylish and graceful

emotive meaning: the aura of favourable or unfavourable feeling that hovers about a word

emotivism: the view that ethical claims are an expression of feeling and emotion

empathy: the ability to imagine and understand the feelings and viewpoint of another person

empirical: based on and verified by observation and experience

empiricism: a school of thought which claims that all knowledge must ultimately be based on sense perception

empiricist: a supporter of empiricism

enlightenment: a state of perfect knowledge about existence, perfect wisdom and infinite compassion

epidemiology: the study of the origins and spread of diseases

epistemic injustice: injustice that happens when knowledge is ignored, not believed or not understood

epistemology: the philosophical study of how we know what we know, and the exploration of the difference between justified belief and opinion

equality: the state of being equal in terms of status, rights and opportunities

equity: the quality of being fair and impartial

espionage: the practice of spying to obtain political or military information

ethical: conforming to accepted moral standards

ethics: the branch of knowledge to do with right and wrong, and the study of the moral principles that govern our beliefs and behaviours

ethnolinguistics: a field of linguistics that studies the relationship between language and culture

ethology: the study of animal behaviour

Eucharist: a ritual in which Christians remember Jesus's last supper and sacrifice by breaking bread and drinking wine, as symbols of Jesus's body and blood

Euclidean geometry: a system of mathematics attributed to the Greek mathematician, Euclid, based on five axioms

euphemism: a softer-sounding word or phrase used to disguise something unpleasant or not usually talked about in polite conversation

evidence: signs that you can see, hear, experience or read to support the truth of an assertion

evolutionary epistemology: the theory that knowledge evolves by natural selection

exegesis: drawing meaning from a text in a critical way

exegete: a person who engages in exegesis

experiential: based on experience

experimental subjects: the individuals who are experimented on

expert: a person with specialist skills and/or knowledge

expertise: specialised skills and knowledge

explanation: an account or statement that makes something clear; in the context of the study of history, a justification or reason that makes sense of why an event or action took place

explicit: clear, made obvious, openly expressed

extremism: an ideology in which people are prepared to take extreme actions including the use of violence for their religious or political causes

extrinsic religiosity: participating in social worship to conform to a social norm or convention

fabricate: manufacture, make up

factual: containing facts

factual memory: our memory of meanings, facts and information

fallacy: a mistaken belief, an invalid argument

fallible: capable of making mistakes or being wrong

false dichotomy: when a situation is presented as having just two possible options, when other perspectives are not only possible, but highly likely

falsehood: a lie or misrepresentation; something that is put forward as a fact or a truth, but it is not

falsify: to prove something to be false

fantasy: the imagination of impossible or improbable characters, situations or narratives

fideism: reliance on faith for all knowledge; a belief that faith is superior to reason

Fields medal: an award made every four years by the International Congress of Mathematics to recognise outstanding mathematical achievements; it is sometimes described as the equivalent of a Nobel Prize for mathematics

filial piety: showing love, respect and support for one's parents

forest produce: things other than timber that can be found in the forest, including wild honey, fruits, edible plants and firewood

formal system: in mathematics, a system used to deduce theorems from axioms according to a set of logical rules

futurism: an artistic movement that began in Italy and emphasised speed, technology, youth, violence and objects such as the car, the airplane and the industrial city

general revelation: knowledge of God that is discovered through natural ways, such as observing the natural world, observing patterns in history and applying reason

generalisation: making statements that apply to all cases, on the basis of some specific cases

genre: an artistic style or type; it can apply to any of the arts

Gettier case: an example of a justified true belief that does not appear to be knowledge

go native: to adopt the attitudes and behaviour of a foreign group with whom one has lived for an extended period

God's eye view: when a knower assumes that they have access to knowledge that only an omniscient god could have KEY

golden ratio: image a line – divide it into two unequal parts in such a way that the ratio of the whole line to the big part is the same ratio as the big part to the small part. The ratio is 1:1.618; which is known as the golden ratio

Google effect (or Google amnesia): the tendency to forget information that can easily be found online

Gospel: the teachings or revelations of Jesus, meaning 'good news', originally set out in the four gospels in the New Testament, *Matthew*, *Mark*, *Luke* and *John*

grammar: the rules for constructing meaningful phrases and sentences out of words

'great man' theory of history: the belief that history is driven by great individuals

Gross Domestic Product: a measure of the goods and services produced in a country to estimate the size and growth rate of the economy

hacktivism: gaining unauthorised access to computer files or networks to further social or political ends

hegemon: the dominant group, class or state that exercises hegemonic power and promotes hegemonic ideas

hegemony: the dominance of one group supported by a set of ideas, or the dominance of a set of ideas that become the norm in a way that inhibits the circulation of alternative ideas

heretic: a person within a group who has unconventional or unorthodox beliefs

hermeneutics: the science of interpretation

heterogeneous: mixed; composed of different parts

heuristics: when a person finds, discovers or learns something

hindsight bias: mistakenly thinking, after something has happened, that you had known it would happen

historiography: the study of historical perspectives

history from above: also known as 'top-down' history, this focuses on the perspectives of the leaders, rulers and those in power, and the social and cultural elites of the time

history from below: also known as 'bottom-up' history, this focuses on the perspectives of the ordinary people, such as the working class, women, ethnic minorities or any other voices that may have been neglected by a 'top-down' approach

holism: the belief that the best way to understand some things is by looking at them as a whole rather than by analysing them into separate parts

holistic: considering all factors of any situation, in the belief that all aspects are interconnected and can only be understood in relation to the whole

homeopathy: a system of alternative medicine that believes in treating ailments with minute concentrations of substances that in larger amounts would case the same symptoms of the ailment; it is based on the principle that *'like cures like'*

homogeneous: consistent; of uniform structure throughout

host state: a state that governs the national territory in which an indigenous society lives

hyperthymesia: a condition in which a person can remember an abnormally large number of their own life experiences in detail

hypothermia: unusually low body temperature

hypothesis (plural hypotheses): a proposed explanation or starting point, based on limited evidence that can be tested in an investigation

icon: a symbol or representation often uncritically venerated. In Eastern churches, these figures usually represent Christ, the Virgin Mary, or a saint

identity: how a person, group or nation sees themselves in relation to other people, groups, nations, ideas, and the world

idiom: a colloquial expression whose figurative meaning cannot be deciphered from its literal meaning

ignorance: lack of knowledge

illusion of explanatory depth: the illusion that you understand something in detail when you do not

implicit: implied, hidden

in vitro **fertilisation:** a laboratory procedure in which an egg is fertilised outside the body; the term *in vitro* means 'in glass'. In the past, IVF babies have been called 'test-tube babies'

inadvertent: not deliberate, happening without design or intention

indigenous people: literally, 'people belonging to a place', the term is used to refer to people who inherit and practise unique cultures and ways of relating to people and their environment

indigenous rights: the rights of native people who originate from a particular place

inductivism: the use of and preference for inductive methods of reasoning to develop natural laws

infallible: not capable of being wrong or making mistakes

infer: to come to a conclusion reached on the basis of evidence and reasoning

inference: a conclusion based on evidence and reasoning

infinity: something without bounds, often treated as an unreal number

information theory: the mathematical study of the coding of information, and how that information can be quantified, stored and communicated reliably through computer circuits and telecommunications

information: data that has been processed and structured, and can be used to answer *who, what, when* and *where* questions; in the context of technology, facts about something, or the process, storage and spread of data by a computer

inherent: existing in something as a permanent characteristic

innate: something we are born with

instantiation: the representation of an abstraction by an example of the abstraction; for example, 'apple' is an abstract idea; this particular apple is an instantiation of the idea

intangible: nonmaterial and unquantifiable

intellectual property: the ownership of knowledge or unique products that have been created

intellectual capital: the collective knowledge of people in an organisation or society

intellectual virtues: virtues that are required for the pursuit of knowledge

interpolate: to insert something of a different nature into something else

interpretation: an explanation of the meaning

intrinsic religiosity: where religion is the organising principle of an individual's life; a central and personal experience

introspective: looking inside oneself

intuitionism: the theory that mathematical objects are mental constructions, and that as we create mathematical objects, so we create the reality of them

invalid: an argument that does not follow logically from the premises

irony: a figure of speech in which words are used to say one thing and mean the opposite

irrational number: any number that cannot be written as a fraction with one integer over another (e.g. 2, π)

judiciary: the system of courts and collection of judges in a country

justification: in the context of truth, a reason or reasons for a belief or support for a truth claim

justify: to show that a belief or decision is well-founded and reasonable

key concept: in the context of a TOK essay, the central TOK idea specified in the essay title, for example 'certainty', 'justification', 'interpretation' etc.

kitsch: derivative, cliched art

law of large numbers: a statistical principle which says that random variations tend to cancel out when a population is large enough

law: a generalised description of observations about a relationship between two or more things in the natural world; often the description is mathematical

layperson: a person not from the profession; in a religious context, a person without professional or specialised knowledge in their religion

legitimate: genuine; conforming to acknowledged standards

liberalism: an ideology that regards protecting and enhancing individual freedoms to be a central issue for politics, and strives towards social changes that bring about equality and freedom for all

linguistic determinism: the idea that our language and its structures limit and determine what and how we think, and what we can know

linguistic relativity: the idea that language shapes and influences the way we think and what we can know

logic: the principles of – or a system of – rules that govern reason, and a branch of philosophy

logical empiricism: the belief that all human knowledge should be reduced to logical and scientific foundations (it is often regarded as synonymous with logical positivism)

logical positivism: the belief that all knowledge comes from logical inferences based on observable facts, and that a statement can only be meaningful if it can be determined to be true or false

logicism: the theory that mathematics can be derived from logic, without the need of any specifically mathematical concepts

manifest: as an adjective, clear or obvious; as a verb, to become clear, obvious, visible, evident or noticeable

mathematical empiricism: a form of realism that says that we discover mathematical facts by empirical research, just like facts in any of the other sciences

mathematicism: the theory that everything in the universe is ultimately mathematical

matrilineal: passed down through the mother

mental map: a personal mental picture of what is true and false, reasonable and unreasonable, right and wrong, beautiful and ugly

meta-analysis: analysis of data to establish trends based on various different studies

metacognitive: relating to your own thought processes

metaphor: a figure of speech which describes something using words that are not literally true, for example, *'she is an angel'*, *'he is a book-worm'* or *'knowledge is a map'*

metaphysical: abstract, beyond physical, supernatural, independent of physical reality

mimetic: from *mimesis*, the Greek word for 'imitation', associated with the idea that art copies reality

misattribution: when credit is given to the wrong person or source, whether deliberately or mistakenly

misinformation: incorrect information, unintentionally false information

modifier words: words that qualify a seemingly clear and precise statement, and make it vague or ambiguous

monarchy: a form of government that has a monarch (king, queen or emperor) as the supreme authority

monolithic: relating to one large, unchanging entity

monotheistic: having one personal god

moral: following one's personal principles of what is right or wrong

moral absolutism: the belief that there is at least one universal moral principle, which should always be followed, irrespective of the context or their consequences

mother tongue: the first language that you were brought up to speak

myth: an ancient, traditional story about gods, heroes or groups of people, usually concerning the history of a people or explaining a phenomenon. Myths often, but not always, involve supernatural beings

mythology: a collection of traditional stories usually belonging to a particular religious or cultural tradition

nanotechnology: a branch of technology that manipulates individual atoms and molecules

narrative: a story that tells about a series of events. It can be factual, fictitious or a blend of both

natural number: often called the counting numbers, they go from 1, 2, 3 ... infinity (∞)

neutral: unbiased, impartial, not supporting either side of an argument

neutrino: an uncharged sub-atomic particle with zero mass when at rest

noise: unwanted disturbances in electrical signals; meaningless data, including data that cannot be understood or interpreted by machines

non-putrifying bacteria: bacteria that do not help to decompose dead or decaying matter

non-theistic: having no personal god or no gods at all

nuance: subtle difference or shades of meaning

objectivity: a detached way of looking at the world, largely independent of personal feelings or opinions, that expects to be corroborated by a knowledge community

observer effect: in the natural sciences, the observer effect refers to the principle that the act of observing a phenomenon changes the phenomenon being observed (in the human sciences the observer effect refers to the tendency of people to behave differently when they are being observed)

ochlocracy: mob rule, majoritarianism

omnipotent: all-powerful

omnipresent: present everywhere and at all times

omniscient: all-knowing; having an intuitive, immediate awareness of all truth

optical telescope: a telescope that gathers and focuses light, mostly from the visible light spectrum, to create a magnified image that can be viewed directly

outlier: a value or datum very different from others

outrage: intense anger and shock

panacea: a solution or remedy for all difficulties

pantheon: an overview of a culture's gods and goddesses that reflects the culture's values

paradigm: a pattern, model or example that provides a framework of understanding

pathogen: a virus, bacterium or other micro-organism that can cause disease

patrilineal: passed down through the father

peer: a person of equal standing, usually a member of your own tribe

peer review: the evaluation of academic or scientific work by experts working in the same field

percept: what we notice via the process of sense perception

perception: an awareness of something in and through the mind

personal memory: the internal recollection of the various events that make up our lives

perspective: point of view, a particular way of seeing or considering something

pharmaceutical: related to drugs

phenomenon (plural phenomena): an event, experience or occurrence

phlogiston: a hypothetical component of combustible substances

place-value system: a numerical system in which the position of a digit indicates its value as well as the digit itself; therefore in '9', the digit 9 denotes only 'nine'; in '90' because its place has shifted left, it denotes 'ninety' in a decimal system

plagiarism: passing off someone else's idea or work as your own

plane: a flat surface that extends forever in two dimensions but has no thickness

Platonist: relating to the ideas of the Greek philosopher, Plato (c 427–348 BCE)

pluralist theory (of truth): the theory that there are multiple truths, and various meanings of the word 'truth'

pluralistic: relating to a system in which multiple groups, ideas, or practices coexist. In the context of religion, having many different beliefs and practices

pluralistic history: accepting that there are various different perspectives that may be justified, and multiple possible accounts of the past

polarising: in this context, dividing people into two main groups with opposite views

political science: the scientific study of the state, governments, power and political activity

political spectrum (plural spectra): a system of classifying different political positions in relation to different political values

political values: abstract ideas about the needs of the people that drive political positions, for example, equality, freedom, tradition, progress, etc

polymath: a person with expertise in several different fields of knowledge

polytheistic: having many gods

population: in the context of mathematics, the entire group of objects, measurements or events from which a sample is drawn

portrait: a painting, photograph, or other artistic representation of a person which tries to show the personality of the person portrayed

positivism: the belief that the only authentic knowledge is that which can be scientifically verified or proven through logic or mathematics

post hoc ergo propter hoc: the fallacy of confusing a correlation with a causal connection

post-colonial age: the period of time after colonial rule has ended

post-modern: a movement of 20th-century thinkers who thought that knowledge, reason, ethics and truth are a social, cultural and political construction

post-truth: relating to or denoting circumstances in which objective facts are less influential in shaping public opinion than appeals to emotion and personal belief

postulate: a statement underlying a theory; something assumed to be true (they are slightly different to axioms but the two words are frequently used interchangeably)

power: control, influence, strength; the capacity to control and influence situations and people

practical memory: the remembered ability to know how to do something, such as playing the piano

practical or material (knowledge) tool: the device used to complement or enhance cognition, such as a microscope or an iPad

pragmatic theory (of truth): the theory that a proposition is true if it is useful or works in practice

precession: a slow and continuous change in the orientation of the axis of a rotating body pre-colonial (to be added at first proof of Decoding?)

premise: assumption on which an argument is based, or from which a conclusion is drawn

prescriptivism: the view that ethical claims are imperatives

primary emotions: universal emotions which are usually said to comprise happiness, sadness, anger, fear, disgust and surprise

primary source: Any object or written source from the time or based on the time being studied, for example the eyewitness account of a soldier fighting in the Second World War would be a primary source even if it was written fifty years after the event

procedural: related to actions

proof: generally refers to conclusive evidence, leaving little place for doubt; however, a mathematical proof is more than just a general proof – it is a conclusive deduction from axioms that leaves no room for doubt or argument

propaganda: the deliberate manipulation, distortion and spreading of information in order to influence what people think, usually for political purposes

proselytising: evangelising, persuading others to join a particular group or religion

pseudoscience: a system of beliefs and practices that are claimed to be scientific but which are incompatible with the scientific method

psychology: the scientific study of the human mind and behaviour

pulsar: a small, dense, spinning neutron star

Purchasing Power Parity: a standard of measurement used to compare the economic productivity and standards of living of different countries

quaint: pleasantly, amusingly or interestingly strange

qualitative: relating to, measuring or measured by the quality of something, rather than its quantity; qualitative studies use a method to give a detailed narrative about a human phenomenon that describes a culture or shares a story

quantitative: relating to, measuring or measured by the quantity of something, rather than its quality

quantum mechanics: a branch of mechanics describing the motion and interaction of subatomic particles

quantum theory: a theory in physics which explains the behaviour of subatomic particles

radicalism: a political desire to change social structures in radical ways

radio telescope: a telescope that detects radio waves and microwaves which lie outside the visible spectrum

rational number: any number that can be written as a fraction, that is, a ratio of integers

rationalist: a supporter of rationalism, a school of thought which relies on deduction rather than sensory perception to determine truth

rationality: the ability to reason and think clearly, sensibly or logically

reactance: the tendency of people to react against advice, rules and regulations perceived as a threat to their freedom

real number: any number that can represent a position on a number line; real numbers include all rational and irrational numbers

realistic imagination: imagination which is informed and guided by the relevant facts

reductionism: the belief that some subjects can be explained in terms of other more fundamental ones

reductive fallacy: the fallacy of saying that just because *A* is composed of *B*, it follows that *A* is nothing but *B*

redundancy theory (of truth): the theory that truth has no essential property, and the word can be substituted for another or left out altogether

refute: to prove a statement or theory wrong

relativity: recognising that knowledge claims are dependent on contextual factors or frames of reference

religious experience: a temporary experience that defies normal description, in which the person having the experience feels that a power from outside themself is acting to reveal a truth that could not be reached by reason alone

religious fundamentalism: a belief in the absolute authority of a particular sacred text, religious leader and/ or god

replication: the process of repeating

response bias: the tendency to try and please a person interviewing us or a person carrying out a questionnaire, by choosing the answer we feel will please them

responsibility: a duty or moral obligation

retaliatory killings: killings made in revenge for killing people or livestock

retribution: punishment inflicted in response to an action

revelation: something that has been revealed or disclosed, usually by God or God's representatives or messengers

rigour: strictness; the quality of being extremely thorough and careful

ritual: a prescribed ceremonial action or set of actions that have a symbolic meaning for the individual and the community

rule of thumb: an approximation based on experience

rule worship: blindly following moral rules irrespective of whether or not they are appropriate

sacrament: a special ritual which is said to impart God's grace

sacred: holy; entitled to reverence and respect; set apart for the worship of a god or gods

sacrifice: to give up something valuable to help others, or to appease a god or spirit

sage: a wise person

Sapir–Whorf hypothesis: the claim that the language you speak influences or determines the way you see the world

scepticism: an attitude of doubt; a method of obtaining knowledge through systematic doubt and continual testing

scholasticism: a method of learning characteristic of the Middle Ages, and based on logic and traditional beliefs about what is true

scientific method: a method of procedure for the way scientific investigations are conducted

scientific paradigm: a worldview that underlies the theories and methodology in a particular field of science

scientism: an exaggerated trust in the efficacy of the methods of the natural sciences applied to any and all areas of investigation

scriptures: sacred writings; religious texts

secondary emotions: complex emotions which can be thought of as mixtures of primary emotions

secular humanism: a system of belief that believes in human values, consequentialist ethics based on reason, and a commitment to science, democracy and freedom

secular: not concerned with religion

semantic: relating to the meaning of language

sentient: conscious, capable of feeling

shaman: a priest or priestess who uses magic to cure the sick, divine the hidden and control events

Shulba Sutras: a body of Hindu writings regarded as appendices to the Vedas; they are arguably Hinduism's most authoritative scriptures

singularity: in the context of AI, the point when computer intelligence will surpass human intelligence; a moment of irreversible change for humans and human knowledge

social contract: an actual or implicit agreement between rulers and the people they rule, that defines the rights and responsibilities of each

social justice: the idea that all people should have equal access to – and opportunities for – wealth, education, health, and justice

social media: websites and apps that allow people to form a network, and create and share digital content and information with one another, such as Facebook™, Twitter™, WhatsApp™ or Instagram™

socialism: a social system based on public ownership of the means of production, and an equitable distribution of wealth

sociology: the study of the structure and function of society

sound: the property of a syllogism that contains two true premises and a valid argument

special revelation: knowledge of God that is not available through reason; knowledge of God that is revealed in a supernatural way

spin doctor: a person whose role it is to portray a political party in a favourable light, especially to present the media with a positive interpretation of a particular event

spirituality: a concern with the human spirit or soul, rather than with material or physical things

state: a legal entity that has one central government, which is sovereign over a defined territory and a permanent population

stereotype: a fixed, oversimplified and often negative picture of an individual or group, based on their membership of that group

subjectivity: looking at the world from a personal point of view, under the influence of feelings and emotions

subliminal: subconscious

subtle: precise and delicate distinctions

surrealism: an artistic movement that tried to release the creative potential of the unconscious mind by expressing imaginative dreams and visions

syllogism: a deductive argument with two premises and a conclusion

syntax: the arrangement of words to form sentences or phrases – an example of syntax in toddlers might be a word pair such as *'my bed'* or *'biscuits gone'*

synthesis: the placing together of different parts or elements (evidence) to form a connected whole; in the context of dialectics, a connected whole, a resolution, or a new idea which resolves the conflict between thesis and antithesis

tacit: unspoken; implicit but not expressed

tally: to keep count (of things or events)

Talmud: the book of Jewish law and theology

tautology: saying the same thing in two different but completely equivalent ways; repeating something already implied

taxonomy: classification system, categorisation

tenet: principle, important truth

terrorism: the use of violence, especially against civilians, intended to create a climate of fear in the pursuit of political aims

textual analysis: a data-gathering process that analyses choices of words and the ways in which they are used, to try to develop a greater understanding of the meaning of a text and the culture in which it was written

theist: a person who believes in a god or gods who interact with people and the world

theocracy: literally 'government by God' in which God is seen as the supreme leader, acting through religious authorities; in other words, government by religious authorities

theologian: a person who studies the nature of God and religious beliefs, usually within a particular religious tradition

theorem: a principle or statement that can be demonstrated or proved using logic, but is not self-evident

theory: an interconnected system of ideas intended to explain something in depth

tolerance: acceptance of different perspectives and behaviours, even if you disagree with them

totalitarian state: a state in which the ruling authorities have total political, social and cultural control over those living in the state

traditional knowledge: a body of knowledge that is developed, sustained and passed on over generations within a community

traditional medicine: the indigenous knowledge, practices and skills used by indigenous peoples (and others) to diagnose and treat illnesses and injuries, and to maintain health

transcendental power: supernatural power; in this case, the power of art to take us anywhere, show us anything including past lives and let us see into the minds of others

transient: temporary, fleeting

trans-theistic: beyond theism and atheism

treatise: a detailed written account

tribalism: the behaviours and attitudes that arise out of membership of or loyalty to a social group

trickle-down theory: the theory that lowering taxes for wealthy corporations and high-income earners will lead to greater investments, and will expand economic prosperity. The benefits of the expanded economy will then 'trickle down' to the workers

Triptika: a set of three texts that are said to record the words of the Buddha

truth: in accord with fact or reality, a belief accepted as true, or faithfulness to a standard

Turing Test: a test put forward by Alan Turing where if a computer can pass itself off as a human, it would constitute intelligence on the part of the computer

universal grammar: the idea that all human languages, no matter how different they appear, share some fundamental similarities

universals: qualities that can be shared by different individuals at the same time, for example redness, roundness, beauty

utilitarian approach: a perspective that values usefulness above all other considerations

utilitarianism: the belief that ethics can ultimately be reduced to the principle that we should maximise happiness

vagueness: when something is not clear or has no distinct boundaries, is imprecise and defies exact definition

validity: the property of an argument in which the conclusion follows logically from the premises

values: standards of behaviour; regard for things of important moral worth

veneration: the act of worship or showing great respect

verification: the process of establishing the validity or accuracy of something

***Verstehen* position:** the belief that the main aim of the human sciences is to understand the meaning of various social practices as they are understood by the agents themselves

vigilante: a citizen who enforces the law in their community without legal authority, and often breaks the law when doing so

viral: spreading widely and quickly

virtual reality: the technology that generates a computer simulation of an environment, such as a headset that shows images of a 'virtual' world

virtue ethics: the theory that an ethical action is one performed by a virtuous person for the right reason

***wabi-sabi* (侘寂):** finding beauty in the imperfect, impermanent and incomplete

wallet: in terms of cryptocurrency, a software program that allows users to send and receive digital currency and monitor their balance

weak artificial intelligence: also known as applied AI or narrow AI, the use of software for a specific problem solving or reasoning task

whistleblowing: when a person or group makes public or passes on information about wrongdoing usually by or within an organisation

wisdom of repugnance: the claim that we can validly appeal to our feelings of disgust to justify our moral beliefs

wise nature fallacy: the false assumption that because something is natural it is therefore good

worldview: an overarching theory about the nature of the universe and human beings' place in it

> Acknowledgements

The authors would like to thank: Alison Evans, Micaela Inderst and Jayne Sly at Cambridge University Press for their organisation, advice and support and Richard van de Lagemaat for his fantastic second edition. Margaret Haynes, Michelle Daley and Caroline Mowatt for their tireless work on the text. Wendy would particularly like to thank Susan for being a wonderful co-author; Carl, William and Rosie Heydorn and Judy and Geoff Worham and David and Mary Heydorn for their support and patience; Beryl Maggs and Martin Otero Knott for intellectual inspiration; Katy Ricks and Tim Jones for their encouragement; David Hall, Neetha Kunaratnam, Anna Mack, Alex Colenso, Sue MacLeay and Oliver Barratt, for their insights and feedback. Susan would particularly like to thank Wendy Heydorn for her enthusiasm and easy collaboration; Beryl Potter for her support and understanding when time was short; John Puddefoot for his tireless support and his invaluable insights, suggestions and corrections; and last but not least, Zachary Puddefoot for ensuring a healthy work-life balance was maintained throughout the project and agreeing to model for some of the photographs.

Cambridge University Press would like to thank Tomas Duckling for his invaluable reviewing of the text

The authors and publishers acknowledge the following sources of copyright material and are grateful for the permissions granted. While every effort has been made, it has not always been possible to identify the sources of all the material used, or to trace all copyright holders. If any omissions are brought to our notice, we will be happy to include the appropriate acknowledgements on reprinting.

Excerpt from *Nineteen Eighty-Four* by George Orwell (Copyright © George Orwell, 1949), reproduced by permission of Bill Hamiltonas the Literary Executive of the Estate of the Late Sonia Brownell Orwell, and copyright © 1949 by Houghton Mifflin Harcourt Publishing Company, renewed 1977 by Sonia Brownell Orwell. Reprinted by permission of Houghton Mifflin Harcourt Publishing Company. All rights reserved.

Thanks to the following for permission to reproduce images:

Cover image: Jekaterina Nikitina/Getty Images Inside: Fig 1.02 Zu Sanchez Photography/GI; Fig. 1.1 william87/GI; Fig. 1.2 Xesai/GI; David Sipress/The New Yorker Collection/The Cartoon Bank; Fig 1.3 Maury Phillips/GI; Fig 1.5 Johnhain/PIXABAY; Fig 1.6 Martin Novak/GI; Fig 1.7 Don Mason/GI; Fig 1.8 Tony Marturano/GI; Fig 1.9 Kamil Krzaczynski/GI; Fig 2.0 Chris Gould/GI; Fig 2.1 B.G. Carter via Flickr; Fig 2.2 NNehring/GI; Fig 2.3 Matt Anderson Photography/GI; Fig 2.4 Blend Images - Mike Kemp/GI; Fig 2.5 Witthaya Prasongsin/GI; Fig 2.7 Arman Zhenikeyev/GI; © Punch Limited; Fig 2.8 Bettmann/GI; Fig 2.9 ChrisMilesPhoto/GI; Fig 2.10 Iurii_Au/GI; Fig 2.11 Goddard, Clive/CartoonStock.com; Fig 3.0 Patric Sandri/GI; Fig 3.1 Compassionate Eye Foundation/Three Images/GI; Jack Ziegler/The New Yorker Collection/The Cartoon Bank; Fig 3.4 CSA Images/GI; Fig 3.5 Hank Grebe/Stocktrek Images/GI; Fig 3.6 Adam Gault/GI; Fig 3.7 ullstein bild Dtl./GI; Fig 3.8 PC Plus Magazine/GI; Fig 3.9 Chris Madden/GI; Fig 3.10 Ponsulak Kunsub/EyeEm/GI; Fig 3.11 Karl Tapales/GI; Fig 3.12 Fuse/GI; Fig 3.13 NurPhoto/GI; Fig 3.14 LOIC VENANCE/GI; Fig 4.0 Chalffy/GI; Fig 4.1 Peter Macdiarmid/GI; Fig 4.2 Hannelore Foerster/GI, Magritte, Rene © ADAGP, Paris and DACS, London 2020; Fig 4.3 Robert Niedring/GI; David Sipress/The New Yorker Collection/The Cartoon Bank; Fig 4.4 omgimages/GI; Fig 4.5 Andy Rouse/GI; Fig 4.6 10'000 Hours/GI; Fig 4.7 Mike Hill/GI; Fig 4.8 Lev Savitskiy/GI; Fig 4.9 NASA/GI; Fig 4.10 THOMAS LOHNES/GI; Fig 5.0 Steve Cicero/GI; Fig 5.1 DEA PICTURE LIBRARY/GI; Fig 5.2 urbazon/GI; Fig 5.4 TOBIAS SCHWARZ/GI; Fig 5.5 SOPA Images/GI; Fig 5.6 Chesnot/GI; Fig 5.7 Artyom Geodakyan/GI; Fig 5.8 Smith Collection/Gado/GI; Fig 5.9 VCG/GI; Fig 5.10 Mikhail Tereshchenko/GI; Fig 5.11 NurPhoto/GI; Julia Suits/The New Yorker Collection/The Cartoon Bank; Fig 5.12 NurPhoto/GI; Fig 5.13 hocus-focus/GI; Fig 6.0 Eliza Rowe/EyeEm/GI; Fig 6.1 Arterra/GI; Carolita Johnson/The New Yorker Collection/The Cartoon Bank; Fig 6.2 BSIP/GI; Fig 6.3 WILLIAM WEST/GI; Fig 6.4 China Photos/GI; Fig 6.5 INDRANIL MUKHERJEE/GI; Fig 6.6 NurPhoto/GI; Fig 6.7 MyLoupe/GI; Fig 6.8 SammyVision/GI; Fig. 6.9 ullstein bild/GI; Fig 6.10 Frederick M. Brown/GI; Fig 7.0 Onfokus/GI; Fig 7.1 Bridgeman Images; Ed Fisher/The New Yorker Collection/The Cartoon Bank; Fig 7.2 VCG/GI; Fig 7.4 hadynyah/GI; Fig 7.7 Phil Roeder/GI; Fig 7.8 Malcolm Linton/GI; Fig 8.0 Stuart Dee/GI; Fig 8.1 Ernio48 via Wikimedia

Commons; Fig 8.2 Pew Research Center demographic projections 'The Changing Global Religious Landscape'; Fig 8.3 MANJUNATH KIRAN /GI; Fig 8.4 Arctic Circle © Alex Hallatt, Dist. by King Features Syndicate, Inc.; Seth Fleishman/The New Yorker Collection/The Cartoon Bank; Fig 8.5 Xavier ROSSI/GI; Fig 8.6 MyLoupe/GI; Fig 8.7 Pascal Deloche/GI; Fig 8.8 Craig Ferguson/GI; Fig 8.9 Alison Wright/GI; Fig 8.10 Igor Palkin/GI; Fig 9.0 Werner Van Steen/GI; Victoria Roberts/The New Yorker Collection/The Cartoon Bank; Fig 9.1 fotoVoyager/GI; Fig 9.3 Hakan Hjort/GI; Fig 9.4 Ingetje Tadros/GI; Fig 9.5 Andrea Pistolesi/GI; Fig 9.6 Paul Raffaele/Shutterstock; Fig 9.7 NurPhoto /GI; Fig 9.8 RODRIGO BUENDIA /GI; Fig 10.0 Richard Baker/GI; Campbell, Martha/ CartoonStock.com; Fig 10.2 a & b AFP/GI; Fig 10.3 Time Life Pictures/GI; Fig 10.4 Marco Simoni/GI; Fig 10.5 AWAD AWAD/GI; Fig 10.6 sedmak/GI; Fig 10.7 Heritage Images/GI; Fig 10.8 IWM/GI; Fig 10.10 Archive Photos/ GI; Fig 10.11 VCG/GI; Fig 10.12 Photographer is my life./GI; Fig 11.0 Imagebook/Theekshana Kumara/GI; Fig 11.1 Jean Marc CHARLES/GI; Fig 11.1 Jean Marc CHARLES/GI © Cy Twombly Foundation; Fig 11.2 Richard Stonehouse/GI © Tracey Emin. All rights reserved, DACS 2019; Fig 11.3 Imagno/GI; Fig 11.4 Print Collector/GI; Fig 11.5 The Washington Post/Getty Images; Fig 11.6 The Picture Art Collection/Alamy Stock Photo; Bruce Eric Kaplan/The New Yorker Collection/The Cartoon Bank; Fig 11.7 © The Pollock-Krasner Foundation ARS, NY and DACS, London 2020; Fig 11.8 Science & Society Picture Library/GI; Fig 11.9 Alireza Firouzi/GI; Fig 11.10 Used by permission of Esther Honig; Fig 11.11 Frank Bienewald/GI; Fig. 11.13 RBB/Getty Images; Fig 11.14a © Victoria and Albert Museum, London; Fig 11.14b View of Derwentwater from 'The Silent Traveller in Lakeland' by Chiang Yee, Country Life, London 1938, used by permission of Chien-fei Chiang; Fig 11.15 Auscape/Universal Images Group via GI; Fig 11.16 Grayson Perry Matching Pair, 2017 Glazed ceramic Diptych, each: 105 x 51 cm 41 3/8 x 20 1/8 in © Grayson Perry, Courtesy the artist and Victoria Miro, London/Venice; Fig 11.17a Fratelli Alinari IDEA S.p.A./GI; Fig 11.17b Leemage/GI; Fig 11.17c Fratelli Alinari IDEA S.p.A./GI; Fig 11.18 wynnter/GI; Fig 11.19 duncan1890/GI; Fig 11.20 AFP/GI; Fig 11.21 Meckseper, Josephine, © DACS 2020; Fig 11.22 Aaron Geddes Photography/GI; Fig 11.23 Historic Collection/Alamy Stock Photo; Fig 12.0 oxygen/GI; Fig 12.1 4FR/GI; Fig 12.2 kbeis/GI; Fig 12.3EXTREME-PHOTOGRAPHER/GI; Fig 12.5 lukaves/GI; Fig 12.6 Encyclopaedia Britannica/ UIG/GI; Barbara Smaller/The New Yorker Collection/The Cartoon Bank; Fig 12.7 SDI Productions/GI; Fig 12.8 SEBASTIAN KAULITZKI/SCIENCE PHOTO LIBRARY/GI; Fig 12.9 Sparky/GI; Fig 12.10 Pam Wright/EyeEm/ GI; Fig 12.11 marcoventuriniautieri/GI; Fig 12.13 AFP/GI; Fig 13.0 Sky Noir Photography by Bill Dickinson/GI; Fig 13.2 DEA/S. MONTANARI/GI; Fig 13.3 YinYang/GI; Fig 13.4 Alex Potemkin/GI; Fig 13.5 Paul Kay/GI; Fig 13.6 SDI Productions/GI; Fig 13.7 Education Images/GI; Fig 13.8 iurii Konoval/GI; Fig 13.9 FABRICE COFFRINI/ GI; Farley Katz/The New Yorker Collection/The Cartoon Bank; Fig 13.10 Portra/GI; Fig 13.11 Chris Ryan/GI; Fig 13.12 Adam Gault/GI; Fig 14.0 Laguna Design/GI; Fig 14.1 erhui1979/GI; Fig14.2 Tara Moore/GI; Dana Fradon/ The New Yorker Collection/The Cartoon Bank; Fig 14.4 DNY59/GI; Fig 14.6 Juice Images/GI; Fig 14.8 LIONEL BONAVENTURE /GI; Fig 14.9 BSIP /GI; Fig 14.10 Zhilal El Furqaan/EyeEm/GI; Fig 14.11 Laurence Dutton/ GI; Fig 14.12 NurPhoto/GI; Fig 14.13 andriano_cz/GI; Fig 1 Susan Jesudason; Fig 15.0 Klaus Vedfelt/GI; Fig 15.1 Caitlin Cass/The New Yorker Collection/The Cartoon Bank; Fig 15.2 STR/GI; Fig 15.3 Tetra Images/GI; Fig 15.4 Malcolm P Chapman/GI; Fig 16.0 GaudiLab/GI; Harley L. Schwadron/The New Yorker Collection/The Cartoon Bank; Fig 16.1 aydinmutlu/GI; Fig 16.2 Paul Taylor/GI

GI = Getty Images

> Index

Bailey, David 176
Bailey, Thomas A. 144
ballpark 514
Banksy 472
barbarian 402
Barthes, Roland 457
Bartholdi 426
Basu, Aparna 413
bear market 600
Beard, Mary 391
Beer Street (Hogarth) 472
Beethoven, Ludwig van 461, 467
Beevor, Anthony 417–18
beliefs 9, 21, 39–41, 54, 90, 109, 111
    coherent system 137
    culturally relative 143
    false 143
    justification 159
    language 244
    objectivity and subjectivity
        158–9, 541–4
    political 476
    religion 300, 303–5, 325, 335
    truth 135
Bell Burnell, Jocelyn 564–5
Belley, Jean-Baptiste 407
benevolent leaders 272
benign 24
Bentham, Jeremy 117, 118, 568
Berkeley, George 95
Bertrand, Joseph 515
Bertrand's box paradox 515
Betts, Paul 520
Bhargava, Rajeev 283
biases 3
Big Bang theory 326, 327, 546
big data 172, 198, 510
    in human sciences 590, 601–4
    and internet of things 201–3
    as knowledge tool 189–90
bioavailability 566
Birchall, Clare 155
bit 493
bitcoin™ and Ethereum™
        187, 596, 600
Blake, William 461
Bletchley Park
        (codebreaking) 153–4
blind faith 324
block chain 187
blocking 58
BlockSidewalk™ 201

Bloom, Benjamin 52, 53
Bloomberg™ 590
*bodhisattva*s 323
body language 217
Boghossian, Peter 153
The Book of Judges 312
Book of Nature 326
Book of Scripture 326
The Book Thief (Zusak) 465
Bordisky, Lera 242
Bose, Jagadish Chandra 327
Boserup, Ester 596
bot 64
'bottom-up' history 409
Bouguereau, William-Adolphe 440–1
bourgeoisie 405
Box, George 537
Boyle, Robert 553
Brahmagupta 488
Brahmasputha Siddhanta
        (Brahmagupta) 488
Brave New World (Huxley) 420
breadth of knowledge 52
*Breakfast Table with Blackberry
        Pie* (Heda) 436
The Broken Pitcher (Bouguereau)
        440, 441, 478
The Broken Pitcher (Greuze) 478
The Broken Spears
        (León-Portilla) 386
Brosnan, Pierce 474
Bruguera, Tania 476
Buddhism 301, 307, 316, 454–5
bull market 600
bureaucratic administration 289
Butler, Samuel 417

C

Caesar, Julius 389, 403
Caillois, Roger 61
Canning, George 508
canon 311, 461
Cantor, Georg 516
Cao Xueqin 80
capitalism 405
capitalist 408
Caravaggio 474
Cardano, Gerolomo 494
cardinality 486
caricature 29

Carlyle, Thomas 413
Carr, E.H. 393, 398, 400
Carroll, Lewis 4, 221
cave paintings 432
Caxton, William 204
censorship 399
    arts 475–6
    science 563
centipede effect 47
The Centipede's Dilemma
        (Craster) 47
certain knowledge 103
certainty 10
Chabris, Christopher 580
'change blindness,' concept
        538, 580
chatbot 190, 222
Chenchu 363
cherry-picking texts 318
China
    communism 398
    cultural association 219
    culture 24
    inventions 80
    politics 273–5
    religion 333
    rice-fish farming 349–50
    traditional medicines 353, 560
Chomsky, Noam 8, 45, 216
Christianity 301, 304–5, 333–4
Churchill, Winston 272, 411
Cicero 553
Clemens, Samuel Langhorne.
        see Twain, Mark
Cleopatra 63, 419–20
clickbait 174
Clinton, Bill 110
Clinton, Hillary 62, 183
cognitive bias 605
cognitive science 49–50
cognitive (knowledge) tool 94
coherence theory
        (of truth) 136–8
Cold War 409, 411–12
collaboration 556, 650, 651, 652
Collingwood, R.G. 384, 389,
        399–400, 421
command word 649
common sense 29–31
    caricature 29
    fallacy 30
    judgement, role 32